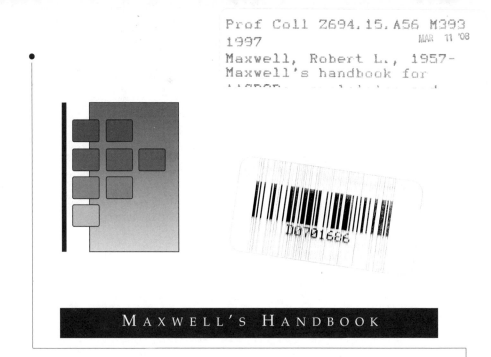

Maxwell's Handbook

for AACR2R

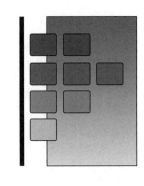

MAXWELL'S HANDBOOK
for AACR2R

Explaining
and Illustrating
the Anglo-American
Cataloguing Rules
and the 1993
Amendments

ROBERT L. MAXWELL

WITH

MARGARET F. MAXWELL

American Library Association
Chicago and London 1997

Design by Image House

Composition by Clarinda in Palatino and Optima

Printed on 50-pound white offset, a pH-neutral stock, and bound in 12-point C1S cover stock by Data Reproductions Corporation

The paper used in this publication meets the minimum requirements of American National Standard for Information Sciences—Permanence of Paper for Printed Library Materials, ANSI Z39.48-1992. ∞

Library of Congress Cataloging-in-Publication Data
Maxwell, Robert L., 1957-
      [Handbook for AACR2R]
      Maxwell's handbook for AACR2R : explaining and illustrating the Anglo-American cataloguing rules and the 1993 amendments / Robert L. Maxwell with Margaret F. Maxwell.
          p.   cm.
      Rev. ed. of: Handbook for AACR2 / by Margaret F. Maxwell. 1989.
      Includes bibliographical references and index.
      ISBN 0-8389-0704-0
      1. Anglo-American cataloguing rules—Handbooks, manuals, etc.   2. Descriptive cataloging—Rules—Handbooks, manuals, etc.   I. Maxwell, Margaret F., 1927- . II. Maxwell, Margaret F., 1927-   Handbook for AACR2. III. Title.
      Z694.15.A56M393 1997
      025.3'2—dc21   97-1449

01   00   99   98   97   5   4   3   2   1

CONTENTS

ABBREVIATIONS

AACR *Anglo-American Cataloguing Rules*

AACR1 *Anglo-American Cataloging Rules, North American Text* (Chicago: American Library Association, 1967)

AACR2 *Anglo-American Cataloguing Rules*, 2nd edition (Chicago: American Library Association; Ottawa: Canadian Library Association, 1978)

AACR2R *Anglo-American Cataloguing Rules*, 2nd edition, 1988 revision (Ottawa: Canadian Library Association; London: Library Association Publishing; Chicago: American Library Association, 1988)

AACR Chapter 6 (1974) *Anglo-American Cataloging Rules, North American Text, Chapter 6* (Chicago: American Library Association, 1974)

APPM *Archives, Personal Papers, and Manuscripts: A Cataloging Manual for Archival Repositories, Historical Societies, and Manuscript Libraries*, 2nd edition, comp. Steven L. Hansen (Chicago: Society of American Archivists, 1989)

CSB *Cataloging Service Bulletin* (quarterly) (Washington, D.C.: Library of Congress Processing Services, 1978–)

Howarth Lynne C. Howarth, comp., *AACR2 Decisions and Rule Interpretations*, 6th edition (Ottawa: Canadian Library Association; Chicago: American Library Association, 1994)

LC The Library of Congress

LCRI *Library of Congress Rule Interpretations*, 2 vols. (Washington, D.C.: Library of Congress Cataloging Distribution Service, 1990 [latest update, 1996])

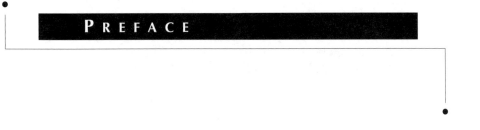

When the first edition of the *Handbook for AACR2* was issued, the *Anglo-American Cataloguing Rules,* second edition, was new and untried. Most catalogers were familiar with the first edition of the *Anglo-American Cataloging Rules (AACR1)* (1967); many had used the preceding code for cataloging, the ALA 1949 rules. All were apprehensive about the possible effect the new cataloging code would have on existing library catalogs. The *Handbook*, therefore, was designed to assist experienced catalogers as well as library school students in the application of the most commonly used rules for description, choice of access points, and form of heading as set forth in the 1978 code, which came to be known as *AACR2.*

Although the principles on which the 1978 code was based have not changed in the nearly two decades since the appearance of *AACR2,* many modifications have been made, either by decision of the Joint Steering Committee for Revision of AACR (JSC) or by the interpretations and policy decisions of the major Anglo-American national libraries (the Library of Congress, the National Library of Canada, the British Library, and the National Library of Australia). The publication of the 1988 revision of *AACR2 (AACR2R),* which incorporated both published and unpublished JSC revisions and added a number of new rules and examples, necessitated a thorough revision of the *Handbook.* The 1989 edition, *Handbook for AACR2 1988 Revision,* reflected the new features in *AACR2R.*

The appearance of the 1993 amendments to *AACR2R*[1] was the impetus for this new edition, *Maxwell's Handbook for AACR2.* At about the same time, however, the author of the original edition, Margaret F. Maxwell, retired from her position at the University of Arizona Library School and desired to pass on the authorship of future editions. The main author of the current edition, Robert L. Maxwell, has reconsidered the entire book in the light of the 1993 amendments and the current rule interpretations. Margaret F. Maxwell has read the manuscript and provided useful guidance.

The most obvious change between the second and this edition of the *Handbook* is the conversion of the cataloging examples to machine-readable (MARC) format.[2] Because most catalogers now work in an on-line environment, it was felt that examples in MARC format would be more useful than those in card format, even though *AACR2R* is written with the card format in mind. A general overview of the MARC bibliographic format is provided in the introduction. Specific information about the fields in the descriptive portion of the catalog is provided in this *Handbook*, chapter 1; and information about the coding of main and added access points is found in chapter 14. An explanation of the MARC authorities format is given in chapters 15, 17, and 18.

A new feature of this edition is a chapter on the cataloging of archival materials, corresponding to *AACR2R* chapter 4. In addition, chapter 9 ("Computer Files") has been completely rewritten, including information on the cataloging of interactive multimedia and Internet resources.

In this edition consideration has been taken of the rule interpretations of the major Anglo-American national libraries, rather than just those of the Library of Congress.[3] The cataloging examples conform to the Library of Congress's rule interpretations; where other national libraries differ from these, it is noted in the text. In the interest of providing usable shared cataloging, U.S. catalogers, particularly those contributing to national databases such as RLIN and OCLC, should conform to LC practice as much as possible. Catalogers in other countries should follow the rule interpretations of their own national libraries.

Although explanations and examples in this *Handbook* have been revised and brought into line with current practice, the basic premises of the first edition of the *Handbook for AACR2* remain the same. The editors of *AACR2R* include frequent examples to illustrate the rules; these examples are not in full catalog entry format. Catalogers as well as library school students may find these examples mystifying in their brevity. The present text therefore attempts not only to explain the rules, but also to give full cataloging examples to illustrate each rule discussed. Furthermore, experience teaching cataloging has demonstrated that one of the most difficult concepts for beginning catalogers is the translation of the title page (or other chief source) into a catalog entry. Therefore, in as many instances as possible, a transcription of the title page or other prescribed source material has been included with each entry.

Many of the readers of this book are experienced catalogers. Others using this text will be library school students, just beginning their study of cataloging theory and practice. For this reason, the preponderance of examples selected to illustrate *AACR2R* chapter 1 in this text are books. In addition, most of the examples are English-language materials. These choices have been made deliberately, in order to provide a comfortable frame of reference for inexperienced catalogers, most of whom have more acquaintance with books as library materials than with their nonprint counterparts. Representative examples of nonprint library materials are also included in chapter 1, "General Information"; nonprint materials are covered in detail in the following chapters.

The reader will notice that chapter numbering in *AACR2R* is not entirely consecutive, skipping from chapter 13 to chapter 21 to leave space for possible future additions and also to accommodate the mnemonic structure of the text. Although the chapters in the *Handbook* are numbered consecutively, discussions of individual rules are numbered to correspond with *AACR2R*. Limitations of space have made it necessary to omit discussion of those rules whose meanings seem self-evident and of certain specialized forms of library materials (such as early printed monographs) not acquired by most libraries. In addition, no chapter in this *Handbook* corresponds to *AACR2R* chapter 26 ("References"). *AACR2R* chapter 26 is a summary of required references already found in *AACR2R* chapters 22–25; these are discussed in the corresponding *Handbook* chapters (15–18).

Maxwell's Handbook for AACR2 is designed as a supplement to, not a substitute for, the text of the *Anglo-American Cataloguing Rules.* It is assumed that the reader will have *AACR2R* (1988) at hand, as well as the 1993 Amendments. In addition, the *Handbook's* provisions and examples will need to be updated by issues of the Library of Congress's *Cataloging Service Bulletin (CSB)* or the cumulative loose-leaf compilation of *Library of Congress Rule Interpretations (LCRI).* It must be emphasized that this *Handbook* is not meant as a self-help manual for beginning catalogers, although with more and more library schools dropping cataloging requirements (or course work altogether), it is probably inevitable that it will be so used. It is therefore designed to address problems beginners often find puzzling. It is our hope that the following pages may serve as a helpful introduction and a guide to the second Anglo-American cataloging code.

Maxwell's Handbook for AACR2 had its inception as long ago as 1967, when Margaret Maxwell attended Seymour Lubetzky's seminar on *AACR1* at the University of Illinois. Lubetzky's exposition of cataloging principles as enunciated at the seminar and on later occasions and his written discussions of rules and theory form the basis for much of the theory presented in this text. The idea of a detailed handbook to the *Anglo-American Cataloging Rules* developed over the next decade into an unpublished manuscript in much the same format as the *Handbook.* The present work has its roots in this earlier manuscript.

Many individuals contributed in various ways to *Maxwell's Handbook for AACR2.* Thanks go first to Margaret F. Maxwell, the author of the first two editions of the *Handbook,* for entrusting me with the project and giving encouragement along the way. Many thanks must also be given to Robert B. Ewald, of the Library of Congress, for countless e-mail and faxed responses to questions about *AACR2R* and LC practice. I am also particularly grateful to numerous catalogers at the Harold B. Lee Library, Brigham Young University, including Janet Bradford, Irene Halliday, Richard Soares, Dale Swensen, and John Wright, for reading various parts of the manuscript and offering helpful suggestions. I must also thank the head of the catalog department, Carla Kupitz, as well as the administration of the Lee Library, for allowing me time away from my regular duties for the final preparation of this book.

Finally, thanks to an understanding wife, Mary Ann Maxwell, who has taken to referring to herself as an "AACR2 widow," and to my children, Carrie, Rachel, and William, who at times wondered if they had a father. I dedicate this book to them.

Robert L. Maxwell
Harold B. Lee Library
Brigham Young University
Provo, Utah

NOTES

1. Joint Steering Committee for Revision of AACR, *Anglo-American Cataloguing Rules, Second Edition, 1988 Revision, Amendments 1993* (Chicago: American Library Association, 1993).
2. Because the author is a U.S. cataloger, USMARC format is used throughout. There are two other manifestations of MARC in the English-speaking world, UKMARC (United Kingdom) and CAN/MARC (Canada). Efforts are currently underway to reconcile the three into a single format, which will be called "IMARC" (for "International MARC"). Details of MARC coding are constantly changing. The examples in this *Handbook* reflect coding practice as of the time of its publication. Two major changes have occurred that have not yet been implemented by the Library of Congress, RLIN, or OCLC, and therefore are not followed in this *Handbook*. These are the elimination of first indicator "2" (for multiple surname) in X00 bibliographic fields (all surnames will be coded "1" when this change is implemented) and the elimination of the second indicator entirely for 100, 110, 111, and their corresponding 4XX and 5XX fields in authorities format.
3. For the National Library of Canada, the British Library, and the National Library of Australia, this information has been found in Lynne C. Howarth, comp., *AACR2 Decisions and Rule Interpretations,* 6th ed. (Ottawa: Canadian Library Association; Chicago: American Library Association, 1994). For the Library of Congress, the *Library of Congress Rule Interpretations,* most recently updated in 1996, have been used. These are referred to in the text as "Howarth" and *"LCRI."*

INTRODUCTION

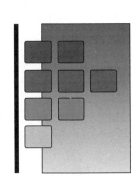

When the *Anglo-American Cataloging Rules* appeared in 1967, the code was heralded as a new departure in cataloging, a unified set of rules based on principle rather than on the enumeration of specific problems. And indeed this was the case. The 1967 rules, like the present code, were based on the "Statement of Principles adopted at the International Conference on Cataloguing Principles, Paris, October 1961."[1] This brief statement, usually referred to as the Paris Principles, is of such overriding importance to the full understanding of *AACR2R* as well as its predecessors that it is abridged below.

1. SCOPE OF STATEMENT
   The principles here stated apply only to the choice and form of headings and entry words. . . .

2. FUNCTIONS OF THE CATALOGUE
   The catalogue should be an efficient instrument for ascertaining
   2.1 whether the library contains a particular book specified by
       a. its author and title, *or*
       b. if the author is not named in the book, its title alone, *or*
       c. if author and title are inappropriate or insufficient for identification, a suitable substitute for the title; *and*
   2.2 a. which works by a particular author *and*
       b. which editions of a particular work are in the library.

3. STRUCTURE OF THE CATALOGUE
   To discharge these functions the catalogue should contain
   3.1 at least one entry for each book catalogued, *and*
   3.2 more than one entry relating to any book, whenever this is necessary in the interests of the user or because of the characteristics of the book. . . .

1

4. KINDS OF ENTRY
Entries may be of the following kinds: main entries, added entries, and references. . . .

5. USE OF MULTIPLE ENTRIES
The two functions of the catalogue (see 2.1 and 2.2) are most effectively discharged by
5.1 an entry for each book under a heading derived from the author's name or from the title as printed in the book, *and*
5.2 when variant forms of the author's name or of the title occur, an entry for each book under a *uniform heading,* consisting of one particular form of the author's name or one particular title . . . *and*
5.3 appropriate added entries and/or references.

6. FUNCTION OF DIFFERENT KINDS OF ENTRY
6.1 The *main entry* for works entered under authors' names should normally be made under a *uniform heading.* The main entry for works entered under title may be *either* under the title as printed in the book, with an added entry under a uniform title, *or* under a uniform title, with added entries . . . under the other titles. . . .
6.4 *Added entries* . . . should also be made under the names of joint-authors, collaborators, etc., and under the titles of works having their main entry under an author's name, when the title is an important alternative means of identification.

7. CHOICE OF UNIFORM HEADING
The *uniform heading* should normally be the most frequently used name (or form of name) or title appearing in editions of the works catalogued or in references to them by accepted authorities. . . .

8. SINGLE PERSONAL AUTHOR
8.1 The main entry for every edition of a work ascertained to be by a single personal author should be made under the author's name. . . .

9. ENTRY UNDER CORPORATE BODIES
9.1 The main entry for a work should be made under the name of a *corporate body* (i.e., any institution, organized body or assembly of persons known by a corporate or collective name)
9.11 when the work is by its nature necessarily the expression of the collective thought or activity of the corporate body . . . *or*
9.12 when the wording of the title or title-page, taken in conjunction with the nature of the work, clearly implies that the corporate body is collectively responsible for the content of the work. . . .

9.4 The *uniform heading* for works entered under the name of a corporate body should be the name by which the body is most frequently identified in its publications, *except that* . . .

    9.44 for states and other territorial authorities the uniform heading should be the currently used form of the name of the territory concerned in the language best adapted to the needs of the users of the catalogue. . . .

9.5 Constitutions, laws and treaties, and certain other works having similar characteristics, should be entered under the name of the appropriate state or other territorial authority, with formal or conventional titles indicating the nature of the material. . . .

9.6 A work of a corporate body which is subordinate to a superior body should be entered under the name of the subordinate body [i.e., as an independent entity] *except that*

    9.61 if this name itself implies subordination . . . or is insufficient to identify the subordinate body, the heading should be the name of the superior body with the name of the subordinate body as a subheading. . . .

10. MULTIPLE AUTHORSHIP

When two or more authors shared in the creation of a work,

10.1 if one author is represented in the book as the *principal author* . . . the *main entry* for the work should be made under [this] name. . . .

10.2 if no author is represented as the principal author, the *main entry* should be made under

    10.21 the *author named first on the title-page,* if the number of authors is two or three, *added entries* being made under the name(s) of the other author(s);

    10.22 the *title of the work,* if the number of authors is more than three, *added entries* being made under the author named first in the book. . . .

10.3 Collections

The main entry for a collection consisting of independent works or parts of works by different authors should be made

    10.31 under the title of the collection, if it has a collective title;

    10.32 under the name of the author, or under the title, of the first work in the collection, if there is no collective title. . . .

11. WORKS ENTERED UNDER TITLE

11.1 Works having their main entry under the title are

    11.11 works whose authors have not been ascertained;

    11.12 works by more than three authors, none of whom is principal author (see 10.22);

    11.13 collections of independent works or parts of works, by different authors, published with a collective title;

11.14 works (including serials and periodicals) known primarily or conventionally by title rather than by the name
of the author.

11.2 An added entry . . . should be made under the title for
11.21 anonymous editions of works whose authors have been
ascertained;
11.22 works having their main entry under the name of the
author, when the title is an important alternative means
of identification. . . .

11.5 When a serial publication is issued successively under different titles, a main entry should be made under each title for the
series of issues bearing that title, with an indication of at least
the immediately preceding and succeeding titles.

12. ENTRY WORD FOR PERSONAL NAMES
When the name of a personal author consists of several words, the
choice of entry word is determined so far as possible by agreed
usage in the . . . language which he generally uses.

AACR1, although it was based on the Paris Principles, suffered from a
number of deficiencies that were only partially resolved through a series of
revisions in the years between 1967 and the publication of *AACR2*. In the
first place, although, as its name suggests, *AACR1* was intended to be a
joint British-American code, one that would unify cataloging practice
throughout the English-speaking world, this was never actually achieved.
Supported by the Association of Research Libraries, the North American
contingent of the *AACR1* code committee decided on two special exceptions
to the principle of entry of a corporate body under the name by which it
chooses to identify itself (Paris Principles 9.4). Local churches and "certain
other corporate bodies" (i.e., educational institutions, libraries, galleries,
museums, agricultural experiment stations, airports, botanical and zoolog-
ical gardens, and hospitals) were, under very carefully specified conditions,
to be entered under place (*AACR1* 98 and 99). The British representatives
on the code committee refused to accept this partial return to ALA 1949
cataloging rules; they also rejected *AACR1* 23, 24, and 25 (court rules and
rules for treaties). *AACR1* was finally issued in two versions, a *North American Text* and a *British Text*.

Almost as serious, from the point of view of international unification
of cataloging practice, was the refusal of the Anglo-American code makers
to accept the majority position on Paris Principle 10.3, which called for the
entry of a collection under title when such a work had a collective title. The
Anglo-American preference was for entry under compiler when such a
name was openly expressed; *AACR1* 4 and 5 at first reflected this position.
A change was made in the rule in 1975 (*CSB* 112, winter 1975, p. 1–8) to
bring Anglo-American practice into conformity with Paris Principle 10.3.
The lamentable exceptions for entry under place of *AACR1* 98 and 99 were
eliminated by *CSB* 109 (May 1974), p. 3–4.

A continuing problem even after the adoption of *AACR1* was the Library of Congress's policy of superimposition. Under superimposition,

headings established by the Library of Congress before *AACR1* went into effect continued to be used for current cataloging, even though these headings had not been formulated according to provisions of the 1967 code. This led to a mixture of headings, some cataloged by "old" and some by "new" rules. Librarians who wished to take advantage of Library of Congress cataloging in their own libraries had to be familiar with ALA 1949 rules, at least to the extent of understanding how ALA 1949 differed from *AACR1*, so that they could interpret Library of Congress headings and assist patrons in their use of the library's catalog. This problem was partially solved by LC's decision to "de-superimpose" certain headings, as announced in *CSB* 106 (May 1973), p. 2–3.[2]

Clearly it was time for an end to ad hoc patchwork, time for a rethinking of the entire structure of the code. The second edition of the *Anglo-American Cataloguing Rules* had its genesis in a meeting of cataloging experts held in March 1974, at which time it was agreed that a new edition of the cataloging code was needed. The Joint Steering Committee for Revision of AACR (JSC), composed of representatives from each of the five bodies most directly affected by the code—the American Library Association, the Library of Congress, the (British) Library Association, the British Library, and the Canadian Committee on Cataloguing—was set up at this meeting (the Australian Committee on Cataloguing has since joined the JSC). Direct implementation of code revision was to be handled by ALA's RTSD Catalog Code Revision Committee (CCRC), the Canadian Committee on Cataloguing, and the Library Association/British Library Committee on Revision of AACR.

The charge to these groups was fourfold: (1) The new code was to incorporate all changes authorized since the appearance of *AACR1*; (2) like the first edition, *AACR2* was to conform to the Paris Principles governing choice of access points and form of heading; (3) rules for bibliographic description were to be based on *International Standard Bibliographic Description for Monographs (ISBD(M))*; and (4) committee members were to keep in mind developments in machine processing of catalog records that might affect cataloging.[3]

The committees set about almost immediately. In the three years that followed, members spent countless hours in careful study and revision of each part of the 1967 *AACR1*. The Paris Principles and *AACR1* were oriented firmly in the concept of the library as a collection of books. Rules for entry and heading did not mention nonprint library materials; *AACR1* Part III, rules for descriptive cataloging of nonbook materials, was a hodgepodge of confusing rules based on format of material rather than type of bibliographic problem. The new rules would be based on principles applicable to all types of library materials, both book and nonbook alike. In 1976, the IFLA Working Group on International Standard Bibliographic Description (General) (ISBD(G)) assigned Michael Gorman to work out a framework for the descriptive cataloging of all types of library materials. This pattern, which was based on the 1974 *ISBD(M)*, served as the basis of *AACR2* Part I, the rules for descriptive cataloging.

The 1988 revision and the 1993 amendments to the *Anglo-American Cataloguing Rules* include all rule revisions and modifications made by the Joint

Steering Committee during the nearly two decades since the first appearance of *AACR2*. Despite these changes, the basic premises that governed *AACR2* remain the same. The 1988 revision and 1993 amendments do not constitute a new edition (cf. *AACR2R* p. xiv).

AACR2R Part I begins with a general chapter that sets out rules applying to all types of library materials, both print and nonprint. This general chapter is an effort to approach the ideal enunciated by Eric Hunter in 1975 at the Anglo-Nordic Seminar on the Revision and International Use of AACR held in York, England. "What is really required," said Hunter, "is one International Standard Bibliographic Description which will cover all media and within which the basis of main entry will be title."[4]

While the present code is still based on the concept of main entry under the person or body responsible for the intellectual or artistic content of the item, it is obvious that the shift toward increasing use of title main entry for catalog records will continue. Under *AACR Chapter 6* (1974), 134D1 alternative rule, the cataloger could, under certain conditions, omit the author statement in the body of the entry. *AACR2R* virtually eliminates this option. Under no circumstances (unless the cataloger chooses to adopt "first level" descriptive cataloging; see *AACR2R* 1.0D1) will the statement of responsibility be omitted, as long as it appears "prominently" in the item (*AACR2R* 1.1F1). This, in effect, makes the catalog entry created according to *AACR2R* Part I rules a possible title unit entry, to which various access points may be added, with no distinction as to "main" and "added" entries. As a matter of fact, this was an option that *AACR2* Part II, chapter 21, "Choice of Access Points," originally allowed. However, this option was dropped in the final version of *AACR2*, chiefly because of the firm grounding of the Paris Principles in the principle of main entry and authorship responsibility, and the charge of the *AACR2* Joint Steering Committee to adhere to the Paris Principles.

AACR2R chapter 1, as already mentioned, deals with general principles of bibliographic description applicable to all kinds of library materials. Following this general chapter is a series of chapters, each dealing with a special form of library material and special rules to be applied in addition to the general rules. These special chapters refer to applicable rules in the general chapter whenever possible rather than repeating general principles already given. Each special chapter is arranged, like chapter 1, in the following order:

1. Rules for sources of information: the part of the work being cataloged that is to be preferred in transcribing the catalog entry
2. Punctuation: prescribed punctuation that must be used between areas and elements of the catalog entry
3. Organization of the description: rules governing the transcription of each of the following:
   a. Title and statement of responsibility area
   b. Edition area
   c. Material (or type of publication) specific details (used only when cataloging cartographic materials, music, computer files, and serials)

   d. Publication, distribution, etc., area
   e. Physical description area
   f. Series area
   g. Note area
   h. Standard number and terms of availability area

The 1967 *AACR1* was criticized on the international level for a number of reasons. First, it came under fire for its deviations from the Paris Principles, including too broad a concept of personal authorship, for an unacceptable approach to corporate authorship, and for an unacceptable concept of entry of serials under corporate body.[5] Some cataloging experts, among them Michael Gorman, criticized *AACR1* for its emphasis on the concept of main entry, which Gorman called "a relic of outdated technology" made obsolete by computer-based catalogs with multiple access points for all works contained in the database.[6] Part II of *AACR2R*, rules for access points and headings, addresses itself to these problems, and in some instances makes substantive and worthwhile contributions toward solving them.

Rules for form of name of personal author in *AACR2* are fundamentally the same as in *AACR1*, which followed the guidelines of the Paris Principles in most cases. However, *AACR1* rules for both form and choice of entry for corporate bodies were not considered satisfactory. *AACR2* rules for entry under corporate body show the influence of Eva Verona's definitive study of corporate bodies, in limiting main entry under corporate heading to works of an administrative nature dealing with the corporate body, its staff, its resources, or official statements recording the collective thought or activity of the body.[7] Entry under government heading is limited to administrative regulations, decrees, laws, court rules, legislative hearings, treaties, charters, and constitutions.

Even before its first publication in 1978, *AACR2* was criticized by some cataloging experts as being too traditional in its approach, too firmly rooted in the premachine-processing era of bibliographic control. It is possible that it may, indeed, be the last catalog code based on the concept of main entry; it may be an interim code on the way to a truly revolutionary concept of computer-oriented bibliographical control. However, as it stands, it still represents a great step forward toward the ideal of universal bibliographic exchange of cataloging data.

Machine-Readable Cataloging (MARC)

All the cataloging examples in this edition of the *Handbook* are given in machine-readable, or MARC, format. When the application of the computer to library tasks began in the early 1960s, cataloging was one of the obvious candidates for automation. The computer could not simply digest a catalog record in card format, however, and still produce a sensible product; furthermore, the possibilities of access to computerized records far surpassed access to the traditional card catalog, but only if the records were properly coded so that the machine could distinguish, for example, between a title and an author, or between a series and a subject heading. Thus various systems of encoding bibliographic data have grown up around the world.

In addition to improved access to the records, computerization of cataloging has also opened the possibility of shared cataloging. Large international databases (for example, RLIN and OCLC) have appeared, containing catalog records contributed by member libraries for most of the world's current publishing and a large percentage of earlier works. Such a project requires standardization of the computerized cataloging format used by the various libraries. Currently there is no single internationally accepted format, but efforts are underway for the reconciliation of formats so that the goal of easily exchangeable cataloging records around the world can be realized. The mechanism for worldwide transmission of data, the Internet, is already in place and has become a catalyst for more serious efforts at standardization than have taken place in the past.

The Library of Congress was one of the first organizations to develop a machine-readable format for catalog records, and this format has evolved into what is currently called "USMARC." USMARC is used almost universally throughout the United States and in many other countries in the world. Canada and the United Kingdom have their own, similar, versions, CAN/MARC and UKMARC, and international efforts to reconcile the three are underway. The resulting international MARC, or "IMARC," is expected within the next several years and should improve the ease of information exchange in the Anglo-American cataloging world.

All examples in this *Handbook* are coded in USMARC format, henceforth referred to simply as "MARC." Details about the coding of the descriptive portion of the catalog record will be found in chapter 1; an explanation of the coding of access points (main and added entries) is given in chapter 14. MARC authorities format is described in chapters 15, 17, and 18. A general introduction follows.

The MARC catalog record is divided into "fields," which in turn are divided into "subfields." These correspond to various aspects of the *AACR2R* catalog record. The fields are all numbered with a three-digit numeric "tag." Although not all numbers are used, there is a theoretical possibility of up to 999 fields (from 001 to 999). Following the field tag in the MARC record are two numeric digits called "indicators." Each of these may either be blank or may contain a number, which normally instructs the machine to manipulate the data in some way (e.g., for display or indexing purposes). Following the indicators are the subfields, which contain the actual cataloging data. Each subfield is preceded by a delimiter mark (in this *Handbook* shown by a double dagger, "‡") and a single letter or number, which tells what type of subfield is being used. This system can obviously become extremely complex, but it is organized in a logical fashion and incorporates a system of mnemonics that are very helpful.

(In the following discussion, the letter *X* in a field tag represents any number from 0 to 9. For example, 1XX can represent 100, 110, 130, etc.; X11 can represent 111, 711, 811, etc.)

The theoretically possible 999 MARC tags are divided into groups of 100.

0XX fields comprise mainly control fields and record various types of identification and classification numbers. A common field from this group found in this *Handbook* is the 020 field, where the International Standard Book Number (ISBN) is recorded (see figure 1-1).

1XX fields record the main entry, including personal authors, corporate names, meeting names, and uniform titles. Because there may only be one main entry per catalog record, there will never be more than one 1XX field in a record.

2XX fields mainly contain title information. The most common of these are the 245 field, the title and statement of responsibility, and the 246 field, where variations on the title are recorded. Another 2XX field, not containing title information, is the 260 field, where imprint information is recorded (see figure 1-1).

3XX fields, which may be repeated, contain the physical description of the item (see figure 1-1, 300 field).

4XX fields record series statements as found on the item; if the series has been established differently from that given on the item, the 4XX field is combined with an 8XX field (see discussion in this *Handbook* at *AACR2R* 1.6 and figure 1-40).

5XX fields contain various types of notes (see figure 1-1).

6XX fields contain subject headings. Because *AACR2R* does not address subject access, these fields are not as a rule found in the cataloging examples in this *Handbook*.

7XX fields contain added access points to the record, which may include headings for coauthors, illustrators, translators, etc.

8XX fields contain series added entries (see 4XX, above).

9XX fields are locally defined fields; each library may define these as it wishes in accord with its own policies. The number 9 in other positions, also, means locally defined: X9X fields (e.g., 590) are reserved for local use as well.

In addition to the division of the 999 numbers into ten blocks, certain mnemonic devices exist that cross these blocks. In the 1XX, 4XX, 6XX, 7XX, and 8XX fields, the second and third digits of the tag have parallel meanings. The most common of these used in this *Handbook* follow:

X00 signifies a personal name. For example, the 100 field contains a main entry heading that is a personal name (see figure 1-1).

X10 signifies a corporate name. For example, the 710 field contains an added entry heading that is a corporate name (see figure 1-11).

X11 signifies a meeting or conference name. A 111 field contains a main entry that is the name of a conference or meeting (see figure 1-11).

X30 signifies a uniform title not linked to an author (see figure 1-19 for a uniform title as main entry).

The MARC record also includes numerous fields that are not explained in this *Handbook*. Only MARC fields that contain data called for by *AACR2R* are included (the figures, therefore, contain no "fixed fields").[8]

A Note on Headings Used in This Handbook

The first thirteen chapters of *AACR2R* and this *Handbook* treat the rules for the "descriptive" cataloging of the item. Rules for access points (main and added entries) aside from subject headings (which are not considered in *AACR2R*) are found in chapters 21–25 of *AACR2R* and are discussed in chapters 14–18 of the *Handbook*. The examples throughout the *Handbook*, however, are fully cataloged, including both the descriptive portion of the record and the access points. It is expected that the user will consult both parts of the *Handbook* (and, indeed, *AACR2R*) in order to fully understand the cataloging of the examples. In addition, the index should be consulted under "MARC fields" for fields not explained with a particular figure. All added access points have been checked against the National Authority File as it appeared at the time of publication; if found, the form there has been used in the *Handbook*. If not found, the heading has been formulated using the item cataloged as its source. On the concept of "authority" and the National Authority File, see *Handbook* chapters 15, 17, and 18.

NOTES

1. The Paris Principles have been reprinted many times. The definitive text dealing with the Paris Principles is International Conference on Cataloguing Principles, Paris, 1961, *Statement of Principles,* annotated edition with commentary and examples by Eva Verona (London: IFLA Committee on Cataloguing, 1971).
2. Superimposition was abandoned by the Library of Congress in 1981 with the freezing of its existing catalog. All new headings are now established according to *AACR2R,* regardless of former practice.
3. For an excellent summary of the background of *AACR2,* see Carol R. Kelm, "The Historical Development of the Second Edition of the Anglo-American Cataloging Rules," *LRTS* 22 (winter 1978): 22–29.
4. "Anglo-Nordic Seminar on the Revision and International Use of AACR, York, 1975," *Catalogue & Index* 37 (summer 1975): 8.
5. Ibid., p. 2.
6. "Rules for Entry and Heading," *Library Trends* 25 (Jan. 1977): 596.
7. *Corporate Headings* (London: IFLA Committee on Cataloguing, 1975).
8. For complete information on USMARC coding, see the latest edition of *USMARC Format for Bibliographic Data, Including Guidelines for Content Designation* (Washington, D.C.: Cataloging Distribution Service, Library of Congress), or the USMARC home page, on the World Wide Web at http://lcweb.loc.gov/marc/marc.html. Because it has not yet been implemented by the Library of Congress, RLIN, or OCLC, the recent elimination of first indicator "2" (multiple surname) in X00 fields and its replacement by "1" have not been followed in this *Handbook*.

GENERAL INFORMATION

Part I of the *Anglo-American Cataloguing Rules* deals with descriptive cataloging: the identification and description of a work in such a fashion that it can be distinguished from all other works and from other editions of the same work. As Paul Dunkin put it, this is the part of the catalog entry that tells what the work looks like—rather than who is responsible for it.[1] Rules in *AACR2R* Part II tell the cataloger how to choose the person or corporate body chiefly responsible for the intellectual content of the work described by rules in *AACR2R* Part I. They also tell the cataloger how to construct a heading for the "main entry" thus chosen, as well as correct format for added entries.

In the example shown in figure 1-1, the 100 field of the entry (Mather, Paul D.) is called the main entry.[2] The main entry is always found in the 1XX field of the MARC record unless the title is the main entry. The choice of Mather as main entry rather than, for instance, the title, is governed by *AACR2R* Part II, chapter 21. *AACR2R* chapter 22, "Headings for Persons," gives rules for the form in which this entry must appear. Part I includes rules for everything else in the above example. Subject headings and classification, which are outside the province of the *Anglo-American Cataloguing Rules*, will not be included in cataloging samples in this *Handbook*.

As mentioned in the introduction, the descriptive cataloging rules of Part I are based on *International Standard Bibliographic Description (ISBD)*. This is an internationally agreed upon framework for cataloging rules for description that has established essential items of information that must appear in the entry, the order in which these items will be given, and a system of arbitrary punctuation that must be used. The purpose of this standardized format is "to facilitate the international exchange of bibliographic information, whether in written or machine-readable form . . . [and to] permit quick identification of the elements [of a catalog entry] even by the catalog user who is totally unfamiliar with the language of the description."[3]

Figure 1-1.   A simple catalog entry

```
020      ‡a 0160363918
100 1    ‡a Mather, Paul D., ‡d 1938-
245 10   ‡a M.I.A. : ‡b accounting for the missing in Southeast Asia / ‡c Paul D. Mather.
246 3    ‡a MIA
260      ‡a Washington, DC : ‡b National Defense University Press, ‡c 1994.
300      ‡a xxiii, 207 p. : ‡b ill., map ; ‡c 23 cm.
500      ‡a Includes index.
```

Title page   M.I.A.
                                          Accounting for
                                            the Missing
                                          in Southeast Asia

                                          Paul D. Mather

                                               1994
                                National Defense University Press
                                          Washington, DC

1.0B. Organization of the description

Elements to be included in the descriptive part of the catalog entry are divided into areas (an area is a major section of the *ISBD*). If these appear in the item being cataloged, they must be transcribed in the following order:

1. Title and statement of responsibility area. This will be discussed in detail under *AACR2R* 1.1. This area appears in the MARC 245 field.
2. Edition area. To be discussed under *AACR2R* 1.2. This area appears in the MARC 250 field.
3. Material (or type of publication) specific details area. This area is used only with cartographic materials (see discussion under *AACR2R* chapter 3), music (see discussion under *AACR2R* chapter 5), computer files (see discussion under *AACR2R* chapter 9), and serials (see discussion under *AACR2R* chapter 12).
4. Publication, distribution, etc., area. To be discussed under *AACR2R* 1.4. This area appears in the MARC 260 field.
5. Physical description area. To be discussed under *AACR2R* 1.5. This area appears in the MARC 300 field.
6. Series area. To be discussed under *AACR2R* 1.6. This area appears in the MARC 440, 490, or 8XX field.
7. Note area. To be discussed under *AACR2R* 1.7. This area appears in MARC 5XX fields.
8. Standard number and terms of availability area. This is the last area in the *AACR2R* catalog entry, but appears early in the MARC record (see discussion under *AACR2R* 1.8 for details). This area appears in the MARC 020 or 022 field.

1.0C. Punctuation

In the card format prescribed by *AACR2R*, except for the first area, each area is preceded by a full stop (period) - space - dash - space (. --). (In typing, a dash consists of two hyphens: --.) This prescribed punctuation is omitted only when the next area is paragraphed. North American cataloging practice calls for a new paragraph at the beginning of the physical description area and at the beginning of each note in the note area as well as the standard number and terms of availability area. Do not use full stop - space - dash - space to separate these areas from those preceding them.

Except for the full stop at the end of an area, punctuation and formatting between areas is not entered as a part of the MARC record.

Elements within each of the areas also have prescribed punctuation. This punctuation will be included in the detailed discussion of each area that follows (1.1 through 1.8).

1.0D. Levels of detail in the description

AACR2R offers a number of options. One of these allows the cataloger to choose among three levels of detail in cataloging description.

1.0D1. First-level description. The first level is brief cataloging. The cataloger is to include only the title proper, omitting other title information. The statement of responsibility may also be omitted if it is the same as the main entry heading (see *Handbook* at 1.1 for a discussion and explanation of the title and statement of responsibility area). The edition statement is included, but not an accompanying statement of responsibility (see *Handbook* at 1.2). A material (or type of publication) specific details statement is included if appropriate. Publication data include only the name of the first publisher and the date of publication. Pagination (for books), notes, and standard number, if available, complete the entry. First-level description would probably be sufficient to identify items in a small library collection (see figure 1-2a).

1.0D2. Second-level description. The second level includes all of the information given in level 1 cataloging. In addition, the cataloger will include general material designation (1.1C) after the title proper if the library has decided to use it for this type of library material. Parallel titles (1.1D) and other title information (1.1E) will be included. They will be followed by all pertinent statements of responsibility (1.1F). The edition statement

Figure 1-2a.   First-level description

```
020        ‡a 9004103066 (alk. paper)
100 1      ‡a Smith, P. A. ‡q (Paul Allan)
245 10     ‡a Rhetoric and redaction in Trito-Isaiah.
260        ‡b E.J. Brill, ‡c 1995.
300        ‡a 228 p.
504        ‡a Includes bibliographical references (p. [208]-217) and indexes.
```

together with its first statement of responsibility is included if it is found in the work (1.2). First place, first publisher, and date of publication are given (1.4). The physical description area will include all items specified in applicable rules (1.5) except that accompanying material, if any, will not be given as a part of this area. The series statement is recorded (1.6). Notes and standard number are included as appropriate. This level might appropriately be used in medium-sized libraries (see figure 1-2b).

The Library of Congress has stated that most of its cataloging will be at the second level, "although the implementation of certain options automatically means that the third level has been achieved" (*Cataloging Service Bulletin* [hereinafter *CSB*] 13, summer 1981, p. 4). The National Library of Canada also catalogs at the second level "for the most part . . . with supplementary data added as required" (Lynne C. Howarth, comp., *AACR2 Decisions and Rule Interpretations*, 6th ed. [1994] [hereinafter "Howarth"], at 1.0D).

1.0D3. Third-level description. The third level includes all the rules applicable to the item being cataloged. Third-level description is appropriate to large libraries and research collections (see figure 1-2c).

No matter which of the three levels of description the cataloger decides to use, choice of access points for main entry and form of headings will be the same (see *AACR2R* Part II). For this reason, it is quite feasible to interfile any or all of the different levels of description into one catalog. Thus, libraries that use LC cataloging data can continue to do so, even though they may decide to use one of the simpler levels for original cataloging done in the home library.

1.0E. Language and script of the description

The Library of Congress has amplified provisions of this rule in regard to transcription of the letters u/v, uu, or vv/w in Latin works published after 1800. When these letters are used without regard to their vocalic value (e.g., v is used for u medially, etc.), the cataloger will transcribe

v for consonants (vox)

u for vowels (historiarum)

w for consonantal uu or vv.

I and j should be transcribed as they appear (*Library of Congress Rule Interpretations* [hereinafter *LCRI*], May 1995) (see figure 1-3).

1.1. TITLE AND STATEMENT OF RESPONSIBILITY AREA

As previously mentioned, the first cataloging area is called the title and statement of responsibility area. General rules for the transcription of this area are included in *AACR2R* 1.1, excluding rules for prescribed punctuation, which are covered in section 1.0C.

Figure 1-2b.   Second-level description

```
020        ‡a 9004103066 (alk. paper)
100 1      ‡a Smith, P. A. ‡q (Paul Allan)
245 10     ‡a Rhetoric and redaction in Trito-Isaiah : ‡b the structure, growth, and authorship of
           Isaiah 56-66 / ‡c by P.A. Smith.
260        ‡a Leiden : ‡b E.J. Brill, ‡c 1995.
300        ‡a xi, 228 p. ; ‡c 25 cm.
440  0     ‡a Supplements to Vetus Testamentum, ‡x 0083-5889 ; ‡v v. 62
504        ‡a Includes bibliographical references (p. [208]-217) and indexes.
```

Figure 1-2c.   Third-level description

```
020        ‡a 9004103066 (alk. paper)
100 1      ‡a Smith, P. A. ‡q (Paul Allan)
245 10     ‡a Rhetoric and redaction in Trito-Isaiah : ‡b the structure, growth, and authorship of
           Isaiah 56-66 / ‡c by P.A. Smith.
260        ‡a Leiden ; ‡a New York : ‡b E.J. Brill, ‡c 1995.
300        ‡a xi, 228 p. ; ‡c 25 cm.
440  0     ‡a Supplements to Vetus Testamentum, ‡x 0083-5889 ; ‡v v. 62
504        ‡a Includes bibliographical references (p. [208]-217) and indexes.
```

Title page   Rhetoric and Redaction in Trito-Isaiah
                   The Structure, Growth and Authorship of Isaiah 55-66
                                        by
                                    P.A. Smith
                                    E.J. Brill
                              Leiden New York Köln
                                      1995

Series title page

                                  Supplements
                                       to
                                Vetus Testamentum
                                   Edited by
                          the Board of the Quarterly
                                 Volume LXII

1.1A2. Sources of information. In general, the cataloger transcribes what he or she sees, in the order in which it appears on the title page or other chief source of information (for nonbook materials). However, if the elements of this area are not in prescribed order on the title page, they are transposed to bring them into correct order, which must be as follows: title

Figure 1-3.   Transcription of u/v

```
020       ‡a 0842523294 (pbk. : alk. paper)
100 1     ‡a Angerhofer, Paul J., ‡d 1960-
245 10    ‡a In aedibus Aldi : ‡b the legacy of Aldus Manutius and his press / ‡c Paul J. Angerhofer,
          Mary Ann Addy Maxwell, Robert L. Maxwell ; with binding descriptions by Pamela
          Barrios.
260       ‡a Provo, Utah : ‡b Friends of the Harold B. Lee Library, Brigham Young University,
          ‡c 1995.
300       ‡a ix, 172 p. : ‡b ill., maps ; ‡c 28 cm.
500       ‡a Catalog to accompany an exhibition at the Harold B. Lee Library.
504       ‡a Includes bibliographical references (p. 129-135) and indexes.
700 1     ‡a Maxwell, Mary Ann Addy, ‡d 1960-
700 1     ‡a Maxwell, Robert L., ‡d 1957-
700 1     ‡a Barrios, Pamela.
710 2     ‡a Harold B. Lee Library.
```

Title page	IN
	The Legacy of
	AEDIBVS
	Aldus Manutius
	ALDI
	and His Press
	Paul J. Angerhofer
	Mary Ann Addy Maxwell
	Robert L. Maxwell
	with binding descriptions by Pamela Barrios
	Friends of the Harold B. Lee Library
	Brigham Young University
	Provo, Utah
	1995

/ statement of responsibility (see figure 1-4). See also *AACR2R* 1.1F3, which specifies transposing a statement of responsibility to its proper position "unless it is an integral part of the title proper."

The title and statement of responsibility area is to be transcribed from the appropriate source as given in chapters following chapter 1 exactly as to wording and spelling but not necessarily as to capitalization and punctuation, which follow conventional library rules. For titles in the English language, capitalize the first word of the title and any proper names thereafter. Do not omit any words. Except where specifically authorized, do not add any words. Do not abbreviate any words in the title and statement of responsibility area.

As seen in the example in figure 1-5, the title proper is separated from other titles by space - colon - space. The entire title element (title proper and other titles) is separated from the statement of responsibility by space - slash - space.

This area appears in the 245 field of the MARC record. The first indicator determines the tracing of the title. Generally, if the title is also the

Figure 1-4.   Title and statement of responsibility area—transposition of elements from title page

```
100 1     ‡a Lander, Jeannette, ‡d 1931-
245 14    ‡a Ein Spatz in der Hand-- : ‡b Sachgeschichten / ‡c Jeannette Lander.
250       ‡a 1. Aufl.
260       ‡a Frankfurt am Main : ‡b Insel, ‡c 1973.
300       ‡a 107 p. ; ‡c 20 cm.
```

> **Title page**
>
> Jeannette Lander
> Ein Spatz in der Hand . . .
> Sachgeschichten
>
> Insel

Figure 1-5.   Title and statement of responsibility area

```
020       ‡a 0684800039
100 1     ‡a Dunning, John, ‡d 1942-
245 14    ‡a The bookman's wake : ‡b a mystery with Cliff Janeway / ‡c John Dunning.
260       ‡a New York : ‡b Scribner, ‡c c1995.
300       ‡a 351 p. ; ‡c 25 cm.
```

> **Title page**
>
> The Bookman's Wake
> A Mystery with Cliff Janeway
>
> John Dunning
>
> Scribner
> New York London Toronto Sydney Tokyo Singapore

main entry (i.e., there is no 1XX field), this indicator is "0." Otherwise, it normally is "1." The second indicator gives the number of "nonfiling characters" (i.e., the number of characters that the machine must skip in order for the title to file properly in the system). Thus, in figure 1-5, in order for the system to file on the word "bookman's" rather than "The," this indicator is coded "4." Initial articles are normally to be ignored in filing (unless, for example, they are part of a proper name); in languages that have case, they are ignored for filing purposes whether or not they are in the nominative case (e.g., "dem" and "des" are ignored in German) (see *CSB* 52, spring 1991, p. 26).

Field 245 is, in general, divided into three subfields. Subfield ‡a contains the title proper and any alternative titles. Subfield ‡b contains the remainder of the title (e.g., parallel titles or other title information). The statement of responsibility is contained in subfield ‡c (see figures 1-4 and

1-5). Field 245 always ends with a full stop, even if the recorded data end with a parenthesis or bracket (see figure 1-6).

1.1B. Title proper

Transcribe the words of the title proper (main title) exactly as they appear on the work. Except for extremely long titles (see 1.1B4), do not omit any words. Except when correcting an inaccuracy (see 1.0F), do not add any words. Capitalization follows normal usage for the language of the title. Figure 1-4 is capitalized according to German-language practice, which calls for the capitalization of the first word of the title and all nouns thereafter. English-language titles are not capitalized according to usual citation practice, as they would be listed in a bibliography. When transcribing the title of a work in the English language, capitalize the first word and all proper names thereafter. Figures 1-1, 1-2, and 1-5 illustrate standard cataloging practice for capitalization (see *AACR2R* Appendix A for detailed rules).

Punctuation between elements (i.e., title proper, parallel title, other title information, and statement of responsibility) is prescribed (1.1A1). Within the title proper, however, punctuation other than the prescribed marks may generally be transcribed from the source or added as necessary to the transcription. For an exception, note that according to 1.1B1 both ellipses (. . .) and square brackets ([ ]) if present within the title proper must be replaced (see figure 1-4). Interestingly, one mark of more or less normal punctuation is prescribed in 1.1B9, which requires a full stop (.) to separate

Figure 1-6.   Prescribed punctuation—title transcription ending in parenthesis

```
020      ‡a 0838900844
245 02   ‡a A biographical directory of librarians in the United States and Canada : ‡b (formerly
         Who's who in library service).
250      ‡a 5th ed. / ‡b Lee Ash, editor ; B. A. Uhlendorf, associate editor.
260      ‡a Chicago : ‡b American Library Association, ‡c 1970.
300      ‡a xviii, 1250 p. ; ‡c 26 cm.
500      ‡a "Sponsored by the Council of National Library Associations"--Publisher's foreword.
500      ‡a First-4th ed. published under title: Who's who in library service.
700 1    ‡a Ash, Lee.
700 1    ‡a Uhlendorf, Bernhard A. ‡q (Bernhard Alexander), ‡d 1893-
710 2    ‡a Council of National Library Associations.
740 0    ‡a Who's who in library service.
```

Title page   (formerly Who's Who in Library Service)
A Biographical Directory of Librarians
in the United States and Canada
Fifth Edition
Lee Ash, Editor
B.A. Uhlendorf, Associate Editor
American Library Association
Chicago 1970

Figure 1-7.   Title proper

```
020       ‡a 0689301286
100 1     ‡a Anderson, Mary, ‡d 1929-
245 10    ‡a I'm nobody! Who are you? / ‡c Mary Anderson.
250       ‡a 1st ed.
260       ‡a New York : ‡b Atheneum, ‡c 1974.
300       ‡a 215 p. ; ‡c 22 cm.
```

Title page	
	I'm Nobody!
	Who Are You?
	Mary Anderson
	Atheneum
	1974 New York

the parts of certain titles proper. The full stop, as well as any other mark of normal punctuation retained within the title proper, is given with normal spacing (i.e., no space preceding). The comma represents the most frequent example of this phenomenon, as in the cases of alternative titles or such titles as the following: *Herblock, his influence on cartoon art.*

An exclamation point (!) or a question mark (?) occurring as part of a title proper will be retained. Sometimes, as in figure 1-7, the title proper consists of two parts separated by such punctuation, which will be transcribed. Note that standard prescribed punctuation separates the title proper from the following element, even though this results in double punctuation.

An alternative title (a second title introduced by "or" or the equivalent in another language, e.g., *Hans Brinker, or, The silver skates*) is part of the title proper. It is punctuated and capitalized as shown in figure 1-8.

The entire title proper, including an alternative title, is recorded in subfield ‡a of the 245 field in the MARC record.

1.1B2. Transcribe the title proper just as it appears in the chief source of information. If the name of the author, the publisher, etc., appears as an integral part of the title (not simply out of prescribed order, as with figure 1-4), transcribe it as shown in figure 1-9.

Note the capitalization in figure 1-9. *AACR2R* Appendix A.4A1 (1993 amendments) calls for the capitalization of the first word of a title proper, alternative title, parallel title, or quoted title (a title embedded within other text). If a title proper begins with the author's name in a possessive case (in any language), the cataloger must decide whether the proper name is the first word of the title (as, for example, *Shepherd's historical atlas*), or whether the name introduces a quoted title (e.g., *Milton's Paradise lost*) (see the examples in *AACR2R* Appendix A.4A1 and those given with *AACR2R* 1.1B2).

1.1B3. The title proper is usually different from the name of the person or body responsible for the item, but this is not always the case, as seen in

Figure 1-8.   Title proper includes alternative title

```
100 0    ‡a Old Sleuth, ‡d 1839?-1898.
245 10   ‡a Detective Dale, or, Conflicting testimonies : ‡b a weird detective experience / ‡c by
         Old Sleuth.
246 30   ‡a Detective Dale
246 30   ‡a Conflicting testimonies
260      ‡a New York : ‡b J.S. Ogilvie Pub. Co., ‡c c1898.
300      ‡a 84 p. ; ‡c 18 cm.
440  0   ‡a Old Sleuth's own ; ‡v no. 116
```

Title page	Detective Dale: or Conflicting Testimonies. A Weird Detective Experience. By Old Sleuth. Copyright, 1898, by Parlor Car Publishing Company. New York: J. S. Ogilvie Publishing Company.

Figure 1-9.   Title proper includes statement of responsibility

```
100 1    ‡a Téramond, Béhotéguy de.
240 10   ‡a 300 recettes culinaires pour maigrir (par la méthode des basses-calories). ‡l English
245 10   ‡a Béhotéguy de Téramond's low-calorie French cookbook : ‡b with season-by-season
         diet menus / ‡c illustrations by Dorothy Ivens.
246 30   ‡a Low-calorie French cookbook
260      ‡a New York : ‡b Grosset & Dunlap, ‡c c1964.
300      ‡a 224 p. : ‡b ill. ; ‡c 25 cm.
500      ‡a Translation of: 300 recettes culinaires pour maigrir (par la méthode des basses-calories).
500      ‡a Includes index.
```

Title page	Béhotéguy de Téramond's Low-Calorie French Cookbook with Season-by-Season Diet Menus Illustrations by Dorothy Ivens Grosset & Dunlap • Publishers New York
Verso of title page	Copyright © 1964 Editions Pallas First published in France under the title: "300 Recettes Culinaires pour Maigrir (par la Méthode des Basses-Calories)," Editions de la Pensée Moderne, éditeurs, Paris

Figure 1-10. Title proper the same as main entry

```
028 02    ‡a 19129-2 ‡b Atlantic
110 2     ‡a Led Zeppelin (Musical group)
245 10    ‡a Led Zeppelin ‡h [sound recording].
260       ‡a New York : ‡b Atlantic, ‡c p1971.
300       ‡a 1 sound disc : ‡b digital ; ‡c 4 3/4 in. + ‡e 1 booklet ([8] p.)
511 0     ‡a Jimmy Page, Robert Plant, John Bonham, John Paul Jones, Memphis Minnie.
518       ‡a Recorded at Headley, Grange, Hampshire; Island Studios, London; and Sunset Sound,
          Los Angeles, Calif.
500       ‡a Compact disc.
530       ‡a Also issued as analog disc and cassette.
505 0     ‡a Black dog (4:55) -- Rock and roll (3:40) -- The battle of evermore (5:38) -- Stairway to
          heaven (7:55) -- Misty mountain hop (4:39) -- Four sticks (4:49) -- Going to California
          (3:36) -- When the levee breaks (7:08).
```

Disc label   Led Zeppelin

1. Black Dog (4:55)
2. Rock and Roll (3:40)
3. The Battle of Evermore (5:38)
4. Stairway to Heaven (7:55)
5. Misty Mountain Hop (4:39)
6. Four Sticks (4:49)
7. Going to California (3:36)
8. When the Levee Breaks (7:08)

Produced by Jimmy Page
℗1971 Atlantic
Made in USA

Atlantic
19129-2
(250 008)
1120141D

figures 1-10 and 1-11. Transcribe the title information as it appears in the chief source.

1.1B4. This rule authorizes the abridgment of a long title proper. Caution: only in rare instances is it appropriate to abbreviate the title proper. In the nineteenth century and earlier, title pages were often crowded with extraneous information, because they often doubled as an advertisement that was printed as a broadside and distributed separately. But even in these instances, the title proper was generally concise. "Other title" information is more likely to be overly lengthy and in need of abridgment than is the title proper (see *Handbook* at 1.1E3 for discussion and example).

1.1B6. A title proper that includes separate letters or initials, with or without full stops between them, is transcribed as it appears, without any internal spaces (see figure 1-1 for transcription of a title including initials with full stops; see figure 1-12 for a title including initials without full stops between them).

Figure 1-11.   Title proper the same as main entry

```
111 2    ‡a Conference on the Acquisition of Material from Africa ‡d (1969 : ‡c University of
         Birmingham)
245 1    ‡a Conference on the Acquisition of Material from Africa, University of Birmingham, 25th
         April 1969 : ‡b reports and papers / ‡c compiled by Valerie Bloomfield.
260      ‡a Zug, Switzerland : ‡b Inter Documentation Co., ‡c c1969.
300      ‡a vii, 154 p. ; ‡c 21 cm.
500      ‡a At head of title: Standing Conference on Library Materials on Africa.
700 1    ‡a Bloomfield, Valerie.
710 2    ‡a Standing Conference on Library Materials on Africa.
```

Title page   Standing Conference on Library Materials on Africa

Conference
on the Acquisition of Material from Africa
University of Birmingham 25th April 1969
Reports and Papers compiled by Valerie Bloomfield

Inter Documentation Company Ag Zug Switzerland

Figure 1-12.   Title proper including initials

```
020      ‡a 0865544778
100 1    ‡a Lamphere, Robert J.
245 14   ‡a The FBI-KGB war : ‡b a special agent's story / ‡c Robert J. Lamphere and Tom
         Shachtman.
250      ‡a New ed. / ‡b with a post-Cold War afterword.
260      ‡a Macon, Georgia : ‡b Mercer University Press, ‡c c1995.
300      ‡a 350 p. : ‡b ill. ; ‡c 24 cm.
504      ‡a Includes bibliographical references and index.
700 1    ‡a Shachtman, Tom, ‡d 1942-
```

Title page   The
FBI-KGB War
A Special Agent's Story

Robert J. Lamphere
and Tom Shachtman

Mercer University Press
Macon, Georgia

1.1B7. Items lacking a title. If the cataloger must go beyond the prescribed sources of information to find a title for an item being cataloged or if the cataloger makes up a title for an item (typically something homemade), enclose this title in brackets (see figure 1-13).

1.1B10. Sometimes the chief source of information includes a collective title together with individual titles for works included in the item. In this

Figure 1-13. A "made-up" title in brackets

```
245 00   ‡a [Stomach of a frog, tangential section] ‡h [microscope slide].
260      ‡c [1955]
300      ‡a 1 microscope slide : ‡b stained ; ‡c 3 × 8 cm.
500      ‡a Title supplied by cataloger.
500      ‡a Made by Robert M. Craig.
500      ‡a Ten microns; stained with Zenker's stain.
700 1    ‡a Craig, Robert M.
```

Figure 1-14. Title proper—collective and individual titles

```
020       ‡a 033033560X
100 1     ‡a Dexter, Colin.
245 14    ‡a The third Inspector Morse omnibus / ‡c Colin Dexter.
260       ‡a London : ‡b Pan Books, ‡c 1994, c1991.
300       ‡a 530 p. : ‡b ill., maps ; ‡c 20 cm.
505 0     ‡a Last bus to Woodstock -- The wench is dead -- The jewel that was ours.
700 12    ‡a Dexter, Colin. ‡t Last bus to Woodstock.
700 12    ‡a Dexter, Colin. ‡t Wench is dead.
700 12    ‡a Dexter, Colin. ‡t Jewel that was ours.
```

Title page	The Third
	Inspector Morse
	Omnibus
	Last Bus to Woodstock
	The Wench is Dead
	The Jewel That Was Ours
	Colin Dexter
	Pan Books
	In Association With Macmillan London

case, the collective title serves as the title proper. Individual titles are omitted from the title and statement of responsibility area and listed instead as a contents note (see figure 1-14).

1.1C. *Optional addition.* **General material designation**

The general material designation (GMD) is a generic term used to identify the general category of material to which an item belongs and to distinguish one general category from another in a catalog containing records for more than one type of material. The area for physical description (1.5) describes the special nature of the item, whether it be a sound recording, a slide, or a printed text. But catalogers have long felt that it is helpful to alert library users almost immediately to the fact that some items, such as microfilms or sound recordings, require special equipment for their use, or that other items, such as maps or pictures, are stored and handled in a special manner. For this reason, it has long been customary in many North American libraries to add a medium designator immediately following the title in the catalog entry for nonbook items.

AACR2R includes two lists of GMDs, one for libraries in the United Kingdom and one for libraries in North America. Two lists are used because in the United Kingdom there is a strong emphasis on the general character of terms to be used as GMDs, while in North America there is a preference for certain terms even though they tend to the specific rather than the generic in character. Thus, no single list was found to be completely acceptable on both sides of the Atlantic.[4]

AACR2R is based on the premise of a fully integrated library collection, with all types of materials being cataloged under the same rules and principles regardless of physical format. Following this premise, *AACR2R* allows the cataloger the option of adding a general material designation not only to nonprint items but also to books. If the cataloger chooses to add GMDs to all types of library materials, figure 1-15 shows how figure 1-5 would be modified.

For materials currently cataloged by the Library of Congress, LC will add the following GMDs, as appropriate (*LCRI* 1.1C, Jan. 5, 1989):

computer file [formerly machine-readable data file]	motion picture
	slide
	sound recording
filmstrip	transparency
kit	videorecording
microform	

Although the *LCRI* has not been changed, since implementation of the 1994 *Guidelines for Bibliographic Description of Interactive Multimedia* (Chicago: American Library Association, Committee on Cataloging: Description and Access, 1994), the Library of Congress also uses a GMD new to *AACR2R*, "interactive multimedia" (see discussion in chapter 9, "Computer Files," of this *Handbook*).

Most North American libraries omit GMDs from catalog records for the following types of materials:

braille	manuscript	music
globe	map	text

Figure 1-15.   General material designation—books

```
020      ‡a 0684800039
100 1    ‡a Dunning, John, ‡d 1942-
245 14   ‡a The bookman's wake ‡h [text] : ‡b a mystery with Cliff Janeway / ‡c John Dunning.
260      ‡a New York : ‡b Scribner, ‡c c1995.
300      ‡a 351 p. ; ‡c 25 cm.
```

This text will not add GMDs for these materials.

Traditional North American practice is to display GMDs for the following materials in addition to those specified by LC, and this text will follow this practice:

art original (includes collages, drawings, paintings, sculpture, and other one-of-a-kind objects that, in the judgment of the cataloger, qualify as "art" rather than "realia")

art reproduction

chart (includes graphic and tabular wall charts, flip charts, and calendars, but *not* cartographic charts; these are regarded as maps)

diorama

flash card

game (includes puzzles and simulations)

microscope slide

model (includes mock-ups)

picture (includes any item covered by rules in *AACR2R* chapter 8 and not subsumed under another term from list 2)

realia (includes naturally occurring objects, machines, stitchery, clothing, sculpture, puppets, rubber stamps, pattern stencils, jewelry, pottery, musical instruments, etc.[5] Compare with art original. Some one-of-a-kind craft items may preferably, in the cataloger's judgment, be qualified as "art original" rather than "realia."

technical drawing (for definition, see *AACR2R* Appendix D [Glossary])

toy.

Some illustrations of GMDs displayed after the title proper of other categories of material are shown in figures 1-16 and 1-17. Note that the GMD is recorded in the 245 field immediately following the title proper or the first title in the case of an item having no collective title. It is enclosed within brackets and preceded by subfield ‡h.

Figure 1-16.   General material designation—game

```
100 1    ‡a Patterson, A. J.
245 10   ‡a Flinch ‡h [game] / ‡c by A.J. Patterson.
260      ‡a Salem, Mass. : ‡b Parker, ‡c c1938.
300      ‡a 1 game (150 cards) ; ‡c in box 12 × 14 × 3 cm.
500      ‡a Includes leaflet: Rules for playing.
710 2    ‡a Parker Brothers, inc.
```

Figure 1-17.   General material designation—slide

```
245 00    ‡a West Germany ‡h [slide] : ‡b the land and its people.
260       ‡a Chicago : ‡b Society for Visual Education, ‡c [196-?]
300       ‡a 25 slides : ‡b col. + ‡e 1 booklet.
710 2     ‡a Society for Visual Education.
```

Figure 1-18.   Parallel title

```
110 2     ‡a Metropolitan Toronto Central Library. ‡b Languages Centre.
245 10    ‡a Spanish books = ‡b Libros en español : a catalogue of the holdings of the Languages
          Centre, Metropolitan Toronto Central Library.
246 31    ‡a Libros en español
260       ‡a [Toronto, Ont.] : ‡b Metropolitan Toronto Library Board, ‡c 1974.
300       ‡a 299 p. ; ‡c 27 cm.
546       ‡a Prelim. matter in English and Spanish.
500       ‡a Includes index.
```

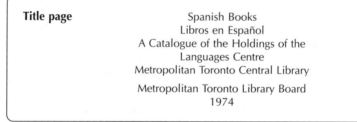

Title page

Spanish Books
Libros en Español
A Catalogue of the Holdings of the
Languages Centre
Metropolitan Toronto Central Library

Metropolitan Toronto Library Board
1974

1.1D. Parallel titles

Sometimes the chief source of information shows a repetition of the title proper in other languages (the item may or may not contain text matching the languages of the titles). If this is the case, the first title is usually re-garded as the title proper of the item. Succeeding repetitions of this title in the other languages are usually regarded as parallel titles. Libraries follow-ing LC decisions will record parallel titles according to second-level de-scription: record the first parallel title and any subsequent parallel title that is in English.

Parallel titles are separated from the title proper and from one another by space - equals sign - space (see figure 1-18). The first parallel title is preceded by subfield ‡b unless subfield ‡b has already occurred.

1.1D3. Sometimes the chief source of information for a translated work gives the original title as well as the title of the translation. This is regarded as a parallel title (separated from the title proper by space - equals sign - space) if the work includes not only the translated text but also "all or some of the text in the original language." In other words, the work must include text in languages to match the titles as given in the chief source. Figure 1-19 is an example of such a text.

Whether or not a translation includes some of the original text, an original title will be recorded as a parallel title if it *precedes* the title proper in the chief source of information. On the other hand, if the chief source of information for a translated work includes the original title *following* the title of the translation and the work contains only the translation, the title of the translation will be given as the title proper and the original title will be listed as a note (see figure 1-20).

Sometimes a work may be reissued under a new title but not translated to another language. If both the new title and the original title are included in the chief source of information, record the original title as "other title" information, separated from the title proper by space - colon - space (see figure 1-21). However, if the chief source of information lists only the new title under which a work is reissued, this is all that will appear in the title element. If the cataloger knows the original title, this information will appear in a note (*AACR2R* 1.7A4). Information about earlier titles, original titles, and so on is often found, as in figure 1-22, on the verso of the title page.

Figure 1-19.   Translated title and parallel title

```
130 0    ‡a Bhagavadgītā. ‡l English & Sanskrit.
245 10   ‡a Bhagavad Gita = ‡b The song celestial / ‡c the Sanskrit text translated into English
         verse by Sir Edwin Arnold ; with an introduction by Sri Prakasa ; illustrated with paintings
         by Y.G. Srimati.
246 31   ‡a Song celestial
260      ‡a New York : ‡b Heritage Press, ‡c c1965.
300      ‡a xx, 128 p. : ‡b col. ill. ; ‡c 26 cm.
546      ‡a Text given in Sanskrit and English on opposite pages.
700 1    ‡a Arnold, Edwin, ‡c Sir, ‡d 1832-1904.
700 1    ‡a Srimati, Y. G.
```

Title page

Bhagavad Gita
The Song Celestial
The Sanskrit Text
Translated into English Verse by Sir Edwin Arnold
With an Introduction by Shri Sri Prakasa
Illustrated with Paintings by
Y.G. Srimati

The Heritage Press   New York

Figure 1-20.   Original title follows translated title on title page

```
020        ‡a 1870007018
100 1      ‡a Tieck, Ludwig, ‡d 1777-1853.
240 10     ‡a Blonde Eckbert. ‡l English
245 14     ‡a The fair-haired Eckbert / ‡c Ludwig Tieck ; in the translation by Thomas Carlyle ;
           illustrated by Jill Heberden.
260        ‡a Henley on Thames [England] : ‡b Langtry Press, ‡c 1988.
300        ‡a 30 p. : ‡b ill. ; ‡c 18 cm.
500        ‡a Translation of: Der blonde Eckbert.
500        ‡a "This is a limited edition of 100 copies, signed by the artist"--Colophon.
590        ‡a Library has copy no. 2, signed by Jill Heberden.
700 1      ‡a Carlyle, Thomas, ‡d 1795-1881.
700 1      ‡a Heberden, Jill.
```

Title page	The Fair-Haired Eckbert (Der blonde Eckbert) Ludwig Tieck In the translation by Thomas Carlyle illustrated by Jill Heberden Langtry Press Henley on Thames 1988

Figure 1-21.   Original title as other title information

```
100 1      ‡a Langton, Jane.
245 10     ‡a Her majesty, Grace Jones : ‡b formerly The majesty of Grace / ‡c by Jane Langton ;
           pictures by Emily Arnold McCully.
260        ‡a New York : ‡b Harper & Row, ‡c c1972.
300        ‡a 189 p. : ‡b ill. ; ‡c 22 cm.
700 1      ‡a Langton, Jane. ‡t Majesty of Grace.
```

Title page	Her Majesty, Grace Jones formerly The Majesty of Grace by Jane Langton pictures by Emily Arnold McCully Harper & Row, Publishers New York Evanston San Francisco London

Figure 1-22.   Original title given as a note

```
020      ‡a 0528820974
020      ‡a 0528801988 (lib. bdg.)
100 1    ‡a Roberts, Elisabeth.
245 10   ‡a Jumping jackdaws! : ‡b Here comes Simon / ‡c by Elisabeth Roberts ; illustrated by
         Prudence Seward ; cover illustrated by Muriel Collins.
260      ‡a Chicago : ‡b Rand McNally, ‡c [1975], c1973.
300      ‡a 192 p. : ‡b ill. ; ‡c 23 cm.
500      ‡a Original title: All about Simon and his grandmother.
700 1    ‡a Roberts, Elisabeth. ‡t All about Simon and his grandmother.
```

Title page

Jumping Jackdaws!
Here Comes Simon
By Elisabeth Roberts
Illustrated by Prudence Seward
Cover Illustrated by Muriel Collins

Rand McNally & Company
Chicago • New York • San Francisco

Verso of title page

First published 1973 under the title
All About Simon and His Grandmother
Illustrations copyright © 1973
Methuen Children's Books Ltd.

1.1E. Other title information

Other title information (see *AACR2R* Appendix D [Glossary]) is to be transcribed, as is the title proper, exactly as to order, wording, and spelling, but (as with the title proper) not necessarily with the capitalization and punctuation given in the chief source of information. Other title information is separated from the title proper by space - colon - space and preceded by subfield ‡b unless it has already appeared, as shown in figure 1-23.

A catalog entry may contain more than one segment of other title information. Each segment is preceded by space - colon - space (see figure 1-24) (see also figure 1-18: subfield ‡b has already been used before the parallel title and is not repeated before the other title information).

1.1E3. Lengthy other title information. If other title information is lengthy, and if it contains no essential information, part of it may be omitted. Indicate omissions by ellipses (...), as shown in figure 1-25. Never omit the first five words of other title information, and do not abbreviate individual words.

Figure 1-23.   Other title information

```
020        ‡a 0670427381
100 1      ‡a Monjo, F. N.
245 10     ‡a Letters to Horseface : ‡b being the story of Wolfgang Amadeus Mozart's journey to
           Italy, 1769-1770, when he was a boy of fourteen / ‡c by F.N. Monjo ; illustrated &
           designed by Don Bolognese & Elaine Raphael.
250        ‡a 1st ed.
260        ‡a New York : ‡b Viking, ‡c 1975.
300        ‡a 91 p. : ‡b ill. ; ‡c 25 cm.
504        ‡a Includes bibliographical references (p. 91).
700 1      ‡a Bolognese, Don.
700 1      ‡a Raphael, Elaine.
```

Title page	Letters to Horseface
	being the story of
	Wolfgang Amadeus Mozart's
	journey to Italy 1769-1770
	when he was a boy of fourteen
	by F. N. Monjo
	illustrated & designed by
	Don Bolognese & Elaine Raphael
	The Viking Press • New York

Figure 1-24.   More than one segment of other title information

```
020        ‡a 290026992X
100 1      ‡a André, Marie-Sophie.
245 14     ‡a Papus : ‡b biographie : la belle epoque de l'occultisme / ‡c Marie-Sophie André,
           Christophe Beaufils.
260        ‡a Paris : ‡b Berg International, ‡c c1995.
300        ‡a 354 p. ; ‡c 24 cm.
440  0     ‡a Faits et représentations
504        ‡a Includes bibliographical references (p. [343]-351).
700 1      ‡a Beaufils, Christophe.
```

Title page	Marie-Sophie André — Christophe Beaufils
	Papus
	biographie
	la Belle Epoque de l'occultisme
	«Faits et Représentations»
	Berg International

Figure 1-25.   Other title information abridged

```
100 1    ‡a Frost, John, ‡d 1800-1859.
245 10   ‡a Border wars of the West : ‡b comprising the frontier wars of Pennsylvania, Virginia,
         Kentucky, Ohio, Indiana, Illinois, Tennessee, and Wisconsin ... / ‡c by John Frost.
260      ‡a New York : ‡b Miller, Orton & Mulligan, ‡c 1856.
300      ‡a 608 p. : ‡b ill. ; ‡c 24 cm.
500      ‡a Added t.-p., engraved, in color.
```

Title page

Border Wars of the West: comprising the
Frontier Wars of Pennsylvania, Virginia, Kentucky,
Ohio, Indiana, Illinois, Tennessee, and Wisconsin;
and embracing
Individual Adventures among the Indians,
and exploits of
Boone, Kenton, Clark, Logan, Brady, Poe, Morgan,
the Whetzels, and other border heroes of the west.
By John Frost, LL.D.
With Numerous Engravings.
New York and Auburn:
Miller, Orton & Mulligan   1856.

Lengthy other title information pertaining to the bibliographic history of the work may more appropriately be included as a note (see figure 1-26). In this case, do not indicate omission by ellipses.

1.1E4. Statement of responsibility included with other title information. This rule has a parallel in 1.1B2. If a statement of responsibility appears anywhere in the title element, whether as part of the title proper or as part of the other title information, and if it is an integral part of the title, transcribe it as it appears (see figure 1-27).

1.1F. Statements of responsibility

The statement of responsibility is separated from the title by space - slash - space. Subfield ‡c appears immediately after the slash in the MARC record. There are generally no further subfields in the 245 field.

The statement of responsibility is transcribed just as it appears in the chief source of information. Do not add words such as "by" or "and" unless these appear in the chief source of information. But if these appear in the source, transcribe them as you see them. That is, "and" must be transcribed as "and"; the ampersand "&" will be transcribed as "&" (see figure 1-28).

A statement of responsibility appearing in the chief source of information will always be recorded, unless the cataloger is following the provisions of first-level description (1.0D1) and the statement of responsibility is the same as the main entry heading. No abbreviations may be used in the statement of responsibility unless they appear in the item, in which case

Figure 1-26.   Other title information dropped to note area

```
020      ‡a 0030206618
100 1    ‡a Schulz, Charles M.
245 10   ‡a How long, Great Pumpkin, how long? / ‡c by Charles M. Schulz.
260      ‡a New York : ‡b Holt, Rinehart and Winston, ‡c 1977.
300      ‡a 1 v. (unpaged) : ‡b all ill. ; ‡c 26 cm.
490 1    ‡a Peanuts parade paperbacks ; ‡v 16
500      ‡a Subtitle: Cartoons from You're the guest of honor, Charlie Brown, and, Win a few, lose
         a few, Charlie Brown.
830  0   ‡a Peanuts parade ; ‡v 16.
```

Title page

Peanuts Parade 16
How Long, Great Pumpkin, How Long?
Cartoons from You're the Guest of Honor, Charlie Brown
and Win a Few, Lose a Few, Charlie Brown
by Charles M. Schulz
Holt, Rinehart and Winston / New York

Series title page

Peanuts Parade Paperbacks
1. Who's the Funny-Looking Kid with the Big Nose?
2. It's a Long Way to Tipperary
3. There's a Vulture Outside
4. What's Wrong with Being Crabby?
5. What Makes You Think You're Happy?
6. Fly, You Stupid Kite, Fly!
7. The Mad Punter Strikes Again
8. A Kiss on the Nose Turns Anger Aside
9. Thank Goodness for People
10. What Makes Musicians So Sarcastic?
11. Speak Softly, and Carry a Beagle
12. Don't Hassle Me with Your Sighs, Chuck
13. There Goes the Shutout
14. Always Stick Up for the Underbird
15. It's Hard Work Being Bitter
16. How Long, Great Pumpkin, How Long?

Figure 1-27.   Other title information including statement of responsibility

```
100 1    ‡a Doré, Gustave, ‡d 1832-1883.
245 12   ‡a A Doré treasury : ‡b a collection of the best engravings of Gustave Doré / ‡c edited
         and with an introduction by James Stevens.
260      ‡a [New York] : ‡b Bounty, ‡c c1970.
300      ‡a ix, 246 p. : ‡b chiefly ill. ; ‡c 32 cm.
700 1    ‡a Stevens, James.
```

```
Title page                     A Doré Treasury
                        A Collection of the Best Engravings
                               of Gustave Doré
                        edited and with an introduction by
                                James Stevens

                                 Bounty Books
                        A Division of Crown Publishers, Inc.
```

Figure 1-28.   Statement of responsibility

```
100 1    ‡a Foeken, D.
245 10   ‡a Tied to the land : ‡b household resources and living conditions of labourers on large
         farms in Trans Nzoia District, Kenya / ‡c Dick Foeken & Nina Tellegen.
260      ‡a [Aldershot, England] : ‡b Avebury, ‡c c1994.
300      ‡a xii, 152 p. : ‡b ill., maps ; ‡c 24 cm.
490 1    ‡a African Studies Centre research series ; ‡v 1/1994
504      ‡a Includes bibliographical references (p. 155-157).
700 1    ‡a Tellegen, Nina.
830  0   ‡a African Studies Centre research series ; ‡v 1994/1.
```

```
Title page                     African Studies Centre
                                 Research Series
                                    1/1994
                                Tied to the land
                        Household resources and living conditions of
                       labourers on large farms in Trans Nzoia District,
                                     Kenya
                           Dick Foeken & Nina Tellegen

                                   Avebury
```

they are to be transcribed exactly as they appear. The statement of responsibility may include, in addition to or instead of names of authors, names of persons or bodies having other responsibility for the work, such as editors, translators, writers of prefaces, illustrators, etc. Names of persons or bodies performing different functions are separated from one another by space - semicolon - space, unless joined grammatically. In addition to this treatment of punctuation, shown in figure 1-29, note the transcription of initials in the statement of responsibility. They are to be recorded with full stops if present in the original source, but without spaces between them.

Although in most cases all personal names appearing in the chief source of information will be recorded in the statement of responsibility, the cataloger should be alert for instances in which an individual's name is included on the source simply because he or she happens to head an agency responsible for the production or publication of the work. If this individual

Figure 1-29.   Statement of responsibility—subsidiary author

```
100 1    ‡a Finberg, A. J. ‡q (Alexander Joseph), ‡d 1866-1939.
245 10   ‡a Turner's sketches and drawings / ‡c A.J. Finberg ; introduction by Lawrence Gowing.
250      ‡a 1st Schocken ed.
260      ‡a New York : ‡b Schocken, ‡c 1968.
300      ‡a xxviii, 163 p., 87 p. of plates ; ‡b ill. ; ‡c 21 cm.
534      ‡p Reprint. Originally published: ‡c New York : Scribner, 1910.
500      ‡a Includes index.
700 1    ‡a Turner, J. M. W. ‡q (Joseph Mallord William), ‡d 1775-1851.
```

Title page	Turner's Sketches and Drawings
	A.J. Finberg
	Introduction by Lawrence Gowing
	Schocken Books • New York
Verso of title page	
	First Schocken Edition 1968
	Copyright © 1968 by Schocken Books, Inc.

Figure 1-30.   Names not part of statement of responsibility omitted

```
110 2    ‡a Myers Demonstration Library Project.
245 14   ‡a The Myers Demonstration Library : ‡b an ESEA Title III project.
260      ‡a Phoenix : ‡b Arizona Dept. of Education, ‡c [1971].
300      ‡a 1 v. (unpaged) ; ‡c 28 cm.
500      ‡a Cover title.
710 1    ‡a Arizona. ‡b Dept. of Education.
```

Title page	The Myers Demonstration Library
	An ESEA Title III Project
	Arizona
	Department of Education
	W.P. Shofstall, Ph.D., Superintendent

has not functioned in the capacity of author or had subsidiary responsibility, or has not worked in some capacity (as, for instance, chair) with a corporate body having some sort of authorship responsibility for the work, his or her name will not be included in the catalog entry (see figure 1-30).

Record in the statement of responsibility only names that are of "bibliographic significance," that is, names associated with the intellectual and artistic content of an item (*LCRI* 1.1F1, Jan. 5, 1989; see also National Library of Canada rule interpretation, Howarth, at 1.1F; and *AACR2R* Appendix D [Glossary], *s.v.* "Statement of responsibility"). These include editors, translators, and writers of introductions and prefaces. Excluded are staff members of publishing companies, such as "in-house" editors, book and layout designers, and production managers. Thus, in figure 1-31, K. C. Den-Dooven, the book designer, is not included in the statement of responsibility. A cataloger familiar with KC Publications will also recognize Mary L. Van Camp as an "in-house" editor and exclude her name from the statement of responsibility. However, if the cataloger is in doubt about the status of a name, he or she should transcribe it if it appears in the chief source.

1.1F1. A statement of responsibility will be recorded only if it appears "prominently" in the item being cataloged. "Prominently" is defined, according to *AACR2R* 0.8, as "a formal statement found in one of the prescribed sources . . . for areas 1 and 2" (the title and statement of responsibility area and the edition area). These prescribed sources will be different for each of the various types of library media. They are listed under .0B in the chapters dealing with special kinds of library materials (e.g., 2.0B2 states that for a book, the prescribed source of information for the title and statement of responsibility is the title page or title page substitute); in addition,

Figure 1-31.   Omission from statement of responsibility of certain names in chief source

```
020       ‡a 0887140645
100 1     ‡a Murphy, Dan.
245 10    ‡a Oregon Trail : ‡b voyage of discovery / ‡c text by Dan Murphy ; photography by Gary
          Ladd.
260       ‡a Las Vegas, NV : ‡b KC Publications, ‡c c1992.
300       ‡a 64 p. : ‡b col. ill. ; ‡c 31 cm.
490 1     ‡a The story behind the scenery
504       ‡a Includes bibliographical references (p. 64).
700 1     ‡a Ladd, Gary.
830  0    ‡a Story behind the scenery
```

Title page

Oregon
Trail
Voyage of Discovery

The Story Behind the Scenery®

The only real
voyage of discovery
consists in not seeking
new landscapes
but in having
new eyes.
Marcel Proust

text by Dan Murphy
photography by Gary Ladd

[two paragraphs listing qualifications of the authors]

Edited by Mary L. Van Camp. Book design by K.C. DenDooven.
Second printing, 1992
©1992 KC Publications, Inc.

information appearing "prominently" (i.e., in the prescribed source listed for the edition area) can be transcribed as part of the statement of responsibility. *AACR2R* 6.0B1 states that the label on a sound recording disc is the chief source of information (i.e., the prescribed source of information for transcribing the title and statement of responsibility for such an item). In addition, a statement appearing "prominently" (i.e., on accompanying textual material or the container, the prescribed source for the edition area) can be transcribed as part of the statement of responsibility. If such "prominent" information (i.e., information taken from prescribed sources for the edition area) is included as part of the statement of responsibility, it must be enclosed in square brackets.

The cataloger should exercise judgment about whether to include "prominent" information *not* appearing in the chief source of information as part of the statement of responsibility. Transcribe it only if it is significant (i.e., of such a nature that an added entry will be made based on the information). In figure 1-32, data about illustrators appear on the verso of the title page, which, because it is one of the prescribed sources of information for the edition area, is a "prominent" location. The illustrations, however, are relatively unimportant, and responsibility for these illustrations is diffuse. The information will not be transcribed. On the other hand, see figure 1-33 for an instance where important information appearing on the verso of the title page should be bracketed as part of the statement of responsibility.

1.1F2. Do *not* construct a statement of responsibility if none appears "prominently" in the item (see figures 1-30 and 1-34).

Figure 1-32.   Statement of responsibility

```
020        ‡a 067121604X
245 14     ‡a The magic of Lewis Carroll / ‡c edited by John Fisher.
260        ‡a New York : ‡b Simon and Schuster, ‡c c1973.
300        ‡a 288 p. : ‡b ill. ; ‡c 25 cm.
504        ‡a Includes bibliographical references (p. 276-279) and index.
700 1      ‡a Fisher, John, ‡d 1945-
```

Title page	The Magic of Lewis Carroll
	Edited by
	John Fisher
	Simon and Schuster
	New York
Verso of title page	
	Line illustrations by Sir John Tenniel,
	Henry Holiday, Arthur B. Frost,
	Harry Furniss and Lewis Carroll;
	diagrams by Laura Potter.
	The book has been designed by
	John Lewis

Figure 1-33.   Statement of responsibility—omission

```
130      ‡a Anglo-American cataloging rules (North American text)
245 10   ‡a Anglo-American cataloging rules : ‡b North American text / ‡c prepared by the
         American Library Association ... [et al. ; general editor, C. Sumner Spalding].
260      ‡a Chicago : ‡b A.L.A., ‡c 1967.
300      ‡a xxi, 400 p. ; ‡c 27 cm.
500      ‡a Includes index.
700 1    ‡a Spalding, C. Sumner ‡q (Charles Sumner), ‡d 1912-
710 2    ‡a American Library Association.
```

```
Title page              Anglo-American Cataloging Rules
                    Prepared by the American Library Association
                           The Library of Congress
                         The Library Association and
                        The Canadian Library Association
                             North American Text
                 American Library Association    Chicago 1967

Verso of title page
                              General Editor
                            C. Sumner Spalding
```

Figure 1-34.   No statement of responsibility

```
245 00   ‡a Population ‡h [game] : ‡b a game of man and society.
260      ‡a Cambridge, Mass. : ‡b Urban Systems, ‡c c1971.
300      ‡a 1 game (various pieces) ; ‡c in box 51 × 27 × 5 cm.
520      ‡a A simulation game designed to acquaint players with the problem of population growth
         and control.
710 2    ‡a Urban Systems (Cambridge, Mass.)
```

1.1F3. If a statement of responsibility precedes the title proper, transpose it to its proper position in the entry (see figures 1-4 and 1-24 for examples). However, if such a name is connected grammatically to the title proper, do not transpose it (see figure 1-9). In such a case, the statement of responsibility following the slash may consist solely of names of persons or bodies performing subsidiary functions. Even though it does not include the name of the author, a statement of responsibility is still to be separated from the title element by space - slash - space (see again figure 1-9).

1.1F5. When more than three persons or bodies performing the same function are named in the source used to record the statement of responsibility, give only the first named, followed by "... [et al.]" (see figures 1-33 and 1-35).

1.1F6. More than one statement of responsibility. Often the chief source of information lists more than one type of bibliographic responsibility. For example, in addition to an author's name on the title page of a

Figure 1-35.   Statement of responsibility—omission

```
020       ‡a 0412453002
245 00    ‡a Introductory microbiology / ‡c Trevor Gross ... [et al.].
250       ‡a 1st ed.
260       ‡a London : ‡a New York ; ‡b Chapman & Hall, ‡c 1995.
300       ‡a xiv, 414 p. : ‡b ill. ; ‡c 25 cm.
500       ‡a Includes index.
700 1     ‡a Gross, Trevor.
```

Title page	Introductory Microbiology

Trevor Gross
Principal Lecturer
Department of Biological Sciences
The Manchester Metropolitan University
Manchester, UK

Jane Faull
Department of Biology
Birbeck College
University of London
London, UK

Steve Ketteridge
Staff Development Officer
Queen Mary and Westfield College
University of London
London, UK

and

Derek Springham
Queen Mary and Westfield College
University of London
London, UK

Chapman & Hall
University and Professional Division
London Glasgow Weinheim New York Tokyo Melbourne Madras

book, the cataloger may find names of editors, writers of prefaces or introductions, illustrators, etc. These names are to be recorded in the order in which they appear in the source (see figure 1-3). Separate names of persons or bodies having different kinds of responsibility by space - semicolon - space, unless these names are linked grammatically.

Contrast figure 1-3 with figure 1-35. Names of one to three persons or bodies performing the same function will be transcribed in the entry; if four or more perform the same function, all but the first will be omitted. (This holds true for those performing subsidiary functions such as illustrators, etc., as well as persons or bodies having primary responsibility for the work.)

1.1F7. Titles included with names in the statement of responsibility. Certain titles, if they appear prominently, in conjunction with the names of persons, will be transcribed as part of the catalog entry. Among titles thus to be transcribed are titles of nobility or British titles of honor (Sir, Dame, Lord, Lady) (see figures 1-36 and 1-37).

Always transcribe a title of address if it is necessary grammatically (see figure 1-38). Include a title of address, etc., when its omission would leave only the person's given name, as shown in figures 1-37 and 1-39. Such a title of address is also retained when its omission would leave only the person's surname (see figure 1-40).

Figure 1-36.   British title of honor included in statement of responsibility

020	‡a 0134341503
100 1	‡a Cadbury, Adrian, ‡c Sir.
245 14	‡a The company chairman / ‡c Sir Adrian Cadbury ; foreword by Sir John Harvey-Jones.
250	‡a 2nd ed.
260	‡a Cambridge, England : ‡b Director Books, ‡c 1995.
300	‡a xiv, 225 p. ; ‡c 24 cm.
500	‡a Includes bibliographical references (p. 218-222) and index.

| Title page | The
Company Chairman

Second edition

Sir Adrian Cadbury
Foreword by Sir John Harvey-Jones

Director Books
Published in association with the Institute of Directors |
|---|---|

Figure 1-37.   Title of nobility included in statement of responsibility

020	‡a 0835420008
100 0	‡a Philip, ‡c Prince, consort of Elizabeth II, Queen of Great Britain, ‡d 1921-
245 14	‡a The evolution of human organisations / ‡c by His Royal Highness the Prince Philip, Duke of Edinburgh, K.G.
260	‡a Southampton [England] : ‡b University of Southampton, ‡c 1967.
300	‡a 27 p. ; ‡c 22 cm.
440 0	‡a Fawley Foundation lecture ; ‡v 14th
500	‡a At head of title: The Fawley Foundation.

| Title page | The Fawley Foundation
The Evolution of Human Organisations
by
His Royal Highness the Prince Philip
Duke of Edinburgh, K.G.
University of Southampton
1967 |
|---|---|

Figure 1-38.   Title necessary grammatically (following "del")

```
020       ‡a 8474839815
100 2     ‡a Olmos Romera, Ricardo.
245 10    ‡a Catálogo de los vasos griegos del Museo Nacional de Bellas Artes de La Habana / ‡c
          por Ricardo Olmos ; con la colaboración de Ernesto Cardet Villegas y Miguel Luis Núñez
          Gutiérrez y de María Castro ; con la inclusión de las listas del profesor Dietrich Von
          Bothmer ; y con apéndice sobre los grafitos de la colección del Dr. Alan W. Johnston.
250       ‡a 1. ed.
260       ‡a Madrid : ‡b Ministerio de Cultura, Dirección General de Bellas Artes y Archivos,
          Instituto de Conservación y Restauración de Bienes Culturales, ‡c 1993.
300       ‡a 306 p. : ‡b ill. (some col.) ; ‡c 26 cm.
504       ‡a Includes bibliographical references.
710 2     ‡a Museo Nacional de Bellas Artes (Cuba)
```

Title page

Catálogo de los Vasos Griegos
del Museo Nacional de Bellas Artes
de La Habana
por Ricardo Olmos
Investigador Científico del Centro de Estudios Históricos, C.S.I.C.
Con la colaboración de Ernesto Cardet Villegas y Miguel Luis Núñez Gutiérrez,
Investigadores del Museo Nacional de Bellas Artes de La Habana; y de
la Dra. María Castro, profesora de la Universidad de La Habana.
Con la inclusión de las listas del Profesor Dietrich Von Bothmer, Distinguished
Research Curator of Greek and Roman Art, Metropolitan Museum de
Nueva York; y con apéndice sobre los grafitos de la colección del Dr.
Alan W. Johnston, University College, Londres.
Ministerio de Cultura
Dirección General de Bellas Artes y Archivos
Instituto de Conservación y Restauración de Bienes Culturales
1993

Figure 1-39.   Title with given name only

```
020       ‡a 0192817795
100 0     ‡a Augustine, ‡c Saint, Bishop of Hippo.
240 10    ‡a Confessiones. ‡l English
245 10    ‡a Confessions / ‡c Saint Augustine ; translated with an introduction and notes by Henry
          Chadwick.
260       ‡a Oxford ; ‡a New York : ‡b Oxford University Press, ‡c 1991.
300       ‡a xxviii, 311 p. ; ‡c 23 cm.
500       ‡a Translation of: Confessiones.
504       ‡a Includes bibliographical references and index.
700 1     ‡a Chadwick, Henry, ‡d 1920-
```

Title page

Saint Augustine
Confessions
translated with an
introduction and notes by
Henry Chadwick
Oxford University Press
1991

Figure 1-40.   Title with surname only

```
020        ‡a 0860687236 (pbk.)
100 1      ‡a Oliphant, ‡c Mrs. ‡q (Margaret), ‡d 1828-1897.
245 10     ‡a Salem Chapel / ‡c Mrs. Oliphant ; with a new introduction by Penelope Fitzgerald.
260        ‡a London : ‡b Virago, ‡c 1986.
300        ‡a xiii, 461 p. ; ‡c 20 cm.
490 1      ‡a Virago modern classic ; ‡v no. 228
490 1      ‡a Chronicles of Carlingford / Mrs. Oliphant ; ‡v 2
800 1      ‡a Oliphant, ‡c Mrs. ‡q (Margaret), ‡d 1828-1897. ‡t Chronicles of Carlingford ; ‡v 2.
830  0     ‡a Virago modern classics (London, England) ; ‡v no. 228.
```

Title page	Chronicles of Carlingford Salem Chapel Mrs Oliphant with a new introduction by Penelope Fitzgerald Virago

Figure 1-41.   Title needed for proper identification

```
020        ‡a 0932218075
100 1      ‡a Reinhardt, Robert M., ‡c Mrs.
245 10     ‡a Nubian history : ‡b America and Great Britain / ‡c by Mrs. Robert M. Reinhardt.
250        ‡a 2nd ed. / ‡b Alice Hall ; sketches by Dorothy Schott.
260        ‡a San Bernardino, CA : ‡b Hall Press, ‡c c1978.
300        ‡a xiv, 119, [5] p. : ‡b ill. ; ‡c 22 cm.
500        ‡a "First edition, 1947."
504        ‡a Includes bibliographical references (p. [124]).
700 1      ‡a Hall, Alice.
```

Title page	Nubian History: America and Great Britain by Mrs. Robert M. Reinhardt first edition, 1947 and Alice Hall second edition sketches by Dorothy Schott

For a married woman who writes under her husband's name plus the term of address, it is necessary to include the term of address in order to identify the author correctly (see figure 1-41).

Words indicating relationship (junior, filho, etc.) *are* included in the statement of responsibility when they appear in the chief source of information. Such words are not included in the list of titles to be omitted in 1.1F7 (see figure 1-42).

Figure 1-42.   Words indicating relationship included

```
020       ‡a 0471372919
100 1     ‡a Henry, Rene A.
245 10    ‡a How to profitably buy and sell land / ‡c Rene A. Henry, Jr.
260       ‡a New York : ‡b Wiley, ‡c c1977.
300       ‡a xix, 203 p. : ‡b ill. ; ‡c 24 cm.
440  0    ‡a Real estate for professional practitioners
500       ‡a "A Wiley-Interscience publication."
500       ‡a Includes index.
500       ‡a Glossary: p. 166-198.
```

Title page	How to Profitably Buy and Sell Land
	Rene A. Henry, Jr.
	A Wiley-Interscience Publication
	John Wiley & Sons
	New York • London • Sydney • Toronto

Figure 1-43.   Religious title omitted

```
020       ‡a 560850752
100 1     ‡a Colton, Albert J., ‡d 1925-1988.
245 12    ‡a A grace observed : ‡b sermons / ‡c by Albert J. Colton ; edited by Bradley S. Wirth ;
          with a foreword by William F. Maxwell, Jr.
260       ‡a Salt Lake City : ‡b All Saints Trust, ‡c 1994.
300       ‡a li, 551 p. ; ‡c 24 cm.
504       ‡a Includes bibliographical references.
700 1     ‡a Wirth, Bradley S., ‡d 1955-
```

Title page	A Grace Observed
	Sermons by The Reverend Canon
	Albert J. Colton
	Edited by
	Bradley S. Wirth
	With a foreword by The Very Reverend
	William F. Maxwell, Jr.
	The All Saints Trust
	Salt Lake City
	1994

Other than exceptions noted above, titles are omitted from names of persons in statements of responsibility. It is particularly necessary to exercise caution when dealing with religious titles because the associated names often consist solely of a forename or a surname. If the person's name includes a surname and forename(s), omit titles, as shown in figure 1-43. Religious titles such as "cardinal," "bishop," "brother," and "father" will be omitted if the person's name includes a surname and forename(s). This practice is shown in figures 1-43 and 1-44. Likewise, initials standing for the religious order to which the individual belongs will be omitted when the name includes a surname and forename(s) (see figure 1-45). Note, however, the retention of "Jr." in the transcription of the statement of responsibility in figure 1-45.

Figure 1-44.   Religious title omitted

```
100 1   ‡a Newman, John Henry, ‡d 1801-1890.
245 10  ‡a Apologia pro vita sua / ‡c John Henry Newman ; introduction by Anton C. Pegis.
260     ‡a New York : ‡b Modern Library, ‡c 1950.
300     ‡a xiv, 430 p. ; ‡c 19 cm.
490 0   ‡a The modern library of the world's best books
```

Title page

Apologia
Pro Vita Sua
John Henry Cardinal Newman
"Commit thy way to the Lord, and trust in Him,
and He will do it.
And He will bring forth thy justice as the light,
and thy judgment as the noon-day"
Introduction by
Anton C. Pegis
President, Pontifical Institute of Medieval Studies
The Modern Library • New York

Figure 1-45.   Initials of religious order omitted

```
245 00  ‡a Introduction to the great religions / ‡c Jean Danielou ... [et al.] ; translated by Albert J.
        La Mothe, Jr.
260     ‡a Notre Dame, Ind. : ‡b Fides, ‡c c1964.
300     ‡a 142 p. ; ‡c 21 cm.
505 0   ‡a Christianity and the non-Christian religions / Jean Danielou -- The religions of nature /
        Andre Retif -- Islam / Joseph Hours -- Buddhism / François Houang -- Hinduism / Maurice
        Queguiner -- The religions of Japan / R.P. Dunoyer -- Judaism / R.P. Demann --
        Contemporary atheism / Gaston Fessard -- The transcendence of Christianity / Jean
        Danielou.
700 1   ‡a Daniélou, Jean.
700 1   ‡a La Mothe, Albert J.
```

Title page   Introduction to the Great Religions
Jean Danielou, S.J.   Maurice Queguiner, P.F.M.
Andre Retif, S.J.   R.P. Dunoyer, P.F.M.
Joseph Hours, S.J.   R.P. Demann
François Houang   Gaston Fessard, S.J.
Translated by Albert J. La Mothe, Jr.
Fides Publishers, Inc.
Notre Dame, Indiana

Chapter opening
1. Jean Danielou, S.J.
Christianity and the Non-Christian Religions

1.1F8. Additions to statement of responsibility. As previously mentioned, the cataloger is not to add words such as "by" or "and" that simply serve to link the statement of responsibility to the title or one collaborating author with another, unless these words are found in the chief source of information. However, if the statement of responsibility as it appears in the source is not clear, or perhaps is misleading, a word or short phrase may be added to clarify it (see figure 1-46).

1.1F12. If a word appearing in the source of information or a word added, according to directions in 1.1F8, to a statement of responsibility is to appear as part of the statement of responsibility, it should be "indicative of the role of the person(s) or body (bodies) named in the statement of responsibility rather than of the nature of the work." A noun or noun phrase "indicative of the nature of the work" is to be regarded as other title information. Such nouns typically are as follows: an anthology, a report, a collection, a tribute, etc. Note the example shown in figure 1-47.

A word of caution: while it is true that a participle (edited, written, collected, etc.) is generally indicative of the role of the person and a noun is generally indicative of the nature of the work, this is not always the case. Sometimes a noun indicates the role of the person, and when it does, the noun should be included as part of the statement of responsibility. In case of doubt, include it (see figure 1-19).

1.1F13. If the author's name is transcribed as part of the title element under *AACR2R* 1.1B2, it is not necessary for the cataloger to bracket in a further author statement. The chief source of information is transcribed as it appears. However, if, in addition to the author's name appearing in the title, the name also appears in a separate statement of responsibility in the chief source of information, this is transcribed (see figure 1-48).

Figure 1-46.   Addition to the statement of responsibility

```
020      ‡a 0486220419
245 00   ‡a Pictures and stories from forgotten children's books / ‡c [selected] by Arnold Arnold.
260      ‡a New York : ‡b Dover, ‡c c1969.
300      ‡a viii, 170 p. : ‡b ill. ; ‡c 21 X 23 cm.
440  0   ‡a Dover pictorial archive series
504      ‡a Includes bibliographical references.
700 1    ‡a Arnold, Arnold.
```

Title page	Pictures and Stories from Forgotten Children's Books By Arnold Arnold Dover Publications, Inc., New York

Figure 1-47.   "Nature of the work" vs. "role of the persons"

```
245 00   ‡a William Warner Bishop : ‡b a tribute, 1941 / ‡c edited by Harry Miller Lydenberg and
         Andrew Keogh.
260      ‡a New Haven : ‡b Yale University Press, ‡c 1941.
300      ‡a vi, 204 p. : ‡b ill. ; ‡c 24 cm.
505 0    ‡a William Warner Bishop / Frederick Paul Keppel -- Reflections from Ingonish / Herbert
         Putnam -- William Warner Bishop / Harry Miller Lydenberg -- Rinaldo Rinaldini (Capo
         Brigante) and George Washington / Jens Christian Bay -- The Federation of Library
         Associations / A.C. de Breycha-Vauthier -- Some rare Americana / Isak Gustaf Alfred
         Collijn -- Monsieur William Warner Bishop et la Fédération internationale des associations
         de bibliothécaires / Marcel Godet -- Book divisions in Greek and Latin literature / Sir
         Frederic George Kenyon -- The Yale Library in 1742 / Andrew Keogh -- Palm leaf books /
         Otto Kinkeldey -- Sir Henry Ellis in France / Gerhard Richard Lomer -- Some trends in
         research libraries / Keyes DeWitt Metcalf -- De Bibliotheca Neerlandica Manuscripta de
         Vreese in Leiden / Tietse Pieter Sevensma -- The preparation of a main index for the
         Vatican Library manuscripts / Eugene, Cardinal Tisserant -- Optima in library service for
         the south by 1950 / Louis Round Wilson.
700 1    ‡a Lydenberg, Harry Miller, ‡d 1874-1960.
700 1    ‡a Keogh, Andrew, ‡d b. 1869.
700 1    ‡a Bishop, William Warner, ‡d 1871-1955.
```

Title page	William Warner Bishop
	A Tribute
	1941
	Edited by Harry Miller Lydenberg and
	Andrew Keogh
	New Haven
	Yale University Press
	London • Humphrey Milford
	Oxford University Press

1.1F14. Statements that would be considered statements of authorship if a person or body were named are transcribed. "Unnamed bodies" are included as part of the statement of responsibility, even though, according to the catalogers' definition (*AACR2R* 21.1B1), such corporate bodies cannot be said to function as a unit and will not be given an entry in the catalog (see figure 1-49).

But note the inclusion of "words or phrases that are neither names nor linking words" when they are concise and when they provide useful bibliographical information. In the example shown in figure 1-50, "compiled in June 1946" should be retained. The names of the heads of the two agencies listed as part of the statement of responsibility are omitted because they had no authorship responsibility for the work (see also figure 1-30).

A word of caution: excluded from provisions of 1.1F14 are statements of this nature that deal with illustrations. For these, see 1.1F15.

1.1F15. This rule has been interpreted by the Library of Congress as follows: "When illustration statements such as '117 photogravure plates, 26

Figure 1-48.   Author statement repeated

```
020      ‡a 0670845515
100 1    ‡a Young, Coleman A.
245 10   ‡a Hard stuff : ‡b the autobiography of Coleman Young / ‡c Coleman Young and Lonnie
         Wheeler.
246 30   ‡a Autobiography of Coleman Young
260      ‡a New York : ‡b Viking, ‡c 1994.
300      ‡a xxii, 344 p. : ‡b ill. ; ‡c 24 cm.
504      ‡a Includes bibliographical references (p. 333-334) and index.
700 1    ‡a Wheeler, Lonnie.
```

First part of double title page   Hard
                                             Stuff

Second part of double title page
                                    The Autobiography of
                                           Coleman
                                            Young
                                              •
                                    Coleman Young and
                                     Lonnie Wheeler
                                          Viking

Figure 1-49.   Unnamed bodies in statement of responsibility

```
245 00   ‡a General education in school and college : ‡b a committee report / ‡c by members of
         the faculties of Andover ... [et al.] ; the committee, Alan R. Blackmer, chairman ... [et al.].
260      ‡a Cambridge, Mass. : ‡b Harvard University Press, ‡c 1953, c1952.
300      ‡a v, 142 p. ; ‡c 22 cm.
710 2    ‡a Andover Academy.
700 1    ‡a Blackmer, Alan R.
```

First part of double title page
                                    The Committee
                              Alan R. Blackmer, chairman
                                  Henry W. Bragdon
                                   McGeorge Bundy
                                  E. Harris Harbison
                                  Charles Seymour, Jr.
                                  Wendell H. Taylor

Second part of double title page
                                   General Education
                                 in School and College
                                  A Committee Report
                               By Members of the Faculties of
                              Andover, Exeter, Lawrenceville,
                               Harvard, Princeton, and Yale
                                 Harvard University Press
                                 Cambridge, Massachusetts
                                          1953

Figure 1-50.   Phrase in statement of responsibility included

```
245 02   ‡a A survey of the recreational resources of the Colorado River Basin / ‡c compiled in
         June 1946, United States Department of the Interior, National Park Service.
260      ‡a Washington, D.C. : ‡b U.S. G.P.O., ‡c 1950.
300      ‡a xxiv, 242 p. : ‡b ill. (some col.), maps ; ‡c 30 cm.
500      ‡a Part of illustrative matter in pocket.
504      ‡a Includes bibliographical references (p. 224-232) and index.
710 1    ‡a United States. ‡b National Park Service.
```

Title page	A Survey of the Recreational Resources of the Colorado River Basin United States Department of the Interior Oscar L. Chapman, Secretary National Park Service Newton B. Drury, Director Compiled in June 1946 United States Government Printing Office Washington • 1950 For sale by the Superintendent of Documents, Washington, D.C. Price $3.25

Figure 1-51.   Statement of responsibility—omission of illustration statement

```
020      ‡a 0387979883 (acid-free paper)
245 00   ‡a Adaptive control, filtering, and signal processing / ‡c K.J. Åström, G.C. Goodwin,
         P.R. Kumar, editors.
260      ‡a New York : ‡b Springer-Verlag, ‡c c1995.
300      ‡a xviii, 396 p. : ‡b ill. ; ‡c 25 cm.
440  0   ‡a IMA volumes in mathematics and its applications ; ‡v v. 74
504      ‡a Includes bibliographical references.
700 1    ‡a Åström, Karl J. ‡q (Karl Johan), ‡d 1934-
700 1    ‡a Goodwin, Graham C. ‡q (Graham Clifford), ‡d 1945-
700 1    ‡a Kumar, P. R.
```

Title page	K.J. Åström G.C. Goodwin P.R. Kumar Editors Adaptive Control, Filtering, and Signal Processing With 48 Illustrations Springer-Verlag New York Berlin Heidelberg London Paris Tokyo Hong Kong Barcelona Budapest

colour plates,' 'with 115 illustrations,' 'illustrated with 10 woodcuts,' etc., appear in the chief source, omit them unless (1) an artist or illustrator is named in the phrase, or (2) the phrase is inseparable from the title proper or other title information" (*LCRI* 1.1F15, Jan. 5, 1989).

In other words, only include an illustration statement as part of the statement of responsibility if it names the person responsible for the illustrations (see figures 1-25, 1-51, and 1-52 for examples of the omission of an illustration statement found in the chief source).

Figure 1-52.   Omission of illustration statement

```
100 1    ‡a Defoe, Daniel, ‡d 1661?-1731.
240 10   ‡a Robinson Crusoe
245 14   ‡a The life and adventures of Robinson Crusoe, of York, mariner.
260      ‡a Philadelphia : ‡b Lippincott, ‡c [186-?]
300      ‡a viii, 312 p. : ‡b ill. ; ‡c 20 cm.
500      ‡a Written by Daniel Defoe.
```

Title page	The Life and Adventures of Robinson Crusoe, of York, Mariner Illustrated with One Hundred and Ten Wood Engravings. Philadelphia J.B. Lippincott & Co.

Figure 1-53.   Statement of responsibility

```
020      ‡a 088494901X
100 1    ‡a Packer, Boyd K.
245 12   ‡a A Christmas parable / ‡c Boyd K. Packer ; illustrated by the author.
250      ‡a 2nd ed.
260      ‡a Salt Lake City, Utah : ‡b Bookcraft, ‡c 1993.
300      ‡a 1 v. (unpaged) : ‡b col. ill. ; ‡c 16 cm.
```

Title page	A Christmas Parable Second Edition Boyd K. Packer Illustrated by the Author Bookcraft Salt Lake City, Utah

In contrast to the examples of omission of illustration statement (figures 1-51 and 1-52), a statement of responsibility will be transcribed if it includes a phrase referring to a person, even though the person is not specifically named in the statement (see figure 1-53).

The chief source of information sometimes includes extraneous matter such as mottoes and bits of verse. If these have no connection with the bibliographical information needed to identify the item, they should be ignored (see figures 1-31 and 1-44). Do not use ellipses to indicate their omission.

Figure 1-54.   Title of address omitted

```
100 2   ‡a Cotarelo y Mori, Emilio, ‡d 1857-1936.
245 10  ‡a Diccionario biográfico y bibliográfico de calígrafos españoles / ‡c por Emilio Cotarelo
        y Mori.
260     ‡a Madrid : ‡b Tip. de la "Revista de Arch., Bibl. y Museos," ‡c 1913-1916.
300     ‡a 2 v. : ‡b ill. ; ‡c 28 cm.
500     ‡a Includes indexes.
```

Title page

Diccionario Biográfico y Bibliográfico
de Calígrafos Españoles por
Don Emilio Cotarelo y Mori
De la Real Academia Española
Obra Premiada por la Biblioteca Nacional en el
Concurso Público de 1906
É Impresa á Expensas del Estado
«Los españoles han sido los mejores
escribanos
del mundo.»
(El Herm. Lorenzo Ortiz, en su Maestro
de escribir, 1696.)
Madrid 1913
Tip. de la «Revista de Arch., Bibl. y Museos»

Figure 1-54 includes two extraneous pieces of information that the cataloger will properly ignore in transcribing the title and statement of responsibility area. The first one, which follows the author's name, states that this work won a prize in a contest sponsored by the Biblioteca Nacional in 1906 and that it has been printed at the expense of the national government. The second is a quotation from the Spanish author Lorenzo Ortiz claiming that the Spanish people have produced the best writers in the world. Neither statement has any place in the bibliographic framework of the catalog entry.

1.1G. Items without a collective title

Most items that include a number of separate works have a collective title on the chief source of information. Such materials present no problem for the cataloger. But some items simply list a number of separate titles, with or without their authors, on the chief source of information. *AACR2R* 1.1G gives rules for transcription of such materials. 1.1G1 deals with the relatively rare instance in which one of the separate works named in the chief source of an item without a collective title is predominant. An example of such a work is found in figure 1-55, which gives prominence to the first item by the typography. However, as noted in *LCRI* 1.1G1 (Mar. 5, 1990), application of this rule is usually to be restricted to "cases in which the secondary titles do not appear in the same source as the predominant title." In most instances, record such titles according to rule 1.1G3.

Figure 1-55.   Item without a collective title—one part predominant

100 1	‡a Wiggin, Kate Douglas Smith, ‡d 1856-1923.
245 14	‡a The birds' Christmas carol / ‡c by Kate Douglas Wiggin.
250	‡a Autograph ed.
260	‡a Boston : ‡b Houghton Mifflin, ‡c c1917.
300	‡a xix, 330 p. : ‡b ill. (some col.) ; ‡c 22 cm.
490 1	‡a The writings of Kate Douglas Wiggin ; ‡v v. 1
500	‡a Illustrated t.p.
505 0	‡a The birds' Christmas carol -- The story of Patsy -- Timothy's quest -- A child's journey with Dickens -- Fleur-de-lis.
590	‡a Library's copy signed by the author.
700 12	‡a Wiggin, Kate Douglas Smith, ‡d 1856-1923. ‡t Story of Patsy.
700 12	‡a Wiggin, Kate Douglas Smith, ‡d 1856-1923. ‡t Timothy's quest.
700 12	‡a Wiggin, Kate Douglas Smith, ‡d 1856-1923. ‡t Child's journey with Dickens.
700 12	‡a Wiggin, Kate Douglas Smith, ‡d 1856-1923. ‡t Fleur-de-lis.
800 1	‡a Wiggin, Kate Douglas Smith, ‡d 1856-1923. ‡t Works. ‡f 1917 ; ‡v v.1.

Half-title page	The Writings of Kate Douglas Wiggin Autograph Edition Volume I
Title page	The Birds' Christmas Carol The Story of Patsy, Timothy's Quest, and Other Stories by Kate Douglas Wiggin Houghton Mifflin Company Boston and New York

1.1G3. If a title page lacks a collective title, record each of the titles in the order in which they are given. Separate the titles by semicolons, even if they are joined by a connecting word or phrase. Precede the second title (including a connecting word or phrase) by subfield ‡b (see figure 1-56). If the separate parts are by different authors, give each title with its statement of responsibility. Separate each part by a full stop, as shown in figure 1-57. Do not insert any subfield coding subsequent to the first statement of responsibility.

1.2. EDITION AREA

An edition may be defined as being "one of the differing forms in which a . . . work . . . is published, e.g., as applied to text, original, revised, enlarged, corrected, etc. . . . ; [or] as applied to format: de luxe, library, paperbound, large-paper, illustrated, etc."[6]

The cataloger is required to include the edition statement as found, but a statement such as "35th impression" or "9th printing" may be ignored,

Figure 1-56.   Item without a collective title—no part predominant

```
100 1    ‡a Martineau, Harriet, ‡d 1802-1876.
245 10   ‡a Feats on the fjord ; ‡b and, Merdhin / ‡c by Harriet Martineau.
260      ‡a London : ‡b Dent ; ‡a New York : ‡b Dutton, ‡c 1910.
300      ‡a xi, 239 p. : ‡b ill. ; ‡c 18 cm.
490 0    ‡a Everyman's library ; ‡v no. 429
504      ‡a Includes bibliographical references (p. viii).
700 12   ‡a Martineau, Harriet, ‡d 1802-1876. ‡t Merdhin.
```

Title page	Feats on the Fjord and Merdhin by Harriet Martineau London & Toronto Published by J.M. Dent & Sons Ltd & in New York by E.P. Dutton & Co.

Figure 1-57.   Item without a collective title—no part predominant, works by more than one author

```
100 1    ‡a Tauber, Maurice Falcolm, ‡d 1908-
245 10   ‡a Cataloging and classification / ‡c by Maurice F. Tauber. Subject headings / by Carlyle J.
         Frarey.
260      ‡a New Brunswick, N.J. : ‡b Graduate School of Library Service, Rutgers, the State
         University, ‡c 1960.
300      ‡a 271, 92 p. ; ‡c 23 cm.
490 1    ‡a The state of the library art ; ‡v v. 1, pt. 1-2
700 12   ‡a Frarey, Carlyle J. ‡q (Carlyle James). ‡t Subject headings.
830  0   ‡a State of the library art ; ‡v v. 1, pt. 1-2
```

Title page	The State of the Library Art edited by Ralph R. Shaw Volume 1, part 1. Cataloging and Classification by Maurice F. Tauber Volume 1, part 2. Subject Headings by Carlyle J. Frarey Graduate School of Library Service Rutgers—The State University New Brunswick, N.J. 1960

because it usually simply means that more copies of the work have been made. Such a statement would only be recorded if the cataloger knew that there was some significant difference, either in content or format, between one printing or impression and another.

Printers and publishers have no regard for the cataloger's convenience in their use of bibliographical terminology. Not even when the publisher uses the word "edition" or its equivalent in another language can the cataloger assume that the work in hand is indeed different from other issues of the work. This is especially true in regard to many French and Latin American publications. The cataloger is not required to compare copies to verify the validity of an edition statement. Take the word "edition" or its equivalent at face value and record it as it appears (see figure 1-58). The edition statement is transcribed in the 250 field of the MARC record.

1.2B3. This rule simply reiterates long-standing cataloging practice: in case of doubt, if a statement appears to be an edition statement (see definition given above under 1.2; see also *AACR2R* Appendix D [Glossary]), record it in the edition area.

However, not all items include an edition statement. Do not add "1st ed." or any other such statement unless you find it in your source (but see 1.2B4, "Optional addition"). On the other hand, if the item includes an edition statement, transcribe the wording and order just as you find it. Thus, if the item reads:

Second edition, revised and corrected

transcription will be:

250   ‡a 2nd ed., rev. and corr.

However, if the edition statement reads:

Revised and corrected second edition

transcription will be:

250   ‡a Rev. and corr. 2nd ed.

Note in the preceding examples the use of abbreviations and the transcription of numbers spelled as words to arabic ordinal numerals. You will

Figure 1-58.   Edition statement

```
020      ‡a 0750618647
100 1    ‡a Brydson, J. A.
245 10   ‡a Plastics materials / ‡c J.A. Brydson.
250      ‡a 6th ed.
260      ‡a Oxford ; ‡a Boston : ‡b Butterworth-Heinemann, ‡c 1995.
300      ‡a xxvii, 896 p. : ‡b ill. ; ‡c 24 cm.
504      ‡a Includes bibliographical references and index.
```

Title page   Plastics
                                    Materials
                                  Sixth Edition
                                  J.A. Brydson
            Former Head of the Department of Physical Sciences
                                  and Technology,
              Polytechnic of North London (now known as the
                          University of North London)
                            Butterworth-Heinemann

recall that no abbreviations are allowed in the title and statement of responsibility area. Beginning with the edition area, abbreviations should be used when the word is found in *AACR2R* Appendix B (Abbreviations) (all sections except B.13). Numbers written as words or as roman numerals are to be transcribed as arabic numerals, following directions in *AACR2R* Appendix C (Numerals).

1.2B4. *Optional addition.* The cataloger is given the option of adding, in brackets, a made-up edition statement if he or she knows that the work being cataloged includes "significant changes from other editions." The Library of Congress rarely follows this practice, because it puts a considerable burden of research and comparison on the cataloger. It will, however, apply the option if the differences are "manifest" and the statement is necessary to distinguish between otherwise identical descriptions (*LCRI* 1.2B4, Jan. 5, 1989). The National Library of Australia applies the option in the same way. The National Library of Canada and the British Library do *not* apply the option (see Howarth, at 1.2B4).

1.2C. Statements of responsibility relating to the edition

Occasionally an edition statement is followed by a statement of responsibility pertaining only to the edition in hand (e.g., it may name a reviser, an illustrator, or someone who has performed some other function just for the particular edition). If this is the case, such a statement of responsibility will be transcribed, following space - slash - space, as part of the edition area. Precede the statement of responsibility by subfield ‡b. In transcribing this statement of responsibility, follow all applicable rules for transcription, punctuation, spacing, etc., as given in 1.1F. Unlike the edition statement proper, *no* abbreviations not appearing in the source may be used in recording the statement of responsibility (see figure 1-59).

1.2C2. Many works that lack a formal edition statement are clearly revisions of an earlier work. A cataloger who chooses to follow the option given in 1.2B4 may create an edition statement and include the statement of revision as a statement of responsibility following the bracketed edition statement, if this statement relates to the edition in hand but not to all editions of the work (see example given in *AACR2R* under 1.2C1). When in doubt, however, do not do this. In almost every case, if the item does not include an edition statement, information about revision, etc., of the text will form part of the title and statement of responsibility area (see figure 1-60).

1.2D. Statement relating to a named revision of an edition

This rule gives guidance about what to do when an item includes more than one edition statement. Both statements are included in the edition area, separated by a comma; the first word of each statement is capitalized unless it is a number (see figure 1-61).

In most cases a reissue is identical to the first printing of a particular edition. Note information about a reissue as a subsequent edition statement only if the reissue contains significant changes. This will not often be the case.

Figure 1-59.   Statement of responsibility related to the edition

```
020      ‡a 013814088X
020      ‡a 0138140960 (pbk.)
100 1    ‡a Sisson, A. F. ‡q (Albert Franklin), ‡d 1901-
245 10   ‡a Sisson's word and expression locater / ‡c A.F. Sisson.
246 30   ‡a Word and expression locater
250      ‡a 2nd ed. / ‡b revised by Barbara Ann Kipfer.
260      ‡a Englewood Cliffs, N.J. : ‡b Prentice Hall, ‡c c1994.
300      ‡a xi, 404 p. ; ‡c 24 cm.
500      ‡a Includes index.
700 1    ‡a Kipfer, Barbara Ann.
```

Title page	Sisson's Word and Expression Locater Second edition A.F. Sisson revised by Barbara Ann Kipfer, Ph.D. Prentice Hall Englewood Cliffs, New Jersey 07632

Figure 1-60.   Revision with no edition statement

```
100 1    ‡a Hulbert, James R. ‡q (James Root), ‡d 1884-
240 10   ‡a Anglo-Saxon reader
245 10   ‡a Bright's Anglo-Saxon reader / ‡c revised and enlarged by James R. Hulbert.
260      ‡a New York : ‡b Holt, ‡c c1935.
300      ‡a cxxxii, 395 p. ; ‡c 20 cm.
700 1    ‡a Bright, James Wilson, ‡d 1852-1926. ‡t Anglo-Saxon Reader.
```

Title page	Bright's Anglo-Saxon Reader Revised and Enlarged by James R. Hulbert New York Henry Holt and Company

Figure 1-61.   Two edition statements

```
100 0    ‡a Lady.
245 14   ‡a The child's guide to knowledge : ‡b being a collection of useful and familiar questions
         and answers on every-day subjects / ‡c adapted for young persons and arranged in the
         most simple and easy language by a Lady.
250      ‡a Authorized ed., 57th ed.
260      ‡a London : ‡b Simpkin, Marshall, ‡c 1888.
300      ‡a v, 480 p. ; ‡c 15 cm.
```

Title page

Authorized Edition.
The Child's
Guide to Knowledge;
Being a Collection of
Useful and Familiar Questions and Answers
on Every-day Subjects,
Adapted for Young Persons,
and Arranged in the Most Simple and Easy
Language.
By a Lady.
Fifty-seventh Edition.
London:
Published by Simpkin, Marshall, & Co.
and Sold by All Booksellers.
MDCCCLXXXVIII
Price Two Shillings
The right of Translation and Reproduction is reserved.

1.3. MATERIAL (OR TYPE OF PUBLICATION) SPECIFIC DETAILS AREA

This area appears in catalog entries for cartographic items, music, computer files, and serials (see discussion in this *Handbook,* chapters 3, 5, 9, and 12 for examples and explanation).

1.4. PUBLICATION, DISTRIBUTION, ETC., AREA

For information included in this area, the basic order and punctuation are Place [i.e., City] : Publisher, date. This area is transcribed in the 260 field of the MARC record.

1.4B4. This rule is based on one of the cardinal principles of descriptive cataloging: transcribe what you see. However, the publication, etc., area includes several exceptions to this principle. Some words are normally omitted from the transcription of information in this area. Thus, prepositional phrases may be omitted unless case endings would be affected (see figure 1-62).

1.4C. Place of publication, distribution, etc.

1.4C1. The place name is transcribed in subfield ‡a. Do not translate a place name into an English-language form that might be more familiar to English-speaking users of your library. Transcribe the name as you find it. That is, if the chief source of information gives "Milano," do not translate it to "Milan" (see figure 1-63).

1.4C2. However, if the place as transcribed seems likely to be obscure to your library's users, you may, *at your discretion,* add a more familiar form in brackets (see figure 1-64).

1.4C3. Additions to place names. This rule directs the cataloger to add the name of the larger jurisdiction (country, state, province, etc.) to the name of the city of publication "if it is considered necessary for identification, or if it is considered necessary to distinguish the place from others of the same name."

Figure 1-62.   Phrase omitted, publisher statement

```
245 00   ‡a English madrigal verse, 1588-1632 / ‡c edited from the original song books by
         E.H. Fellowes.
250      ‡a 2nd ed.
260      ‡a Oxford : ‡b Clarendon Press, ‡c 1929.
300      ‡a xxiv, 644 p. ; ‡c 20 cm.
500      ‡a Includes index.
700 1    ‡a Fellowes, Edmund Horace, ‡d 1870-1951.
```

Title page	English Madrigal Verse
	1588-1632
	Edited from the Original
	Song Books by
	E.H. Fellowes
	Oxford
	At the Clarendon Press
	M CM XXIX

Figure 1-63.   Place of publication in vernacular

```
020      ‡a 8804336064
100 1    ‡a D'Annunzio, Gabriele, ‡d 1863-1938.
245 10   ‡a Di me a me stesso / ‡c Gabriele d'Annunzio ; a cura di Annamaria Andreoli.
250      ‡a 1. ed.
260      ‡a Milano : ‡b A. Mondadori, ‡c 1990.
300      ‡a lix, 282 p. ; ‡c 22 cm.
440  0   ‡a Saggi di letteratura
500      ‡a Includes index.
700 1    ‡a Andreoli, Annamaria.
```

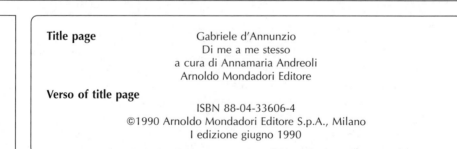

Title page	Gabriele d'Annunzio
	Di me a me stesso
	a cura di Annamaria Andreoli
	Arnoldo Mondadori Editore
Verso of title page	
	ISBN 88-04-33606-4
	©1990 Arnoldo Mondadori Editore S.p.A., Milano
	I edizione giugno 1990

Many of the major publishers of the world are located in large cities, such as New York, Chicago, London, etc. As illustrated by figure 1-65, title pages or other sources for transcription of publication information customarily give the names of such well-known cities without including the larger

Figure 1-64.   Place of publication with translation added

```
100 1    ‡a Milne, A. A. (Alan Alexander), ‡d 1882-1956.
240 10   ‡a Winnie-the-Pooh. ‡l Latin
245 10   ‡a A.A. Milnei Winnie ille Pu : ‡b liber celeberrimus omnibus fere pueris puellisque notus
         / ‡c nunc primum de Anglico sermone in Latinum conversus auctore Alexandro Lenardo.
246 30   ‡a Winnie ille Pu
260      ‡a Novi Eboraci [New York] : ‡b Sumptibus Duttonis, ‡c 1960.
300      ‡a 121 p. : ‡b ill., map ; ‡c 19 cm.
500      ‡a Translation of: Winnie-the-Pooh.
500      ‡a Map on endpapers.
700 1    ‡a Leonard, Alexander.
```

Title page	
	A.A. Milnei
	Winnie ille Pu
	Liber celeberrimus omnibus fere
	pueris puellisque notus
	nunc primum de anglico sermone
	in Latinum conversus
	auctore Alexandro Lenardo
	Novi Eboraci: Sumptibus Duttonis
	MCMLX

Figure 1-65.   Well-known city for which addition to place may be omitted in the publication area

```
020      ‡a 0688132960
100 1    ‡a Noonuccal, Oodgeroo, ‡d 1920-
245 10   ‡a Dreamtime : ‡b aboriginal stories / ‡c by Oodgeroo ; illustrated by Bronwyn Bancroft.
250      ‡a 1st U.S. ed.
260      ‡a New York : ‡b Lothrop, Lee & Shepard, ‡c 1994.
300      ‡a 95 p. : ‡b col. ill. ; ‡c 29 cm.
500      ‡a "First published in Australia by Angus & Robertson [in 1972] as Stradbroke dreamtime"
         --T.p. verso.
700 1    ‡a Bancroft, Bronwyn.
700 1    ‡a Noonuccal, Oodgeroo, ‡d 1920- ‡t Stradbroke dreamtime.
```

Title page	
	Dreamtime
	Aboriginal stories
	by
	Oodgeroo
	Illustrated by Bronwyn Bancroft
	Lothrop, Lee & Shepard Books New York

jurisdiction (e.g., state). By long-standing cataloger custom, names of these well-known cities are transcribed in the publication area without further addition.

It is left up to the cataloger's judgment to determine whether a larger jurisdiction appearing in the prescribed source should be transcribed after the name of the place.[7] If the cataloger chooses to transcribe a larger juris-diction appearing in the prescribed source, abbreviations found in *AACR2R* Appendix B should be used. Thus, if the source gives Tucson, Arizona, as the place, the cataloger will transcribe Tucson, Ariz. Note, however, that if an abbreviation appears in the prescribed source it should not be changed. If the source reads Tucson, AZ, transcribe it as it appears; do not change AZ to Ariz. to make it conform to Appendix B. Abbreviate only the "larger jurisdiction." Do not abbreviate, for example, the names of the cities of New York or Washington, even though these words appear in Appendix B.14. These abbreviations apply only to the names of the states.

Figures 1-66 and 1-67 are examples of place with larger jurisdiction added in the publication area.

Figure 1-66.   Larger jurisdiction transcribed as found in prescribed source

```
100 1    ‡a Halifax, George Savile, ‡c Marquis of, ‡d 1633-1695.
240 10   ‡a Works
245 10   ‡a Complete works / ‡c Halifax ; edited with an introduction by J.P. Kenyon.
260      ‡a Baltimore, Md. : ‡b Penguin, ‡c 1969.
300      ‡a 342 p. ; ‡c 18 cm.
490 0    ‡a The pelican classics ; ‡v AC6
700 1    ‡a Kenyon, J. P. ‡q (John Philipps), ‡d 1927-
```

Title page	Halifax
	Complete Works
	Edited with
	an Introduction by
	J.P. Kenyon
	Penguin Books
	Baltimore • Maryland

Figure 1-67.   Larger jurisdiction transcribed as found in prescribed source

```
245 10   ‡a Forwarded and finished : ‡b an amusement concerning bookbinders / ‡c edited by
         Nick Howell & Graham Moss.
246 18   ‡a Forwarded & finished
260      ‡a Oldham, England : ‡b Incline Press, ‡c 1995.
300      ‡a vii, 40 p. : ‡b ill. ; ‡c 26 cm.
500      ‡a Limited ed. of 300 copies.
590      ‡a Library's copy is no. 30.
700 1    ‡a Howell, Nick.
700 1    ‡a Moss, Graham.
```

Title page   An Amusement Concerning Bookbinders
                                FORWARDED
                                    and
                                 FINISHED
                   Edited by Nick Howell & Graham Moss
                              Incline Press
                                   1995

Title page verso
                 Printed and published by Incline Press of 11A Printer Street
                           Oldham OL1 1PN England

Following the general guidelines of *AACR2R* 1.4C3, if the name of the larger jurisdiction does *not* appear together with the place of publication in the source from which transcription is made and if the city is *not* well known, or conflicts with the name of another city, the larger jurisdiction should be added in square brackets by the cataloger (see, for example, figure 1-20: England should be added in order to identify the city of Henley on Thames).

1.4C5. Two or more places of publication. As a general rule, the publication area includes one place (city) and one publisher, distributor, etc. Normally, if a work is published in more than one city, the cataloger transcribes only the first named place from the prescribed source for the publication area (see figure 1-68).

Figure 1-68.   More than one place

```
020      ‡a 0520088565
100 1    ‡a Shapiro, Gary, ‡d 1941-
245 10   ‡a Earthwards : ‡b Robert Smithson and art after Babel / ‡c Gary Shapiro.
260      ‡a Berkeley : ‡b University of California Press, ‡c c1995.
300      ‡a xiv, 271 p. : ‡b ill. ; ‡c 21 cm.
504      ‡a Includes bibliographical references and index.
```

Title page   Earthwards
                    Robert Smithson and Art after Babel
                                Gary Shapiro
            University of California Press • Berkeley / Los Angeles / London

The cataloger will add a second place if a city outside the cataloger's country (for most readers of this text, the United States) is named first, followed by a city in the "home" country (see figure 1-69).

Note that publication area information generated under the stipulations of this rule will vary, depending on the country of the cataloging agency. Referring again to figure 1-69, a Dutch library would transcribe the publication area:

260   ‡a Dordrecht : ‡b Kluwer Academic Publishers, ‡c c1989.

(The first city is in the home country.) A British library would transcribe it:

260   ‡a Dordrecht [Netherlands]; ‡a London : ‡b Kluwer Academic Publishers, ‡c c1989.

(The first place is transcribed, followed by the place in the cataloger's home country.) A cataloger using *AACR2R* in Australia or any other country other than the three countries specified above would give publication area as:

260   ‡a Dordrecht : ‡b Kluwer Academic Publishers, ‡c c1989.

(No place in home country; list first place only.)

To summarize: always transcribe the first place. If this place is a city outside the country of your cataloging agency and if the item includes the name of a city in your home country, transcribe this second city also.

This practice holds true even if the name of the "home" city appears in a different place in the item than the source being used to transcribe the publication data. Prescribed sources should be used in the order in which they are listed in .0B2 of the appropriate *AACR2R* chapter; for example, for the publication area of an item cataloged under chapter 2, use title page information first, supplementing it with information from other preliminaries and finally the colophon, if appropriate (see figure 1-70).

1.4C6. For published materials, the place of publication element in the publication area must always contain something. If the name of the place

Figure 1-69.   Two places in publication area

```
020      ‡a 0792304284
100 1    ‡a Ziegler, Peter A.
245 10   ‡a Evolution of Laurussia : ‡b a study in late Palaeozoic plate tectonics / ‡c by Pieter A.
         Ziegler.
260      ‡a Dordrecht [Netherlands] ; ‡a Boston : ‡b Kluwer Academic Publishers, ‡c c1989.
300      ‡a viii, 102 p., 13 folded leaves of plates : ‡b ill. (some col.) ; ‡c 27 cm.
500      ‡a "Designated publication no. 0163 of the International Lithosphere Programme."
500      ‡a "Published with the co-operation of and on behalf of the Royal Geological and Mining
         Society of the Netherlands (K.N.G.M.G.)."
504      ‡a Includes bibliographical references (p. [79]-102).
```

Title page

Evolution of Laurussia
A Study in Late Palaeozoic Plate Tectonics
by Pieter A. Ziegler
Geological-Paleontological Institute,
University of Basel, Switzerland
(formerly Shell Internationale Petroleum Maatschappij B.V.,
The Hague, The Netherlands)
Designated publication no. 0163 of the International Lithosphere Programme.
Published with the co-operation of and on behalf of
the Royal Geological and Mining Society of the Netherlands (K.N.G.M.G.)
Kluwer Academic Publishers
Dordrecht / Boston / London

Figure 1-70.   City from home country in publication area

```
020        ‡a 0198158882 (alk. paper)
100 1      ‡a Doherty, Justin.
245 14     ‡a The Acmeist movement in Russian poetry : ‡b culture and the word / ‡c Justin Doherty.
260        ‡a Oxford : ‡b Clarendon Press ; ‡a New York : ‡b Oxford University Press, ‡c 1995.
300        ‡a viii, 316 p. ; ‡c 23 cm.
440 0      ‡a Oxford modern languages and literature monographs
500        ‡a Originally presented as the author's thesis (doctoral--Oxford) under the title: Culture
           and the word.
504        ‡a Includes bibliographical references (p. [287]-306) and index.
700 1      ‡a Doherty, Justin. ‡t Culture and the word.
```

Title page	The Acmeist Movement in Russian Poetry Culture and the Word Justin Doherty Clarendon Press • Oxford 1995
Verso of title page	Published in the United States by Oxford University Press, Inc., New York

Figure 1-71.   Place supplied in publication area

```
028 02     ‡a MGJ 54826 ‡b MGM Records
110 2      ‡a Osmonds (Musical group)
245 14     ‡a The Osmonds "live" ‡h [sound recording].
260        ‡a [Culver City, Calif.] : ‡b MGM Records, ‡c 1972.
300        ‡a 1 sound cassette (42 min.) ; ‡b analog, 1 7/8 ips, stereo.
511 0      ‡a The Osmonds, vocal and instrumental ensemble.
518        ‡a Recorded in concert at the Forum, Los Angeles, California, December 4, 1971.
505 0      ‡a Intro -- Motown special -- My world is empty without you -- I'm gonna make you love
           me -- I can't get next to you, babe -- Double lovin' -- Your song -- Sweet and innocent --
           You've lost that lovin' feelin' -- Proud Mary -- Free -- Go away, little girl -- Sometimes I
           feel like a motherless child -- Where could I go but to the Lord -- Everytime I feel the
           spirit -- We gotta live together -- Trouble -- I got a woman -- Hey girl -- Down by the lazy
           river -- Yo-yo -- One bad apple.
```

does not appear on the item, it may be taken from appropriate reference sources or other materials.

In the example shown in figure 1-71, the *Directory of Inter-Corporate Ownership* (New York: Simon & Schuster, 1974; v. 1, p. 833) gave information that in 1972 MGM Records was a subsidiary of Metro-Goldwyn-Mayer in Culver City, California. The place is definite. If the cataloger is not certain of the place, he or she may give a probable city with a question mark. Always use the English form of the name in these situations.

The cataloger need not do extensive research to learn the location of a publisher. However, if the reference sources are at hand, they should be used. In addition, the place can often be discovered in an on-line system by searching for other records containing the publisher's name.

The cataloger may, if a probable city is not known but a probable country or state is, give the country or state alone as the place element. The rationale for this rule is plain; the addition of a country or state name is preferable to the third alternative, adding "[S.l.]" (*sine loco*, meaning "without place"), which is done if the cataloger has no idea at all where the item originated. Under no other circumstances is state or country ever given *alone* in the publication area. In all but this instance, "place" means city or town.

The book used as the basis of figure 1-72 illustrates several cataloging problems. As can be seen from the facsimile of the title page, no publication information is given in the chief source of information. A careful search of the volume failed to turn up any hint as to place of publication or name of either publisher or printer. The only indication of date of publication is the statement in the preface that "Mrs. W. J. Crowley of Kingman is now serving (1944)." This is enough evidence for the cataloger to bracket [1944?] as publication date (see *AACR2R* 1.4F7).

As for place of publication, the Arizona Federation of Women's Clubs has never had a permanent headquarters, and so no help can come from this source. Furthermore, nothing in the book suggests that the Federation served as publisher of the book, although this is highly probable. The author's place of residence is not known. However, it is an entirely reasonable supposition that she lived in Arizona when the book was issued and that the book was printed and published somewhere in Arizona. Therefore, the

Figure 1-72.   State alone used as place

100 1	‡a Ross, Margaret Wheeler, ‡d 1867-1953.
245 10	‡a History of the Arizona Federation of Women's Clubs and its forerunners / ‡c written and compiled by Margaret Wheeler Ross.
246 1	‡i Spine and cover title: ‡a Tale is told
260	‡a [Arizona? : ‡b s.n., ‡c 1944?]
300	‡a 401 p. : ‡b ill. ; ‡c 24 cm.
500	‡a Subtitle: Forerunners, 1889 to 1901 : Federation history, November 18, 1901 to April 12th, 1944, inclusive.

Title page   History of the Arizona Federation
of Women's Clubs and Its Forerunners
Written and Compiled by
Margaret Wheeler Ross
Forerunners
1889 to 1901
Federation History
November 18, 1901 to April 12th, 1944
Inclusive

name of the state should be used alone as place of publication, qualified with a question mark because the information is not certain.

1.4C7. The cataloger may *optionally* add the full address of the publisher to the name of the place. The decision of the Library of Congress on this option is to add full address on a case-by-case basis when information is readily available for items covered by *AACR2R* chapters 2 and 5, published in the United States within the last three years, and that do not bear an ISBN or an ISSN (*LCRI* 1.4C7, Jan. 5, 1989). The British Library will only apply the option when the publisher's address is not readily available elsewhere. The National Library of Canada and the National Library of Australia will not apply the option (Howarth, at 1.4C7).

1.4D. Name of publisher, distributor, etc.

1.4D1. The name of the publisher, distributor, etc., is the second element of the publication area. It is separated from the first element (place of publication) by space - colon - space and preceded by subfield ǂb.

1.4D2. The publisher's or distributor's name is shortened in the publication area as much as possible, but not so much that it duplicates the name of another publisher or that it cannot be identified internationally. Previous catalog codes gave elaborate guidelines for shortening publishers' names. The present rules are not as explicit. The cataloger must have a knowledge of publishers not only in the United States but also abroad to know that A. S. Barnes & Co. must be distinguished from John W. Barnes, Jr. Publishing, Inc., and therefore that one must be A. S. Barnes in the one publication statement and J. W. Barnes in the other. On the other hand, W. H. Freeman and Co. can be shortened to Freeman, because there is only one Freeman in the publishing business. *Books in Print* and its British counterpart have publisher lists that can be used to ascertain whether a publisher's name is unique and therefore susceptible to being truncated to a single word.

A few guidelines can be given.

1. Omit the initial article.

    The Canadian Record   *becomes*   Canadian Record.

2. Normally omit terms meaning "incorporated" or "limited."

    Caxton Printers, Ltd.   *becomes*   Caxton Printers.

    Artabras, Inc.   *becomes*   Artabras.

3. Omit words or phrases that show the publisher function.

    Bindford & Mort, Publishers   *is shortened to*   Bindford & Mort.

4. Omit words that simply indicate commercial organization.

Dodd, Mead & Co.	*is shortened to*	Dodd, Mead.
Macmillan Publishing Co., Inc.		Macmillan.
Meredith Corp.		Meredith.
Charles Scribner's Sons		Scribner.
Bramhall House		Bramhall.
Fratelli Treves, Editori		Treves.
Penguin Books		Penguin.
Dover Books		Dover.
Avenel Books		Avenel.
The Horn Book, Inc.	*is only shortened to*	Horn Book.

Use care in shortening names; do not change the meaning of the phrase.

5. Unless two or more publishers have the same surname, forenames of well-known publishers may be omitted entirely.

Thomas Y. Crowell Co., Inc.	*is shortened to*	Crowell.
Franklin Watts, Inc.	*is shortened to*	Watts.

Alternately, and perhaps more safely, forenames may be shortened to initials.

Frederick Warne & Co., Ltd.	*is shortened to*	F. Warne.

Now a word of caution. Certain elements of firm names may *not* be shortened.

1. Never omit multiple surnames. Transcribe what appears on the chief source of information with which you are working. These surname combinations may vary from one book to another for we are in a period of publishing house mergers.

Harper & Brothers, Publishers *is shortened to* Harper.
Harper & Row, Publishers, Inc. *is shortened to* Harper & Row.
Coward, McCann & Geoghegan, Inc. *becomes* Coward, McCann & Geoghegan.

2. Do not shorten a firm name when the entire name is descriptive of the type of material produced by the firm or of its viewpoint.

Aviation Book Co.	*is not shortened.*	
Architectural Book Pub. Co.	*is not shortened.*	
The Feminist Press	*becomes*	Feminist Press.
Random House, Inc.	*becomes*	Random House.

(The name is indicative of the founder's desire to choose titles for publication "at random.")

Remember that this is left entirely up to the cataloger's judgment, who should not agonize over the decision but do what is most "efficient and effective in the particular case" (see *LCRI* 1.4D2, Dec. 11, 1989).

Occasionally the name of the publisher, distributor, etc., is given in the prescribed source in more than one language. (This is particularly likely to be so for bilingual or multilingual books.) *AACR2R* 1.4D2 stipulates that the cataloger is to record the form that is in the language of the title proper (see figure 1-73).

Figure 1-73. Publisher's name in more than one language

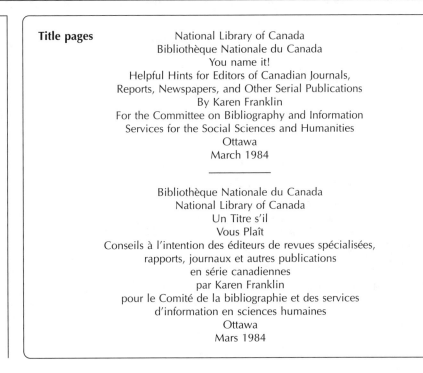

020	‡a 0662527747 (pbk.)
100 1	‡a Franklin, Karen.
245 10	‡a You name it! : ‡b helpful hints for editors of Canadian journals, reports, newspapers, and other serial publications / ‡c by Karen Franklin for the Committee on Bibliography and Information Services for the Social Sciences and Humanities.
246 1	‡i Title on added t.p.: ‡a Titre s'il vous plaît
260	‡a Ottawa : ‡b National Library of Canada, ‡c 1984.
300	‡a 41, 42 p. : ‡b ill. ; ‡c 23 cm.
546	‡a Text in English and French with French text on inverted pages.
500	‡a DSS Cat. no. NS3-196/1984.
710 2	‡a National Library of Canada. ‡b Advisory board. ‡b Committee on Bibliography and Information Services for the Social Sciences and Humanities.

Title pages

National Library of Canada
Bibliothèque Nationale du Canada
You name it!
Helpful Hints for Editors of Canadian Journals,
Reports, Newspapers, and Other Serial Publications
By Karen Franklin
For the Committee on Bibliography and Information
Services for the Social Sciences and Humanities
Ottawa
March 1984

———————

Bibliothèque Nationale du Canada
National Library of Canada
Un Titre s'il
Vous Plaît
Conseils à l'intention des éditeurs de revues spécialisées,
rapports, journaux et autres publications
en série canadiennes
par Karen Franklin
pour le Comité de la bibliographie et des services
d'information en sciences humaines
Ottawa
Mars 1984

Sometimes the name of a publisher is part of a hierarchy. *For commercial publishers only*, omit parts of the hierarchy that are not needed for identification (see, for example, figure 1-74).

1.4D3. Words and phrases to be retained in publisher, distributor, etc., element. Sometimes, as in figure 1-75, the prescribed source includes a phrase indicating that the corporate body named in the publication area has performed a function other than publishing. This phrase should be transcribed.

Figure 1-74.   Parts of commercial publisher hierarchy omitted

```
020        ‡a 0831742593
245 02     ‡a A treasury of North American fiction : ‡b a collection from Harper's magazine.
260        ‡a New York : ‡b Gallery Books, ‡c 1991.
300        ‡a 542 p. : ‡b ill. ; ‡c 23 cm.
500        ‡a Facsims. of original fiction from the archives of Harper's magazine.
730 0      ‡a Harper's magazine.
```

Title page

A Treasury of
North
American
Fiction
A Collection from
Harper's Magazine

Gallery Books
An Imprint of W. H. Smith Publishers, Inc.
112 Madison Avenue
New York City 10016

Figure 1-75.   Phrase indicating distribution

```
110 1      ‡a United States. ‡b President (1963-1969 : Johnson)
245 10     ‡a No retreat from tomorrow : ‡b President Lyndon B. Johnson's 1967 messages to the
           90th Congress.
260        ‡a Garden City, N.Y. : ‡b Distributed to the book trade by Doubleday, ‡c [1968?]
300        ‡a 241 p. : ‡b ill. (some col.) ; ‡c 29 cm.
700 1      ‡a Johnson, Lyndon B. ‡q (Lyndon Baines), ‡d 1908-1973.
710 1      ‡a United States. ‡b Congress ‡n (90th, 1st session : ‡d 1967).
```

Title page

No Retreat from Tomorrow
President Lyndon B. Johnson's
1967 Messages to the
90th Congress
Distributed to the book trade by
Doubleday & Company, Inc.
Garden City, New York

Therefore, the following may *not* be omitted from the name of a publisher, distributor, etc.:

3. Words or phrases needed to indicate a function other than publishing performed by a body.

Asia House Gallery	*remains the same.*
American Camping Association	*remains the same.*
American Library Association	*remains the same.*
Boston Public Library	*remains the same.*

The word "press" needs careful consideration. Literally, it indicates a printing function, yet many publishers who do no printing include the word "press" as part of their corporate name. Furthermore, the word "press" sometimes is needed to differentiate between two different corporate bodies; for example:

University of Illinois Press   *remains the same.*

(The University of Illinois may also be a publisher.)

Yet "press" may be omitted from the names of such publishers as

The Viking Press, Inc.	*which becomes*	Viking.
Bradbury Press, Inc.	*which becomes*	Bradbury.

Phrases or words that simply indicate a publishing function should be omitted (see figure 1-61).

1.4D4. If the name of the publisher, etc., appears in the title and statement of responsibility area in "recognizable" form, it may be shortened in the publication area. The Library of Congress has interpreted "recognizable" to mean full form (*CSB* 11, winter 1981, p. 9). However, it need not be identical to the form given in the publisher statement on the work. Thus, when a parent body serves as publisher for one of its subordinate units and the name of the subordinate unit is given as part of the title and statement of responsibility area, the name of the parent body as publisher may be shortened in the publication area (see figure 1-76).

Initials may be used, as in figure 1-76, to abbreviate the publisher's name if the agency is familiarly known by an acronym. *CSB* 13 (summer 1981), p. 10, gives a useful caution regarding this practice: use such an acronym "only if it appears in the item or is one that is known by the cataloger to be in common use for the body." If in doubt, give a generic term standing for the name of the agency (see figure 1-77).

When using the generic term (The Museum, The Society, The Library, etc.), the term should be spelled out in full, regardless of whether the word is found in Appendix B (Abbreviations), e.g., The Company (*CSB* 13, summer 1981, p. 10).

As mentioned previously, *AACR2R* calls for the inclusion of some word or phrase representing the name of the publisher as the second element of the publication, etc., area even when such a name is not explicitly given in the item. When a corporate body named only in the title and statement of

Figure 1-76.   Publisher's name abbreviated

```
110 2    ‡a Library of Congress. ‡b Processing Dept.
245 14   ‡a The cataloging-in-source experiment : ‡b a report to the Librarian of Congress / ‡c by
         the director of the Processing Department.
260      ‡a Washington : ‡b L.C., ‡c 1960.
300      ‡a xxiv, 199 p. : ‡b ill. ; ‡c 27 cm.
710 2    ‡a Library of Congress.
```

Title page
　　　　　　　　　　　　　　　　　The
　　　　　　　　　　　　Cataloging-in-Source
　　　　　　　　　　　　　　　Experiment
　　　　　　　　A Report to the Librarian of Congress
　　　　　　　　　　　　　　　by the
　　　　　　　Director of the Processing Department
　　　　　　　　　　　Library of Congress
　　　　　　　　　　　Washington : 1960

Figure 1-77.   Publisher's name abbreviated

```
110 2    ‡a American Philosophical Society.
245 12   ‡a A catalogue of portraits and other works of art in the possession of the American
         Philosophical Society.
260      ‡a Philadelphia : ‡b The Society, ‡c 1961.
300      ‡a viii, 173 p., 1 leaf of plates : ‡b ill. (some col.) ; ‡c 24 cm.
490 1    ‡a Memoirs of the American Philosophical Society held at Philadelphia for Promoting
         Useful Knowledge ; ‡v v. 54
830  0   ‡a Memoirs of the American Philosophical Society ; ‡v v. 54.
```

Half-title page
　　　　　　　　　　　　　　Memoirs of the
　　　　　　　　　　American Philosophical Society
　　　　　　　　　　　　Held at Philadelphia
　　　　　　　　　for Promoting Useful Knowledge
　　　　　　　　　　　　　Volume 54

Title page
　　　　　　　　　　　　　　A Catalogue of
　　　　　　　　　　　　　　　Portraits
　　　　　　　　　　　　　　　　and
　　　　　　　　　　　　　Other Works of Art
　　　　　　　　　　　in the Possession of the
　　　　　　　　　　American Philosophical Society

　　　　　　　　　The American Philosophical Society
　　　　　　　Independence Square • Philadelphia
　　　　　　　　　　　　　　　1961

responsibility is the publisher, apply 1.4D4; give this name in shortened form, without brackets, in the publication area (see figure 1-78).

1.4D5. Two or more publishers, distributors, etc. If an item has two or more publishers, distributors, etc., describe it in terms of the first one named and the corresponding place (see figure 1-79).

The name of a subsequently named publisher, etc., along with its corresponding place (if different from the place already named) will be given if the two names are linked, as frequently happens when the first name is that of a distributor, releasing agent, etc., and the second is that of the publisher (see figures 1-80 and 1-81). The name of a subsequently named publisher and its place will also be recorded if the first named publisher is outside the cataloger's home country and the subsequently named publisher is in the home country. This parallels rule 1.4C5 (see figures 1-56 and 1-70).

Motion pictures and videorecordings frequently have more than one distributor, releasing agent, etc., involved with the publication of such a work. In many instances it is appropriate to add a second named place, distributor, releasing agent, etc. (see figure 1-82).

1.4D7. Publisher not named. Except when cataloging unpublished items (see *AACR2R* 1.4D9), something must always appear in the publisher, etc., element of the publication area. If the cataloger does not know and cannot infer the name of the publisher, the abbreviation "s.n." (*sine nomine*,

Figure 1-78.   Publisher not named in publication area

245 00	‡a Occupational employment outlook, 1993-1998 : ‡b Colorado Denver-Boulder area, Vocational Planning Region III / ‡c prepared by Colorado Department of Labor and Employment, Division of Employment and Training, Labor Market Information Section, Occupational Employment Survey (OES) Unit.
260	‡a Denver, Colo. : ‡b The Unit, ‡c 1993.
300	‡a i, 59 p. : ‡b ill. ; ‡c 28 cm.
500	‡a "December, 1993"--Cover.
504	‡a Includes bibliographical references.
710 1	‡a Colorado. ‡b Labor Market Information. ‡b Occupational Employment Survey Unit.

Title page

Occupational Employment Outlook
1993-1998
Colorado
Denver-Boulder Area, Vocational Planning Region III
Prepared by:
Colorado Department of Labor and Employment
Division of Employment and Training
Labor Market Information Section
Occupational Employment Survey (OES) Unit

Figure 1-79.   More than one place and publisher

```
100 0    ‡a John, ‡c Uncle.
245 14   ‡a The boy's book of sports and games : ‡b containing rules and directions for the
         practice of the principal recreative amusements of youth / ‡c by Uncle John.
260      ‡a Philadelphia : ‡b Appleton, ‡c 1851.
300      ‡a 192 p. : ‡b ill. ; ‡c 15 cm.
```

Title page	The Boy's Book of
	Sports and Games,
	Containing
	Rules and Directions
	for the Practice of the
	Principal Recreative Amusements of Youth.
	By Uncle John,
	Author of "The Little Boy's Own Book," etc. etc.
	With Illustrations
	Philadelphia:
	George S. Appleton
	New York:
	D. Appleton & Co.
	1851.

Figure 1-80.   Names of two agents included

```
020      ‡a 0807822078 (cloth : alk. paper)
020      ‡a 0807845213 (pbk. : alk. paper)
100 1    ‡a Conroy, David W.
245 10   ‡a In public houses : ‡b drink & the revolution of authority in colonial Massachusetts / ‡c
         David W. Conroy.
260      ‡a Chapel Hill [N.C.] : ‡b Published for the Institute of Early American History and
         Culture, Williamsburg, Virginia, by the University of North Carolina Press, ‡c c1995.
300      ‡a xiii, 351 p. : ‡b ill., maps ; ‡c 24 cm.
504      ‡a Includes bibliographical references (p. 327-340) and index.
710 2    ‡a Institute of Early American History and Culture (Williamsburg, Va.)
```

Title page	In
	Public
	Houses
	Drink & the Revolution
	of Authority in Colonial
	Massachusetts
	David W. Conroy
	Published for the Institute of Early American
	History and Culture, Williamsburg, Virginia,
	by the University of North Carolina Press,
	Chapel Hill & London

Figure 1-81.   Names of two agents included

```
245 00   ‡a Scrabble ‡h [game].
260      ‡a New York : ‡b Manufactured by Selchow & Righter Co. for Production & Marketing
         Co., ‡c 1953.
300      ‡a 1 game (board, 4 racks, 100 letter tiles) ; ‡c in box, 19 × 37 × 4 cm.
500      ‡a A word game for 2, 3, or 4 players.
710 2    ‡a Production & Marketing Co. (New York, N.Y.)
```

Figure 1-82.   Names of two agents included

```
245 00   ‡a Navajo ‡h [videorecording] : ‡b the fight for survival.
260      ‡a London : ‡b BBC-TV ; ‡a New York : ‡b Released in the U.S. by Time-Life Video, ‡c
         [1972?]
300      ‡a 1 videocassette (50 min.) : ‡b sd., col. ; ‡c 3/4 in.
500      ‡a Released in Great Britain under title: Navaho : the last of the red Indians.
520      ‡a Details the demise of Native American culture from the time of the earliest European
         explorers, and reports efforts to preserve Navajo culture.
538      ‡a U-matic.
710 2    ‡a British Broadcasting Corporation. ‡b Television Service.
710 2    ‡a Time-Life Video.
740 0    ‡a Navaho : the last of the red Indians.
```

meaning "without a name") in brackets is transcribed following the place element and before the date (see figure 1-83).

Not all publications include a conventionally arranged title page or other chief source. For a book, the title page usually includes the name of the publisher near the bottom of the page. However, sometimes the title page lacks such information. In these cases, if a corporate body is named at the head of title, it may be regarded as the publisher and moved to the appropriate position in the catalog entry (*CSB* 25, summer 1984, p. 24) (see figure 1-73).

LCRI 1.4D1 (Jan. 5, 1989) directs the cataloger to treat the person or the group for which a privately printed work has been issued as the publisher, whether named as such in the work or not (see figure 1-84).

It is not always possible to ascertain without research and correspondence whether a corporate body listed in one of the appropriate sources of information has, indeed, functioned as a publisher (i.e., an agency that edits, designs, distributes, sells, etc., books, music, etc.) rather than simply as a printer or manufacturer. Many publishers include the word "press" as a part of their name; some of these "presses" have no facilities for printing; others do. In case of doubt, it is better to record the name of an agency appearing in one of the prescribed sources for the publisher statement rather than use "s.n." in the statement, although in reality the agency may only have functioned as a printer (see figure 1-85).

Figure 1-83.   Publisher not known

```
100 1    ‡a Reynolds, George, ‡d 1842-1909.
245 10   ‡a Commentary on the Book of Mormon / ‡c by George Reynolds and Janne M. Sjodahl ;
         edited and arranged by Philip C. Reynolds.
250      ‡a 1st ed.
260      ‡a Salt Lake City, Utah : ‡b [s.n.], ‡c 1955-1961.
300      ‡a 7 v. ; ‡c 24 cm.
500      ‡a Includes index.
500      ‡a v. 3-7: From the notes of George Reynolds and Janne M. Sjodahl. Arranged and
         amplified by Philip C. Reynolds ; v. 3-4: with David Sjodahl King.
505 0    ‡a v. 1. The small plates of Nephi -- v. 2. The words of Mormon and the Book of Mosiah
         -- v. 3. The Book of Alma, Chapters 1-26 -- v. 4. The Book of Alma, Chapters 27-44 -- v. 5.
         The Book of Alma, Chapters 45-63 -- v. 6. The Book of Ether -- v. 7. III-IV Nephi, Mormon
         and Moroni.
700 1    ‡a Sjodahl, Janne M. ‡q (Janne Mattson), ‡d 1853-1939.
700 1    ‡a Reynolds, Philip C.
700 1    ‡a King, David S., ‡d 1927-
730 02   ‡a Book of Mormon.
```

Title page	Commentary on the Book of Mormon by George Reynolds and Janne M. Sjodahl Volume 1—The Small Plates of Nephi Edited and Arranged by Philip C. Reynolds Salt Lake City

Figure 1-84.   Privately printed work

```
100 1    ‡a Martin, Lowell Arthur, ‡d 1912-
245 10   ‡a Development plan for the Tucson Public Library, 1974-1984 : ‡b preliminary
         recommendations and alternatives for library service in Tucson and Pima County,
         presented for discussion / ‡c Lowell A. Martin.
260      ‡a [Tucson, Ariz. : ‡b The Library, ‡c 1974]
300      ‡a 31 leaves ; ‡c 28 cm.
710 2    ‡a Tucson Public Library.
```

Title page	Development Plan for the Tucson Public Library 1974-1984 Preliminary recommendations and alternatives for library service in Tucson and Pima County, presented for discussion. Lowell A. Martin Director of the 1973-1974 study of the Tucson Public Library

Figure 1-85.   Printer or publisher?

```
100 1    ‡a Stillwell, Margaret Bingham, ‡d 1887-
245 10   ‡a Rhythm and rhymes : ‡b the songs of a bookworm / ‡c by Margaret B. Stillwell.
250      ‡a Keepsake ed.
260      ‡a Mount Vernon, N.Y. : ‡b Press of A. Colish, ‡c 1977.
300      ‡a xii, 97 p. : ‡b ill. ; ‡c 24 cm.
500      ‡a Limited ed. of 500 copies.
590      ‡a Library's copy signed by the author.
```

Title page

Rhythm and Rhymes
The Songs of a Bookworm
By Margaret B. Stillwell
Mount Vernon, New York
MDCCCCLXXVII

Verso of title page

Copyright © 1977, Margaret B. Stillwell
From The Press of A. Colish,
Mount Vernon, New York

In the absence of indications to the contrary, a government printer or printing office is to be recorded as a publisher (see figure 1-50 and *LCRI* 1.4D1, Jan. 5, 1989).

1.4D9. For many items that are one-of-a-kind materials not intended for widespread distribution, the name of a publisher, etc., as well as the listing of a place of publication is inappropriate. Simply omit both of these elements from the publication statement. Do not record "s.l." or "s.n." (see, for example, figure 1-13 and discussion in *Handbook* chapter 10, at 10.4).

1.4E. *Optional addition.* Statement of function of publisher, etc.

A term may be added in square brackets to clarify the function of the publisher, distributor, etc. The list of terms in 1.4E1 is not exclusive and has been removed by the 1993 amendments. The Library of Congress will apply this option whenever it is necessary to clarify the function of the particular body.

1.4F. Date of publication, distribution, etc.

The third element of the publication area is the date of the item. It is preceded by a comma and subfield ‡c. The date is the year of publication, distribution, etc., of "the edition . . . named in the edition area." This means the date of the first impression or printing of an edition. An impression consists of all of the copies of a publication run at one time from a set of photographic plates, type, etc. Frequently, if the publication sells well, the publisher will decide at a later date to run more copies from the same plates or forms of type. Customarily, although not always, a second run of a publication will be referred to as a "second impression" or "second printing." This information will usually be printed, possibly along with a date, on the title page or its verso. Generally speaking, succeeding impressions or printings are identical to the first; catalogers treat them as copies of the first impression of that particular edition. As discussed above under 1.2B, these impression or printing statements are usually ignored in the edition area. They are likewise ignored in the publication area, as in figure 1-86. Except for the verso of the title page, this book is a photographic reprint of the 1889 edition. Because it is a book in relatively high demand, it has been reprinted in this way every few years. The date for any of these impressions should be recorded in the 260 field as 1889. If a library feels it is important to record which printing it has, the cataloger may include a note in a 590 field such as "The library's copy is the 1991 impression." Alternately, if the library does not have copies with differing impression dates, the cataloger may add "(1991 printing)" after the date in the 260 field.

Figure 1-86.   Printing or impression omitted in recording date

```
020      ‡a 0199102066
100 1    ‡a Liddell, Henry George, ‡d 1811-1898.
245 13   ‡a An intermediate Greek-English lexicon : ‡b founded upon the seventh edition of Liddell
         and Scott's Greek-English lexicon.
250      ‡a 1st ed.
260      ‡a Oxford : ‡b Clarendon Press ; ‡a New York : ‡b Oxford University Press, ‡c 1889.
300      ‡a 910 p. ; ‡c 23 cm.
700 1    ‡a Scott, Robert, ‡d 1811-1887.
```

Title page

An Intermediate
Greek-English Lexicon
Founded upon
the Seventh Edition of
Liddell and Scott's
Greek-English Lexicon
Oxford
At the Clarendon Press

Verso of title page

Oxford University Press, Walton Street, Oxford OX2 6DP
Oxford New York Toronto
Delhi Bombay Calcutta Madras Karachi
Petaling Jaya Singapore Hong Kong Tokyo
Dairobi Dar es Salaam Cape Town
Melbourne Aukland
and associated companies in
Berlin Ibadan
Impression of 1991
First edition 1889

Sometimes, as shown in figure 1-86, specific statements indicating a date of publication will be found in the item being cataloged. A statement such as "First Schocken Edition 1968," which appears as part of the cataloging data for figure 1-29, is also evidence of publication date for a particular edition.

Few items include such a specific statement of publication date, however. If no such statement appears, the cataloger simply records whatever information is available in the prescribed source for publication area information. A date appearing in the imprint position on the title page may normally be accepted as the publication date, particularly if it is the same as the copyright date given on the verso of the title page, as is the case in figure 1-87.

The date in the publication area is limited to the year of publication. Do not transcribe month, day, etc., even if this information is found on the chief source of information. The date is always transcribed in arabic numerals, even if it is found in the chief source in roman numerals (see figure 1-61).

1.4F5. *Optional addition.* The latest copyright date is not always the same as the actual date of publication. If the two differ, the Library of Congress gives both dates unless the copyright date is later than the publication date, for example, 1970, c1969, but not 1993, c1994 (*LCRI* 1.4F5, Dec. 11, 1989). Examples in this text also follow this option, figure 1-88 being one. The British Library, National Library of Australia, and National Library of Canada also apply the option (Howarth, at 1.4F5).

1.4F6. Many works do not specify a date of publication. Give latest copyright date if this is the case (see figure 1-89). For works first copyrighted before 1978, the Library of Congress will ignore the copyright re-

Figure 1-87.   Publication date the same as copyright date

```
020       ‡a 0195093453 (pbk. : alk. paper)
100 1     ‡a Auyang, Sunny Y.
245 10    ‡a How is quantum field theory possible? / ‡c Sunny Y. Auyang.
260       ‡a New York : ‡b Oxford University Press, ‡c 1995.
300       ‡a viii, 280 p. ; ‡b ill. ; ‡c 24 cm.
504       ‡a Includes bibliographical references and index.
```

Title page
How Is
Quantum Field Theory
Possible?
Sunny Y. Auyang
New York Oxford
Oxford University Press
1995

Verso of title page
Copyright © 1995 by Oxford University Press, Inc.

Figure 1-88.   Copyright date in addition to the publication date when the two differ

```
100 2    ‡a Pryce-Jones, David, ‡d 1936-
245 10   ‡a Next generation : ‡b travels in Israel / ‡c David Pryce-Jones.
250      ‡a 1st ed.
260      ‡a New York : ‡b Holt, Rinehart and Winston, ‡c 1965, c1964.
300      ‡a 195 p. : ‡b map ; ‡c 22 cm.
500      ‡a "Chapter 1 was originally published as 'Israel's Three Cities' in Commentary, and a
         much-abbreviated article on 'The Yossele Case' appeared in the New Statesman. Passages
         from Chapter 10 were included in an article for the Spectator"--T.p. verso.
```

Title page	Next Generation
	Travels in Israel
	David Pryce-Jones
	Holt, Rinehart and Winston
	New York Chicago San Francisco
Verso of title page	
	Copyright © 1964 by David Pryce-Jones
	First published in the United States in 1965.
	Chapter 1 was originally published as "Israel's
	Three Cities" in *Commentary,* and a much-abbre-
	viated article on "The Yossele Case" appeared in
	the *New Statesman.* Passages from Chapter 10
	were included in an article for the *Spectator.*
	First Edition

Figure 1-89.   Copyright date in publication area

```
020      ‡a 0671881779
100 1    ‡a Blauner, Peter.
245 10   ‡a Casino moon : ‡b a novel / ‡c Peter Blauner.
260      ‡a New York : ‡b Simon & Schuster, ‡c c1994.
300      ‡a 249 p. ; ‡c 24 cm.
```

Title page	Casino
	Moon
	a novel
	Peter Blauner
	Simon & Schuster
	New York London
	Toronto Sydney
	Tokyo Singapore
Verso of title page	
	Copyright © 1994 by Peter Blauner

newal dates, giving only the original copyright date (*LCRI* 1.4F6, Dec. 11, 1989).

1.4F7. Except for naturally occurring objects (see *AACR2R* 1.4F9 and discussion in this *Handbook* at 10.4F2), the publication, distribution, etc., area must *always* include a date, even if it can only be a conjectural interpolation by the cataloger. All dates taken from other than prescribed sources, whether derived from the item, reference sources, or the cataloger's conjecture, must be bracketed. (See the various chapters in *AACR2R* for specific kinds of library materials. In each chapter, rule .0B2 prescribes the sources from which data may be taken without bracketing.) If no date can be transcribed from any source, then the cataloger must guess at the date. In such a case the cataloger's interpolation is not only enclosed within square brackets, but also displayed as one type of conjecture or another: [1971 or 1972], [1969?], [ca. 1960], [197-], etc. In the example shown in figure 1-90, the date was taken from the preface.

Usually the cataloger cannot find a dated preface to use for the year of publication. In the example shown in figure 1-75, the title itself is evidence that the book cannot have been published before 1967. Because the book is

Figure 1-90. Date not from a prescribed source

110	1	‡a United States.
240	10	‡a Constitution
245	14	‡a The Constitution of the United States of America : ‡b with a summary of the actions by the States in ratification of the provisions thereof : to which is appended, for its historical interest, the Constitution of the Confederate States of America / ‡c prepared and distributed by the Virginia Commission on Constitutional Government.
260		‡a [Richmond, Va.] : ‡b The Commission, ‡c [1961]
300		‡a 94 p. ; ‡c 22 cm.
440	0	‡a Historic statements and papers expounding the role of the States in their relation to the central government ; ‡v 8
500		‡a Cover title.
500		‡a Pref. dated 1961.
710	1	‡a Virginia. ‡b Commission on Constitutional Government.
710	12	‡a Confederate States of America. ‡t Constitution.

Title page

The Constitution of the
United States of America
With a Summary of the Actions by the States
in Ratification of the Provisions Thereof
to Which is Appended, for its Historical Interest
the Constitution of the
Confederate States of America
Prepared and Distributed by the
Virginia Commission on Constitutional
Government

not copyrighted, there is no copyright statement to refer to. The table of contents lists President Johnson's speeches with the dates of delivery, ranging between January 10 and May 25, 1967. It is possible, though not likely, that this book could have appeared toward the end of 1967. But the LC catalog card number is listed as 68-23394 on the verso of the title page. The first two digits of the LC number normally stand for the last two digits of the year in which the publisher applied for a preassigned number. It is rather likely that the book appeared in 1968. Therefore the date is recorded in the catalog entry as [1968?].

Few books furnish this much internal evidence about probable date of publication. Particularly when dealing with nineteenth-century reprint editions, the cataloger may fail to find the slightest clue to the date. Under normal circumstances the cataloger will not search beyond the item itself. But, as with the example shown in figure 1-91, it is only sensible to do the minimum amount of research necessary to discover that Mayne Reid (1818–1883) was a nineteenth-century American writer of stories for boys and that *The Young Voyageurs* first appeared in 1853, which gives at least a minimum parameter for the date. Both Dutton and Routledge were well-established nineteenth-century publishers. Reid's novels were widely reprinted until the end of the nineteenth century but lost popularity after that. Therefore, one can make a safe guess that this edition appeared in the nineteenth century, but, without more research than the item warrants, one cannot say more.

1.4F8. If a work appearing in more than one part does not appear to be complete, the cataloger gives in the date element of the publication area, if possible, the date of the earliest part, or if not, the earliest date of whatever parts of the item the library has, followed by a hyphen. Figure 1-92 is an example of such a work. When the date is followed by a hyphen in this fashion, the catalog record is known as an "open entry." When the item is

Figure 1-91.   Conjectural date

```
100 1   ‡a Reid, Mayne, ‡d 1818-1883.
245 14  ‡a The young voyageurs, or, The boy hunters in the north / ‡c by Mayne Reid.
246 30  ‡a Young voyageurs
246 30  ‡a Boy hunters in the north
260     ‡a London : ‡b G. Routledge ; ‡a New York : ‡b Dutton, ‡c [18--]
300     ‡a viii, 471 p. : ‡b ill. ; ‡c 20 cm.
```

Title page	The Young Voyageurs or the Boy Hunters in the North by Captain Mayne Reid London George Routledge and Sons, Limited New York: E.P. Dutton and Co.

Figure 1-92. Open entry

```
020      ‡a 1850752443 (v. 1)
245 04   ‡a The dictionary of classical Hebrew / ‡c David J.A. Clines, editor.
260      ‡a Sheffield [England] : ‡b Sheffield Academic Press, ‡c 1993-
300      ‡a v. ; ‡c 26 cm.
504      ‡a Includes bibliographical references (v.1, p. 51-54) and index.
505 1    ‡a v. 1. [Aleph] -- v. 2 [Beth]-[Vav]
700 1    ‡a Clines, David J. A.
```

Title page	The Dictionary of Classical Hebrew David J.A. Clines Editor Volume I [Aleph] John Elwolde Executive Editor Sheffield Sheffield Academic Press 1993

finally completed (this may take a number of years), the cataloger adds the latest date and closes the entry (see figure 1-93).

A word of caution: obviously, the cataloger will not "close" an entry unless he or she has evidence that the work is complete or that no more will be published. In addition, the cataloger must be aware that not all bibliographical items are issued beginning with part 1. The date in the publication area is the earliest followed by the latest date of publication, whether or not the earliest date is the date of part 1.

Library of Congress cataloging practice allows the recording of "temporary" data in angle brackets. Thus, an LC cataloger might record the dates of a multivolume set that is only partially complete as follows: "1991-<1993>." This is not standard *AACR2R* practice, nor is it covered in the *LCRIs*. It will not be followed in this *Handbook*.

1.4G. Place of manufacture, name of manufacturer, date of manufacture

Information about manufacture will be given if possible when the name of the publisher is not known. See also *AACR2R* 1.4D8 for guidance in this matter.

1.4G4. The cataloger may optionally add the place, name, date of manufacture, printing, etc., in addition to the place, name, and date of publication if, in the opinion of the cataloging agency, this information is considered important. One instance in which this optional rule might be followed would be the addition of a date of printing to the date of publi-

Figure 1-93.   Closed entry

```
020       ‡a 3411047321 (set)
245 00    ‡a Duden, das grosse Wörterbuch der deutschen Sprache in acht Bänden.
246 30    ‡a Grosse Wörterbuch der deutschen Sprache
250       ‡a 2., völlig neu bearb. und stark erw. Aufl. / ‡b herausgegeben und bearbeitet
          vom Wissenschaftlichen Rat und den Mitarbeitern der Dudenredaktion unter der Leitung
          von Günther Drosdowski.
260       ‡a Mannheim : ‡b Dudenverlag, ‡c c1993-1995.
300       ‡a 8 v. ; ‡c 25 cm.
504       ‡a Includes bibliographical references (Bd. 1, p. 32-49).
700 1     ‡a Drosdowski, Günther.
710 2     ‡a Dudenredaktion (Bibliographisches Institut).
710 2     ‡a Dudenredaktion (Bibliographisches Institut). ‡b Wissenschaftlicher Rat.
```

Title page	Duden
	Das große Wörterbuch
	der deutschen Sprache
	in acht Bänden
	2., völlig neu bearbeitete
	und stark erweiterte Auflage
	Herausgegeben und
	bearbeitet vom Wissenschaftlichen Rat
	und den Mitarbeitern der
	Dudenredaktion unter der Leitung von
	Günther Drosdowski
	Band 1: A-Bim
	Dudenverlag
	Mannheim • Leipzig • Wien • Zürich

cation when significant changes have been made in the particular printing. The Library of Congress will follow this optional rule when it seems appropriate.

1.5. PHYSICAL DESCRIPTION AREA

The physical description area includes, as applicable, four elements:

1. The extent of the item and the specific type of material being described
2. Other physical data such as color, type of illustrations, etc.
3. Physical dimensions (size)
4. Accompanying materials, if any.

1.5A1. Punctuation. The physical description area is recorded in the 300 field of the MARC record. The first element begins with subfield ‡a and is separated from the second by space - colon - space. The second element begins with subfield ‡b and is separated from the third by space - semicolon - space. The third element, size, is recorded in subfield ‡c. It is normally the last element in the physical description area, but if the item includes accompanying materials, description of these materials will be separated from the third element by space - plus sign - space. This fourth element is preceded by subfield ‡e.

The physical description area, because it describes the physical format of the item being cataloged, is unique for each type of library material. For this reason, specific rules have been set forth for the physical description area of each type of material, following general principles of *AACR2R* chapter 1. Examples and further discussion of the physical description area will be found in succeeding chapters of this *Handbook*.

1.5E. Accompanying material

One aspect of *AACR2R* 1.5 that is not dependent on the physical format of the item, however, is the treatment of accompanying material. The cataloger is given four choices. He or she may (a) make a separate entry for the accompanying material; (b) analyze it using multilevel description (*AACR2R* 13.6); (c) simply mention the material in a note; or (d) give details about the accompanying material as the final element of the physical description area.

The Library of Congress, the National Library of Australia, and the National Library of Canada have issued fairly detailed instructions to their catalogers for choosing between these four, which should be of use to catalogers at other institutions as well.

Option (a), separate entry, will be chosen if the material is not issued at the same time as the main work or has a significantly different title or statement of responsibility from that of the main work.

Option (b) will never be chosen by any of these libraries.

If the item is of little bibliographic importance, or its title is not generic enough for option (d), or it is a supplement usable only in connection with the main work, choose option (c).

Option (d) may be chosen if the accompanying item satisfies all of the following: (1) it is issued at the same time by the same publisher as the main work and is of use only in conjunction with the main work; (2) it is by the same author as the main work or makes no mention of an author; and (3) its title is generic (e.g., "teacher's manual" or "plates") or lacks a title (or bears the same title as the main work) (*LCRI* 1.5E1, Aug. 14, 1990; Howarth, at 1.5E).

For an example of option (d), see figure 1-94.

The example shown in figure 1-95 is a straightforward monograph that in itself offers no problems to the cataloger.

The publisher has also issued a "Teacher's resource book" to supplement the main volume (see figure 1-96). Because the supplement has a different title and different author from the main volume, it may be given a separate catalog entry, option (a) of 1.5E1. (See also *AACR2R* 21.28B for instructions for access points in this situation.)

If the supplement title were entirely different from that of the main work, the description of the supplement would present no problem. But if the title proper of the supplement consists of the title of the main volume

Figure 1-94.   Accompanying material

```
100 1    ‡a Green, Nancy.
245 14   ‡a The bigger giant : ‡b an Irish legend / ‡c retold by Nancy Green ; pictures by Betty
         Fraser.
260      ‡a New York : ‡b Scholastic Book Services, ‡c c1963.
300      ‡a 1 v. (unpaged) : ‡b ill. ; ‡c 23 cm. + ‡e 1 sound disc (13 min. : analog, 33 1/3 rpm,
         mono. ; 7 in.)
700 1    ‡a Fraser, Betty.
```

Title page	The Bigger Giant
	An Irish Legend
	Retold by Nancy Green
	Pictures by Betty Fraser
	Scholastic Book Services
	New York • Toronto • London • Auckland • Sydney

Figure 1-95.   Monograph

```
100 1    ‡a Current, Richard Nelson.
245 10   ‡a United States history / ‡c Richard N. Current, Alexander DeConde, Harris L. Dante.
260      ‡a Glenview, Ill. : ‡b Scott, Foresman, ‡c c1967.
300      ‡a 832 p. : ‡b ill. (some col.), col. maps ; ‡c 24 cm.
500      ‡a "Scott, Foresman program in United States history."
504      ‡a Includes bibliographical references (p. 777-781).
700 1    ‡a DeConde, Alexander.
700 1    ‡a Dante, Harris L.
```

Title page	United States History
	Richard N. Current
	Alexander DeConde
	Harris L. Dante
	Scott, Foresman and Company

and title of supplement, or if the two titles are grammatically independent of each other, the cataloger follows a special procedure. Record the title and statement of responsibility of the main volume first. Close this part of the entry with a full stop. Do not separate title and statement of responsibility of the main volume with space - slash - space, because this is not a catalog entry for the main volume. The supplement's title is transcribed following main volume information.

The cataloger must disregard the order in which the foregoing elements are presented in the chief source of information (the title page of the supplement). The order must be: Main volume information. Supplement title.

Figure 1-96.   Title proper—supplement

100 1	‡a Dante, Harris L.
245 10	‡a United States history, [by] Richard N. Current, Alexander DeConde, Harris L. Dante. Teacher's resource book / ‡c Harris L. Dante, Robert F. Harris.
260	‡a Glenview, Ill. : ‡b Scott, Foresman, ‡c c1967.
300	‡a 159 p. ; ‡c 23 cm.
500	‡a A guide to the use of the text United States history by Richard N. Current, Alexander DeConde, and Harris L. Dante.
504	‡a Includes bibliographical references.
700 1	‡a Harris, Robert F.
700 1	‡a Current, Richard Nelson. ‡t United States history.

Title page	United States History
	Richard N. Current
	Alexander DeConde
	Harris L. Dante
	Teacher's Resource Book
	Harris L. Dante
	Robert F. Harris
	Scott, Foresman and Company

All of this information constitutes the title proper of the supplement. Note figure 1-96. The title proper consists of everything before the space - slash - space. See also the final example in *AACR2R* 2.1B1.

1.6. SERIES AREA

The series area is recorded in the 4XX and 8XX MARC fields. A series associated with an item is one of the headings that requires authority work; that is, because the series title appears in many items, the library must "establish" the form of the series title that will always be used to trace the series (a series may appear in slightly different forms in differing items and still be considered the same series) (for more information on the concept of authority, see chapter 15 of this *Handbook*). The library will also want to establish the treatment it wishes to apply to a series: will it be traced or untraced? Will every item in a series be analyzed (cataloged separately)? Will all the items be classed at the same call number or not? These decisions are made in the authority record for the series, which will be kept in the library's authority file and must be consulted each time a new item in the series is cataloged to determine its proper form and treatment.

In the MARC record, the 4XX fields are used to record the series *as it appears in the prescribed source in the item at hand.* If this presentation matches the form found in the authority record for the series, the series title is recorded in the 440 field (see figure 1-97). The first indicator is blank; the second gives the number of nonfiling characters. This should always be

Figure 1-97.   Omit names of editors in series statement

```
020       ‡a 0405044593
100 1     ‡a Gilman, Charlotte Perkins, ‡d 1860-1935.
245 14    ‡a The living of Charlotte Perkins Gilman : ‡b an autobiography / ‡c by Charlotte Perkins
          Gilman.
250       ‡a Reprint ed.
260       ‡a New York : ‡b Arno Press, ‡c 1972, c1935.
300       ‡a xxxviii, 341 p. : ‡b ill. ; ‡c 23 cm.
440  0    ‡a American women : images and realities
534       ‡p Reprint. Originally published: ‡c New York : Appleton-Century, 1935.
```

Series title page	American Women Images and Realities Advisory Editors Annette K. Baxter Leon Stein
Title page	The Living of Charlotte Perkins Gilman An Autobiography by Charlotte Perkins Gilman Arno Press New York • 1972

coded "0" and the initial article dropped (*LCRI* 21.30L, Aug. 27, 1990). This applies whether the article is in the nominative case or not for languages that distinguish by case (*CSB* 52, spring 1991, p. 26). The 440 field "traces" (i.e., it is an access point in the record that may be looked up by the user of the catalog).

If the presentation of the series in the item does not match precisely the form found in the authority record, or if the library has chosen not to trace the series (this information will also be found in the authority record), the form of the series title found in the item is recorded in the 490 field, which does not trace. If the library does not trace the series, the first indicator is coded "0" (see figure 1-98). If the library does trace the series, but differently from the form found in the prescribed source, the first indicator of the 490 field is "1" and the authorized form of the series is recorded in an 8XX field, which traces (see, e.g., figures 1-26 [series traced differently], 1-40 [series qualified to distinguish it from another of the same name], and 1-55 [series traced under the author's name]). 4XX fields are *not* closed with a period, nor are parentheses manually added by the cataloger, because the parentheses are supplied by the system. 8XX fields, on the other hand, should be closed with a period unless a closing parenthesis is present.

As it appears in the work being cataloged, the series statement typically includes several different elements. Primary, of course, is the series title and

Figure 1-98.   Varying form of series title

```
100 0    ‡a Thomas, ‡c Aquinas, Saint, ‡d 1225?-1274.
245 10   ‡a Introduction to Saint Thomas Aquinas / ‡c edited, with an introduction, by Anton C.
         Pegis.
260      ‡a New York : ‡b Random House, ‡c c1948.
300      ‡a xxx, 690 p. ; ‡c 19 cm.
490 0    ‡a The modern library of the world's best books ; ‡v [259]
504      ‡a Includes bibliographical references (p. 682-690).
700 1    ‡a Pegis, Anton Charles, ‡d 1905-
```

Verso of title page   Copyright, 1948, by Random House, Inc.
                          Random House is the publisher of
                                The Modern Library

Half-title page (series title page)
                                The Modern Library
                              of the world's best books

Title page
                                  Introduction to
                                Saint Thomas Aquinas
                             Edited, with an Introduction, by
                                   Anton C. Pegis
                             President, Pontifical Institute of
                               Mediaeval Studies, Toronto
                           The Modern Library • New York

the volume numbering, if any, of the series. This information will be transcribed. Names of editors may also appear with the series title in the work. These are not included as part of the series statement in the catalog entry (see figure 1-97).

1.6B. Title proper of series

The series title is transcribed exactly as to order, wording, and spelling in the 4XX field, following the same rules that govern transcription of the title of the work (*AACR2R* 1.1B).

1.6B2. Sometimes the series title appears in more than one form in the publication. *AACR2R* has clarified the somewhat confusing statement in the original *AACR2* rules. If differing forms of the series title appear, the cataloger is to "choose the title given in the first of the prescribed sources for the series area." This means, for a book (see *AACR2R* 2.0B2), that the cataloger will prefer the series title page, "a source at the beginning of the item that is devoted solely to the series (or to the series and the analytic title) and contains a formal presentation of the series title; it usually, though not necessarily, also contains a statement of responsibility, an expression of numbering, and the name of the publisher, etc." (*CSB* 34, fall 1986, p. 21). See figure 1-98 for an example of a book including a series given in different forms. In this example, the phrase "The Modern Library" appears on the title page of the book. The half-title page (page preceding the title page) serves as the series title page, following the *CSB* definition given above. The series statement as given in this source reads "The Modern Library of the world's best books." The cataloger will choose the form found on the series title page.

Figure 1-26 is a further example of a book that includes variant forms of the series statement. The title page for Schulz's *How Long, Great Pumpkin, How Long?* lists the series as "Peanuts Parade 16." The book's cover calls it "A Peanuts Parade Book." Facing the title page is a page headed "Peanuts Parade Paperbacks" that gives, in addition to the series title, a list of titles of books in the series with their numbering. According to the *CSB* definition, this page constitutes the series title page and will be chosen for transcription in the series area (here, the 490 field) of the catalog entry. Note, however, that a different form of the series title has been chosen in this case as the authorized form (probably because of differing presentations among the various items in the series); the series is therefore traced via the 830 field.

1.6D. Other title information of series

Include only "other title information" that significantly helps identify the series. If other title information is included in the series statement, it is separated from the title proper by space - colon - space, as explicitly shown in *AACR2R* 1.6D1. Unlike the 245 field, there is no subfield coding for other title information in a series field (see figure 1-97 for an example of a series statement that includes other title information).

1.6E. Statements of responsibility relating to series

A series is a group of "separate and successive publications . . . , having a collective series title and usually all issued in a uniform format by the same publisher."[8] If, as sometimes happens, all of the parts of a series are by the same author, a statement of responsibility will be included as part of the series area. Such a statement is necessary if it appears in conjunction with the title and is considered necessary for the identification of the series. Sometimes, as with a statement of responsibility for a work, the statement of responsibility is joined grammatically to the title proper. If this is the case, transcribe it as it appears (see figures 1-55 and 1-77 for examples).

In the example shown in figure 1-99, the name of the responsible body is part of the series title, although in this case the name has been abbreviated in the prescribed source to an acronym. This acronym is regarded as an integral part of the series title and is so transcribed.

Sometimes the name of the entity responsible for the series has no grammatical connection with the series title, but appears in relatively close proximity to it. If in such a case the name is considered necessary for the identification of the title, the statement of responsibility will be given according to the general rules for transcription of the title and statement of

Figure 1-99. Responsible body's name part of series

```
111 2     ‡a Symposium on Laboratory Shear Testing of Soils ‡d (1963 : ‡c Ottawa)
245 10    ‡a Laboratory shear testing of soils : ‡b a symposium / ‡c sponsored by the National
          Research Council of Canada and the American Society for Testing and Materials,
          Ottawa, Canada, Sept. 9, 1963.
260       ‡a Philadelphia : ‡b A.S.T.M., ‡c c1964.
300       ‡a vii, 505 p. : ‡b ill. ; ‡c 24 cm.
440   0   ‡a ASTM special technical publication ; ‡v no. 361
504       ‡a Includes bibliographical references.
710 2     ‡a National Research Council of Canada.
710 2     ‡a American Society for Testing and Materials.
```

```
Title page              Laboratory Shear Testing
                               of Soils
                        A symposium sponsored by the
                 National Research Council of Canada and the
                   American Society for Testing and Materials
                        Ottawa, Canada, Sept. 9, 1963
                 ASTM Special Technical Publication No. 361
                             Published by the
                 American Society for Testing and Materials
```

responsibility area (see *AACR2R* 1.1F). However, no subfield coding follows the slash. As a series title is never established with such a statement of responsibility, a series title transcribed with a statement of responsibility will always be recorded in a 490 field. If the library traces the series, the authorized form will be recorded in an 8XX field.

The first of the two series in the example given in figure 1-100 includes a formal statement of responsibility. The second series also includes the name of the responsible body, but in this case the statement of responsibility is included as part of the title proper of the series. Caution: in *no case* will the cataloger transcribe the name of the *series editor* as part of a series statement of responsibility (see discussion under 1.6 and figure 1-97).

1.6F. International Standard Serial Number (ISSN)

A series is closely related to a serial, which has been defined as "a publication . . . issued in successive parts bearing numeric or chronological designations and intended to be continued indefinitely. . . ."[9] Some series are of such a nature that they could be cataloged as a serial under the series title (see *Handbook* chapter 12 for further discussion and explanation). Some items that show a series statement also show an ISSN, a number often used to identify serials. This information will be recorded immediately after the series title and before the series number, if any. The ISSN is preceded by a comma and subfield ‡x. The letters "ISSN" are *not* transcribed in the MARC record; they will be supplied by the system (see figure 1-101 for an example of a series that includes an ISSN).

Figure 1-100.   Series includes statement of responsibility

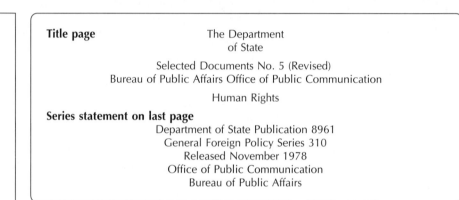

```
245 00    ‡a Human rights.
260       ‡a Washington, D.C. : ‡b Dept. of State, Bureau of Public Affairs, Office of Public
          Communication : ‡b For sale by the Supt. of Docs., U.S. G.P.O., ‡c 1978.
300       ‡a 63 p. ; ‡c 27 cm.
490 1     ‡a Selected documents / Bureau of Public Affairs, Office of Public Communication ; ‡v
          no. 5, rev.
490 1     ‡a Department of State publication ; ‡v 8961. ‡a General foreign policy series ; ‡v 310
500       ‡a Caption title.
500       ‡a At head of title: The Department of State.
710 1     ‡a United States. ‡b Dept. of State.
830  0    ‡a Selected documents (United States. Dept. of State. Bureau of Public Affairs) ; ‡v no. 5,
          rev.
830  0    ‡a Department of State publication ; ‡v 8961.
830  0    ‡a Department of State publication. ‡p General foreign policy series ; ‡v 310.
```

Title page	The Department of State
	Selected Documents No. 5 (Revised) Bureau of Public Affairs Office of Public Communication
	Human Rights
Series statement on last page	
	Department of State Publication 8961 General Foreign Policy Series 310 Released November 1978 Office of Public Communication Bureau of Public Affairs

1.6G. Series numbering

If the series includes a number, the number is recorded in the series statement. It is separated from the series title by space - semicolon - space and
is preceded by subfield ‡v. The cataloger is to transcribe the number as an
arabic numeral no matter how it appears in the source (but see an important
exception to this in *AACR2R* Appendix C.2B2). Include whatever descriptive term (volume, part, etc.) appears with it, using abbreviations from
AACR2R Appendix B (see figure 1-102). However, if the descriptive term
is abbreviated in the source, transcribe it as it appears. Do not modify it to
make it conform to Appendix B. If the series number is listed on the item
without a descriptive term, do not make one up (see, for example, figure
1-100).

1.6H. Subseries

Sometimes a main series may have a number of subordinate parts. If so,
the title of the main series is given first, followed by its series numbering,

Figure 1-101.   International Standard Series Number (ISSN) in series area

```
020      ‡a 9004103589 (alk. paper)
245 04   ‡a The public treasury of the Muslims : ‡b monthly budgets of the Mahdist state in the
         Sudan, 1897 / ‡c edited and translated by Ahmad Ibrahim Abu Shouk and Anders
         Bjørkelo.
260      ‡a Leiden ; ‡b New York : ‡b E.J. Brill, ‡c 1996.
300      ‡a xl, 371 p. : ‡b ill. ; ‡c 30 cm.
440   0  ‡a Ottoman Empire and its heritage, ‡x 1380-6076 ; ‡v v. 5
500      ‡a One source in Ahmad Abu Shouk's thesis (master's)--University of Bergen, 1991.
546      ‡a English and Arabic.
504      ‡a Includes bibliographical references (p. [365]-366) and index.
700 2    ‡a Abu Shouk, Ahmad Ibrahim.
700 1    ‡a Bjørkelo, Anders J.
```

Title page   The Public Treasury of the Muslims
            Monthly Budgets of the Mahdist State in the Sudan, 1897
                        Edited and Translated by
                        Ahmad Ibrahim Abu Shouk
                                and
                           Anders Bjørkelo

                             E.J. Brill
                    Leiden • New York • Köln
                                1996

Series title page

                          The Ottoman Empire
                           and Its Heritage
                       Politics, Society and Economy
                               edited by
                     Suraiya Faroqhi and Halil Inalcik
                               volume 5

Title page verso
ISSN 1380-6076
ISBN 90 04 10358 9

if any. If the main series is numbered, it is separated from the subseries by a full stop and subfield ‡a and recorded in a 490 field. If it is not, it is normally traced in a 440 field, with the subseries preceded by subfield ‡p. If the main series is numbered, both series and subseries must be recorded in 8XX fields if the library wishes to trace them (see figure 1-100 for treatment of a subseries).

1.6J. More than one series statement

If a work is part of more than one independent series, each series is recorded in a separate 4XX field. If it is possible to make such a distinction, give the more specific series first (see figure 1-100).

Figure 1-102.   Series numbering

```
020      ‡a 3110137445 (library binding : alk. paper)
111 2    ‡a International Conference on the History of Jewish Mysticism ‡n (5th : ‡d 1991 : ‡c
         Frankfurt am Main, Germany)
245 00   ‡a Mysticism, magic, and kabbalah in Ashkenazi Judaism : ‡b international symposium
         held in Frankfurt a.M. 1991 / ‡c edited by Karl Erich Grözinger and Joseph Dan.
260      ‡a Berlin ; ‡a New York : ‡b Walter de Gruyter, ‡c 1995.
300      ‡a vi, 331 p. ; ‡c 24 cm.
490 1    ‡a Studia Judaica ; ‡v Bd. 13
500      ‡a "Fifth International Conference on the History of Jewish Mysticism ... met in Frankfurt
         a.M. in December 1991"--Introd.
504      ‡a Includes bibliographical references.
700 1    ‡a Grözinger, Karl-Erich.
700 1    ‡a Dan, Joseph, ‡d 1935-
830  0   ‡a Studia Judaica (Walter de Gruyter & Co.) ; ‡v Bd. 13.
```

Title page	Mysticism, Magic, and Kabbalah in Ashkenazi Judaism International Symposium Held in Frankfurt a.M. 1991 Edited by Karl Erich Grözinger and Joseph Dan Walter de Gruyter • Berlin • New York 1995
Series title page	Studia Judaica Forschungen zur Wissenschaft des Judentums Herausgegeben von E.L. Ehrlich Basel Band XIII

1.7. NOTE AREA

Information to be recorded in the first five areas of the catalog entry is, for the most part, standardized in content and presentation. Notes amplify the formal description given in previous areas, providing information that cannot be included there. Some notes are regarded as indispensable; others are given at the discretion of the cataloger, depending on the intrinsic importance of the work and the needs of a particular library's users.

Notes are recorded in 5XX fields in the MARC record. There are currently more than forty different types of note fields, and new fields are constantly being added. Only the most common fields and their subfield coding will be discussed in this book. The cataloger is referred to the latest edition of *USMARC Format for Bibliographic Data* for details of other note fields.

One of the basic premises of cataloging is that the main entry and each added entry (not subject entry) must be justified by some statement in the catalog entry. Such information can be included in the body of the entry only if it appears prominently (see *AACR2R* 0.8 for definition of "prominently"). If the information does not appear in the body of the entry (the first five areas: title and statement of responsibility area through physical description area), it must be given in the note area. For example, it is customary to give an added entry to a corporate body that sponsors a conference, a publication, or some other type of intellectual or artistic activity, as long as this relationship is indicative of something more than financial responsibility. Such information can be included in the body of the entry only if it is found in one of the prescribed sources of information. In the example shown in figure 1-6 the sponsorship information was found in the publisher's foreword, a source that may not be used for the title and statement of responsibility area. Because the sponsorship statement was needed to justify an added entry, it is given as a note.

1.7A1. Punctuation. *AACR2R* gives the cataloger the option of either starting a new paragraph for each note, or simply continuing the entry without paragraphing, separating notes with a full stop, space, dash, space. It is nearly universal practice, however, to start a new paragraph for each note. In MARC-tagged records, this means that each note is recorded in a separate 5XX field (see, e.g., figure 1-103). Notes always end with a full stop (.). This will be done even when a note closes with parentheses or square

Figure 1-103.   Notes in separate 5XX fields

```
100 1    ‡a Baudelaire, Charles, ‡d 1821-1867.
240 10   ‡a Fleurs du mal. ‡l English & French
245 14   ‡a The flowers of evil and other poems of Charles Baudelaire / ‡c translated by Francis
         Duke.
260      ‡a [Charlottesville] : ‡b University of Virginia Press, ‡c 1961.
300      ‡a 294 p. ; ‡c 24 cm.
546      ‡a English translation, with original French text, of: Les fleurs du mal.
504      ‡a Includes bibliographical references (p. 294).
590      ‡a Errata slip tipped in.
700 1    ‡a Duke, Francis, ‡d 1906-
```

Title page	The Flowers of Evil and other poems of Charles Baudelaire Translated by Francis Duke University of Virginia Press : 1961

brackets (*LCRI* 1.7A1, Feb. 1, 1989; National Library of Canada rule inter-pretation, Howarth, at 1.7A1) (see figure 1-9, etc.).

1.7A3. Form of notes. Use of prescribed punctuation (space - colon - space; space - slash - space; space - semicolon - space) in the notes area is limited to actual cataloging data that include such punctuation. But space - dash - space (the punctuation prescribed for use between cataloging areas) is not to be used in notes citing cataloging data. If more than one area is included in a citation in a note, separate the two areas by a full stop and one space. The note in figure 1-104 shows proper punctuation.

Words found in *AACR2R* Appendix B (Abbreviations) are abbreviated, except in quoted notes. Numbers are transcribed as arabic numerals, except when the number begins the note, in which case it is spelled out as a word (see note 3 in figure 1-13 for an example).

Statements in notes should be as concise and brief as is consistent with clarity. A quotation from the item itself or from another source may be given if it is concise. If a quotation is used, enclose it in quotation marks and cite the source, unless the information is found on the chief source of information. For such a quoted note, with its citation, see figure 1-88. For an example of a note using abbreviation, see figure 1-85.

1.7A4. A note that shows the relationship of the work being cataloged to another work is generally recorded as a formal note in a 500 field. Such a note is prefaced by a brief, standard explanatory word or phrase followed by a colon and the necessary information in standard cataloging format (except for the dash between areas). There is no subfield coding (see figure 1-104).

Figure 1-104.   Punctuation of a note citing cataloging data

020	‡a 0838902057
100 1	‡a Sheehy, Eugene P. ‡q (Eugene Paul), ‡d 1922-
245 10	‡a Guide to reference books.
250	‡a 9th ed. / ‡b compiled by Eugene P. Sheehy, with the assistance of Rita G. Keckeissen and Eileen McIlvaine.
260	‡a Chicago : ‡b American Library Association, ‡c 1976.
300	‡a xviii, 1015 p. ; ‡c 28 cm.
500	‡a Rev. ed. of: Guide to reference books / Constance M. Winchell. 8th ed. 1967.
500	‡a Includes index.
700 1	‡a Keckeissen, Rita G.
700 1	‡a McIlvaine, Eileen.
700 1	‡a Winchell, Constance M. ‡q (Constance Mabel), ‡d 1896- ‡t Guide to reference books.

Title page	Guide to Reference Books Ninth Edition Compiled by Eugene P. Sheehy with the assistance of Rita G. Keckeissen and Eileen McIlvaine American Library Association Chicago 1976

1.7B. Notes

This rule gives guidance about various types of notes that may be included in the note area. When more than one type of note is needed, give them in the order in which *AACR2R* lists them, except when a particular note is very important.

1.7B1. Nature, scope, or artistic form. If the nature, scope, or literary or artistic form of the item is not apparent from the information in the formal part of the catalog entry, and if the cataloger feels that such information would be useful, a note may be given. Figures 1-3, 1-105, and 1-106 show typical notes dealing with nature, scope, and form. This type of note is recorded in a 500 field.

Figure 1-105.   Literary form note

```
020        ‡a 2760901971
100 1      ‡a Tremblay, Michel, ‡d 1942-
245 10     ‡a Marcel poursuivi par les chiens / ‡c Michel Tremblay.
260        ‡a Montréal : ‡b Leméac, ‡c 1992.
300        ‡a 69 p. ; ‡c 20 cm.
490 1      ‡a Théâtre ; ‡v 195
500        ‡a Play.
830  0     ‡a Collection Théâtre Leméac ; ‡v 195.
```

Title page	Michel Tremblay Marcel Poursuivi Par les Chiens Leméac

Figure 1-106.   Scope note

```
100 1      ‡a Rheault, Charles A.
245 10     ‡a SP at 75 : ‡b the Society of Printers, 1955-1980 / ‡c Charles A. Rheault, Jr.
246 3      ‡a S.P. at 75
246 3      ‡a SP at seventy-five
260        ‡a Boston : ‡b The Society, ‡c 1981.
300        ‡a 114 p. : ‡b ill. ; ‡c 25 cm.
500        ‡a "This book is a record of the society in the period 1955-1980, and differs from its more
           historically-oriented predecessor, Printing as an art, by Ray Nash (Cambridge, 1955)"--P. 1.
500        ‡a 350 copies printed.
500        ‡a Includes bibliographical references and index.
```

Title page	S•P at 75 The Society of Printers 1955-1980 Charles A. Rheault, Jr. Boston 1981

1.7B2. Language of the item and/or translation or adaptation. Give a note about the language if the information is not evident from the catalog entry (see figure 1-103). Language notes are recorded in the 546 field.

If it is not evident from the formal part of the description, make a note in a 500 field to indicate that the work is an adaptation from another work. A name-title added entry is made for the earlier work (see figure 1-107).

1.7B3. Source of title proper. Give this note if the title proper is not taken from the chief source of information for the item. This is a required note (see *AACR2R* 1.1B1). For a book, this means that if the item lacks a title page, the source used as a substitute will be specified (see figures 1-90, 1-100, and 1-108). See also figure 1-13 for an additional example of an item in need of a note to explain the source of the title data. This note is recorded in a 500 field.

1.7B4. Variations in title. The title must be taken from the chief source of information; in a book, for instance, this is the title page. A variant title will sometimes appear elsewhere in the item, on the spine or cover of the book, for example. Because some library users are likely to think of the item by its variant title, a note should be made of the variant, if it is different enough from the title recorded in the 245 field that it would file in a different place in the library catalog. Significant variations in title within the item itself are traced from the 246 field. The indicators in this field may be used to generate notes automatically. If the cataloger wishes the system to generate a note as well as trace the variant title, the first indicator should be set to "1." The second indicator generates various types of notes. "4" generates the display "Cover title: [title]"; "5" generates "Added title page: [title]"; "6" generates "Caption title: [title]"; "7" generates "Running title: [title]"; "8" generates "Spine title: [title]". *No* 5XX note should be included

Figure 1-107.   Adaptation note

```
020      ‡a 0690007345
020      ‡a 0690006764 (lib. bdg.)
100 1    ‡a Green, Norma.
245 14   ‡a The hole in the dike / ‡c retold by Norma Green ; pictures by Eric Carle.
260      ‡a New York : ‡b Crowell, ‡c c1974.
300      ‡a 1 v. (unpaged) : ‡b col. ill. ; ‡c 28 cm.
500      ‡a Adapted from a story in: Hans Brinker, or, The silver skates / by Mary Mapes Dodge.
520      ‡a A little boy's courage saves Holland from destruction by the sea.
700 1    ‡a Carle, Eric.
700 1    ‡a Dodge, Mary Mapes, ‡d 1830-1905. ‡t Hans Brinker.
```

Title page

The Hole in the Dike
Retold by Norma Green
Pictures by Eric Carle
Thomas Y. Crowell Company • New York
Copyright © 1974 by Norma B. Green
Illustrations copyright © 1974 by Eric Carle

Figure 1-108.   Source of title proper

```
110 1    ‡a Tucson (Ariz.). ‡b Mayor.
245 12   ‡a A city in action, 1951 to 1955 : ‡b four years of progress / ‡c City of Tucson, Office of
         the Mayor.
260      ‡a [Tucson] : ‡b Office of the Mayor, [1955]
300      ‡a 7 leaves ; ‡c 28 cm.
500      ‡a Caption title.
500      ‡a Text signed: "Fred Emery, Mayor, April 29, 1955."
700 1    ‡a Emery, Fred.
```

Caption title	City of Tucson
	Office of the Mayor
	A City in Action—1951 to 1955
	Four Years of Progress

in addition to a correctly coded 246 field in the above cases. If the variant title falls outside of these five cases, the cataloger may create whatever note is appropriate by leaving the second indicator blank. The field then begins with subfield ‡i, which contains the wording of the note, then subfield ‡a, which contains the variant title. Subfield ‡a traces. Because the 246 field does not contain provisions for nonfiling characters, initial articles must be dropped. Do not end this field with a full stop. (Detailed guidelines regarding the use of the 246 field may be found in *LCRI* 21.30J, Nov. 1995.)

Figure 1-67 is an example of the use of the 246 field. The title appears in a different form on the spine from that of the title page; if no provision is made for this and the patron types in a search containing "&" instead of "and," he or she will not find the item in many systems. Therefore, the cataloger adds a 246 field. Because the indicators are coded "18," the system will generate the note "Spine title: Forwarded & finished."

In the example shown in figure 1-72, the title "The Tale Is Told," a much more memorable and distinctive title than the title-page title, is both on the spine and the cover of the book. This is a more complex situation than provided for by any of the 246 indicators; therefore, the cataloger will use subfield ‡i. The note generated will display exactly as the cataloger enters the information (without displaying the subfield delimiters).

Field 246 is also used for variant titles for which no note is necessary (e.g., for alternative titles or parallel titles). In such cases, the first indicator is coded "3"; this tells the system not to generate a note. The second indicator is "0" for portions of the title (see figures 1-8 and 1-9), "1" for parallel titles (see figure 1-19), and left blank for other variations that need tracing (see figure 1-106).

It should be kept in mind that field 246 is for *variations* in the title proper and is used to record both the variant and its source. If the source of the title proper itself, as recorded in the 245 field, must be noted, it is recorded in a 500 field (see discussion of 1.7B3).

If the title of a work is changed but the text remains the same (not revised or translated), make an "original title" note (see figure 1-22 for format). This note is recorded in a 500 field, and an added entry for the original title is made, entered as it would have been in the original item. If the original was entered under author, the added entry in the record for the later item would be a name-title entry, as in figure 1-22. If the original was entered under title, the added entry would be recorded in a 740 field, first indicator "0", second indicator blank. In either case, an initial article is omitted from the title.

See *AACR2R* 1.1D3 for the rare instance in which an original title of a translated work will appear as part of the title proper and thus not appear in the note area (see figure 1-19).

The original title of a work that has been translated will be given, preceded by the words "Translation of:". Unless the names of the languages involved are a part of the wording of the note, this is not a "language" note and thus is recorded in a 500, not a 546, field. The original title of a translated work is normally the uniform title of the work. If so, it is traced from the 240 or 130 field, as in figures 1-9, 1-19, and 1-20. If it is not, it is traced in the 740 field.

For a related discussion of variant titles, including the use of the 740 field, see this *Handbook* at 21.30J.

1.7B5. Parallel titles and other title information. *AACR2R* 1.1D4 directs the cataloger to record parallel titles in a note if they are found outside the chief source of information; likewise, 1.1E3 indicates that lengthy other title information pertaining to the bibliographic history of the work may more appropriately be included in the note area (see figures 1-26 and 1-72 for examples). These notes are recorded in the 500 field.

1.7B6. Statements of responsibility. If an added entry is to be made for persons or bodies having responsibility for the item being cataloged and if this information cannot, according to rules for the title and statement of responsibility area, be included in that area, a note will be made, generally in a 500 field, giving the necessary information (see, for examples, figures 1-6 and 1-100).

In the example shown in figure 1-109 information about the composer of the music is found in the preface, which is not a prominent source. The information would not be transcribed in the title and statement of responsibility area. Because the statement is concise, it is quoted.

1.7B7. Edition and history. These notes serve to show the bibliographical relationship of one item to another when it is not evident from the formal part of the catalog entry. Such notes are of various types. For instance, when a revision is entered under a different author, or when a revision has a changed title, give sufficient information about the earlier edition so that it may be identified (see figure 1-104).

A literary work that is continued by another work is given a sequel note (see figure 1-110). A literary work that continues another story is given a slightly different note, an example of which is shown in figure 1-111. Unlike other types of "related works," a sequel by the same author does not call for an added entry in addition to this note (see *AACR2R* 21.28B1, footnote 8).

Most "edition and history" notes are recorded in 500 fields. Information about reprints, including facsimile reprints, may be recorded in the 534 field

Figure 1-109.   Statement of responsibility note

100 1	‡a Stein, Gertrude, ‡d 1874-1946.
245 10	‡a Four saints in three acts : ‡b an opera to be sung / ‡c Gertrude Stein ; introduction by Carl Van Vechten.
260	‡a New York : ‡b Random House, ‡c 1934.
300	‡a 57 p. ; ‡c 22 cm.
500	‡a "Orchestrated by Virgil Thomson"--Pref.
500	‡a Without music.
700 1	‡a Thomson, Virgil, ‡d 1896- ‡t Four saints in three acts.

Title page	Gertrude Stein Four Saints in Three Acts An Opera to be Sung Introduction by Carl Van Vechten New York • Random House 1934

Figure 1-110.   Sequel note

020	‡a 0312932081
100 1	‡a Card, Orson Scott.
245 10	‡a Ender's game / ‡c Orson Scott Card.
250	‡a Rev. ed.
260	‡a New York : ‡b Tor, ‡c 1991.
300	‡a xxi, 226 p. ; ‡c 24 cm.
500	‡a Sequel: Speaker for the dead.
500	‡a "A Tom Doherty Associates book."

Title page	Orson Scott Card Ender's Game Tor A Tom Doherty Associates book

("original version note") (see, e.g., figure 1-112). LC does not use this field, recording such information in the 500 field.

For works other than works of the imagination, use "continues" or "continued by" as appropriate. This wording is much used with serials particularly (see discussion of notes in *Handbook* chapter 12 for examples).

1.7B8. Material specific details. This note is appropriate only with cartographic materials, music, computer files, or serials (see *AACR2R* chapters 3, 5, 9, and 12).

1.7B9. Publication, distribution, etc. Important information regarding publication, etc., that is not included in the publication area may be given as a note in a 500 field (see figure 1-113). Caution: compare this note with 1.7B7, which covers previous publication, revisions, etc.

Figure 1-111.   Sequel note

```
020        ‡a 0312853254 (pbk.)
100 1      ‡a Card, Orson Scott.
245 10     ‡a Speaker for the dead / ‡c Orson Scott Card.
250        ‡a Rev. ed.
260        ‡a New York : ‡b Tor, ‡c 1992, c1991.
300        ‡a xxii, 280 p. ; ‡c 24 cm.
500        ‡a "A Tom Doherty Associates Book."
500        ‡a "Revised trade paperback edition: September 1992."
500        ‡a Sequel to: Ender's game.
```

Title page	Orson Scott Card
	Speaker
	for the Dead
	Tor
	A Tom Doherty Associates book

Figure 1-112.   Edition and history note

```
100 1      ‡a Blades, William, ‡d 1824-1890.
245 10     ‡a Numismata typographica : ‡b the medallic history of printing / ‡c by William Blades ;
           with a foreword by Henry Morris.
246 30     ‡a Medallic history of printing
246 18     ‡a Printers' register 1883
260        ‡a Newtown, Pa. : ‡b Bird & Bull Press, ‡c 1992.
300        ‡a xvii, 144 p., xxiv p. of plates : ‡b ill. ; ‡c 29 cm.
500        ‡a Includes index.
534        ‡p Facsimile reprint. Originally published: ‡t Numismata typographica, or, The medallic
           history of printing / by William Blades. ‡c London : "Printers' Register" Office, 1883.
500        ‡a One of three hundred copies.
```

Title page of facsimile	Numismata
	Typographica
	The Medallic History of Printing
	by William Blades
	with a foreword by Henry Morris
	Bird & Bull Press • Newtown, Pennsylvania
	1992
Title page of original (reprinted with the facsimile)	
	Numismata Typographica
	or, The
	Medallic History of Printing
	Reprinted from the "Printers' Register."
	by William Blades
	London: "Printers' Register" Office.
	1883

Figure 1-113.   Publication note

```
100 1    ‡a Milne, A. A. ‡q (Alan Alexander), ‡d 1882-1956.
245 10   ‡a Winnie-the-Pooh / ‡c A.A. Milne ; with decorations by Ernest H. Shepard.
260      ‡a New York : ‡b Dutton, ‡c c1926.
300      ‡a ix, 161 p. : ‡b ill. ; ‡c 21 cm.
500      ‡a Published simultaneously in Great Britain by Methuen.
520      ‡a The adventures of Christopher Robin, Pooh Bear, Piglet, and Eeyore, including the
         stories of the honey tree, the Heffalump, and Eeyore's birthday.
700 1    ‡a Shepard, Ernest H. ‡q (Ernest Howard), ‡d 1879-1976.
```

Title page	A. A. Milne
	Winnie-the-Pooh
	with decorations by
	Ernest H. Shepard
	E. P. Dutton & Co., Inc.
	Publishers : New York

Figure 1-114.   Note that amplifies physical description

```
020      ‡a 0151000611
100 1    ‡a Walker, Alice, ‡d 1944-
245 10   ‡a Warrior marks : ‡b female genital mutilation and the sexual blinding of women /
         ‡c Alice Walker and Pratibha Parmar.
250      ‡a 1st ed.
260      ‡a New York : ‡a Harcourt Brace, ‡c c1993.
300      ‡a 373 p. : ‡b ill., map ; ‡c 24 cm.
500      ‡a Map on lining papers.
700 1    ‡a Parmar, Pratibha.
```

Title page	Alice Walker and
	Pratibha Parmar
	Warrior Marks
	Female Genital Mutilation and
	the Sexual Blinding of Women
	Harcourt Brace & Company
	New York San Diego London

1.7B10. Physical description. Important information not brought out in the title and statement of responsibility area that is of a type that, according to rule, cannot be included in the physical description area should be given in a note in a 500 field. A note may also be given to amplify information that has been transcribed in any of the preceding areas. Give a note, for instance, to record the presence of a map on the endpapers of a book, because such a map could be removed from a copy of the book when it is rebound. If the map is duplicated on front and back endpapers, as in the example shown in figure 1-114, say ''Map on lining papers.'' If the maps are different, say ''Maps on lining papers.''

A note is often appropriate to amplify the physical description area for a nonbook item. See the following chapters and the example shown in figure 1-115.

Notes of limitation of edition also fall under this rule. For an example, see figure 1-20.

1.7B11. Accompanying material and supplements. Material accompanying the work that cannot be described with a simple word or phrase should be listed in a note in a 500 field rather than included at the end of the physical description area (*AACR2R* 1.5E). The second note in figure 1-116 is of this type. For other methods of recording supplements and accompanying materials, see *AACR2R* 1.5E, 1.9, and 13.6.

1.7B12. Series. A series statement of such complexity that it requires explanation may be given as a note rather than in the series area. This will be done only rarely. A note about the series may also be given when cataloging a reprint if the original work was part of a series (see *AACR2R* 11.7B12 and figure 1-117).

Figure 1-115.   Note that amplifies physical description

245 00	‡a Faces and feelings ‡h [slide] / ‡c author, George A. Lane ; produced by Society for Visual Education, Inc., in cooperation with Loyola University Press.
260	‡a Chicago : ‡b Singer Education & Training Products, ‡c c1971.
300	‡a 20 slides : ‡b col. + ‡e 1 teacher's guide.
490 1	‡a Slodeas [sic] for creative expression ; ‡v SD 10
500	‡a Slides in flat plastic holder (28 × 23 cm.) punched for insertion in 3-ring binder.
530	‡a Also issued with phonotape in cassette.
520	‡a Slide set designed to encourage children to express themselves imaginatively by depicting people of different ages showing various emotions.
700 1	‡a Lane, George, ‡d 1934-
710 2	‡a Society for Visual Education.
830 0	‡a Slideas for creative expression ; ‡v SD 10.

Title page in teacher's guide   Faces and Feelings
Slodeas for creative expression
Author: George A. Lane, S.J., Associate Director,
Loyola University Press
Singer Education & Training Products
Produced by Society for Visual Education, Inc.
in cooperation with Loyola University Press
Chicago, Ill. 60657

Figure 1-116. Accompanying material

```
100 1    ‡a Jones, Patricia.
245 10   ‡a Rumpelstiltskin : ‡b an adaptation from Grimms' fairy tales / ‡c by Patricia Jones ;
         pictures by Jan B. Balet.
260      ‡a [Chicago] : ‡b Container Corp. of America, ‡c c1954.
300      ‡a 31 p. : ‡b col. ill. ; ‡c 25 cm.
490 0    ‡a Slottie library books
500      ‡a "A Concora book."
500      ‡a Cardboard punch-out figures tipped into back cover.
700 1    ‡a Balet, Jan B., ‡d 1913-
730 0    ‡a Rumpelstilzchen (Grimm version).
```

Title page	An Adaptation from Grimms' Fairy Tales
	by Patricia Jones
	Rumpelstiltskin
	Pictures by Jan B. Balet
	A Concora Book
	Published by Container Corporation of America

Figure 1-117. Reprint of an item from a series

```
020      ‡a 0313232423 (lib. bdg.)
100 1    ‡a Schlesinger, Rudolf.
245 10   ‡a Central European democracy and its background : ‡b economic and political group
         organization / ‡c by Rudolf Schlesinger.
260      ‡a Westport, Conn. : ‡a Greenwood Press, ‡c 1981.
300      ‡a xiv, 402 p. ; ‡c 23 cm.
534      ‡p Reprint. Originally published: ‡c London : Routledge & K. Paul, 1953. ‡f (International
         library of sociology and social reconstruction).
504      ‡a Includes bibliographical references (p. 390-395) and index.
830 0    ‡a International library of sociology and social reconstruction (Routledge & Kegan Paul)
```

Title page	Central European Democracy
	and Its Background
	Economic and Political
	Group Organization
	by
	Rudolf Schlesinger
	Author of Soviet Legal Theory, Changing
	Attitudes in Soviet Russia
	Greenwood Press
	Westport, Connecticut

1.7B13. Dissertations. The fact that an item is a dissertation or thesis is recorded in the 502 field. Use the word "thesis" to designate all types of academic theses, dissertations, etc. Qualify this term with the degree (M.A. or Ph.D.), the name of the university, and the date, as shown in figure 1-118. If these qualifications do not apply, the cataloger is to add "Thesis (doctoral)" or "Thesis (master's)," as appropriate. This designation will most commonly be used when cataloging European dissertations. A somewhat different note is used for a thesis revised for publication (see figure 1-119). This note is recorded in a 500 field, not a 502 field.

1.7B14. Audience. If the information is stated in the item, a note in the 521 field about the intended audience may be given. In the example shown in figure 1-120, information regarding the earlier edition and the intended audience was taken from the foreword. The 521 field with the first indicator blank will generate in the local system the term "Audience:" at the beginning of the note. First indicator "0" generates "Reading grade level:"; "1" generates "Interest age level:"; "2" generates "Interest grade level:"; "3" generates "Special format characteristics:"; "4" generates "Motivation/interest level:". If the first indicator is coded "8", no display constant will be generated. The note generated from the 521 field of figure 1-120, because the first indicator is blank, will display to the public: "Audience: High school students."

1.7B15. References to published descriptions. These notes are ordinarily used in connection with the cataloging of early printed or rare books.

Figure 1-118.   Thesis note

100 1	‡a Maxwell, Margaret F., ‡d 1927-
245 10	‡a Anatomy of a book collector : ‡b William L. Clements and the Clements Library / ‡c by Margaret Nadine Finlayson Maxwell.
260	‡c1971.
300	‡a viii, 420 leaves : ‡b col. ill. ; ‡c 28 cm.
500	‡a Typescript (photocopy).
500	‡a Published as: Shaping a library : William L. Clements as collector. Amsterdam : N. Israel, 1973.
500	‡a Abstract (3 leaves) bound with copy.
502	‡a Thesis (Ph.D.)--University of Michigan, 1971.
504	‡a Includes bibliographical references (leaves 412-419).
700 1	‡a Maxwell, Margaret F., ‡d 1927- ‡t Shaping a library.

Title page	Anatomy of a Book Collector: William L. Clements and the Clements Library by Margaret Nadine Finlayson Maxwell A dissertation submitted in partial fulfillment of the requirements for the degree of Doctor of Philosophy (Library Science) in the University of Michigan 1971

Figure 1-119.   Thesis note

```
020        ‡a 9060726316
100 1      ‡a Maxwell, Margaret F., ‡d 1927-
245 10     ‡a Shaping a library : ‡b William L. Clements as collector / ‡c by Margaret Maxwell.
260        ‡a Amsterdam : ‡b N. Israel, ‡c 1973.
300        ‡a 364 p. : ‡b ill. ; ‡c 21 cm.
500        ‡a Originally presented as the author's thesis (Ph.D.--University of Michigan) under title:
           Anatomy of a book collector.
504        ‡a Includes bibliographical references (p. 348-356).
700 1      ‡a Maxwell, Margaret F., ‡d 1927- ‡t Anatomy of a book collector.
```

Title page	Shaping a Library: William L. Clements as Collector by Margaret Maxwell Nico Israel/Amsterdam 1973

Figure 1-120.   Audience note

```
245 14     ‡a The record of mankind / ‡c A. Wesley Roehm ... [et al.].
260        ‡a Boston : ‡b Heath, ‡c c1956.
300        ‡a vi, 754 p. : ‡b ill. (some col.) ; ‡c 24 cm.
500        ‡a Revision of: World civilization / by Hutton Webster and Edgar Bruce Wesley.
521        ‡a High school students.
504        ‡a Includes bibliographical references and index.
700 1      ‡a Roehm, A. Wesley.
700 1      ‡a Webster, Hutton, ‡d 1875-1955. ‡t World civilization.
```

Title page	The Record of Mankind A. Wesley Roehm • Morris R. Buske Hutton Webster Edgar B. Wesley D.C. Heath and Company • Boston

A reference to one of the detailed descriptions in one of the standard bibliographies of such materials makes exact identification for these often complex bibliographical entities possible in a manner not possible for the cataloger following *AACR2R* (see *AACR2R* 2.12–2.18). Such notes are recorded in the 510 field. The title of the bibliography or other source should be recorded as succinctly as possible followed by the location (page or item number) of the citation. The first indicator should be coded "4" and the page or citation number recorded in subfield ‡c (see figure 1-121). Guidance

Figure 1-121.   Reference to published description

245 00	‡a BR today : ‡b a selection of his books, with comments.
246 3	‡a B.R. today
260	‡a New York : ‡b The Grolier Club, ‡c 1982.
300	‡a xiv, 41 p. ; ‡c 22 cm.
500	‡a "This book is the catalogue of an exhibition [devoted to Bruce Rogers] at The Grolier Club of New York, December 15, 1982 to January 15, 1983"--T.p. verso.
500	‡a Consists of 35 entries selected from the work of Bruce Rogers, with commentaries on each item by "selected bibliophiles and typographers."
500	‡a "450 copies of this catalogue, designed by Bert Clarke, have been printed for the Grolier Club at The Press of A. Colish December 1982"--Colophon.
510 4	‡a The Grolier Club 1884-1984, ‡c p. 154, no. 143
710 2	‡a Grolier Club.

Title page	BR Today A Selection of His Books, With Comments The Grolier Club • New York 1982

for abbreviation of the names of the most common sources will be found in *Standard Citation Forms for Published Bibliographies and Catalogs Used in Rare Book Cataloging,* 2nd ed. (Washington: Library of Congress, 1996).

1.7B17. Summary. A brief summary may be included if it amplifies and clarifies the catalog record. Summaries are particularly useful for entries for nonbook materials as such items often are not easily accessible for browsing (see, for example, figure 1-34). Summaries are also frequently included as part of the cataloging data for stories for adolescents and children (see, for example, figure 1-113). Summary notes are recorded in the 520 field. This field, with the first indicator blank, automatically generates in the local system the term "Summary:" at the beginning of the note. The note generated from the 520 field of figure 1-113 will appear to the public: "Summary: The adventures of Christopher Robin, Pooh Bear, Piglet, and Eeyore, including the stories of the honey tree, the Heffalump, and Eeyore's birthday."

1.7B18. Contents. A contents note should be given when required by a specific rule, such as 1.1B10 (see figure 1-14). When the cataloger creates a bibliographic record from a number of publications (a made-up collection), a contents note should be made (see figure 1-122). Unless a collection (*AACR2R* 21.7B) contains a large number of items (usually interpreted to mean more than twelve), a contents note will be given (see figure 1-123).

Give a list of the titles of individual works contained in an item. Add to these titles statements of responsibility not included in the title and statement of responsibility area. Individual items are separated by space - dash

Figure 1-122.   Contents note for a made-up collection

245 00   ‡a [Miscellaneous newspapers and newsmagazines concerning the assassination of John F.
              Kennedy, November 22, 1963].
260   ‡a [S.l. : ‡b s.n.], ‡d 1963-1964.
300   ‡a 48 pieces : ‡b ill. ; ‡c 28-65 cm.
505 0   ‡a B.Z. (Berlin, Germany) (Nov. 23, 25-26, 1963) -- Berliner Morgenpost (Nov. 23, 26,
              1963) -- Bild Zeitung (Berlin, Germany) (Nov. 23, 25, 30, 1963) -- Boston globe (Nov. 23,
              1963) -- Chicago daily news (Nov. 22, 25, 1963) -- Daily herald (Provo, Utah) (Nov. 22,
              1963) -- Daily sentinel (Grand Junction, Colo.) (Nov. 22, 1963) -- Daily universe (Provo,
              Utah) (Nov. 22, 25-26, 1963) -- Deseret news (Salt Lake City, Utah) (Nov. 22, 25-26,
              1963) -- Guardian (Manchester, England) (Nov. 15, 23, 25-28, 1963) -- Houston post (Nov.
              23, 1963) -- Life (Nov. 29, Dec. 6, 1963) -- Nacht-Depesche (Berlin) (Nov. 23, 25, 1963)
              -- National observer (Nov. 25, 1963) -- New York times (Nov. 23, 26, Dec. 2, 1963; Sept.
              28, 1964) -- Newsweek (Dec. 2, 1963) -- Record American (Boston) (Nov. 23, 1963) --
              Salt Lake tribune (Nov. 23, 25-26, 1963) -- Spandauer Volksblatt (Berlin, Germany) (June
              27, Nov. 23-24, 26-28, 1963) -- Time (Nov. 29, 1963) -- U.S. news and world report (Dec.
              2, 1963).

Figure 1-123.   Contents note for a collection

020   ‡a 0385255144
245 00   ‡a Making it : ‡b the business of film and television production in Canada / ‡c Barbara
              Hehner and Andra Sheffer, editors.
250   ‡a Rev., updated ed.
260   ‡a Toronto : ‡b Doubleday Canada, ‡c c1995.
300   ‡a 374 p. ; ‡c 22 cm.
504   ‡a Includes bibliographical references and index.
500   ‡a "The Academy of Canadian Cinema and Television."
505 0   ‡a So you want to be a producer / Alexandra Raffé -- Developing a property / Laël McCall
              with Richard Craven -- The budget / Charles Zamaria -- Financing your own production /
              Steve Ord -- Pre-production, production, and post-production / Tom Dent-Cox --
              Television Distribution / Marie-Claude Poulin -- Co-production / W. Paterson Ferns --
              Publicity / Kevin Tierney -- Production and the law / Diana Cafazzo and Douglas Barrett --
              The wrap / Seaton McLean.
700 1   ‡a Hehner, Barbara, ‡d 1947-
700 1   ‡a Sheffer, Andra.
710 2   ‡a Academy of Canadian Cinema & Television.

Title page   Making It
                        The Business of Film and Television Production
                                      in Canada

                        Barbara Hehner and Andra Sheffer, editors

                        The Academy of Canadian Cinema and Television

                                Doubleday Canada Limited

- space; if statements of responsibility are included, they are separated from their titles by space - slash - space. For further examples of contents notes, see figures 1-45 and 1-47. The contents note is recorded in field 505. If the cataloger is recording the complete contents of the item, the first indicator will be coded "0." If the cataloger is unable to record the complete contents, for example because a multivolume set is not yet finished, the first indicator will be coded "1" (see figure 1-92). Introductory terms or phrases such as "Contents:" should not be included, as these are system generated. For detailed guidelines on LC policy for contents notes, see *LCRI* 2.7B18 (Dec. 11, 1989, and May 8, 1991).

See also discussion under 2.7B18 in this *Handbook* for other types of contents notes.

1.7B19. Numbers borne by the item. Numbers such as the Superintendent of Documents (SUDOC) number on United States government publications serve as important means of identifying the item; in some libraries, government documents are arranged by SUDOC number. Always list this number in a 500 field if it is available (see figure 1-73 for an example of a Canadian government publication). Other items, such as technical reports, also show important numbers that must be transcribed (see figure 1-124). Other miscellaneous numbers sometimes included by commercial publishers are of no particular significance and can safely be ignored.

1.7B20. Copy being described and library's holdings. A note may record matters unique to the library's copy in a 590 field.[10] For example, the

Figure 1-124.   Technical report number

020	‡a 0833024671 (alk. paper)
100 1	‡a Dixon, Lloyd S.
245 10	‡a Drought management policies and economic effects in urban areas of California, 1987-1992 / ‡c Lloyd S. Dixon, Nancy Y. Moore, Ellen M. Pint.
260	‡a Santa Monica, CA : ‡b RAND, ‡c 1996.
300	‡a xx, 131 p. : ‡b ill. ; ‡c 28 cm.
504	‡a Includes bibliographical references (p. 129-131).
500	‡a "MR-813-CUWA/CDWR/NSF"--P. [4] of cover.
700 1	‡a Moore, Nancy Y., ‡d 1947-
700 1	‡a Pint, Ellen M. ‡q (Ellen Marie), ‡d 1960-

Title page

Drought Management Policies
and Economic Effects
in Urban Areas of California,
1987-1992

Lloyd S. Dixon
Nancy Y. Moore
Ellen M. Pint

Supported by the California Urban Water Agencies
California Department of Water Resources
National Science Foundation

RAND

fact that the library's copy is autographed is usually noted (see figure 1-55). The presence of a tipped-in errata slip should also be noted, as such a slip may not be in all copies of the book (see figure 1-103). If the library has a numbered copy of a limited edition, this may appropriately be recorded in a 590 field (see figure 1-20). Other local notes would include a description of the binding (particularly if it is in disrepair) or notation of missing parts from the library's copy.

1.7B21. "With" notes. The presence of an item that is physically inseparable from the item being described is noted unless this has been brought out in the formal description for the work. This statement is made whether (as with books) the items were separately published and later bound together (in a 590 field) or they were originally issued together as a unit (in a 501 field). The distinction is between items issued together at the time of publication and those bound together at a later date, for example, by the library (see figure 1-125 for an example of separate items issued together by the publisher). A note of this type is also used when the description is of a separately titled part of an item lacking a collective title (see figures 1-126 and 1-127, showing records for two of three works issued together in a single binding by the publisher).

1.8. STANDARD NUMBER AND TERMS OF AVAILABILITY AREA

The last area of the *AACR2R* catalog entry is standard number and terms of availability. Publishers began using International Standard Book Numbers (ISBN) about 1968; International Standard Serial Numbers (ISSN) fol-

Figure 1-125.   "With" note

100 1	‡a Carroll, Lewis, ‡d 1832-1898
240 10	‡a Through the looking-glass
245 10	‡a Through the looking-glass, and what Alice found there / ‡c Lewis Carroll ; with fifty illustrations by John Tenniel.
260	‡a London : ‡b Folio Society, ‡c 1962 (1993 printing).
300	‡a 131 p. : ‡b ill. ; ‡c 23 cm.
501	‡a Issued with: Alice's adventures in Wonderland / Lewis Carroll. London : Folio Society, 1961 (1993 printing).
700 1	‡a Tenniel, John, ‡c Sir, ‡d 1820-1914.

Title page	Lewis Carroll
	Through the Looking-Glass
	and What Alice Found There
	with fifty illustrations by John Tenniel
	The Folio Society
	London 1962

Figure 1-126.   "With" note

```
100 1    ‡a Burn, A. E. ‡q (Andrew Ewbank), ‡d 1864-1927.
245 14   ‡a The Athanasian creed and its early commentaries / ‡c by A.E. Burn.
260      ‡a Cambridge [England] : ‡b University Press, ‡c 1896.
300      ‡a xcix, 68 p. ; ‡c 23 cm.
490 1    ‡a Texts and studies ; ‡v vol. 4, no. 1
500      ‡a Includes index.
501      ‡a With: Coptic apocryphal gospels : translations together with the texts of some of them /
         by Forbes Robinson -- The Old Latin and the Itala : with an appendix containing the text
         of the S. Gallen palimpsest of Jeremiah / by F.C. Burkitt.
830  0   ‡a Texts and studies (Cambridge, England) ; ‡v vol. 4, no. 1.
```

Title page	
	The Athanasian Creed
	and Its Early Commentaries
	by
	A.E. Burn M.A.
	Trinity College Cambridge
	Rector of Kynnersley Wellington Salop
	Cambridge
	At the University Press
	1896
	[All Rights Reserved]

lowed a year or so later. Therefore, materials that appeared before 1968 will not have such numbers. Because publishers include these numbers on a voluntary basis, not all materials with publication dates after 1968 will have them. If a book has a standard number, in most instances the number will be found on the verso of the title page. Record ISBN in the 020 field; record ISSN in the 022 field. Do not enter the acronym "ISBN" or "ISSN"; for ISBN, do not record the standard hyphens. These are all system generated. Do not close 020 or 022 fields with a period (see figure 1-124).

1.8D. Terms of availability

LC does not record the terms of availability (i.e., price) of the item (see *LCRI* 1.8, May 1995). Do, however, add qualifiers such as "pbk." or "acid-free paper" in parentheses following the ISBN if they are succinct and are found in the item (see figures 1-2a-c, 1-3, and 1-22). Qualifiers are particularly important to distinguish between separate ISBNs for different manifestations (e.g., paperback and hard-bound) of the same edition of an item (see figure 1-80). The National Library of Canada, the British Library, and the National Library of Australia do record terms of availability for "current" items (Howarth, at 1.8D and 1.8D1). If given, terms of availability are recorded in subfield ‡c of the 020 field.

Figure 1-127. "With" note

```
245 00   ‡a Coptic apocryphal Gospels : ‡b translations together with the texts of some of them /
         ‡c by Forbes Robinson.
260      ‡a Cambridge [England] : ‡b University Press, ‡c 1896.
300      ‡a xxxii, 264 p. ; ‡c 23 cm.
490 1    ‡a Texts and studies ; ‡v vol. 4, no. 2
546      ‡a Coptic texts with English translation.
500      ‡a Includes indexes.
501      ‡a With: The Athanasian creed and its early commentaries / by A.E. Burn -- The Old Latin
         and the Itala : with an appendix containing the text of the S. Gallen palimpsest of
         Jeremiah / by F.C. Burkitt.
700 1    ‡a Robinson, Forbes, ‡d 1864-1904.
830  0   ‡a Texts and studies (Cambridge, England) ; ‡v vol. 4, no. 2.
```

Title page

Coptic
Apocryphal Gospels

translations
together with the texts
of some of them

by
Forbes Robinson M.A.
lecturer in theology at
Christ's College Cambridge

Cambridge
At the University Press
1896

1.9. SUPPLEMENTARY ITEMS

This rule covers the description of such materials as separately issued continuations, supplements, indexes, or other materials so closely related to another work as to be more or less dependent on it. If in the cataloger's judgment the supplementary material is important in its own right, the item may be cataloged as a separate work (see *AACR2R* 21.28). Supplementary material of lesser importance may be cataloged as part of the entry for the larger work. Two methods of describing accompanying material have been discussed and illustrated already.

1. The supplementary item may be added as accompanying material at the end of the physical description area (see *AACR2R* 1.5E and figure 1-115).
2. If supplementary material is of minor importance but of such nature that it cannot be listed succinctly in the physical description area, it may be added as a note (see *AACR2R* 1.7B11 and figure 1-116).

A third method of describing supplementary items dependently is by using multilevel description (13.6). By this method one or more parts of a multipart work that has been cataloged as a unit may be brought out (i.e., "analyzed"). This technique was developed for national bibliographies, for which some kind of separate entry must be prepared for each part of an ongoing work.

1.10. ITEMS MADE UP OF SEVERAL TYPES OF MATERIAL

Many library items are made up of several parts (e.g., an encyclopedia in twenty-four volumes, a set of filmstrips, or four sound recordings that form a unit). For cataloging, such items are described as a unit; description of the parts is basically a simple enumeration of their physical extent.

But in many instances library items clearly designed to function as a unit are made up of components that belong to different types of material (e.g., a book with an accompanying sound recording, a plastic model of a cuneiform tablet with a printed pamphlet of explanation).

1.10B. If such a multimedia item has one predominant part, the cataloger will make the catalog record from this part. Subsidiary parts will be added as accompanying materials, either at the end of the physical description area or as a note (*AACR2R* 1.5E and 1.7B11) (see figure 1-128).

1.10C. Sometimes a package of different kinds of media, all of the components of which are related and intended to be used together, has no predominant component. Such a package is called a "kit" using North American terminology, or "multimedia" by British GMD. A kit is commonly issued in a container with a title on it that will serve as a collective title for the entire item. In most instances, use rule 1.10C2a for describing kits (see figure 1-129).

Figure 1-128.   Multimedia item with one predominant component

245 10	‡a Learning "look-it-up" skills with an encyclopedia ‡h [transparency] / ‡c prepared by the Department of Educational Services in cooperation with Audio-Visual Services, Field Enterprises Educational Corporation.
260	‡a Chicago : ‡b The Corporation, ‡c c1966.
300	‡a 8 transparencies : ‡b col. ; ‡c 26 × 26 cm.
500	‡a "Directions for teachers" included on folder.
710 2	‡a Field Enterprises Educational Corporation. ‡b Dept. of Educational Services.
710 2	‡a Field Enterprises Educational Corporation. ‡b Audio-Visual Services.

Figure 1-129.   Physical description of a kit

```
245 00   ‡a Touchphonics ‡h [kit] : ‡b the manipulative multi-sensory phonics system.
260      ‡a Newport Beach, CA : ‡b Touchphonics Reading Systems, ‡c [1995?]
300      ‡a 1 guidebook, 1 word list, 50 phonics inventory cards, 1 videocassette, 200 plastic letter
         combinations, 4 trays, 1 whiteboard ; ‡c in container 41 × 52 × 10 cm.
500      ‡a "T100 kit".
710 2    ‡a Touchphonics Reading Systems.
```

1.11. FACSIMILES, PHOTOCOPIES, AND OTHER REPRODUCTIONS

Most libraries own many reprint editions of books, and libraries will increasingly acquire them as reprint publishers and reprint editions proliferate. Therefore, it is important that catalogers understand the provisions of this rule.

Basically, the rule stipulates that the catalog entry must describe the item in hand (i.e., the reprint). Any information pertaining to the original edition, even if it appears in the chief source of information, will be omitted from the body of the entry. Do not indicate such omission by ellipses. All necessary information about the original edition will be given in a single note in the note area.

Note, however, that LC and most North American libraries do not follow the stipulations of 1.11 for "reproductions of previously existing materials that are made for preservation purposes" (*LCRI* 1.11A, May 28, 1993). This includes photocopies and reproductions published on demand (e.g., from University Microfilms International in Ann Arbor, Michigan). For such items the bibliographic data are transcribed as for the original work; details relating to the reproduction are recorded in a 533 field. The examples described below do *not* fall into this category, but are formally published reprints. They exemplify the most common reprint publishing practices.

In the most straightforward situation, the publisher creates a new title page for the reprint, using its own imprint, sometimes rewording the title, and usually also reprinting the original title page, as in figure 1-112. In this case the title and statement of responsibility and publication areas are transcribed from the new title page. The cataloger will ignore the original title page for most purposes, although in this case the original makes it clear that the phrase "the medallic history of printing" is an alternative title, so it will be given an added entry in the 246 field. A formal note pertaining to the original publication is recorded in a 500 or 534 field (see discussion at 1.7B7). For the form of this note, see *AACR2R* 1.7A3 and 1.7B7. Another example of this situation may be seen in figure 1-130.

Sometimes the original title page is reproduced as the title page of the reprint edition, with the reprint publisher's imprint added to it. Such is the

Figure 1-130.   Reprint—new title page

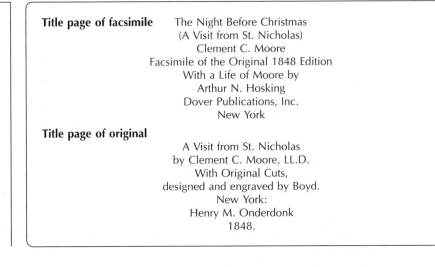

020	‡a 0486227979 (pbk.)
020	‡a 0486220834 (cloth)
100 1	‡a Moore, Clement Clarke, ‡d 1779-1863.
245 14	‡a The night before Christmas : ‡b (A visit from St. Nicholas) / ‡c Clement C. Moore ; with a life of Moore by Arthur N. Hosking.
246 30	‡a Visit from St. Nicholas
260	‡a New York : ‡b Dover, ‡c 1971.
300	‡a [16], 36 p. : ‡b ill. ; ‡c 16 cm.
440 0	‡a Dover books for children
520	‡a An important Christmas Eve visitor pays a call.
500	‡a "Facsimile of the original 1848 edition."
534	‡p Facsimile reprint. Originally published: ‡c New York : H.M. Onderdonk, 1848.
504	‡a "Bibliography of the works of Clement Clarke Moore": p. 34-36.
700 1	‡a Hosking, Arthur N. ‡q (Arthur Nicholas), ‡d b. 1874.

Title page of facsimile

The Night Before Christmas
(A Visit from St. Nicholas)
Clement C. Moore
Facsimile of the Original 1848 Edition
With a Life of Moore by
Arthur N. Hosking
Dover Publications, Inc.
New York

Title page of original

A Visit from St. Nicholas
by Clement C. Moore, LL.D.
With Original Cuts,
designed and engraved by Boyd.
New York:
Henry M. Onderdonk
1848.

case with the example shown in figure 1-131. In this example, "1891" at the bottom of the title page is reproduced from the original. It should be ignored in the transcription and given in a note (see *AACR2R* 1.11C).

Often a publisher will reproduce the original title page exactly, adding its own imprint information in another place, such as the verso of the title page, as in figure 1-132. Again, the imprint of the original is *not* transcribed in the 260 field, even though it and no other publication data appear on the title page. It will be recorded in a note.

Figure 1-131.   Reprint—original title page reprinted with new publisher information

```
020        ‡a 1897853424 (pbk.)
100 1      ‡a Moore, A. W. ‡q (Arthur William), ‡d 1853-1909.
245 14     ‡a The folk-lore of the Isle of Man : ‡b being an account of its myths, legends,
           superstitions, customs, & proverbs / ‡c collected from many sources ; with a general
           introduction and with explanatory notes to each chapter by A.W. Moore.
260        ‡a Felinfach [Wales] : ‡b Llanerch, ‡c 1994.
300        ‡a xii, 192 p. : ‡b ill. ; ‡c 21 cm.
534        ‡p Facsimile reprint. Originally published: ‡c Douglas, Isle of Man : Brown & Son, 1891.
```

Title page	The
	Folk-Lore
	of the
	Isle of Man,
	Being an Account of Its
	Myths, Legends, Superstitions,
	Customs, & Proverbs,
	Collected from many sources; with a General Introduction;
	and with Explanatory Notes to each Chapter;
	by
	A.W. Moore, M.A.;
	Author of "Manx Names," &c.
	Facsimile reprint 1994 by Llanerch publishers,
	Felinfach. ISBN 1 897853 42 4
	1891

Caution: give information in the note that corresponds to data found in the original work in the format appropriate to the original work. The work cataloged in figure 1-132 is a facsimile of an early printed monograph (book published before 1801). Cataloging data for the original would be transcribed according to *AACR2R* 2.12–2.18 or *Descriptive Cataloging of Rare Books* (Washington, D.C.: Cataloging Distribution Service, Library of Congress, 1991) (see discussion in chapter 2 at 2.12–2.18). Publication area data as given in the 534 note of figure 1-132 follow 2.16D.

In some cases a publisher will reprint an item giving little or no information about the reprint itself. Nevertheless, here, too, the reprint information is recorded in the publication area. In the case of figure 1-133 the name of the reprint publisher, the University of Notre Dame Press, appears only on the back cover. A new preface has been added, which claims that this is a "new, second edition" (although, in fact, no changes have been made) and states that the book has been out of print "for some three-score years." Given publishing practices of the period, this book probably would have been in print until at least the mid-1930s; in addition, the book arrived as a new book in the library in 1995, sixty years later. The cataloger is thus justified in estimating a publication date of 1995.

Figure 1-132.   Reprint—original title page reprinted unchanged

```
020      ‡a 1899373004
100 1    ‡a Harris, Walter, ‡d 1686-1761.
245 14   ‡a The history and antiquities of the city of Dublin : ‡b from the earliest acounts / ‡c
         compiled ... by Walter Harris ; with an appendix containing an history of the cathedrals of
         Christ-Church and St. Patrick, the university, the hospitals and other public buildings ; also
         two plans, one of the city as it was in the year 1610 ..., the other as it is at present ...
260      ‡a Ballynahinch, Northern Ireland : ‡b Davidson Books, ‡c 1994.
300      ‡a 509 p. : ‡b ill. (some folded), maps ; ‡c 21 cm.
534      ‡p Facsimile reprint. Originally published: ‡c Dublin : Printed for Laurence Flinn ... and
         James Williams ..., 1766.
```

Title page   The
                          History and Antiquities
                          of the City of Dublin,
                       from the earliest acounts:
                            compiled from
             Authentick Memoirs, Offices of Record, Manuscript
             Collections, and other unexceptionable Vouchers.
                      By the late Walter Harris, Esq;
                                with an
                               Appendix,
                              Containing,
             An History of the Cathedrals of Christ-Church and
                St. Patrick, the University, the Hospitals and
                         other Public Buildings.
            Also two Plans, one of the City as it was in the Year 1610,
            being the earliest extant; the other as it is at Present, from
             the accurate Survey of the late Mr. Rocque; with several
                           other Embellishments.
                                Dublin:
                   Printed for Laurence Flinn, in Castle-street;
                   and James Williams, in Skinner-row
                              M DCC LXVI.

Verso of title page
                   This is an exact photolithographic facsimile of the first
                         and only edition of 1766.
                   The maps and plans are reproduced to the same size
                              as the originals
                          ISBN 1-899373-00-4
                   Printed and published, 1994 by Davidson Books
             Ballynahinch, County Down, Northern Ireland BT24 8QD

The most difficult case is that of a publisher attempting to reproduce an original in every detail. There may be nothing at all in the item identifying the publisher or the date of publication. In figure 1-134, the item has been scrupulously reproduced, including a simulation of the original binding. The library's copy came with a publisher's advertisement telling about the facsimile, but a copy of this book could easily arrive in the collection without this small slip of paper. The cataloger is still required to describe the facsimile, not the original, in the publication and physical description areas.

Figure 1-133.   Reprint—original title page reprinted unchanged

```
020       ‡a 0268011095
100 1     ‡a O'Dea, John.
245 10    ‡a History of the Ancient Order of Hibernians and Ladies' Auxiliary / ‡c by John O'Dea.
246 14    ‡a History of the Ancient Order of Hibernians in America and Ladies' Auxiliary.
260       ‡a Notre Dame, Ind. : ‡b University of Notre Dame Press, ‡c [1995?]
300       ‡a 3 v. (1505 p.) ; ‡c 22 cm.
500       ‡a "New, second edition"--Pref.
534       ‡p Facsimile reprint. Originally published: ‡c Philadelphia : Keystone, 1923.
504       ‡a Includes bibliographical references and indexes.
```

Title page to volume 1	History of the Ancient Order of Hibernians and Ladies' Auxiliary by John O'Dea Volume 1 Published by authority of the National Board of the A. O. H. 1923

Figure 1-134.   Reprint—original title page reprinted unchanged

```
130 0     ‡a Book of Mormon.
245 14    ‡a The book of Mormon : ‡b an account written by the hand of Mormon, upon plates
          taken from the plates of Nephi ... / ‡c by Joseph Smith, Junior.
260       ‡a [Salt Lake City : ‡b Deseret Book Company, ‡c 1980]
300       ‡a 588 p. ; ‡c 20 cm.
534       ‡p Facsimile reprint. Originally published: ‡c Palmyra [N.Y.] : E.B. Grandin, 1830.
500       ‡a "Deseret Book Company ... produce[d] this limited facsimile edition on the 150th
          anniversary of the publication of the Book of Mormon"--Publisher's prospectus laid in.
700 1     ‡a Smith, Joseph, ‡d 1805-1844.
```

Title page	The Book of Mormon: An Account Written by the Hand of Mor- mon, upon Plates Taken from the Plates of Nephi. Wherefore it is an abridgment of the Record of the People of Nephi; and also of the Lamanites, which are a remnant of the House of Israel; and also to Jew and Gentile; written by way of commandment, and also by the spirit of Prophesy and of Revelation. Written, and sealed up, and hid up unto the Lord, that they might not be destroyed; to come forth by the gift and power of God unto the interpretation thereof by the gift of God ... By Joseph Smith, Junior, Author and Proprietor. Palmyra: Printed by E.B. Grandin, for the Author. 1830.

NOTES

1. Paul S. Dunkin, *Cataloging U.S.A.* (Chicago: American Library Association, 1969), p. 23, 48.
2. General information about MARC coding is found in the introduction to this *Handbook*. Details about coding the descriptive portion of the record are found throughout this chapter; information about the coding of main and added access points is found at the beginning of chapter 14. An explanation of the MARC authorities format is given in *Handbook* chapters 15, 17, and 18. Information about specific MARC fields may be found by consulting the index under "MARC fields."
3. *CSB* 105 (Nov. 1972): 2.
4. At the present time, the British Library does not use GMD (see Howarth, at 1.1C). Other British libraries should use terms from list 1.
5. Definition from *Bits & Tidbits* (Nov. 1986): 10–11.
6. *Bookman's Glossary*, 6th ed. (New York: Bowker, 1983), p. 77.
7. Between 1981 and 1991 it was the Library of Congress's practice to transcribe all larger jurisdictions if they appeared in the prescribed source, whether the city was "well-known" or not (*CSB* 12, spring 1981, p. 10). This policy was canceled in *CSB* 55 (winter 1992), p. 14, leaving the decision up to the cataloger.
8. *Bookman's Glossary*, p. 185. See also *AACR2R* Appendix D (Glossary), *s.v.* "Series."
9. *AACR2R* Appendix D (Glossary), *s.v.* "Serial."
10. Ten MARC fields, 590-599, have been reserved for local notes and may be locally defined. At the present time, the near-universal practice is to use only 590 for this purpose.

BOOKS, PAMPHLETS, AND PRINTED SHEETS

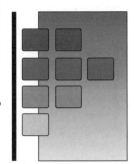

A book, by definition, is a printed "non-periodical literary publication containing forty-nine or more pages, not counting covers."[1] A pamphlet has less than forty-nine pages; a printed sheet (otherwise called a broadside or broadsheet) is "a sheet of paper printed on one side only, usually intended to be posted, publicly distributed or sold."[2] Librarians call the type of material included in *AACR2R* chapter 2 monographic. As opposed to a serial, a monograph is a work that either is complete as it is issued or has a projected termination point (e.g., an encyclopedia issued in parts).

For the description of a printed work issued in microform reproduction, see *AACR2R* chapter 11. For printed material issued serially, see *AACR2R* chapter 12 in addition to rules in *AACR2R* chapter 2.

Most of the cataloging examples and discussion in *Handbook* chapter 1 are purposely geared toward the cataloging of books, in order to provide a familiar frame of reference to the inexperienced cataloger. Information already supplied in *Handbook* chapter 1 is not repeated in detail in chapter 2, and most of the explanations in chapter 2 are illustrated with figures from chapter 1. For this reason the user of the *Handbook* is advised to begin with chapter 1 for details about monographic cataloging, and then proceed to chapter 2.[3]

The cataloging of books will be governed by all appropriate rules in *AACR2R* chapter 1, "General Rules for Description." Additional special rules that apply only to books, pamphlets, and printed sheets, and not to other types of library materials, are contained in *AACR2R* chapter 2.

2.0B. Sources of information

The title page is the chief source of information. If a book has no title page, the cover, half-title page, caption, colophon, or running title may be used as a substitute; preference should be given to the source with the most complete information. Make a note if you have used a substitute for a title page (see figure 1-108).

If title page information is spread over two facing pages without repetition, it is transcribed as if it were found on one page (see figures 1-48 and 1-49).

2.0H. Items with several title pages

Sometimes a book has more than one title page. Follow guidelines under *AACR2R* 1.0H. Prefer a title page giving a later publication date or, as with the example shown in figure 2-1, prefer a printed title page with a publication date rather than an engraved title page without a publication date (1.0H1b).

A bilingual dictionary often has separate facing title pages in two languages. Following guidelines under 1.0H1diii, choose the title page in order of languages listed in the rule. If one of the title pages is in English, use that title page (see figure 2-2).

2.1. TITLE AND STATEMENT OF RESPONSIBILITY AREA

See general discussions in this text under 1.1B and 1.1F1. The prescribed source of information for transcription of the title and statement of responsibility area in a monograph is the title page or, if the book lacks a title page, the title page substitute (cf. 2.0B1). In addition, statements of responsibility appearing "prominently" (*AACR2R* 0.8, i.e., in the preliminaries and the colophon as well as the title page, all prescribed sources for the edition area) may be recorded as part of the statement of responsibility, if, in the cataloger's judgment, they are significant. The title and statement of responsibility are recorded in the 245 field of the MARC record.

2.1B. Title proper

Transcribe the title proper in subfield ‡a exactly as it appears in the chief source of information. Generally, do not omit or add words. For general comments and rules covering the recording of the title proper, as well as supporting examples, see this *Handbook* at 1.1B.

2.1C. *Optional addition.* General material designation

See discussion of general material designation under 1.1C. If a library chooses to add GMDs to materials covered by chapter 2, GMD "text" will be added, in brackets, immediately after the title proper and following subfield ‡h (see figure 1-15). Examples in this text will follow traditional North American library practice of displaying GMDs for nonbook materials but not for materials covered by rules in *AACR2R* chapter 2.

Figure 2-1.   More than one title page

```
100 1    ‡a Bishop, Frederick.
245 14   ‡a The illustrated London cookery book : ‡b containing upwards of fifteen hundred first-
         rate receipts selected with great care, and a proper attention to economy ... : combined
         with useful hints on domestic economy ... / ‡c by Frederick Bishop.
260      ‡a London : ‡b J. Haddon, ‡c 1852.
300      ‡a xxxi, 460 p. : ‡b ill. (some folded) ; ‡c 23 cm.
500      ‡a Includes index.
500      ‡a Added t.p., engraved.
```

Printed title page

The
Illustrated London
Cookery Book,
containing upwards of
fifteen hundred first-rate receipts
selected with great care, and a proper attention to economy;
and embodying all the latest improvements in the culinary art:
accompanied by important remarks and counsel on the
arrangement and well-ordering of the kitchen,
combined with
useful hints on domestic economy.
The whole based on many years' constant practice and experience;
and addressed to
Private Families as well as the Highest Circles.
By
Frederick Bishop.
Late cuisinier to St. James's Palace, Earl Grey, the Marquis of Stafford,
Baron Rothschild, Earl Norbury, Captain Duncombe, and
Many of the first families in the Kingdom.
Profusely illustrated with engravings on wood.
London: 227, Strand.
MDCCCLII.

Engraved title page

The
Illustrated
London Cookery
Book
&
Complete Housekeeper.
250 engravings.
London: 227, Strand.

2.1D. Parallel titles

Precede a parallel title by space - equals sign - space and subfield ‡b unless
it has already occurred. Transcribe it exactly as it appears in the chief source
of information. See *Handbook* at 1.1D for general instructions, discussion,
and examples.

Figure 2-2.   More than one title page

```
020        ‡a 0671774018
100 1      ‡a Dubois, Marguerite-Marie.
245 10     ‡a Larousse's French-English, English-French dictionary / ‡c by Marguerite-Marie Dubois,
           Denis J. Keen, Barbara Shuey, with the assistance of Jean-Claude Corbeil, Lester G.
           Crocker.
246 1      ‡i Added t.p. in French: ‡a Dictionnaire français-anglais, anglais-français Larousse
250        ‡a Rev. and enl.
260        ‡a New York : ‡b Pocket Books, ‡c 1971.
300        ‡a 565 p. ; ‡c 16 cm.
700 1      ‡a Keen, Denis J.
700 1      ‡a Shuey, Barbara.
```

First title page

Dictionnaire
Français-Anglais Anglais-Français
Larousse
par
Marguerite-Marie Dubois
Denis J. Keen   Barbara Shuey
avec la collaboration de
Jean-Claude Corbeil   Lester G. Crocker
Édition revue et augmentée
Published by Pocket Books New York

Second title page

Larousse's
French-English English-French
Dictionary
by
Marguerite-Marie Dubois
Denis J. Keen   Barbara Shuey
with the assistance of
Jean-Claude Corbeil   Lester G. Crocker
Revised and enlarged
Published by Pocket Books New York

2.1E. Other title information

Precede other title information by space - colon - space and subfield ‡b
unless it has already occurred. Transcribe it as it appears in the chief source.
See *Handbook* at 1.1E for discussion and examples.

2.1F. Statements of responsibility

Precede the statement of responsibility by space - slash - space and subfield
‡c. Transcribe it exactly as it appears in the chief source of information. See
Handbook at 1.1F for general instructions, discussion, and examples.

2.1F2. Additions to statement of responsibility. This rule is identical
to 1.1F8, which see. See also discussion of figure 1-46.

2.2. Edition Area

The prescribed sources for books, pamphlets, and printed sheets for information for this area are the title page, other preliminaries (half-title page, verso of title page, cover), and colophon. Information taken from other sources must be bracketed.

The edition area is recorded in the 250 field. Transcribe the edition statement in subfield ‡a exactly as it appears in the source. However, abbreviations from *AACR2R* Appendix B should be used if available. See *Handbook* at 1.2 for discussion and examples.

2.2C. Statements of responsibility relating to the edition

Record a statement of responsibility relating to an edition following space - slash - space in subfield ‡b. See discussion and examples under 1.2C in this *Handbook*. For additional examples, see figures 1-6, 1-41, etc.

2.2D. Statement relating to a named revision of an edition

If more than one edition statement is present on an item, record both, separated by a comma. Capitalize the first word in each statement. See this *Handbook* at 1.2D for discussion and examples.

2.4. Publication, Distribution, etc., Area

The prescribed sources of information for the publication area of *AACR2R* chapter 2 materials are the title page, other preliminaries (half-title page, verso of title page, cover), and colophon. If information is taken from a source other than these, it must be enclosed in brackets (see *AACR2R* 2.0B2).

This area is recorded in the 260 field of the MARC record. Prescribed order and basic punctuation for information included in the publication area are as follows:

260   ‡a Place : ‡b Publisher, ‡c date.

All three elements must be given. See discussion and examples in this *Handbook* at 1.4C6, 1.4D7, and 1.4F7 for procedure when one or more of these elements does not appear. For a general discussion and examples, see this *Handbook* at 1.4, 1.4C, 1.4D, and 1.4F. Abbreviations are used in the publication area if they are found in *AACR2R* Appendix B.

2.4C. Place of publication, distribution, etc.

Record the place of publication in subfield ‡a as it appears in the source. The cataloger will always list the first place appearing in the prescribed source of information. If this place is in the country of the cataloging agency (for catalogers in the United States, a city in the U.S.A.), all subsequent places are ignored. If a city in another country is given first, it will be recorded. But if a city in the country of the cataloging agency is also named, it will be given in addition to the first city. For a general discussion and examples, see *Handbook* at 1.4C.

2.4D. Name of publisher, distributor, etc.

Transcribe the name of the publisher, distributor, etc., following space - colon - space in subfield ‡b. The name may be shortened, but must remain identifiable. See extensive discussion and examples under 1.4D in this *Handbook*.

2.4E. *Optional addition.* Statement of function of publisher, distributor, etc.

See *Handbook* at 1.4E for discussion of this statement.

2.4F. Date of publication

Transcribe the date found in the source, preceded by a comma, in subfield ‡c. If the date is given as a roman numeral, convert it to an arabic numeral. See *Handbook* at 1.4F for discussion and examples.

2.5. Physical Description Area

Chapter 2 gives special rules for describing books, pamphlets, and printed sheets. The prescribed source for this area is the whole publication. The physical description area is recorded in the 300 field of the MARC record.

2.5B. Number of volumes and/or pagination

Single volumes

2.5B1. Extent of the item. The extent is always the first element of the physical description area and is introduced in the 300 field by subfield ‡a. A single book is described in terms of the number of its pages or leaves (see 2.5B2, etc.). Roman numerals should be recorded as such, lowercase (see *AACR2R*, Appendix C.2B3).

Although books are the most numerous class of materials covered by *AACR2R* chapter 2, the chapter also covers other printed materials. Posters showing predominantly written material, handbills, and other separately published sheets defined in *AACR2R* Appendix D as broadsides are also included in *AACR2R* chapter 2 (see figure 2-3), as are portfolios (two covers joined at the back holding loose sheets of paper). The number of pieces included in a portfolio (bracketed unless numbered on the pieces) and the type of material are designated (see figure 2-4).

2.5B2. A broadside, a portfolio, or one or more loose sheets are described as such in the physical description area. A single volume book is

Figure 2-3.   Broadside

245 00 ‡a Poesia = ‡b Poetry : Friday, March 17, 7:30 p.m., El Pueblo Community Center, 6th
        and Irvington : mecha dance following poetry, 9:00 p.m. / ‡c Fernando Tápia ... [et al.] ; a
        Campo-El Pueblo/Gonzalez co-production.
246 31 ‡a Poetry
260   ‡a [Tucson, Ariz.] : ‡b The Producers, ‡c [1978]
300   ‡a 1 broadside : ‡b ill. ; ‡c 44 × 28 cm.
700 1   ‡a Tápia, Fernando.

Broadside   Poesia/Poetry
                                        fernando tápia
                                        chocolate brown
                                        marta bermudez
                                        miguel mendez
                                        elena parra
                                        aristeo brito

                            Friday, March 17, 7:30 p.m.
                            El Pueblo Community Center
                                6th and Irvington
                        Mecha dance following poetry, 9:00 p.m.
                        A Campo-El Pueblo/Gonzalez Co-Production

Figure 2-4.   Portfolio

100 1   ‡a Nelson, Stan.
245 10 ‡a Typefounding by hand : ‡b a suite of prints / ‡c by Stan Nelson.
260   ‡a Kalamazoo, Mich. : ‡b Private Press & Typefoundry of P.H. Duensing, ‡c 1977.
300   ‡a 1 portfolio (5 sheets) : ‡b ill. ; ‡c 42 cm.
500   ‡a Previously published in: Typefounding / by Stanley Nelson. 1972.
500   ‡a Limited ed. of 25 signed and numbered copies.
590   ‡a Library copy is no. 15.
700 1   ‡a Nelson, Stan. ‡t Typefounding.

Title page   Typefounding by Hand
                                        A Suite of Prints
                                        By Stan Nelson
                                        Privately Printed
                                        1977

Colophon
This suite of five prints first appeared in *Typefounding* by Stanley Nelson ... The
original blocks have been reprinted on handmade Kome paper, in an edition of
25 copies at The Private Press & Typefoundry of Paul Hayden Duensing,
Kalamazoo, Michigan in September, 1977, of which this is no. 15.

described in terms of pages or leaves. Record the last *numbered* page or leaf of each section. A leaf is a single sheet in a book. It consists of two pages, one on each side. If the leaf is printed on both sides, the book is described in terms of pages (e.g., ix, 67 p.). Most modern trade books are printed and the pages numbered in this fashion. The cataloger must be alert, however, for works printed or numbered only on one side of the leaf. These are described in terms of leaves; that is, if we may speak of ordinary books as being "paged," these books are "foliated" (from Latin "folium," leaf) (see, for example, figure 1-108).

2.5B3. Books published in the second half of the nineteenth century often included a several-page list of other books issued by the publisher. The book illustrated in figure 2-1 has such a list on three unnumbered pages following page 460. Such publishers' advertisements are to be disregarded in the pagination of the volume.

2.5B5. The cataloger is directed in 2.5B2 to "give the last numbered page, leaf, or column in each sequence." 2.5B5 is a caution: a book whose pages are numbered i-xxx and then 1-500 is said to have two sequences; however, a book whose pages are numbered i-xxx and then 31-500 has only one sequence, because the only change has been from roman to arabic numerals in the same sequence. Hence, the pagination of the first book would be recorded xxx, 500 p., but the second would simply be recorded 500 p.

2.5B6. Sometimes a publication may be an extract from a larger work. Inclusive paging is given for such a publication. In figure 2-5, the final two sequences of numbers (519-542, 260-273) represent two articles by the author of the book added as an appendix. Because their pagination is reproduced from the original printing, it is so recorded.

Figure 2-5.   Complicated pagination

020	‡a 0824074491 (alk. paper)
100 1	‡a Reeds, Karen.
245 10	‡a Botany in medieval and Renaissance universities / ‡c Karen Meier Reeds.
260	‡a New York : ‡b Garland, ‡c 1991.
300	‡a xix, 316 p., 10 p. of plates, p. 519-542, 260-273 : ‡b ill. ; ‡c 24 cm.
440 0	‡a Harvard dissertations in the history of science
500	‡a Thesis (Ph. D.)--Harvard University, 1975.
500	‡a "Annex: 'Renaissance humanism and botany,' Annals of science 33 (1976), 519-542 [and] 'Publishing scholarly books in the sixteenth century,' Scholarly publishing, April 1983, 259-274."
504	‡a Includes bibliographical references (p. 261-283) and index.

Title page	Botany in Medieval and Renaissance Universities Karen Meier Reeds Garland Publishing, Inc. New York & London 1991

2.5B7. The Library of Congress has modified the provisions of this rule. Pages or leaves of unpaged or unfoliated books will no longer be counted. Instead, the cataloger will use "1 v. (unpaged)" (see, for example, figure 1-30). For rare books, however, the Library of Congress, and libraries that follow LC practice, will count pages as before (what constitutes "rare" is, naturally, the decision of the cataloging agency) (*LCRI* 2.5B7, Feb. 4, 1991). This means that if such a work is neither paged nor foliated, the pages or leaves should be counted and the number recorded in brackets. Begin the count with the first page containing either printing or illustration; end it with the last such page (see figure 2-6). Generally do not count pages for items longer than 100 pages. For these, give the estimated number preceded by "ca.", without brackets.

2.5B8. A volume with complicated paging. If there are various (i.e., more than three) main numbered sections in a single volume monograph, record the pagination as "1 v. (various pagings)." (LC will apply only method "c" of *AACR2R* 2.5B8; see *LCRI*, Jan. 5, 1989) (see figure 2-7).

If there are not more than three main numbered sections, record pagination as shown in figure 2-8.

2.5B10. Leaves and pages of plates. The following Library of Congress policy decision should be substituted for *AACR2R* 2.5B10: give the number of leaves or pages of plates after the paging only if the leaves or pages of plates are numbered by the printer (see figure 2-5). Do not count leaves or pages of plates. If leaves or pages of plates are unnumbered, ignore them as part of the first element of the physical description (*LCRI* 2.5B10, Nov. 27, 1990). When recording numbered leaves or pages of plates, do not substitute arabic for roman numerals when the publisher numbers the plates with roman numerals; but record roman numerals lowercase, regardless of the publisher's practice (see *AACR2R*, Appendix C.2B1 and C.2B3).

Figure 2-6.   Unpaged work (rare book)

100 1	‡a Wakoski, Diane.
245 14	‡a The ice queen / ‡c Diane Wakoski ; illustrations by Margaret Prentice.
260	‡a [Tuscaloosa, Alabama] : ‡b Parallel Editions, ‡c 1994.
300	‡a [31] p. : ‡b ill. (some col.) ; ‡c 34 cm.
500	‡a "This limited edition book was designed and produced by Eileen Wallace, Steve Miller, Paula Marie Gourley, Timothy Geiger, Shari DeGraw and Inge Bruggeman in the MFA in the Book Arts Program at the University of Alabama"--Colophon.
500	‡a Two colored illustrations on double leaves.
500	‡a Edition limited to 70.
590	‡a Library copy no. 11, signed by author.
700 1	‡a Prentice, Margaret.

Title page

The Ice Queen
Diane Wakoski

Illustrations by Margaret Prentice
Parallel Editions 1994

Figure 2-7.   Complicated pagination

```
020       ‡a 0316770671
245 04    ‡a The AIDS knowledge base : ‡b a textbook on HIV disease from the University of
          California, San Francisco and San Francisco General Hospital / ‡c edited by P.T. Cohen,
          Merle A. Sande, Paul A. Volberding ; associate editors, Mark B. Feinberg ... [et al.].
250       ‡a 2nd ed.
260       ‡a Boston : ‡b Little, Brown, ‡c c1994.
300       ‡a 1 v. (various pagings) : ‡b ill. (some col.) ; ‡c 27 cm.
504       ‡a Includes bibliographical references and index.
700 1     ‡a Cohen, P. T. ‡q (Philip T.), ‡d 1940-
700 1     ‡a Sande, Merle A., ‡d 1939-
700 1     ‡a Volberding, Paul.
710 2     ‡a University of California, San Francisco.
710 2     ‡a San Francisco General Hospital (Calif.)
```

Title page	The AIDS Knowledge Base A Textbook on HIV Disease from the University of California, San Francisco, and San Francisco General Hospital Second Edition Edited by P.T. Cohen, Merle A. Sande, Paul A. Volberding Associate Editors Mark B. Feinberg, Lawrence D. Kaplan, Sharon Safrin Julie Louise Gerberding, Dennis H. Osmond, Constance B. Wofsy Little, Brown and Company Boston/New York/Toronto/London

Figure 2-8.   Complicated pagination

```
110 2     ‡a Catholic Church.
240 10    ‡a Liber usualis
245 14    ‡a The liber usualis : ‡b with introduction and rubrics in English / ‡c edited by the
          Benedictines of Solesmes.
260       ‡a Tournai, Belgium ; ‡a New York : ‡b Society of St. John the Evangelist : ‡b Desclée, ‡c
          c1956.
300       ‡a xlix, 1880, 100, 80 p. : ‡b ill. ; ‡c 19 cm.
500       ‡a Edition with complete musical notation.
710 2     ‡a Abbaye Saint-Pierre de Solesmes.
```

Title page	The Liber Usualis With Introduction and Rubrics in English Edited by the Benedictines of Solesmes Society of St. John the Evangelist Desclée & Cie Tournai (Belgium) New York, N.Y.

The type of paper used for printing has nothing to do with whether a leaf is a plate or not. The important thing to watch for is that "plate" material must be outside the regular numbering of the book. Plates are recorded either as "leaves of plates" or "pages of plates," depending on whether they are printed on both sides of the leaf or only on one. However, to reiterate, if the enumeration by the printer does not accurately reflect the number of pages or leaves of plates, or if the plates are not numbered, the cataloger should ignore them. Unpaged plates are regarded simply as illustrations, to be recorded as part of the second element of the physical description area (see *AACR2R* 2.5C).

In summary, a plate, by cataloger definition, does *not* form part of the original physical makeup of the folded signature or gathering that makes up the book. A plate *interrupts* the regular sequence of pagination of the book. Plates may be gathered together in one place in the book, or they may be scattered through the book. The number of plates must be recorded following the number of pages, as part of the physical extent (first) element of the physical description area. Give the number of leaves or pages of plates after the paging *only* if the leaves or pages of plates are numbered by the printer. Do not count leaves or pages of plates. If leaves or pages of plates are unnumbered, ignore them as part of the first element of the physical description.

2.5B11. Folded leaves. For an example, see figure 1-69.

Publications in more than one volume

2.5B17. Generally speaking, if a monograph consists of more than one physical volume, record the number of volumes (e.g., 3 v.). If a multivolume set is incomplete, give the specific material designation alone without a number (see figure 1-92). In Library of Congress practice, catalogers record the volumes of incomplete sets within angle brackets (e.g., "v. <1-3 >"). This practice is not called for in *AACR2R* and is not reflected in the *LCRIs*; it is not used in this *Handbook*.

2.5B18. See the definition of "volume" in *AACR2R* Appendix D (Glossary). If the term "volume" is not appropriate for a multipart monograph, one of the terms listed under 2.5B18 may be used. This is an inclusive list. Do not use terms other than these in describing multipart monographs.

2.5B19 and **2.5B20.** The item on which figure 2-9 is based is paged continuously, beginning with volume 1 and ending with the last page of volume 6. The set is in six bibliographical volumes, bound in three physical volumes.

2.5B23. Braille or other tactile systems. Materials for the visually handicapped occupy a more prominent position in the revised *AACR2R*. A new GMD, "braille," has been devised as an optional addition (not used by the Library of Congress) following the title proper (1.1C1). In the first element of the physical description, the cataloger will add "of braille" or a similar term as appropriate to the statement of pages, leaves, or volumes (see figure 2-10).

Figure 2-9.   More than one volume

```
130 0    ‡a Arabian nights. ‡l English.
245 14   ‡a The book of the thousand nights and a night : ‡b a plain and literal translation of the
         Arabian nights entertainments / ‡c made and annotated by Richard F. Burton ; decorated
         with illustrations by Valenti Angelo.
246 18   ‡a Arabian nights entertainments
260      ‡a New York : ‡b Heritage Press, ‡c c1934.
300      ‡a 6 v. in 3 (xvi, 3975 p.) : ‡b ill. ; ‡c 22 cm.
500      ‡a Edited by Emile Van Vliet.
504      ‡a Includes bibliographical references and index.
700 1    ‡a Burton, Richard Francis, ‡c Sir, ‡d 1821-1890.
700 1    ‡a Van Vliet, Emile.
700 1    ‡a Angelo, Valenti, ‡d 1897-
```

Title page

The Book Of
The Thousand Nights and a Night
A Plain and Literal Translation of the
Arabian Nights Entertainments
Made and Annotated by Richard F. Burton
Decorated with Illustrations by Valenti Angelo

The Heritage Press, New York

Figure 2-10.   Braille

```
245 00   ‡a Understanding AIDS / ‡c [prepared by the Surgeon General and the Centers for
         Disease Control, U.S. Public Health Service] ; transcribed and embossed by National
         Braille Press, Inc.
260      ‡a Boston, Mass. : ‡b The Press, ‡c [1988]
300      ‡a 1 v. of braille (unpaged) ; ‡c 32 cm.
440 0    ‡a HHS publication ; ‡v no. (CDC) 88-8407
500      ‡a Cover title.
500      ‡a C. Everett Koop, Surgeon General, U.S. Public Health Service.
700 1    ‡a Koop, C. Everett ‡q (Charles Everett), ‡d 1916-
710 2    ‡a Centers for Disease Control (U.S.)
```

Title page

Understanding AIDS
Transcribed and embossed by National Braille Press, Inc.
Free additional Braille copies can be ordered from
U.S. Department of Health and Human Services
Public Health Service
Centers for Disease Control
P.O. Box 6003
Rockville, Maryland

HHS Publication No. (CDC) HHS-88-8407

Back cover

This brochure has been prepared by the Surgeon General and the
Centers for Disease Control, U.S. Public Health Service.

2.5C. Illustrative matter

This is the second element of the physical description area. It is separated from the first element (number of volumes or pages of a book) by space - colon - space. In the MARC record, subfield ‡b follows the colon. The abbreviation "ill." is used to describe all types of illustrations unless one of the special types listed in *AACR2R* 2.5C2 is considered to be important. The Library of Congress has ceased indicating particular types of illustration in most cases. If a book contains illustrations of any type, including those listed under 2.5C2, the Library of Congress, and other libraries following LC policy, will simply use "ill." Maps, however, should also be noted (*LCRI* 2.5C2, Nov. 22, 1990) (see, e.g., figure 1-1). Note, however, that this change does not affect the provisions of 2.5C3. Catalogers will continue to describe a book in which all illustrations are colored as "col. ill." or one that contains a mix of colored and black-and-white illustrations as "ill. (some col.)" (see figure 2-6). Examples in this text follow Library of Congress policy for illustrations.

2.5D. Size

Size is measured in centimeters, except for items measuring less than ten centimeters, which are measured in millimeters. For a book, measure the height of the cover. Fractions of a centimeter are rounded up to the next centimeter.

2.5D2. Give height followed by width if width is less than half the height or greater than the height (see figure 1-46).

2.5D4. A single sheet or broadside is measured height by width (see figure 2-3). Note under rule 2.5D4 instructions for designating folded sheets.

2.5E. Accompanying material

There are numerous ways to deal with accompanying material under *AACR2R*. See *Handbook* at 1.5E for general discussion and examples.

2.6. SERIES AREA

A series statement found in an item is recorded exactly as it appears in a 440 or 490 field; if its authority form differs from the form found, the series is traced from an 8XX field. See discussion and examples under 1.6 in this *Handbook*.

2.7. NOTE AREA

Follow instructions on format and order of notes as given in 1.7A. In addition, use categories of notes stipulated under 2.7B.

2.7B1. Nature, scope, or artistic form. See discussion in this *Handbook* at 1.7B1; for an example, see figure 1-105. This note is recorded in MARC field 500.

2.7B2. Language of item and/or translation or adaptation. See discussion under 1.7B2 in this *Handbook* and figure 1-103. This note is recorded in MARC field 546.

2.7B3. Source of title proper. See discussion in this *Handbook* at 1.7B3; see also figure 1-108. This note is recorded in MARC field 500.

2.7B4. Variations in title. See discussion under 1.7B4; see also figure 2-2 for an example of this type of note. Many of these notes are generated from a 246 field.

2.7B6. Statements of responsibility. See discussion under 1.7B6. An "At head of title" note is given in a 500 field for a name not transcribed in the statement of responsibility that appears at the top of the title page. The most frequent "At head of title" information is the name of a corporate body appearing in this position whose relationship to the work is not certain, but for whom an added entry should be given because of its prominent position on the title page (21.30E) (see figure 2-11).

2.7B7. Edition and history. For discussion and an example of this kind of note, see this *Handbook* at 1.7B7 and figure 1-104.

Notice the absence in *AACR2R* chapter 2 of a rule numbered 2.7B8. The omission of this number is not accidental. As previously pointed out, the rules in *AACR2R* chapters 2–12 are correlated with the general rules in *AACR2R* chapter 1 (e.g., 2.7B7 is a particular application for monographs of general principles governing edition and history notes set forth in 1.7B7).

Figure 2-11.   "At head of title" note

020	‡a 0903043009
111 2	‡a International Conference on Cataloguing Principles ‡d (1961 : ‡c Paris, France)
245 10	‡a Statement of principles adopted at the International Conference on Cataloguing Principles, Paris, October 1961.
250	Annotated ed. / ‡b with commentary and examples by Eva Verona ; assisted by Franz George Kaltwasser, P.R. Lewis, Roger Pierrot.
260	‡a London ; ‡b IFLA Committee on Cataloguing, ‡c 1971.
300	‡a xviii, 119 p. ; ‡c 25 cm.
500	‡a At head of title: International Federation of Library Associations.
504	‡a Includes bibliographical references (p. x-xii).
700 1	‡a Verona, Eva.
710 2	‡a International Federation of Library Associations.

Title page	International Federation of Library Associations
	Statement of Principles
	Adopted at the International Conference on Cataloguing Principles
	Paris, October, 1961
	Annotated Edition
	with commentary and examples
	by Eva Verona
	assisted by Franz George Kaltwasser, P.R. Lewis, Roger Pierrot
	London
	IFLA Committee on Cataloguing
	1971

Rule 1.7B8 has to do with notes pertaining to the "material specific details" area, a special area found only in entries for cartographic materials, music, computer files, and serials. Because a monograph entry does not include the material specific details area, this sort of note is not pertinent to monographs. Therefore the number is skipped in *AACR2R* chapter 2.

2.7B9. Publication, distribution, etc. See *Handbook* at 1.7B9. This note is given in a 500 field.

2.7B10. Physical description. For discussion, see *Handbook* at 1.7B10; for an example, see figure 2-4. Record this note in a MARC 500 field.

2.7B11. Accompanying material. See figure 1-16 and *Handbook* at 1.7B11. This note is recorded in a MARC 500 field.

2.7B13. Dissertations. See discussion under 1.7B13. Note that unless a thesis or dissertation has been published (i.e., issued for public sale or distribution), such a work will be cataloged following the rules for manuscripts (*AACR2R* chapter 4). See discussion of the matter of dissertations in *CSB* 118:8 (summer 1976). Dissertation notes are given in the MARC 502 field.

2.7B14. Audience. See discussion in this *Handbook* at 1.7B4 and figure 1-120 for an example of such a note. The appropriate MARC field is 521.

2.7B17. Summary. See discussion in this *Handbook* at 1.7B17. Summary notes are given in a 520 field.

2.7B18. Contents. See *Handbook* at 1.7B18 for a discussion of formal contents notes. These are given in a 505 field.

Informal contents notes are made when the publication includes features of particular importance, such as indexes, that should be brought out. These are recorded in a 500 field.

Bibliographical citations are noted. *AACR2R* rule 2.7B18 includes examples of such notes. The Library of Congress will not follow these examples (see *LCRI* 2.7B18, May 8, 1991). Instead, if a publication contains bibliographical citations in any form (including footnotes, etc.), use the following note in a 504 field:

    504   ‡a Includes bibliographical references.

However, if the publication contains a single bibliography, add pagination to the note:

    504   ‡a Includes bibliographical references (p. 310-325).

If the publication contains an index or indexes to its own contents, use one of the following notes in a 500 field:

    500   ‡a Includes index.
    500   ‡a Includes indexes.

If a publication contains bibliographical citations and an index or indexes, the two notes may be combined in a single 504 field, as in the following example:

    504   ‡a Includes bibliographical references (p. 530-555) and indexes.

2.7B20. Copy being described. See discussion under 1.7B20 in this *Handbook*; also see the last note for figure 2-4. This is a local note and as such is recorded in a 590 field.

2.7B21. "With" notes. See figure 1-125. Depending on the situation, these notes are recorded in a 590 or a 501 field. See discussion at *Handbook* 1.7B21.

2.8. STANDARD NUMBER AREA

See discussion under 1.8 in this *Handbook.* ISBN is recorded in an 020 field.

2.12–2.18. EARLY PRINTED MONOGRAPHS

These rules, which apply to books published before 1801, should not be used. Instead, catalogers should follow rules formulated by the Library of Congress and the Bibliographic Standards Committee of the Rare Books and Manuscripts Section (Association of College and Research Libraries) for such items: *Descriptive Cataloging of Rare Books* (Washington, D.C.: Cataloging Distribution Service, Library of Congress, 1991).

NOTES

1. *Bookman's Glossary,* 6th ed. (New York: Bowker, 1983), p. 29.
2. Ibid., p. 39.
3. General information about MARC coding is found in the introduction to this *Handbook*; details about coding the descriptive portion of the record are found throughout chapter 1; information about the coding of main and added access points is found at the beginning of chapter 14. An explanation of the MARC authorities format is given in *Handbook* chapters 15, 17, and 18. Information about specific MARC fields may be found by consulting the index under "MARC fields."

CARTOGRAPHIC MATERIALS

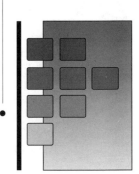

AACR2R chapter 3 covers cartographic materials of all sorts. The most common variety of cartographic material is a map, which may be defined as any kind of graphic representation of any place in the universe, on the earth or in the heavens, real or imaginary. Relief maps, globes, atlases, and the photographs and surveys that are the raw materials from which conventional maps are made are all regarded as cartographic materials and are also covered by rules in *AACR2R* chapter 3.

Many nonspecialist catalogers in general libraries find the vocabulary and techniques of cartography daunting. Such individuals will find much aid and comfort in a manual issued by the Anglo-American Cataloguing Committee for Cartographic Materials (AACCCM). Entitled *Cartographic Materials: A Manual of Interpretation for AACR2* (Chicago: ALA, 1982), the manual consists of a rule-by-rule discussion and elucidation of all *AACR2* rules that apply to map cataloging. In addition, helpful appendixes discuss such mysteries as determination of the scale of a map and the date of situation, and treatment of map series. Many examples of map cataloging are provided by the national libraries making up the membership of the AACCCM. Although originally prepared for *AACR2* (1978), the manual forms an invaluable companion to *AACR2R* chapter 3, "Cartographic Materials," and should be used along with materials presented in this chapter.

Once again it must be emphasized that none of the chapters in *AACR2R* Part I, including chapter 3, says anything about main or added entries. These rules are to be found in *AACR2R* Part II, chapter 21. Specific mention of maps was made in the original version of *AACR2* 21.1A1, which stated "cartographers are the authors of their maps." This statement, together with other specifically listed examples of personal authorship, has been eliminated in *AACR2R*, being subsumed under a more general statement now to be found under 21.1A1. This definition does not eliminate all instances of a cartographer being regarded as the "author" of a map, but it does place the burden of choice on the cataloger's judgment as to whether the cartographer is "chiefly responsible for the creation of the intellectual or artistic content" of the item.

In addition, when determining main entry for cartographic material, the cataloger should consult *AACR2R* 21.1B2f, the rule governing entry of a cartographic work under the heading for a corporate body. This rule states that 21.1B2 may be applied to "cartographic materials emanating from a corporate body other than a body that is merely responsible for their publication or distribution."

Official Anglo-American cataloging preference for entry under person or body primarily responsible for the intellectual, etc., content of a work is of long standing, going back at least as far as Charles Ammi Cutter's *Rules for a Dictionary Catalogue,* which states, "The designer or painter copied is the author of engravings; the cartographer is the author of maps."[1]

Entry under cartographer may have fit in nicely with the principle of authorship responsibility, but it does not seem to have been a very helpful method of arrangement for most library users. The average library user generally comes to the library with a request for a map of Boston, or a literary map of Great Britain, or a map showing Arizona's weather patterns—a topographic or topographic-subject approach rather than an author approach. As early as 1921, Sir Herbert Fordham summarized the difficulty in his statement, "A map lies in character between a book and a picture, and combines the features of both. The classification and the bibliographical description of maps are thus difficult, and require a good deal of attention."[2]

Fordham presented the difficulty but offered no real suggestion other than that title main entry for maps should be preferred, a position adopted by the Royal Geographical Society in the next decade.[3] As for librarians in the United States, in most cases, unless they were map specialists, they controlled maps in a number of different homemade, informal fashions, usually keeping them apart from the rest of the library's collection.

It was not until 1945 when Samuel W. Boggs and Dorothy C. Lewis presented their monumental *The Classification and Cataloging of Maps and Atlases* that anyone gave concentrated attention to the solution of the problem of proper identification and collocation of maps in a general library catalog. Boggs and Lewis discarded the concept of author entry for maps in favor of an entry that was "to present that information which the experienced map user is entitled to find, taking into account the essential characteristics of maps (e.g., scale and map projection); and . . . to make the map catalog cards conform to present library practice. . . . This should make it possible to consolidate the map catalog with the book catalog."[4] Boggs and Lewis suggested that cataloging should be based on a title unit entry consisting of title followed by author, edition (if any), place, publisher, and date. Added entries to bring out geographic area and date, or area, subject, and date, would be added as needed.

Boggs and Lewis's work had a great impact on practical library cataloging of maps; it had little impact on official catalog code makers. The *ALA Cataloging Rules for Author and Title Entries,* published four years later, still prescribed entry for maps under "the name of the person or corporate body responsible for the content of the map, as cartographer, editor, publisher, government bureau, society or institution."[5] But an almost apologetic footnote following the rule recognized at least that such author entry presented problems for both cataloger and library user. It stated, "Small libraries may . . . find that an entry under subject (i.e., area mapped) is all that is necessary . . . and special collections may prefer a main entry under area, a scheme for which is worked out in the Boggs and Lewis Manual."[6]

Map librarians remained unhappy with the official cataloging rules. Among the articles written during the period between the appearance of the 1949 ALA rules and the formulation of *AACR1* was one by Bill M. Woods, entitled "Map Cataloging: Inventory and Prospect."[7] Woods summarized some of the differences between maps and books that should be reflected in their bibliographical control. Among these differences was "the primary identification of maps with area rather than with authority or author." Also different from books and of importance for identification of a map, said Woods, were subject information, date, scale, size of the map, projection, and color. Not only was entry under author illogical for maps, but also, because most map titles tend to be vague, title entry was of little value. Woods's conclusion agreed with that of the final report of the Special Libraries Association's Geography and Map Division Committee on Map Cataloging, which he summarized. Maps, said Woods and the committee, require their own cataloging rules, which should be based on area-subject-date rather than the principle of authorship.[8]

Presumably SLA's suggestion was considered by the editors of the 1967 *Anglo-American Cataloging Rules.* As it turned out, though, the editors were under pressure to get *AACR1* into print, and so the rules for nonbook materials, which made up Part III, are, for the most part, a reprint of the Library of Congress's own rules for handling these materials. *AACR1* chapter 11, "Maps, Atlases, etc.," is firmly based in ALA 1949 rule 10. *AACR1* rule 210 states, "A map, a series or set of maps, an atlas, a relief model, or a globe is entered under the person or corporate body that is primarily responsible for its informational content" if this responsibility is explicit (211A). If it is not explicit, main entry might be, in order of preference, under "the individual whose survey provided the basis for the cartography . . . the cartographer . . . the engraver . . . the corporate body . . . that prepared the maps," or, as a last choice, the title of the map (21.1B).

Map catalogers in the period following the appearance of *AACR1* continued to be unhappy with the official rules for entry. The Library of Congress, of course, followed the official rules. However, their coverage of maps as reflected in the National Union Catalog was not adequate to assure libraries of LC copy for maps in local libraries. Many map librarians disregarded *AACR1* rules and adopted Boggs and Lewis's manual, the American Geographical Society's *Cataloging and Filing Rules for Maps and Atlases in the Society's Collections* (New York: American Geographical Society, 1969), or the simpler rules advocated by the Canadian Library Association[9] or the Association for Educational Communications and Technology.[10]

The appearance of *AACR2* solved some of these problems. Fewer maps are entered under corporate author and more entered under title as main entry than was the case with previous cataloging codes. The addition of a new area preceding the publication area, the mathematical data area, gives emphasis to scale and projection by including this important information as a part of the formal catalog entry rather than as a note. But the overriding concern of *AACR2* with the principle of authorship responsibility governing main entry for all types of library materials continues to mandate main entry under cartographer or corporate body when appropriate. In a fully integrated catalog, one that includes entries for all types of library materials, such entry would seem necessary.

3.0B. Sources of information

Bibliographical information for map catalog entries has not been standardized on the face of maps in the same fashion as it has been for books, where most of the information may usually be found on the title page. Cataloging information may be taken from *any* part of the map, its container, or, for areas other than the title and statement of responsibility, other accompanying materials. Punctuation and arrangement of data follow the general pattern set forth in *AACR2R* chapter 1; rules given there should be followed as applicable.

3.0J. Description of whole or part

Many maps are issued as a set, sometimes over a long period of time in many parts, sometimes at one time. A library may decide to catalog each of the individual maps that make up the set, or it may decide to catalog the set as a unit, possibly making a separate entry for one or more individual parts of the set if this seems useful. The Geological Survey of Great Britain issues several sets of this kind, of considerable complexity. Another example of a map set is that cataloged at figures 3-1a and 3-1b.[11]

3.1B. Title proper

Record the title proper for a map as instructed in *AACR2R* 1.1B, following wording and order exactly, but using conventional library capitalization and punctuation rules.

3.1B2 and **3.1B3**. A map may bear more than one title. If this is the case, follow instructions under 1.1B8.

The title sometimes includes information about the scale of the map. Although the scale statement is given formally as part of the mathematical data area, it will still be transcribed as part of the title proper if appropriate (see figure 3-2).

3.1B4. Supplied title. See discussion under 3.1G5.

Figure 3-1a.   Description of part

```
110 1    ‡a Arizona. ‡b Office of the State Climatologist.
245 10   ‡a National Weather Service stations as of March 1975 : ‡b [Arizona] / ‡c prepared under
         the direction of the State Climatologist, the Laboratory of Climatology, Arizona State
         University.
246 1    ‡i Title on cover letter: ‡a Climatology maps of Arizona
255      ‡a Scale 1:1,000,000 ; ‡b Lambert conformal conic proj.
260      ‡a [Phoenix] : ‡b Available from ARIS, ‡c 1975.
300      ‡a 1 map : ‡b col. ; ‡c 81 × 64 cm.
490 1    ‡a Cooperative publication / Arizona Resources Information System ; ‡v no. 5
500      ‡a "Satellite image base, 1972-1973, prepared and published by the U.S. Geological
         Survey in cooperation with the National Aeronautics and Space Administration (ERTS-1,
         Proposal SR 211) ... 1927 North American Datum. Highway and name base by Arizona
         Department of Transportation, 1974."
710 2    ‡a Arizona State University. ‡b Laboratory of Climatology.
710 2    ‡a Arizona Resources Information System.
830  0   ‡a Cooperative publication (Arizona Resources Information System) ; ‡v no. 5.
```

```
Information from map face
              National Weather Service Stations as of March 1975
        Satellite Image Base 1972–1973 prepared and published by the U.S. Geological
        Survey in cooperation with the National Aeronautics and Space Administration
                          (ERTS-1, Proposal SR 211)
           Imagery from NASA Earth Resources Technology Satellite (ERTS-1)
                     Controlled to photoidentified ground positions
                           1927 North American Datum
        Highway and name base by Arizona Department of Transportation, 1974
                  Prepared under the direction of the State Climatologist
                            The Laboratory of Climatology
                  Arizona State University, Tempe AZ 85281 May 1975
                               Scale 1:1,000,000
                          Lambert conformal conic projection
                       Arizona Resources Information System
                             Cooperative publication no. 5
           Available at a nominal cost from ARIS or the Laboratory of Climatology
```

Figure 3-1b.   Description of whole

```
245 10   ‡a [Climatology maps of Arizona] / ‡c prepared under the direction of the State
         Climatologist, the Laboratory of Climatology, Arizona State University.
255      ‡a Scale 1:1,000,000 and [ca. 1:3,000,000] ; ‡b Lambert conformal conic proj.
260      ‡a [Phoenix] : ‡b Available from ARIS, ‡c 1975.
300      ‡a 16 maps on 5 sheets : ‡b col. ; ‡c 81 × 64 cm. and 23 × 20 cm.
490 1    ‡a Cooperative publication / Arizona Resources Information System ; ‡v no. 5
505 0    ‡a [1] National Weather Service stations as of March 1975 -- [2] Evaporation and
         evapotranspiration -- [3] Arizona precipitation -- [4] Solar energy -- [5] Arizona
         temperatures.
710 2    ‡a Arizona State University. ‡b Laboratory of Climatology.
710 1    ‡a Arizona. ‡b Office of the State Climatologist.
710 2    ‡a Arizona Resources Information System.
830  0   ‡a Cooperative publication (Arizona Resources Information System) ; ‡v no. 5.
```

Figure 3-2.   Scale as part of title transcription

020	‡a 0851523625 (paper)
020	‡a 0851523633 (cloth)
110 2	‡a John Bartholomew and Son.
245 10	‡a Bartholomew one inch map of the Lake District.
250	‡a Rev.
255	‡a Scale 1:63,360. 1 in. to 1 mile.
260	‡a Edinburgh : ‡b Bartholomew, ‡c 1971.
300	‡a 1 map : ‡b col. ; ‡c 70 × 82 cm. folded to 21 × 12 cm.
500	‡a Relief shown by gradient tints.

Information from map
Bartholomew One Inch Map of the Lake District
Revised 1971   Scale 1:63360—1 inch to the mile
© John Bartholomew & Son Ltd, Edinburgh
SBN 85152 362 5 paper
85152 363 3 cloth

3.1C. *Optional addition.* **General material designation**

The general material designation "map" or "globe" in brackets may be added immediately following the title proper in subfield ‡h, if the library chooses to use GMDs. Following Library of Congress practice, examples in this text do not show GMDs for cartographic materials.

3.1D. Parallel titles

A parallel title will be recorded as instructed in 1.1D (see figure 3-3). The order of the titles is governed by the layout of the map; record titles from top to bottom, or left to right, as given on the chief source.

3.1E. Other title information

Other title information will be recorded following general rules 1.1E (see figure 3-4).

3.1E2. Because the most prominent unit of the catalog record for many maps will be the title, add the geographic area covered by the map as bracketed other title information, if the title gives no indication of the geographic area (see figure 3-5).

3.1F. Statements of responsibility

The statement of responsibility, as indicated in 1.1F, includes names of all persons or corporate bodies that have some responsibility other than for

Figure 3-3.   Parallel title

```
110 2     ‡a Trigonometrical Survey (South Africa).
245 10    ‡a Suidelike Afrika / ‡c Driehoeksmeting = Southern Africa / Trigonometrical Survey.
250       ‡a 3. uitgawe.
255       ‡a Scale 1:2,500,000 ; ‡b Albers equal area proj., standard parallels 18° South and 32°
          South ‡c (E100--E370/S170--S360).
260       ‡a Pretoria : ‡b Staatsdrukker, ‡c 1972 (1977 printing).
300       ‡a 1 map : ‡b col. ; ‡c 96 × 68 cm.
440 0     ‡a T.S.O. Misc. ; ‡v 4793
500       ‡a Relief shown by contours and color.
500       ‡a Base map: Trigonometrical Survey, 1962.
500       ‡a Includes glossary in Afrikaans, English, and Portuguese.
```

Information from map face   Suidelike Afrika
Derde Uitgawe 1972
1:2 500 000
Albers se vlaktroue projeksie,
standaard parallele 18° Suid en 32° Suid.
Herdruk En Uitgegee Deur Die Staatsdrukker,
Privaatsak X85, Pretoria, 1977.

Driehoeksmeting
Trigonometrical Survey
T.S.O. Misc. 4793

Southern Africa
Third Edition 1972
1:2 500 000
Albers equal-area projection,
standard parallels
18° South and 32° South.
Reprinted and Published by the
Government Printer
Private Bag X85, Pretoria 1977

simple publication or distribution of the item, as long as these names appear "prominently" (i.e., in the chief source of information or accompanying printed material, the prescribed sources for areas 1 and 2 of cartographic materials) (see figure 3-6; see also discussion in this text under 1.1F1).

Refer to discussion of figures 1-30 and 1-50 in this *Handbook* at 1.1F and 1.1F14 for the rationale for omission of names of Doyle and Grosvenor from the catalog entry in figure 3-6.

3.1G. Items without a collective title

An item lacking a collective title may be described in several different fashions.

Figure 3-4.   Other title information

```
100 1    ‡a Wintle, William.
245 10   ‡a Highway map of the northern & southern mines : ‡b the Mother Lode / ‡c delineation
         and cartography by William Wintle.
246 1    ‡i Panel title: ‡a California's golden chain : ‡b the Mother Lode highway
246 3    ‡a Mother Lode highway
255      ‡a Scale [1:700,000].
260      ‡a Murphys, Calif. : ‡b Golden Chain Council of the Mother Lode, ‡c [1971?]
300      ‡a 1 map : ‡b col. ; ‡c 57 × 43 cm. folded to 22 × 10 cm.
500      ‡a At head of title: The Golden Chain Council.
500      ‡a Relief shown by spot heights.
500      ‡a Includes 16 insets, ill. of early mining operations and mileage charts. On verso: text
         and photos. of area by county.
710 2    ‡a Golden Chain Council of the Mother Lode.
```

Information from map face
The Golden Chain Council
Highway Map of the Northern & Southern Mines
The Mother Lode
Delineation & Cartography
by William Wintle

Verso of map
California's
Golden
Chain
The
Mother
Lode
Highway
published by
The Golden Chain Council®
of the Mother Lode, Inc.,
Murphys, California
© The Golden Chain Council of the Mother Lode

Figure 3-5.   Area added as other title information

```
110 2    ‡a Tulsa Metropolitan Area Planning Commission.
245 10   ‡a Existing land use, 1964 : ‡b [in Tulsa, Oklahoma] / ‡c Tulsa Metropolitan Area
         Planning Commission.
255      ‡a Scale [ca. 1:140,000].
260      ‡a [Tulsa] : ‡b The Commission, ‡c 1965.
300      ‡a 1 map : ‡b col. ; ‡c sheet 48 × 40 cm.
```

Information from map
October, 1965   Scale in Miles
Tulsa Metropolitan Area Planning Commission
Existing Land Use—1964

Figure 3-6.   Statement of responsibility

```
110 2   ‡a National Geographic Society (U.S.). ‡b Cartographic Division.
245 10  ‡a British Columbia, Alberta, and the Yukon Territory / ‡c produced by the Cartographic
        Division, National Geographic Society ; William T. Peele, chief cartographer, Richard K.
        Rogers, assistant chief cartographer.
255     ‡a Scale 1:3,500,000. 1 cm. = 35 km. 1 in. = 55.2 miles ; ‡b Lambert conformal conic
        proj., standard parallels 62°20′ and 51°40′.
260     ‡a Washington : ‡b The Society, ‡c 1978.
300     ‡a 1 map : ‡b col. ; ‡c 89 × 58 cm. folded to 23 × 15 cm.
440  0  ‡a Close-up : Canada
500     ‡a Suppl. to: National geographic magazine, v. 153, no. 4, April 1978, p. 548A.
500     ‡a On verso: Canada's Rocky Mountain parks. Scale 1:2,375,000 -- Yukon Territory. Scale
        1:4,900,000 -- Victoria and Vancouver. Scale 1:1,750,000 -- Beauty to flaunt and bounty
        to grow on [text].
700  1  ‡a Peele, William T.
```

Information from map face   Close-up: Canada
British Columbia
Alberta
and the Yukon Territory
Produced by the Cartographic Division
National Geographic Society
Robert E. Doyle, President
National Geographic Magazine
Gilbert M. Grosvenor, Editor
William T. Peele, chief cartographer
Richard K. Rogers, assistant chief cartographer
Washington April 1978

Supplement to the National Geographic
April 1978, Page 548A, Vol. 153, No. 4
Close-up: Canada
Lambert Conformal Conic Projection
Standard Parallels 62° 20′ and 51° 40′
Scale 1:3,500,000
1 centimeter = 35.0 kilometers or 1 inch = 55.2 miles
Copyright © 1978 National Geographic Society
Washington, D.C.

3.1G2. Such an item may be described as a unit, following directions in 3.1G1. The example shown in figure 3-7a has been cataloged in this fashion. This item has two maps, one on each side of a sheet. The folded title of the item is "The earth's fractured surface." On one side of the sheet is a map of the world showing fault lines; on the other side is a map of the West Coast of the United States, entitled "Living on the edge." The folded title information in conjunction with the position of the map of the world makes that side of the map the predominant part of the item. Thus, the entry begins with this map.

3.1G4. Each of the separately titled parts of the map, the cataloging for which has been shown in figure 3-7a, may alternately be cataloged as a

Figure 3-7a.   Item without a collective title cataloged as a unit

110 2	‡a National Geographic Society (U.S.). ‡b Cartographic Division.
245 14	‡a The earth's fractured surface ; ‡b Living on the edge : [West Coast of U.S.] / ‡c produced by the Cartographic Division, National Geographic Society ; John F. Shupe, chief cartographer.
255	‡a Scale 1:48,000,000. 1 in. = 758 miles. At equator ; ‡b Winkel tripel proj. ‡c (W 1800--E 1800/N 900--S 900).
255	‡a Scale 1:2,380,000. 1 in. = 38 miles ; ‡b Albers conic equal-area proj., standard parallels 20°30′ and 45°30′.
260	‡a Washington, D.C. : ‡b The Society, ‡c 1995.
300	‡a 2 maps on 1 sheet : ‡b both sides, col. ; ‡c sheet 57 × 93 cm.
500	‡a "... April 1995."
500	‡a Relief shown by satellite imagery, gradient tints, and spot heights. Depth shown by satellite imagery, shading, and soundings.
500	‡a Includes text, indexed ancillary map showing major plates, indexes to earthquakes and volcanic eruptions, cross section, 2 graphs, and 5 ancillary maps.
700 1	‡a Shupe, John F.
710 2	‡a National Geographic Society (U.S.). ‡b Cartographic Division. ‡t Living on the edge.

Figure 3-7b.   Item without a collective title—titles cataloged separately

110 2	‡a National Geographic Society (U.S.). ‡b Cartographic Division.
245 14	‡a The earth's fractured surface / ‡c produced by the Cartographic Division, National Geographic Society ; John F. Shupe, chief cartographer.
255	‡a Scale 1:48,000,000. 1 in. = 758 miles. At equator ; ‡b Winkel tripel proj. ‡c (W 1800--E 1800/N 900--S 900).
260	‡a Washington, D.C. : ‡b The Society, ‡c 1995.
300	‡a 1 map on 1 side of 1 sheet : ‡b col. ; ‡c 51 × 83 cm.
500	‡a "... April 1995."
500	‡a Relief shown by satellite imagery, gradient tints, and spot heights. Depth shown by satellite imagery, shading, and soundings.
500	‡a Includes text, indexed ancillary map showing major plates, and indexes to earthquakes and volcanic eruptions.
501	‡a Issued with: Living on the edge / produced by the Cartographic Division, National Geographic Society.
700 1	‡a Shupe, John F.

Information from map   The Earth's Fractured Surface
Produced by the Cartographic Division
National Geographic Society
Gilbert M. Grosvenor, President and Chairman
William L. Allen, editor, National Geographic Magazine
John F. Shupe, chief cartographer
Washington, D.C., April 1995
Winkel Tripel Projection
Scale 1:48,000,000 or 1 inch = 758 miles
at the equator

separate unit. If it is, the other map will be named in a "with" note (see figures 3-7b and 3-7c).

A collection of separate maps lacking a collective title may also be cataloged separately, following stipulations of 3.1G4. The example shown in figure 3-1a is based on five climatology maps issued as a set by the Arizona Resources Information System, described in figure 3-1b.

3.1G5. If a set lacking a collective title is to be kept together and cataloged as a unit, and if it consists of a large number of items (more than three), the cataloger may supply a collective title descriptive of the entire set. According to instructions in *AACR2R* 3.1B4, the title must include the name of the area covered.

The example shown in figure 3-1b illustrates cataloging for the set from which figure 3-1a was taken. The collective title was taken from descriptive information about the set from the issuing body. Because it was not found on the chief source, it is enclosed in brackets. Each of the five maps in the set has an identical statement of responsibility and series statement (including series number). Each map is titled separately.

Figure 3-7c.   Item without a collective title—titles cataloged separately

110 2	‡a National Geographic Society (U.S.). ‡b Cartographic Division.
245 10	‡a Living on the edge : ‡b [West Coast of U.S.] / ‡c produced by the Cartographic Division, National Geographic Society ; John F. Shupe, chief cartographer.
255	‡a Scale 1:2,380,000. 1 in. = 38 miles ; ‡b Albers conic equal-area proj., standard parallels 20°30′ and 45°30′.
260	‡a Washington, D.C. : ‡b The Society, ‡c 1995.
300	‡a 1 map on 1 side of 1 sheet : ‡b col. ; ‡c 57 : 93 cm.
500	‡a "... April 1995."
500	‡a Relief shown by satellite imagery, gradient tints, and spot heights. Depth shown by satellite imagery, shading, and soundings.
500	‡a Includes text, cross section, 2 graphs, and 5 ancillary maps.
501	‡a Issued with: The earth's fractured surface / produced by the Cartographic Division, National Geographic Society.
700 1	‡a Shupe, John F.

Information from map   Living on the Edge
Produced by the Cartographic Division
National Geographic Society
Gilbert M. Grosvenor, President and Chairman
William L. Allen, editor, National Geographic Magazine
John F. Shupe, chief cartographer
Washington, D.C., April 1995
Albers Conic Equal-Area Projection, Standard Parallels 20°30′ and 45°30′
Scale 1:2,380,000 or 1 inch = 38 miles
Elevations in feet, soundings in fathoms

3.2. EDITION AREA

If a cartographic item includes an edition statement, it will be transcribed according to general directions given in *AACR2R* 1.2.

3.2B4. If an item contains an edition statement in more than one language, give the statement that matches the language of the title proper. Figure 3-3 includes such a statement. The title proper on this map is in Afrikaans; therefore the Afrikaans-language edition statement is recorded rather than the English-language statement.

3.2C. Statements of responsibility relating to an edition

Record a statement of responsibility that relates to a particular edition, but not to all editions, according to *AACR2R* 1.2C. Note, however, figure 1-60 and the discussion at *Handbook* 1.2C2. If the chief source of information does not include an edition statement, such a revision statement forms a part of the title and statement of responsibility area for the entire work. The example shown in figure 3-8 illustrates this.

3.2D. Statement relating to a named revision of an edition

A map may be reissued with partial revisions pertaining to a particular edition. The edition statement should be transcribed following provisions of *AACR2R* 1.2D.

Figure 3-8.   Revision statement

245 10	‡a Earthquake fault map of a portion of Salt Lake County, Utah / ‡c revised in 1976 by Bruce N. Kaliser.
255	‡a Scale [1:160,000].
260	‡a Salt Lake City : ‡b Distributed by Utah Geological and Mineral Survey, ‡c 1976.
300	‡a 1 map ; ‡c 26 × 20 cm.
490 1	‡a Map / State of Utah, Department of Natural Resources, Utah Geological and Mineral Survey ; ‡v 42.
500	‡a "Originally issued in 1968 as map 18."
700 1	‡a Kaliser, Bruce N.
710 2	‡a Utah Geological and Mineral Survey.
830 0	‡a Map (Utah Geological and Mineral Survey) ; ‡v 42.

Information from map   Map 42
State of Utah
Department of Natural Resources
Utah Geological and Mineral Survey
Originally issued in 1968 as Map 18
Revised in 1976 by Bruce N. Kaliser

Earthquake Fault Map of a Portion of
Salt Lake County, Utah
Distributed by
Utah Geological and Mineral Survey
Donald T. McMillan, Director
606 Black Hawk Way
Salt Lake City, Utah 84108

3.3. MATHEMATICAL DATA AREA

The mathematical data area is used only with cartographic materials. Such essentials as scale, projection, and coordinates are to be included in this area.[12] This area is recorded in the 255 field.

3.3B. Statement of scale

The first element of the mathematical data area is the statement of scale. It is recorded in subfield ‡a of field 255.

3.3B1. No matter how the statement may be given in the item, scale is expressed in the mathematical data area as a representative fraction with a ratio 1:x (e.g., 1:250 means that one inch on the map represents 250 inches of area). Note that even if the scale has been recorded as part of the title proper, it will be repeated—translated into the proper representative fraction if necessary—in the mathematical data area (see figure 3-2).

If only a verbal scale is given, translate this into a representative fraction. Enclose the figure in square brackets (see figures 3-1b and 3-8).

Sometimes, as in the basis for figure 3-5, a map includes a bar graph rather than a scale statement. Scale can be arrived at by using a scale indicator (a device for measuring bar graphs and grids to convert them into a representative fraction) or a conversion formula.

If no grid, bar graph, or verbal statement is found on a map, compare the map to another of known scale and give an approximate scale. Useful instructions for conversion of map scales to representative fractions are found in *Cartographic Materials: A Manual of Interpretation for AACR2* (Chicago: ALA, 1982), Appendix B, p. 164–74.

Scale statements computed from a bar graph or grid, or estimated by comparison with another map of known scale, should be bracketed and preceded by "ca."

3.3B2. Optional addition. If it seems appropriate, the fractional scale statement may be followed by additional scale information found on the item. If the cataloger chooses to do this, each element is separated by a full stop. For an example, see figure 3-6. The Library of Congress will apply this option.

3.3B3. Sometimes the scale used on a single item varies, especially on small-scale maps (those covering large areas). If this is the case, give the largest fraction followed by the smallest fraction, connecting the two by a hyphen (see figure 3-9). Note here, by the way, that English-language terms are always used in the mathematical data area.

3.3B4. If an item with more than one part is collected under one title, the scale statement must fit all of the parts of the item. If the scales vary and there are not more than two scales for all the parts of the item, show the scale statement as stipulated in the rule. Figure 3-1b is an example with added complications. (The scale for the first map was stated on the map; the scale for the other maps, which were all the same size, was approximated following 3.3B1.) Alternately, the entire 255 field may be repeated for an item lacking a collective title and cataloged as a unit (see figure 3-7a).

Figure 3-9.   Scale statement

```
110 2    ‡a Falk-Verlag.
245 10   ‡a Frankfurt a. M., Offenbach / ‡c Falk-Verlag.
246 3    ‡a Frankfurt am Main, Offenbach
246 14   ‡a Frankfurt, Offenbach-Hanau
246 18   ‡a Falkplan Frankfurt
250      ‡a 31. Aufl.
255      ‡a Scale 1:16,500-1:27,500 ; ‡b hyperboloid proj.
260      ‡a Hamburg ; ‡a New York : ‡b Falk-Verlag, ‡c [1970]
300      ‡a 1 map : ‡b col. ; ‡c 75 × 103 cm. folded in cover 21 × 11 cm.
490 0    ‡a Falk Plan ; ‡v 118
546      ‡a Legend in German, English, and French.
500      ‡a Imprint on label pasted on cover: New York : French and European Publications.
500      ‡a Contains: Index map of Frankfurt and Strassenverzeichnis. Nordweststadt. Scale
         1:8,000 -- Hanau. Scale 1:28,000, inserted in Strassenverzeichnis.
```

Information from map   Falk Plan
                        Frankfurt a. M. Offenbach
            In Hyperboloid — Projektion mit Kilometernetz
                    Maßstab 1:16 500 - 1:27 500
                            Falk-Verlag
                 Hamburg • Den Haag • Paris
                 Berlin • London • New York

Figure 3-10.   "Bird's-eye view"

```
100 1    ‡a Clarke, Roger D. ‡q (Roger Dean), ‡d 1969-
245 00   ‡a [Brigham Young University campus, Provo, Utah] / ‡c Clarke & B.W.
255      ‡a Not drawn to scale.
260      ‡a [Provo, Utah] : ‡b BYU Student Auxiliary Services, ‡c [1993]
300      ‡a 1 view : ‡b col. ; ‡c 39 × 56 cm.
500      ‡a Pictorial bird's-eye view illustrating campus activities at various locations and buildings.
500      ‡a Includes text and illustrations advertising the Brigham Young University signature card.
700 1    ‡a Williams, Bethany, ‡d 1974-
710 2    ‡a Brigham Young University. ‡b Student Auxiliary Services.
```

3.3B5. If maps in a collected set are drawn to more than two scales, use the statement "Scales vary."

3.3B7. For some cartographic items, scale would be inappropriate. Such items include imaginary maps. Often a pictorial "bird's-eye view" of an area is not drawn to an accurate scale. If no scale is stated on such an item, do not try to approximate one. Use the statement "Not drawn to scale" (see figure 3-10).

Some maps, particularly those designed for tourists, are deliberately not drawn to scale, in order that certain areas or features may be highlighted. The same statement, "Not drawn to scale," is appropriate for such items (see figure 3-11).

Figure 3-11.   Not drawn to scale

110 1	‡a Saint John (N.B.) ‡b Dept. of Promotion.
245 10	‡a Tour map, metro Saint John, New Brunswick, Canada / ‡c produced by the Saint John Department of Promotion.
246 1	‡i Panel title: ‡a Saint John, New Brunswick, tour map : ‡b Canada's loyalist city
255	‡a Not drawn to scale.
260	‡a Saint John, N.B. : ‡b The Dept., ‡c 1973.
300	‡a 1 map : ‡b col. ; ‡c 41 × 46 cm., folded to 23 × 11 cm.
500	‡a Includes 3 insets. On verso: Points of interest in Saint John.

Information from map   Tour Map—Metro Saint John
New Brunswick, Canada
Produced by the Saint John Department of Promotion
This map is not to scale

3.3C. Statement of projection

If a map includes a statement of projection, record it following the statement of scale, separating the two statements by space - semicolon - space and subfield ‡b (see, for example, figures 3-6 and 3-9).

3.4. PUBLICATION, DISTRIBUTION, ETC., AREA

Data to be included in this area are recorded according to the general rules given in *AACR2R* 1.4.

3.5. PHYSICAL DESCRIPTION AREA

The physical description area consists of the number of items (qualified by one of the terms included in the list under 3.5B1), color (if any), material (if other than paper), mounting (if any), and size. It is recorded in the 300 field.

3.5B3. Atlases. An atlas shares the characteristics of both book and cartographic material. The source of information for an atlas is, as for a book, the title page (3.0B1; cf. 2.0B). In most cases, scale statement will be given according to 3.3B3 (see figure 3-12).

3.5B4. A cartographic item that is physically a *part* of another item but cataloged separately from it under *AACR2R* 3.1G4 should include a statement of the fractional extent of the *whole* in this area. For an example, see figures 3-7b and 3-7c.

Figure 3-12.   Atlas

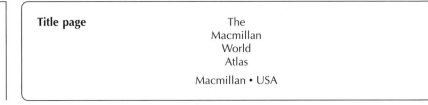

```
020        ‡a 0028608127
245 04     ‡a The Macmillan world atlas.
246 30     ‡a World atlas
250        ‡a 1st U.S. ed.
255        ‡a Scale varies.
260        ‡a New York : ‡b Macmillan, ‡c 1996.
300        ‡a 1 atlas (xv, 415 p.) : ‡b col. ill., col. maps ; ‡c 35 cm.
500        ‡a Includes index.
710 2      ‡a Macmillan Publishers.
```

Title page	
	The
	Macmillan
	World
	Atlas
	Macmillan • USA

3.5C. Other physical details

As with other library materials, the presence of color in a cartographic item is noted with the abbreviation "col." as part of the second element of the physical description area in subfield ‡b. Some special features of maps may be noted: if a map is printed on material other than paper, this is indicated; if the item has been mounted, this is noted. For atlases (3.5C2) the number of maps will be specified if the maps are numbered or if they are listed in such a fashion that the number can easily be ascertained. If this is not the case, describe the maps that make up the atlas as otherwise stipulated under 3.5C.

3.5D. Dimensions

For maps, give, in subfield ‡c, height by width in centimeters, measuring between the neat lines (the innermost of a series of lines that frame the map). If a map lacks such lines, or if it is extremely irregularly shaped, give dimensions of the sheet (see figure 3-5). (Note: 3.5D1 stipulates that the map itself should be measured in such a case, if this is feasible.) For a map designed to be folded, include the dimensions of the folded map as well as the dimensions of the sheet (see figure 3-2, etc.).

   3.5D2. Atlases. Measure atlases according to the rules for books (i.e., give the height of the cover in centimeters) (see figure 3-12).

3.5E. Accompanying material

See 1.5E for methods of handling various types of materials issued with a map and intended to be used with it.

3.6. SERIES AREA

Maps are frequently issued as part of a series. Series statements will be recorded following instructions in 1.6. For examples of map series, see the following:

> Figure 3-1b, the series as an important unifying element for the five maps of the set. Each of them bears the statement: Arizona Resources Information System cooperative publication no. 5.

> Figure 3-6, a series with other title information.

> Figure 3-8, a series that includes a statement of responsibility (1.6E1).

> Figure 3-9, a numbered publisher series.

3.7. NOTE AREA

Notes follow the general pattern stipulated in *AACR2R* 1.7. In addition to directions on the order of notes given in 1.7B, follow the order of notes indicated in 3.7B.

3.7B1. Nature and scope. If the map contains any features not evident from the rest of the description, which one would not expect to find in such an item, make a note in the 500 field. Make a note of the method of showing the relief on the map (see figures 3-13 and 3-14).

Figure 3-13.   Scope note

110	‡a Nevada. ‡b Dept. of Transportation.
245 10	‡i 1995/1996 official highway map of Nevada / ‡c Nevada Department of Transportation.
246 1	‡i Panel title: ‡a Nevada official state map 1995-96
246 30	‡a Official highway map of Nevada
255	‡a Scale [ca. 1:1,500,000].
260	‡a [Carson City, Nevada] : ‡b The Dept., ‡c c1995.
300	‡a 1 map : ‡b col. ; ‡c 57 × 41 cm. on sheet folded to 23 × 11 cm.
500	‡a Relief shown by shading and spot heights.
500	‡a Includes text, indexes, distance chart, and ancillary maps of Lake Tahoe region, Reno-Sparks region and Las Vegas region.
500	‡a Text, ill. and 5 pictorial maps of various highways on verso.

Information from map

1995/1996 Official Highway Map of
Nevada
Nevada Department of Transportation
Free distribution
Copyright © 1995 by Nevada Department of Transportation

Figure 3-14.   Nature of the item

```
110 1      ‡a United States. ‡b Forest Service.
245 10     ‡a Payette National Forest : ‡b non-commercial firewood map : free use and charge /
           ‡c USDA--Forest Service.
246 30     ‡a Non-commercial firewood map, Payette National Forest
250        ‡a Rev.
255        ‡a Scale [1:168,960]. 3/8″ = 1 mile.
260        ‡a [Ogden, Utah?] : ‡b The Service, ‡c [1995]
300        ‡a 1 map ; ‡c 73 × 90 cm. on sheet 56 × 77 cm. folded to 28 × 19 cm.
500        ‡a Relief shown by hachures and spot heights.
500        ‡a Panel title.
500        ‡a Shipping list no.: 95-0106-P.
500        ‡a Includes text, woodcutting regulations, and ill.
505 0      ‡a East half -- West half.
```

Information from map

Non-Commercial Firewood Map
Free use and charge
USDA-Forest Service
Payette
National Forest
Rev. 1/95

3.7B11. Accompanying material. If material issued with a map and intended to be used with it is too complex in its nature to be added at the end of the physical description area (see discussion in this text under 1.5E for criteria), in many cases it may appropriately be added in the note area in a 500 field (see figure 3-15).

Figure 3-15. Accompanying material

100 1	‡a Lemmon, Robert E.
245 10	‡a Geologic map of the Fruitland quadrangle, North Carolina / ‡c prepared in cooperation with Tennessee Valley Authority by Robert E. Lemmon and David E. Dunn.
246 1	‡i In envelope bearing title: ‡a Geological map and mineral resources summary of the Fruitland quadrangle, North Carolina
255	‡a Scale 1:24,000.
260	‡a [Raleigh] : ‡b State of North Carolina, Dept. of Natural and Economic Resources, Office of Earth Resources, ‡c 1973.
300	‡a 1 map : ‡b col. ; ‡c 58 × 48 cm.
500	‡a Accompanied by pamphlet: Mineral resources summary of the Fruitland quadrangle, North Carolina / by Robert E. Lemmon
500	‡a Includes insets listing mineral resources and linear features of the quadrangle.
500	‡a Publisher's no.: GM 202-NW (map). -- MRS 202-NW (pamphlet).
700 12	‡a Lemmon, Robert E. ‡t Mineral resources summary of the Fruitland quadrangle, North Carolina.
700 1	‡a Dunn, David E., ‡d 1935-
710 2	‡a Tennessee Valley Authority.
710 1	‡a North Carolina. ‡b Office of Earth Resources.

Information from map face   Scale 1:24000
Geologic Map of the Fruitland Quadrangle,
North Carolina
by Robert E. Lemmon and David E. Dunn 1973
State of North Carolina
Department of Natural and Economic Resources
Office of Earth Resources
Prepared in cooperation with
Tennessee Valley Authority

Information from envelope   Geologic Map
and
Mineral Resources Summary
of the
Fruitland Quadrangle
North Carolina

Raleigh
1973

Title page of pamphlet   Mineral Resources Summary
of the
Fruitland Quadrangle
North Carolina
by
Robert E. Lemmon

NOTES

1. *Rules for a Dictionary Catalogue* (Washington, D.C.: GPO, 1876), rule 6 1/2, p. 19.
2. *Maps: Their History, Characteristics, and Uses* (Cambridge: University Press, 1921), p. 4–5.
3. R. G. Crone, "The Cataloguing and Arrangement of Maps," *Library Association Record*, ser. 4, no. 3 (March 1936): 98–104.
4. *The Classification and Cataloging of Maps and Atlases* (New York: Special Libraries Association, 1945), p. 3.
5. *ALA Cataloging Rules for Author and Title Entries* (Chicago: ALA, 1949), rule 10, p. 26.
6. Ibid.
7. *LRTS* 3 (fall 1959): 257–73.
8. Ibid., p. 268–69.
9. Canadian Library Association, *Nonbook Materials* (Ottawa: Canadian Library Association, 1973).
10. Association for Educational Communications and Technology, *Standards for Cataloging Non-print Materials*, 4th ed. (Washington, D.C.: AECT, 1976).
11. General information about MARC coding is found in the introduction to this *Handbook;* details about coding the descriptive portion of the record are found throughout chapter 1; information about the coding of main and added access points is found at the beginning of chapter 14. An explanation of the MARC authorities format is given in *Handbook* chapters 15, 17, and 18. Information about specific MARC fields may be found by consulting the index under "MARC fields."
12. Catalogers who find the technicalities of map interpretation intimidating will find John V. Bergen's "Map Reading and Map Appreciation" (*Illinois Libraries* 56 (May 1974): 349–59) helpful. Another good general discussion for nonspecialists of map librarianship is the *Drexel Library Quarterly* 9 (Oct. 1973). The entire issue is devoted to various aspects of the subject.

MANUSCRIPTS (INCLUDING MANUSCRIPT COLLECTIONS)

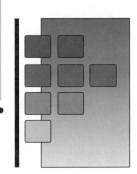

One of the more problematic and controversial aspects of *AACR2* is the cataloging of manuscripts, covered in chapter 4. *AACR2* was not at first accepted by archivists as a guide for their cataloging. In 1983 the first edition of *Archives, Personal Papers, and Manuscripts: A Cataloging Manual for Archival Repositories, Historical Societies, and Manuscript Libraries* (Washington, D.C.: Library of Congress) was published in an attempt to adapt archival description to the standards of *AACR2*. This was followed by a second edition in 1989, and this has become the standard guide for archival cataloging.[1] It will be referred to in the following discussion as *APPM*.

This chapter is not intended to present a detailed account of archival cataloging. This is a complex and specialized area, involving much more than simple cataloging (papers and groups of records must be inventoried and organized before cataloging can even be attempted), and librarians with large collections are referred to the detailed discussion in *APPM*. Rather, this chapter is written with the intent of helping a library that may have a few collections of letters or business documents to make catalog records that will be helpful to its patrons.

Archival and manuscript cataloging deals with unique, unpublished materials. Usually the catalog record deals with a *collection* of manuscript or archival materials, but this is not always so. A manuscript book, for example, can be dealt with quite successfully under *AACR2R* chapter 4. Figure 4-1 is an example of *AACR2R* cataloging of a seventeenth-century manuscript.[2] The title has been transcribed from a title page exactly as would be the case with a monograph (see *AACR2R* chapter 2). Other unpublished items, such as theses, are also cataloged under *AACR2R* chapter 4 (see figure 1-118).

AACR2R chapter 4 treats area 4, normally the publication area, differently from treatment elsewhere because manuscripts are by nature unpub-

Figure 4-1.   Manuscript book (*AACR2R* cataloging)

```
100 1    ‡a Flamsteed, John, ‡d 1646-1719.
254 14   ‡a The description and uses of an instrument for finding [th]e true places of [th]e sun &
         Jupitor [sic] with the eclipses of 4's [i.e., Jupiter's] satellites and their configurations at all
         times / ‡c by John Flamsteed.
260      ‡a 1685.
300      ‡a 23 p. : ‡b vellum, ill. ; ‡c 21 cm.
500      ‡a Dated at end: The Observatory August [th]e 4th of 1685.
500      ‡a Written at Greenwich, England.
```

lished materials. It is called instead the date area, and contains only the date of the manuscript (see figure 1-118). If the place where the manuscript was written is known, it may be recorded in a note (see figure 4-1).

The physical description area for such a manuscript is similar to that for a monograph. Begin with the extent of the item: in this case, the leaves have been paginated, so they are recorded as such. If the manuscript is written on anything other than paper, record this in the "other physical details" part of the area, along with the presence of illustrations. The dimensions are calculated just as for a monograph: give the height to the nearest centimeter up; include the width if it is less than half of or greater than the height.

It is in the cataloging of archival *collections* that *AACR2R* falls short and must be supplemented by *APPM*. As outlined in *APPM* 0.8, archival cataloging is based on three assumptions not common to other types of cataloging: (1) the *provenance* of the materials is often the most significant aspect; (2) the materials exist in *groups* rather than as single items; and (3) the materials are generally *unpublished* and unique. These three considerations have some important effects on archival interpretations of the rules.

Archival collections may be accumulated "organically" (e.g., the records collected by a business recording its activities) or "artificially" (e.g., materials gathered by a collector around a particular subject area). In either case the link tying the collection together is the creator of the collection. The importance of provenance is reflected in archival rules for choice of access points, which may differ from those prescribed under *AACR2R*. Main entry is frequently under the creator of the collection. Provenance also is reflected in a number of customary notes used in archival cataloging and not used elsewhere, including historical notes about the creator (*APPM* 0.9).

Cataloging implications for the collective nature of archives include the fact that the title will almost always be supplied by the cataloger. Detailed rules are given for the formulation of this title. In addition the rules for physical description include description of aspects of the collection such as the amount of space occupied by it as well as the number of individual items (*APPM* 0.10).

The fact that archival materials are for the most part unpublished means that *AACR2R* concepts of chief and prescribed sources of information are stretched to the limit and become in some cases nearly meaningless.

Also, given the lack of imprint, publication, and distribution information, the publication area is omitted from the catalog record (*APPM* 0.11).

Among the aspects of *AACR2R* cataloging that initially caused controversy among archivists were the rules for formulation of headings (*AACR2R* chapters 22–25). Because archival catalogs are now usually integrated with the overall catalog of the library (which, unless it is solely an archival library, will include cataloging of materials covered by other chapters in *AACR2R*), it is imperative that all contributors to the catalog, including archivists, follow the same rules for forming headings and use established forms.

APPM 1.0B (*AACR2R* 4.0B). Sources of information

The *APPM* chief sources of information for an archival collection are (in this order): (a) the finding aid prepared for the materials; (b) provenance and accession records; and (c) the materials themselves. The sources listed in *AACR2R* (title page, colophon, etc.) are geared toward individual items and are not useful guidance for the cataloging of collections.

APPM 1.1 (*AACR2R* 4.1)
TITLE AND STATEMENT OF RESPONSIBILITY AREA

If a manuscript has a formal title, use it. This will only be the case with individual manuscripts (see figure 4-1). In the case of collections and manuscripts without a formal title, the cataloger must supply the title. In a departure from *AACR2R* rules, because supplied titles will occur in nearly all of archival cataloging, a supplied title is *not* to be enclosed in square brackets.

A title statement may be taken from a formally prepared inventory or finding aid. More normally, however, the title will consist of generic terms characterizing the form of the material. Use "papers" for the personal papers of a person or persons (see figure 4-2; "papers" is also used in figure 4-3, which includes a mixture of DeMille's personal papers and his business archives). Use "records" for the archival records of a business or other corporate body (see figure 4-4). Use "collection" for an artificially gathered collection of materials, centered around a person (as in figure 4-5), subject, or activity. These three terms are standard but very general; more specific terms should be used if the nature of the collection allows. For example, the collection cataloged in figure 4-6 consists entirely of an artist's sketches; hence, the term "sketches" is appropriate.

Optionally, a "name element" may be added to this supplied title, in which the name predominantly associated with the collection is incorporated into the title. Figure 4-3, under this option, might have been titled "The Cecil B. DeMille papers." Figure 4-6 might have been titled "Seth Eastman sketches." In the case of figure 4-5, the name element is necessary to clarify the nature of the collection.

Figure 4-2.   Personal papers

```
100 1    ‡a Alcott, Louisa May, ‡d 1832-1888.
245 00   ‡k Papers, ‡f 1862-1888.
300      ‡a 50 items.
300      ‡a 30 typescripts.
300      ‡a 61 photocopied items.
300      ‡a 2 cassette tapes.
300      ‡a 5 publications.
545      ‡a American poet, novelist, and short story writer best known for her classic "Little
         Women."
520      ‡a Handwritten and signed correspondence of Louisa May Alcott and her sister, May
         Alcott Nieriker and various other family members and writers. The letters are of both a
         private and professional nature, and discuss social engagements, familial affairs, writing
         schedules, and upcoming publications. Also included are two portraits, a sound recording
         with transcript of a radio adaptation of "Little Women," the poem "Lines to a Robin," and
         the short story "A Free Bed." Also included are various other writings by Alcott.
540      ‡a The copyright of this collection rests with the Estate of Theresa W. Pratt and the Harold
         B. Lee Library, Brigham Young University. Permission from the Curator of Archives and
         Manuscripts is necessary to publish any item in its entirety.
555      ‡a A finding aid is available in the repository.
700 1    ‡a Alcott, May, ‡d 1840-1879.
700 12   ‡a Alcott, Louisa May, ‡d 1832-1888. ‡t Little women.
700 12   ‡a Alcott, Louisa May, ‡d 1832-1888. ‡t Lines to a robin.
700 12   ‡a Alcott, Louisa May, ‡d 1832-1888. ‡t Free bed.
```

Figure 4-3.   Personal papers and business archive

```
100 1    ‡a DeMille, Cecil B. ‡q (Cecil Blount), ‡d 1881-1959.
245 00   ‡k Papers, ‡f 1863-1983.
246 1    ‡i Title from finding aid: ‡a Cecil B. DeMille archives
300      ‡a 1,263 boxes.
300      ‡a 275 v.
545      ‡a American motion picture producer and director, considered the archetype of the
         American film mogul. His 70 films reflect changing American tastes and values, and he
         was particularly noted for his multimillion-dollar spectacles.
520      ‡a Personal and business papers generated by DeMille (1881-1959), his family, and his
         motion picture and other activities from 1863 to 1983 including correspondence, audio-
         and videotape recordings, financial ledgers, and memorabilia. Also with the collection are
         more than 8,000 pieces of production-related artwork, more than 10,000 motion picture
         still photographs, 275 volumes of scrapbooks (1919-1962), sound recordings, and
         videotapes of 36 motion pictures from DeMille's personal film collection.
555      ‡a Finding aid available in repository.
```

A supplied title consisting of more than simply a generic term is recorded in subfield ‡a of the 245 field (see figure 4-5). If it consists only of
generic, form terms, use subfield ‡k (see figures 4-2, 4-4, etc.).

If parallel titles, other title information, or statements of responsibility
are present, they may be added as outlined in this *Handbook* at 1.1D–F. This
will occur only rarely (cf. *APPM* 1.1D–F).

Figure 4-4.   Records

```
110 2    ‡a Charles Redd Center for Western Studies.
245 00   ‡k Records, ‡f 1972-1980.
300      ‡a 3 linear ft.
545      ‡a Center established at Brigham Young University for the study of Western American
         culture and history.
520      ‡a Includes correspondence, reports, news clippings, budgets and other financial records,
         monographs, manuscripts of lectures, proposals and agreements.
555      ‡a Register available at repository.
```

Figure 4-5.   Collection

```
100 1    ‡a Whittaker, David J., ‡d 1945- , ‡e collector.
245 14   ‡a The Mark Hofmann case collection, ‡f 1985-[ongoing].
300      ‡a 7 boxes (3 linear ft.)
545      ‡a Historian, author, and archivist at Brigham Young University.
520      ‡a Photocopies of all known printed items relating to the Mark Hofmann case, including
         articles, transcripts, and newspaper clippings. Hofmann (1954-    ) was a forger of
         documents relating primarily to Mormon Church history. He murdered two individuals
         presumably to keep from being exposed as a fraud.
520      ‡a The collection also contains a biographical file on Hofmann, a chronological file from
         15 Oct. 1985 when the individuals were murdered to 29 Jan. 1988, the date of the
         Hofmann parole hearing. Another section is topical and contains folders on each of the
         major forgeries as well as various official and unofficial publications relating to the case.
         Popular and scholarly articles are included. A detailed chronology as well as a
         bibliographical guide to the Hofmann case are also with the collection. Craig Foster aided
         in creating the collection.
555      ‡a A guide to the collection is available in the repository.
700 1    ‡a Foster, Craig L., ‡d 1959-
```

Figure 4-6.   Specific term

```
100 1    ‡a Eastman, Seth, ‡d 1808-1875.
245 00   ‡k Sketches, ‡f ca. 1850.
300      ‡a 59 items.
545      ‡a American illustrator, painter, landscape artist, and army officer.
520      ‡a Sketches made with pen and ink. The materials depict scenes of the Mississippi River
         and of the Mississippi River Valley and nearby areas. The collection consists of two boxes
         individually matted and numbered.
541      ‡c Purchase; ‡a Art gallery of W. Graham Arader III; ‡d 1990.
555      ‡a Finding aid available in repository.
```

An additional element in the *APPM* title area, not present in *AACR2R*, is the date element (*APPM* 1.1B5). This is the last element of the area. End the title/statement of responsibility portion of the area with a comma; in subfield ‡f, record the inclusive dates of the materials (i.e., the years of the earliest and latest items in the collection). In the case of a collection that is continuing to grow (as with a current business archive), add "[ongoing]" in the place of the closing date (e.g., "1969-[ongoing]") (see figure 4-5). For other examples of the date element, see figures throughout this chapter. If more specificity than years is possible, record the dates in the order year, month, day:

> 245 00 ‡k Letters, ‡f 1896 June 15-1903 May 5.

APPM 1.1C (AACR2R 4.1C). General material designation

The general material designation (GMD) may be added to the titles of archival cataloging in accordance with the library's policy. For example, an archival collection consisting solely of computer data might have the GMD "computer file." If used, the GMD should be added immediately after the title proper in subfield ‡h.

APPM 1.2 (AACR2R 4.2). EDITION AREA

The edition area is used in archival cataloging only when describing individual items, if the item is a different version of another item (e.g., various drafts of a literary author's manuscript). If the item includes an edition statement (e.g., "3rd draft"), use it. AACR2R abbreviations should be used. If the item lacks an edition statement but it is known that it includes significant changes from another version, the cataloger should supply an edition statement, in the language of the title proper, within brackets (e.g., "[4th revision]").

AACR2R 4.4. DATE AREA

This area is not used in archival cataloging, because the dates of the material have already been included in the title area (cf. APPM 1.4).

APPM 1.5 (AACR2R 4.5). PHYSICAL DESCRIPTION AREA

APPM 1.5B (AACR2R 4.5B). Statement of extent

Give a statement in subfield ‡a of the 300 field either in terms of number of items (see figures 4-2 and 4-3), in terms of the number of linear or cubic feet (meters in Canada) occupied (see figure 4-4), or both (see figure 4-5). With the latter option, give the second part in parentheses. The parts can be given in either order (the statement of extent of figure 4-5 could have been given "3 linear ft. (7 boxes)"). Separate statements of extent may also be given if the collection consists of more than one type of material (see figure 4-2). The elements included in the statement of extent and their order are determined by the policy of the cataloging agency. This policy should be "internally consistent and clearly indicate to a potential user the size of the collection" (*APPM* 1.5B1).

APPM 1.5C (*AACR2R* 4.5C). Other physical details

APPM instructs the cataloger to give "any other physical details that the repository considers important (e.g., the type of paper, the presence of illustrations or maps, or the type of binding)." This allows more latitude than the equivalent *AACR2R* rule, which is similar to the rule for monographs (although it does allow naming the material on which the item is written if it is other than paper; see 4.5C1).

APPM 1.5D (*AACR2R* 4.5D). Dimensions

This element of the physical description area is optional under *APPM*. It is not optional under *AACR2R*. If used, give the size rounding up to the nearest centimeter. In the case of a collection, if the sizes are not uniform, give the largest size followed by "or smaller" (e.g., "45 cm. or smaller"). Dimensions have not been given in examples in this *Handbook*.

APPM 1.7 (*AACR2R* 4.7). NOTE AREA

APPM 1.7B1. **Biographical/Historical** (partially covered in *AACR2R* 4.7B1). Make a *brief* statement about the creator of the archival materials, including dates, if relevant. This statement is recorded in a 545 field (see examples throughout this chapter).

APPM 1.7B2. **Scope and content/Abstract** (*AACR2R* 4.7B1, 4.7B17). Describe the content, nature, and scope of the materials. The note is given in a 520 field (see figures throughout this chapter).

APPM 1.7B4. **Additional physical form available.** If the library has, in addition to the original materials, copies in another physical form (e.g., a microfilm), make a note of it in a 530 field (see figure 4-7).

APPM 1.7B9. **Provenance;** *APPM* 1.7B10. **Immediate source of acquisition** (*AACR2R* 4.7B7). Make a note detailing the custodial history of the materials; if earlier custodial history is known in addition to the immediate source of acquisition, make two notes. A custodial history note is recorded in a 561 field; an immediate source of acquisition note is recorded in a 541 field (see figures 4-6 and 4-7 for examples of a 1.7B10 immediate source of acquisition note and 4-7 for a 1.7B9 provenance/custodial history note).

APPM 1.7B11. **Restrictions on access** (*AACR2R* 4.7B14). If there are any restrictions on access to the materials, it is important that the patron be aware of this. This should be recorded in a 506 field. Such a note might read

506   ‡a Not available until 2010 except by permission of the donor.

For another example, see figure 4-7.

Figure 4-7.   Additional physical form

```
100 1    ‡a Camp, Walter Mason, ‡d 1867-1925.
245 04   ‡a The Walter Mason Camp papers, ‡f 1905-1925.
300      ‡a 8 boxes (3 linear ft.)
545      ‡a Railway engineer, editor, and historian of the Indian wars of the U.S. Plains, 1864-
         1890. He avidly researched the Indian wars from 1890 to 1925, including conducting
         interviews with surviving Indian and White participants; his heaviest activity was from
         1900 to 1920.
520      ‡a The collection consists of correspondence, interview notes, general research and field
         notes, drafts of writings, photographs, maps, news clippings and miscellaneous research
         and reference materials created and collected by Camp, and pertaining to the Indian Wars
         of the plains (1864-1890). The bulk of the collection consists of the correspondence
         (1908-1923), interviews, general research and field notes (1890-1924). Chief interviewees
         and correspondents were the officers, enlisted men, and Indian scouts of the U.S. 7th
         Cavalry, and the Indians who fought at the Battle of Little Bighorn. Significant information
         on the other battles is also present in the papers, including the following: Slim Buttes,
         Washita, Beecher Island, Wounded Knee, Wagon Box, Adobe Walls, Rosebud, Redwater
         Creek, Platte Bridge and Red Buttes, Nez Perce Campaign, Hayfield Fight, Dull Knife
         Fight, Fetterman Massacre, Conner-Cole Expedition and the Battle of Buffalo Wallow.
530      ‡a Microfilmed copies available; ‡d MSS FM 5.
561      ‡a Custody assumed by Camp's widow in 1925; sold to William Carey Brown in 1933,
         who organized and apparently misplaced some of the papers. Some materials were added
         by Brown and Robert Ellison. Some of the materials were removed from the collection by
         Brown; these are now at the University of Colorado Library. The bulk of the papers went
         to Ellison; on his death, most of these went to the Lilly Library and the Denver Public
         Library; the remaining papers were purchased by Fred Rosenstock.
541      ‡c Gift and purchase; ‡a Fred Rosenstock; ‡d 1968-1981.
506      ‡a Use of the original Camp interview notes and notes is restricted. Only those scholars
         requiring access in order to authenticate a particular note or to verify a transcription will
         be allowed to use them and then only under the supervision of the curator of manuscripts.
         All others must use the microfilmed copies found in box 8 of the collection.
555      ‡a Finding aid available in the repository.
524      ‡a The Walter Mason Camp Papers, ca. 1890-1925.
581      ‡a Camp, Walter Mason. Custer in '76 : Walter Camp's notes on the Custer fight / edited
         by Kenneth Hammer. -- Provo, Utah : Brigham Young University Press, 1976.
```

APPM **1.7B12. Terms governing use and reproduction** (*AACR2R* 4.7B14). Here is recorded information about copyright, film rights, etc. Record the note in a 540 field (see figure 4-2).

APPM **1.7B13. Cumulative index/finding aids** (*AACR2R* 4.7B11). The catalog record, as such, is only a part of the processing of an archival collection and usually only gives very general information about the collection. Especially in the case of a large collection, the researcher needs an index or finding aid (a detailed description of the collection, giving information about each individual item) in order to use the materials. If such an aid has been prepared, it should be noted in a 555 note (see examples throughout this chapter).

APPM **1.7B15. Preferred citation of described materials.** Record the format of citation preferred by the custodian of the materials in a 524 note. The system should generate the introductory phrase "Cite as:" from this field (see figure 4-7).

APPM **1.7B16. Publications.** If publications have resulted from the use of the collection, cite them in a 581 note. The system should generate the display "Publications:" from this field (see figure 4-7).

Choice of access points

APPM departs somewhat from *AACR2R* on rules for choice of access points, particularly in the determination of main entry. However, if the collection is considered as a whole and the person or body responsible for assembling the collection (i.e., the intellectual content of the activity) is thought of as the author, archival practice can make sense to a cataloger used to the philosophy underlying *AACR2R* on the question.

APPM directs the cataloger to make entry under personal name if a collection consists of the personal papers of an individual (*APPM* 2.1A1; see figures 4-2, 4-3, and 4-6) or, in the case of an individual manuscript, if the item is of known authorship (see figure 4-1).

Family papers are to be entered under the family name (*APPM* 2.1A3).

Collections "artificially accumulated around a person, subject, activity, etc., without regard to the archival integrity or provenance of the materials" are to be entered under the name of the collector. In this case, add the relator term "collector" in subfield ‡e following the heading for the person (see figure 4-5).

Interviews of individuals are to be entered under the name of the interviewee, with added entry for the interviewer(s) (*APPM* 2.1A6).

The records of a corporate body are to be entered under the heading for that body. Records "consist of any documentation created in the course of fulfilling the purposes and functions of the corporate body" (*APPM* 2.1B2; see figure 4-4). This is a much more inclusive rule than the restrictive rules for entry under corporate body in *AACR2R* chapter 21.

In contrast to *AACR2R* practice, if the corporate body's name changed during the period covered by the collection, enter under the latest name covered and give added entries for other names used during the period (*APPM* 2.1B3).

The following should be entered under title: artificial collections better known under the name of the collection than the name of the collector (*APPM* 2.1C2); the personal papers of more than one individual where no one person is identified as predominating (*APPM* 2.1C3); collections emanating from corporate bodies but not falling under the definition of "records," above (*APPM* 2.1C4); family papers of more than one family (*APPM* 2.1C5); and manuscripts and collections of unknown authorship (*APPM* 2.1C6).

NOTES

1. *Archives, Personal Papers, and Manuscripts: A Cataloging Manual for Archival Repositories, Historical Societies, and Manuscript Libraries,* 2nd ed., comp. Steven L. Hansen (Chicago: Society of American Archivists, 1989).

2. General information about MARC coding is found in the introduction to this *Handbook;* details about coding the descriptive portion of the record are found throughout chapter 1; information about the coding of main and added access points is found at the beginning of chapter 14. An explanation of the MARC authorities format is given in *Handbook* chapters 15, 17, and 18. Information about specific MARC fields may be found by consulting the index under "MARC fields."

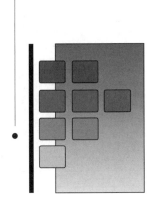

CHAPTER 5

MUSIC

(*AACR2R* Chapters 5, 21.18–21.22, and 25.25–25.35)

AACR2R chapter 5 covers the description of published music. Rules in chapter 5 do not deal with choice and form of main and added entries. These are covered in *AACR2R* chapters 21 through 24. Nor does chapter 5 concern itself with rules for uniform titles that are usually needed to organize entries for musical works. These rules are contained in *AACR2R* chapter 25, particularly rules 25.25 through 25.35.

This chapter of the *Handbook* will first discuss choice of access points for music (*AACR2R* chapter 21), next, the bibliographic description of music (*AACR2R* chapter 5), and finally, the formulation of uniform titles (*AACR2R* chapter 25).[1]

AACR2R Chapter 21.   CHOICE OF ACCESS POINTS

The cataloging of music, because of the special nature of the material, presents unique problems. Indicative of these problems is the fact that a fairly substantial section of *AACR2R* chapter 21 (rules 21.18–21.22) is given over to specific rules for choice of entry for musical works. All of these special rules are based on general rule 21.9, "Works That Are Modifications of Other Works." If a musical work has been modified in such a way that "the modification has substantially changed the nature and content of the original," entry will be under the heading appropriate to the new work. Otherwise, entry is under the heading for the original work. The special rules in *AACR2R* chapter 21 for music help the cataloger to make the proper decision in this regard.

It must be emphasized that the general principles governing choice of main entry for other types of library materials apply equally to musical works. For instance, the composer of a musical work is regarded as the author and, according to 21.1A1, will be given main entry (see figure 5-1).

Figure 5-1.   Entry under composer

```
028 32   ‡a FSB 597 ‡b Jalni
100 1    ‡a Bernstein, Leonard, ‡d 1918-
245 10   ‡a Jeremiah : ‡b symphony no. 1 for orchestra and mezzo-soprano / ‡c Leonard
         Bernstein ; Hebrew text from Lamentations.
250      ‡a Corr. ed.
254      ‡a Full score.
260      ‡a [United States] : ‡b Jalni : ‡b Boosey & Hawkes, ‡c 1992, c1943.
300      ‡a 1 score (84 p.) ; ‡c 31 cm.
546      ‡a Hebrew words romanized; printed also as text with English translation.
500      ‡a Duration: 24 min.
505 0    ‡a Prophecy -- Profanation -- Lamentation.
```

Title page

Leonard Bernstein
Jeremiah
Symphony no. 1
For Orchestra and Mezzo-Soprano
Hebrew Text from Lamentations

I. Prophecy .... p. 1
II. Profanation .... p. 17
III. Lamentation .... p. 63

Full Score
Jalni Publications, Inc.
Boosey & Hawkes

21.18. MUSICAL WORKS: GENERAL RULE

This rule concerns itself with choice of entry for musical arrangements, free transcriptions, and other arrangements that in some way are different from the composer's original work.

21.18B. Arrangements, transcriptions, etc.

This rule is analogous to 21.12, "Revisions of Texts." A simple arrangement (not a paraphrase or free transcription) will be entered under the name of the original composer (see figure 5-2).

21.18C. Adaptations

This rule is analogous to 21.10, "Adaptations of Texts." If the nature or content of a musical work has been modified so much that it is substantially changed, main entry will be under the heading for the adapter. Name-title added entry will be made under the name of the original (see figure 5-3).

Figure 5-2.   Transcription for another instrument under original composer

100 1	‡a Martini, Giovanni Battista, ‡d 1706-1784.
240 10	‡a Toccata, ‡m organ; ‡o arr.
245 10	‡a Toccata / ‡c Giovanni Battista Martini ; arranged for brass quintet by Peter Knudsvig.
260	‡a Columbia, S.C. : ‡b International Trumpet Guild, ‡c c1994.
300	‡a 1 score (5 p.) + 5 parts ; ‡c 28 cm.
500	‡a Cover title.
500	‡a For 2 trumpets, horn, trombone, and tuba; originally for organ.
500	‡a "Special supplement to the May 1994 ITG Journal"--Cover.
700 1	‡a Knudsvig, Peter.

Cover	Giovanni Battista Martini
	Toccata
	Arranged for Brass Quintet
	by
	Peter Knudsvig
	Special Supplement to the May 1994 ITG Journal
	International Trumpet Guild
Foot of first page of music	
	©1994 by Peter Knudsvig

Figure 5-3.   Entry under name of adapter

020	‡a 0895792753
100 0	‡a Rudolph, ‡c Archduke of Austria, ‡d 1788-1831.
240 10	‡a Aufgabe von Ludwig van Beethoven gedichtet, vierzig Mahl verändert
245 10	‡a Forty variations on a theme by Beethoven : ‡b for piano ; Sonata in F minor for violin and piano / ‡c Archduke Rudolph of Austria ; edited by Susan Kagan.
260	‡a Madison, Wis. : ‡b A-R Editions, ‡c c1992.
300	‡a 1 score (xiv, 136 p.) : ‡b ill. + ‡a 1 part (23 p.) ; ‡c 31 cm.
440　0	‡a Recent researches in the music of the nineteenth and early twentieth centuries, ‡x 0193-5364 ; ‡v v. 21
500	‡a The theme of the variations is Beethoven's O Hoffnung, WoO 200.
500	‡a Includes Beethoven's emendations to the variations and an earlier version of the sonata.
700 1	‡a Kagan, Susan.
700 1	‡a Beethoven, Ludwig van, ‡d 1770-1827. ‡t O Hoffnung.
700 0	‡a Rudolph, ‡c Archduke of Austria, ‡d 1788-1831. ‡t Sonatas, ‡m violin, piano, ‡r F minor.
740 02	‡a Sonata in F minor for violin and piano.

Title page	Recent Researches in the Music of the Nineteenth and Early Twentieth Centuries • volume 21
	Archduke Rudolph of Austria
	Forty Variations on a Theme by Beethoven for Piano
	Sonata in f Minor for Violin and Piano
	Edited by Susan Kagan
	A-R Editions, Inc.
	Madison

21.19. MUSICAL WORKS THAT INCLUDE WORDS

This rule is somewhat analogous to rule 21.11, "Illustrated Texts." A vocal work that includes music and words will have main entry under the name of the composer (as appropriate under 21.1–21.6). If the words are "fully represented," give their author an added entry (see figure 5-4).

For a musical work with words based on a previously published text, give name-title added entry for the original text (see figure 5-5).

21.19C. Writer's works set by several composers

This rule, which calls for entry of a collection of musical settings of songs, etc., with text by one writer and music by more than one composer as a collection, is based on *AACR2R* 21.7. Entry will be under title if such a musical collection has a collective title (see figure 5-6). Added entries are made for the author of the text and the editor, if any.

21.20. MUSICAL SETTINGS FOR BALLETS, ETC.

Main entry for such works will be under the name of the composer of the music; an added entry will be given to a choreographer, etc., whose name appears in the chief source of information. Martha Graham is the choreographer for the work on which figure 5-7 is based.

21.21. ADDED ACCOMPANIMENTS, ETC.

Sometimes a composer writes only the basic structure of the music, leaving it up to the performer to "realize," or fill in the harmony, of a piece. This is particularly common in music of the baroque period. In figure 5-8, a piece for harp sketched out by Handel has been realized and published. The item receives the same main entry, Handel, as the original, even though it has received extensive arrangement. The composer of the realization is given an added entry.

AACR2R Chapter 5. MUSIC

AACR2R rules 21.18–21.22 are concerned with special problems of entry of musical works. The rules in *AACR2R* chapter 5 deal with the description of such works.

5.0B1. Chief source of information. As with printed books (*AACR2R* chapter 2), the chief source of information for a musical work is the title page. One type of title page, a "list" title page, is simply a list of the composer's works issued by the publisher or lists of related music from the publisher. Included in the list will be the title of the work being cataloged. When dealing with a title page of this type, the cataloger is directed to use either the "list" title page, a caption title page (title on first page of musical text), or a cover title page, whichever provides the fullest information. The

Figure 5-4.   Musical work with words

```
028 32    ‡a 46127 ‡b G. Schirmer
100 1     ‡a Schubert, Franz Peter, ‡d 1797-1828.
240 10    ‡a Schöne Müllerin. ‡l English & German
245 14    ‡a The lovely milleress = ‡b (Die Schöne Müllerin) : for voice and piano / ‡c by Franz
          Schubert ; English words by Richard Dyer-Bennet.
260       ‡a New York : ‡b G. Schirmer, ‡c c1967.
300       ‡a 76 p. of music ; ‡c 28 cm.
500       ‡a German words by Wilhelm Müller.
700 1     ‡a Müller, Wilhelm, 1794-1827.
700 1     ‡a Dyer-Bennet, Richard.
```

Title page	The Lovely Milleress (Die Schöne Müllerin) For Voice and Piano by Franz Schubert English Words by Richard Dyer-Bennet G. Schirmer, Inc./New York

Figure 5-5.   Text based on previously published text

```
020       ‡a 0852493339
028 32    ‡a B 333 ‡b Galliard
100 1     ‡a Butterworth, George, ‡d 1885-1916.
240 10    ‡a Songs from A Shropshire lad
245 10    ‡a Eleven songs from A Shropshire lad / ‡c by George Butterworth ; with an introduction
          by Peter Pirie.
260       ‡a London : ‡b Stainer & Bell ; ‡a New York : ‡b Galaxy Music Corp., ‡c c1974.
300       ‡a 1 score (46 p.) ; ‡c 24 cm.
500       ‡a Words by A.E. Housman.
505 0     ‡a Six songs from A Shropshire lad. Loveliest of trees. When I was one-and-twenty. Look
          not in my eyes. Think no more, lad. The lads in their hundreds. Is my team ploughing? --
          Bredon Hill and other songs. Bredon Hill. O fair enough are sky and plain. When the lad
          for longing sighs. On the idle hill of summer. With rue my heart is laden.
700 12    ‡a Butterworth, George, ‡d 1885-1916 ‡t Bredon Hill and other songs.
700 1     ‡a Housman, A. E. ‡q (Alfred Edward), ‡d 1859-1936. ‡t Shropshire lad.
```

Title page	Eleven Songs from A Shropshire Lad by George Butterworth with an introduction by Peter Pirie Contents [table of contents] Stainer & Bell Ltd 82 High Road, London N2 9PW Galaxy Music Corporation 2121 Broadway, New York, NY 10023 SBN85249 333 9 ©1974 Stainer & Bell Ltd

Figure 5-6.   Collection of musical settings, text by one author

```
020        ‡a 0895793075
245 00     ‡a Anthology of Goethe songs / ‡c edited by Richard D. Green.
260        ‡a Madison, Wis. : ‡b A-R Editions, ‡c c1994.
300        ‡a 1 score (xxxviii, 105 p., 2 p. of plates) : ‡b ill. ; ‡c 31 cm.
440   0    ‡a Recent researches in the music of the nineteenth and early twentieth centuries,
           ‡x 0193-5364 ; ‡v v. 23
500        ‡a "Texts and translations": p. xxvi-xxxviii.
504        ‡a Includes bibliographical references.
505 0      ‡a Sehnsucht / Carl Zelter -- Das Blümlein wunderschön / Johann Rudolf Zumsteeg --
           Nähe des Geliebten ; Das Veilchen / Wenzel Johann Tomaschek -- Die Spinnerin /
           Ferdinand Ries -- Mignons Lied / Louis Spohr -- Der Fischer / Moritz Hauptmann --
           Der Erlkönig / Bernhard Klein -- Der König von Thule / Heinrich Marschner -- Der
           Zauberlehrling / Carl Loewe -- Nähe des Geliebten / Ferdinand Hiller -- Wonne der
           Wehmut / Robert Franz -- Clärchens Lied / Anton Rubinstein -- Freisinn / Hans von
           Bülow -- Nachtgesang / Joseph Rheinberger -- Wer sich der Einsamkeit ergibt ; Am Flusse
           / Arnold Mendelssohn -- Lied des Mephistopheles / Ferruccio Busoni -- Mailied / Hans
           Pfitzner -- An den Mond / Justus Hermann Wetzel -- Geweihter Platz / Nikolay Karlovich
           Medtner -- Rastlose Liebe / Othmar Schoeck.
700 1      ‡a Green, Richard D., ‡d 1944-
700 1      ‡a Goethe, Johann Wolfgang von, ‡d 1749-1832.
```

Title page	Recent Researches in the Music of the Nineteenth and Early Twentieth Centuries • Volume 23 Anthology of Goethe Songs Edited by Richard D. Green A-R Editions, Inc. Madison

Figure 5-7.   Music for ballet

```
028 22     ‡a B. & H. 9054 ‡b Boosey & Hawkes
100 1      ‡a Copland, Aaron, ‡d 1900-
240 10     ‡a Appalachian spring; ‡o arr.
245 10     ‡a Appalachian spring : ‡b (ballet for Martha) / ‡c Aaron Copland.
246 30     ‡a Ballet for Martha
260        ‡a London ; ‡a New York : ‡b Boosey & Hawkes, ‡c c1945.
300        ‡a 1 score (82 p.) ; ‡c 26 cm.
490 0      ‡a Hawkes pocket scores ; ‡v no. 82
500        ‡a "The original scoring called for a chamber ensemble of thirteen instruments. The
           present arrangement for symphony orchestra was made by the composer in the spring
           of 1945. It is a condensed version of the ballet."
500        ‡a Duration: about 20 min.
700 1      ‡a Graham, Martha.
```

Title page	Aaron Copland Appalachian Spring (Ballet for Martha) Boosey & Hawkes

Figure 5-8.   Added accompaniment, etc.

```
100 1    ‡a Handel, George Frideric, ‡d 1685-1759.
240 10   ‡a Saul. ‡p Sinfonie pour les carillons; ‡o arr.
245 10   ‡a Two sinfonias from "Saul" : ‡b (1738) / ‡c by G.F. Handel ; arranged and realized by
         Ellis Schuman.
260      ‡a Ellensburg, WA : ‡b F C Pub. Co., ‡c c1990.
300      ‡a 1 score (7 p.) ; ‡c 28 cm.
440  0   ‡a Solo series. ‡p Harp
505 0    ‡a Carillon sinfonia -- David's harp interlude.
700 1    ‡a Schuman, Ellis.
```

Title page
                    Two sinfonias from "Saul" (1738)
                         by G.F. Handel
                arranged and realized by Ellis Schuman
                        I Carillon Sinfonia
                      II David's Harp Interlude
            On the Aria "Oh Lord Whose Mercies Numberless"
      F C Publishing Co., 309 West 6th Avenue, Ellensburg, WA 98926

Foot of first page of music
                       © 1990 by Ellis Schuman

list title page furnished the information for the example shown in figure 5-9. Note the omission from the catalog entry of the other titles listed on the page.

5.1. TITLE AND STATEMENT OF RESPONSIBILITY AREA

5.1B. Title proper

The chief source of information must be used in transcribing the title proper. General rule 1.1B governs the transcription of titles of musical works. In addition, because musical works are frequently issued in different editions with varying titles, and because in many cases the titles of published works are not adequate for a proper organization of a composer's file, the cataloger often interposes a uniform title between the main entry heading and the title proper as it appears on a single work. See discussion of *AACR2R* 25.25–25.35 at the end of this chapter for rules for uniform titles for musical works.

   5.1B1. Determination of the length of the title proper can be a problem in music cataloging, because so many pieces of music are given titles consisting of a generic term (the name of a type of composition, such as "symphony" or "concerto") followed by a medium of performance (e.g., "for flute"), key (e.g., "in B flat"), opus number (e.g., "no. 3"), etc. In such a case, all of this information is included as part of the title proper (see figure 5-10). On the other hand, if the title is not generic (e.g., "Don Giovanni"), or consists of a generic term modified by a nongeneric adjective (e.g.,

Figure 5-9.   "List" title page

```
028 32    ‡a E.C.S. no. 3136 ‡b E.C. Schirmer
100 1     ‡a Ashforth, Alden
245 10    ‡a Hodie Christus natus est : ‡b (Christ is born today) : for unaccompanied mixed voices /
          ‡c Alden Ashforth.
260       ‡a Boston, Mass. : ‡b Ione Press : ‡b Sole selling agent, E.C. Schirmer, ‡c c1988.
300       ‡a 1 score (16 p.) ; ‡c 28 cm.
490 1     ‡a Three Christmas motets / Alden Ashforth ; ‡v 1
500       ‡a For chorus (SATB); includes keyboard accompaniment for rehearsal only.
800 1     ‡a Ashforth, Alden. ‡t Three Christmas motets ; ‡v 1
```

> **List title page**   Alden Ashforth
>   Three Christmas Motets
>   * 1. Hodie Christus natus est (Christ is born today) E.C.S. No. 3136
>   2. O magnum mysterium (O Greatest of Mysteries) E.C.S. No. 3137
>   3. Viderunt omnes (All Peoples Witness) E.C.S. No. 3138
>   For Unaccompanied Mixed Voices

Figure 5-10.   Generic term title

```
020       ‡a 0793542022
028 32    ‡a HL00120015 ‡b Hal Leonard
100 1     ‡a Starer, Robert.
240 10    ‡a Sonatas, ‡m piano, ‡n no. 3
245 10    ‡a Sonata for piano, no. 3 / ‡c Robert Starer.
260       ‡a Milwaukee, WI : ‡b MCA Music : ‡b Distributed by Hal Leonard, ‡c c1994.
300       ‡a 1 score (23 p.) ; ‡c 31 cm.
500       ‡a Cover title.
```

> **Cover**   Robert Starer
>   Sonata for Piano, No. 3
>   A publication of MCA music publishing
>   A division of MCA Inc.
>   7777 W. Bluemound Rd., Milwaukee, WI 53213
>   Distributed by Hal Leonard
>
> **Foot of first page of music**
>   © Copyright 1994 by MCA Music Publishing, A Division of MCA Inc.

"The Pastoral Symphony"), any mention of medium of performance, key, etc., on the chief source will be treated as other title information (see figure 5-11).

Figure 5-11.   Nongeneric title
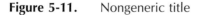

```
028 32    ‡a K 163 ‡b Keturi Musikverlag
100 1     ‡a Baumann, Herbert, ‡d 1925-
245 10    ‡a Sonata serena : ‡b für Hackbrett (oder Marimba/Xylophon) und Harfe (ersatzweise
          Klavier) / ‡c Herbert Baumann.
250       ‡a Faksimile-Ausg.
260       ‡a Rimsting/Chiemsee : ‡b Keturi Musikverlag, ‡c c1993.
300       ‡a 1 score (24 p.) + 1 part (11 p.) ; ‡c 30 cm.
500       ‡a Cover title.
```

Cover   Herbert Baumann
                            Sonata Serena
             für Hackbrett (oder Marimba/Xylophon)
                und Harfe (ersatzweise Klavier)
                        Faksimile-Ausgabe
                        Keturi Musikverlag
             Höhenweg 36, D-8219 Rimsting/Chiemsee
Foot of first page of music
       © Copyright 1993 by Keturi Musikverlag, D-83251 Rimsting/Chiemsee
                      Alle Rechte vorbehalten

5.1C. *Optional addition.* General material designation

The cataloger may optionally add the general material designation "music" in brackets immediately following the title proper. Following Library of Congress practice, examples of music in this text do not include GMDs.

5.1D. Parallel titles

Parallel titles are recorded according to stipulations of general rule 1.1D (see figure 5-4 for an example).

5.1E. Other title information

This information is recorded following general rule 1.1E (see figure 5-7, etc.).

5.1F. Statements of responsibility

These statements follow general instructions given under 1.1F.

5.2. EDITION AREA

5.2B. Edition statement

Music title pages frequently use the word "edition" to indicate the arrangement or form of the work, as "edition for 2 pianos," in figure 5-12. Such statements are *not* editions statements in the *AACR2R* sense. The cataloger must use caution in determining if a statement is in fact an edition statement. For a true edition statement in music cataloging, see figure 5-13.

5.3. *Optional area.* MUSICAL PRESENTATION STATEMENT AREA

This area is to be used to indicate the special format of a musical work when such a work has appeared in more than one format and when the information regarding the format appears on the chief source of informa-

Figure 5-12.   Word "edition" does not trigger edition statement

```
024 2    ‡a M003027920
028 22   ‡a H.S. 2287 ‡b H. Sikorski
100 1    ‡a Prokofiev, Sergey, ‡d 1891-1953.
240 10   ‡a Concertos, ‡m piano, 1 hand, orchestra, ‡n op. 53, ‡r B♭ major; ‡o arr.
245 10   ‡a Konzert Nr. 4 für Klavier (linke hand) und Orchester, B-Dur, opus 53 / ‡c Sergej
         Prokofjew ; Ausgabe für 2 Klaviere von Anatoli Wedernikow = Concerto no. 4 for piano
         (left hand) and orchestra, B-flat major, opus 53 / Sergei Prokofiev ; edition for 2 pianos by
         Anatoly Vedernikov.
246 31   ‡a Concerto no. 4 for piano (left hand) and orchestra, B-flat major, opus 53
260      ‡a Hamburg ; ‡b H. Sikorski ; ‡a New York ; ‡b G. Schirmer, ‡c c1995.
300      ‡a 1 score (55 p.) ; 32 cm.
440  0   ‡a Sikmuz
500      ‡a Duration: ca. 24 min.
700 1    ‡a Vedernikov, Anatoliĭ
```

Title page

Sergej Prokofjew	Sergei Prokofiev
Konzert Nr. 4	Concerto No. 4
für Klavier (linke Hand)	for Piano (left hand)
und Orchester	and Orchestra
B-Dur opus 53	B flat major Opus 53
Ausgabe für 2 Klaviere	Edition for 2 Pianos
von Anatoli Wedernikow	By Anatoly Vedernikov

Boosey & Hawkes Music Publishers Ltd., London
G. Schirmer Inc., New York

MUSIKVERLAG HANS SIKORSKI, HAMBURG

Foot of first page of music
        ©1995 by Musikverlag Hans Sikorski, Hamburg

Figure 5-13. Edition statement

```
028 32    ‡a 042 ‡b Comus Edition
100 1     ‡a Richardson, Alan, ‡d 1904-
245 10    ‡a Sussex lullaby : ‡b for viola (or cello) and piano / ‡c Alan Richardson.
250       ‡a Rev. ed. / ‡b prepared by John White.
260       ‡a Colne, Lancashire, Great Britain : ‡b Comus Edition, ‡c c1995.
300       ‡a 1 score (7 p.) + 2 parts ; ‡c 30 cm.
500       ‡a Viola and cello parts printed in opposite sides of a single leaf.
500       ‡a Duration: ca. 3 min.
700       ‡a White, John.
```

Title page

Cat. no. 042
Alan Richardson
Sussex Lullaby
for Viola (or Cello) and Piano

Revised edition prepared by John White

Comus Edition, Heirs House Lane, Colne, Lancashire, Great Britain

Foot of first page of music

© Copyright 1995 Comus Edition

tion, caption, cover, colophon, or other preliminaries. Examples of such statements would be "playing score," "study score," "miniature score," or other statements referring to the physical presentation of the music. This is recorded in field 254, subfield ‡a (see figure 5-14). If the statement implies a changed version from the original ("vocal score," for example), or is associated with a statement of responsibility, the information should be recorded as part of the statement of responsibility rather than in the musical presentation statement area. LC will adopt the use of optional area 5.3.

5.4. PUBLICATION, DISTRIBUTION, ETC., AREA

General rule 1.4 is to be followed in transcribing this area. Note, however, that the prescribed sources of information for the publication area for *AACR2R* chapter 5 include the first page of the music (see 5.0B2). It is common practice in music publishing to put a copyright date at the foot of the first page of the music, and this is frequently the only date found in the publication (see figures 5-2 and 5-8).

5.5. PHYSICAL DESCRIPTION AREA

The physical description area follows the general pattern for other types of library materials.

Figure 5-14.   Musical presentation statement

```
020        ‡a 0486252175 (pbk.)
100 1      ‡a Tchaikovsky, Peter Ilich, ‡d 1840-1893.
240 10     ‡a Romeo et Juliette (Fantasy-overture)
245 10     ‡a Romeo and Juliet overture ; ‡b and, Capriccio italien / ‡c Peter Ilyitch Tchaikovsky.
254        ‡a In full score.
260        ‡a New York : ‡b Dover, ‡c 1986.
300        ‡a 1 score (201 p.) ; ‡b 29 cm.
500        ‡a For orchestra.
534        ‡p Reprint (1st work). Originally published: ‡c Moscow : Gosudarstvennoe muzykal'noe
           izdatel'stvo, 1950.
534        ‡p Reprint (2nd work). Originally published: ‡c Moscow : Gosudarstvennoe muzykal'noe
           izdatel'stvo, 1961.
700 12     ‡a Tchaikovsky, Peter Ilich, ‡d 1840-1893. ‡t Capriccio italien.
```

Title page	Peter Ilyitch Tchaikovsky
	Romeo and Juliet Overture
	and
	Capriccio Italien
	in Full Score
	Dover Publications, Inc., New York

5.5B. Extent of item and specific material designation

The number of physical units is stated together with the specific format of music (e.g., 1 score (32 p.); 4 parts). See *AACR2R* Appendix D (Glossary) for definition of terms listed under 5.5B1. If none of the listed terms is appropriate, use, as appropriate, "v. of music," "p. of music," or "leaves of music."

   5.5B2. If the item consists of a score and parts, these are recorded separately, the score being listed first (see figures 5-3, 5-11, etc.).

5.5C. Illustrations

Illustrations are recorded following stipulations of 2.5C.

5.5D. Dimensions

The height of the musical work is measured, following stipulations of 2.5D.

5.6. SERIES AREA

Rules for the series statement follow general rule 1.6.

5.7. NOTE AREA

Notes follow the general order and are of the same type as those listed under 1.7.

5.7B1. Form of composition and medium of performance. Make a note about the form of the work if it is not evident from the rest of the description (see figures 5-2, 5-7, 5-9, etc.).

5.7B8. Notation. If a piece is written in an unusual or unexpected notation, make a note of this (see figure 5-15).

5.7B10. Duration of performance. If the item states how long the piece lasts, make a note (see figures 5-1, 5-7, 5-13, etc.).

5.7B18. Contents. Formulate contents notes as explained at 1.7B18 (see figures 5-1, 5-5, 5-6, etc.).

5.7B19. Publishers' numbers and plate numbers. Plate numbers appear at the bottom of each page of music when the music is reproduced by engraving. The publisher's number is a number that usually appears on the title page. These numbers serve as one method of approximating the publication date of music that appears with no indication of this information. In addition, because they are often included in listings of music in publishers' catalogs, such numbers serve as a means of identification. If they are found, they should be recorded in the 028 field, with the first indicator coded "2" for a plate number or "3" for a publisher's number. If the second indicator is coded "2," a note will be generated with the display "Pl. no.:" or "Publisher's no.:", as appropriate. The number is recorded in subfield ‡a; its source (usually the name of the publisher) is recorded in subfield ‡b (see figures 5-1, 5-7, etc.).

5.8. STANDARD NUMBER AND TERMS OF AVAILABILITY AREA

See discussion in *Handbook* at 1.8.

5.8B2. The cataloger is instructed to "give any other number [than ISBN or ISSN] in a note." There is, however, a MARC field for the International Standard Music Number (ISMN): the 024 field with the first indicator coded

Figure 5-15.   Notation

```
028 32   ‡a SBB 3 ‡b Boosey & Hawkes
100 1    ‡a Druckman, Jacob, ‡d 1928-
245 10   ‡a Valentine : ‡b for solo contrabass / ‡c Jacob Druckman.
260      ‡a [United States] : ‡b MCA Music : ‡b Boosey & Hawkes, sole agent, ‡c 1993, c1970.
300      ‡a 9 p. of music ; ‡c 28 × 36 cm.
500      ‡a "Written in analog notation ... Employs vocal sounds and sounds made with a soft, felt
         headed timpani stick."
500      ‡a Duration: 9 min.
```

Title page   Jacob Druckman
                  Valentine
                  for solo Contrabass

"2." Thus ISMNs should be recorded there rather than in a note field (see figure 5-12).

AACR2R Chapter 25.   UNIFORM TITLES

For a general discussion of uniform titles, see this *Handbook*, chapter 18. Discussed here are specific rules for music uniform titles.

Uniform titles in music serve the same purpose as uniform titles for other types of materials. However, because of the special nature of music titling practice, uniform titles are particularly crucial to music cataloging, and the majority of music catalog records will contain a uniform title. According to *AACR2R* 25.1A, a uniform title is used (1) to bring together in the catalog all entries for the same work, even though they may have been published under differing titles; (2) to identify a work that is known by a different title than that under which it was published; (3) to differentiate between different works published under the same title; and (4) to aid in the organization of the bibliographic file in a logical manner. These are all important in music cataloging. Music is published and republished, and often the same work is issued under many different titles; frequently, famous works come to have a different name than that under which they are published (for example, should the catalog user look for Beethoven's Third Symphony under "Symphony no. 3" or "Eroica"?); and the differentiation function is extremely important (a composer may write many pieces titled "sonata" or "trio," and the catalog user must be guided to the one he or she wants).

25.25.   MUSICAL WORKS: GENERAL RULE

This rule simply directs the cataloger to use the special rules for music uniform titles (25.26–25.35) rather than the more general rules in the rest of the chapter. As with other uniform titles, music uniform titles are recorded in the 240 field if there is an author main entry (a 1XX field) or in the 130 field if the work is entered under title (in which case the uniform title becomes the main entry). If the 240 field is used, the first indicator is coded "1" if the cataloger wishes the uniform title to display; if it is coded "0" it will not display. The second indicator gives the number of nonfiling characters. For uniform titles formulated using *AACR2R*, this will always be "0," because initial articles are dropped. If the 130 field is used to record the uniform title, the first indicator shows the number of nonfiling characters, which again will always be "0" under *AACR2R*. The second indicator is blank.

The Library of Congress's *Music Cataloging Decisions* (hereinafter *MCD*) instruct the cataloger not to add a uniform title to a catalog record if it would be identical to the title proper (*MCD* 25.25, May 1989). Obviously, however, the cataloger must still formulate a uniform title for every work in order to know whether it would be identical to the title proper, so it is important to understand the following rules.

25.26. GENERAL RULE (Individual titles)

25.26 instructs the cataloger to "formulate the initial title element" and make required additions. The concept of the initial title element is unique to music cataloging and may be somewhat difficult to grasp. The initial title element is "the word or words selected from the title of a musical work and placed first in the uniform title for that work" (see *AACR2R* Appendix D [Glossary], *s.v.* "Initial title element"). The complication is deciding which word or words to select from the title to place in the uniform title. This will be discussed under 25.28–25.29.

25.27. SELECTION OF TITLE

Before attempting to formulate the initial title element, the cataloger must choose the title to use as the basis of this initial title element. 25.27A instructs the cataloger to choose the composer's original title in the language in which the work was presented (note that this is not necessarily the composer's native language) (see figure 5-4). However, if another title *in the same language* has become better known, this other title should be selected. This may be discovered by checking for the work in a thematic catalog or a reference source in the language in question. The title referred to in 25.27 is the entire title proper, that is, everything preceding any other title information. However, in the case of alternative titles, only one of the alternative titles is to be used as the selected title (although this will not necessarily be the first of the alternative titles) (*MCD* 25.27, May 1989). If the title chosen under 25.27 is particularly long, it may be shortened (see 25.27C1 for details).

25.28. ISOLATION OF INITIAL TITLE ELEMENT

Once the appropriate title is selected, manipulate it by removing certain elements. Most of these elements will be replaced in a logical order following the stipulations of rules 25.30 and 25.31.

1. Remove any statement of medium of performance. For example, in figure 5-10, the title selected under 25.27 would be "Sonata for piano, no. 3". Remove "for piano", leaving "Sonata no. 3." Remove "voor fluit, altviool en piano" from figure 5-16, leaving "Trio, 1992."
2. Remove the name of the key. The title selected under 25.27 for 5-12 would be "Konzert Nr. 4 für Klavier (linke Hand) und Orchester, B-Dur, opus 53." Remove the medium of performance ("für Klavier (linke Hand) und Orchester") and the key ("B-Dur"), leaving "Konzert Nr. 4, opus 53."
3. Remove the serial, opus, and thematic index numbers. The partially manipulated example from figure 5-12 becomes "Konzert Nr. 4" by removing "opus 53."
4. Remove numbers unless they are an integral part of the title (i.e., grammatically connected to the rest of the title). Figure 5-12, now

shortened to "Konzert Nr. 4" becomes simply "Konzert." Figure 5-10, already shortened to "Sonata no. 3" becomes "Sonata." "Eleven songs from A Shropshire lad," figure 5-5, becomes "Songs from A Shropshire lad."

5. Remove a date of composition present in the title. Figure 5-16, already reduced to "Trio, 1992" becomes "Trio."

6. Remove adjectives and epithets not part of the original title of the work. "A favorite waltz," figure 5-17, becomes "A waltz."

7. Remove an initial article. "Die schöne Müllerin" (figure 5-4) becomes "Schöne Müllerin"; "A waltz" (figure 5-17) becomes "Waltz." Initial articles are to be removed whether or not they appear in the nominative case in languages that distinguish by case (see *CSB* 52, spring 1991, p. 26).

25.29. FORMULATION OF INITIAL TITLE ELEMENT

Once the initial title element has been isolated, it must be further manipulated. Frequently, the application of rule 25.28 leaves nothing but the name of a type of composition. In the above examples, figure 5-12 has become "Konzert" and figure 5-10 "Sonata," both simply the names of types of composition. If this happens, 25.29 instructs the cataloger to translate this name into the accepted English form of the name if it is cognate (etymologically related) to the French, German, or Italian forms of the name. "Konzert" becomes "Concerto"; "Sonata" remains the same. Next, the cataloger is instructed to give the name in the plural unless it is known that the composer only wrote one piece in this form. "Concerto" becomes "Concertos"; "Sonata" becomes "Sonatas." *LCRI* 25.29A (Feb. 1, 1989) points out that the medium of performance has nothing to do with the decision about whether to use the singular or plural. In the case of figure 5-10, it is not a matter of whether the composer wrote more than one *piano* sonata or not, but whether he wrote more than one *sonata*. In the case of living composers,

Figure 5-16.   Date of composition in title

```
100 1    ‡a Otten, Ludwig.
240 10   ‡a Trios, ‡m piano, flute, viola
245 10   ‡a Trio voor fluit, altviool en piano, 1992 / ‡c Ludwig Otten.
260      ‡a Amsterdam : ‡b Donemus, ‡c c1993.
300      ‡a 1 score (50 p.) + 2 parts ; ‡c 35 cm.
500      ‡a Duration: ca. 12 min.
```

Title page

Ludwig Otten
Trio
voor fluit, altviool en piano
1992

Donemus Amsterdam

Figure 5-17.   Adjective/epithet not part of original title of the work

```
028 32   ‡a AL-16 ‡b A. Lawson
100 1    ‡a Gallenberg, Robert, ‡c Graf von, ‡d 1783-1839.
240 10   ‡a Waltzes, ‡m harp; ‡o arr.
245 12   ‡a A favorite waltz / ‡c by Count Gallenburg [sic] ; arranged by Robert Nicholas Charles
         Bochsa for the harp ; edited by Alice Lawson.
260      ‡a San Anselmo, Calif. : ‡b A. Lawson, ‡c c1970.
300      ‡a 3 p. of music ; ‡c 31 cm.
700 1    ‡a Bochsa, Robert Nicolas Charles, ‡d 1789-1856.
700 1    ‡a Aber, Alice Lawson.
```

Title page	A Favorite Waltz by Count Gallenburg Arranged by Robert Nicholas Charles Bochsa (1789-1856) for the Harp Edited by Alice Lawson This edition is respectfully dedicated to Melanie Rogers

LC will use the singular unless there is evidence (such as a serial number on the piece or catalog records of other pieces of the same type) that the composer has written or intends to write more than one work of the type. If the composer later, in fact, writes a second work of the same type, LC will revise the earlier uniform title headings (*LCRI* 25.29A, Feb. 1, 1989).

25.30. ADDITIONS TO INITIAL TITLE ELEMENTS CONSISTING OF THE NAME(S) OF ONE OR MORE TYPE(S) OF COMPOSITION

The initial title element is the first part of the uniform title. It is recorded, as explained above, in either the 240 or the 130 field of the MARC record, in subfield ‡a. Rules 25.30–25.31 instruct the cataloger to make various additions to the initial title elements in certain cases. Each of these additions will be preceded by specific subfield coding in the MARC record. Because the subfield coding and punctuation is the same for both the 240 and the 130 fields (with the exception that the 130 field ends with a full stop while the 240 does not), no distinction will be made between the fields in the explanation below.

Rule 25.30 applies to initial title elements that have been reduced by the application of rule 25.28 to nothing but the name (or names) of a type (or types) of composition. It does not, therefore, apply to manipulated initial title elements such as "Schöne Müllerin" (figure 5-4) or "Songs from A Shropshire lad" (figure 5-5). It does, on the other hand, apply to "Concertos" (figure 5-12) and "Sonatas" (figure 5-10). 25.30 instructs the cataloger to add to the initial title element most of the items that were stripped off in the formulation of the initial title element, but in a prescribed order, with each element preceded by a comma. This procedure results in a tight organization of the bibliographic file and produces a very useful tool to the library user, especially in the case of voluminous composers.

25.30B. Medium of performance

The first addition is medium of performance. In the MARC record, it is preceded by comma - subfield ‡m. In figure 5-10, "Sonatas" becomes "Sonatas, ‡m piano"; in figure 5-12, "Concertos" becomes "Concertos, ‡m piano, 1 hand, orchestra" (for the formulation "piano, 1 hand," see 25.30B4). The subcategories of 25.30B give standard terms that are to be used, standard groupings of instruments or voices, prescribed orders when listing more than one instrument or voice, etc., and should be consulted for complex situations. The cataloger should be specific, but should not list more than three elements under the medium of performance subsection of the uniform title (for an exception, see 25.30B3). If more than three elements are present, it should be possible to group them under a more general heading. Elements should be listed in the following order: voices, keyboard instrument (if there is more than one non-keyboard instrument—otherwise the keyboard instrument is listed after the non-keyboard instrument), other instruments in score order, continuo.

Do not add medium of performance to the uniform title when (a) the medium is implied by the title (e.g., "Symphonies" implies "orchestra," so there is no need to add this to the uniform title; on the other hand, if a composer writes something called a symphony for organ, the cataloger should add "organ" to the uniform title because "organ" is *not* implied by the title); (b) the work is a set of compositions for different media or is part of a series with the same title but for differing media; (c) the composer has not designated the medium; or (d) stating the medium would be so complex that another method of identifying the piece would be more useful.

25.30B4. Individual instruments. The rules give a choice of names for certain instruments. LC, and libraries following LC, will use "violoncello," "English horn," "contrabassoon," and "timpani" (*LCRI* 25.30B4, Feb. 15, 1994). *MCD* 25.30B4 (Jan. 1990) states that the list of terms for keyboard instruments is not restrictive and other terms may be used if necessary. The key wording of *AACR2R* 25.30B4 is that the entire list is to be used as a *guide* to naming the instruments.

25.30C. Numeric identifying elements

Add (if readily ascertainable) in the following order (a) serial number and (b) opus number or thematic index number. This element is preceded by comma - subfield ‡n. Figure 5-10 now expands to "Sonatas, ‡m piano, ‡n no. 3"; figure 5-12 becomes "Concertos, ‡m piano, 1 hand, orchestra, ‡n op. 53".

25.30D. Key

The next element that may be added to the uniform title is the key. It is preceded by comma - subfield ‡r. The cataloger is instructed to ascertain the key for any piece composed before 1900; for pieces composed after 1899, the cataloger need add the key only if it is "stated prominently in the item being cataloged." "Key" includes mode (major or minor). Figure 5-12 now becomes "Concertos, ‡m piano, 1 hand, orchestra, ‡n op. 53, ‡r B♭ major." English terms should be used in stating the key (*LCRI* 25.30D, Jan. 5, 1989).

25.30E. Other identifying elements

If the preceding three additional elements still do not suffice to distinguish between two or more works by the same composer, the cataloger may further add in parentheses, in the following order, (a) the year of completion of the work, (b) the year of its first publication, or (c) any other identifying elements, such as place of composition, etc. A mass by a composer who wrote more than one mass in the same key might have a uniform title such as:

    240 10 ‡a Masses, ‡r D minor ‡n (1811)

25.31. ADDITIONS TO OTHER INITIAL TITLE ELEMENTS

The additions given in 25.30 are prescriptive; that is, when the initial title element consists solely of a type or types of composition, the cataloger *must* add all of the prescribed elements that are available. 25.31 addresses the situation where the initial title element is *not* solely a type or types of composition (as "Schöne Müllerin" [figure 5-4] or "Songs from A Shropshire lad" [figure 5-5]). In this case, all of the elements of 25.30 *may* be added to the uniform title, but *only* if they are needed to resolve a conflict between uniform titles entered under the same heading (see *AACR2R* 25.31B1). The preferred method is to add either the medium of performance (as instructed in 25.30B) or a descriptive phrase within parentheses (with no subfield coding). If neither of these resolves the conflict, add other elements as instructed in 25.30.

25.32. PARTS OF A WORK

AACR2R 25.32 is based on 25.6 and deals with the publication of only a part, rather than the whole, of a work. The uniform title itself is identical to that of the whole work. The cataloger will add to the uniform title a designation of the part, whether that be a title or a number. If the part has a title, the cataloger should add a name [i.e., that of the composer]-title reference for the subsidiary title to the authority record for the uniform title for the part.

If the part is identified by a number, the number should be preceded by a full stop - subfield ‡n. The example in *AACR2R* 25.32A1(a) would be coded as follows:

240 10 ‡a Ungarische Tänze. ‡n Nr. 5

If the part is identified by a title, the title should be preceded by a full stop - subfield ‡p. The two examples in *AACR2R* 25.32A1(b) would be coded as follows:

240 10 ‡a Aïda. ‡p Celeste Aïda
240 10 ‡a Symphonies, ‡n no. 1, op. 21, ‡r C major. ‡p Andante cantabile
    con moto

Generally, if the part is designated both by a title and a number, prefer the title. See, however, 25.32A1(c–d) for exceptions.

If a publication contains more than one part of a work, follow the instructions given in 25.6B. However, if the composer uses the name "Suite" for a group of his works, use that term rather than "Selections."

25.34. COLLECTIVE TITLES

These are generally the same as those of 25.8. However, music uniform title practice includes a number of collective titles for broad media that do not exist for other types of materials. The lists in 24.34C1–3 are examples of such collective titles; however, these lists are not exclusive. They are meant to be examples on which the cataloger may pattern collective titles to fit the item in hand.

25.35. ADDITIONS FOR MUSICAL WORKS

The following additions to uniform titles for musical works should be made in the order given in 25.35.

25.35C. Arrangements

This rule requires the cataloger to distinguish between "classical" and "popular" music, assuming that such a distinction can be made. It deals with an original work that has been republished in a different arrangement, whether by the original composer or by another. In the case of "classical" music, the piece will be cataloged under the heading for the original composer, with the same uniform title as the original composition. The uniform title will have "arr." added to it preceded by semicolon - ‡o. An added entry will be made for the arranger (unless the arranger is also the original composer) (see figures 5-2, 5-7, 5-8, and 5-12). In the case of "popular" music, "arr." is added only if an instrumental work has been arranged for voices or if a vocal work has been arranged for instruments.

The Library of Congress will not consider a work to be "arranged" for purposes of this rule if a composer revises his own work, retaining the original title and opus number, and the arrangement remains in the same broad medium and is not an "extensive overall revision [with] the introduction of new material." The same uniform title, in these cases, is to be used for both the original and the revised versions (*MCD* 25.35C, Apr. 1990). Such a work may, however, require an edition statement in the edition area if one appears on the work.

25.35D. Vocal and chorus scores

Add "Vocal score(s)" or "Chorus score(s)" to the uniform title following full stop - ‡s if appropriate. As defined in *AACR2R* Appendix D (Glossary), a vocal score is "a score showing all vocal parts, with accompaniment, if any, arranged for keyboard instrument." A chorus score is "a score of a vocal work showing only the chorus parts, with accompaniment, if any, arranged for keyboard instrument." The distinction is that a vocal score will show, in addition to the chorus parts of a work, any solo vocal parts as well. The uniform titles given as examples in *AACR2R* 25.35D1 would be coded as follows:

    240 10 ‡a Messiah. ‡s Vocal score
    240 10 ‡a Mikado. ‡s Chorus score
    240 10 ‡a Operas. ‡s Vocal scores

These terms will be added to a uniform title whenever the item has been so described in the physical description area (*MCD* 25.35D1, May 1989).

25.35E. Librettos and song texts

"Libretto" or "Text" should be added to the uniform title as appropriate following full stop - ‡s. Both terms refer to the publication of the words alone of vocal or choral work. The distinction is that "libretto" is used for the words of an opera, operetta, oratorio, etc., and "text" is used for the words of a song. The examples in *AACR2R* 25.35E1 would be coded as follows:

    240 10 ‡a Forza del destino. ‡s Libretto
    240 10 ‡a Crocodile rock. ‡s Text
    240 10 ‡a Operas. ‡s Librettos

25.35F. Language

If the text of a vocal or choral work has been translated, the name of the language(s) should be added following full stop - subfield ‡l (the letter l, not the number 1) (see figure 5-4). This is the same as *AACR2R* 25.5C. Note that if the work is in its original language only, the cataloger is *not* to add the language to the uniform title. This is so that all the copies of the work in its original language will file before any translations.

25.35F2. Liturgical works. This section was deleted under the 1993 amendments to *AACR2R*. The name of the language, formerly added whether a liturgical work was in its original language or not, will now only be added if the work contains a translation from the original language.

NOTE

1. General information about MARC coding is found in the introduction to this *Handbook*; details about coding the descriptive portion of the record are found throughout chapter 1; information about the coding of main and added access points is found at the beginning of chapter 14. An explanation of the MARC authorities format is given in *Handbook* chapters 15, 17, and 18. Information about specific MARC fields may be found by consulting the index under "MARC fields."

SOUND RECORDINGS

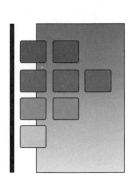

AACR2R chapter 6 includes rules for the description of all types of sound recordings. Once again it must be emphasized that the rules in chapter 6 have nothing to say about choice of main or added entries. For guidance on these matters the cataloger must turn to *AACR2R* chapter 21 ("Choice of Access Points"). Main entry for sound recordings is based on the same principles of authorship governing other types of library materials: entry will be under "the person chiefly responsible for the creation of the intellectual or artistic content of a work." This means, for the most part, that main entry will be under the composer of a musical work that has been recorded, or the writer of a book or other material that is being narrated, applying rules 21.1 through 21.22 as appropriate. In some instances, an individual performer or performing group is regarded as the author of a sound recording and will be given main entry (21.23C). Because entry for sound recordings presents special difficulties, a separate section in *AACR2R* chapter 21 is devoted to rules governing this type of material. These may be briefly summarized.

21.23A. Sound recording of one work

Enter a sound recording of one work under the person or body chiefly responsible for the intellectual or musical content of the work, following general rules as indicated above.

A sound recording of a single work of a composer will be entered under the name of the composer. Form for entry of the composer's name is governed by *AACR2R* chapter 22, ("Headings for Persons"). Transcription of the title is governed by chapter 5 ("Music"). Sound recordings of music require uniform title in the same situations as printed music. A uniform title brings all the editions, versions, etc., of a musical composition together in the same place in the catalog. See *AACR2R* chapter 25 ("Uniform Titles"), and discussion in chapter 5 of this *Handbook,* for specific rules and guidance

Figure 6-1.   A recorded musical work with uniform title

```
028 02   ‡a CAL 50914 ‡b Calig
100 1    ‡a Cherubini, Luigi, ‡d 1760-1842.
240 10   ‡a Masses, ‡r D minor ‡n (1811)
245 10   ‡a Missa solemnis ‡d [sound recording] : ‡b Nr. 2 d-moll = D minor / ‡c Luigi Cherubini.
260      ‡a München : ‡b Calig-Verlag, ‡c p1992.
300      ‡a 1 sound disc (66 min., 10 sec.) : ‡b digital, stereo. ; ‡c 4 3/4 in.
500      ‡a Compact disc.
500      ‡a Program notes in German and English (20 p.) inserted.
511 0    ‡a Monika Wiebe, soprano ; Helena Jungwirth, alto ; Rodrigo Orrego, tenor ; Wolf
         Matthias Friedrich, bass ; Münchner MottetenChor ; Münchner Symphoniker ; Hans
         Rudolf Zöbeley, conductor.
518      ‡a Recorded 17-21 March, 1992, Bavaria Musikstudios München.
700 1    ‡a Wiebe, Monika.
700 1    ‡a Zöbeley, Hans Rudolf.
710 2    ‡a Münchner MottetenChor.
710 2    ‡a Münchner Symphoniker.
```

Disc label

CALIG
Luigi Cherubini (1760-1842)
Missa Solemnis
Nr. 2 d-moll/D minor
Monika Wiebe • Helena Jungwirth
Rodrigo Orrego • Wolf Matthias Friedrich
Der Münchner MottetenChor
Münchner Symphoniker
Leitung: Hans Rudolf Zöbeley

Digital DDD CAL 50914
℗1992 Calig-Verlag GmbH 8000 München 2

in this matter (see figure 6-1 for an example of a musical title for which a uniform title is required).[1]

A sound recording made from a book will be entered under the heading appropriate to the book, as long as the narrator retains the original words of the book (see figure 6-2). And, of course, a recording may be an original work never intended for any other medium (see figure 6-3). What more effective way could there be for a master storyteller to reveal some of her secrets than orally, on tape?

Figure 6-2.   A recorded literary work

```
028 02   ‡a SDP 22 ‡b Riverside
100 1    ‡a Carroll, Lewis, ‡d 1832-1898.
240 10   ‡a Alice's adventures in Wonderland
245 10   ‡a Alice's adventures in Wonderland ‡h [sound recording] : ‡b the Lewis Carroll classic,
         complete / ‡c music composed by Alec Wilder.
260      ‡a New York : ‡b Released by Bill Grauer Productions, ‡c [1957?]
300      ‡a 4 sound discs : ‡b analog, 33 1/3 rpm, mono. ; ‡c 12 in. + ‡e 1 book (192 p. : ill. ;
         20 cm.)
511 0    ‡a Read and sung by Cyril Ritchard; directed by Barrett Clark.
500      ‡a Original music by Alec Wilder, played by the New York Woodwind Quintet with
         Arthur Marotti, percussion.
518      ‡a Recorded in New York City, spring and summer 1957.
500      ‡a Includes facsimile volume of "the rare 1865 first edition of the book," with 42
         illustrations by John Tenniel.
500      ‡a Program notes on inside top cover of container.
520      ‡a Alice goes down a rabbit hole to a strange world of fantasy.
700 1    ‡a Ritchard, Cyril, ‡d 1897-1977.
700 1    ‡a Clark, Barrett.
700 1    ‡a Wilder, Alec. ‡t Alice's adventures in Wonderland.
700 1    ‡a Marotti, Arthur.
700 1    ‡a Tenniel, John, ‡c Sir, ‡d 1820-1914.
710 2    ‡a New York Woodwind Quintet.
```

Disc label
```
                 Riverside
      Alice's Adventures in Wonderland
      The Lewis Carroll classic—complete
         read and sung by Cyril Ritchard
 Long Playing SDP 22     Side 1 Microgroove
    Music composed by Alec Wilder; played by
        the New York Woodwind Quintet
           Bill Grauer Productions
              New York City
```

21.23B. Two or more works by the same person(s) or body (bodies)

This rule is analogous to 21.4A. It states that a sound recording of two or more works by one individual or body will be entered under the name of that individual or group (see figure 6-4).

21.23C. Works by different persons or bodies. Collective title

Main entry for recordings with a collective title containing works by different persons will be under the principal performer of those works. Figure 6-5 is a clear example of entry under the name of the performer.

Such a sound recording containing performances by two or three different persons or groups will be entered under the name of the first performer or first performing group listed if no one of these can be called the

Figure 6-3.   Single work

```
028 02   ‡a Album 6 ‡b Listener Corp.
100 1    ‡a Tooze, Ruth.
245 10   ‡a Storytelling ‡h [sound recording] / ‡c Ruth Tooze.
260      ‡a Hollywood, Calif. : ‡b Listener Corp., ‡c [1971]
300      ‡a 4 sound cassettes : ‡b analog, 2 track, mono.
440  0   ‡a Listener in-service cassette library ; ‡v album 6
500      ‡a In container (24 cm.).
500      ‡a Title from container.
500      ‡a Synopsis and biographical note on container.
505 0    ‡a 1. Why we tell stories. What makes a story good to tell -- 2. How to tell a story --
         3. Selected stories -- 4. Poetry for today's child.
```

Container   Listener
                        In-Service Cassette Library
                              Album 6
                             Storytelling
                              Ruth Tooze
                          Listener Corporation
            6777 Hollywood Boulevard, Hollywood, California 90028

Figure 6-4.   Entry under composer—two or more works by one person

```
028 02   ‡a PCD 863 ‡b Pickwick
100 1    ‡a Palestrina, Giovanni Pierluigi da, ‡d 1525?-1594.
240 10   ‡a Masses, ‡n book 2. ‡p Missa Papae Marcelli
245 10   ‡a Missa Papae Marcelli ‡h [sound recording] ; ‡b Stabat Mater / ‡c Palestrina.
260      ‡a London : ‡b Innovative Music Productions, ‡c p1987.
300      ‡a 1 sound disc (58 min., 10 sec.) : ‡b digital, stereo. ; ‡c 4 3/4 in.
500      ‡a Compact disc.
500      ‡a Program notes in English inserted.
511 0    ‡a Pro Cantione Antiqua ; Mark Brown, director ; Charles Brett, Timothy Penrose, Ashley
         Stafford, countertenors ; Wynford Evans, James Griffeth, Neil Jenkins, tenors ; David
         Beavan, Michael George, Gordon Jones, Christopher Keyte, basses.
518      ‡a Recorded 31 January-1 February, 1987, St. Alban's Church, Brook St., London.
700 12   ‡a Palestrina, Giovanni Pierluigi da, ‡d 1525?-1594. ‡t Stabat mater, ‡m voices (8).
700 1    ‡a Brown, Mark, ‡c conductor.
710 2    ‡a Pro Cantione Antiqua.
```

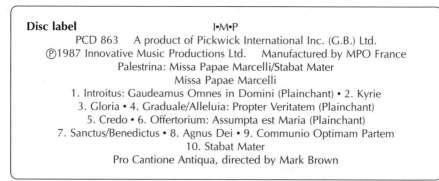

Disc label   I•M•P
         PCD 863   A product of Pickwick International Inc. (G.B.) Ltd.
         ℗1987 Innovative Music Productions Ltd.   Manufactured by MPO France
                  Palestrina: Missa Papae Marcelli/Stabat Mater
                          Missa Papae Marcelli
         1. Introitus: Gaudeamus Omnes in Domini (Plainchant) • 2. Kyrie
         3. Gloria • 4. Graduale/Alleluia: Propter Veritatem (Plainchant)
         5. Credo • 6. Offertorium: Assumpta est Maria (Plainchant)
         7. Sanctus/Benedictus • 8. Agnus Dei • 9. Communio Optimam Partem
                             10. Stabat Mater
                  Pro Cantione Antiqua, directed by Mark Brown

Figure 6-5.   Entry under performer—collection of songs by different persons

```
028 02   ‡a Criss 1024 CD ‡b Criss Cross Jazz
110 2    ‡a Jimmy Knepper Quintet.
245 10   ‡a Dream dancing ‡h [sound recording] / ‡c Jimmy Knepper Quintet.
260      ‡a Eschede, Holland : ‡b Criss Cross Jazz, ‡c p1986.
300      ‡a 1 sound disc (59 min., 38 sec.) : ‡b digital, stereo. ; ‡c 4 3/4 in.
500      ‡a Jazz.
500      ‡a Program notes by Frank van Dixhoom inserted.
511 0    ‡a Jimmy Knepper Quintet (Jimmy Knepper, trombone ; Ralph Moore, tenor sax ; Dick
         Katz, piano ; George Mraz, bass ; Mel Lewis, drums).
518      ‡a Recorded at Van Gelder Recording Studio, Englewood Cliffs, N.J., Apr. 3, 1986.
530      ‡a Also issued on LP.
505 0    ‡a Dream dancing / Cole Porter (6:57) -- Goodbye / Gordon Jenkins (6:18) -- All through
         the night / Cole Porter (5:14) -- In the interim / Jimmy Knepper (6:37) -- Of things past /
         Jimmy Knepper (6:33) -- This time the dream is on me / Harold Arlen (7:11) -- In the
         interim (take 3) / Jimmy Knepper (5:52) -- Dream dancing (take 1) / Cole Porter (7:09)
         -- Night vision / Jimmy Knepper (6:58).
```

Disc label

Criss Cross Jazz
Dream Dancing
Jimmy Knepper Quintet
℗ © 1986 Criss Cross Jazz
Recorded April 3, 1986
Produced by Gerry Teekens
Criss 1024 CD
Digital, stereo
1. Dream dancing 6.57   2. Goodbye 6.18   3. All through the night 5.14
4. In the interim 6.37   5. Of things past 6.33
6. This time the dream is on me 7.11   7. In the interim (take 3) 5.52*
8. Dream dancing (take 1) 7.09*   9. Night vision 6.58*
*Does not appear on L.P. configuration

principal performer. Make added entries for the other performer(s) or group(s) (see figure 6-6).

A sound recording collection with four or more performing individuals or groups, or one in which no performing individual or group is listed, will be entered under title. The example shown in figure 6-7 includes a solid gold hit from each of twenty different performing groups and individuals, from Love Unlimited Orchestra and Hog Heaven to Aretha Franklin.

The cataloger should be reminded that a sound recording may be issued as a serial. In most instances, a serial sound recording will include works by more than one person or group, performed by more than three performers or groups, because a serial by definition is a publication intended to be continued indefinitely (see *AACR2R* chapter 12). Such a serial will be entered under title, following stipulations of 21.23D. For an example of a serial sound recording, see figure 6-8.

Figure 6-6.   A collection recorded by three groups

```
028 02   ‡a H 71095 ‡b Nonesuch Records
110 2    ‡a N.C.R.V. Vocaalensemble.
245 10   ‡a Renaissance choral music for Christmas ‡h [sound recording].
260      ‡a New York : ‡b Nonesuch Records, ‡c [1965]
300      ‡a 1 sound disc (33 min.) : ‡b analog, 33 1/3 rpm, stereo. ; ‡c 12 in.
500      ‡a "A Camerata recording."
546      ‡a Sung in Latin or German.
511 0    ‡a N.C.R.V. Vocaal Ensemble, Marinus Voorberg, conductor ; Kaufbeurer Martinsfinken,
         Ludwig Hahn, conductor ; Niedersächsicher Singkreis, Willi Träder, conductor.
500      ‡a Texts, with English translations, on container.
505 0    ‡a Praeter rerum seriem / Josquin Desprez (6:54) -- Egredietur virga-Radix Jesse / Jacobus
         Gallus (Handl) (2:28) -- Quem vidistis pastores / Andrea Gabrieli (2:55) -- Der Engel
         sprach zu den Hirten / Heinrich Schütz (3:05) -- Hodie Christus natus est / Giovanni
         Gabrieli (2:33) -- O Jesu mi dulcissime / Giovanni Gabrieli (6:14) -- Joseph lieber, Joseph
         mein / Johann Walther (1:45) -- Ein Kind geborn zu Bethlehem / Bartholomäus Gesius,
         Michael Praetorius, Melchior Vulpius (1:23) -- Es ist ein Ros entsprungen / Michael
         Praetorius (2:42) -- In dulci jubilo / Samuel Scheidt (3:05).
710 2    ‡a Kaufbeurer Martinsfinken.
710 2    ‡a Niedersächsischer Singkreis.
```

Disc label

```
                    Nonesuch Records
                Renaissance Choral Music
                      for Christmas
                         Stereo
                       H-71095-A
                        Side One
       1. Josquin Desprez: Praeter rerum seriem 6:54
         N.C.R.V. Vocaal Ensemble, Hilversum,
              Marinus Voorberg, conductor
   2. Jacobus Gallus (Handl): Egredietur virga-Radix Jesse 2:28
        3. Andrea Gabrieli: Quem vidistis pastores 2:55
     4. Heinrich Schütz: Der Engel sprach zu den Hirten 3:05
       5. Giovanni Gabrieli: Hodie Christus natus est 2:33
       6. Giovanni Gabrieli: O Jesu mi dulcissime 6:14
        Kaufbeurer Martinsfinken, Ludwig Hahn, conductor
                  a Camerata recording
           Nonesuch Records, 15 Columbus Circle,
                      New York, N.Y.
```

Figure 6-7.   More than three artists or groups—title main entry

```
028 02   ‡a 8016 ‡b Adam VIII Ltd.
245 00   ‡a 20 solid gold hits ‡h [sound recording] : ‡b original hits / ‡c by original artists.
246 3    ‡a Twenty solid gold hits
260      ‡a [S.l.] : ‡b Adam VIII Ltd., ‡c p1975.
300      ‡a 1 sound cartridge : ‡b analog, quad.
```

Figure 6-8.   Serial sound recording

```
245 00    ‡a Radio news service.
260       ‡a [Salt Lake City, Utah] : ‡b Church of Jesus Christ of Latter-day Saints, ‡c 1993-
300       ‡a sound cassettes : ‡b 1 7/8 ips, mono.
310       ‡a Weekly.
362 0     ‡a Aug. 14-20, 1993-
500       ‡a Weekly radio broadcast.
710 2     ‡a Church of Jesus Christ of Latter-day Saints.
780 00    ‡a News from the Church of Jesus Christ of Latter-day Saints
```

Cassette label

Radio News Service
for broadcast Aug. 14-20, 1993
running time: 14:50
In cue: "I'm . . ."   Out cue: ". . . City."
©The Church of Jesus Christ of Latter-day Saints

6.0. GENERAL RULES

Rule 21.23 addresses itself to special problems of main entry for sound recordings. Rules in *AACR2R* chapter 6 deal with the description of such works.

6.0B1. Chief source of information. Although chapter 6 includes rules for diverse types of sound recordings, the chief source of information is the same in all cases. The label affixed to the recording is the preferred source. If the item includes more than one label (as, for instance, a phonograph disc), both labels are regarded as one source. For a disc, the disc itself is also part of the chief source. For tape, the reel, cassette, or cartridge is also considered part of the chief source. For film, the container as well as the label is the chief source. For any type of sound recording, accompanying textual material or a container may be used as the chief source of information whenever it furnishes a collective title not found on the parts or their labels. In this case, make a note to indicate the source.

6.1B. Title proper

The chief source of information must be used in transcribing the title proper (see *AACR2R* 1.1B for general rules governing such transcription). The title proper is transcribed in subfield ‡a of the 245 field.

In addition, when transcribing the title of a musical work, refer to 5.1B. In the example shown in figure 6-9, the title proper consists of the generic term "Concerto," the key, and the thematic index number. As previously mentioned, a uniform title is included with sound recordings under the same circumstances as in music cataloging (see 25.25–25.35 for rules on uniform titles for music, discussed in chapter 5 in this *Handbook*).

Figure 6-9. Title proper

```
028 02   ‡a S 36189 ‡b Angel
100 1    ‡a Mozart, Wolfgang Amadeus, ‡d 1756-1791.
240 10   ‡a Concertos, ‡m flute, harp, orchestra, ‡n K. 297c (299) ‡r C major
245 10   ‡a Concerto in C major, K. 299 ‡h [sound recording] / ‡c Mozart.
260      ‡a [London] : ‡b Angel, ‡c p1964.
300      ‡a on side 1 of 1 sound disc (30 min., 47 sec.) : ‡b analog, 33 1/3 rpm, stereo. ; ‡c 12 in.
500      ‡a Program notes by Charles Reid on container.
501      ‡a With: Suite in A minor / Telemann.
511 0    ‡a Elaine Shaffer, flute ; Marilyn Costello, harp ; Philharmonia Orchestra ; Yehudi
         Menuhin, conductor.
518      ‡a Recorded in England.
700 1    ‡a Shaffer, Elaine.
700 1    ‡a Costello, Marilyn.
700 1    ‡a Menuhin, Yehudi, ‡d 1916-
710 2    ‡a Philharmonia Orchestra (London, England)
```

Disc labels

Angel
Side 1   Stereo
S. 36189
(2YEA-X-834) 33 1/3
Mozart—Concerto in C major, K.299
(1) - 1st Movement: Allegro - Cadenza (by Flothuis)
(2) - 2nd movement: Andantino - Cadenza (by Flothuis)
(3) 3rd movement: Rondo (Allegro) - Cadenza (by Flothuis)
Elaine Shaffer (flute) & Marilyn Costello (harp)
and the Philharmonia Orchestra
conducted by Yehudi Menuhin
Recorded in England
Mfd. in U.S.A.
Mfd. by Capitol Records, Inc.,
a subsidiary of Capitol Industries, Inc., U.S.A.

Angel
Side 2   Stereo
S. 36189
(2YEA-X-835) 33 1/3
Telemann—Suite in A minor
Ouverture
Les Plaisirs
Air à l'Italien
Menuet 1 & 2
Réjouissance
Passepied 1 & 2
Polonaise
Elaine Shaffer (flute)
and the Philharmonia Orchestra
conducted by Yehudi Menuhin
Recorded in England
Mfd. in U.S.A.
Mfd. by Capitol Records, Inc.,
a subsidiary of Capitol Industries, Inc., U.S.A.

Figure 6-10.   Other title information

```
028 02    ‡a 010 12201 ‡b Motivational Programming Corp.
245 10    ‡a Genesis of a novel ‡h [sound recording] : ‡b a documentary on the writing regimen of
          Georges Simenon.
260       ‡a Tucson, Ariz. : ‡b Motivational Programming Corp., ‡c p1969.
300       ‡a 1 sound cassette (24 min.) : ‡b analog, 2 track, mono.
440  0    ‡a 20th century European authors
520       ‡a An account of the development of Georges Simenon's book, Le président.
504       ‡a Bibliography on container.
700  1    ‡a Simenon, Georges, ‡d 1903-        ‡t Président.
710  2    ‡a Motivational Programming Corporation
```

Cassette label   010 12201
                              Genesis of a novel
              A documentary on the writing regimen of Georges Simenon
                      Motivational Programming Corporation
                 512 Transamerica Building, Tucson, Arizona 85701

6.1C. *Optional addition.* **General material designation**

Following Library of Congress practice, most catalogers will use the GMD "sound recording" for all types of sound recordings. It is added immediately following the title proper in subfield ‡h.

6.1E. **Other title information**

Other title information follows the GMD (see figure 6-10, etc.). See general rules under 1.1E for punctuation and transcription.

6.1F. **Statements of responsibility**

The statement of responsibility is to be transcribed according to general instructions found in 1.1F. However, a special exception to the general rules is made for the transcription of statements of responsibility for sound recordings. Names of narrators or performers are in most cases omitted and given in the note area (see *AACR2R* 6.7B6). The statement of responsibility is limited to writers, composers, and collectors of field material if these names appear prominently (see, for instance, figures 6-1 and 6-2). The rule does allow performers who do more than perform to be named in the statement of responsibility. The Library of Congress instructs its catalogers to accept only the most obvious cases of this situation (*LCRI* 6.1F1, Jan. 5, 1989).

6.1F3. A short phrase may be added to clarify an ambiguous statement of responsibility as shown in figure 6-11.

6.1G. **Items without a collective title**

Items without a collective title may be handled in either of two ways. According to 6.1G2, such an item may be described as a unit (see figure 6-12).

Figure 6-11.   Statement of responsibility

```
028 02   ‡a E 3464 ST ‡b M-G-M
100 1    ‡a Arlen, Harold, ‡d 1905-1986.
240 10   ‡a Wizard of Oz. ‡k Selections
245 14   ‡a The Wizard of Oz ‡h [sound recording] : ‡b musical and dramatic selections recorded
         directly from the sound track of M-G-M's technicolor film / ‡c [lyrics by] Harburg ; [music
         by] Arlen.
260      ‡a [New York] : ‡b M-G-M Records, ‡c [1939?]
300      ‡a 1 sound disc : ‡b analog, 33 1/3 rpm, mono. ; ‡c 12 in.
511 0    ‡a Starring Judy Garland and others ; M-G-M Studio Orchestra and Chorus, Herbert
         Stothart and George Stoll, conductors.
500      ‡a Selections from the motion picture adaptation of: The wizard of Oz / by L. Frank
         Baum.
500      ‡a Also issued in stereo as: SE 3996 ST ; previously issued as: E 3464.
500      ‡a Descriptive notes and summary of story in container.
505 0    ‡a Over the rainbow -- If I only had a brain -- If I only had a heart -- If I only had the
         nerve -- Ding, dong! the witch is dead -- We're off to see the wizard -- If I were king of
         the forest.
700 1    ‡a Harburg, E. Y. ‡q (Edgar Yipsel), ‡d 1898-1981.
700 1    ‡a Garland, Judy.
700 1    ‡a Baum, L. Frank ‡q (Lyman Frank), ‡d 1856-1919. ‡t Wizard of Oz.
710 2    ‡a MGM Studio Orchestra.
```

Disc label

M-G-M
"The Wizard of Oz"
E3464 ST   (Harburg-Arlen)   Side 1
Starring
Judy Garland, Ray Bolger, Bert Lahr,
Jack Haley and Frank Morgan
with Billie Burke, Margaret Hamilton
Over the Rainbow — Judy Garland
If I Only Had a Brain — Ray Bolger
If I Only Had a Heart — Jack Haley
If I Only Had the Nerve — Bert Lahr
Ding, Dong! The Witch is Dead
We're Off to See the Wizard
M-G-M Studio Orchestra and Chorus
Conducted by Herbert Stothart and George Stoll
Musical and dramatic selections recorded directly from the sound track of
M-G-M's Technicolor Film
MGM Records—A division of Loew's Incorporated
Made in U.S.A.

See 1.1G for general instructions on procedures and for prescribed punctuation. If all of the selections are by a single composer, the titles are separated by space - semicolon - space.

If, on the other hand, selections on a sound recording lacking a collective title are by more than one composer, and if the item is to be described as a unit, make entry as shown in figure 6-13.

The cataloger should remember that when the disc label does not provide a collective title, but the container or accompanying textual material

Figure 6-12.   Item without a collective title—one composer

```
028 02   ‡a NI 5096 ‡b Nimbus Records
100 1    ‡a Haydn, Joseph, ‡d 1732-1809.
240 10   ‡a Symphonies, ‡n H. I, 104, ‡r D major
245 10   ‡a Symphony no. 104 in D major ‡h [sound recording] : ‡b "London" ; Symphony no.
         100 in G major : "Military" / ‡c Joseph Haydn.
246 30   ‡a London
246 30   ‡a Military
260      ‡a Wyastone Leys, Monmouth : ‡b Nimbus Records, ‡c c1988, p1987.
300      ‡a 1 sound disc (50 min.) : ‡b digital, stereo. ; ‡c 4 3/4 in.
511 0    ‡a Hanover Band ; Roy Goodman, director.
518      ‡a Recorded Mar. 16-17, 1987, at All Saints', Tooting.
500      ‡a Compact disc.
500      ‡a Program notes by Robert Maycock ([10] p. : ports) inserted in container.
700 12   ‡a Haydn, Joseph, ‡d 1732-1809. ‡t Symphonies, ‡n H. I, 100, ‡r G major.
700 1    ‡a Goodman, Roy.
710 2    ‡a Hanover Band.
740 02   ‡a Symphony no. 100 in G major.
```

Disc label

Nimbus Records
Made in England
Digital recording
Stereo Ambisonic
NI 5096
Joseph Haydn
Symphony No. 104 in D major 'London'
Symphony No. 100 in G major 'Military'
The Hanover Band
directed by Roy Goodman
℗1987 © 1988 Nimbus Records Ltd.

Figure 6-13.   Item without a collective title—two composers

```
028 02   ‡a S 36189 ‡b Angel
100 1    ‡a Mozart, Wolfgang Amadeus, ‡d 1756-1791.
240 10   ‡a Concertos, ‡m flute, harp, orchestra, ‡n K. 297c (299) ‡r C major
245 10   ‡a Concerto in C major, K. 299 ‡h [sound recording] / ‡c Mozart. Suite in A minor /
         Telemann.
260      ‡a [London] : ‡b Angel, ‡c p1964.
300      ‡a 1 sound disc (59 min.) : ‡b analog, 33 1/3 rpm, stereo. ; ‡c 12 in.
500      ‡a Durations: 30 min., 47 sec.; 27 min., 40 sec.
500      ‡a Program notes by Charles Reid on container.
511 0    ‡a Elaine Shaffer, flute ; Marilyn Costello, harp ; Philharmonia Orchestra ; Yehudi
         Menuhin, conductor.
518      ‡a Recorded in England.
700 12   ‡a Telemann, Georg Philipp, ‡d 1681-1767. ‡t Suite, ‡m flute, string orchestra, ‡r A minor.
700 1    ‡a Shaffer, Elaine.
700 1    ‡a Costello, Marilyn.
700 1    ‡a Menuhin, Yehudi, ‡d 1916-
710 2    ‡a Philharmonia Orchestra (London, England)
```

does, the latter should be treated as the chief source for purposes of transcribing the title and statement of responsibility (see *AACR2R* 6.0B1). Figure 6-14 is an example of such a situation.

Figure 6-14.   Collective title from accompanying textual material

```
028 02   ‡a 80395-2 ‡b New World Records
100 1    ‡a Harbison, John.
240 10   ‡a Flight into Egypt
245 14   ‡a The flight into Egypt and other works ‡h [sound recording] / ‡c by John Harbison.
260      ‡a New York : ‡b New World Records, ‡c p1990.
300      ‡a 1 sound disc (48 min.) : ‡b digital, stereo. ; ‡c 4 3/4 in.
490 1    ‡a Meet the Composer orchestra residencies series
500      ‡a Title from accompanying textual material.
500      ‡a Compact disc.
504      ‡a Includes discography and bibliographical references (p. 10 of accompanying text).
511 0    ‡a Cantata Singers and ensemble, David Hoose, conductor (1st work) ; Janice Felty,
           mezzo-soprano, Roberta Anderson, soprano, Sanford Sylvan, baritone, Los Angeles
           Philharmonic New Music Group, John Harbison, conductor (2nd work) ; Los Angeles
           Philharmonic Orchestra, André Previn, conductor (3rd work).
518      ‡a Recorded May 31, 1990, Methuen Memorial Music Hall, Methuen, Mass. (1st work);
           Nov. 14, 1989, Little Bridges Auditorium, Claremont College, Calif. (2nd work); May 1,
           1990, Royce Hall, UCLA, Calif. (3rd work).
500      ‡a Program notes and text (11 p. : ill.) inserted in container.
505 0    ‡a The flight into Egypt (12 min., 32 sec.) -- The natural world (14 min., 40 sec.) --
           Concerto for double brass choir and orchestra (20 min.)
700 12   ‡a Harbison, John. ‡t Natural world.
700 12   ‡a Harbison, John. ‡t Concertos, ‡m brasses, orchestra.
700 1    ‡a Hoose, David.
700 1    ‡a Previn, André.
710 2    ‡a Cantata Singers.
710 2    ‡a Los Angeles Philharmonic New Music Group.
710 2    ‡a Los Angeles Philharmonic Orchestra.
830  0   ‡a Meet the Composer orchestra residency series.
```

Disc label   John Harbison
               Made in USA ℗1990 Recorded Anthology of American Music, Inc.
                      New World Records 80395-2 DIDX 008881
                              1. The Flight into Egypt
                              2-5. The Natural World
                  6-8. Concerto for Double Brass Choir and Orchestra

Cover of accompanying booklet
                            The Flight into Egypt
                            and other works by
                              John Harbison
                      Los Angeles Philharmonic Orchestra
                         André Previn, conductor
                      Cantata Singers and ensemble
                         David Hoose, conductor
                  Los Angeles Philharmonic New Music Group
                      Janice Felty, mezzo-soprano
                      Roberta Anderson, soprano
                       Sanford Sylvan, baritone
                    New World Records 80395-2

6.1G4. Optionally, the cataloger may make a separate catalog entry for each item without a collective title. One side of the sound recording cataloged as a unit in figure 6-13 appears in figure 6-9. The other side of the recording would be cataloged as shown in figure 6-15 if the cataloger chooses to follow this optional practice. The Library of Congress will not implement this option, but will always catalog the item as a unit under 6.1G2 (see *LCRI* 6.1G1, Jan. 5, 1989, and 6.1G4, Dec. 11, 1989).

6.4. PUBLICATION, DISTRIBUTION, ETC., AREA

6.4C. Place of publication, distribution, etc.

General rules under 1.4C are to be followed. The prescribed sources of information for the entire publication area include the chief source of information, any accompanying textual material, or the container, in that order of preference. If place or other elements of this area are taken from sources other than these, they must be enclosed in brackets.

The cataloger must often search to find the place of publication, distribution, etc., because this information is frequently omitted from the recording and its accompanying material. The following reference sources should prove helpful:

> *Billboard International Buyer's Guide* (annual). New York: Billboard Publications, 1970– . Popular recording companies.

> *British Music Yearbook* (annual). London: [various publishers], 1975– . British classical recording companies.

> *Musical America: International Directory of the Performing Arts* (annual). Great Barrington, Mass.: ABC Leisure Magazines, 1974– . North American recording companies.

> Pavlakis, Christopher. *The American Music Handbook*. New York: Free Press, 1974. Chiefly classical music, American sources.

Figure 6-15. Separate entry for a single item from recording without a collective title

028 02	‡a S 36189 ‡b Angel
100 1	‡a Telemann, Georg Philipp, ‡d 1681-1767.
240 10	‡a Suite, ‡m flute, string orchestra, ‡r A minor
245 10	‡a Suite in A minor ‡h [sound recording] / ‡c Telemann.
260	‡a [London] : ‡b Angel, ‡c p1964.
300	‡a on side 2 of 1 sound disc (27 min., 40 sec.) : ‡b analog, 33 1/3 rpm, stereo. ; ‡c 12 in.
500	‡a Program notes by Charles Reid on container.
501	‡a With: Concerto in C major, K. 299 / Mozart.
511 0	‡a Elaine Shaffer, flute ; Philharmonia Orchestra ; Yehudi Menuhin, conductor.
518	‡a Recorded in England.
700 1	‡a Shaffer, Elaine.
700 1	‡a Menuhin, Yehudi, ‡d 1916-
710 2	‡a Philharmonia Orchestra (London, England)

Sandberg, Larry, and Dick Weissman. *The Folk Music Sourcebook.* New, updated ed. New York: Da Capo Press, 1989. Recording companies specializing in folk music.

6.4D2. Name of publisher, distributor, etc. Prefer a trade or brand name rather than the name of the publisher if both appear on the label. Prefer label information rather than information appearing in accompanying material or container (see, for instance, figure 6-9). The brand name "Angel" will be preferred to the name of the manufacturer, Capitol Records, Inc. In figure 6-11, MGM Records is listed as "A division of Loew's Incorporated." Prefer the name of the division to that of the parent body.

6.4D3. Trade name as series. The example shown in figure 6-16 includes a trade name that appears to be a series. It should be recorded as such, rather than used as the name of the publisher.

6.4F. Date of publication, distribution, etc.

Follow general instructions under 1.4F.

6.4F2. If no date of publication is available, the date of recording may be used as the basis for a conjectural publication date. Make a note of the recording date, however, when known, whether this date has been used as a conjectural publication date or not (see figure 6-2, etc.).

If the pressing date is being transcribed, precede it by a lowercase "p" (see figures 6-1, 6-5, etc.).

Figure 6-16.   Trade name as series title

```
028 02   ‡a 2280 ‡b Audio Fidelity
100 1    ‡a Shakespeare, William, ‡d 1564-1616.
240 10   ‡a Selections
245 10   ‡a John Barrymore reads Shakespeare ‡h [sound recording].
260      ‡a [New York] : ‡b Audio Fidelity, ‡c [195-?]
300      ‡a sound discs : ‡b analog, 33 1/3 rpm, mono. ; ‡c 12 in.
440  0   ‡a Audio rarities
500      ‡a Program notes on container.
505 1    ‡a v.1. Scenes from Hamlet. Scenes from Twelfth night. Scenes from Richard III. Scenes
         from Macbeth
700 1    ‡a Barrymore, John, ‡d 1882-1942.
```

Disc label   Audio Rarities
              John Barrymore Reads Shakespeare   2280-1
              Audio Fidelity   Side 1
              Audio Fidelity Enterprises, inc.   33 1/3 rpm
                  1. Scenes from "Hamlet"   Long Play
                  2. Scenes from "Twelfth Night"
                      (Mr. Barrymore reads both
                      Sir Toby Belch and Malvolio)

6.5. PHYSICAL DESCRIPTION AREA

6.5B1. Extent of item (including specific material designation). State the number of physical units, together with the specific type of sound recording, using terms listed under 6.5B1 in subfield ‡a of the 300 field. Libraries that do not choose to include the general material designation "sound recording" as part of the catalog entry should include the word "sound" as part of the specific designation. Optionally, if "sound recording" has been included as the GMD in the entry, the word "sound" may be dropped as being redundant from the specific material designation. Following Library of Congress decision, this will not be done in cataloging examples in this text.

6.5B2. In many cases, playing time is included on the item as part of the information on the label, container, or accompanying material. If this is the case, such information should be included in the physical description area, following instructions under *AACR2R* 1.5B4 (see, e.g., figure 6-1). If the total duration does not appear on the item, but the durations of all its parts do, the cataloger may add them together, rounding to the nearest minute. Do not add "ca." to a duration calculated in this manner (*LCRI* 6.5B2, Jan. 5, 1989) (see figure 6-6).

If playing time is not stated on the item, give it only if it is "readily ascertainable." In most cases where playing time is not listed, it will not be included in the physical description of the item. Rule 1.5B4c indicates that, optionally, the cataloger may give an approximate time, with minutes preceded by the abbreviation "ca." The Library of Congress will not implement this option and will only use "ca." if it appears on the item (*LCRI* 6.5B2, Jan. 5, 1989).

6.5B3. If a separately titled part of a sound recording has been cataloged as an independent work, give the physical extent as shown in figures 6-9 and 6-15.

6.5C. Other physical details

Whereas for visual materials, such as a book, it is appropriate to give details such as the presence of illustrations or color as part of this element, for a sound recording the analogous items are type of recording (analog or digital), playing speed, number of tracks, number of sound channels, etc. These details are separated from the physical extent by space - colon - space and preceded by subfield ‡b.

All sound recordings requiring analog playback equipment (12-inch long-playing discs, cassettes, etc.) must be described as "analog" (see figure 6-2). Discs requiring digital playback equipment ("compact" or "laser" discs) are described as "digital" (see figure 6-1). Sometimes a note is added to clarify the type of playback equipment required. See figure 6-17 for an example of this type of note (the "compact disc" note is still routinely added, even though the compact disc has now become nearly the exclusive format for disc recordings).

Figure 6-17.   Physical description and note

```
028 02    ‡a CHAN 8369 ‡b Chandos
100 1     ‡a Chausson, Ernest, ‡d 1855-1899.
240 10    ‡a Symphony, ‡n op. 20, ‡r B♭ major
245 10    ‡a Symphony in B flat, op. 20 ‡h [sound recording] ; Soir de fête : op. 32 ; La tempête :
          op. 18 : 2 scenes / ‡c Ernest Chausson.
260       ‡a London : ‡b Chandos Records, ‡c 1985.
300       ‡a 1 sound disc (56 min.) : ‡b digital, stereo. ; ‡c 4 3/4 in.
500       ‡a 2nd work is a symphonic poem; 3rd work is composer's own arrangement of 2 dances
          from his incidental music to a marionnette theater production of Shakespeare's Tempest,
          originally for voices, violin, flute, harp, and celesta.
530       ‡a Also issued on LP.
511 0     ‡a Orchestre Symphonique de la R.T.B.F. ; José Serebrier, conductor.
518       ‡a Recorded at the Maison de la Radio, Brussels, September 1984.
500       ‡a Compact disc.
500       ‡a Program notes by Robert Maycock and notes on the conductor ([8] p. : ill.) inserted in
          container.
700 1     ‡a Serebrier, José, ‡d 1938-
700 12    ‡a Chausson, Ernest, ‡d 1855-1899. ‡t Soir de fête.
700 12    ‡a Chausson, Ernest, ‡d 1855-1899. ‡t Tempête. ‡k Selections; ‡o arr.
710 2     ‡a Orchestre symphonique de la R.T.B.F.
```

6.5D. Dimensions

The size of the item is always the last element in the physical description area (unless, of course, accompanying material is present). It is separated from the other physical details element by space - semicolon - space and subfield ‡c. Unlike most other library items, sound recording discs are measured in inches, because this is the standard measurement used in the recording industry.[2] Dimensions are omitted for rolls, cartridges, and cassettes if they are standard size.

6.5E. Accompanying material

As explained under 1.5E, accompanying material may be added as the last element of the physical description area if its description is simple. Figure 6-18 shows an example of a recording issued as a serial. Each disc is accompanied by a booklet containing the text of the disc so that the child listener can read along with the recording. Because the booklets were issued regularly with the recordings, they may be added as the last element of the physical description area (12.5E1).

However, if authorship or publication details are different from those on the main item being cataloged, either give the accompanying material a separate entry (1.5E1; see figure 1-96) or list the accompanying material in a note (6.7B11; see figure 6-2).

Figure 6-18.   Accompanying material

```
100 0    ‡a Miranda, ‡d 1912-
245 10   ‡a Reading records ‡h [sound recording].
260      ‡a Memphis, Tenn. : ‡b Reading Records, ‡c p1963-
300      ‡a sound discs : ‡b analog, 33 1/3 rpm, mono. ; ‡c 12 in. + ‡e booklets.
362 0    ‡a Vol. 1- = RR1001- .
500      ‡a Series: RR1000. Each v. numbered separately in addition to general number.
500      ‡a "(ASCAP-Muhoberac-Huddleston) with Mary Shelton."
521      ‡a Preschool children.
520      ‡a Stories and poems, told by Miranda, with booklet for the child to read along with the
         recording.
700 1    ‡a Shelton, Mary.
```

Disc label

Reading Records   RR1001
Monaural   33 1/3 RPM
Vol. 1   Side 1
(ASCAP-Muhoberac-Huddleston) with Mary Shelton
Copyright 1963 by Reading Records, Inc.
Memphis, Tenn.

6.6. SERIES AREA

See *Handbook* at 1.6 for general directions and examples; see also figures 6-3 and 6-16.

6.7. NOTE AREA

Notes follow the general order and are of the same type as notes listed under 1.7; see discussion at 1.7 in this *Handbook*.

6.7B1. Nature or artistic form and medium of performance. If the form or medium of performance for a musical work is not evident from the title or the uniform title, a note should be given (see figure 6-5). This is recorded in a 500 field.

6.7B2. Language. Such a note is appropriate either for spoken or sung recordings unless the language is evident from the rest of the description (see figure 6-6 for an instance in which a note about the language is appropriate). Use a 546 field for this note.

6.7B3. Source of title proper. See discussion under 6.0B1 for circumstances in which the cataloger should give a note in a 500 field indicating the source of the title proper (see figure 6-14).

6.7B4. Variations in title. Rather frequently, title information on the record sleeve or other container will differ, sometimes markedly, from title information on the label of the item. If the difference is enough to affect filing, give it a separate title added entry (see figure 6-19). A note will be generated from the 246 field (see discussion in the *Handbook* at 1.7B4).

6.7B5. Parallel titles and other title information. A long subtitle may be omitted from the body of the catalog entry and given as a note in a 500 field (see *AACR2R* 1.1E3 and 1.7B5 for guidance).

6.7B6. Statements of responsibility. As already noted, names of performers ordinarily are not transcribed as part of the formal statement of responsibility in the body of the entry. If, in the cataloger's opinion, names of singers, readers, orchestra, etc., are important, these names should be given in a note. The note may be quoted from the prescribed source if it is concise; otherwise, the cataloger should make up a brief descriptive note. This note is recorded in the 511 field (see figures 6-1, 6-2, etc.). Make added entries for the principal performers.

6.7B7. Edition and history. Note the date and place of recording in a 518 field if it is readily ascertainable (i.e., if it is mentioned on the disc or in the accompanying material) (see figures 6-1, 6-2, etc.).

Figure 6-19.   Variant title

```
028 02   ‡a LM 2268 ‡b RCA Victor
100 1    ‡a Fox, Virgil, ‡d 1912-1980.
245 10   ‡a Virgil Fox playing the organ at the Riverside Church ‡h [sound recording].
246 1    ‡i Title on container: ‡a Virgil Fox encores
260      ‡a [New York] : ‡b RCA Victor, ‡c p1959.
300      ‡a 1 sound disc : ‡b analog, 33 1/3 rpm, mono. ; ‡c 12 in.
500      ‡a Program notes by C. O'Connell on container.
505 0    ‡a Fugue in G minor (the little) / J.S. Bach -- Canon in B minor / Schumann -- Jesu, joy of
         man's desiring / J.S. Bach -- Concerto no. 4 in F. First movement. Allegro / Handel -- Ye
         sweet retreat / Boyce -- Thou art the rock / Mulet -- Trumpet tune and air / Purcell -- Trio
         sonata no. 6 in G / J.S. Bach -- Tenth concerto for strings. Aria / Handel -- Now thank we
         all our God / J.S. Bach -- Air on the G string / J.S. Bach -- Symphony no. 5 in F minor, op.
         42, no. 1. Toccata / Widor.
```

```
Disc label                        RCA Victor
                          "New Orthophonic" High Fidelity
                             LM-2268    Side 1
                           (J2RP-8490)    Red Seal
                  Band 1—J.S. Bach    Fugue in G minor (the Little)
                     Band 2—Schumann    Canon in B minor
                  Band 3—J.S. Bach    Jesu, Joy of Man's Desiring
                     Band 4—Handel    Concerto no. 4 in F
                        First Movement: Allegro
                     Band 5—Boyce    Ye Sweet Retreat
                         (Arr.: Harold Bauer)
                     Band 6—Mulet    Thou Art the Rock
                            Virgil Fox
                 Playing the Organ at The Riverside Church
                              Monaural
                Tmk(s) Registered—Marca(s) Registrada(s)—
                      Radio Corporation of America
                            Made in U.S.A.
```

6.7B10. Physical description. In addition to other important physical details, duration times may be given for a multipart item without a collective title that has been described as a unit (see figure 6-13). Notes on physical description are recorded in 500 fields.

Many libraries are now formulating a note incorporating the three-letter code found on compact discs, e.g., "Compact disc (ADD)." Such a note assumes that the catalog user understands the meaning of the code, which may become more and more a valid assumption as people become accustomed to the terminology of compact discs. There are basically three codes, DDD, ADD, and AAD. In any of the three positions, "D" stands for "digital" and "A" stands for "analog." The letter in the first position indicates the type of recording made at the original recording session; the second position indicates the type of equipment used during mixing and editing; the third position indicates the type of equipment used in mastering the disc itself. Thus, DDD means that all aspects of the recording, from the original session to the mastering, are digital; ADD means that the original recording was analog, but mixing, editing, and mastering were digital; and AAD means that the original recording and the mixing or editing were analog, but the final disc mastering was digital.

6.7B11. Accompanying material. See figures 6-1, 6-2, etc., for appropriate notes.

6.7B14. Audience. As for other types of materials, an audience note may be appropriate for a sound recording (see figure 6-18 and discussion in *Handbook* at 1.7B14).

6.7B16. Other formats. If other formats (disc, cartridge, cassette, etc.) are known, this information is given in a 530 note (see figure 6-5). The Schwann catalog is one of the sources for this kind of information. The cataloger should not do extensive research to discover this, however.

6.7B17. Summary. A brief summary may be given in the 520 field for the contents of a spoken sound recording (see figures 6-2, 6-10, and 6-18).

6.7B18. Contents. List titles of individual works cataloged under a collective title in a 505 note if these are considered important. Follow title and statement of responsibility pattern as directed in 1.7B18. If time is given for individual works, include this information (see, for example, figure 6-5).

6.7B19. Publishers' numbers. According to *AACR1* rule 252C1, serial album and record numbers were recorded as part of the imprint (publication area). With *AACR2* (1978) these numbers were removed from this area; they are listed as a note. In MARC format, however, publishers' numbers for sound recordings are not recorded in a note (5XX) field; rather they are recorded in the 028 field with the indicators "02." The number is recorded in subfield ‡a; the source (usually the name of the record company) is recorded in subfield ‡b. The indicators "02" cause the system to generate a note to the patron with the display "Publisher no.:". See figures throughout this chapter.

6.7B21. "With" notes. See figures 6-9 and 6-15 for examples.

NOTES

1. General information about MARC coding is found in the introduction to this *Handbook;* details about coding the descriptive portion of the record are found throughout chapter 1; information about the coding of main and added access points is found at the beginning of chapter 14. An explanation of the MARC authorities format is given in *Handbook* chapters 15, 17, and 18. Information about specific MARC fields may be found by consulting the index under "MARC fields."

2. The National Library of Canada has made a policy decision to use metric measurements throughout the catalog record, including the dimensions of sound recordings. A Canadian library should therefore record, for example, "30 cm." rather than "12 in." for a standard LP, "12 cm." rather than "4 3/4 in." for a CD. Other libraries will continue to measure sound recordings in inches (Howarth, at 6.5).

CHAPTER 7

MOTION PICTURES AND VIDEO-RECORDINGS

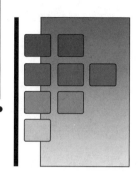

AACR2R chapter 7 includes rules for the descriptive cataloging of all types of media involving a sequence of images projected in rapid succession so that they create the illusion of movement. These include videorecordings with all of their manifestations. Also included are motion pictures, which come in many packages such as film cartridges and film cassettes as well as film reels. Filmstrips are not included in this chapter. For rules governing filmstrips, see *AACR2R* chapter 8, "Graphic Materials."

The problem of main entry for motion pictures has troubled catalogers for many years. British cataloging authority Anthony Croghan feels that a film "is a collaborative work, and there are essentially three authors: the director, the cameraman, and the scriptwriter. The director is the principal author, and the cameraman and scriptwriter are secondary authors."[1] Following Croghan's line of reasoning, main entry for films would be the name of the director. But Croghan's idea has had little support among catalogers. Previous cataloging codes were in agreement in stipulating title main entry for all motion pictures.

The present rules for choice of access points (*AACR2R* chapter 21) make no specific mention of motion pictures as such; the same rules of authorship responsibility that govern other types of library materials are to be applied to motion pictures and videorecordings. In most instances, numerous people and many different groups contribute in various ways to the creation of the intellectual or artistic content of a motion picture or videorecording (see figures 7-1 and 7-2).[2] Because of this diffusion of responsibility, main entry for most motion pictures will continue to be under title according to *AACR2R* practice as it was under previous rules.

A film may be sponsored by a society, corporation, institution, or other corporate body.[3] If the content of the film is "of an administrative nature dealing with the corporate body," its procedures, or its operations, main entry will be under the name of the sponsoring body (21.1B2a). Figure 7-3 is of this type. The example shown in figure 7-4 is not; entry is under title.

Figure 7-1.   Motion picture—entry under title

```
245 00   ‡a Japanese tea ceremony ‡h [motion picture] / ‡c Walt Disney Productions.
260      ‡a Santa Ana, Calif. : ‡b Doubleday Multimedia, ‡c 1971.
300      ‡a 1 film cartridge (4 min.) : ‡b si., col. ; ‡c super 8 mm. + ‡e 1 study guide.
440  0   ‡a Japan series
500      ‡a From the 1961 motion picture entitled: Japan harvests the sea.
500      ‡a Released by International Communications Films in 1968.
520      ‡a Shows the teahouse and the complete ritual, including trained young ladies as
         hostesses, the preparation of tea, and proper etiquette.
710 2    ‡a Walt Disney Productions.
740 0    ‡a Japan harvests the sea.
```

Figure 7-2.   Motion picture—entry under title

```
020      ‡a 0792814223
245 00   ‡a I am a fugitive from a chain gang ‡h [videorecording] / ‡c Warner Bros. Pictures, Inc. ;
         by Robert E. Burns.
260      ‡a Culver City, Calif. : ‡b MGM/UA Home Video : ‡b Turner Entertainment, ‡c [1992]
300      ‡a 1 videodisc (93 min.) : ‡b sd., b&w ; ‡c 12 in.
511 1    ‡a Paul Muni, Glenda Farrell, Helen Vinson, Noel Francis.
508      ‡a Director, Mervyn LeRoy ; screenplay, Howard J. Green, Brown Holmes ; photography,
         Sol Polito.
538      ‡a LaserDisc CLV.
520      ‡a An ex-soldier wrongly condemned to hard labor on a Georgia chain gang suffers
         cruelty and misery.
500      ‡a Videodisc release of the 1932 motion picture by Warner Bros. Pictures, Inc.
500      ‡a Based on the novel I am a fugitive from a Georgia chain gang by Robert Elliott Burns,
         who in real life was sentenced to a chain gang after taking part in a minor robbery. The
         brutalities of the chain gang were so emphatically exposed that there was a public outcry
         when this film was shown, resulting in drastic reforms of the system.
500      ‡a Videodisc LD70.
700 1    ‡a Muni, Paul, ‡d 1895-1967.
700 1    ‡a LeRoy, Mervyn, ‡d 1900-1987.
700 1    ‡a Green, Howard J., ‡d 1893-1965.
700 1    ‡a Holmes, Brown.
700 1    ‡a Polito, Sol, ‡d 1892-1960.
700 1    ‡a Burns, Robert Elliott. ‡t I am a fugitive from a Georgia chain gang.
710 2    ‡a Warner Bros. Pictures.
```

Figure 7-3.   Main entry under corporate body

```
110 2    ‡a TRW Electronics Group.
245 10   ‡a Beats reading the annual report ‡h [motion picture] / ‡c [sponsored by] TRW
         Electronics Group ; produced for TRW Electronics Group by TRW Systems Group,
         Motion Picture Department.
260      ‡a [Redondo Beach, Calif. : ‡b Distributed by TRW Systems Group, ‡c 1970]
300      ‡a 1 film reel (ca. 15 min.) : ‡b sd., col. ; ‡c 16 mm.
520      ‡a Shows electronic products manufactured by TRW Electronics Group operations for the
         previous year.
710 2    ‡a TRW Systems Group. ‡b Motion Picture Dept.
```

Figure 7-4.   A sponsored motion picture

```
245 00   ‡a Boeing 737 ‡h [motion picture].
260      ‡a Seattle : ‡b Cameron Film Productions Co., ‡c 1967.
300      ‡a 1 film reel (ca. 6 min.) : ‡b sd., col. ; ‡c 16 mm.
500      ‡a Sponsored by Boeing Company.
520      ‡a Describes the flight testing program of the twin engine, short range Boeing 737 jet
         liner.
710 2    ‡a Boeing Company.
710 2    ‡a Cameron Film Productions.
```

Motion pictures are frequently based on books. Entry for such works normally is covered by 21.9, because in virtually every instance such versions involve substantial changes in the nature and content of the original, to say nothing of the fact that the medium of expression is different. *AACR2R* rule 21.9 stipulates that main entry will be under the heading "appropriate to the new work." Because many individuals normally are involved in the production of films, entry under the name of an adapter is usually not possible. Title main entry should be made, with a name-title added entry for the original work (see figures 7-2 and 7-5).

The example shown in figure 7-6 is an unusual twist on the standard pattern of a motion picture adaptation of a previously published book. In this case, the motion picture was produced first, followed a year later by a faithful reproduction in book format under the same title, *Arrow to the Sun.* The film and the book, which won the Caldecott Award, are both by Gerald McDermott. He wrote the script of the motion picture, designed and drew the animated cartoons, and directed and produced the entire film. His responsibility for the intellectual and artistic content of the film is clear. Entry is under his name. In the record for the book, a note is made to indicate publication of the film version (see figure 7-7).

Examples given above illustrate several ways of entering a motion picture in the library catalog. The rules for main entry for motion pictures may be summarized by stating once again that general principles governing authorship apply to motion pictures as well as to other types of library materials. If authorship responsibility can be attributed by definitions and rules of 21.1, entry will be under personal or corporate author. However, the difficulties involved in ascribing authorship or creator responsibility for most motion pictures mean that, as a general rule, they will be entered under title.

7.0B. Sources of information

The chief source of information for films, as it is for other library items, is the item itself. When a book is cataloged, the title page is the chief source of information. By analogy the chief source of information for a film is the title frame(s). If the film is permanently encased in a cassette or cartridge, a label appearing on this container is also regarded as a chief source.

Figure 7-5.   Motion picture adaptation of a book

```
028 32   ‡a 36 VS ‡b Walt Disney Home Video
245 00   ‡a Alice in Wonderland ‡h [videorecording] / ‡c Walt Disney Productions ; story, Winston
         Hibler ... [et al.] ; directors, Clyde Geronimi, Hamilton Luske, Wilfred Jackson.
260      ‡a Burbank, Calif. : ‡b Walt Disney Home Video, ‡c [1983?]
300      ‡a 1 videocassette (75 min.) : ‡b sd., col. ; ‡c 1/2 in.
508      ‡a Musical score by Oliver Wallace.
500      ‡a Based on: Alice's adventures in Wonderland / Lewis Carroll.
500      ‡a Originally issued as motion picture in 1951.
500      ‡a Closed-captioned for the hearing impaired.
520      ‡a Alice falls through a rabbit hole and ends up in Wonderland.
700 1    ‡a Carroll, Lewis, ‡d 1832-1898. ‡t Alice's adventures in Wonderland.
700 1    ‡a Hibler, Winston.
700 1    ‡a Geronimi, Clyde.
700 1    ‡a Luske, Hamilton S.
700 1    ‡a Jackson, Wilfred.
700 1    ‡a Wallace, Oliver, ‡d 1887-1963.
710 2    ‡a Walt Disney Productions.
```

Title frames   The Classics
                              Walt Disney Home Video
                              ──────────

                              Walt Disney Presents
                              ──────────

                              Alice in Wonderland
                          an adaptation of Lewis Carroll's
                       The Adventures of Alice in Wonderland
                          and Through the Looking Glass
                              color by Technicolor
                              ──────────

                          [very long list of credits,
        including various types of editors and others involved in the production]
                              ──────────

                      Copyright MCMLI Walt Disney Productions
                              ──────────

                        Musical score by Oliver Wallace
                              ──────────

                Story by Winston Hibler [and about a dozen others]
                              ──────────

            Directors, Clyde Geronimi, Hamilton Luske, Wilfred Jackson
                    Production supervisor Ben Sharpsteen

Container (outer box)   The Classics
                              Walt Disney Home Video
                         Walt Disney's Alice in Wonderland
                          Running time: 75 minutes/color
                    Closed-captioned for the hearing impaired by
                         the National Captioning Institute
            Distributed by Buena Vista Home Video, Burbank, California 91521

Figure 7-6.   Motion picture entered under creator

100 1	‡a McDermott, Gerald.
245 10	‡a Arrow to the sun ‡h [motion picture] : ‡b a Pueblo Indian tale / ‡c designed and directed by Gerald McDermott ; produced by Gerald McDermott & Texture Films, inc.
260	‡a [New York] : ‡b Texture Films, ‡c c1973.
300	‡a 1 film reel (ca. 15 min.) : ‡b sd., col. ; ‡c 16 mm.
500	‡a With study guide.
508	‡a Music, Thomas Wagner; camera, Frank Koenig; voice of the boy, Joquin Brant; story and research consultant, Charles Hofmann.
520	‡a Pueblo Indian myth about a boy's search for his father, the Lord of the Sun, including his voyage to the sky and back to the earth.
710 2	‡a Texture Films, inc.

Figure 7-7.   Book version of a film

020	‡a 0670133698
100 1	‡a McDermott, Gerald.
245 10	‡a Arrow to the sun : ‡b a Pueblo Indian tale / ‡c adapted and illustrated by Gerald McDermott.
260	‡a New York : ‡b Viking, ‡c c1974.
300	‡a 1 v. (unpaged) : ‡b col. ill. ; ‡c 25 x 29 cm.
520	‡a Pueblo Indian myth about a boy's search for his father, the Lord of the Sun, including his voyage to the sky and back to the earth.
500	‡a Book version of the 1973 film produced by Gerald McDermott and Texture Films, inc.

Some films lack title frames. If no printed information appears on the film, accompanying material may furnish information or a title presented orally on the film may be used.

7.1. TITLE AND STATEMENT OF RESPONSIBILITY AREA

The title must be transcribed from the chief source—in most cases, the title frame(s) of the film. The statement of responsibility may also include information from accompanying material; such information should be enclosed in brackets (1.1F1). Title frames at the beginning of the film and frames at the end may include pertinent information to be recorded in the title and statement of responsibility area. Some information on the title or end frames may be given about individuals whose contribution to the film is best included in the note area (7.1F1). Other information may be ignored if it is not important to the cataloging agency (7.7B6). If material is omitted from transcription of title and end frames, do not indicate such omission by ellipses.

7.1B. Title proper

Transcribe the title in subfield ‡a of the 245 field as it appears on the title frames, following the general rules under 1.1B. If the title on the title frame includes a statement of responsibility, transcribe it as it appears (see figure 7-6). In a departure from the general rules of transcribing the title exactly as it appears (see discussion at 1.1B2), the Library of Congress has instructed its catalogers not to consider credits for performer, author, director, producer, etc., that precede or follow the title or part of the title proper, even though they are grammatically an integral part of the title. The title proper of "Twentieth Century Fox presents Star Wars" is "Star Wars"; that of "Steve McQueen in Bullitt" is "Bullitt" (see *LCRI* 7.1B1, Feb. 1, 1989, for further details). In figure 7-5, the title proper of "Walt Disney presents Alice in Wonderland" is "Alice in Wonderland."

7.1C. *Optional addition.* General material designation

Add in brackets "motion picture" or "videorecording" as appropriate, immediately following the title proper and subfield ‡h.

7.1C2. A sound track is considered a part of a motion picture or videorecording even if it is physically separate from the film, so long as it is "synchronized with the item and intended to be played with it." The GMD appropriate to the film should be used. A large film library may, however, have sound track film not accompanied by visual material. These should be cataloged using the rules of *AACR2R* chapter 6, with GMDs appropriate to that chapter (see 7.0A1).

The National Library of Australia will catalog interactive videodiscs under this chapter rather than chapter 9 ("Computer Files") (Howarth, at 7.1C2). Other national libraries have not made an official decision on this matter. However, U.S. libraries should use *Guidelines for Bibliographic Description of Interactive Multimedia* (Chicago: American Library Association, 1994), discussed in *Handbook* chapter 9.

7.1E. Other title information

Other title information is transcribed, following general rule 1.1E, as it appears in the chief source of information (see figure 7-8).

7.1F. Statements of responsibility

Ordinarily, three types of activity enter into the creation of a motion picture. The sponsor, if the film has one, has a primary role that often includes promoting the initial idea of the film, financing the production, and arranging for production. Boeing Company is the sponsor of the film illustrated by figure 7-4. The producer or production company is responsible for the mechanics of making the motion picture. In figure 7-2, Warner Bros. Pictures is a production company. A releasing agent issues the completed motion picture to the public. In figure 7-5, Walt Disney Home Video is a releasing agent.

Figure 7-8. Other title information—a videorecording

```
245 00   ‡a Governance in the academic library ‡h [videorecording] : ‡b a program / ‡c presented
         under the auspices of the Committee on Academic Status of the Association of College
         and Research Libraries.
260      ‡a Chicago : ‡b Distributed by ACRL, ‡c 1974.
300      ‡a 1 videocassette (ca. 40 min.) : ‡b sd., b&w ; ‡c 3/4 in.
500      ‡a Participants: David Laird, Jane Flener, Ellsworth Mason, Stuart Forth, and Frederick
         Duda; moderator, Eldred Smith.
520      ‡a Patterns of administration in academic libraries, a panel discussion.
538      ‡a Sony U-Matic, UC-60.
710 2    ‡a Association of College and Research Libraries. ‡b Committee on Academic Status.
```

7.1F1. This rule limits information included in the statement of responsibility to persons or bodies actually involved in the production of the film. While flexible and allowing for cataloger judgment, the rule generally limits persons or bodies named in the statement of responsibility to producers, directors, and writers (see *LCRI* 7.1F1, Jan. 5, 1989, and *LCRI* 7.7B6, Mar. 5, 1990). The name of the releasing agent or distributor is given as part of the publication area; names of other persons or groups, such as principal performers, etc., are given in a note, even if they appear in the chief source of information. The rationale for this distinction is that the sponsoring body, the producer, etc., have a type of author-creator responsibility; thus, these names, if they are listed "prominently," should be transcribed as part of the statement of responsibility. If such names are not listed "prominently," and their relationship to the film should be brought out, give the information in a note (see figure 7-4: the title frame for this film gives title only. Sponsor information was found in *Educator's Guide to Free Films,* 1973). The releasing agent and the distributor perform different functions; these names should appear in the publication area.

7.1F2. If the relationship between the work and a person or body named in the statement of responsibility is not clear, add a word or phrase in brackets (see figure 7-3).

7.1F3. If the names of both the sponsor and the producer are given in a single statement of responsibility, the information will be so transcribed. Whether the sponsor's name is given as the main entry depends, obviously, on the nature of the material (see *AACR2R* 21.1B2 for guidance). In the example shown in figure 7-3, main entry is under the name of the sponsor (agency for which the film was produced) because the film concerns itself with the activities of the sponsor (21.1B2a).

7.1G. Items without a collective title

7.1G1. The Library of Congress will use either method of cataloging (describing the item as a unit or making a separate description for each separately titled part), depending on the situation (*LCRI* 7.1G1, Jan. 5, 1989). The National Library of Canada's decision is to describe the item only as a unit (Howarth, at 7.1G1). Other national libraries have not made a decision on 7.1G1.

7.4. PUBLICATION, DISTRIBUTION, ETC., AREA

7.4C. Place of publication, distribution, etc.

Place is always included as the first element of the publication, distribution, etc., area. However, this information is not always given on the film, nor is it always included with the material that may accompany the film. The following are good sources of general information about films that will be helpful in giving the location of distributors, releasing agents, etc.

> *The American Film Institute Catalog of Motion Pictures Produced in the United States.* New York: R. R. Bowker, 1971– .
>
> *The Film Daily Year Book* (later titled *The Film Daily Year Book of Motion Pictures* and *Film TV Daily Yearbook*) (annual). New York: J. W. Alicoate, 1928– .
>
> *International Motion Picture Almanac* (also titled *Motion Picture Almanac* and *Motion Picture and Television Almanac*) (annual). New York: Quigley Pub. Co., 1929– .
>
> *International Television Almanac* (later titled *International Television and Video Almanac*) (annual). New York: Quigley Pub. Co., 1956– .
>
> *Variety* (weekly). New York: Variety Pub. Co., 1905– .

7.4D. Name of publisher, distributor, etc.

As previously mentioned, note that the name of the releasing agent and distributor are among the types of bodies that should be included as the second element of this area (see figure 7-5).

7.4F. Date of publication, distribution, release, etc.

The date is recorded as the last element of the area. A date of original production that is different from the distribution date may optionally be given in the note area (see figure 7-1, note 2). The Library of Congress will apply this option if the difference in dates is more than two years (*LCRI* 7.4F2, Jan. 5, 1989).

7.5. PHYSICAL DESCRIPTION AREA

The physical description area for motion pictures and videorecordings, like the physical description area for other types of library materials, is divided into the three major elements described in 7.5B–7.5D.

7.5B. Extent of item

The number of physical units followed by one of the specific material designators listed under 7.5B1 is the first element in the physical description area. If the GMD is used following the title proper, the words "film" and "video" may be omitted from the specific material designators. Following Library of Congress decision, "film" and "video" have not been omitted from specific material designation in this text.

7.5B2. If the playing time is stated on the item, on the container, or elsewhere, it is listed following the extent of the item (see 1.5B4).

7.5C. Other physical details

For all types of motion pictures and videorecordings, indicate whether the film is sound or silent, and whether it is in color or black and white. In addition, give special characteristics as stipulated in the rules.

7.5D. Dimensions

The critical dimension for a motion picture or a videorecording, because it affects hardware used for playback, is the width of the film. A motion picture film is measured in millimeters, a videotape in inches or millimeters, as appropriate; videodiscs (laser discs) are measured in inches.[4] Figure 7-1 is an example of the stipulation in 7.5D2 for 8 mm. films.

7.5E. Accompanying material

Follow directions in 1.5E for recording accompanying material at the end of the physical description area. For example, see figure 7-1.

7.7. NOTE AREA

Notes follow the general order and are based on types given under 1.7, which see for guidance.

7.7B2. Language. Notes indicating the presence of a foreign language not evident from the rest of the description are recorded in the 546 field.

Also included under this type of note is the presence of closed-captioning. If the film is closed-captioned, give the note "Closed-captioned for the hearing impaired" (*LCRI* 7.7B2, Jan. 5, 1989; see figure 7-5) in a 500 field.

7.7B6. Statements of responsibility. This note lists performers and other individuals not directly involved with the production of the film or with its sponsorship and, thus, according to 7.1F1, not to be given in the title and statement of responsibility area in the formal part of the description. This note is flexible; list names considered by the cataloging agency to be of importance (see, e.g., figures 7-5, 7-6, and 7-8). If these notes are from credits in the film, they should be recorded in a 508 field, which automatically generates the display constant "Credits:" at the beginning of the note; otherwise use a 500 field. Sometimes the statement of responsibility note may be combined with the summary note in a 520 field (see figure 7-9 for an example).

7.7B7.   Edition and history. For examples of this type of note, see figures 7-1, 7-5, etc.

7.7B10.   Physical description. (7.7B10f, *Videorecording system.*) Because motion pictures and videorecordings are produced in so many different formats, the cataloger should inform the catalog user what system will be necessary to play the film for unusual formats. This information is recorded in a MARC 538 field. For examples, see figures 7-2 and 7-8.[5]

7.7B17. Summary. Because film and videorecording collections are not easy to browse through, a brief summary note is important unless the content of the item is evident from other parts of the catalog entry (see previous examples). Sometimes such a note may combine information about the content of the film and persons responsible for it, as in the example shown in figure 7-9. A summary note is recorded in the 520 field.

7.7B19. Numbers. Most numbers borne by an item and considered important by the cataloging agency should be given in a 500 field. Publishers' numbers, however, should be given in the 028 field with the indicators coded "32" (see figure 7-5).

Figure 7-9.   Summary note

245 00	‡a Apollo 11 ‡h [motion picture] : ‡b man on the moon : official NASA footage.
260	‡a [Burbank, Calif.] : ‡b U. S. National Aeronautics and Space Administration ; ‡b Released by Columbia Pictures 8 mm Division, ‡c 1969.
300	‡a 1 film reel (9 min.) : ‡b si., b&w ; ‡c super 8 mm.
500	‡a Issued in standard 8 mm. and in super 8 mm.
500	‡a Also issued in col.
520	‡a Motion pictures taken by Neil Armstrong and Michael Collins during the first moon landing, July 1969.
700 1	‡a Armstrong, Neil, ‡d 1930-
700 1	‡a Collins, Michael, ‡d 1930-
710 1	‡a United States. ‡b National Aeronautics and Space Administration.

NOTES

1. "A Feasibility Study of a Multimedia Catalog," in *Bibliographic Control of Nonprint Media,* ed. Pierce Grove (Chicago: American Library Association, 1972), p. 134.
2. General information about MARC coding is found in the introduction to this *Handbook*; details about coding the descriptive portion of the record are found throughout chapter 1; information about the coding of main and added access points is found at the beginning of chapter 14. An explanation of the MARC authorities format is given in *Handbook* chapters 15, 17, and 18. Information about specific MARC fields may be found by consulting the index under "MARC fields."
3. A sponsor is "the company, institution, organization, or individual other than the producer who finances the production of the material. Sponsorship often involves the promotion, either directly or indirectly, of a product or point of view" (Alma M. Tillin and William J. Quinly, *Standards for Cataloging Nonprint Materials,* 4th ed. [Washington, D.C.: AECT, 1976], p. 16).
4. As allowed under *AACR2R* 0.28, the National Library of Canada will use only metric measurements throughout the record. Canadian libraries will not use inches in area 7.5.
5. In addition to the note required by 7.7B10f, the National Library of Australia has authorized Australian catalogers to include this information in the extent of item part of the physical description area (7.5B1), as "1 videocassette (VHS)" (Howarth, at 7.5B2). This practice had been authorized under certain circumstances by *AACR2* (1978) rules, but was discontinued under *AACR2R*, so catalogers outside of Australia should only give the note.

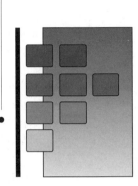

GRAPHIC MATERIALS

AACR2R chapter 7 dealt with rules for the description of pictures that give the illusion of movement when projected. In contrast, chapter 8 covers all kinds of two-dimensional graphic materials, both opaque and transparent. Chapter 10 deals with three-dimensional materials.

The full rules given in chapter 8, as in other sections of *AACR2R* Part I, are appropriate only for the description and identification of materials felt to be of significance and of some permanent importance to the library's collection. Some of the kinds of graphic materials included in chapter 8 may be ephemeral in nature; these may be more appropriately cataloged according to minimum levels of description (see 1.0D) or possibly kept in a vertical file without cataloging. Examples and discussion in this text assume full cataloging.

Elizabeth W. Betz's *Graphic Materials: Rules for Describing Original Items and Historical Collections* (Washington, D.C.: Library of Congress, 1982) is designed to be used as a supplement to the rules contained in *AACR2* chapter 8. Betz's guide should be referred to when cataloging original materials or those that are historical in nature. *AACR2R* chapter 8 is primarily designed to cover published graphic materials of a current nature. However, its rules provide adequately for the identification of most original material that would be found in general libraries. See, for instance, figure 8-1, which

Figure 8-1. Entry under artist—art original

```
100 1    ‡a Mosley, Shelley.
245 00   ‡a [Black cat with yellow flower] ‡h [art original] / ‡c SM.
260      ‡c [1977]
300      ‡a 1 art original : ‡b acrylic on poster board ; ‡c 16 × 27 cm.
500      ‡a Title supplied by cataloger.
500      ‡a Unmounted.
```

has been cataloged according to *AACR2R* chapter 8, as have all examples in this chapter of the *Handbook*.[1]

The general rules for main and added entries as given in *AACR2R* chapter 21 apply to graphics as they do to other types of library materials. For example, in cataloging an original art work, the artist is regarded as the "author" of the work. Entry will be under the name of the artist (21.1A1) as shown in figure 8-1.

Following the same principles of authorship responsibility, a photographic or other photomechanical reproduction of an art work will be entered under the name of the original artist (21.16B) (see figure 8-2).

The rationale behind entry of a photographic or other photomechanical reproduction of an art work under the original artist's name is the same as that governing other facsimile reproductions also entered under the heading for the original work. However, art librarians feel that other forms of reproduction involving another artist's intervention (e.g., a person who executes the engraving, the lithograph, etc.) constitute adaptations in the same sense that a literary work rewritten in a different literary form (e.g., a novel adapted as a play) is an adaptation (*AACR2R* 21.10). Thus, if an art work is adapted from one medium to another (e.g., an engraving is made from an oil painting), such a work will be entered under the heading for the adapter (see the examples under *AACR2R* 21.16A).

In the examples shown in figures 8-3 and 8-4, Phillipe Galle made an engraving from Pieter Bruegel's tempera painting *Death of the Virgin*. Although placement of the figures is the same, it is evident that Galle's work is an adaptation of the original, not a reproduction.

Except for 21.16, chapter 21 does not refer specifically to graphic materials. The basic assumption of the Paris Principles, which calls for main

Figure 8-2.   Entry under artist—art reproduction

```
100 1    ‡a Manet, Edouard, ‡d 1832-1883.
245 14   ‡a The fifer ‡h [art reproduction] / ‡c Manet.
260      ‡a [New York] : ‡b Shorewood Press, ‡c [19--]
300      ‡a 1 art reproduction : ‡b photogravure, col. ; ‡c 57 × 70 cm.
500      ‡a Original in Musée du Louvre, Paris.
500      ‡a Unmounted.
710 2    ‡a Musée du Louvre.
```

Figure 8-3.   Entry under artist—art original

```
100 1    ‡a Bruegel, Pieter, ‡d ca. 1525-1569.
245 14   ‡a [The death of the Virgin] ‡h [art original].
260      ‡c [1564]
300      ‡a 1 art original : ‡b tempera on wood, col. ; ‡c 26 × 55 cm.
```

Figure 8-4.   Entry under adapter—engraving based on art original

```
100 1    ‡a Galle, Philippe, ‡d 1537-1612.
245 14   ‡a [The death of the Virgin] ‡h [art reproduction].
260      ‡a [1574]
300      ‡a 1 art print : ‡b engraving, b&w ; ‡c 31 × 42 cm.
500      ‡a Based on the tempera painting by Pieter Bruegel the Elder.
700 1    ‡a Bruegel, Pieter, ‡d ca. 1525-1569. ‡t Death of the Virgin.
```

entry under author or creator responsible for the intellectual or artistic content of a work when this can be determined, holds true equally for graphic materials as it does for books. And, as with other materials, if authorship responsibility is diffuse or indeterminate, main entry will be under title.

8.0B1. Chief source of information. As with other types of library materials, the chief source of information for a graphic item is the item itself. Only if the chief source does not include necessary information will cataloging data be taken from the container, accompanying textual material, or other sources. However, if an item consists of a number of physical parts with individual titles in a container that furnishes a collective title for the set, the container is to be preferred as the chief source of information. Rule 8.0B1 instructs the cataloger to make a note when the container is used as the chief source of information (see figure 8-5).

8.1. TITLE AND STATEMENT OF RESPONSIBILITY AREA

The prescribed source of information for transcription of this area is the chief source of information—in most cases, the item itself.

8.1B. Title proper

Follow general guidelines given in 1.1B for transcribing the title proper. Transcribe the title as it appears in the chief source of information. The title for the example shown in figure 8-6 was transcribed from the chart itself.

8.1C. *Optional addition.* General material designation

The GMD is to be added immediately following the title proper. British catalogers using the GMD will use "graphic" for all graphic materials. North American catalogers should select one of the following terms, as appropriate: activity card, art original, art reproduction, chart, filmstrip, flash card, picture, slide, technical drawing, or transparency (see list given under 1.1C1). Use the GMD "kit" (North American) or "multimedia" (British) in brackets when cataloging a set of two or more different types of media, designed to be used together, none of which is the dominant type (see figure 8-7).

Figure 8-5.   Container as chief source of information

```
245 00   ‡a Subtraction ‡h [flash card].
260      ‡a Racine, Wis. : ‡b Western Pub. Co., ‡c c1962.
300      ‡a 43 flash cards : ‡b col. ; ‡c 9 × 6 cm.
440  0   ‡a Whitman help yourself flash cards for home and school ; ‡v no. 4571:39
500      ‡a Title from container.
520      ‡a Prepares the child for abstract thinking in arithmetic.
```

Figure 8-6.   Title proper from chief source

```
245 04   ‡a The great ages of man ‡h [chart].
260      ‡a [New York : ‡b Time Inc., ‡c 1967]
300      ‡a 1 chart : ‡b col. ; ‡c 53 × 63 cm. folded to 27 × 21 cm.
520      ‡a Shows, in tabular form, principal events in western, central, and eastern civilizations
         from 4500 B.C. to the 20th century.
710 2    ‡a Time, inc.
```

Figure 8-7.   Kit as GMD

```
100 1    ‡a Bishop, Dorothy Sword.
245 10   ‡a Leonardo y Ramon ‡h [kit] : ‡b the story of the lion and the mouse / ‡c told in Spanish
         and English.
260      ‡a Skokie, Ill. : ‡b National Textbook Co., ‡c c1972.
300      ‡a 1 booklet, 1 filmstrip, 1 sound cassette, 1 teacher's guide ; ‡c in container 24 × 38 ×
         4 cm.
490 1    ‡a Fábulas bilingües = ‡a Bilingual fables
500      ‡a Adaptation by Dorothy Sword Bishop of the Aesopic fable, The lion and the mouse.
521 3    ‡a Designed for children who are in a language development program.
520      ‡a A tiny mouse saves the mighty lion when he becomes tangled in a net.
730 0    ‡a Lion and the mouse.
830  0   ‡a Fábulas bilingües.
```

Box cover

Leonardo y Ramon
The Story of the Lion and the Mouse
Told in Spanish and English

© National Textbook Company, Skokie, Illinois 60076

Bilingual Fables   Fábulas bilingües
A Series of Fables in Spanish and English
Una serie de fábulas en español e inglés

See 1.10 for special rules governing the cataloging of kits; see figure 1-129 for a further example of a kit.

8.1D. Parallel titles

Follow general directions under 1.1D for the transcription of parallel titles. Figure 8-8 shows an item in which the parallel title also includes "other title" information (see *AACR2R* 1.1E5 and discussion in this *Handbook* for general directions).

8.1F. Statements of responsibility

Follow general guidelines in 1.1F in transcribing the statements of responsibility. The title frame of the filmstrip cataloged in figure 8-9 furnished all of the information in the title and statement of responsibility area.

8.1F2. A word or phrase may be added if needed to clarify the relationship to the work of a person or corporate body included in the state-

Figure 8-8.   Parallel title

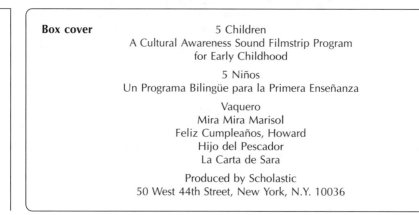

245 00	‡a 5 children ‡h [kit] : ‡b a cultural awareness sound filmstrip program for early childhood = 5 niños : un programa bilingüe para la primera enseñanza.
246 3	‡a Five children
246 30	‡a 5 niños
246 3	‡a Cinco niños
260	‡a New York : ‡b Scholastic, ‡c c1974.
300	‡a 5 filmstrips, 5 sound cassettes, 2 teacher's guides, 1 wallchart ; ‡c in container 21 × 22 × 5 cm.
546	‡a Sound recordings in Spanish; text on filmstrips in Spanish; teacher's guides in English.
521 1	‡a 003-008.
530	‡a Also available with sound discs.
520	‡a Teaches children to appreciate cultural differences.
505 0	‡a Vaquero = Cowboy (56 fr.) -- Mira mira Marisol = Mira mira Marisol (46 fr.) -- Feliz cumpleaños, Howard = Happy birthday, Howard (66 fr.) -- Hijo del pescador = Fisherman's son (61 fr.) -- La carta de Sara = Sara's letter (56 fr.).
710 2	‡a Scholastic Magazines, inc.

Box cover

5 Children
A Cultural Awareness Sound Filmstrip Program
for Early Childhood

5 Niños
Un Programa Bilingüe para la Primera Enseñanza

Vaquero
Mira Mira Marisol
Feliz Cumpleaños, Howard
Hijo del Pescador
La Carta de Sara

Produced by Scholastic
50 West 44th Street, New York, N.Y. 10036

Figure 8-9.   Statement of responsibility

245 00	‡a Media programs for individual schools ‡h [filmstrip] / ‡c produced by the American Library Association and the National Education Association.
260	‡a [Washington] : ‡b ALA and NEA, ‡c c1969.
300	‡a 1 filmstrip (75 fr.) : ‡b col. ; ‡c 35 mm. + ‡e 1 sound tape reel (10 min. : 3 3/4 ips, 1 track, mono. ; 5 in.) + 1 guide + 1 script.
500	‡a Based on the book: Standards for school media programs / prepared by the American Association of School Librarians and the Department of Audiovisual Instruction of the National Education Association ... [et al.].
520	‡a Stresses the usefulness and importance of school media programs.
710 2	‡a Joint Committee of the American Association of School Librarians and the Department of Audiovisual Instruction of the National Education Association. ‡t Standards for school media programs.
710 2	‡a American Library Association.
710 2	‡a National Education Association of the United States.

ment of responsibility. In the example shown in figure 8-10, each of the sixty posters in the set has a picture and some explanatory text. John M. Carroll wrote the text and selected the pictures. A brief phrase is added to clarify his responsibility. Because the posters have no common title, the guide accompanying the set has been used as the chief source (8.0B1).

8.2. EDITION AREA

The edition statement may be transcribed from the chief source of information, the container, or any accompanying material (8.0B2). Record the edition statement following general directions given in 1.2.

In the example shown in figure 8-11, each of the thirty-five presidential portraits includes a series statement, an edition statement, and the name of the publisher. Because the pictures do not have a collective title, this information has been transcribed from the booklet accompanying the pictures.

8.4. PUBLICATION, DISTRIBUTION, ETC., AREA

The three standard elements of the publication area (place, publisher [etc.], and date) will be transcribed following the general rules under 1.4.

8.4C2, 8.4D2. The conventional elements (place, publisher, date) of the publication area are inappropriate for the catalog entry for certain types of materials that are, in most instances, unique items. These include manuscripts (*AACR2R* chapter 4), some types of realia (*AACR2R* chapter 10), original art works, and unpublished photographs. For such items the publication area includes only the date of production (see 8.4F2 and 8.4F3; see also figures 8-1, 8-3, and 8-4).

Figure 8-10.   Phrase added to statement of responsibility

```
100 1    ‡a Carroll, John M.
245 10   ‡a American Indian posters ‡h [picture] / ‡c [text by] John M. Carroll.
260      ‡a [United States?] : ‡b Class National Pub., ‡c c1971.
300      ‡a 60 posters : ‡b b&w ; ‡c 28 × 43 cm. + ‡e 1 guide.
500      ‡a Title from guide.
```

Title page of guide	American Indian Posters
	John M. Carroll
	Copyright 1971 by Class National Publishing, Inc.

Figure 8-11.   Edition area

```
245 04   ‡a The Perry pictures of our thirty-five presidents ‡h [picture] / ‡c biographies by Olive M.
         Spring.
250      ‡a Boston ed.
260      ‡a Malden, Mass. : ‡b Perry Pictures, ‡c [196-]
300      ‡a 35 pictures : ‡b b&w ; ‡c 21 × 15 cm. + ‡e 1 booklet.
490 0    ‡a The Perry pictures
500      ‡a Title from booklet.
500      ‡a Portraits of U.S. presidents, George Washington through Lyndon B. Johnson.
700 1    ‡a Spring, Olive M.
710 2    ‡a Perry Pictures, inc.
```

Title page of booklet	The Perry Pictures of
	Our Thirty-Five Presidents
	Biographies by
	Olive M. Spring
	Perry Pictures, Inc.
	Malden, Mass.

8.5. PHYSICAL DESCRIPTION AREA

Following the general pattern of 1.5, the physical description area includes three elements, with a possible fourth if the item includes accompanying material.

8.5B. Extent of item (including specific material designation)

As with other types of library materials, the first element is the extent of the item and the specific material designation. A list of terms is given under 8.5B1. These terms are designed to describe the type of material more specifically, in most instances, than the GMD (see 1.1C1) allows. Preceded by the number of items, one of these terms appears as the first element of the physical description area.

Optionally, a more specific term may be used, phrased as concisely as possible. The Library of Congress will apply this option.

The terms defined and discussed below are among those listed as specific material designators (see also *AACR2R* Appendix D [Glossary]).

Art original. Generally speaking, an art original is a unique item. The GMD is "art original." The following rules specifically mention art originals: 8.5B1, 8.5C1, 8.5D4 (see figures 8-1 and 8-3 for examples of art originals).

Art print. An art print is a work reproduced from a plate, a woodblock, etc., that has been prepared by an artist. Lithographs, etchings, engravings, woodcuts, linoleum block prints, etc., are subsumed under this term. The GMD will be "art reproduction." It will not be "art original," according to the definition of the term given in Appendix D, unless the cataloger is cataloging the actual woodblock, etching plate, etc.

Sometimes an art print is a copy of an art original in another medium (see figure 8-4). In other cases, the original artist and the etcher, engraver, etc., are one and the same. In either case, main entry is under the name of the etcher, engraver, lithographer, etc.

If an art print is not commercially published, publication area data will appear as given in figure 8-4, even though the engraving may exist in a number of copies. On the other hand, some art prints are issued by commercial publishers. Conventional publication area data are appropriate for such an item (see the example shown in figure 8-12). Rules that may apply are 8.5B1, 8.5C1, 8.5C2, and 8.5D4.

Art reproduction. Any sort of photomechanical reproduction of an original art work or art print is called an art reproduction. Obviously, the qual-

Figure 8-12.   Art print

100 1	‡a Josset, Lawrence.
245 14	‡a The George Inn, Southwark ‡h [art reproduction] / ‡c drawn and etched by Lawrence Josset.
260 0	‡a Godalming [England] : ‡b Stevens & Brown, ‡c 1978.
300	‡a 1 art print : ‡b etching, b&w ; ‡c 17 × 24 cm.
500	‡a Extracted from: Calendarium Londinense, or, The London almanack for the year 1978.
710 2	‡a B.F. Stevens & Brown, Ltd.
740 0	‡a Calendarium Londinense.

Calendar   Calendarivm Londinense
or the London Almanack for the Year 1978
The George Inn
Southwark
drawn and etched by Lawrence Josset, A.R.C.A. (Lond.), R.E.
published by Stevens & Brown, Ltd.
Ardon House, Mill Lane, Godalming, Surrey.

ity of an art reproduction may vary according to the quality of the equipment used for the reproduction, but the end product is still regarded as being a representation of the original. The GMD "art reproduction" is used for an art reproduction (see figure 8-2 for an example of an art reproduction). Most art reproductions are commercially produced, as is this one; publication area will include all three of the conventional elements.

Some of the rules that may apply to art reproductions are 8.5B1, 8.5C1, 8.5C2, and 8.5D4.

Chart. See *AACR2R* Appendix D (Glossary) for definition. If a chart is designed with large print and illustrations in such a way that it can successfully be interpreted at a distance, and if it is meant to be displayed on a wall, use the specific material designation "wall chart" rather than "chart." The GMD "chart" will appear following the title proper for both charts and wall charts (see, for example, figure 8-6). Some of the rules for charts are 8.5B1 and 8.5D6.

Filmslip. As might be guessed, a filmslip is a short filmstrip, sometimes mounted so as to lie flat instead of being rolled, as a filmstrip generally is. The GMD "filmstrip" is used for both filmslips and filmstrips. All rules for filmstrips apply also to filmslips (e.g., 8.5B1, 8.5B2, 8.5B5, 8.5C1, 8.5C2, and 8.5D2).

The chief source of information for a filmslip, as for a filmstrip, is the film itself. Generally a title frame at the beginning and possibly a frame at the end will furnish information. Title and statement of responsibility information should come from either of these sources if possible. The container or accompanying material may be used for data for other parts of the catalog entry. In the example shown in figure 8-13, all of the cataloging

Figure 8-13.   Filmslip

245 00	‡a Different kinds of plants ‡h [filmstrip] / ‡c collaborator, Illa Podendorf ; produced by Encyclopaedia Britannica Films.
260	‡a [Wilmette, Ill.] : ‡b Encyclopaedia Britannica Films, ‡c c1963.
300	‡a 1 filmslip (14 fr.) : ‡b col. ; ‡c 35 mm. + ‡e 1 student guide.
440　0	‡a Plants around us
500	‡a Filmslip and student guide in plastic envelope 28 × 13 cm.
520	‡a Describes differences among plants, including size, age, and color.
700　1	‡a Podendorf, Illa.
710　2	‡a Encyclopaedia Britannica Films, inc.

Title frame   Plants Around Us

Different Kinds of Plants
Collaborator: Illa Podendorf
The University of Chicago Laboratory School
Produced by Encyclopaedia Britannica Films
©1963 by Encyclopaedia Britannica Films
Copyright and all rights of reproduction,
including by television, reserved.

information except for the location of Encyclopaedia Britannica Films appears on the title frame of the filmslip.

Filmstrip. See *AACR2R* Appendix D (Glossary) for definition. The GMD "filmstrip" is used following the title proper. The number of frames is to be added to the specific material designation "filmstrip" in the physical description area (see figure 8-14). If the frames are not numbered, count them, beginning with the first content frame and ending with the last content frame (8.5B2). Other special rules for filmstrips include 8.5B1, 8.5B5, 8.5C1, 8.5C2, and 8.5D2.

Flash card. See *AACR2R* Appendix D (Glossary) for definition. The GMD "flash card" is used following the title proper. The cards themselves are the chief source of information if they include a collective title. If not, use information on a container or accompanying material. The container served

Figure 8-14.   Filmstrip

245 00	‡a Walt Disney's Kidnapped ‡h [filmstrip] / ‡c adapted from the Walt Disney motion picture version of the novel by Robert Louis Stevenson ; produced by Encyclopaedia Britannica Films in cooperation with Walt Disney Productions and in collaboration with Paul A. Witty ; Oscar E. Sams, producer.
246 30	‡a Kidnapped
260	‡a [Wilmette, Ill.] : ‡b Encyclopaedia Britannica Films, ‡c c1960.
300	‡a 1 filmstrip (54 fr.) : ‡b col. ; ‡c 35 mm.
440 0	‡a Walt Disney famous stories retold
520	‡a David Balfour's perilous venture to claim his inheritance from a villainous and miserly Scottish uncle.
700 1	‡a Stevenson, Robert Louis, ‡d 1850-1894. ‡t Kidnapped.
710 2	‡a Walt Disney Productions.
710 2	‡a Encyclopaedia Britannica Films, inc.

Frame 1	Encyclopaedia Britannica Films presents
Frame 2	Walt Disney Famous Stories Retold a series of filmstrips
Frame 3	Walt Disney's Kidnapped adapted from the Walt Disney motion picture version of the novel by Robert Louis Stevenson © MCMLX by Walt Disney Productions Copyright and all rights of reproduction, including by television, reserved
Frame 4	Produced by Encyclopaedia Britannica Films in cooperation with Walt Disney Productions and in collaboration with Paul A. Witty, Ph.D., Northwestern University Oscar E. Sams, producer.

as the chief source for the flash cards cataloged as figure 8-5. In the example shown in figure 8-15, title information is found on the back of each card; this source was used for transcription of the title proper. The container furnished publication area information, the series, and a publisher's number. Information about the creator and designer of the cards was taken from the guide.

Flip chart. A flip chart is a set of charts hinged at the top so that information may be presented in a logical sequence. The GMD "chart" follows the title proper (see figure 8-16). The entire flip chart is used as the chief source of information. Special rules for flip charts are 8.5B1, 8.5B3, 8.5C1, and 8.5D1.

Photograph. As with other unpublished graphic items, a complete publication area is inappropriate to a photograph. Unless the photograph has been reproduced commercially for public sale or distribution, give only the date of creation in the publication area (8.4F2). In most cases, the GMD for a photograph will be "picture." The photograph itself is the chief source of information. Unless a title is given on the item, the cataloger will make up a brief descriptive title, bracketing it in the title and statement of responsibility area. Special rules for photographs are 8.5B1, 8.5C1, 8.5C2, and 8.5D1.

Picture. This term is used as the specific material designation in the physical description area when the item cannot appropriately be called by another of the more specific pictorial terms under 8.5B1. In addition, "pic-

Figure 8-15.   Flash card

```
100 1    ‡a Brown, Esther.
245 10   ‡a Parts and wholes ‡h [flash card] / ‡c [by Esther Brown].
260      ‡a Boston : ‡b Teaching Resources Corp., ‡c c1973.
300      ‡a 69 flash cards : ‡b col. ; ‡c 10 × 8 cm. + ‡e 1 guide.
440  0   ‡a Language skills
520      ‡a Designed to develop an understanding of the relationship of parts to wholes.
500      ‡a Catalog no. 84-310.
710 2    ‡a Teaching Resources Corporation.
```

Back of card (chief source of information)
Parts and Wholes

Guide title page   Guide
Language Skills Development
Parts and Wholes
Picture Cards
by Esther Brown
Teaching Resources Corporation
100 Boylston Street, Boston, Massachusetts 02116

Container   Language Skills
Parts and Wholes
Catalog no. 84-310

Figure 8-16.   Flip chart

```
100 1   ‡a Bergwall, Charles.
245 10  ‡a Vicalog ‡h [chart] : ‡b Eye Gate visual card catalog / ‡c conceived and designed by
        Charles Bergwall and Sherwin S. Glassner.
260     ‡a Jamaica, N.Y. : ‡b Eye Gate House, ‡c [196-]
300     ‡a 1 flip chart (6 sheets) : ‡b b&w ; ‡c 22 × 36 cm.
500     ‡a 2 heavy cardboard sheets with 4 transparencies hinged at the top.
500     ‡a Shows the parts of a catalog card.
700 1   ‡a Glassner, Sherwin S.
710 2   ‡a Eye Gate House, inc.
```

Coversheet

Vicalog
Eye Gate Visual Card Catalog
Another Eye Gate Audio Visual Product
Eye Gate House, Inc.
146-01 Archer Ave., Jamaica 35, N.Y.

Instructions for using "Vicalog"
[text]
Conceived and designed by Charles Bergwall
and Sherwin S. Glassner

ture" may be used to describe a collection that is a mixture of different types of reproduction. For example, the thirty-five presidential pictures of figure 8-11 include photographs of more recent presidents and black-and-white reproductions of oil paintings and drawings of earlier presidents. The term "picture" embraces all of these variations and should be used. Special rules for pictures are 8.5B1, 8.5C2, and 8.5D1.

Postcard. Like "picture," the term "postcard" may be used as the specific material designation in the physical description area when one is cataloging an item as a postcard. Although this case is not explicitly mentioned in *AACR2R* chapter 8, "postcard" would be particularly appropriate as the designation for a collection of items all of which are postcards but of varying content (e.g., art reproductions, photographs, technical drawings). For particular items, 8.5B1 lists the various specific designations and includes an option allowing the cataloger to substitute one designation for another or to use a term of his or her own formulation if a very specific statement is appropriate. This means that optionally one may use "art reproduction," "organization chart," etc., in place of "postcard" as the specific material designation. The GMD "picture" is normally used with postcards.

In the example shown in figure 8-17, "postcard" is the most appropriate designation for the group of postcards, each of which is a photomechanical reproduction of sculpture. Each postcard bears the same statement on the verso: "Fernand Hazen, éditeur, Paris. Printed in France. Distributed in USA by Artext Prints Inc. Westport Conn." The postcards have no common title; a brief descriptive title appropriate to the collection has been supplied by the cataloger (8.1B2).

Figure 8-17.   Postcard

245 00	‡a [Sculpture] ‡h [picture].
260	‡a Paris : ‡b F. Hazen ; ‡a Westport, Conn. : ‡b Distributed in USA by Artext Prints, ‡c [19--]
300	‡a 4 postcards : ‡b b&w ; ‡c 11 × 15 cm.
500	‡a Title supplied by cataloger.
505 0	‡a Sculpture grecque : Victoire de Samothrace -- Sculpture égyptienne : groupe de Sennefer et de sa femme -- L'homme-cactus / Julio González -- La danseuse de quatorze ans / Degas.

Poster. A poster is a large sheet intended for display. A poster that contains only printed text, or one in which text is the dominant element, is called a "broadside." A broadside is cataloged according to *AACR2R* chapter 2. For an example of broadside cataloging, see figure 2-3 and discussion.

However, if the emphasis of the poster is pictorial or otherwise graphic, use the rules in chapter 8 for cataloging. A chart, an art print, an art reproduction, etc., may be a poster (i.e., a large sheet intended for display). Use these more specific material designations in preference to "poster" if they are applicable.

Figure 8-10 is a set of graphic materials, each of which is about half pictorial and half text. However, the chief intent of the set seems to be illustrative; therefore, it should be cataloged as graphic material rather than as a set of broadsides (*AACR2R* chapter 2). The pictures are of different media: one photograph of an American Indian woman; several reproductions of paintings of American Indians, which would be called "art reproductions"; and engravings that are adaptations of paintings (21.16A). Taking all factors into consideration, it seems appropriate to use the generic term "poster" for the specific material designation for the set.

Radiograph. The most familiar type of material subsumed under the term "radiograph" is an x-ray negative. See the illustration of physical description for a radiograph under 8.5D1, *AACR2R*.

Slide. A slide is a small, transparent image made of film or glass and mounted for projection. A microscope slide is not considered to be a graphic item. Because it usually is made up of a bit of "realia" sandwiched between two pieces of glass, such a slide is categorized as realia (see *AACR2R* chapter 10).

The chief source of information for a slide is the slide itself. In the example shown in figure 8-18, the slides are obviously designed to be used as a unit, in sequence, almost as one would use a filmstrip. Each of the four sets included in the collection begins with a slide that gives title information; for example:

GERMAN PAINTING
OF THE
TWENTIETH CENTURY
Set 1

Figure 8-18.   Slide

245 00	‡a German painting of the twentieth century ‡h [slide].
260	‡a East Providence, R.I. : ‡b H.E. Budek Co., ‡c c1962.
300	‡a 122 slides : ‡b col. + ‡e 1 commentary.
500	‡a In flat plastic holders (28 × 23 cm.) punched for insertion in 3-ring binder.
520	‡a Chronological development of German painting from the beginning of the century to the post-war period of the 1950s. The works of Kubin, Kokoschka, Kandinsky, Klee, etc.

In each set, the last slide has the following information:

THE END
Copyright 1962, by
Herbert E. Budek Company Inc.

If individual slides in a slide set do not provide a collective title for the entire set, the container or material accompanying the slides may be used as the chief source. In the slide set entitled "West Germany" (figure 1-17), each slide bears the name and address of the producer and a title descriptive of the subject matter of the particular slide. The commentary with the slide set furnished the collective title for the set.

For a further example of slide cataloging, see figure 1-115.

Stereograph. By definition a stereograph is "a picture composed of two superimposed stereoscopic images prepared so as to give a three-dimensional effect when viewed with a stereoscope or with special spectacles."[2] One type of stereograph is the postcard-sized, opaque, double-image photograph of the late nineteenth and early twentieth century that was designed to be viewed through Grandpa's stereoscope. The modern version of the old stereoscope and its double-image photographs is the View-Master viewer with its double-frame stereoscopic slides. The chief source of information for this and other types of stereographic material is the item itself, which in the case of View-Master reels usually includes a label (see figure 8-19).

Special rules for stereographs include 8.5B1, 8.5B2, 8.5B5, 8.5C2, and 8.5D3.

Study print. A study print is a graphic item that has been prepared specifically for teaching purposes. It is generally pictorial; it may or may not include text. The specific material designation "study print" rather than one of the other terms listed under 8.5B1 should be assigned to an item or a collection of items if the term reflects the intent of the author or creator of the material (see figure 8-20).

Transparency. A transparency is a transparent image, either mounted or unmounted, designed for use on an overhead projector. The chief source of information is the transparency itself. It should be used as the source for transcribing the title and statement of responsibility. In addition, information appearing "prominently" (i.e., on the container or accompanying material) may be given in brackets as part of the statement of responsibility

Figure 8-19.   Stereographic reel

```
245 00   ‡a Cairo, Egypt ‡h [slide].
260      ‡a Portland, Or. : ‡b Sawyer, ‡c c1950.
300      ‡a 1 stereograph reel (7 pairs of fr.) : ‡b col. + ‡e 1 commentary.
440  0   ‡a View-master travelogue ; ‡v reel no. 3301
710 2    ‡a Sawyer's Inc.
```

Container	Cairo, Egypt Reel No. 3301 View-Master Travelogue
Reel label	3301 Cairo View-Master Reel Egypt Copyright 1950 Sawyer's Inc. Portland 7, Oregon

Figure 8-20.   Study print

```
100 1    ‡a Fegely, Tom.
245 10   ‡a How does your organic garden grow? ‡h [picture] / ‡c photos by Tom Fegely, Tom
         Gettings ; text by Bud Souders, Tom Fegely ; edited by Rita Reemer.
260      ‡a Emmaus, Pa. : ‡b Rodale Press, Educational Services Division, ‡c c1973.
300      ‡a 14 study prints : ‡b col. ; ‡c 34 × 46 cm. + ‡e 1 booklet.
440  0   ‡a Organic classroom series
700 1    ‡a Gettings, Tom.
700 1    ‡a Souders, Bud.
700 1    ‡a Reemer, Rita.
```

Guide title page	Organic Classroom Series How Does Your Organic Garden Grow? Rodale Press Educational Services Division Photos by Tom Fegely, Tom Gettings Text by Bud Souders, Tom Fegely Edited by Rita Reemer

(1.1F1). Each of the transparencies in the set shown in figure 8-21 bears the title "Africa." The statement of responsibility is found on the accompanying material.

If individual transparencies in the set do not have a common title, the container or material accompanying the transparencies may be used as the chief source for the entire title and statement of responsibility.

Special rules for transparencies include 8.5B1, 8.5B4, 8.5B5, 8.5C2, and 8.5D4. For another example of cataloging of a transparency, see figure 1-128.

Wall chart. See under "chart" for discussion.

8.7. NOTE AREA

Follow general instructions under 1.7. Notes are to be listed in the order in which they appear in 8.7B. For specifics on MARC coding, see the corresponding discussion in 1.7.

8.7B2. Language. Give a note on the language of the item unless it is evident from the rest of the description (see, for example, figure 8-8, note 1).

8.7B7. Edition and history. As with other notes, make this note only if the information is not evident elsewhere in the entry. The note connects the work being cataloged with other versions, editions, etc. (see, for example, figures 8-4, 8-7, and 8-9). Because information about the adaptation appears

Figure 8-21.   Transparency

245 00	‡a Africa ‡h [transparency] / ‡c [collaborators, Nadine I. Clark, Herbert S. Lewis ; producers, Weking Schroeder, Penelope Wilmot ; produced by Encyclopaedia Britannica Films in cooperation with Compton's pictured encyclopedia].
260	‡a Chicago : ‡b Encyclopaedia Britannica Educational Corp., ‡c c1963.
300	‡a 16 transparencies : ‡b some col. ; ‡c 22 × 22 cm.
500	‡a Teacher's guide on envelope.
500	‡a With plastic frame, 27 × 26 cm.
521 2	‡a Junior and senior high schools.
505 0	‡a unit 1. The land (8 transparencies) -- unit 2. The people (3 transparencies) -- unit 3. Africa, past and present (5 transparencies).
500	‡a Series 30040.
700 1	‡a Clark, Nadine I.
700 1	‡a Lewis, Herbert S.
710 2	‡a Encyclopaedia Britannica Films, inc.
710 2	‡a Compton's pictured encyclopedia.

Transparency   Series: Africa   Unit I: The Land
Encyclopaedia Britannica Educational Corporation
425 North Michigan Avenue • Chicago, Illinois 60611
©1963 by Encyclopaedia Britannica
Educational Corporation

Envelope   Series 30040 Africa
Unit I, 8 transparencies
The Land
Produced by Encyclopaedia Britannica Films
in cooperation with Compton's Pictured Encyclopedia
Collaborators: Nadine I. Clark, Herbert S. Lewis
Producers: Weking Schroeder, Penelope Wilmot

in the statement of responsibility, such a note is not necessary in figure 8-14.

8.7B10. Physical description. See figures 8-1, 1-115, etc.

8.7B11. Accompanying material. See discussion under 1.7B11 for guidance about when this note is needed.

8.7B14. Audience. Give this note only if the information is stated on the item, the container, or accompanying material (see figures 8-7, 8-8, etc.). This note is given in a 521 field. For MARC coding and display, see discussion in this *Handbook* at 1.7B14.

8.7B17. Summary. Because graphic materials are often stored so that they are difficult to browse, a summary of the content of the item is particularly useful unless content is obvious from the rest of the entry. This note is recorded in a 520 field (see, for instance, figures 8-5, 8-8, etc.).

8.7B18. Contents. See *Handbook* at 1.7B18 for guidance on format for contents note (see, e.g., figures 8-8, 8-17, etc.).

8.7B19. Numbers. Give important numbers that may serve to identify the item (but not series numbers, ISBNs, or ISSNs) (see, for example, figure 8-21).

8.10. ITEMS MADE UP OF SEVERAL TYPES OF MATERIAL

Items consisting of various types of material, if they lack a predominant component, take the GMD "kit" (North American) or "multimedia" (British). See discussion in *Handbook* at 1.10 for instructions; see also figures 8-7 and 8-8 for examples of kits.

NOTES

1. General information about MARC coding is found in the introduction to this *Handbook*; details about coding the descriptive portion of the record are found throughout chapter 1; information about the coding of main and added access points is found at the beginning of chapter 14. An explanation of the MARC authorities format is given in *Handbook* chapters 15, 17, and 18. Information about specific MARC fields may be found by consulting the index under "MARC fields."

2. *Webster's Third New International Dictionary of the English Language Unabridged* (Springfield, Mass.: Merriam, 1993), p. 2238.

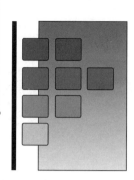

Computer Files

AACR2R chapter 9 contains the rules for the cataloging of computer files of all types. Because computer files may contain elements of other media—for example, text, graphics, maps, music, sound—other chapters in *AACR2R* may also need to be consulted.

Because the technology associated with computer files is developing so rapidly, the cataloging rules for certain parts of this section of *AACR2R* are subject to change. In many cases the cataloger may need to go beyond *AACR2R*. Two such cases are the treatment of interactive multimedia and Internet resources. (Guidelines that have been established for these will be discussed below.) However, the general chapter of *AACR2R* (chapter 1) was written with the intention of providing for the cataloging of media not envisioned at the time of its writing. Thus, for the most part, the basic cataloging of a computer file follows the general rules used for any other type of medium.

Catalogers should not be put off from attempting to catalog computer files by the fact that the technology is complex and only fully understood by computer scientists. Little more than the ability to run the program—and sometimes not even this—is required to do basic computer file cataloging.[1]

9.0. General Rules

Computer files are defined in *AACR2R* as data or programs, which are either stored on a physical carrier (e.g., a floppy disk or the hard drive of a computer) or available by remote access (e.g., from a Local Area Network [LAN] or via the Internet). A "program" is an electronic file containing a set of instructions that tells a computer to perform certain tasks. "Data" comprise electronic text (which may be, for example, sets of numbers or

233

blocks of alphabetic text) that is manipulated by a program. A program may stand alone (for example, a game); data always require an underlying program to be usable. Figure 9-1 is an example of a computer program, a tax preparation program. Figure 9-2 catalogs text data (the entire text of Migne's *Patrologia Latina*) along with the software program necessary to index, retrieve, and display items from the data. Figure 9-3 shows cataloging of graphic data (an elaborate world atlas), along with its necessary program.

Computer files differ from most other media covered by *AACR2R* in that they cannot be directly accessed by the user; an intermediate machine (computer hardware) is required to use the file. The multiplicity of computer systems and hardware required to run various types of computer files presents a challenge to the cataloger, who cannot be expected to have at his or her disposal all of the possible types of machinery necessary to run or read any given computer file. Some account of this is taken in the rules for this chapter.

Caution: chapter 9 does *not* cover self-contained electronic devices such as calculators, even though they, too, may use computer technology. Nor is system software, the basic computer file necessary to run the machine (as opposed to the computer file comprising the program being run *by* the machine), cataloged under chapter 9. If it is thought necessary to catalog such materials, they should be described along with the device containing them under chapter 10, "Three-Dimensional Artifacts and Realia."

Figure 9-1.   Computer program

245 00	‡a MacInTax ‡h [computer file].
250	‡a Tax year 1994, v94.01.
256	‡a Computer program.
260	‡a Tucson, Ariz. : ‡b Intuit, ‡c c1995.
300	‡a 4 computer disks ; ‡c 3 1/2 in. + ‡e 1 manual (viii, 100 p.)
538	‡a System requirements: Macintosh Plus or better; 2 MB RAM; System 6.0.7 or greater; hard disk with at least 15 MB; high-density diskette drive; 100% Apple-compatible printer; Hayes-compatible modem.
500	‡a Title from title screen.
500	‡a Manual title: MacInTax : the easiest way to do your taxes.
500	‡a "Personal/1040 final."
520	‡a Personal tax return preparation software, including 1994 tax forms.
710 2	‡a Intuit (Firm)

Title screen	Intuit Tax year 1994 © copyright 1994, 1995 MacInTax
Label to disk 1	MacInTax Personal/1040 Final Tax Year 1994 v94.01 To Install: Insert Disk 1 into your disk drive. Double click on the MacInTax 94 installer icon © 1994, 1995 Intuit Inc. Licensed material property of Intuit Inc. All rights reserved

Figure 9-2.   Computer data and program

```
020       ‡a 0898871131
245 00    ‡a Patrologia Latina database ‡h [computer file].
250       ‡a Release 4.
256       ‡a Computer data and program.
260       ‡a Alexandria, VA : ‡b Chadwyck-Healey, ‡c c1995.
300       ‡a 4 computer optical discs ; ‡c 4 3/4 in. + ‡e 2 computer disks (3 1/2 in.) + 1 user
          manual and supplement (2 v. : ill. ; 21 cm.) + 1 installation sheet ([4] p. : ill. ; 21 cm.)
538       ‡a System requirements: IBM or compatible 386 or 486 PC running at 25MHz; 4 MB
          RAM; DOS version 3.3 or higher; Microsoft Windows version 3.1; hard disk with at least
          6 MB free; VGA card and monitor; Microsoft or compatible mouse; CD-ROM drive with
          Microsoft CD-ROM extensions version 2.1 or higher.
500       ‡a Title from disc label.
500       ‡a Computer disks: Installation software version 4.0; User manual: 2nd ed., c1994; User
          manual supplement: 2nd ed., c1995.
520       ‡a Online version of Migne's Patrologia Latina, v. 1-129 and 158-185.
700 1     ‡a Migne, J.-P. ‡q (Jacques-Paul), ‡d 1800-1875.
710 2     ‡a Chadwyck-Healey, Inc.
730 0     ‡a Patrologiae cursus completus. ‡p Series Latina.
```

Figure 9-3.   Computer data and program

```
245 04    ‡a The Software Toolworks world atlas ‡h [computer file].
246 30    ‡a World atlas
250       ‡a [Version] 2.1.1.
256       ‡a Computer data and program.
260       ‡a Novato, CA : ‡b Software Toolworks, ‡c c1992.
300       ‡a 10 computer disks : ‡b col. ; ‡c 3 1/2 in.
538       ‡a System requirements: Macintosh.
500       ‡a Title from disk label.
500       ‡a Copyright by Software Toolworks.
530       ‡a Issued also in Windows and DOS versions.
520       ‡a Contains color maps of all types, comparison graphs, comprehensive city data, area
          codes and mileage between cities.
710 2     ‡a Software Toolworks (Firm)
```

Label to disk 1

The Software Toolworks®
World Atlas
2.1.1
Macintosh®   Disk 1
The Software Toolworks
60 Leveroni Ct • Novato CA • (415) 883-3000
Copyright ©1991, 1992 The Software Toolworks, Inc. All Rights Reserved

Note that the rules for main entry and other access points are the same for computer files as for any other medium cataloged under *AACR2R*, and are found in chapter 21. Because the responsibility for computer files is usually diffuse, they more often than not are entered under title. However, if it is clear that no more than three persons have responsibility for a computer file, main entry may be under author. Figure 9-4, *HyperMyth*, is a computer file comprising data written entirely by Randy Stewart; main entry is therefore under his name. On the other hand, the program that runs *HyperMyth*, called *HyperCard*, is the product of the collaborative effort of programmers at Apple Computer. Although a statement of responsibility naming the chief programmer, Dan Allen, is found on the title screen, entry will be under title with added entry for Allen (see figure 9-5).

Interactive multimedia

A new form of computer file has developed over the past decade that is now referred to as "interactive multimedia." As implied by its name, interactive multimedia combines computer technology with other media, such as graphics and sound. Interactive multimedia should be cataloged according to the *Guidelines for Bibliographic Description of Interactive Multimedia*, which, though based on *AACR2R*, occasionally departs from those rules in order to meet the needs of the new medium.[2] The definition of interactive multimedia, as given in the *Guidelines*, is as follows:

Figure 9-4.   Personal author

100 1	‡a Stewart, Randy.
245 10	‡a HyperMyth ‡h [computer file] : ‡b classical mythology made simple / ‡c by Randy Stewart.
246 3	‡a Hyper myth
246 30	‡a Classical mythology made simple
250	‡a Version 2.0.
256	‡a Computer data (1 file).
260	‡a Salt Lake City, Utah : ‡b Hermes Pub. Co., ‡c c1991.
300	‡a 1 computer disk ; ‡c 3 1/2 in. + ‡e 1 reference and study guide (137 p. ; 23 cm.) + 1 instruction booklet.
538	‡a System requirements: Macintosh; at least 1 MB RAM; System 6.0.5 or higher; HyperCard 2.0; drive that reads high-density disks (or a hard drive).
500	‡a Title from title screen.
520	‡a Classical mythology presented in a HyperCard stack.

Title screen	HyperMyth: Classical Mythology Made Simple by Randy Stewart Version 2.0 ©1991 by Randy Stewart Hermes Publishing Company
Disk label	HyperMyth: Classical Mythology Made Simple Version 2.0 © 1991 by Randy Stewart Hermes Publishing Company

Figure 9-5.   Authorship diffuse

```
245 00   ‡a HyperCard ‡h [computer file] / ‡c by Dan Allen.
246 3    ‡a Hyper card
250      ‡a Version 2.1.
256      ‡a Computer program.
260      ‡a Cupertino, CA : ‡b Apple Computer, Inc., ‡c c1991.
300      ‡a 7 computer disks ; ‡c 3 1/2 in.
538      ‡a System requirements: Macintosh Plus or better; two 800K disk drives, or one floppy
         drive and hard drive (hard drive recommended); minimum 1 MB of memory (minimum 2
         MB memory for Multifinder; minimum 2.5 MB memory for System 7); System software
         6.0.5 or later.
500      ‡a Title from title screen.
500      ‡a Copyright by Apple Computer, Inc.
700 1    ‡a Allen, Dan.
710 2    ‡a Apple Computer, Inc.
```

Title screen   HyperCard by Dan Allen
                    Version 2.1 © 1987-91 Apple Computer, Inc.
                    Management Ron Metzker and Kevin Calhoun
                    Engineering Leads Kevin Calhout and Alam Paal
                        Hypertalk Language Dan Winkler
                            [and about 50 other names]
                    Based on HyperCard 1.0 by Bill Atkinson and friends

Label to disk 1   HyperCard Program
                                    HyperCard®
                                        7

Interactive multimedia: media residing in one or more physical carriers (video-discs, computer disks, computer optical discs, computer audio discs, etc.) or on computer networks. Interactive multimedia must exhibit both of these characteristics: (1) user-controlled, nonlinear navigation using computer technology; and (2) the combination of two or more media (audio, text, graphics, images, animation, and video) that the user manipulates to control the order and/or nature of the presentation. (*Guidelines*, p. 1)

While this definition leaves some ambiguity, the two parts of the definition that differentiate interactive multimedia from other types of computer files seem to be (a) the fact that the work allows a considerable level of user control; and (b) the work allows nonlinear navigation (i.e., the user controls the direction and order of the unfolding of the program). A good example is the computer game *Myst*, which allows the user to explore a set of fantasy worlds at his or her whim (see figure 9-6). On the other hand, the Carmen Sandiego computer games are *not* nonlinear: although the user is given a limited set of choices and to a certain extent has control over the direction of the game, each game follows a definite direction and has a predictable outcome. These games should be cataloged as computer files (see figures 9-7 and 9-8). Another popular type of interactive multimedia is the various interactive encyclopedias, such as Microsoft Encarta '95 (see figure 9-9).

Figure 9-6.   Interactive multimedia

```
100 1     ‡a Miller, Rand.
245 10    ‡a Myst ‡h [interactive multimedia].
250       ‡a Version 1.01.
256       ‡a Computer data and program.
260       ‡a Novato, Calif. : ‡b Brøderbund, ‡c c1993.
300       ‡a 1 computer optical disc : ‡b sd., col. ; ‡c 4 3/4 in. + ‡e 1 user's manual + 1 journal.
538       ‡a System requirements: 256 color Macintosh; 4 MB RAM; system 7.0.1 or higher;
          QuickTime 1.6 and Sound Manager 3.0; hard disk with 3 MB free; CD-ROM drive.
500       ‡a Title and ed. statement from title screen.
508       ‡a "Designed and directed by Rand Miller and Robyn C. Miller"--Final credits.
500       ‡a Copyright by Brøderbund Software and Cyan, Inc.
500       ‡a Issued also in Windows version.
520       ‡a Adventure game; player explores five fantasy worlds searching for the vanished
          inhabitants of Myst Island.
700 1     ‡a Miller, Robyn.
710 2     ‡a Brøderbund Software.
710 2     ‡a Cyan, Inc.
```

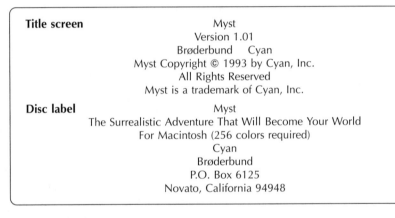

Title screen   Myst
                                    Version 1.01
                                Brøderbund   Cyan
                          Myst Copyright © 1993 by Cyan, Inc.
                               All Rights Reserved
                          Myst is a trademark of Cyan, Inc.

Disc label   Myst
                   The Surrealistic Adventure That Will Become Your World
                        For Macintosh (256 colors required)
                                      Cyan
                                  Brøderbund
                                 P.O. Box 6125
                            Novato, California 94948

Figure 9-7.   Computer file

```
245 00    ‡a Where in the world is Carmen Sandiego? ‡h [computer file] / ‡c by Gene Portwood,
          Lauren Elliott, Chris Jochumson ; graphics by Don Albrecht and Michelle McBride.
250       ‡a V[ersion] 1.3.
256       ‡a Computer program (3 files)
260       ‡a San Rafael, Calif. : ‡b Brøderbund Software, ‡c c1991.
300       ‡a 1 computer disk : ‡b sd., col. ; ‡c 3 1/2 in. + ‡e 1 user's manual (24 p.) + 1 book
          (960 p.).
538       ‡a System requirements: Macintosh.
500       ‡a Title from title screen.
500       ‡a Copyright by Brøderbund Software.
500       ‡a Includes book: World almanac and book of facts, 1991. New York : World Almanac,
          c1990.
520       ‡a Students learn geography and map reading, research skills, and historical, economic
          and cultural facts by tracking down notorious criminals.
700 1     ‡a Portwood, Gene.
700 1     ‡a Elliott, Lauren.
700 1     ‡a Jochumson, Chris.
710 2     ‡a Brøderbund Software.
740 02    ‡a World almanac and book of facts, 1991.
```

Title screen

Where in the World is
Carmen Sandiego?
by Gene Portwood
Lauren Elliott
Chris Jochumson
Graphics by Don Albrecht
and Michelle McBride
Copyright © 1985-1991 Brøderbund Software, Inc. v1.3
All rights reserved

Disk label

Macintosh
Where in the World is
Carmen Sandiego?
Brøderbund
17 Paul Drive • San Rafael • California 94903-2101

Figure 9-8.   Computer file

245 00	‡a Where in the U.S.A. is Carmen Sandiego? ‡h [computer file] / ‡c designed by Gene Portwood and Lauren Elliott ; programmed by Chris Jochumson ; graphics by Don Albrecht, Mark Schlicting and Michelle McBride ; music and sound by Tom Rettig ; update by Scott Luther.
250	‡a V[ersion] 1.2
256	‡a Computer program (27 files)
260	‡a Novato, Calif. : ‡b Brøderbund, ‡c c1991.
300	‡a 2 computer disks : ‡b sd., col. ; ‡c 3 1/2 in. + ‡e 1 user's manual (20 p.) + 1 book (xiii, 879 p.) + 1 map.
538	‡a System requirements: Macintosh.
500	‡a Title from title screen.
500	‡a Copyright by Brøderbund Software.
500	‡a Includes book: Fodor's USA. Brøderbund ed. New York : Fodor's Travel Guides, c1985.
700 1	‡a Portwood, Gene.
700 1	‡a Elliott, Lauren.
710 2	‡a Brøderbund Software.
740 02	‡a Fodor's USA.

Title screen

Where in the U.S.A. is
Carmen Sandiego?
Designed by Gene Portwood and Lauren Elliott
Programmed by Chris Jochumson
Graphics by Don Albrecht
Mark Schlicting and Michelle McBride
Music and sound by Tom Rettig
Update by Scott Luther
Copyright © 1986, 1991 Brøderbund Software, Inc. v1.2
All Rights Reserved

Label to disk 1

Disk 1
Macintosh
Where in the U.S.A. is
Carmen Sandiego?
CLASSIFIED
Brøderbund®
P.O. Box 6125 • Novato • California • 94948-6125
© 1989, 1992, Brøderbund Software, Inc. All rights reserved

Figure 9-9.   Interactive multimedia

245 00   ‡a Microsoft Encarta '95 ‡h [interactive multimedia] : ‡b the complete interactive multimedia encyclopedia.
246 3   ‡a Microsoft Encarta 1995
246 1   ‡i Title on spine of jewel case: ‡a Encarta '95
250   ‡a 1995 ed.
256   ‡a Computer data and program.
260   ‡a [Redmond, Wash.] : ‡b Microsoft, ‡c c1994.
300   ‡a 1 computer optical disc : ‡b sd., col. ; ‡c 4 3/4 in. + ‡e 1 user's guide + 1 quick reference card.
440 0   ‡a Microsoft Home
538   ‡a System requirements: Multimedia PC or compatible with 386SX microprocessor or higher; 4 MB RAM; MS-DOS 3.1 or later; Microsoft Windows 3.1 or later; SVGA graphics capabilities; hard disk with 3.5 MB free space; CD-ROM drive; audio board; Microsoft-compatible mouse or compatible pointing device; headphones or speakers.
500   ‡a Title and ed. statement from disc label.
520   ‡a Funk & Wagnalls new encyclopedia plus assorted sounds, music, spoken text, etc.
710 2   ‡a Microsoft Corporation.
730 02   ‡a Funk & Wagnalls new encyclopedia.

Disc label
Microsoft® Encarta '95
The Complete Interactive Multimedia Encyclopedia
1995 Edition
© and ℗ 1992-1994 Microsoft Corporation
Microsoft Home

Title screen
Encarta '95
copyright © 1992-94

In case of doubt, do not consider the work to be interactive multimedia (*Guidelines*, p. 4). Specific applications of the guidelines will be treated below at the appropriate *AACR2R* rule.

Internet resources

Another important recent development is the rise of the Internet, a worldwide conglomeration of interconnected computer networks. The Internet allows libraries and their users to gain access to computer files all over the world without actually physically holding the file in the library. This was partially anticipated in *AACR2R* chapter 9 with rules govening the cataloging of computer files available only by remote access, but the Internet has introduced a new level of complexity to the area, and new guidelines are under consideration. The most recent summary of these proposed guidelines is Nancy Olson's *Cataloging Internet Resources*, available (where else?) on the Internet.[3] Examples of catalogable resources on the Internet include journals (see figure 9-10), World Wide Web home pages (see figure 9-11), "gopher" sites (see figure 9-12), and text files (see figure 9-13).

Like interactive multimedia, Internet resources can be cataloged according to *AACR2R* chapter 9; specific difficulties will be treated below.

Figure 9-10.   Internet journal

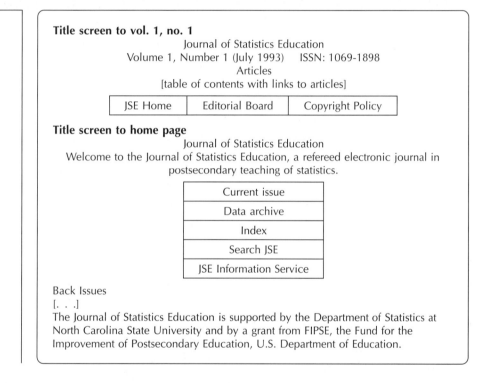

```
022 0     ‡a 1069-1898
245 00    ‡a Journal of statistics education ‡h [computer file]
246 1     ‡i Also known as: ‡a JSE
256       ‡a Computer data.
260       ‡a [S.l. : ‡b s.n.], ‡c 1993-
310       ‡a Quarterly
362 0     ‡a Vol. 1, no. 1 (July 1993)-
538       ‡a Mode of access: Internet.
500       ‡a Title from title screen of vol. 1, no. 1.
856 7     ‡u http://www2.ncsu.edu/ncsu/pams/stat/info/jse/homepage.html ‡2 http
```

Title screen to vol. 1, no. 1

Journal of Statistics Education
Volume 1, Number 1 (July 1993)   ISSN: 1069-1898
Articles
[table of contents with links to articles]

| JSE Home | Editorial Board | Copyright Policy |

Title screen to home page

Journal of Statistics Education
Welcome to the Journal of Statistics Education, a refereed electronic journal in postsecondary teaching of statistics.

| Current issue |
| Data archive |
| Index |
| Search JSE |
| JSE Information Service |

Back Issues
[. . .]
The Journal of Statistics Education is supported by the Department of Statistics at North Carolina State University and by a grant from FIPSE, the Fund for the Improvement of Postsecondary Education, U.S. Department of Education.

One important problem is that of the volatility of the medium. For example, the publication date for figure 9-11 was taken from the statement on the title display "Last updated on February 20, 1997." This will change the next time the home page "owner" makes changes, and the February 20, 1997, version will disappear permanently from the Internet. Must the cataloger of this site constantly update the record to match its current state? Not only that, the "addresses" of Internet resources are also constantly changing as "host" computers come and go. Change and impermanence are problems inherent in the medium and should be considered before a decision is made to catalog an item.

Figure 9-11.   World Wide Web home page

```
110 2    ‡a Iowa Center for the Book.
245 14   ‡a The University of Iowa Center for the Book ‡h [computer file].
256      ‡a Computer data.
260      ‡a [S.l. : ‡b s.n.], ‡c 1997.
500      ‡a Home page.
538      ‡a Mode of access: Internet.
500      ‡a Title from title display.
505 0    ‡a About the Center -- Directory -- Graduate program -- Courses -- Windhover Press --
         The offset workshop -- Handmade paper -- Center for the Book editions -- Conservation
         lab -- Book Arts Club -- Other Internet resources -- Counter.
856 7    ‡u http://www.uiowa.edu/~ctrbook/ ‡2 http
```

Title display	The University of Iowa Center for the Book	
About the Center	Directory	Graduate Program
Courses	Windhover Press	The Offset Workshop
Handmade Paper	Center for the Book Editions	Conservation Lab
Book Arts Club	Other Internet Resources	Counter

Last updated on February 20, 1997 by H Pedelty.

Figure 9-12.   Gopher site

```
245 00   ‡a The master plan : ‡b the Baal Shem Tov's unique conception of Divine Providence.
256      ‡a Computer data.
260      ‡a [S.n. : ‡b s.l., ‡c 1992]
500      ‡a Gopher site maintained by Chabad Lubavitch.
500      ‡a Foreword to article dated: 3 Sivan, 5752 (1992).
504      ‡a Includes bibliographical references.
538      ‡a Mode of access: Internet, gopher.
500      ‡a Title from article caption.
710 2    ‡a Chabad Lubavitch (Organization)
856 7    ‡u gopher://gopher.chabad.org:70/00/chabad/mastrpln/ ‡2 gopher
```

Caption title to article	The Master Plan The Baal Shem Tov's Unique Conception of Divine Providence

Figure 9-13.   Text file

```
245 00   ‡a In aedibus Aldi : ‡b the legacy of Aldus Manutius and his press ‡h [computer file].
246 3    ‡a In aedibvs Aldi
256      ‡a Computer data.
260      ‡a [S.l. : ‡b s.n., ‡c 1996]
500      ‡a Exhibition catalog in electronic format.
538      ‡a Mode of access: Internet.
500      ‡a Title from title display.
500      ‡a Based on a catalog by Paul J. Angerhofer, Mary Ann Addy Maxwell, and Robert L.
         Maxwell accompanying an exhibit held at the Harold B. Lee Library in 1995. Web version
         constructed by Robert Espinosa.
504      ‡a Includes bibliographical references.
505 0    ‡a Preface -- Intro[duction] -- Greek & Latin -- Humanists -- Rome -- Manutii -- New
         World -- Checklist.
700 1    ‡a Angerhofer, Paul J., ‡d 1960-
700 1    ‡a Maxwell, Mary Ann Addy, ‡d 1960-
700 1    ‡a Maxwell, Robert L., ‡d 1957-
700 1    ‡a Espinosa, Robert.
710 2    ‡a Harold B. Lee Library.
856 7    ‡u http://www.lib.byu.edu/~aldine/aldus.html ‡2 http
```

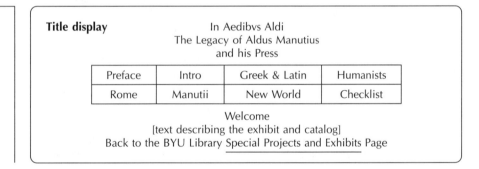

Title display

In Aedibvs Aldi
The Legacy of Aldus Manutius
and his Press

Preface	Intro	Greek & Latin	Humanists
Rome	Manutii	New World	Checklist

Welcome
[text describing the exhibit and catalog]
Back to the BYU Library Special Projects and Exhibits Page

9.0B. Sources of information

There are two sources of information for computer files; internal (those that display when the file is being run) and external (e.g., the container, the disk label, etc.). Internal sources are preferred under *AACR2R* chapter 9, and the chief source is the title screen. This is the screen that displays when the computer file begins to run. (In the case of a Macintosh computer file, the title screen is displayed by choosing "About . . ." under the Apple menu.) Frequently, however, the title screen either does not exist or disappears from view almost immediately, too quickly to be usable for cataloging purposes. In this case, "other formally presented internal evidence" may be used, such as information from menus.

In many cases the required information is not available in internal sources (note: "available" explicitly includes a cataloger's inability to access the file due to lack of hardware, etc.). If so, the cataloger is to go (in this order) to (1) the carrier (disk or disc) and its labels; (2) documentation provided by the publisher; (3) information printed on the box the file came in; or, as a last resort, (4) the cataloger may use any other source, such as a published description of the file.

The chief source of information for interactive multimedia is the entire work, including both internal and external sources. A source giving information that applies to the entire work and includes a collective title is preferred; if there is more than one such source, that giving the most complete information is chosen (*Guidelines,* p. 4; see figure 9-9: the disc label provides more complete information than the title screen).

The chief source for an Internet resource follows (in order of priority): (1) the title screen; (2) information from the file itself (e.g., a "readme" file); (3) other sources (e.g., another home page leading to the cataloged resource, menus, etc.).[4]

9.1. TITLE AND STATEMENT OF RESPONSIBILITY AREA

9.1B. Title proper

Having chosen a source of information (see above), the cataloger is to transcribe the title as instructed in 1.1B. One peculiarity of computer files is that they may be given titles with unusual spelling or capitalization, and words are often run together. These are to be transcribed exactly as they appear, including odd capitalization. Do not change, for example, "Mac-InTax" to "Mac in tax" or "Macintax" (see figure 9-1). If it is thought that the user might attempt to look the words up separately, give an added entry for the differing form in a 246 field (see figures 9-4 and 9-5).

9.1B2. Because there are so many possible sources for information in this chapter, a note must *always* be given recording the source of the title (see figures throughout this chapter). If at all possible, the cataloger should attempt to at least examine the title screen and other internal sources. These often differ markedly from information available on external sources, both with respect to the wording of the title proper and to the availability of statement of responsibility information.

9.1C. *Optional addition.* General material designation

AACR2R prescribes a single GMD for materials covered by chapter 9: "computer file" (1.1C1). A new GMD, "interactive multimedia," has also been proposed in *Guidelines,* but has not yet appeared either as an *LCRI* or as a rule revision to *AACR2R* 1.1C. The Library of Congress currently uses it, however, and it will be used in this *Handbook.* In addition, "kit" may be used if appropriate.

9.1E–9.1F. Other title information/Statements of responsibility

Like other types of media cataloged under *AACR2R,* the source of information chosen for a computer file may include, in addition to the title proper, other title information and statements of responsibility. If so, these should be transcribed as usual. Because complex computer files are usually the result of collaborative efforts, they often display long lists of contributors. The cataloger should therefore be cautious in the transcription of statements of responsibility and limit it to major contributors. *Guidelines* explicitly instructs the cataloger:

> Transcribe statements of responsibility relating to those persons or bodies responsible *for the entire content* of the interactive multimedia work. . . . Give all other statements of responsibility, including those confined to the creation of specific parts of the interactive multimedia work in a note. (p. 7, emphasis added)

While this rule is confined to the cataloging of interactive multimedia, it may be good advice for the cataloging of other computer files as well, especially those that display extensive statement of responsibility information.

Figure 9-7 shows a manageable statement of responsibility, which will be transcribed just as it would if it appeared on the title page of a book. The title screen on which figure 9-14 is based shows other title information, which is transcribed; it also shows statement of responsibility information. However, this information lists about two dozen persons, all of whom contributed to the program but none of whom was responsible for the entire content. In addition, although the rest of the title screen remains stationary, the statement of responsibility scrolls in the fashion of film credits, and too quickly for the cataloger to transcribe the information. The statement of responsibility is not transcribed.

Figure 9-14.   Other title information; statement of responsibility omitted

```
245 00   ‡a SAM ‡h [computer file] : ‡b Symantec AntiVirus for Macintosh.
246 30   ‡a Symantec antivirus for Macintosh
250      ‡a Version 4.0.
256      ‡a Computer program.
260      ‡a Cupertino, CA : ‡b Symantec Corp., ‡c c1994.
300      ‡a 2 computer disks; ‡c 3 1/2 in.
500      ‡a Virus protection program for the Macintosh.
538      ‡a System requirements: Macintosh Plus or higher; System 6.0 and Finder 6.1 or higher;
         hard disk drive and 1 1.4 K floppy disk drive.
500      ‡a Title from title screen.
500      ‡a Copyright by Symantec Corporation
710 2    ‡a Symantec Corporation.
```

Title screen   SAM
                          Symantec AntiVirus for Macintosh
                                Version: 4.0
                   [scrolling list of about two dozen contributors]
                       copyright © 1989-94 Symantec Corporation
                               All rights reserved

9.2. EDITION AREA

9.2B. Edition statement

An edition statement, if found, is to be transcribed as instructed at 1.2B. The definition of "edition" is quite inclusive in the case of computer files, and because almost all commercially produced computer files are either new versions of older files or anticipate future versions, an edition statement will almost always be present. Words within a statement, such as "edition," "issue," "release," "level," "update," or most commonly, "version" (often abbreviated to "v"), are evidence that the statement is an edition statement (see, e.g., figure 9-2). If "version" or a similar word has been abbreviated, the cataloger may expand the word within brackets if it is thought that leaving it abbreviated may cause confusion (see figure 9-8). Unusual statements, or a number standing alone, may also constitute edition statements. In the latter case, a bracketed word such as "[Version]" should be added (see figure 9-3).

The source of an edition statement should be given in a note if it differs from that of the title proper. In the case of interactive multimedia, the source of the edition statement should always be given (*Guidelines*, p. 8). This may be combined with the note giving the source of the title proper (see figure 9-6, etc.).

Be careful to distinguish between the name of the edition of the file being cataloged and the name of the edition of the operating system required to run the computer. Software often includes statements such as "runs on System 7.0" or "requires MS-DOS version 3.1." These are statements about the edition of the *operating system,* not the program itself. This information is recorded in the system requirements note (9.7B1, recorded in a 538 field), not the edition statement (see figure 9-1, etc., and discussion under 9.7B1b).

9.2C, 9.2E. Statements of responsibility relating to the edition/Statements of responsibility relating to a named revision of an edition

If a statement of responsibility accompanies an edition statement, transcribe it following space - slash - space as usual (see discussion at 1.2C and figure 9-15).

9.2D. Statement relating to a named revision of an edition

Treat a named revision of an edition as discussed at 1.2D. Give the name of the edition first followed by a comma; then give the name of the revision. Capitalize both names. In figure 9-15, the edition is "Macintosh version" (the program is available for other systems as well); the revision of this edition is "Version 1.1."

Figure 9-15.   Statement of responsibility in edition statement

```
245 04   ‡a The Chessmaster 3000 ‡h [computer file].
246 3    ‡a Chessmaster three thousand
246 3    ‡a Chess master 3000
250      ‡a Macintosh version, Version 1.1 / ‡b Troy Heere & Steven Roth ; art direction Vicki
         Sidley ; artwork Cesar de Castro.
256      ‡a Computer program.
260      ‡a Novato, CA : ‡b Software Toolworks, ‡c c1994.
300      ‡a 2 computer disks : ‡b col. ; ‡c 3 1/2 in. + ‡e 1 user's guide (iv, 41 p.) + 1 quick start
         card.
538      ‡a System requirements: Macintosh Classic II, Mac Color Classic, Mac II, LC, Performa,
         Centris, Quadra, or PowerBook; 1.5 MB of RAM (monochrome); 2 MB RAM (color); hard
         disk with 3.4 MB free memory; system 7.0 or later.
500      ‡a Title from title screen.
500      ‡a Copyright by The Software Toolworks Inc.
530      ‡a Issued also for the Multimedia PC, Apple II series and IIGS, Commodore 64/128, and
         Amiga systems.
520      ‡a Teaches chess to the beginner, and offers games at the newcomer through grandmaster
         level; user plays against the computer, another human, or watches the program play
         against itself.
700 1    ‡a Heere, Troy.
700 1    ‡a Roth, Steven.
710 2    ‡a Software Toolworks (Firm)
```

Title screen

The
Chessmaster
3000
copyright © 1986-1994 The Software Toolworks Inc.
Macintosh Version
Troy Heere & Steven Roth
version 1.1
Art direction Vicki Sidley
Artwork Cesar de Castro

Label to disk 1

The
Chessmaster
3000
Macintosh® Disk 1
The Software Toolworks
60 Leveroni Court • Novato, CA 94949 • (415) 883-3000

9.3. FILE CHARACTERISTICS AREA

This area is used to record information about the type of file being cataloged, specifically, whether the file contains data, programs, or both. The file characteristics area is recorded in the 256 field of the MARC record; the only subfield is subfield ‡a (see figures throughout this chapter).

The area may also contain information about the number of records, etc., contained within a file. This information is recorded within parentheses. Information about the number of records, etc., is only to be given if it is "readily available." Computer files have exhibited a tendency toward greater and greater complexity in recent years, and because of this, this information is rarely "readily available." If it is, however, it should be recorded (see figures 9-4 and 9-7; the number of files in figure 9-8 was revealed by a statement on the screen when the cataloger copied the program from one drive to another).

If the computer file is a serial, area 3 for the serial (*AACR2R* 12.3) is recorded in addition to that for the computer file, just as for any other serial. This is recorded in MARC field 362 (see figure 9-16 and discussion at 12.3). Depending on the nature of the computer file, it may also be possible to have additional fields recording area 3 for the other *AACR2R* chapters using this area (cartographic items [MARC field 255] and music [MARC field 254]).

9.4. PUBLICATION, DISTRIBUTION, ETC., AREA

The publication area for published computer files is recorded exactly as for any other published material (see discussion at 1.4, and 260 fields of figures throughout this chapter). The prescribed source includes the chief source, the disk or disc label, documentation accompanying the computer file, and the container the file came in. The cataloger may have to consult all of these in order to find full information.

Figure 9-16.   Serial computer file

```
022 0    ‡a 1084-1164
130 0    ‡a Time almanac (Multimedia ed. for Macintosh)
245 00   ‡a Time almanac ‡h [interactive multimedia].
246 1    ‡i Title on disc label: ‡a Time magazine almanac
246 1    ‡i Title on main menu screen: ‡a Compact almanac
250      ‡a Multimedia ed., Version 1.0.4.
256      ‡a Computer data and program.
260      ‡a Washington, D.C. : ‡b Compact Pub., ‡c c1993-
300      ‡a computer laser optical discs : ‡b sd., col. ; ‡c 4 3/4 in.
310      ‡a Annual
362 0    ‡a 1993-
500      ‡a Title and ed. statement from title screen.
538      ‡a System requirements: Macintosh; CD-ROM drive.
520      ‡a Features the full text of: Time, with photos and videos, from 1989-   in addition to
         information from: World factbook (Washington, D.C.); and: United States. Congress.
         Official congressional directory.
580      ‡a Also available for DOS and for Windows.
787 1    ‡t Time ‡x 0040-781X
787 1    ‡t World factbook (Washington, D.C.) ‡x 0277-1527
787 1    ‡a United States. Congress. ‡t Official congressional directory ‡x 0160-9890
```

Title screen	Time Almanac 1993 version 1.0.4 multimedia edition

9.4C2, 9.4D2, 9.4F2. If a computer file is unpublished, do not record a place of publication or name of publisher. *Do* record the date of creation of the file. The definition of "published" is quite broad for computer files. If a file has been (a) issued in multiple copies (b) for distribution (including public domain software such as "shareware"), it is considered published; if it has been mounted for remote access (e.g., on the Internet), it is usually considered published. Unpublished items include theses and locally written computer files.[5]

9.5. PHYSICAL DESCRIPTION AREA

9.5B. Extent of item (including specific material designation)

AACR2R 9.5B1 gives four specific material designations available for computer files: "computer cartridge," "computer cassette," "computer disk," and "computer reel." A fifth term, "computer disc," should now be used although it is not found in *AACR2R*.[6] A distinction is made between a computer *disk*, used for magnetic storage devices (for example, a floppy disk) (see figure 9-1), and a computer *disc*, used for optical storage devices (e.g., a CD-ROM) (see figure 9-2). Because the average library patron cannot be expected to be aware of this distinction, a computer disc should normally be referred to in this area as a "computer optical disc" or a "computer laser optical disc" (note that the spelling in the example under *AACR2R* 9.5B1 should be changed to reflect this new usage). Given the current state of computer technology, "computer disk" and "computer [optical] disc" are likely to be the most common specific material designations for cataloged computer files.

9.5C. Other physical details

Following space - colon - space, record "sd." if the computer file produces sound and "col." if it displays in more than one color (see figure 9-8). Optionally, give the number of sides used on the disk (e.g., "double sided"), its recording density (e.g., "double density"), and sectoring (e.g., "soft sectored"). The Library of Congress and the British Library will apply this option on a case-by-case basis; the National Library of Canada will not apply the option (see *LCRI* 9.5C2, Dec. 11, 1989; Howarth, at 9.5C2).

9.5D. Dimensions

The dimensions of disks, discs, cartridges, and cassettes should be given in inches as instructed, rounding up to the nearest 1/4 inch for disks, discs, and cartridges, and rounding up to the nearest 1/8 inch for cassettes; dimensions of reels are not given; the dimensions of other carriers are to be given in centimeters. The most common sizes for computer disks are 3 1/2 in. and 5 1/4 in. The most common size for a computer optical disc (CD-ROM) is 4 3/4 in. This measurement is of the disk or disc itself, *not* the envelope or cartridge it is contained in.

The National Library of Canada, by policy decision, will not use inches anywhere in its catalog records. Therefore, Canadian catalogers should measure the dimensions of all types of computer file carriers in centimeters (Howarth, at 1.5, 9.5).

9.5E. Accompanying material

Computer files are frequently accompanied by manuals, command charts, etc. The presence of such materials may be recorded here, following space - plus - space (see figure 9-1 and discussion at 1.5).

9.5E2. Computer files that are available only by remote access (e.g., mounted on a Local Area Network or accessible via the Internet) do not have any physical format to describe. In such cases, omit the physical description area (see *AACR2R* p. 231, footnote 3; for examples see figures 9-10, 9-11, 9-12, and 9-13). If the library possesses accompanying materials in a physical format for this type of computer file, details should be given in a note.

9.6. SERIES AREA

As with other media, computer files may be published in series. For an example, see figure 9-17.

Figure 9-17.   Series

```
245 00   ‡a Microsoft Word ‡h [computer file].
246 1    ‡i Container title: ‡a Microsoft Word for the Macintosh
250      ‡a Version 5.1a.
256      ‡a Computer program.
260      ‡a Redmond, WA : ‡b Microsoft Corp., ‡c c1992.
300      ‡a 6 computer disks : ‡b col. ; ‡c 3 1/2 in. + ‡e What's new guide (55 p.) + Getting
         started manual (136 p.) + Equation editor user's guide (104 p.) + User's guide (829 p.) +
         Graph user's guide (118 p.)
440  0   ‡a Apple Macintosh series
500      ‡a Word processing program.
538      ‡a System requirements: Macintosh Plus, SE, Classic, Portable, PowerBook, LC, Apple II
         series, or Quadra; 1 MB RAM for System 6, 3 MB for System 7 (additional 1 MB required
         to run grammar checker); System 6.02 or higher (System 7 required for Microsoft Graph
         module); Finder 6.1 or later; one 800K disk drive and a hard drive; Macintosh-compatible
         printer.
500      ‡a Title from title screen.
500      ‡a Copyright by Microsoft Corporation.
710 2    ‡a Microsoft Corporation.
```

Title screen   Microsoft®
                          Microsoft Word Version 5.1a
                              November 4, 1992
                          © 1987-1992 Microsoft Corporation

9.7. NOTE AREA

9.7B1. Nature and scope and system requirements. (a) *Nature and scope.* If it is not apparent from the rest of the description, make a note about the nature of the computer file. This note is recorded in a MARC 500 field (see figures 9-11, 9-13, 9-14, and 9-17).

(b) *System requirements.* This is probably the most important note of all, and it, or a mode of access note, is mandatory. Because computer files will only operate using the computer hardware and operating system they were designed for, it is essential that the library patron know what kind of equipment is needed. Record this note in a MARC 538 field, in subfield ‡a. Begin the note with the words "System requirements:". The wording may be copied from system requirements notes, which usually are included with the documentation accompanying the computer file, but the order of the characteristics should be that prescribed by the rule: (1) the make and model of the computer (e.g., "Macintosh Plus", "IBM PC"); (2) the amount of memory required; (3) the name of the operating system (e.g., "System 7", "DOS version 3.3"); (4) software requirements (e.g., "HyperCard"); and (5) required or recommended peripherals (such as modem, printer, CD-ROM drive, etc.). The cataloger should be as complete as possible in this note, although if nothing beyond the model of computer required is known, that is all the information that can be recorded.

(c) *Mode of access.* Files available only by remote access should give mode of access here. Because access to remote computer files is often not dependent on the user having a particular type of hardware or system, a mode of access note may replace the system requirements note for this type of computer file. The appropriate MARC field is 538. The note may be prefaced by the words "Mode of access:", although other wording may be used (see figure 9-10).

The mode of access note is normally given in conjunction with an 856 field, which gives the "address" at which the file resides. Because the details will be found in the 856 field, the mode of access note itself may be brief (see figure 9-11).

The 856 field contains the information needed to locate electronic resources. The field has been designed so that the local system (if it is adequately programmed) can allow the patron to go directly to the resource from the catalog record. At the least, it should display so that the patron can copy down the address and approach the resource through a different program.

856 can serve as a locator for many types of electronic resources, including "in-house" resources that may reside on the library's Local Area Network. Examples in this *Handbook* are for computer files located at World Wide Web sites on the Internet. For information about other uses of the 856 field, see the latest edition of *USMARC Format for Bibliographic Data* (Washington, D.C.: Library of Congress).

To record an Internet address in an 856 field, make the first indicator "7"; the URL (Uniform Resource Locator, i.e., the "address") is recorded *exactly* (this is critical) in subfield ‡u. The field is completed by subfield ‡2, which gives the access method, i.e., the URL scheme. This is often "http" or "gopher." The access method will usually appear as the first element of the URL. For examples of 856 fields, see figures 9-10, 9-11, 9-12, and 9-13.

9.7B2. Language and script. This refers to *spoken* language, not a programming language. Programming language, if necessary, is recorded in the system requirements note.

9.7B3. Source of title proper. Because there are so many possible sources for the transcription of the title for computer files, it is necessary to note the source used. This is a required note (see examples throughout this chapter).

9.7B6. Statements of responsibility. Make a note for any person or body not already mentioned (e.g., in the statement of responsibility of the title area) who has a significant degree of responsibility for the work. It is customary to give an added entry for the publisher of software; this should be justified by a statement of responsibility note. Often this is simply a note stating that the copyright is held by the publisher (see figure 9-3).

9.7B11. Accompanying material. Notes elaborating the accompanying material recorded in the physical description area may be given here. The "Carmen Sandiego" computer games normally come with a reference book that the player is required to use to discover the whereabouts of the criminal. Details about the book are recorded in this note (see figures 9-7 and 9-8).

9.7B14. Audience note. Educational software is frequently geared to a specific audience level. Record this information in a MARC 521 field (see figure 9-18 and discussion in this *Handbook* at 1.7B14).

Figure 9-18.   Audience note

```
245 00  ‡a New math blaster plus! ‡h [computer file] / ‡c program design, Cathy B. Siegel, David
        D. Ely, Kristine R. Sato ; programming, David D. Ely, Kristine R. Sato ; graphics, Jarvis Eto.
246 30  ‡a Math blaster plus!
250     ‡a V[ersion] 1.0.2.
256     ‡a Computer program.
260     ‡a Torrance, CA : ‡b Davidson, ‡c c1991.
300     ‡a 1 computer disk : ‡b col. ; ‡c 3 1/2 in.
538     ‡a System requirements: Macintosh.
500     ‡a Title from title screen.
521 1   ‡a Ages 6 to 12.
700 1   ‡a Siegel, Cathy B.
700 1   ‡a Ely, David D.
700 1   ‡a Sato, Kristine R.
710 2   ‡a Davidson & Associates
```

Title screen

New Math Blaster Plus! v1.0.2
program design: Cathy B. Siegel
David D. Ely
Kristine R. Sato
programming: David D. Ely
Kristine R. Sato
graphics: Jarvis Eto
copyright © 1991 Davidson & Associates, Inc.

9.7B16. Other formats. The majority of computer files have versions for more than one format. If this information is known to the cataloger, it should be recorded in a note. The MARC 530 field is used (see figure 9-3).

9.7B17. Summary. A brief summary of the purpose or contents of the computer file is often helpful to the library user. This should be recorded in a MARC 520 field (see figures 9-1, 9-2, 9-3, etc.).

9.7B18. Contents. If it is possible to list the contents of a computer file and there are less than about 12 parts, list them in a 505 MARC field, each part separated by space - dash - space (see figure 9-19).

9.8. STANDARD NUMBER AND TERMS OF AVAILABILITY AREA

Occasionally a computer file is assigned an ISBN by its publisher. If an ISBN is found, record it in the 020 MARC field (see figures 9-2 and 9-20).

21.29. ADDED ENTRIES. GENERAL RULE

Computer files are treated no differently from any other medium with respect to the chapter 21 rules for main and added entry. However, one type

Figure 9-19.   Contents note

245 00	‡a Finale ‡h [computer file] : ‡b the art of music notation.
250	‡a Version 3.0.1.
256	‡a Computer programs and data.
260	‡a Eden Prairie, MN : ‡b Coda Music Technology, ‡c c1993.
300	‡a 4 computer disks : ‡b sd., col. ; ‡c 3 1/2 in. ‡e +1 manual (3 v.) + quick reference card (8 p.)
538	‡a System requirements: Macintosh Plus or higher; 2 MB RAM; system 6.0.7 or higher; hard disk with 5 MB free; any Macintosh compatible printer.
500	‡a Title from title screen.
500	‡a On documentation and container: 3.0 for Macintosh.
500	‡a May be used with MIDI instrument (MIDI interface required).
500	‡a Accompanied by 3 v. manual: v. 1. Installation & tutorials -- v. 2. Finale encyclopedia -- v. 3. Finale reference.
520	‡a Program for music transcription, notation, playback, and publishing.
505 0	‡a Program -- Install -- Fonts -- Help.
710 2	‡a Coda Music Technology.

Title screen	Finale The Art of Music Notation © 1987, 1989, 1993 by Coda Music Technology All rights reserved U.S. Patent 4,945,804 and 4,960,031
Label to disk 1	Finale Install Version 3.0.1 For Macintosh® Coda Music Software

Figure 9-20. ISBN

```
020      ‡a 0789400901
100 1    ‡a Macaulay, David.
245 14   ‡a The way things work ‡h [interactive multimedia] / ‡c David Macaulay.
256      ‡a Computer data.
260      ‡a New York : ‡b Dorling Kindersley Multimedia, ‡c c1995.
300      ‡a 1 computer laser optical disc : ‡b sd., col. ; ‡c 4 3/4 in.
538      ‡a System requirements: Macintosh; System 7 or later; 4 MB of Ram (6 MB
         recommended); 14 inch monitor displaying 256 colors; CD-ROM drive.
500      ‡a Title from title screen.
500      ‡a Based on the author's book published by Houghton Mifflin in 1988.
520      ‡a Scientific and mechanical principles of various types of technology are humorously
         demonstrated through text and animation.
710 2    ‡a Dorling Kindersley Multimedia (Firm)
```

Title screen   The Way Things Work
                                       David Macaulay

Disc label
CD-ROM for Macintosh® • Copyright © 1994 Dorling Kindersley Multimedia and
Houghton Mifflin Company • All Rights Reserved • ISBN 0-7894-0090-1
David Macaulay • The Way Things Work

of added entry is somewhat unique to computer files. The custom of giving an added entry for the publisher has been mentioned above, at 9.7B6. This may be justified by 21.29D, which allows added entries "in the context of a given catalogue" for headings other than those prescribed in 21.30.

It has been customary to make an entry for the system details in a 753 field. The name of the make and model of the machine are entered in subfield ‡a; the operating system is recorded in subfield ‡c, as for example:

```
753      ‡a Macintosh Classic ‡c System 6.
```

Because this simply repeats information already found in the system requirements note (538 field; see discussion in this *Handbook* at 9.7B1b) and there is little justification for it as an added entry (it is not called for in *AACR2R*, nor is it under authority control), the Library of Congress will no longer use this field and has proposed that it be made obsolete.[7] Although commonly found in computer file records, it has not been used in this *Handbook*.

21.30G. Related works

Computer files, particularly games and educational software, may be based on a printed book. The computer game "The hitchhiker's guide to the galaxy" is based on the book of the same name by Douglas Adams. Because Adams did not write the computer program, he is not given main entry. A name-title related works added entry is given instead (see figure 9-21). On

Figure 9-21.   Related work

```
245 04   ‡a The hitchhiker's guide to the galaxy ‡h [computer file] : ‡b Infocom interactive fiction :
         a science fiction story.
250      ‡a Release 56
256      ‡a Computer program (5 files)
260      ‡a Cambridge, MA : ‡b Infocom, Inc., ‡c c1984.
300      ‡a 1 computer disk ; ‡c 3 1/2 in. + ‡e 1 instructional manual + 1 cotton fluff ball +
         1 destruct order for home planet + 1 "don't panic" button + 1 pair of black paper glasses
         + 1 microscopic space fleet + 1 reference card.
538      ‡a System requirements: Macintosh.
500      ‡a Title from title screen.
500      ‡a Copyright by Infocom, Inc.
500      ‡a Based on: Adams, Douglas, 1952-    The hitchhiker's guide to the galaxy.
700 1    ‡a Adams, Douglas, ‡d 1952-    ‡t Hitchhiker's guide to the galaxy.
710 2    ‡a Infocom (Firm)
```

Title screen   The Hitchhiker's Guide to the Galaxy
              Infocom Interactive Fiction -- A Science Fiction Story
                     Copyright © 1984 by Infocom, Inc.
                           All rights reserved
                             Release 56

the other hand, the computer disc "The Way Things Work" is represented as being by David Macaulay, also the author of the book by the same name. Although no doubt Macaulay did not do all the programming for the disc, he is responsible for the text and graphics, and so is given main entry; because the title in the catalog record is the same as the title of the book, no further added entry is necessary for the related work (see figure 9-20).

NOTES

1. Two books that are useful in cataloging computer files are Nancy B. Olson, *Cataloging Microcomputer Software: A Manual to Accompany AACR2 Chapter 9, Computer Files* (Englewood, Colo.: Libraries Unlimited, 1988) (hereinafter referred to as Olson 1988), and Nancy B. Olson, *Cataloging Computer Files* (Lake Crystal, Minn.: Published for the Minnesota AACR2 Trainers by Soldier Creek Press, 1992) (hereinafter referred to as Olson 1992). The second book is basically a second edition of the first, but the earlier book contains much useful general information about computer files omitted from the 1992 volume.

   General information about MARC coding is found in the introduction to this *Handbook*; details about coding the descriptive portion of the record are found throughout chapter 1; information about the coding of main and added access points is found at the beginning of chapter 14. An explanation of the MARC authorities format is given in *Handbook* chapters 15, 17, and 18. Information about specific MARC fields may be found by consulting the index under "MARC fields."

2. Interactive Multimedia Guidelines Review Task Force, *Guidelines for Bibliographic Description of Interactive Multimedia* (Chicago: American Library Association,

Committee on Cataloging: Description and Access, 1994) (hereinafter referred to as *Guidelines*). This publication explicitly takes precedence over *AACR2R* in case of conflict (*Guidelines*, p. vi). *Guidelines* contains a useful glossary of computer file terms not found in the *AACR2R* Glossary (see *Guidelines*, Appendix D). The Library of Congress will apply the *Guidelines*, including the new GMD "interactive multimedia" (*CSB 67*, winter 1995, p. 22).

3. Nancy B. Olson, editor, *Cataloging Internet Resources: A Manual and Practical Guide* (OCLC Online Computer Library Center, Inc., 1995) (available at URL http://www.uccs.edu/~ddodd/internet.html/#9.6) (hereinafter referred to as Olson 1995).

4. Olson 1995, at 9.0B1.

5. See Olson 1988, p. 54, and Olson 1995, at 9.4.

6. See *LCRI* 9.5B1 (Feb. 15, 1994). The new edition of *International Standard Bibliographic Description for Computer Files (ISBD (CF))*, to be published in 1997 (draft published 1995), is also expected to include this distinction (see John D. Byrum, "ISBD (CF) Review Group, Meeting of April 24–26, 1995, Summary Report," *International Cataloging and Bibliographic Control* 24, no. 3 [July–Sept. 1995]: 51). The new edition will be called *ISBD (ER)* (Electronic Resources).

7. Announced at the Association for Library Collections and Technical Services Committee on Cataloging: Description and Access meeting at the American Library Association, July 8, 1996.

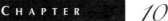

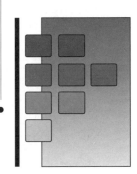

THREE-DIMENSIONAL ARTIFACTS AND REALIA

AACR2R chapter 10 gives rules for the description of all kinds of three-dimensional items—handmade, manufactured, and natural—with the exception of those covered in other chapters. Globes and relief maps, for example, are considered cartographic materials and are covered in *AACR2R* chapter 3.

AACR2R chapter 21 has no specific rules for main and added entries for three-dimensional objects. Thus, general principles governing authorship responsibility as set forth in *AACR2R* 21.1A1 indicate that a sculptor will be given main entry for his or her work (see figure 10-1).[1]

In addition, *AACR2R* 21.16B states that a reproduction of an art original (e.g., a painting, drawing, or sculpture; see *AACR2R* Appendix D [Glossary]) will be entered under the heading for the original work. Thus, replicas of sculpture that are intended to simulate the appearance of the original piece are entered under the heading for the original work, whether they are the same size as the original or not.

10.0B1. Chief source of information. Descriptive cataloging rules that govern other types of library materials will be applied to the cataloging of three-dimensional objects. The object itself or a label permanently attached to it serves as the chief source of information, along with any accompanying

Figure 10-1.   Main entry under creator

```
100 1    ‡a Maxwell, Robert.
245 10   ‡a Pig 10 ‡h [art original] / ‡c Robert Maxwell.
260      ‡c [196-?]
300      ‡a 1 sculpture : ‡b unglazed clay, brown ; ‡c 8 × 9 cm.
500      ‡a Stylized wide-mouth pig designed as a container for small objects.
```

textual material and a container issued by the "publisher" or manufacturer (see figure 10-2).

10.0H. Many of the three-dimensional items covered by *AACR2R* chapter 10 have more than one part. If the individual items in the set do not bear a common title, take cataloging information from the container. The container furnished all the information for the example shown in figure 10-3.

10.1. TITLE AND STATEMENT OF RESPONSIBILITY AREA

Record the information according to general guidelines in 1.1. In figure 10-1 the title of the sculpture and the name of the sculptor were incised on the base of the object. The information was transcribed accordingly. But many, if not most, noncommercially produced three-dimensional artifacts will not be labeled in this fashion. If no title appears on the object, a con-

Figure 10-2.   Object as chief source

245 00	‡a Tok-bak ‡h [realia].
260	‡a [Niles, Ill.] : ‡b Developmental Learning Materials, ‡c [197-]
300	‡a 1 sound intensifier : ‡b plastic, blue ; ‡c 20 × 12 cm.
500	‡a Device that fits over the ears and mouth so as to intensify the sound of the wearer's voice.
710 2	‡a Developmental Learning Materials (Firm)

Figure 10-3.   Container as chief source

100 1	‡a Ploutz, Paul F.
245 10	‡a Evolution ‡h [game] : ‡b geologic time chart : the historical record of life on earth ... / ‡c by Paul F. Ploutz.
246 30	‡a Geologic time chart
260	‡a Athens, Ohio : ‡b Union Print. Co., ‡c c1972.
300	‡a 1 game (board, cards, 4 tokens, 1 die, chips, glossary) ; ‡c in box 37 × 39 × 4 cm.
521 1	‡a Ages 10 to adult.
520	‡a Game traces the development of life from algae to modern man.
500	‡a For 2-6 players.

Chart	Geologic Time Chart The historical record of life on earth becomes a simplified playing board for a fun educational game for science entitled Evolution by Paul F. Ploutz, Ed.D. © Copyright 1972

tainer, or accompanying textual material, the cataloger makes up a brief descriptive title, which is transcribed within brackets as the first part of the title and statement of responsibility area (1.1B7). No statement of responsibility will be given unless the item was signed or the information appeared on one of the locations considered part of the chief source. This information, if taken from another source, appears in a note (see figure 10-4).

10.1C. *Optional addition.* **General material designation**

See discussion under *AACR2R* 1.1C. The GMD will be added immediately following the title proper. Appropriate GMDs for materials covered by *AACR2R* chapter 10 include: art original, art reproduction, diorama, game, microscope slide, model, realia, and toy. A clear-cut distinction between "art original" and "realia" is often difficult to make. See discussion and definitions under 1.1C in this *Handbook*. Follow guidelines given there.

10.4. Publication, Distribution, etc., Area

For commercially produced three-dimensional artifacts the three elements (place, publisher, etc., and date) prescribed by 1.4 will be included and general guidelines under it will be followed. However, place and name of publisher or manufacturer, obviously, are inappropriate for a noncommercial item. Give the year of creation as the sole element in the publication area for such objects (10.4F2) (see figure 10-4).

10.4F2. Date. The date will also be omitted (and thus the entire area) when describing a naturally occurring object (see figure 10-5).

Figure 10-4.   Noncommercial artifact

```
100 1    ‡a Fingal, Ingrid.
245 00   ‡a [Hand weaving] ‡h [art original].
260      ‡c [1978]
300      ‡a 1 sampler : ‡b cotton, col. ; ‡c 125 × 30 cm.
500      ‡a Title supplied by cataloger.
500      ‡a Woven by Ingrid Fingal.
500      ‡a Pattern: Crackle weave.
```

Figure 10-5.   Natural object—no publication area

```
245 00   ‡a [Scorpion] ‡h [realia].
300      ‡a 1 scorpion : ‡b tan ; ‡c in dome 4 cm. high × 10 cm. diameter.
500      ‡a Obtained in Arizona desert, Aug. 1972.
```

10.5. PHYSICAL DESCRIPTION AREA

For the cataloging of three-dimensional artifacts, this area includes the same general elements used to describe other library materials: extent of item, other details, dimensions, and, when appropriate, accompanying material.

10.5B1. Extent of the item. Give the number of units followed by a specific material designation. The terms listed under 10.5B1 are not the only terms that may be used as specific material designators in the physical description area. As already demonstrated, everything from samplers to scorpions may be cataloged by rules given in *AACR2R* chapter 10. If one of the terms listed under 10.5B1 is appropriate to the three-dimensional object being described, use it. Otherwise, give the name of the object as the specific material designator.

Caution: although the specific material designator list may be enlarged at the cataloger's discretion, this is not the case with the GMD given following the title proper. The cataloger is limited to the terms listed in 1.1C1 for the GMD.

Diorama: See *AACR2R* Appendix D (Glossary) for definition of a diorama. The diorama itself is the preferred source for cataloging data. If appropriate information is not found on the object, data may be transcribed from the container or from accompanying material. In the example shown in figure 10-6, the title was transcribed from the envelope in which the folded diorama was stored; publication area information is from the diorama itself.

Exhibit: An exhibit is "a collection of objects and materials arranged in a setting to convey a unified idea."[2] An exhibit may be made up of a number of different types of materials; if so, the GMD will be "kit" (North American) or "multimedia" (British). If the materials are unified, use an appropriate GMD from the list under 1.1C1 (see figure 10-7). An exhibit is to be studied and observed; it is not meant for user interaction.

Game: See *AACR2R* Appendix D (Glossary) for definition. Unless individual pieces in the game bear a common title, the container will be the chief source of information. Supplement this as needed with information from accompanying material (see figure 10-8).

Microscope slide: A microscope slide is a special slide produced for use with a microscope. It is generally made of two pieces of glass put together sandwich fashion, with some realia between the layers. Cataloging information will be taken from the slide itself, a container, or accompanying

Figure 10-6.   Diorama

```
245 00    ‡a Christmas scene ‡h [diorama].
260       ‡a Providence, R.I. : ‡b Providence Lithograph Co., 1959.
300       ‡a 1 diorama (various pieces) : ‡b cardboard, col. ; ‡c 37 × 56 × 26 cm. folded to 26 ×
          38 × 2 cm.
500       ‡a Includes 3 groups of figures: Mary, Joseph, the baby Jesus, and 2 groups of shepherds
          and sheep with stable background; in envelope.
500       ‡a Stock DF 211.
710 2     ‡a Providence Lithograph Co.
```

Figure 10-7.   Exhibit

```
245 00    ‡a Coal ‡h [realia] : ‡b plant life to plastics.
260       ‡a Washington : ‡b Bituminous Coal Institute, Education Dept., ‡c [196-?]
300       ‡a 1 exhibit (12 pieces) : ‡b col. ; ‡c in folder 25 × 17 × 2 cm.
500       ‡a Samples of coal and coal products.
710 2     ‡a Bituminous Coal Institute. ‡b Education Dept.
```

Figure 10-8.   Game

```
245 00    ‡a Alice in Wonderland card game set ‡h [game] : ‡b with the original illustrations in full
          color.
260       ‡a New York : ‡b Merrimack Pub. Corp., ‡c [196-?]
300       ‡a 1 game (48 cards) : ‡b col. ; ‡c 10 × 7 × 2 cm.
500       ‡a Reproduced from the antique original set; featuring John Tenniel illustrations.
500       ‡a No. 1974S.
700 1     ‡a Carroll, Lewis, ‡d 1832-1898. ‡t Alice's adventures in Wonderland.
700 1     ‡a Tenniel, John, ‡c Sir, ‡d 1820-1914.
```

Container	48 Piece Antique Replica Alice in Wonderland Card Game Set with the original illustrations in full color

material. If none of these sources furnishes cataloging data, the cataloger constructs an entry as has been done with figure 1-13. Special rules governing microscope slides are 10.5C1, 10.5C2, and 10.5D1.

Mock-up: See *AACR2R* Appendix D (Glossary) for definition. A mock-up is a teaching device that should involve interaction with the user. Thus, a dummy steering wheel and dashboard used to teach automobile driving is a mock-up; a plastic piano keyboard sometimes used in teaching class piano is a mock-up (figure 10-9).

Model: See *AACR2R* Appendix D (Glossary) for definition. A mock-up (q.v.) is one kind of a model, generally one with moving parts. A model may have moving parts, but it differs from a mock-up in that it is basically noninteractive; it is simply an artifact to be examined, not a training tool.

The chief source of information for a model, as for other three-dimensional objects, is the object itself, together with the container and accompanying textual material (see figure 10-10).

Figure 10-9.   Mock-up

```
245 00   ‡a [Piano keyboard] ‡h [model].
260      ‡a [S.l. : ‡b s.n., ‡c 196-?]
300      ‡a 1 mock-up : ‡b plastic ; ‡c 16 × 36 cm.
500      ‡a Silent keyboard, two octaves, for use in teaching piano.
```

Figure 10-10.   Model

```
245 00   ‡a Pictograph-cuneiform unit ‡h [model] / ‡c prepared by the Educational Division of
         Alva Museum Replicas ; educational consultant, Hyman Kavett.
260      ‡a Long Island City, N.Y. : ‡b Alva Museum Replicas, ‡c c1968.
300      ‡a 6 tablets : ‡b plastic, brown ; ‡c in box 30 × 32 × 6 cm. + ‡e 1 teacher's guide + ‡e
         1 student activity program.
440  0   ‡a Alva class research kit ; ‡v 1/2
500      ‡a Replicas colored to simulate an early Sumerian pictograph (ca. 3000 B.C.) and a
         cuneiform tablet with its 2-part envelope (ca. 1800 B.C.); includes 4 pictographs and 2
         cuneiform tablets.
504      ‡a Includes bibliographical references (p. 8 of teacher's guide).
710 2    ‡a Alva Museum Replicas. ‡b Educational Division.
```

10.6. SERIES AREA

Follow general instructions under 1.6 for transcription of series (see, for instance, figure 10-10).

10.7. NOTE AREA

Notes are of the same type and are listed in the same order as that indicated in 1.7. See discussion of this rule for general guidance and instructions for MARC field coding.

NOTES

1. General information about MARC coding is found in the introduction to this *Handbook;* details about coding the descriptive portion of the record are found throughout chapter 1; information about the coding of main and added access points is found at the beginning of chapter 14. An explanation of the MARC authorities format is given in *Handbook* chapters 15, 17, and 18. Information about specific MARC fields may be found by consulting the index under "MARC fields."
2. Alma M. Tillin and William J. Quinly, *Standards for Cataloging Nonprint Materials,* 4th ed. (Washington, D.C.: AECT, 1976), p. 215.

CHAPTER 11

MICROFORMS

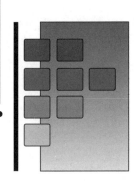

A microform may be defined as "a miniature reproduction of printed or other graphic matter which cannot be utilized without magnification."[1] Because a microform requires special equipment for its use, under *AACR2R* rules it is regarded as a special type of library material rather than as a variant type of book, as was the case under *AACR1* rules. A library collection is likely to include two types of microforms: microform reproductions of works previously published in eye-readable format and microforms that are original publications.

Under *AACR1* rule 191 (1967), a microform was to be described in terms of the original work; that is, a microform that reproduced a monograph would be cataloged according to monographic cataloging rules, including a physical description area, that gave the number of pages, illustration statement, and size of the original book, if this could be determined. Microform publication details were relegated to a note.

AACR Chapter 6 (1974) suggested that a microform edition of an eye-readable work should be added to the catalog entry for the original work as a dashed-on entry (rule 152C). This was to be done if the library owned both the original, hard-copy edition and the microform version. If the library had only the microform, *AACR* Chapter 6 (1974) rule 156A stipulated treatment in the same fashion as *AACR1* rule 191. For an original edition in microform, the instructions in *AACR1* 191C and *AACR* Chapter 6 (1974) 156C were identical. In this instance only, the physical description area gave information about the microform itself.

In contrast to previous rules, *AACR2* chapter 11 rules for the description of microforms are analogous to rules for the cataloging of facsimiles (1.11). In all cases, the cataloger is to describe the microform item. Any data about the original work (except for mathematical data of a cartographic item, 11.3A; physical presentation of music, 11.3B; or numeric and/or chronological or other designation of a serial, 11.3C) will be ignored in transcribing information in the body of the card. Data about the original work are to be given in a note.

Almost immediately, the Library of Congress encountered difficulty in applying the rules of *AACR2* chapter 11 to microreproductions of previously published materials. As part of its preservation program, LC makes or purchases microform replacements of thousands of deteriorating books in its collections each year. The expense for creating unique bibliographic records for each of these microform versions of printed originals proved to be overwhelming, to say nothing of the fact that library patrons, confronted often with two catalog records for the same item—one hard copy and one microform—were confused and dissatisfied. As a result, the Library of Congress, the National Agricultural Library, and the National Library of Medicine determined that they would continue to follow the *AACR1* principle for bibliographic description when cataloging microforms for previously published books and serials (*CSB* 11, winter 1981, p. 15–16; see *LCRI* ch. 11, Sept. 1, 1992).

This decision has had enormous influence on North American cataloging practice. The almost universal practice—based on the author's experience in using the RLIN database—is to follow the *LCRI* rather than *AACR2R* chapter 11 when cataloging microform reproductions of previously published materials.[2]

If a library wishes to follow the Library of Congress policy decision in this matter, the cataloger will catalog a microform that has previously appeared in a different format according to the original format. In the instance of figure 11-1a, unless the library also owns the original hardcopy thesis, the fiche must be checked for pages and types of illustrations, and the size must be figured.[3] This information can often be obtained by consulting a database such as RLIN or OCLC. If the size of the original publication cannot be determined, this portion of the physical description area may be omitted. Figures 11-1a and 11-1b show cataloging first by LC policy decision and second according to *AACR2R* chapter 11. Because a thesis is not formally published, there is no note in figure 11-1b about the original publication.

Figure 11-1a.   Microfiche. LC policy decision

100 1	‡a Beard, Linda Susan, ‡d 1951-
245 10	‡a Precambrian geology of the Cottonwood Cliffs area, Mohave County, Arizona ‡h [microform] / ‡c by Linda Sue Beard.
260	‡c 1986.
300	‡a ix, 115 leaves : ‡b ill., maps ; ‡c 28 cm.
502	‡a Thesis (M.S.)--University of Arizona, 1985.
504	‡a Includes bibliographical references (leaves 109-115).
533	‡a Microfiche. ‡b Ann Arbor, Mich. : ‡c University Microfilms International, ‡d 1986. ‡e 2 microfiches : ill., maps ; 11 X 15 cm.

Figure 11-1b.   Microfiche. *AACR2R* chapter 11

```
100 1    ‡a Beard, Linda Susan, ‡d 1951-
245 10   ‡a Precambrian geology of the Cottonwood Cliffs area, Mohave County, Arizona ‡h
         [microform] / ‡c by Linda Sue Beard.
260      ‡a Ann Arbor, Mich. : ‡b University Microfilms International, ‡c 1986.
300      ‡a 2 microfiches : ‡b ill., maps.
502      ‡a Thesis (M.S.)--University of Arizona, 1985.
504      ‡a Includes bibliographical references (leaves 109-115).
```

11.0B. Sources of information

As with other types of library materials, the chief source for microforms is the item itself. For previously published materials, however, if the cataloger chooses to follow LC policy decision, the chief source will be that prescribed by the *AACR2R* chapter giving rules for cataloging the original.

Microfilm: The title frame at the beginning of the microfilm is the chief source of cataloging data for a microfilm. Figures 11-2a and 11-2b illustrate cataloging of a microfilm done by LC policy decision and by *AACR2R.*

Aperture card: This card, usually 9 × 19 cm., includes an opening for a microfilm insert. Aperture cards are usually punched for machine manipulation and retrieval. The chief source of information is the title card.

Microfiche: See *AACR2R* Appendix D (Glossary) for definition of microfiche. The title frame at the beginning of the microfiche serves as the chief source. The microfiche cataloged as figure 11-3 is an original microform publication. Therefore, the Library of Congress would apply *AACR2R* rules from chapter 11.

Microopaque: See *AACR2R* Appendix D (Glossary) for definition of microopaque. The title frame at the beginning of the microopaque is the chief source; eye-readable data at the top of the card may also be used if necessary. In the example shown in figure 11-4, the title frame furnished the title and statement of responsibility information. The rest of the data—publication area and series—appeared at the top of the card in eye-readable type. Figure 11-4 shows cataloging by *AACR2R* rules.

11.1. TITLE AND STATEMENT OF RESPONSIBILITY AREA

Follow guidelines given in 1.1 for transcribing this area. If the title of the microform is different from that of the original, give the microform title in the title and statement of responsibility area if following *AACR2R;* if following the LC decision, transcribe the original's chief source.

Figure 11-2a.   Microfilm. LC policy decision

```
100 1    ‡a Tuttle, John B. ‡q (John Betley), ‡d 1882-
245 14   ‡a The analysis of rubber ‡h [microform] / ‡c by John B. Tuttle.
260      ‡a New York : ‡b Chemical Catalog Co., ‡c 1922.
300      ‡a 155 p. ; ‡c 24 cm.
490 1    ‡a Monograph series / American Chemical Society
504      ‡a Includes bibliographical references (p. 121-138) and index.
533      ‡a Microfilm. ‡b Ann Arbor, Mich. : ‡c University Microfilms International, ‡d 1976. ‡e 1
         microfilm reel ; 35 mm.
830  0   ‡a Monograph series (American Chemical Society)
```

Figure 11-2b.   Microfilm. *AACR2R* chapter 11

```
100 1    ‡a Tuttle, John B. ‡q (John Betley), ‡d 1882-
245 14   ‡a The analysis of rubber ‡h [microform] / ‡c by John B. Tuttle.
260      ‡a Ann Arbor, Mich. : ‡b University Microfilms International, ‡c 1976.
300      ‡a 1 microfilm reel ; ‡c 35 mm.
504      ‡a Includes bibliographical references (p. 121-138) and index.
534      ‡p Reproduction of: ‡c New York : Chemical Catalog Co., 1922. ‡f (Monograph series /
         American Chemical Society).
```

Figure 11-3.   Microfiche

```
111 2    ‡a Library History Seminar ‡n (4th : ‡d 1971 : ‡c Florida State University)
245 10   ‡a Library history seminar, no.4 ‡h [microform] : ‡b proceedings, 1971 / ‡c edited by
         Harold Goldstein, John M. Goudeau.
260      ‡a Tallahassee, Fla. : ‡b Journal of library history, ‡c c1972.
300      ‡a 4 microfiches : ‡b negative.
700 1    ‡a Goldstein, Harold.
700 1    ‡a Goudeau, John M.
730 0    ‡a Journal of library history.
```

Frame 1	Library History Seminar No. 4, Proceedings, 1971 Edited by Harold Goldstein, John M. Goudeau The Journal of Library History School of Library Science Florida State University Tallahassee, Florida
Frame 2	[blank]
Frame 3	Library History Seminar No.4, Proceedings, 1971 Copyright 1972 by the Journal of Library History

Figure 11-4.   Microopaque

```
100 1    ‡a Georgi, Charlotte.
245 10   ‡a Twenty-five years of Pulitzer prize novels, 1918-1943 ‡h [microform] : ‡b a content
         analysis / ‡c by Charlotte Georgi.
260      ‡a Rochester, N. Y. : ‡b University of Rochester Press for Association of College and
         Research Libraries, ‡c 1958.
300      ‡a 4 microopaques (103 fr.) ; ‡c 8 X 13 cm.
440  0   ‡a ACRL microcard series ; ‡v no. 96
502      ‡a Thesis (M.S.L.S.)--University of North Carolina, 1956.
504      ‡a Includes bibliographical references (frames 67-69).
500      ‡a Microcard: UR-58 RL 22.
```

```
Frame 1                              UR-58
                                     RL 22
                                   Micro Card
Frame 2          Twenty-five years of Pulitzer prize novels, 1918-1943:
                        a content analysis by Charlotte Georgi
             A thesis submitted to the Faculty of the University of North Carolina
                 in partial fulfillment of the requirements for the degree of
                    Master of Science in the School of Library Science
                                  Chapel Hill 1956
```

11.2. EDITION AREA

The edition statement may be transcribed from the chief source of information, the rest of the item, and the container. The edition statement given in the edition area must be that of the microform if cataloging according the *AACR2R*. The item may also include an edition statement pertinent to the original work. Such information will be given in a note.

11.3. SPECIAL DATA FOR CARTOGRAPHIC MATERIALS, MUSIC, AND SERIALS

This information may be transcribed from the chief source of information, the rest of the item, or the container. Data about the original item are to be given in this area; aside from the note area, this is the only place where information about the original work appears in the *AACR2R* chapter 11 entry.

11.3C. Serials

Record numeric and/or other designation area as instructed in 12.3 for a serial in microformat, either an original or a reproduction. See chapter 12 in this *Handbook* for discussion and examples of numeric and/or other designation area.

Cataloging information for the examples shown in figures 11-5a and 11-5b was taken from four consecutive title frames at the beginning of the microfilm reproduction of the periodical.

11.4. PUBLICATION, DISTRIBUTION, ETC., AREA

Publication details are those of the microform, not the original, if the microform is a reproduction of another publication, unless the LC policy decision is followed.

11.5. PHYSICAL DESCRIPTION AREA

As with other types of library materials, the physical description area includes four elements:

11.5B. Extent of item and specific material designation

11.5C. Other physical details

11.5D. Dimensions

11.5E. Accompanying material (if any)

See preceding examples for illustrations of the application of rules for the physical description area. Note that if microfiches are standard sized (11 × 15 cm.), dimensions are omitted (see figures 11-1b and 11-3).

11.6. SERIES AREA

A series statement pertaining to the microform will be included in the series area. As appropriate, a series statement pertaining to the original publication will be given in a note (11.7B12) (see figure 11-2b).

Figure 11-5a.   Periodical on microform. LC policy decision

```
245 00   ‡a Frank Leslie's boys' and girls' weekly ‡h [microform].
260      ‡a New York : ‡b F. Leslie, ‡c 1866-1884.
300      ‡a 36 v. : ‡b ill. ; ‡c 32-41 cm.
310      ‡a Weekly
362 0    ‡a Vol. 1, no. 1 (Oct. 13, 1866)-v. 36, no. 905 (Feb. 9, 1884).
500      ‡a Title from caption.
500      ‡a "An illustrated journal of amusement, adventure, and instruction."
533      ‡a Microfilm. ‡b [Washington] : ‡c Library of Congress Photoduplication Service, ‡d 1969.
         ‡e 11 microfilm reels : ill. ; 35 mm.
700 1    ‡a Leslie, Frank, ‡d 1821-1880.
```

Figure 11-5b.   Periodical on microform. *AACR2R* chapter 11

```
245 00   ‡a Frank Leslie's boys' and girls' weekly ‡h [microform].
260      ‡a [Washington] : ‡b Library of Congress Photoduplication Service, ‡c 1969.
300      ‡a 11 microfilm reels : ‡b ill. ; ‡c 35 mm.
310      ‡a Weekly
362 0    ‡a Vol. 1, no. 1 (Oct. 13, 1866)-v. 36, no. 905 (Feb. 9, 1884).
500      ‡a "An illustrated journal of amusement, adventure, and instruction."
534      ‡p Reproduction of: ‡c New York : F. Leslie, 1866-1884.
700 1    ‡a Leslie, Frank, ‡d 1821-1880.
```

Frame 1	START
Frame 2	Frank Leslie's boys' and girls' weekly New York Shelf no. 20365 (AP 200.F65)
Frame 3	[reproduction of LC card] Microfilmed 1969, Library of Congress Photoduplication Service
Frame 4	October 13, 1866 thru April 25, 1868 (reel 1)

11.7. NOTE AREA

Notes pertaining to the microform come first. Then, as stipulated in 11.7B, give notes relating to the original, combined in a single note. This note may be either a 500 or a 534 note (see discussion at 1.7B7). Catalogers following the LC decision will do the opposite, giving notes pertaining to the original in separate 5XX fields, with a single, combined note in a 533 field giving details relating to the reproduction. See examples throughout this chapter for the formatting of 534 and 533 notes.

11.8. STANDARD NUMBER AREA

Although it seems a contradiction in terms, a microform publication sometimes includes an International Standard Book Number (ISBN). If one appears somewhere on the item, or if the ISBN (or other standard number) pertaining to the item is given in any other source, it is to be transcribed as part of the entry. Figure 11-6 is an example of an original microform publication that includes an ISBN.

Figure 11-6.   ISBN

```
020      ‡a 0226014185
100 1    ‡a Allen, Sue.
245 10   ‡a Victorian bookbindings ‡h [microform] : ‡b a pictorial survey / ‡c Sue Allen.
260      ‡a Chicago : ‡b University of Chicago Press, ‡c c1972.
300      ‡a 4 microfiches : ‡b col. ill.
```

Frame 1   Key to contents
            [fiche number and frame show location of items]

Frame 2   Victorian bookbindings: a pictorial survey   Sue Allen
            The University of Chicago Press, Chicago 60637
            The University of Chicago Press, Ltd. London
            ©1972 by the University of Chicago
            All rights reserved. Published 1972
            Library of Congress Catalog card number 72-94380
            International Standard Book Number 0-226-01-418-5

NOTES

1. Jean Riddle Weihs, *Nonbook Materials,* 1st ed. (Ottawa: Canadian Library Association, 1973), p. 53.
2. The National Library of Australia also follows the *LCRI* for chapter 11 (Howarth, at ch. 11, p. 2). The policy of the National Library of Canada and the British Library is to apply *AACR2R* chapter 11 (correspondence with the British Library and the National Library of Canada dated 26 March 1996 and 28 March 1996, in the author's possession).
3. General information about MARC coding is found in the introduction to this *Handbook;* details about coding the descriptive portion of the record are found throughout chapter 1; information about the coding of main and added access points is found at the beginning of chapter 14. An explanation of the MARC authorities format is given in *Handbook* chapters 15, 17, and 18. Information about specific MARC fields may be found by consulting the index under "MARC fields."

CHAPTER 12

SERIALS

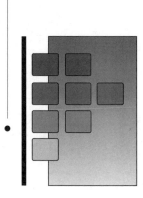

A serial, by definition, is "a publication in any medium issued in successive parts bearing numerical or chronological designations and intended to be continued indefinitely."[1] Serials include everything from annual reports and yearbooks of learned societies through *Mad Magazine, The Perils of Pauline,* and the local newspaper; "serial" is a state of issue, not a kind of material. Anything, print or nonprint, may be a serial, as long as it is issued in successive parts, numbered or dated in some fashion, and as long as it has no planned termination point (see *LCRI* 12.0A, Aug. 27, 1990).

The basic rules and principles governing main entry and added entries for serials are the same as for monographs. These rules are covered in *AACR2R* Part II, chapter 21. *AACR2R* chapter 12, as well as other chapters in Part I, deals only with rules for descriptive cataloging.

Because, as Michael Gorman has correctly pointed out, "serials constitute a type of publication rather than a condition of authorship," there is little specific mention of serials as such in *AACR2R* chapter 21.[2] The only specific directives are in regard to a change in the title proper of a serial (21.2C) and to a change in the name of the person or corporate body responsible for a serial (21.3B). However, in view of the problems that serial publications often pose for catalogers, it seems appropriate to give some attention to the evolution of rules for serials cataloging that has resulted in the present rules.

The *ALA Cataloging Rules for Author and Title Entries* (1949) included a number of separate rules for treatment of various kinds of serials: periodicals and newspapers were covered by 5C; almanacs, yearbooks, and similar materials by 5D; directories by 5E; and series by 5F. As already stated, the International Conference on Cataloguing Principles, Paris, 1961, which resulted in the Paris Principles, was an attempt to arrive at a set of principles governing entry that would eliminate such multiplication of rules. It is possibly significant that almost nothing was said at the conference about serial publications as such, because the fact that a publication may be issued serially has nothing necessarily to do with the question of authorship responsibility. Paris Principle 11.14 says that "works (including serials and periodicals) known primarily or conventionally by title rather than by the name of the author" should be entered under title. Paris Principle 11.5 states: "When a serial publication is issued successively under different titles, a main entry should be made under each title."

Following the International Conference of 1961, the editors of *AACR1* proceeded to draw up a code based on the Paris Principles. The problem of formulating a rule for the entry of serials following the directive of Paris Principle 11.14 was a thorny one that troubled the editors greatly. The result of their efforts, *AACR1* rule 6, was, as Sumner Spalding admitted, rather arbitrary.[3] Briefly, rule 6 divided serials into three groups:

1. Those issued by commercial corporate bodies and not of personal authorship (to be entered under title)
2. Those issued by a corporate body—be it professional, civic, or political—that is in some way more than commercially interested in the publication (chiefly, but not entirely, to be entered under title)
3. Those by a personal author (to be entered under author).

All serials in the first group (rule 6A) were to be given title main entry. But those serials in the second group (rule 6B) proved difficult to categorize. This enormous category of serials issued by a corporate body was subdivided into two parts. The first group (6B1) was limited to periodicals, monographic series, serially published bibliographies, indexes, directories, biographical dictionaries, almanacs, and yearbooks not covered by 6A and 6C. Most of the serials in this group would also be entered under title, with added entry for the sponsoring or issuing corporate body. However, the committee felt that the wording of the serial title had to be taken into consideration, in accordance with Paris Principle 9.12, which directed entry under corporate body "when the wording of the title or title page, taken in conjunction with the nature of the work, clearly implies that the corporate body is collectively responsible for the content of the work . . . e.g., serials whose titles consist of a generic term (Bulletin, Transactions, etc.) preceded or followed by the name of a corporate body, and which include some account of the activities of the body."

It seemed too much to expect the cataloger to decide in each case whether such serials did indeed "include some account of the activities of the body," and so a rather complex set of exceptions to 6B1's general premise of entry under title evolved. Entry would be under the name of the corporate body if the title included the name of the corporate body (*Library of Congress Information Bulletin, Journal of the Optical Society of America*); or if the title included an abbreviation of the name of the corporate body (*NEA Handbook*); or if the title consisted "solely of a generic term [such as journal, newsletter, annals, etc.] that requires the name of the body for adequate identification of the serial" (the American Theological Library Association's publication titled *Newsletter*).

As previously mentioned, serials covered by 6B1 were limited to periodicals, monographic series, serially published directories, indexes, bibliographies, biographical dictionaries, almanacs, and yearbooks. Entry for any other type of serial "issued by or under the authority of a corporate body" was to be under the name of the body (6B2), without exception.

In accordance with Paris Principle 11.5, and in a change from ALA 1949 rule 5, *AACR1* rule 6D stipulated that serials that changed their names would be entered separately under each title. The rationale behind this rule, which is still in effect under *AACR2R* 21.2C and 21.3B, was the fact that a change in the name of a serial, even though it might not be accompanied by a change in the sponsoring organization, generally meant a shift in emphasis, a change of direction for the serial. Such a shift often meant that the serial was in effect a new entity. Thus, under the general principles that governed both the Paris Principles and *AACR1*, the serial should be given a new entry, even though the volume numbering might be continuous.

In the years following publication of *AACR1*, serials catalogers, particularly those concerned with machine-readable records, were increasingly unhappy with the complexities of *AACR1* rule 6. By 1975 many serials experts had rejected the concept of entry under personal or corporate author entirely. Opposing viewpoints were aired at a meeting held at the ALA Midwinter Meeting, January 19, 1975.[4] Those advocating title main entry for all serials won out at the ALA Conference of summer 1975; for several months it seemed that type of format rather than authorship responsibility would be the deciding factor for serials entry rules in the coming revision of *AACR*. In the midst of the turmoil over choice of main entry, a new international code for the bibliographical description of serials, *ISBD(S): International Standard Bibliographic Description for Serials*, was formulated.[5] *ISBD(S)* was the result of the efforts of a joint working group set up by the IFLA Committee on Cataloguing, which was responsible for *ISBD(M)*, together with the IFLA Committee on Serials Publication. *ISBD(S)* was in many respects a close parallel to *ISBD(M)* and its American counterpart, *AACR* Chapter 6 (1974).

Although the rules for cataloging of serials as set forth in *AACR2* chapter 12 bore much resemblance to *ISBD(S)*, the charge of the editors to adhere to the Paris Principles of authorship responsibility meant that serials rules did not satisfy those who preferred title main entry for all serials. However, as Sumner Spalding so ably put it:

> If those who process incoming serial issues and those who store them can do their work better by using the title as the means of organizing the records and the stock of serial issues, they should do so. The present cataloging rule does not prevent this. . . . So this is all the issue seems to hang on: must we undermine a fundamental principle in our existing cataloging system because a certain class of change in serial publications could thereby be handled somewhat more simply? I think not.[6]

To reiterate: when choosing the main entry for a serial, the cataloger will be governed by the general principles given in *AACR2R* chapter 21. In order for main entry to be under the name of a person, 21.1A1 states that this person must be "chiefly responsible for the creation of the intellectual or artistic content of a work." If four or more authors are involved with the creation of a work, main entry will be under title (21.6C2). Only rarely does a serial publication meet the criteria for entry under personal author. *The Forerunner*, one of the rare examples, is a magnificent tour de force, a substantial monthly publication containing poetry, articles, short stories, and even advertisements, every word written by Charlotte Perkins Gilman. But even the indefatigable Gilman ran out of steam (and funds) after seven years of heroic effort, and *The Forerunner* breathed its last (see figure 12-1).[7]

Because of the nature of a serial publication, entry under the name of a personal author is extremely rare. Choice of main entry is usually between entry under the name of a corporate body or entry under the title of the serial. The cataloger should carefully consider *AACR2* 21.1B2 in making this decision. If the serial emanates from a corporate body and if more than half of the material contained in the publication has to do with the policies, operations, resources, etc., of that body, then main entry should be under the name of the corporate body. Otherwise, entry will be under title (21.1B3) (see more detailed discussion at 21.1B2–21.1B3). As with other library materials, the content of the serial, not the name, governs the choice of main entry. See, for example, figure 12-2: the *GARC Newsletter* emanates from the Graphic Arts Research Center. It includes material on general developments in the graphic arts as well as announcements of Graphic Arts Research Center activities. According to 21.1B2, entry under the name of the center is inappropriate. Main entry will be under title with added entry under the name of the center.

In contrast to figure 12-2, the Midwest Inter-Library Center's *Newsletter* is a work with contents dealing almost entirely with the policies, procedures, and operations of the center. Therefore, under the provision of 21.1B2a, main entry will be under the name of the center (see figure 12-3).

As previously mentioned, the basic rules governing main and added entries for serials are the same as for other library materials. However, two rules in *AACR2R* chapter 21 are addressed specifically to serials. One of these deals with a change in the name of the person or corporate body

Figure 12-1.   Main entry under personal author

```
100 1    ‡a Gilman, Charlotte Perkins, ‡d 1860-1935.
245 14   ‡a The forerunner / ‡c by Charlotte Perkins Gilman.
260      ‡a New York : ‡b Charlton Co., ‡c 1909-1916.
300      ‡a 7 v. ; ‡c 25 cm.
310      ‡a Monthly
362 0    ‡a Vol. 1, no. 1 (Nov. 1909)-v. 7, no. 12 (Dec. 1916).
500      ‡a Title from cover.
```

Cover   Volume 1. No. 1   November 1909
                        The Forerunner
                  by Charlotte Perkins Gilman
                     The Charlton Company
                     67 Wall St. New York

Figure 12-2.   Main entry under title

```
022        ‡a 0271-9479
245 00     ‡a GARC newsletter.
246 3      ‡a Graphic Arts Research Center newsletter
260        ‡a Rochester, N.Y. : ‡b Graphic Arts Research Center, Rochester Institute of Technology,
           ‡c 1973-1981.
300        ‡a 9 v. : ‡b ill. ; ‡c 30 cm.
310        ‡a Monthly
362 0      ‡a Vol. 1, no. 1 (Jan. 1973)-v. 9, no. 3 (May 1981).
500        ‡a Title from caption.
500        ‡a Vols. 2-3: 24 cm.
500        ‡a Vol. 2, no. 8 (Sept. 1974) is special issue: Graphic arts experience '74.
710 2      ‡a Rochester Institute of Technology. ‡b Graphic Arts Research Center.
780 01     ‡t Graphic arts progress
785 00     ‡t T & E Center newsletter (Rochester, N.Y. : 1981) ‡x 0276-9611
```

Caption title   January 1973   Volume 1 Number 1
                                      GARC Newsletter
                          Published by Graphic Arts Research Center,
                             Rochester Institute of Technology
                                          [text]

Masthead
The GARC Newsletter is published monthly by the Graphic Arts Research Center,
College of Graphic Arts and Photography, Rochester Institute of Technology.
Subscriptions are free upon request. Contents consist of announcements and
activities at GARC and comments on the events in graphic arts and graphic
                                  communications.
Address all correspondence to: Editor, GARC Newsletter,
                          Graphic Arts Research Center,
                          Rochester Institute of Technology,
                              One Lomb Memorial Drive,
                              Rochester, New York 14623

responsible for a serial (21.3B); the other concerns changes in the title proper of a serial (21.2C).

Under earlier cataloging rules, if volume numbering of a serial was continuous, the serial was considered to be a single serial despite a change in its title or the name of the corporate body under which it was entered. This is no longer the case. Whether or not volume numbering is continuous, *AACR2R* 21.2C and 21.3B direct that a new entry be made for a serial that undergoes either a change in title or, if entered under corporate body, in the corporate body's name during the course of publication. The old entry is closed off; a new entry is started. The reason for this practice is sound. A change in the name of a corporate body most generally is accompanied by a shift in direction, emphasis, or makeup of the entire body. Therefore, even if the name of the serial remains the same and the volume numbering continues, a serial entered under such a corporate body will be given a new entry for issues under the changed name.

Figure 12-3.   Main entry under corporate body

```
110 2     ‡a Midwest Inter-Library Center (U.S.)
245 10    ‡a Newsletter / ‡c issued by the Midwest Inter-Library Center.
260       ‡a Chicago, Ill. : ‡b The Center, ‡c 1949-1964.
300       ‡a 102 v. ; ‡c 28 cm.
310       ‡a Monthly
362 0     ‡a No. 1 (Oct. 31, 1949)-no. 102 (Oct. 1, 1964).
500       ‡a Title from caption.
785 00    ‡a Center for Research Libraries (U.S.). ‡t Newsletter ‡x 0008-9087
```

Caption title

Newsletter
A Monthly Report to Members Issued by the
Midwest Inter-Library Center
at Room E51 • 1116 East Fifty-Ninth Street
Chicago 37, Illinois   No. 1   October 31, 1949
[text]

The *Newsletter* of the Midwest Inter-Library Center is such a serial. In 1966, the Midwest Inter-Library Center changed its name to the Center for Research Libraries. The entry for the *Newsletter* published by the center under its earlier name was closed (see figure 12-3) and a new entry was started for issues of the *Newsletter* published after the center changed its name (see figure 12-4).

The cataloger should read rule 21.3B carefully. A new entry will be made for a serial only if the *main entry* changes in some way. The two conditions listed are (a) the heading for the corporate body under which the serial is entered changes; or (b) the personal or corporate heading under which the serial is entered is no longer responsible for the serial. In the example shown in figure 12-5, *The Journal of Library History*, two changes have occurred in the publisher, one of them being a change in the name of the publisher, the other being a shift to an entirely different publisher. Because these changes do not affect the main entry, they are handled by notes.

Note, however, that the Library of Congress has added two conditions for new entry in addition to those listed in 21.3B. These are (c) main entry is under a uniform title that changes (e.g., because the corporate body used as a qualifier changes); or (d) the physical format of the serial changes (e.g., from paper to an on-line version, as in figures 12-6a and 12-6b) (*LCRI* 21.3B, Nov. 27, 1990). A new entry for the serial will be made in all these cases, even though the title remains the same.

Sometimes the title proper of a serial changes. When this happens, 21.2C stipulates that a new entry will be made for issues under the changed title. The two serials are connected with MARC 780 and 785 fields in a similar fashion to those used in figures 12-7 and 12-8 (see discussion of MARC coding at 12.7B7).

Figure 12-4.   Serial name change

```
022        ‡a 0008-9087
110 2      ‡a Center for Research Libraries (U.S.)
245 10     ‡a Newsletter / ‡c issued by the Center for Research Libraries.
260        ‡a Chicago, Ill. : ‡b The Center, ‡c 1966-1980.
300        ‡a 70 v. ; ‡c 28 cm.
310        ‡a Quarterly
362 0      ‡a No. 103 (Mar. 30, 1966)-no. 172 (May/June 1980).
500        ‡a Title from caption.
780 00     ‡a Midwest Inter-Library Center (U.S.). ‡t Newsletter
785 00     ‡a Center for Research Libraries (U.S.). ‡t Focus on the Center for Research Libraries
           ‡x 0275-4924
```

Caption title	Newsletter
	A Quarterly Report to Members Issued by the
	Center for Research Libraries
	5721 Cottage Grove Avenue • Chicago • Illinois 60637
	Teletype CG 1516
	No. 103 March 30, 1966
	[text]

Figure 12-5.   Serial publisher change

```
022        ‡a 0022-2259
245 04     ‡a The journal of library history.
246 1      ‡i Also known as: ‡a JLH
260        ‡a Tallahassee, Fla. : ‡b Library School, Florida State University, ‡c 1966-1987.
300        ‡a 22 v. ; ‡c 23 cm.
310        ‡a Quarterly
362 0      ‡a Vol. 1, no. 1 (Jan. 1966)-v. 22, no. 4 (fall 1987).
550        ‡a Published: Tallahassee : School of Library Science, Florida State University, Apr. 1968-
           fall 1976; Austin : Graduate School of Library Science, the University of Texas at Austin,
           winter 1977-fall 1987).
710 2      ‡a Florida State University. ‡b Library School.
710 2      ‡a Florida State University. ‡b School of Library Science.
710 2      ‡a University of Texas at Austin. ‡b Graduate School of Library Science.
785 00     ‡t Libraries & culture ‡x 0894-8631
```

Title page	The Journal of Library History
	Philosophy and Comparative Librarianship
	Louis Shores, Editor
	1966 Volume 1
	Library School
	Florida State University
	Tallahassee, Florida

Figure 12-6a.   New entry—format change

```
022 0    ‡a 1055-7660
245 00   ‡a Bryn Mawr classical review.
260      ‡a Bryn Mawr, PA : ‡b Thomas Library, Bryn Mawr College, ‡c c1990-
300      ‡a v. ; ‡c 22 cm.
310      ‡a Five no. a year
362 0    ‡a Vol. 1, no. 1 (Nov. 1990)-
530      ‡a Issued also in an online format.
710 2    ‡a Thomas Library (Bryn Mawr College)
776 1    ‡t Bryn Mawr classical review (Plain text file version) ‡x 1063-2948
```

Figure 12-6b.   New entry—format change

```
022 0    ‡a 1063-2948
130 0    ‡a Bryn Mawr classical review (Plain text file version)
245 00   ‡a Bryn Mawr classical review ‡h [computer file].
246 1    ‡i Listserv name: ‡a BMCR-L
246 1    ‡i Also known as: ‡a BMCR
250      ‡a [Plain text file version.]
260      ‡a [Bryn Mawr, PA : ‡b Bryn Mawr College and University of Pennsylvania], ‡c 1990-
310      ‡a Irregular
362 0    ‡a 1.1.1-
500      ‡a Each issue has a distinctive title.
500      ‡a Description based on printout of online display; title from gopher menu.
516 8    ‡a Electronic serial in ASCII text
530      ‡a Issued also in a print format published five times per year.
538      ‡a Mode of access: Electronic mail, FTP, and gopher. For email subscription, send to:
         majordomo@cc.brynmawr.edu, the message: SUBSCRIBE BMCR-L.
580      ‡a Distributed also with: BMMR (i.e., Bryn Mawr medieval review); as: Bryn Mawr
         reviews.
710 2    ‡a Bryn Mawr College.
710 2    ‡a University of Pennsylvania.
776 1    ‡t Bryn Mawr classical review ‡x 1055-7660
787 1    ‡t BMMR ‡x 1070-3616
787 1    ‡t Bryn Mawr reviews ‡x 1070-9770
856 0    ‡a cc.brynmawr.edu ‡f BMCR-L ‡h majordomo ‡i subscribe ‡z Email subscription
856 1    ‡a ftp.lib.virginia.edu ‡d /pub/alpha/bmcr/ ‡k [your full email address] ‡l anonymous
856 7    ‡u gopher://gopher.lib.virginia.edu:70/11/alpha/bmcr/ ‡2 gopher
856 7    ‡u gopher://gopher.cic.net:2000/11/e-serials/archive/ ‡2 gopher
```

Figure 12-7.   Title proper—changed title

```
022        ‡a 0449-329X
245 04     ‡a The journal of typographic research.
260        ‡a Cleveland, Ohio : ‡b For M.E. Wrolstad by the Press of Western Reserve University,
           ‡c 1967-1970.
300        ‡a 4 v. : ‡b ill. ; ‡c 23 cm.
310        ‡a Quarterly
362 0      ‡a Vol. 1, no.1 (Jan. 1967)-v. 4, no. 4 (autumn 1970).
700 1      ‡a Wrolstad, Merald Ernest.
785 00     ‡t Visible language ‡x 0022-2224
```

Title page   The Journal of Typographic Research
                        January 1967

Masthead
        The Journal of Typographic Research, Volume 1, Number 1, January 1967.
        Published four times a year (January, April, July, and October) for Dr. Merald E.
        Wrolstad by The Press of Western Reserve University, 2029 Adelbert Road,
        Cleveland, Ohio 44106. Copyright ©1967 by The Press of Western Reserve
        University.

Because *AACR2R* chapter 21 mandates main entry under title for many serials, instructions are also given to solve problems created by serials entered under title where the title proper is identical to the title proper of another serial in the catalog. For such a serial a uniform title should be constructed (see *AACR2R* 25.5B1, 1993 Amendments). (For discussion of uniform titles, see *AACR2R* chapter 25 and this *Handbook*, chapter 18.) This uniform title is composed of the title proper of the serial plus a qualifier in parentheses. The Library of Congress directs its catalogers to add the uniform title only to the serial being cataloged; the earlier serial with the same title should not be recataloged simply to make this change (see *LCRI* 25.5B, Aug. 27, 1990). A uniform title for a serial entered under title is recorded in the 130 field.

Figure 12-8.   Title proper—changed title

```
022        ‡a 0022-2224
210 0      ‡a Visible lang.
222 0      ‡a Visible language
245 00     ‡a Visible language.
260        ‡a Cleveland, Ohio : ‡b M.E. Wrolstad, ‡c 1971-
300        ‡a v. : ‡b ill. ; ‡c 23 cm.
310        ‡a Quarterly
362 0      ‡a Vol. 5, no. 1 (winter 1971)-
500        ‡a "The journal for research on the visual media of language expression."
500        ‡a Title from cover.
510 1      ‡a Art index, ‡x 0004-3222
510 2      ‡a Abstracts of English studies, ‡x 0001-3560
510 2      ‡a Computer & control abstracts, ‡b Autumn 1971- , ‡x 0036-8113
510 2      ‡a Electrical & electronics abstracts, ‡b Autumn 1971- , ‡x 0036-8105
510 2      ‡a Electronic publishing abstracts, ‡x 0739-2907
510 2      ‡a LLBA, language and language behavior abstracts, ‡x 0023-8295
510 2      ‡a Mathematical reviews, ‡x 0025-5629
510 2      ‡a MLA international bibliography of books and articles on the modern languages and
           literatures (Complete edition), ‡x 0024-8215
510 2      ‡a Physics abstracts. Science abstracts. Series A, ‡b Autumn 1971- , ‡x 0036-8091
510 2      ‡a Printing abstracts, ‡x 0031-109X
700 1      ‡a Wrolstad, Merald Ernest.
780 00     ‡t Journal of typographic research ‡x 0449-329X
```

Cover	Visible Language The Journal for Research on the Visual Media of Language Expression Volume V, Number 1, Winter 1971
Masthead	Dr. Merald E. Wrolstad, editor and publisher c/o The Cleveland Museum of Art, Cleveland, Ohio USA 44106

Generally, the place of publication of the first issue will be used as the qualifying term. See figure 12-9: there are two serials bearing the title *Directions*.

The name of a corporate body will be used for the qualifier in a few cases, chiefly if the title proper consists *solely* of words indicating the type of publication (*Bulletin, Newsletter, Journal*, etc.) and/or periodicity (*Occasional Paper, Quarterly Journal, Weekly Newsletter*, etc.) and if there is another serial with the same title. Figure 12-10 is such a serial.

In summary, serials cataloging presents many problems, among them the choice of heading for main entry. *AACR2R* chapter 21 gives rules for main entry of serials as well as for all types of library materials. General principles given in chapter 21 will be followed, particularly noting rules 21.2C, changes in titles proper of serials, and 21.3B, changes of persons or bodies responsible for a serial. In addition, uniform titles will be formulated as necessary under 25.5B1 for serials entered under title.

Figure 12-9.   Uniform title with qualifier

```
022       ‡a 0360-473X
130 0     ‡a Directions (New York, N.Y. : 1975)
245 00    ‡a Directions.
260       ‡a New York : ‡b Baker & Taylor, ‡c 1975-
300       ‡a v. : ‡b ill. ; ‡c 28 cm.
310       ‡a Monthly
362 0     ‡a Vol. 1, no. 1 (Aug. 1975)-
500       ‡a Each issue includes Scholarly book publishing record, books available from Baker &
          Taylor.
710 2     ‡a Baker & Taylor Books (Firm)
```

Figure 12-10.   Uniform title with qualifier

```
022       ‡a 0098-6070
130 0     ‡a Bulletin (American College of Radiology).
245 10    ‡a Bulletin / ‡c American College of Radiology.
260       ‡a Reston, Va. : ‡b The College, ‡c 1992-
300       ‡a v. ; ‡b ill., ports. ; ‡c 28 cm.
310       ‡a Monthly
362 0     ‡a Vol. 48, issue 8 (Aug. 1992)-
500       ‡a Title from caption.
780 00    ‡a ACR bulletin ‡x 0098-6070
```

Descriptive Cataloging for Serials

Once the cataloger has decided on the proper main entry for a serial (based on rules given in *AACR2R* chapter 21), the rest of the cataloging will normally be transcribed according to the rules set forth in *AACR2R* chapter 12. However, when cataloging a nonprint serial, the cataloger should remember that the chief source of information is the same as for a corresponding nonprint monographic item. For example, for instructions on the prescribed sources of information for cataloging a cassette serial (see figure 12-11), see *AACR2R* chapter 6, rule 6.0B, which gives sources of information for sound recordings.

12.0B1. Sources of information for printed serials. Chief source of information. For a printed serial, as with a monograph (*AACR2R* chapter 2), the title page, or title page substitute, is the chief source of information. Because a serial is meant to be issued in many parts on a continuing basis, rule 12.0B1 states that the cataloger is to use the title page (or title page substitute) of the first issue, if possible.

In the case of serials such as a yearbook, an annual report, a serially published biographical dictionary, directory, almanac, index, etc., locating a title page poses no problem. The piece in hand usually includes a fairly conventional-looking title page that will serve as the chief source of information (see figure 12-12).

Figure 12-11.   Nonprint serial

```
022        ‡a 0191-2259
245 00     ‡a Black box ‡h [sound recording].
260        ‡a Washington, D.C. : ‡b New Classroom, ‡c 1972-1979.
300        ‡a 34 sound cassettes : ‡b 1 7/8 ips, stereo., Dolby processed + ‡e pamphlets.
310        ‡a Quarterly, ‡b 1978-1979
321        ‡a Bimonthly, ‡b 1972
321        ‡a 6 times a year, ‡b 1974-1977
362 0      ‡a 1-17.
500        ‡a No. 15 called also Breathingspace/77.
500        ‡a Each no. issued in two cassettes.
500        ‡a Poetry, music, radio plays and interviews.
500        ‡a Program notes with each issue.
550        ‡a Vols. for 1972-1976 issued by New Classroom; 1977-1979 by Watershed Foundation.
710 2      ‡a New Classroom (Organization)
710 2      ‡a Watershed Foundation.
730 0      ‡a Breathingspace.
```

Cassette label   Black Box
                        Copyright © 1972 • The New Classroom

Program notes
    Black box is published bi-monthly in Washington, D.C. as a service of The New
                Classroom, a nonprofit educational cooperative.

Figure 12-12.   Biographical dictionary

```
022        ‡a 0270-2940 ‡y 0083-9841
210 0      ‡a Who's who Am. women ‡b (1959)
222  0     ‡a Who's who of American women ‡b (1959)
245 00     ‡a Who's who of American women.
260        ‡a Chicago : ‡b Marquis-Who's Who, ‡c 1958-
300        ‡a 3 v. ; ‡c 28 cm.
310        ‡a Biennial
362 0      ‡a 1st ed. (1958-1959)-3rd ed. (1964-1965).
500        ‡a Subtitle varies.
500        ‡a First and 2nd eds. also called v. 1-2.
785 00     ‡t Who's who of American women and women of Canada ‡x 0270-2800
```

Title page   Who's Who of American Women
                    A Biographical Dictionary of Notable
                        Living American Women
                        Volume 1 (1958-1959)
                            First Edition
                        Marquis—Who's Who
                        Chicago 11, Illinois

When cataloging other types of serials, however, locating the title page may be a problem. Generally speaking, the first issue of a serial does not include a formal title page. The title page is generally issued separately with the last number of the serial in the volume, if the publisher is library-minded enough to furnish a formal title page, that is. Consequently, if the cataloger uses the title page of the first volume as the chief source of information, according to 12.0B1, he or she must usually wait until the completion of that volume of the serial before doing the cataloging.

Except for retrospective cataloging, such a title page, because it is published later than the first issue, is not often used as the chief source. In most instances, the cataloger will take cataloging information from a title page substitute, in this order of preference:

1. The analytical title page of the first issue of the serial (found only in a monographic series)
2. The cover of the first issue
3. The caption page of the first issue (the caption is the title and other information that appears at the head of the first page of text)
4. The masthead of the first issue (this section, usually near the front of the serial, gives details of ownership, advertising, subscription rates, etc.).

When the title proper of a serial has been transcribed from a title page substitute, make a note on the source of the title proper (*AACR2R* 12.7B3) (see, for example, figures 12-1, 12-2, etc.).

Even aside from the lack of uniformity in such matters as title pages, serials pose unique problems simply because they continue over a long period of time. Editors change; the sponsoring body or publisher may change; even the title of the serial itself may change. The catalog entry for a serial publication must show not only the original status of the serial but also changes that have taken place. In order to provide this information, some modifications of the conventional patterns for monographic cataloging are necessary. A special area—the area for numeric, chronological, etc., designations—is included for serials (see 12.3). This numeric area describes volume numbering and dates for the entire serial, beginning with its first issue and leaving a space for information about its ultimate demise. The serial is cataloged from the first issue; notes show later variations such as a change in the name of the publisher or a changed subtitle. The date in the publication area is left open, as stipulated in 1.4F8, because a serial is a multipart item that is not yet complete.

The Journal of Library History changed publishers during its existence. Its catalog entry is shown in figure 12-5. (The record has been simplified for purposes of the illustration. In fact, the journal briefly changed title in 1973, then switched back to its original title, without, however, changing its numbering system. The journal should therefore properly be cataloged on three separate records under *AACR2R* 21.2C.)

12.1. TITLE AND STATEMENT OF RESPONSIBILITY AREA

For details about MARC tagging for the title and statement of responsibility area, see 1.1.

12.1B. Title proper

12.1B1. Transcription of the title proper follows guidelines as given in *AACR2R* rule 1.1B. The title of *The Journal of Library History* was transcribed from the serial's title page, following these guidelines (see figure 12-5).

12.1B7. Normally, the title proper of a serial will be recorded as instructed in *AACR2R* 1.1B. Rule 12.1B7 gives an exception to this general rule. If a serial title includes a variable number or a date, this number or date will be omitted from the title transcription. If it occurs anywhere but at the beginning of the title, omission is indicated by ellipses. However, if the number or date occurs at the beginning of the title, it is simply ignored (see figure 12-13).

12.1E. Other title information

AACR2R states that the cataloger should transcribe other title information according to general provisions of *AACR2R* 1.1E. However, by Library of Congress policy decision (*LCRI* 12.1E1, Jan. 5, 1989), in most cases other title information is not transcribed.

The title page for *The Journal of Library History* includes other title information (*Philosophy and Comparative Librarianship*). Following LC guidelines, other title information has been omitted from cataloging for figure 12-5.

Figure 12-13. Statement of responsibility; title with variable number

```
022 1    ‡a 0363-3292
110 2    ‡a Henry E. Huntington Library and Art Gallery.
245 10   ‡a Annual report / ‡c Henry E. Huntington Library and Art Gallery.
260      ‡a San Marino, Calif. : ‡b The Library, ‡c 1929-
362 0    ‡a 1st (July 1, 1927-June 30, 1928)-
310      ‡a Annual
515      ‡a Report year ends June 30.
```

Title page	Henry E. Huntington Library and Art Gallery First Annual Report July 1, 1927-June 30, 1928 San Marino, California 1929

However, the cataloger should note that following the same Library of Congress policy decision, other title information will be included if a serial carries both an initialism and a full form of the same title. See figure 12-14; also, note examples under *AACR2R* 12.1E1 beginning with Twin Cities : TC. Other title information reflecting the full form of the acronym (or vice versa) will be transcribed as indicated in *AACR2R* in these examples.

In addition, other title information will be included if a statement of responsibility for the serial is inseparably embedded in the other title information (see figure 12-15). Also note examples under *AACR2R* 12.1E1. *The Greenwood Tree* and *941.1* would be transcribed by LC as indicated in *AACR2R*. LC would omit other title information in other examples under 12.1E1.

12.1F. Statements of responsibility

12.1F1. With some exceptions, the statement of responsibility for a serial will be recorded according to the general guidelines of *AACR2R* 1.1F (see figure 12-13).

12.1F2. As instructed under 1.1F, transcribe the title as it appears; if it includes a statement of responsibility or the name of a sponsoring body, etc., transcribe it (see figure 12-16).

As indicated in general rule 1.1F13, a further statement of responsibility will not be transcribed when the title includes a statement of responsibility, unless a separate statement of responsibility appears in the chief source of information. See discussion in this *Handbook* under rule 1.1F13. Conversely, when such a statement does appear in the chief source of information, transcribe the information as it is found (see figure 12-17).

Figure 12-14.   Initialism in title

```
022      ‡a 0090-7324 ‡y 0090-7234
245 00   ‡a RSR : ‡b reference services review.
246 30   ‡a Reference services review
260      ‡a Ann Arbor, Mich. : ‡b Pierian Press, ‡c 1973-
300      ‡a v. ; ‡c 28 cm.
310      ‡a Quarterly
362 0    ‡a Vol. 1 (Jan./Mar. 1973)-
500      ‡a Title from caption.
515      ‡a Vol. 1, no. 1 preceded by a number dated Nov./Dec. 1972, called Pilot issue.
```

Caption title   RSR
                                  Reference Services Review
                          January/March 1973   Volume 1, Number 1

Masthead   Pierian Press
Editorial offices: 931 S. State, Ann Arbor, Michigan 48104. Mailing address: Box 1808, Ann Arbor, Michigan 48106. Cable address: Pierianpress, Ann Arbor, Michigan, U.S.A. 313/662-1777.

Figure 12-15.   Statement of responsibility in other title information

```
022        ‡a 0047-0635
245 00     ‡a International cataloguing : ‡b quarterly bulletin of the IFLA Committee on Cataloguing.
260        ‡a London : ‡b The Committee, ‡c 1972-1987.
300        ‡a 16 v. ; ‡c 30 cm.
310        ‡a Quarterly
362 0      ‡a Vol. 1, no. 1 (Jan./Mar. 1972)-v. 16, no. 4 (Oct./Dec. 1987).
500        ‡a Title from caption.
550        ‡a Vols. for 1972-1976 issued by: IFLA Committee on Cataloguing; 1977-July/Sept. 1984
           by: IFLA International Office for UBC; Oct./Dec. 1984-1986 by: IFLA International
           Programme for UBC; 1987 by: IFLA UBCIM Programme.
555        ‡a Vols. 1 (1972)-5 (1976). 1 v.
710 2      ‡a IFLA Committee on Cataloguing.
710 2      ‡a IFLA International Office for UBC.
710 2      ‡a IFLA International Programme for UBC.
710 2      ‡a IFLA UBCIM Programme.
780 00     ‡t Newsletter of the IFLA Committee on Cataloguing
785 00     ‡t International cataloguing and bibliographic control ‡x 1011-8829
```

Caption title   International Cataloguing
                        Quarterly Bulletin of the IFLA Committee on Cataloguing
                            Volume 1 Number 1 January/March 1972

Masthead
            International Cataloguing is published quarterly by the IFLA Committee on
        Cataloguing, c/o The Department of Printed Books, The British Museum, London
                            WC1B 3DG, Great Britain.

Compare the main entries as given for *The Yale University Library Gazette* and *The Harvard Librarian* (see figures 12-16 and 12-17). Entry is governed by *AACR2R* 21.1B2. Examination of each serial reveals that *The Harvard Librarian* is devoted to Harvard University Library matters; *The Yale University Library Gazette* is not.

12.1F3. This rule specifies that the editor's name is not to be recorded as part of the statement of responsibility. This is because most serials have a series of editors over the life of the serial. If each editor's name were included as part of the entry, the catalog record would need to be constantly updated (see, for example, figure 12-5, *The Journal of Library History*. Note that the name of the editor is not transcribed as part of the catalog record).

However, if, in the cataloger's judgment, library users are likely to iden-

Figure 12-16.   Sponsoring body's name in title

```
022       ‡a 0044-0175
245 04    ‡a The Yale University Library gazette.
260       ‡a [New Haven] : ‡b The Library, ‡c 1926-
300       ‡a v. : ‡b ill. ; ‡c 27 cm.
310       ‡a Quarterly
362 0     ‡a Vol. 1, no.1 (June 1926)-
500       ‡a Title from cover.
510 2     ‡a Abstracts of English studies, ‡x 0001-3560
510 2     ‡a America, history and life, ‡x 0002-7065 ‡b 1965-
510 2     ‡a Annual bibliography of English language and literature, ‡x 0066-3786
510 2     ‡a Artbibliographies modern, ‡x 0300-466X
510 2     ‡a Historical abstracts. Part A. Modern history abstracts, ‡b 1965- , ‡x 0363-2717
510 2     ‡a Historical abstracts. Part B. Twentieth century abstracts, ‡b 1965- , ‡x 0363-2725
510 2     ‡a MLA international bibliography of books and articles on the modern languages and
          literatures (Complete edition), ‡x 0024-8215
510 2     ‡a Writings on American history, ‡x 0364-2887
550       ‡a "Edited and published by the staff of the Yale Library."
555       ‡a Vols. 1-31, 1926-Apr. 1957. 1 v.; Vols. 1-45, 1926-Apr. 1971. 1 v.
710 2     ‡a Yale University. ‡b Library.
```

Cover	The Yale University Library Gazette Volume 1 June 1926 Number 1

Figure 12-17.   Sponsoring body's name in title, repeated in statement
of responsibility

```
022       ‡a 0073-0564
110 2     ‡a Harvard University. ‡b Library.
245 14    ‡a The Harvard librarian / ‡c issued from the office of the director, Harvard University
          Library.
260       ‡a Cambridge, Mass. : ‡b The Library, ‡c 1957-
300       ‡a v : ‡b ill. ; ‡c 28 cm.
310       ‡a Frequency varies
362 0     ‡a Vol. 1, no.1 (Dec. 1957)-
500       ‡a Title from caption.
515       ‡a Suspended June 1966-Sept. 1968.
```

Caption title	The Harvard Librarian issued from the Office of the Director Harvard University Library Cambridge 38, Massachusetts December, 1957

Figure 12-18.   Name of editor omitted from statement of responsibility

```
022      ‡a 0049-514X
245 04   ‡a The unabashed librarian.
260      ‡a New York, N.Y. : ‡b M.H. Scilken, ‡c c1971-
300      ‡a v. : ‡b ill. ; ‡c 28 cm.
310      ‡a Quarterly
362 0    ‡a No. 1 (Nov. 1971)-
500      ‡a Title from cover.
500      ‡a Founded, edited, and published by Marvin H. Scilken.
500      ‡a "A letter for innovators."
700 1    ‡a Scilken, Marvin H.
```

Cover   The
                                        U*n*a*b*a*s*h*e*d
                                           Librarian
                                     A Letter for Innovators
                                    Number 1   November 1971
                               © U.L. 1971 G.P.O. Box 2631, New York, N.Y. 10001

tify the serial by the name of the editor, an added entry for editor may be made. If this is done, the cataloger will give the editor's name in a note, following the guidelines given in 12.7B6 (see figures 12-18 and 12-19). *In no instance will the cataloger include the editor's name as part of the statement of responsibility.*

In the example shown in figure 12-19, Ada P. McCormick served as editor, and indeed did a substantial part of the writing, for *Letter* during the six years of its existence.

12.2. EDITION AREA

For details about MARC tagging for the edition area, see 1.2.

12.2B2. Edition statement. If the edition statement on a serial publication changes with each issue, it is to be regarded as numeric information and included in the numeric area. For an example of such an edition statement, see figure 12-12.

12.3. NUMERIC AND/OR ALPHABETIC, CHRONOLOGICAL, OR OTHER DESIGNATION AREA

The third area of descriptive cataloging for serials is used to record numerical and chronological designations, beginning with the first issue and ending with the last issue of the serial, whenever that issue appears. This will be done (if possible) whether the cataloging library owns the first issue or not. Check *New Serial Titles, Union List of Serials,* or a national database such as RLIN or OCLC to determine the starting date for the serial. If the

Figure 12-19.   Name of editor omitted from statement of responsibility

```
130 0    ‡a Letter (Tucson, Ariz.)
245 10   ‡a Letter.
260      ‡a Tucson, Arizona : ‡b A.P. McCormick, ‡c 1943-1949.
300      ‡a 5 v. : ‡b ill. ; ‡c 20 cm.
310      ‡a Irregular
362 0    ‡a Vol. 1, no. 1 (Jan. 1943)-v. 5, no. 9 (1949).
500      ‡a Title from cover.
500      ‡a Editor: Ada P. McCormick.
700 1    ‡a McCormick, Ada P.
```

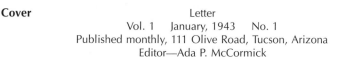

Cover   Letter
                    Vol. 1   January, 1943   No. 1
            Published monthly, 111 Olive Road, Tucson, Arizona
                        Editor—Ada P. McCormick

library does not have a complete run of a serial, this information can be given in a note (12.7B20), or wherever the library records its holdings information.

This area is recorded in the 362 field in the MARC record. The first indicator is "0," the second blank. The entire designation is recorded in subfield ‡a. As may be seen from an examination of cataloging examples included in this chapter of the *Handbook*, designations are given in the form in which they appear on the item, using abbreviations as indicated in *AACR2R* Appendix B. Capitalization is the same as for other areas: the first word is capitalized; in addition, the cataloger will capitalize proper names and terms as given in Appendix A (Capitalization). Note that although names of months in the English language are capitalized, seasons are not (A.23). Note rules for punctuation (12.3A1). Dates following numeric or alphabetic designations are to be enclosed in parentheses, no matter how they appear on the publication.

12.4. PUBLICATION, DISTRIBUTION, ETC., AREA

Follow general rules as given in *AACR2R* 1.4. For instructions in MARC tagging, see this *Handbook* at 1.4.

12.4F. Date of publication will be the year as found on the first issue of the serial. Follow the date with a hyphen as stipulated in 12.4F1. If the serial is completed, the year of publication of the final issue should be added.

12.5. PHYSICAL DESCRIPTION AREA

For instructions in MARC tagging, see *Handbook* at 1.5.

12.5B. Extent of the item (including specific material designation)

Because the extent, like the rest of the physical description area, describes the entire serial, the number in the specific material designation is omitted; this part of the entry is left open until the serial ceases publication. For printed serials, use only the specific material designation "v." (*LCRI* 12.5B1, Nov. 1995). For nonprint serials, use a specific material designation from the appropriate *AACR2R* chapter.

12.5C. Other physical details

If illustrations are a feature of the serial, the general term "ill." is usually sufficient. See the discussion in *Handbook* under 2.5C.

12.5D. Dimensions

See the chapter on the particular type of material (e.g., for printed serials, see *AACR2R* 2.5D) for directions on recording dimensions.

12.5E. Accompanying material

Record accompanying material only if it is issued regularly with the serial.
See figure 12-11; a pamphlet is included with each issue of this serial. Frequency of accompanying material is indicated in a note (12.7B11).

12.7. NOTE AREA

Follow general instructions given in 1.7A concerning format and the order of notes. Also, include any necessary notes pertinent to the specific type of library material being cataloged. For instance, for a cassette serial (see figure 12-11), refer to *AACR2R* chapter 6, rule 6.7.

As a supplement to guidelines and rules in *AACR2R* 12.7, the cataloger will find Nancy G. Thomas and Rosanna O Neil's *Notes for Serials Cataloging* (Littleton, Colo.: Libraries Unlimited, 1986) to be very helpful. Arranged according to MARC format, the notes were taken from *New Serial Titles* (Aug. 1982–May 1984), OCLC serial records, and the authors' own cataloging.

12.7B1. Frequency. In contradiction to *AACR2R*, by Library of Congress and National Library of Canada policy decision, the frequency note must always be given, even when it duplicates information in the title (*LCRI* 12.7B1, Nov. 1995; Howarth, at 12.7B1). Frequency is recorded in the 310 field; the indicators are blank, and the statement is placed in subfield ‡a (see figure 12-15). If the frequency of the serial has changed over its history, the 310 field is used only for the latest publication frequency. Earlier frequencies are recorded in 321 fields. In this case, each field should include the statement of frequency followed by a comma, subfield ‡b, and dates showing the time period for the stated frequency (see figure 12-11).

12.7B3. Source of title proper. If the cataloger has used a title page substitute (see 12.0B1) in the cataloging of a printed serial or, when cataloging a nonprint serial, if the cataloger has used a source other than the chief source of information for transcription of the serial title, a note must be given in a 500 field. The conventional wording of the note is "Title from (source)." See examples in this chapter.

12.7B6. Statements of responsibility. If a statement of responsibility, such as the fact that a serial is the official organ of a society or other corporate body, is not transcribed in the title and statement of responsibility area, give it as a note (see figure 12-20). Use the terminology found in the publication itself if possible. A statement of responsibility note, such as that of figure 12-20, recording the name of the issuing body, is recorded in a 550 field.

For an example of the expansion of a name appearing in abbreviated form as part of the title, see figure 12-21.

A note in a 500 field is made to give the name of an editor of a serial when an added entry is to be made for this individual (see figures 12-18 and 12-19).

12.7B7. Relationships with other serials. The fact that a serial has changed its identity in any fashion is recorded in fields between 760 and 787 (known as linking fields). Depending on the system being used by the

Figure 12-20.   Statements of responsibility as notes

```
022       ‡a 0024-2527
245 00    ‡a Library resources & technical services.
246 3     ‡a Library resources and technical services
260       ‡a [Richmond] : ‡b ALA Resources and Technical Services Division, ‡c 1957-
300       ‡a v. ; ‡c 24 cm.
310       ‡a Quarterly
362 0     ‡a Vol. 1, no.1 (winter 1957)-
500       ‡a Title from cover.
550       ‡a Official publication of: The American Library Association, Resources and Technical
          Services Division.
580       ‡a Merger of: Serial slants, and: Journal of cataloging and classification.
710 2     ‡a American Library Association. ‡b Resources and Technical Services Division.
780 14    ‡t Serial slants ‡x 0559-5258
780 14    ‡t Journal of cataloging and classification
```

Cover	Library Resources & Technical Services Vol. 1 No. 1
Contents page	Library Resources & Technical Services Vol. 1 No. 1 Winter, 1957 ALA Resources and Technical Services Division

Masthead
Library Resources and Technical Services, the quarterly official publication of the Resources and Technical Services Division of the American Library Association, is published at 1407 Sherwood Ave., Richmond 5, Va.

Figure 12-21.   Supplement

```
245 00    ‡a ACRL news.
260       ‡a Chicago : ‡b Association of College and Research Libraries, ‡c 1966.
300       ‡a 9 v. : ‡b ill. ; ‡c 24 cm.
310       ‡a Monthly (except July and Aug. combined)
362 0     ‡a No. 1 (Mar. 1966)-no. 9 (Dec. 1966).
500       ‡a Title from caption.
550       ‡a Issued by: Association of College and Research Libraries.
555       ‡a Vol. 26 (1965)-v. 40 (1979). (Includes index to the later title) 1 v. (Included in the index
          to: College & research libraries).
710 2     ‡a Association of College and Research Libraries.
772 0     ‡t College & research libraries
785 00    ‡t College & research libraries news ‡x 0099-0086
```

Caption title	ACRL News No. 1, March 1966 A Supplement to College & Research Libraries, Vol. 27, No. 2

library, these fields may trace, and they should generate notes according to the coding of the indicators. This has the effect of linking all of the manifestations of a serial in chronological order, as well as linking other relationships (such as editions in different languages).

The 780 field is used to record the title of the immediate predecessor of the serial being cataloged; the 785 field records its immediate successor. The coding of the first indicator should be "0." This will cause the local system to generate a note that will be visible to the patron. (In some cases the generation of a note is not wanted [see below]. In such cases, the first indicator is coded "1.") The second indicator depends on the note wanted. Its operation will be seen in the discussion below of specific situations.

Some 12.7B7 notes are recorded in other fields. These are detailed below.

In all cases, the related serial should be recorded in the linking field in exactly the same way it would be recorded on its own record. For example, if it is entered under a corporate body, it should be so recorded in the linking field; if it is entered under title, the linking field contains this form.

12.7B7a. *Translation.* This is recorded in the 765 field with the first indicator "0" and the second blank. This generates the note "Translation of: [name]."

12.7B7b. *Continuation.* Record this in a 780 field with the indicators coded "00." This generates the note "Continues: [name]." The note generated from the 780 field of figure 12-4 will appear to the patron "Continues: Midwest Inter-Library Center (U.S.). Newsletter."

12.7B7c. *Continued by.* Record this in a 785 field with the indicators coded "00." This generates the note "Continued by: [name]." The note generated from the 785 field of figure 12-3 will appear to the patron "Continued by: Center for Research Libraries (U.S.). Newsletter."

More complex situations are handled by a combination of a 580 field and a 785 field with the indicators coded "10." The second example in *AACR2R* 12.7B7c would be recorded

> 580   ‡a Continued by a section in: Canadian Association of Geographers' newsletter.
>
> 785 10 ‡t Canadian Association of Geographers' newsletter

Because of the complexity involved, the Library of Congress, the National Library of Canada, and the British Library will not implement the option of dating the change (see *LCRI* 12.7B7c, Nov. 1995, and Howarth, at 12.7B7c).

12.7B7d. *Merger.* Because this situation is too complex for the indicators to generate the needed note, it is handled by a combination of a 580 field, which displays as a note, and 780 fields with indicators "14" (see figure 12-20).

"Merged with" is handled in exactly the same way, except the related serial names are recorded in 785 fields with indicators "17."

12.7B7e. *Split.* When a serial is the result of a previous serial splitting into more than one part, record this in a 780 field with indicators "01." This generates the note "Continues in part: [name]." The note generated from the 780 field in figure 12-2 will display "Continues in part: Graphic arts progress." The Library of Congress, the National Library of Canada, and the British Library will not implement the option of recording the names of other "sibling" serials resulting from the split (*LCRI* 12.7B7e, Nov. 1995; Howarth, at 12.7B7e).

The opposite situation, recording the names of the serials a "parent" serial has split into, requires a combination of 580 and 785 fields. The note for the second example in *AACR2R* 12.7B7e would be transcribed in a 580 field; the two serial names would be transcribed into 785 fields with indicators "16."

12.7B7f. *Absorption.* The name of a serial that the serial being cataloged has absorbed is recorded in the 780 field with indicators "05." This generates the note "Absorbed: [name]." If the information is known, the date of absorption is recorded in subfield ‡g following the name of the serial. The second example in *AACR2R* 12.7B7f would be recorded

> 780 05 ‡t Worker's friend ‡g 1936

and would display: "Absorbed: Worker's friend, 1936." The comma is supplied by the system and not recorded in the 780 field. Because of the complexity of coding, the article is dropped in MARC tagging and display.

To record a serial that absorbs the serial being cataloged, use a 785 field with indicators "04," which generates the note "Absorbed by: [name]." The final example given under *AACR2R* 12.7B7f would be coded

> 785 04 ‡t Quarterly review of marketing

and would display: "Absorbed by: Quarterly review of marketing."

12.7B7g. *Edition.* Relationship to another edition is recorded in a 580 field, which displays as a note. The name of the related edition is recorded in a 775 field, first indicator "1," second indicator blank.

12.7B7j. *Supplements.* The name of a serial to which the serial being cataloged is a supplement is recorded in the 772 field, first indicator "0," second indicator blank. This generates the note "Supplement to: [name]." The 772 field in both figures 12-21 and 12-22 would display "Supplement to: College & research libraries."

The name of a serial that supplements the serial being cataloged is recorded in a 770 field, first indicator "0," second indicator blank, which generates the note "Has supplement: [name]." The second example in *AACR2R* 12.7B7j would be coded

770 0   ‡t Journal of the Royal Numismatic Society

and would display "Has supplement: Journal of the Royal Numismatic Society."

More complex situations are handled by combinations of 580 and 770 fields, first indicator "1" (see, for example, figure 12-23).

12.7B8. Numbering and chronological designation. Notes on irregularities in numbering, etc., are given in a note in a 515 field (see, e.g., figure 12-22).

Sometimes an introductory number of a serial will be issued to sound out the market before the new venture is officially launched. Information

Figure 12-22.   Supplement with changed title

```
022      ‡a 0099-0086
245 00   ‡a College & research libraries news.
246 3    ‡a College and research libraries news
260      ‡a Chicago : ‡b Association of College and Research Libraries, ‡c 1967-
300      ‡a v. : ‡b ill. ; ‡c 24 cm.
310      ‡a Monthly (except July and Aug. combined)
362 0    ‡a Jan. 1967-Dec. 1979 ; v. 41, no. 1 (Jan. 1980)-
500      ‡a Title from caption.
550      ‡a Issued by: Association of College and Research Libraries.
515      ‡a Issues for 1967-1979 also numbered 1-11 each year.
515      ‡a Issues for Jan. 1980- assume vol. numbering of College & research libraries.
555      ‡a Vol. 26 (1965)-v. 40 (1979). 1 v.; v. 41 (1980)-50 (1989). (Includes index to the earlier
         title) 1 v. (Included in the index to: College & research libraries).
710 2    ‡a Association of College and Research Libraries.
772 0    ‡t College & research libraries
780 00   ‡t ACRL news
```

Caption title	College & Research Libraries News
	No. 1, January, 1967
	ACRL News Issue (A) of College & Research Libraries
	Vol. 28, no. 1

about such an introductory issue is given in a note, also in a 515 field. Cataloging will not be done from this issue; 12.0B1 stipulates the use of the "first" issue (i.e., first regular issue) (see figure 12-14).

12.7B9. Publication, distribution, etc. A note should be made when a change occurs in the publication or distribution of a serial. The Library of Congress instructs its catalogers to make such a note only if the change involves a change in country or region, or a change in the place when the place has been used as a qualifier in a key title or uniform title (*LCRI* 12.7B9, Nov. 1995). The note is recorded in a 550 field if the publisher is also the issuing body (see figure 12-5), or a 500 field if the change involves a commercial publisher.

1.7B15. Reference to published descriptions. Although there is no specific application mentioned in chapter 12 for the note stipulated at 1.7B15, it is very frequently used in serials cataloging for noting other sources where a serial has been indexed. Academic journals in particular are likely to be included in indexes covering many journals in a given subject area.

Figure 12-23.   Supplement note

022	‡a 0010-0870
245 00	‡a College and research libraries.
246 3	‡a College & research libraries
246 1	‡i Also known as: ‡a C & RL
260	‡a Chicago : ‡b American Library Association, ‡c 1939-
300	‡a v. : ‡b ill. ; ‡c 23-26 cm.
310	‡a Bimonthly, ‡b 1956-
321	‡a Quarterly, ‡b 1939-1955
362 0	‡a Vol. 1, no. 1 (Dec. 1939)-
500	‡a Issues for 1991- have title: College & research libraries : C & RL.
550	‡a Official organ of: Association of College and Reference Libraries (U.S.), 1939-1957; Association of College and Research Libraries, 1958-
550	‡a Official journal of the Association of College and Reference Libraries, 1939-1957; of the Association of College and Research Libraries, 1958-
555	‡a Vols. 1 (1939)-10 (1949) (issued as v. 11, no. 3, pt. 2) with v. 11; v. 11 (1950)-15 (1954) with v. 16; v. 16 (1955)-20 (1959). 1 v.; v. 21 (1960)-25 (1964). 1 v.; v. 26 (1965)-40 (1979). 1 v.; v. 41 (1980)-50 (1989). 1 v.
580	‡a Vol. for 1966 has supplement: ACRL news; vols. for 1967- have supplement: College and research libraries news.
710 2	‡a Association of College and Reference Libraries (U.S.)
710 2	‡a Association of College and Research Libraries.
770 1	‡t ACRL news
770 1	‡t College & research libraries news

Title page	College and Research Libraries Title Page and Index to Vol. 1, 1939-40 Association of College and Reference Libraries
Masthead	College and Research Libraries is the official organ of the Association of College and Reference Libraries. It is published by the American Library Association.

This is very useful information to the library user and should be recorded in 510 fields. In the serials application, the first indicator may be coded "0" if the coverage of the index is unknown; "1" if coverage is complete (i.e., it includes references to all articles in all issues of a serial); or "2" if coverage is selective. Indicator "0" generates the note "Indexed by: [name]"; "1" generates "Indexed in its entirety by: [name]"; "2" generates "Indexed selectively by: [name]." The second indicator is blank. As these indexes are typically serials themselves, they should be recorded in the same way as linking entries for related serials (see discussion at 12.7B7). Dates of coverage are recorded in subfield ‡b; ISSN in subfield ‡x.

Because of space constraints (there can typically be a dozen or more individual 510 fields in the record for a popular journal), these fields are given as an example only in figures 12-8 and 12-16.

12.7B17. Indexes. In contrast to 1.7B15, which notes sources outside a serial where the serial is indexed, 12.7B17 stipulates that the presence of indexes within the serial itself should also be noted. This is done in a 555 field. With both indicators blank, this field generates the note "Indexes: [vol. no.]." For example, the 555 field in figure 12-15 would display "Indexes: Vols. 1 (1972)-5 (1976). 1 v."

12.7B21. "Issued with" notes. If a serial is issued with (not simply bound with) another that is cataloged separately, each should record the name of the other in a 777 field, with the first indicator "0," the second blank. This coding generates the note "Issued with: [name]." If a more complex note is needed, the indicator should be coded "1" and the full note given in a 580 field.

12.7B23. Item described. The cataloger should make every effort to base the bibliographic description on the first regular issue of the serial. If any other issue must be used, a note giving the numbering of the issue used is required. It should be given in the format prescribed in *AACR2R* 12.7B23 in a 500 field (see figure 12-24).

Figure 12-24.   Description based on item other than first

```
245 00   ‡a Zion's messenger and advocate.
260      ‡a Provo, UT : ‡b Fundamental Place, ‡c [1989?]-
300      ‡a v. ; ‡c 28 cm.
500      ‡a Description based on: Vol. 1, no. 3 (Aug. 1989).
500      ‡a Art Bulla, editor.
700 1    ‡a Bulla, Art.
```

Masthead	Zion's Messenger and Advocate
	Art Bulla
	Editor
	Vol. 1, No. 3 August 1, 1989

12.8B. International Standard Serial Number (ISSN)

The ISSN is a number assigned by the National Serials Data Program (NSDP) or the ISSN Network/Canada. It is recorded in the 022 field. Catalogers at other institutions doing original cataloging of serials leave the indicators blank if they record an ISSN (which they may find printed on the item itself). Catalogers using copy ultimately originating from one of these two institutions should use the coding given by them. Examples in this *Handbook* have been coded blank (see figures throughout the chapter).

12.8C. Key-title

The key-title is a unique title assigned to a serial in conjunction with the ISSN. It is often identical to the title proper, but may be qualified to differentiate it from other identical titles. If found on an item or in another record for the serial, it should be recorded in the 222 field. The first indicator is blank; the second gives the number of nonfiling characters in order to give the system instructions to disregard articles in sorting. A second field, 210, records the "abbreviated key-title." This consists of a title using abbreviated forms of the words in the key-title. The first indicator is "1" if the cataloger wishes to produce an added entry for the abbreviated key-title; otherwise it is "0." Because key-title and abbreviated key-title are assigned by an ISSN Network national center, and never by original catalogers at other institutions, only two examples are given in this *Handbook*, figures 12-8 and 12-12. However, these titles should always be recorded if they are known.

Notes

1. *AACR2R* Appendix D (Glossary), *s.v.* "Serial."
2. Michael Gorman, "The Current State of Standardization in the Cataloging of Serials," *LRTS* 19 (fall 1975): 302.
3. Colloquium on the Anglo-American Cataloging Rules, University of Toronto, 1967, *The Code and the Cataloguer* (Toronto: Univ. of Toronto Press, 1969), p. 25.
4. Two of the papers presented at the January 19, 1975, meeting were printed in *LRTS* 19 (fall 1975): "No Special Rules for Entry of Serials" (Michael Carpenter) and "AACR, ISBDS, and ISSN: A Comment" (Paul Fasana). Almost the entire issue is devoted to the serials question.
5. *ISBD(S): International Standard Bibliographic Description for Serials,* 1st standard ed. (London: IFLA International Office for UBC, 1977).
6. "ISBDS and Title Main Entry for Serials," *LC Information Bulletin* 33 (Nov. 22, 1974): A-232.
7. General information about MARC coding is found in the introduction to this *Handbook*; details about coding the descriptive portion of the record are found throughout chapter 1; information about the coding of main and added access points is found at the beginning of chapter 14. An explanation of the MARC authorities format is given in *Handbook* chapters 15, 17, and 18. Information about specific MARC fields may be found by consulting the index under "MARC fields."

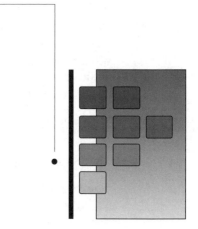

CHAPTER 13

ANALYSIS

13.1. SCOPE

13.1A. The definition of the process of analysis as set down in *AACR2R* has been slightly expanded and clarified by the 1993 amendments. It now reads: "Analysis is the process of preparing a bibliographic record that describes a part or parts of an item for which a comprehensive entry might be made." The former language, which read "for which a comprehensive entry has been made," implied that this technique could only be used if a library had, in fact, made a comprehensive entry for the "parent" item. The amendment makes it clear that analysis may be used even if the library has not made such a comprehensive record.

Both monographs and serials may be analyzed, and additional access points for parts of the larger work may be created by means of the methods gathered in *AACR2R* chapter 13. Some of these methods have already been discussed in previous chapters. All of the "rules" in chapter 13 are to be applied according to the policy of the cataloging agency.

13.2. ANALYTICAL ADDED ENTRIES

Added entries are customarily made for parts of a work named in the title and statement of responsibility area, which are not the title proper. Make such added entries as name-title entries, using the name in *AACR2R* format followed by a uniform title or title proper, as appropriate. Note that when making such analytical (i.e., contained within the work cataloged) added name-title entries, if the title begins with an article, the article is dropped (see, for instance, figure 1-14).[1] 7XX fields containing analytical entries code the second indicator "2" (see also figures 1-83 and 1-90).

At the discretion of the library, analytical added entries may be made for all or part of the items listed in a contents note. If made, they will be constructed under the same guidelines (see figure 1-55).

13.3. ANALYSIS OF MONOGRAPHIC SERIES AND MULTIPART MONOGRAPHS

A monographic series is "a group of monographs, usually related to one another in subject, issued in succession, normally by the same publisher and in uniform style with a collective title applying to the group as a whole."[2] A monographic series is often numbered; in some instances, each monograph in the series is cataloged independently, with the unifying title of the group listed as a series. In other instances, the entire series is cataloged as a serial, following rules in *AACR2R* chapter 12, with all, part, or none of it analyzed (i.e., given a separate access point) depending on the decision of the cataloging agency.

Library Trends is a good example of a monographic series. The set as a whole may be cataloged as a serial. All issues will be given the same classification number and will stand together on the library shelves (see figure 13-1). At the discretion of the library, individual volumes in a monographic series may be analyzed—that is, cataloged as an independent work. Most libraries will want to do this. If it is analyzed, an issue of *Library Trends* will appear in the library's catalog as shown in figure 13-2.

Figure 13-1.   Monographic series

```
022       ‡a 0024-2594
245 00    ‡a Library trends.
260       ‡a Urbana, Ill. : ‡b University of Illinois Library School, ‡c 1952-
300       ‡a v. ; ‡c 23 cm.
310       ‡a Quarterly
362 0     ‡a Vol. 1, no. 1 (July 1952)-
500       ‡a Title from analytical title page.
500       ‡a Each issue is concerned with one aspect of librarianship, and is planned by an invited
          guest editor.
500       ‡a Description based on: Vol. 36, no. 1 (Summer 1987).
550       ‡a Issued by: University of Illinois Library School, 1952-1977; University of Illinois
          Graduate School of Library Science, 1978-1980; University of Illinois Graduate School of
          Library and Information Science, 1981-
710 2     ‡a University of Illinois (Urbana-Champaign campus). ‡b Library School.
710 2     ‡a University of Illinois (Urbana-Champaign campus). ‡b Graduate School of Library
          Science.
710 2     ‡a University of Illinois at Urbana-Champaign. ‡b Graduate School of Library Science.
710 2     ‡a University of Illinois at Urbana-Champaign. ‡b Graduate School of Library and
          Information Science.
```

Analytical title page	Library Trends Volume 36 Number 1 Summer 1987 University of Illinois Graduate School of Library and Information Science

Figure 13-2.   Monographic series analyzed

```
245 00   ‡a Recent trends in rare book librarianship / ‡c Michèle Valerie Cloonan, issue editor.
260      ‡a Champaign, Ill. : ‡b University of Illinois, Graduate School of Library and Information
         Science, ‡c 1987.
300      ‡a 256 p. ; ‡c 23 cm.
440  0   ‡a Library trends, ‡x 0024-2594 ; ‡v v. 36, no. 1
500      ‡a Title from cover.
500      ‡a "Summer 1987".
504      ‡a Includes bibliographical references.
700 1    ‡a Cloonan, Michèle Valerie, ‡d 1955-
```

Cover	Recent Trends in Rare Book Librarianship
	Michèle Valerie Cloonan
	Issue Editor
	Library Trends
	Summer 1987

13.4. NOTE AREA

A contents note is an appropriate way to give details of parts of a monograph (see discussion in *Handbook* under 1.7B18). At the discretion of the library, name-title added entries may be made for part or all of the items included in a contents note, following the format indicated in 13.2.

13.5. "IN" ANALYTICS

Although this method was often used in the past to bring out parts of a larger work, the Library of Congress has instructed its catalogers to use this technique only "in very special cases" (*LCRI* 13.5, Jan. 5, 1989). As an example of one type of cataloging where "in" analytics would be useful, a library that has a comprehensive collection on a particular author may collect everything written about that author, including copies of articles in journals and encyclopedias. If the library wishes to catalog these, the cataloger would base the description on the article itself. The "in" note is recorded in a 773 field, with the first indicator "0," the second blank. This field generates the display "In: [name of analyzed item--location within the item]." The third example in *AACR2R* 13.5 would be coded:

```
245 14 ‡a The loved one / ‡c by Evelyn Waugh.
300     ‡a p. 78-159; ‡c 17 cm.
773 0   ‡t Horizon ‡g Vol. 17, no. 98 (Feb. 1948)
```

The coding of the 773 field can be quite complex. For more information, see the latest edition of *USMARC Format for Bibliographic Data* (Washington, D.C.: Cataloging Distribution Service, Library of Congress).

13.6. MULTILEVEL DESCRIPTION

The Library of Congress does not employ this technique of analysis (*LCRI* 13.6, Jan. 5, 1989).

NOTES

1. General information about MARC coding is found in the introduction to this *Handbook*; details about coding the descriptive portion of the record are found throughout chapter 1; information about the coding of main and added access points is found at the beginning of chapter 14. An explanation of the MARC authorities format is given in *Handbook* chapters 15, 17, and 18. Information about specific MARC fields may be found by consulting the index under "MARC fields."
2. *ALA Glossary of Library and Information Science* (Chicago: ALA, 1983), p. 148. See also *AACR2R* Appendix D (Glossary), *s.v.* "Series. 1."

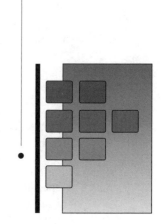

CHAPTER *14*

CHOICE OF
ACCESS POINTS

(*AACR2R* Chapter 21)

AACR2R chapter 21 gives rules for determining the main entry (the principal heading under which a work will be entered in the library's catalog) and added entries (other access points under which the work will be entered in the catalog). The rules in chapter 21 are based on the following general principles:

1. Main entry will be under the heading for the personal author chiefly responsible for the intellectual content or the artistic creation of the work (21.1A).
2. Main entry will be under corporate body if the content of the work is among the six types listed under 21.1B2.
3. Main entry will be under title in the following instances:
   a. if responsibility for intellectual or artistic content is diffuse (four or more authors) or unknown (anonymous) (21.1C1a);
   b. if the work is a collection of works by different persons or bodies (21.1C1b);
   c. if the work emanates from a corporate body, but is not of personal authorship and is not subsumed under the six categories listed under 21.1B2 (21.1C1c);
   d. if the work is regarded as sacred scripture (21.1C1d).

Most libraries today use on-line catalogs. A few, reluctant to abandon the traditional card catalog, still use printed cards, one of which functions as the main entry, with others overprinted with added points of access to the work. In view of the widespread use of on-line catalogs, however, many catalogers have questioned the continued emphasis of *AACR2* on rules for choice of main entry. There are several reasons. Despite the general library custom of multiple entries for most library items, many bibliographical sources, such as union catalogs, book-trade directories, etc., cite works by a single entry. Also, a single entry is needed to identify a work about which something has been written (e.g., a commentary on Milton's *Paradise Lost*).

In addition, index displays in an on-line environment can be clearer when arranged by main entry rather than title, particularly when the user is searching for someone who performed a subsidiary function, such as an editor, translator, or illustrator. Indexing "hits" in such a case by title rather than main entry implies, confusingly, that the person (editor, translator, or illustrator) is the author of the work in question.

Some people nevertheless argue with considerable logic that the title of the work should always serve as main entry, with all other points of access as added entries. Certainly there is something to be said for that, despite the counterargument that many titles are indistinct, such as "complete works," or those beginning with the word "journal" or "proceedings," etc. Early bibliographies in the Western world were customarily arranged by title; oriental practice calls generally for title main entry. However, the Paris Principles, following traditional Western library practice, are based on the concept of author responsibility. As mentioned in the introduction to this *Handbook*, the Joint Steering Committee for Revision of AACR charged the Catalog Code Revision Committee and other organizations involved in shaping the code to adhere to the Paris Principles. The editors of *AACR2R* did so, and in this respect it may be said that *AACR2R* continues to be a conservative code.

MARC Coding of Access Points

The MARC coding of the descriptive portions of the catalog record has been discussed in previous chapters, but except for the coding of series (see *Handbook* at 1.6), the coding of main entry and added access points has not yet been discussed.[1]

The main entry is coded in a 1XX field. As "main" entry, there is only one such field per record. There are four types of 1XX fields:

- 100   Personal name
- 110   Corporate name
- 111   Meeting name
- 130   Uniform title

Added access points are recorded in 7XX fields. There may be many such fields in a bibliographic record. The four same types exist:

- 700   Personal name
- 710   Corporate name
- 711   Meeting name
- 730   Uniform title

The following explanation of field coding has been kept to basic information. There are more subfields for each MARC field than those explained here. For further information, consult the latest edition of *USMARC Format for Bibliographic Data* (Washington, D.C.: Cataloging Distribution Service, Library of Congress).

The 100 and 700 fields contain personal names, established according to *AACR2R* chapter 22. The first indicator is "0" if the name is only a forename (see figure 14-1), "1" if there is a single surname (see figure 14-2), and "2" if the name has been established as a compound surname (see figure 14-3). (First indicator "2" has been recently eliminated from USMARC for X00 fields. Because this change has not yet been implemented by the Library of Congress, RLIN, or OCLC, it is not reflected in the figures in this *Handbook*. After implementation, all surnames should be coded first indicator "1".) The second indicator is normally blank (for the exception, see *Handbook* at 13.2, "Analytical Added Entries"). The name itself is recorded in subfield ‡a, qualifiers in subfield ‡q, titles in subfield ‡c, and dates in subfield ‡d.

Figure 14-1.   Forename alone

```
100 0    ‡a Ovid, ‡d 43 B.C.-17 or 18 A.D.
240 10   ‡a Fasti. ‡l English & Latin
245 10   ‡a Publii Ovidii Nasonis Fastorum libri sex = ‡b The Fasti of Ovid / ‡c edited with a
         translation and commentary by Sir James George Frazer.
246 31   ‡a Fasti of Ovid
246 30   ‡a Fastorum libri sex
260      ‡a London ; ‡a New York : ‡b Macmillan, ‡c 1929.
300      ‡a 5 v. : ‡b ill., maps ; ‡c 23 cm.
500      ‡a Includes bibliographical references and indexes.
505 0    ‡a I. Text and translation -- II. Commentary on books I and II -- III. Commentary on books
         III and IV -- IV. Commentary on books V and VI -- V. Indices. Illustrations. Plans.
700 1    ‡a Frazer, James George, ‡c Sir, ‡d 1854-1941.
```

Title page

Publii Ovidii Nasonis
Fastorum Libri Sex
The *Fasti* of Ovid
edited with a translation and commentary
by
Sir James George Frazer
O.M., F.R.S., F.B.A.
Fellow of Trinity College, Cambridge
Membre de l'Institut de France

In five volumes
vol. 1
Text and Translation

Macmillan and Co., Limited
St. Martin's Street, London
1929

Figure 14-2.   Single surname

```
020       ‡a 0394707893
100 1     ‡a Ledgard, Henry F., ‡d 1943-
245 10    ‡a Elementary Basic, as chronicled by John H. Watson / ‡c edited with commentaries by
          Henry Ledgard and Andrew Singer.
250       ‡a 1st ed.
260       ‡a New York : ‡b Random House, ‡c c1982.
300       ‡a xii, 264 p. : ‡b ill. ; ‡c 24 cm.
500       ‡a Includes index.
700 1     ‡a Singer, Andrew, ‡d 1943-
```

Title page	Elementary Basic as Chronicled by John H. Watson Edited with Commentaries by Henry Ledgard and Andrew Singer Random House New York

Figure 14-3.   Compound surname

```
020       ‡a 071904152X
020       ‡a 0719041538 (alk. paper)
245 03    ‡a An illustrated history of late medieval England / ‡c edited by Chris Given-Wilson.
260       ‡a Manchester [England] ; ‡a New York : ‡b Manchester University Press, ‡c 1996.
300       ‡a xi, 292 p. : ‡b ill. (some col.) ; ‡c 29 cm.
504       ‡a Includes bibliographical references (p. 275-278) and index.
700 2     ‡a Given-Wilson, Chris.
```

Title page	An Illustrated History of Late Medieval England Edited by Chris Given-Wilson Manchester University Press Manchester and New York

The 110 and 710 fields contain corporate names, established according to *AACR2R* chapter 24. The first indicator is "1" if the name begins with that of a jurisdiction (e.g., a country or city) (see figure 14-4), and "2" if it is any other type of corporate name entered in direct order (see figure 14-5). The second indicator is normally blank (for the exception, see *Handbook* at 13.2). The basic name is recorded in subfield ‡a, and subordinate units in subfield ‡b.

Figure 14-4.   Jurisdiction

```
020      ‡a 0835206084
110 1    ‡a United States. ‡b Congress. ‡b House. ‡b Committee on Education and Labor. ‡b
         Special Subcommittee on Education.
240 10   ‡a Discrimination against women. ‡k Selections
245 10   ‡a Discrimination against women : ‡b congressional hearings on equal rights in education
         and employment / ‡c edited by Catharine R. Stimpson in conjunction with the
         Congressional Information Service.
260      ‡a New York : ‡b Bowker, ‡c 1973.
300      ‡a xvii, 558 p. ; ‡c 24 cm.
440  0   ‡a Bowker/CIS congressional document series
500      ‡a Selections from the original ed., 1971, have been rearranged.
700 1    ‡a Stimpson, Catharine R., ‡d 1936-
710 2    ‡a Congressional Information Service.
```

Title page	Discrimination against Women
	Congressional Hearings on Equal Rights
	in Education and Employment
	Edited by Dr. Catharine R. Stimpson, Barnard College
	in conjunction with
	the Congressional Information Service,
	Washington, D.C.
	R.R. Bowker Company
	New York & London, 1973
	A Xerox Education Company
	Xerox
Facing title page	
	Bowker/CIS Congressional Document Series
	Published by R.R. Bowker Co. (A Xerox Education Company)
	1180 Avenue of the Americas, New York, N.Y. 10036
	Copyright © 1973 by Xerox Corporation

Figure 14-5.   Corporate name

```
110 2    ‡a Library of Congress. ‡b Descriptive Cataloging Division.
245 10   ‡a Cooperative cataloging manual for the use of contributing libraries / ‡c the Library of
         Congress, Descriptive Cataloging Division.
260      ‡a Washington, D.C. : ‡b U.S. G.P.O., ‡c 1944.
300      ‡a 104 p. ; ‡c 24 cm.
```

Title page	Cooperative Cataloging Manual
	for the use of contributing libraries
	The Library of Congress
	Descriptive Cataloging Division
	United States Government Printing Office
	Washington, D.C., 1944

The 111 and 711 fields contain the names of meetings, expeditions, fairs, etc. If entered directly under the name, the first indicator is "2." (Other indicators are used for non-*AACR2R* forms.) The second indicator is blank. The name itself is recorded in subfield ‡a, date in subfield ‡d, location in subfield ‡c, and number in subfield ‡n. Figure 14-6 contains a 111 field.

The 130 and 730 fields contain uniform titles not associated with authors. The first indicator indicates the number of nonfiling characters (i.e., the number of characters the machine is to skip before it begins filing). Always code this "0," and drop an initial article from the title (*LCRI* 21.30L, Aug. 27, 1990). This applies in languages that distinguish by case whether the article is in the nominative case or not (see *CSB* 52, spring 1991, p. 26). The second indicator is normally blank (for the exception, see *Handbook* at 13.2). The title is recorded in subfield ‡a, the number of a part in subfield ‡n, the name of a part in subfield ‡p, the language of a work in subfield

Figure 14-6.   Named conference

111 2	‡a Conference on Historical and Bibliographical Methods in Library Research ‡d (1970 : ‡c University of Illinois)
245 10	‡a Research methods in librarianship : ‡b historical and bibliographical methods in library research : papers / ‡c presented at the Conference on Historical and Bibliographical Methods in Library Research ; conducted by the University of Illinois Graduate School of Library Science, March 1-4, 1970 ; edited by Rolland E. Stevens.
260	‡a Urbana : ‡b The School, ‡c c1971.
300	‡a 140 p. ; ‡c 24 cm.
490 1	‡a Monograph ; ‡v no. 10
504	‡a Includes bibliographical references.
700 1	‡a Stevens, Rolland Elwell, ‡d 1915-
710 2	‡a University of Illinois at Urbana-Champaign. ‡b Graduate School of Library Science.
830 0	‡a Monograph (University of Illinois at Urbana-Champaign. Graduate School of Library Science) ; ‡v no. 10.

Title information on two facing pages

First page
> Papers Presented at the
> Conference on Historical
> and Bibliographical Methods
> in Library Research
> Conducted by the University of Illinois
> Graduate School of Library Science
> March 1-4, 1970

Second page
> Research Methods in Librarianship
> Historical and Bibliographical Methods
> in Library Research
> Edited by Rolland E. Stevens
> University of Illinois
> Graduate School of Library Science
> Urbana, Illinois

‡l, the date of a work in subfield ‡f, form subheading in subfield ‡k, and version in subfield ‡s. See figure 14-7 for an example of a 130 field.

Uniform titles that are associated with an author may also constitute an added access point. They are recorded either in a 240 field (when the author is in the 1XX field) or in the title portion (subfield ‡t) of an author-title added entry in a 7XX field. The first indicator in the 240 field is coded "0" if the cataloger does not want the uniform title to display, or, more normally, "1" if the cataloger wants the uniform title to display (see figure 14-4). Depending on the system, this coding can also affect whether or not the field indexes. The second indicator indicates nonfiling characters. Again, code this "0" and drop articles from uniform titles (the article must also be dropped in a 7XX name-title entry). Subfields for 240 fields and the title portion of 7XX name-title entries are the same as for the 130/730 field, except that the title itself in a 7XX name-title entry is recorded in subfield ‡t rather than ‡a (see figure 14-8).

21.0B. Sources for determining access points

The most important source for determining access points—in fact, the most important source for the transcription of the bibliographic description—is the part of the item that may be termed "prominent." For a determination of "prominence" it is necessary to consult *AACR2R* 0.8, where prominence is limited to the sources prescribed for the first two areas of description (the title and statement of responsibility area and the edition area). The prescribed sources for these two areas vary somewhat from category to

Figure 14-7.   Uniform title

130 0	‡a Doctrine and Covenants.
245 10	‡a Book of Doctrine and Covenants / ‡c carefully selected from the revelations of God, and given in the order of their dates by the Reorganized Church of Jesus Christ of Latter Day Saints.
260	‡a Independence, Mo. : ‡b Printed by the Board of Publications of the Church, ‡c 1949.
300	‡a 99 p. ; ‡c 19 cm.
500	‡a Revelations given to Joseph Smith.
710 2	‡a Reorganized Church of Jesus Christ of Latter Day Saints.
700 1	‡a Smith, Joseph, ‡d 1805-1844.

Title page

Book of
Doctrine and Covenants
Carefully selected from the revelations
of God, and given in the order of their dates
by The Reorganized Church of Jesus Christ of Latter Day Saints
Independence, Missouri
Printed by the Board of Publications of the
Reorganized Church of Jesus Christ of Latter Day Saints
1949

Figure 14-8.   Uniform title in 7XX field

```
020      ‡a 0664220177
245 00   ‡a Luther and Erasmus : ‡b free will and salvation.
246 30   ‡a Free will and salvation
260      ‡a Philadelphia : ‡b Westminster Press, ‡c c1969.
300      ‡a xiv, 348 p. ; ‡c 22 cm.
490 1    ‡a The library of Christian classics ; ‡v v. 17
504      ‡a Includes bibliographical references and indexes.
505 0    ‡a De libero arbitrio / Erasmus ; translated and edited by E. Gordon Rupp, in
         collaboration with A.N. Marlow -- De servo arbitrio / Luther ; translated and edited by
         Philip S. Watson, in collaboration with B. Drewery.
700 12   ‡a Erasmus, Desiderius, ‡d d. 1536. ‡t De libero arbitrio diatribe. ‡l English.
700 12   ‡a Luther, Martin, ‡d 1483-1546. ‡t De servo arbitrio. ‡l English.
700 1    ‡a Rupp, Ernest Gordon.
700 1    ‡a Watson, Philip S. ‡q (Philip Saville), ‡d 1909-
830  0   ‡a Library of Christian classics (Philadelphia, Pa.) ; ‡v v. 17.
```

Title page

The Library of Christian Classics

Luther
and Erasmus:
Free Will
and Salvation

Erasmus: De Libero Arbitrio
translated and edited by
E. Gordon Rupp, M.A., D.D.
Dixie Professor of Ecclesiastical History in the University of Cambridge

In collaboration with
A.N. Marlow, M.A.
Senior Lecturer in Latin in the University of Manchester

Luther: De Servo Arbitrio
translated and edited by
Philip S. Watson, M.A., D.D.
Rall Professor of Systematic Theology, Garrett Theological Seminary,
Evanston, Illinois

In collaboration with
B. Drewery, M.A.
Bishop Fraser Lecturer in Ecclesiastical History in the University of Manchester

Philadelphia
The Westminster Press

category of material (see rule designated .0B2 in each chapter; e.g., for microforms, 11.0B2). In some cases these prescribed sources may amount to the whole item. Thus, data that are prominent within an item should furnish the necessary information to determine the main entry and added entries. Only rarely does the cataloger need to read a book, listen to a sound recording, or watch a motion picture to determine appropriate access points.

21.0D. *Optional addition.* **Designations of function**

In view of the fact that the Library of Congress will not normally apply the option of adding a designator for function to added entry headings,[2] it is unlikely that designators will be used by many North American libraries except in specialized fields, such as rare book and archival cataloging, which have their own sets of designators. Designators will not be used in examples in this text.

21.1. General Rule

21.1A. Works of personal authorship

An author is "the person chiefly responsible for the creation of the intellectual or artistic content of a work." This would include such persons as writers of books and composers of music, persons who prepare bibliographies, artists and photographers, and, in certain cases, cartographers. In addition, performers, in some cases, are "authors" of sound recordings, films, and videorecordings (see 21.23C and discussion of this rule in *Handbook* chapter 6, "Sound Recordings").

21.1B. Entry under corporate body

The definition of a corporate body given under 21.1B1 should be read carefully. The important thing to remember is that, for cataloging purposes, a corporate body must (1) be an organization or group of persons (2) that has a formal name. Rule 21.1B1 gives several criteria for deciding whether a group does indeed have a name. The idea is not new, but the careful delineation and explication probably have their roots in Eva Verona's monumental study of corporate headings, a document that had much influence on this section of the code.[3]

21.1B2. General rule. The general rule governing entry under corporate body is much more restrictive than earlier codes, which simply stated that a work should be entered "under the person or corporate body that is the author." Thus, under *AACR1*, many works issued by a corporate body were entered under the body simply because the work lacked a personal author (*AACR1* Rule 1A). As Verona phrased it, "*AACR* [1] avoids, as far as possible, entry under title proper."[4] Verona suggests a definition of corporate authorship that, although not explicitly stated in the stipulations of 21.1B2, obviously enunciates the principle underlying the rule:

> A work should be considered to be of corporate authorship if it may be concluded by its character or nature that it is necessarily the result of the creative and/or organizational activity of a corporate body as a whole, and not the result of an independent creative activity of the individual(s) who drafted it.[5]

Following Verona's lead, 21.1B2 totally abandons the principle of corporate authorship in favor of a very restrictive set of guidelines for corporate responsibility under which entry will be made under the heading for the body.

The cataloger must make two decisions under 21.1B2. First, does a work "emanate" from a corporate body? If so, second, does the nature of the work fall into one of the six categories listed in 21.1B2? If both of these conditions are met, the corporate body will be given main entry. Note that it makes no difference if a personal author is involved, even as the main author of the work. If the conditions of 21.1B2 are met, the corporate body receives main entry (note the ninth and eleventh examples under *AACR2R* 21.4B1, with clear personal authorship of Michael Levey and John W. Hayes; main entry is still under the corporate body).

A work "emanates" from a corporate body if the corporate body has "issued," or published, the work, or if the corporate body has caused the work to be published, or if the work originates with the body (see *AACR2R* 21.1B2, footnote 2; *LCRI* 21.1B2, Dec. 11, 1989). The Library of Congress gives as an example of "originating with" a body the case of a commercial publisher arranging with a library to publish the library's catalog. Although it cannot be said that the library either published the catalog or caused it to be published, it still "originated with" and thus "emanated" from the library (*LCRI* 21.1B2, Dec. 11, 1989).

A work emanating from a corporate body will have main entry under the heading for the body *only* if its content is as follows:

21.1B2a. Official reports, rules and regulations, and catalogs of an institution's resources clearly represent the "creative and/or organizational activity of a corporate body as a whole." These are to be entered under the name of the corporate body. A newsletter reporting activities of the corporate body will be entered under the body (see figure 12-4).

An annual report will be entered under corporate body (see figure 12-13). A manual of procedure reflecting rules and regulations of a corporate body will be entered under the name of the body (see figure 14-5).

A catalog of the resources of an institution will be entered under the name of the institution (see figure 1-77). A report of an official of a corporation, institution, or other corporate body dealing with administrative affairs, procedures, etc., of the corporate body will be entered under the body (see figure 1-76).

To be included in this category, the work must deal with the body itself; such works are generally published "in the first instance" for internal use (cf. *LCRI* 21.1B2a, Dec. 11, 1989).

21.1B2b. Also to be entered under the corporate body responsible for them is a group of works that Verona calls "primary legal acts." Included are laws (21.31), treaties (21.35), and constitutions and charters (21.33); these will be considered later in this chapter. Also entered under corporate heading are decrees of the chief executive (21.31) and administrative regulations (21.32).

A legislative hearing is to be entered under the name of the legislative body that has called the hearing (see figure 14-4).

21.1B2c. A work that records "the collective thought of the body" will be entered under the name of the body (see figures 14-9 and 14-10). Works that fall into this category present official statements or position statements from a corporate body on matters other than those with which the body itself deals. But the subject itself should be related to the corporate body's

Figure 14-9.   Official statements

```
110 2    ‡a American Library Association. ‡b Library Standards for Microfilm Committee.
245 10   ‡a Microfilm norms : ‡b recommended standards for libraries / ‡c prepared by the Library
         Standards for Microfilm Committee of the Copying Methods Section, Resources and
         Technical Services Division, American Library Association ; Peter R. Scott, committee
         chairman.
260      ‡a Chicago : ‡b The Division, ‡c 1966.
300      ‡a 48 p. : ‡b ill. ; ‡c 23 cm.
700 1    ‡a Scott, Peter R.
```

Title page	Microfilm Norms Recommended Standards for Libraries prepared by the Library Standards for Microfilm Committee of the Copying Methods Section Resources and Technical Services Division American Library Association Peter R. Scott, committee chairman ALA Resources and Technical Services Division Chicago, 1966

Figure 14-10.   Official statements—reports

```
110 2    ‡a Incorporated Association of Assistant Masters in Secondary Schools.
245 10   ‡a Teaching in comprehensive schools : ‡b a second report / ‡c issued by the
         Incorporated Association of Assistant Masters in Secondary Schools.
260      ‡a Cambridge [England] : ‡b University Press, ‡c 1967.
300      ‡a vii, 174 p. : ‡b ill. ; ‡c 19 cm.
500      ‡a Includes index.
```

Title page	Teaching in Comprehensive Schools a Second Report Issued by the Incorporated Association of Assistant Masters in Secondary Schools Cambridge at the University Press 1967

activities. It should contain recommendations for action, change, etc. If such a work simply gathers information, without recommendations for action, this does not constitute the type of material that would be entered under the name of the corporate body.

21.1B2d. A work that reports "the collective activity of a [named] conference" will be entered under the name of the conference (see figure 14-6). For discussion of conferences and criteria for determining whether a conference is a named conference, see 24.7.

Named exhibitions, fairs, festivals, expeditions, etc., also fall into the category of works covered by 21.1B2d. However, such events only rarely are named, according to the cataloger's definition of a corporate body. One example of such a formally named event is found in figure 14-11.

For an example of a named expedition, see figure 14-12.

In order for an entity whose work is defined in 21.1B2d to be treated as main entry, LC policy requires that its name appear *on the chief source* of the item being cataloged. 21.1B2d may *only* be applied to the three types of bodies stated in the rule (named conference, expedition, or event) (*LCRI* 21.1B2d, Dec. 11, 1989).

Figure 14-11.   Named exhibition

```
111 2    ‡a Pan-American Exposition ‡d (1901 : ‡c Buffalo, N.Y.)
245 10   ‡a Catalogue of the exhibition of fine arts / ‡c Pan-American Exposition.
260      ‡a Buffalo [N.Y.] : ‡b D. Gray, ‡c 1901.
300      ‡a xii, 179 p., 34 p. of plates : ‡b ill. ; ‡c 22 cm.
```

Title page	Pan-American Exposition Catalogue of the Exhibition of Fine Arts Buffalo, 1901

Figure 14-12.   Named expedition

```
111 2    ‡a Antarctic Walk Environmental Research Expedition ‡d (1991-1993)
245 14   ‡a Scientific results from the Antarctic Walk Environmental Research Expedition 1991-
         1993 / ‡c edited by K. Yoshikawa, K. Harada, S. Ishimaru.
260      ‡a Tokyo : ‡b Antarctic Environmental Research Expedition Organizing Committee,
         ‡c 1995.
300      ‡a 258 p. : ‡b ill., maps ; ‡c 27 cm.
504      ‡a Includes bibliographical references.
700 1    ‡a Yoshikawa, K. ‡q (Kenji)
700 1    ‡a Harada, K. ‡q (Koichiro)
700 1    ‡a Ishimaru, S. ‡q (Satoshi)
```

Title page	Scientific Results from the Antarctic Walk Environmental Research Expedition 1991-1993 Edited by K. Yoshikawa K. Harada S. Ishimaru Antarctic Environmental Research Expedition Organizing Committee Tokyo 1995

21.1B2e. A performing group is also regarded as a corporate body. In certain cases, the performing group will be given the main entry (see 21.23C and its discussion in chapter 6 of this *Handbook*, and figure 6-6).

21.1B2f. Cartographic materials may be entered under a corporate heading, if the issuing body is other than a body that is merely responsible for the publication or distribution of the materials (see figures 3-2, 3-5, 3-6, etc.).

21.1B3. If a work issued by a corporate body does not fit in one of the categories listed under 21.1B2, it will not be entered under the corporate body. If no personal author is given, the work will, in many cases, be entered as a work of unknown authorship—under title. Give added entry to the corporate body (see figure 14-13).

A work issued by a corporate body that is not of a type included in the six categories of 21.1B2 may have a personal author or authors. If so, entry will be governed by the number of persons involved in the intellectual content of the work. The example shown in figure 14-14 is entered under personal author by stipulations of 21.4A. Added entry is made for the issuing corporate body.

Figure 14-15 shows a work issued by a corporate body but that is not one of the six categories of 21.1B2. It has five personal authors who are responsible for the content of the work. Entry is under title by provisions of 21.6C2.

Each of the examples given to illustrate 21.1B3 (figures 14-13, 14-14, and 14-15) would have been entered under corporate body under provisions of previous codes. *AACR2R* rules for entry under corporate body are more restrictive. Unless a work is clearly one of the types listed under 21.1B2, it will not be given main entry under a corporate heading, following guidelines of 21.1B3.

Figure 14-13.   Work emanating from a corporate body not included in 21.1B2

020	‡a 0816503850
245 00	‡a Landscaping with native Arizona plants / ‡c Natural Vegetation Committee, Arizona Chapter, Soil Conservation Society of America.
246 18	‡a Native Arizona plants
260	‡a Tucson, Ariz. : ‡b University of Arizona Press, ‡c 1973.
300	‡a vii, 194 p. ; ‡b ill. ; ‡c 23 cm.
504	‡a Includes bibliographical references (p. 183-184).
710 2	‡a Soil Conservation Society of America. ‡b Arizona Chapter. ‡b Natural Vegetation Committee.

Title page   Landscaping with Native Arizona Plants
Natural Vegetation Committee Arizona Chapter
Soil Conservation Society of America
The University of Arizona Press
Tucson, Arizona

Figure 14-14.   Entry under personal rather than corporate author

```
100 1    ‡a Groben, W. Ellis.
245 10   ‡a Adobe architecture : ‡b its design and construction / ‡c prepared by W. Ellis Groben.
260      ‡a [Washington, D.C.] : ‡b U.S. Dept. of Agriculture, Forest Service, ‡c 1941.
300      ‡a 24 leaves, 11 leaves of plates : ‡b ill. ; ‡c 28 cm.
710 2    ‡a United States. ‡b Forest Service.
```

Title page	United States Department of Agriculture Forest Service Adobe Architecture Its Design and Construction 1941 prepared by W. Ellis Groben Division of Engineering T.W. Norcross, Chief

Figure 14-15.   Entry under title (more than three personal authors)

```
020      ‡a 0833023535 (alk. paper)
245 00   ‡a USFK strategy-to-task resource management : ‡b a framework for resource
         decisionmaking / ‡c John Y. Schrader ... [et al.] ; prepared for the Commander, U.S.
         Forces Korea.
260      ‡a Santa Monica, CA : ‡b RAND, ‡c 1996.
300      ‡a xxiv, 85 p. : ‡b ill. ; ‡c 28 cm.
500      ‡a "National Defense Research Institute."
500      ‡a At head of title: RAND.
500      ‡a "The research described in this report was sponsored by the Commander, United States
         Forces Korea. The research was conducted in RAND's National Defense Research Institute,
         a federally funded research and development center supported by the Office of the
         Secretary of Defense, the Joint Staff, and the defense agencies, Contract no.
         MDA903-90-C-0004"--P. [2] of cover.
500      ‡a "MR-654-USFK"--P. [4] of cover.
504      ‡a Includes bibliographical references (p. 85).
700 1    ‡a Schrader, John Y.
710 2    ‡a National Defense Research Institute (Rand Corporation)
710 2    ‡a United States Forces, Korea.
```

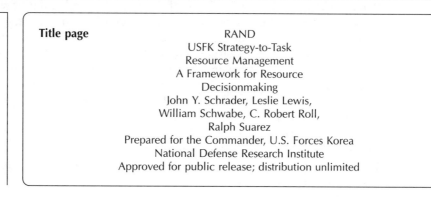

Title page	RAND USFK Strategy-to-Task Resource Management A Framework for Resource Decisionmaking John Y. Schrader, Leslie Lewis, William Schwabe, C. Robert Roll, Ralph Suarez Prepared for the Commander, U.S. Forces Korea National Defense Research Institute Approved for public release; distribution unlimited

21.1B4. Entry under a subordinate unit of a corporate body. If, by terms of 21.1B2, a work would be entered under corporate body, and a subordinate unit of the corporate body is responsible for it, main entry will be under the subordinate unit—if the unit is prominently named (i.e., is listed in the prescribed source for areas 1 and 2) (see discussion under 1.1F1). See figure 14-4 for an example of a subordinate unit of a corporate body that is prominently named; see also figure 14-5.

21.2. CHANGES IN TITLES PROPER

21.2C. Serials

See chapter 12 of this *Handbook* for discussion and examples of proper catalog entry for a serial with a changed title, specifically figures 12-7 and 12-8.

21.3. CHANGES OF PERSONS OR BODIES RESPONSIBLE FOR A WORK

21.3B. Serials

See chapter 12 of this *Handbook* for discussion and figures 12-3 and 12-4 for examples of a serial entered under corporate heading with a change in the name of the corporate body.

21.4. WORKS FOR WHICH A SINGLE PERSON OR CORPORATE BODY IS RESPONSIBLE

Rules 21.1 through 21.3 deal with general principles of authorship responsibility. Rule 21.4 gives guidance for entry of a work that is the responsibility of one person or corporate body.

21.4A. Works of single personal authorship

This simple rule, because it is the foundation of Western cataloging practice, is probably the most important rule in the entire code. As stated in the Paris Principles (8.1), "The main entry for every edition of a work ascertained to be by a single personal author should be made under the author's name." The Paris Principles deal only briefly with the question of determining the form of the author's name that will appear as a heading in the catalog. Some authors use full legal name; some use a nickname; some use one or more pseudonyms; and some simply are not at all consistent about the form of name they use to identify their works. *AACR2R* chapter 22 gives rules for guidance in these problems. Basically, the rule states that the heading will be the name by which the author is commonly known. Thus, entry for a single work by one author may appear under the person's real name (see figure 1-1), a pseudonym (figure 6-2), or a word or phrase (figure 1-61). See this *Handbook*, chapter 15, and *AACR2R* chapter 22 for further discussion and more examples.

A collection or selection of works by one author will also be entered under the name of the author, following guidelines in *AACR2R* chapter 22 for the form of the heading (see figure 14-16).

A work known to be by a single author will be entered under the name of that person even if the name of the person appears nowhere in the work (see figure 14-17).

21.4B. Works emanating from a single corporate body

If a single corporate body is responsible for a work under stipulations of 21.1B2, entry will be under its name (see figure 14-5, for example).

Figure 14-16.   Selections from the work of one author

```
020       ‡a 1562362291
100 1     ‡a Bennion, Lowell Lindsay, ‡d 1908-
245 10    ‡a How can I help? : ‡b final selections by the legendary writer, teacher, and
          humanitarian / ‡c Lowell L. Bennion ; foreword by Emma Lou Thayne.
260       ‡a Murray, UT : ‡b Aspen Books, ‡c c1996.
300       ‡a xvi, 172 p. ; ‡c 21 cm.
500       ‡a "Funeral tributes to Lowell Bennion," p. [147]-172.
```

Title page

How Can
I Help?
Lowell L. Bennion
Final Selections by the Legendary
Writer, Teacher, and Humanitarian
Foreword by Emma Lou Thayne
Aspen Books

Figure 14-17.   Entry under author—name not in book

```
100 1     ‡a Sassoon, Siegfried, ‡d 1886-1967.
245 10    ‡a Memoirs of an infantry officer / ‡c by the Author of Memoirs of a fox-hunting man.
260       ‡a London ; ‡b Faber & Faber, ‡c 1930.
300       ‡a 334 p. ; ‡c 18 cm.
500       ‡a Sequel: Sherston's progress.
500       ‡a "Limited to seven hundred and fifty numbered copies."
590       ‡a Library copy no. 75, signed by the author.
```

Title page

Memoirs of an Infantry Officer
by the Author of Memoirs of a Fox-Hunting Man
London
Faber & Faber Limited
24 Russell Square

21.4C. Works erroneously or fictitiously attributed to a person or corporate body

21.4C1. The correct application of this rule assumes a fair degree of literary sophistication on the part of the cataloger. Normally, catalogers transcribe descriptive cataloging data and assign main and added entries without questioning the validity of information presented in prescribed sources. However, 21.4C1 stipulates that if the cataloger *knows* that responsibility for the work being cataloged is erroneous, or "fictitiously attributed," entry will be under the name of the real author, or under title if the real author is not known. In the examples given under *AACR2R* 21.4C1, because Alice B. Toklas, a real person, is known not to have written the "autobiography," main entry is under the name of the actual author, Gertrude Stein. Because Toklas is a real person, an added entry will be given for her.

As for the second example, it is well known that A. A. Milne is the author of the children's classic entitled *Winnie the Pooh.* He never attempted to disguise his identity by using the name Winnie the Pooh. The book entitled *The Hums of Pooh* is made up of extracts from several of the books about Winnie the Pooh, a teddy bear, written by A. A. Milne. Therefore, main entry will be under Milne's name. An explanatory reference, following the pattern given below for Watson, John H., may be made to explain the relationship between Winnie the Pooh and Milne for library users who may not be aware of it.

The third example given under *AACR2R* 21.4C1 is less obvious. Unless the cataloger happened to be a Sherlock Holmes fan, he or she might take the title page at its face value and give main entry to the fictitious John H. Watson. No harm would be done; it would hardly be the first time that a cataloger has assigned a main entry incorrectly! However, if the cataloger is alert enough to recognize the name of Sherlock Holmes's sidekick and to detect the mild deception of the title page attribution, he or she will apply 21.4C1 and give Farmer the main entry. As with Winnie the Pooh, an explanatory reference may be made to join Watson's name to Farmer's.

Farmer is not the only author who has turned to Sherlock Holmes and his friends for inspiration. The example in figure 14-2 is an imaginative reconstruction of a number of Sherlock Holmes stories, except that this time the great sleuth solves the problems with the application of his newly discovered skill, Basic programming language. As for the cataloging, could Sherlock Holmes have guessed from the title page that main entry would be under the heading for Ledgard? Perhaps not. But he might have been pleased with the explanatory reference generated by the authority record below, which not only clears up the puzzle but also indicates how many authors have assumed the faithful Dr. Watson's mantle since the stories first appeared. The following authority record (a form of which will display to the public) should be added to the catalog, appearing under Watson's name. (For explanation of the MARC authorities format, see chapters 15, 17, and 18 of this *Handbook*.)

100 10 ‡a Watson, John H., ‡c M.D.

663   ‡a For works written by various authors under the name of the
         Holmesian Dr. Watson, search under the heading for the author, e.g.,
         ‡b Ledgard, Henry F., 1943-   , ‡a or ‡b Farmer, Philip José

21.4D. Works by heads of state, etc.

The principle governing 21.4D is basically the same as that of 21.1B2: when
the head of a government speaks or writes in an official capacity, he or she
represents the office in a fashion that is clearly analogous to 21.1B2c. Therefore, entry is under the corporate heading provided for the office that he
or she holds (see 24.20 for form of heading). Such special headings are
provided only for *heads* of government, not for subsidiary officials. Typical
of officials included in this rule would be the queen of England, the president of the United States, the governor of Arizona, and the mayor of Tucson (see figures 1-75 and 1-108 for examples).

A collection of official communications of more than one governmental
head goes under the general heading for the office (see figure 14-18).

Figure 14-18.   Collection of official communications

```
020        ‡a 080503305X
110 1      ‡a United States. ‡b President.
245 14     ‡a The Presidents speak : ‡b the inaugural addresses of the American Presidents from
           Washington to Clinton / ‡c [annotated by] Davis Newton Lott.
260        ‡a New York : ‡b H. Holt and Co., ‡c c1994.
300        ‡a xi, 434 p. : ‡b ports. ; ‡c 29 cm.
440    0   ‡a Henry Holt reference book
504        ‡a Includes index.
500        ‡a Appendices include lists of the presidents and vice presidents, presidents who were not
           inaugurated, the Declaration of Independence, the Act of Confederation, and the
           Constitution.
700 1      ‡a Lott, Davis Newton.
```

Title page   The
                                  Presidents
                                   Speak
              The Inaugural Addresses of the American Presidents,
                         from Washington to Clinton
                           Davis Newton Lott
                       A Henry Holt Reference Book
                        Henry Holt and Company
                              New York

21.4D2. Other works. Any nonofficial communication from a person covered by provisions of 21.4D1 will be entered under personal heading (see figure 14-19).

Because such persons are entered sometimes under personal name and sometimes under the heading for their office, references are needed between the two headings to help the bewildered patron. This is accomplished under *AACR2R*, somewhat confusingly, in a different manner for each heading.

21.4D1, official communications entered under the head of government, requires the cataloger to "make an added entry under the personal heading for the person." This means that each bibliographic record entered under head of government will also include a 700 added entry field containing the head of government's personal heading (see figure 1-75). Thus, the user will retrieve the record whether he or she searches using the official title or the personal name.

On the other hand, rule 21.4D2 requires the cataloger to "make an explanatory reference from the corporate heading to the personal heading." This means that a record entered under the personal name of the head of government will *not* also contain an added entry for the official form. Rather, the reference is achieved through the authority structure of the catalog. An explanatory reference will be written in the authority record for the official title that will direct the patron to search both under the official title and under the personal name, as follows:

```
110 10 ‡a United States. ‡b President (1963-1969 : Johnson)
663     ‡a Here are entered works of the President acting in his official
        capacity. For other works, search under ‡b Johnson, Lyndon B. (Lyndon
        Baines), 1908-1973
```

For reasons of economy, the Library of Congress no longer makes this type of reference. LC catalogers now add only a "see also" reference to the authority heading for the personal name:

```
100 10 ‡a Johnson, Lyndon B. ‡q (Lyndon Baines), ‡d 1908-1973
510 10 ‡a United States. ‡b President (1963-1969 : Johnson)
```

Figure 14-19.   Nonofficial communication from head of government

```
100 1   ‡a Johnson, Lyndon B. ‡q (Lyndon Baines), ‡d 1908-1973.
245 10  ‡a My hope for America / ‡c by Lyndon B. Johnson.
260     ‡a New York : ‡b Random House, ‡c c1964.
300     ‡a 127 p. : ‡b ill. ; ‡c 21 cm.
```

```
Title page          My Hope for America
                    by Lyndon B. Johnson
                    Random House • New York
```

This will display to the patron who searches under the corporate heading as follows:

United States. President (1963-1969 : Johnson)
 search also under
Johnson, Lyndon B. (Lyndon Baines), 1908-1973

Although this type of reference is less helpful to the patron, it serves the same purpose as the explanatory reference called for under 21.4D2.

21.4D3. The provisions for entry under personal name hold true when the work is a mixture of official and nonofficial communications. Because part of the work consists of official communications, an added entry will be made under the appropriate heading for the office. The example shown in figure 14-20 includes speeches made while Lyndon B. Johnson was senator, official speeches to Congress that he made as president, and miscellaneous writings.

A collection containing both official communications and other works by more than one head of a government will be given title main entry under the general rules for collections (21.7).

21.5. WORKS OF UNKNOWN OR UNCERTAIN AUTHORSHIP OR BY UNNAMED GROUPS

21.5A. Enter works of unknown or uncertain authorship under title, assuming that research has not revealed the name of the author. This rule eliminates cataloger-constructed headings such as "Boston. Citizens," which, under ALA 1949 rule 140, would have been given to the second example, "A Memorial to Congress . . . " under *AACR2R* 21.5A. It is obvious that

Figure 14-20. Official and nonofficial communications

```
100 1    ‡a Johnson, Lyndon B. ‡q (Lyndon Baines), ‡d 1908-1973.
245 12   ‡a A time for action : ‡b a selection from the speeches and writings of Lyndon B. Johnson,
         1953-64 / ‡c introduction by Adlai E. Stevenson.
250      ‡a 1st ed.
260      ‡a New York : ‡b Atheneum, ‡c 1964.
300      ‡a xv, 183 p. : ‡b ill. ; ‡c 22 cm.
710 1    ‡a United States. ‡b President (1963-1969 : Johnson)
```

Title page	A Time for Action
	A Selection from the Speeches
	and Writings of
	Lyndon B. Johnson
	1953-64
	Introduction by Adlai E. Stevenson
	Atheneum Publishers
	New York
	1964

such a heading is of no value to the catalog user; title main entry is appropriate. The example shown in figure 14-21 is a book for which the author is unknown. See figure 1-49 for an example of title main entry for a work by an unnamed group.

21.5B. A work that has been attributed to a person will be entered under title, with added entry for the person, unless it is generally assumed that the person is the probable author. In that case, enter under the heading for the person (see figure 14-22).

21.5C. If an author, otherwise unknown, is identified in a work by a characterizing word or phrase, enter under the word or phrase (see figure 14-23).

Note that entry under characterizing word or phrase is limited to one person. A group of persons so characterized is considered an unnamed body (see *AACR2R* 21.5A, "citizens of Boston"; see also 22.11 for further directions on entry under word or phrase).

The only type of device, under *AACR2R*, that cannot be used as a pseudonym, and thus as an entry word, is a nonalphabetic and nonnumeric symbol that cannot be filed. An author who identifies himself or herself entirely by such a device (note that under the 1993 amendments the word "predominantly," as well as the second example, have been deleted from the rule) will be entered under real name if this is known; if real name is not known, the works of such an author will be entered under title.

21.6. WORKS OF SHARED RESPONSIBILITY

Rule 21.6 gives direction about main entry for works produced by two or more authors, whether these authors worked as collaborators in a work of joint authorship or as contributors to a composite work (a work in which

Figure 14-21.   Unknown author

```
020       ‡a 1556159315
245 00    ‡a Supporting Microsoft Windows 95 : ‡b hands-on, self-paced training for supporting
          Windows 95.
246 17    ‡a Microsoft Windows 95 training
260       ‡a Redmond, Wash. : ‡b Microsoft Press, ‡c c1995.
300       ‡a 2 v. (xxii, 1140 p.) : ‡b ill. ; ‡c 23 cm. + ‡e 1 computer laser optical disc (4 3/4 in.)
500       ‡a Issued in case with disc in its own case.
538       ‡a System requirements for computer disc: IBM PC or compatible.
500       ‡a Includes indexes.
710 2     ‡a Microsoft Corporation.
```

Title page	
	Supporting
	Microsoft®
	Windows®95
	Volume One
	Hands-On, Self-Paced Training for Supporting Windows 95
	Microsoft Press

Figure 14-22.   Probable author

```
100 1    ‡a Plantin, Christophe, ‡d ca. 1520-1589.
245 10   ‡a Calligraphy & printing in the sixteenth century : ‡b dialogue / ‡c attributed to
         Christopher Plantin ; edited, with English translation and notes by Ray Nash ; foreword
         by Stanley Morison.
260      ‡a Antwerp : ‡b Plantin-Moretus Museum, ‡c 1964.
300      ‡a 77 p., p. 218-255 : ‡b ill. ; ‡c 19 cm.
546      ‡a Includes French and Flemish facsimile.
700 1    ‡a Nash, Ray, ‡d 1905-
```

Title page	Calligraphy & Printing in the sixteenth century Dialogue attributed to Christopher Plantin in French and Flemish facsimile Edited, with English translation and notes by Ray Nash Foreword by Stanley Morison Antwerp The Plantin-Moretus Museum MCMLXIV

Figure 14-23.   Author not known—entry under word or phrase

```
100 0    ‡a Old Author.
245 10   ‡a Anecdotes illustrative of the power of the Holy Scriptures, &c. ; ‡b to which is
         annexed, The Bible / ‡c from an Old Author.
260      ‡a Aberdeen : ‡b G. and R. King, ‡c 1847.
300      ‡a 72 p. ; ‡c 15 cm.
700 02   ‡a Old Author. ‡t Bible.
```

Title page	Anecdotes Illustrative of the Power of the Holy Scriptures, &c.; To Which is Annexed, "The Bible" from an Old Author Aberdeen: George and Robert King 28, St. Nicholas Street, 1847

each author's contribution is separate and distinct) as long as such a work has a title applicable to the entire work. Paris Principle 10 ("Multiple authorship") governs the rule insofar as personal authors are involved: main entry will be under the name of the person primarily responsible for the intellectual or artistic creation of the work, if this primary responsibility can be determined. If primary responsibility cannot be determined, main entry will be under the heading for the author named first in the prescribed source of information or, if the source lists four or more authors, under title.

In addition to works of personal authorship, rule 21.6 covers entry of works emanating from more than one corporate body if such works are covered by the categories listed under 21.1B2. Also covered are "works resulting from a collaboration or exchange between a person and a corporate body."

Not covered are collections of previously existing works. These are treated under 21.7.

21.6B. Principal responsibility indicated

This rule is closely related to 21.6C; the only instance in which the stipulations of this rule would result in an entry different from that called for under 21.6C is if the layout (type, etc.) of the chief source indicates that a person other than the one named first is principally responsible for the work. Only rarely is a chief source set up in such a fashion. A straightforward and obvious example of the rule is shown in figure 14-24.

21.6C. Principal responsibility not indicated

If the chief source of information does not indicate which author has principal responsibility for the work, give main entry to the first author named if the chief source lists either two or three authors. Give added entries to the author or authors not receiving main entry. Figure 1-3 is an example of this rule.

21.6C2. If the chief source of information lists four or more persons or corporate bodies, none of which has the principal responsibility for the work, make a title main entry. The rationale for this rule is that the user of

Figure 14-24.   Principal responsibility indicated

100 1	‡a Asheim, Lester Eugene, ‡d 1914-
245 14	‡a The humanities and the library : ‡b problems in the interpretation, evaluation and use of library materials / ‡c by Lester Asheim and associates.
260	‡a Chicago : ‡b American Library Association, ‡c 1957.
300	‡a xix, 278 p. ; ‡c 24 cm.
504	‡a Includes bibliographical references.

Title page	The Humanities and the Library Problems in the Interpretation, Evaluation and Use of Library Materials by Lester Asheim and associates American Library Association Chicago • 1957

the catalog in thinking of a book with four or more authors is more likely to remember it by title than by author (i.e., authorship is diffuse). The choice of cutoff point for main entry under author at three authors follows Paris Principle 10.22. Figure 1-33 is an example of this rule, as is figure 1-35. The former shows entry for a work for which four corporate bodies had responsibility.

21.6D. Shared pseudonyms

See figure 14-25 (Maristan Chapman is a pseudonym used by Mary Ilsley Chapman and John Stanton Chapman). See discussion in *Handbook* chapter 15 at 22.2B ("Pseudonyms").

21.7. Collections of Works by Different Persons or Bodies

21.7B. Item with collective title

A collection of independent works by two or more different persons or bodies (21.7A1a) having a collective title will be entered under its title. An encyclopedic dictionary is a familiar type of such a work (see figure 14-26). Figure 14-27 is an example of 21.7A1b, a collection of extracts from independent works by different persons.

Added entries will be made for compilers or editors if not more than three are named prominently (i.e., in the prescribed sources for transcription of the title and statement of responsibility, or for the edition area).

Language referring to works produced under editorial direction was removed from *AACR2R* 21.7 by the 1993 amendments. However, provision is added under both 21.6C2 and 21.7B1 for added entry for up to three "prominently named" editors. Figure 1-33 is an example of a work with a prominently named editor.

Figure 14-25.   Joint pseudonym

```
100 1    ‡a Chapman, Maristan.
245 14   ‡a The weather tree / ‡c by Maristan Chapman.
260      ‡a New York : ‡b Viking, ‡c 1932.
300      ‡a 298 p. ; ‡c 20 cm.
```

Title page	The
	Weather
	Tree
	by Maristan Chapman
	New York
	The Viking Press
	MCMXXXII

Figure 14-26.   Collection entered under title

```
020       ‡a 0393034879
245 04    ‡a The Norton/Grove dictionary of women composers / ‡c edited by Julie Anne Sadie &
          Rhian Samuel.
250       ‡a 1st American ed.
260       ‡a New York : ‡b Norton, ‡c 1994, c1995.
300       ‡a xliii, 548 p. : ‡b ill. ; ‡c 25 cm.
504       ‡a Includes bibliographical references and index.
700 1     ‡a Sadie, Julie Anne.
700 1     ‡a Samuel, Rhian.
```

Title page	The Norton/Grove dictionary of women composers edited by Julie Anne Sadie & Rhian Samuel W.W. Norton & Company New York London

Figure 14-27.   Collection of extracts from independent works

```
020       ‡a 0521431921 (hardback)
020       ‡a 0521437687 (pbk.)
245 00    ‡a Early Greek political thought from Homer to the sophists / ‡c translated and edited by
          Michael Gagarin, Paul Woodruff.
260       ‡a Cambridge [England] ; ‡a New York : ‡b Cambridge University Press, ‡c 1995.
300       ‡a lvi, 324 p. ; ‡c 23 cm.
440  0    ‡a Cambridge texts in the history of political thought
504       ‡a Includes bibliographical references and index.
700 1     ‡a Gagarin, Michael.
700 1     ‡a Woodruff, Paul, ‡d 1943-
```

Title page	Early Greek Political Thought from Homer to the Sophists translated and edited by Michael Gagarin University of Texas Paul Woodruff University of Texas

If more than three editors or compilers are named prominently in a work with a collective title, only the first named (or the principal) editor or compiler's name is transcribed in the statement of responsibility; added entry will be given to that person only (see figure 14-28).

A "collection" may have as few as two works by different authors and still be a collection under the terms of 21.7. If a collection has two or three items in it, enter under title and make name-title added entries for each (see figures 14-8 and 14-29 for examples of such collections). Note that the title in a name-title added entry is the uniform title, not necessarily the title as found in the item. A patron searching under the English title of one of the works collected in figure 14-29 may be directed to the correct form by means of a "search under" reference generated by the authority record for the uniform title (cf. also *LCRI* 21.30M, "Analytical added entries," §4, Nov. 10, 1993). Alternately, as in figure 14-29, the cataloger may make title added entries through the 740 field for "uncontrolled" forms of titles.

Sometimes a collection includes more than three separate items but these items are by either two or three contributors. If a contributor is responsible for only one of the items, make a name-title added entry for that item. For other contributors who are responsible for more than one item, make added entries under the headings for their names. See the example *A Cornish quintette* under *AACR2R* 21.7B1.

Ordinarily, if there are more than three contributors, no added entry is given to any of the names. But if the names of the contributors are listed prominently, the first contributor's name will be transcribed as part of the statement of responsibility; this person will be given an added entry (see figure 14-30). Furthermore, under *AACR2R* chapter 13 ("Analysis"), a library may, according to its own policy, give name-title added entries to any or all contributors, beyond those called for in 21.7B.

Figure 14-28.   More than three editors named prominently

```
020      ‡a 1563964597
245 00   ‡a Research trends in fluid dynamics : ‡b report from the United States National
         Committee on Theoretical and Applied Mechanics / ‡c editors, J.L. Lumley ... [et al.].
260      ‡a Woodbury, New York : ‡b American Institute of Physics, ‡c c1996.
300      ‡a xix, 328 p. ; ‡c 24 cm.
504      ‡a Includes bibliographical references.
700 1    ‡a Lumley, John L. ‡q (John Leask), ‡d 1930-
710 2    ‡a U.S. National Committee on Theoretical and Applied Mechanics.
```

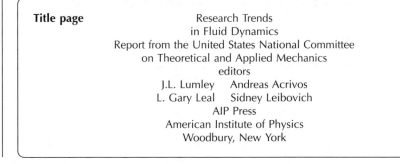

Title page

Research Trends
in Fluid Dynamics
Report from the United States National Committee
on Theoretical and Applied Mechanics
editors
J.L. Lumley   Andreas Acrivos
L. Gary Leal   Sidney Leibovich
AIP Press
American Institute of Physics
Woodbury, New York

Figure 14-29.   Collection with three items

```
245 00   ‡a Three classic Spanish plays / ‡c edited and with introductions by Hymen Alpern.
260      ‡a New York : ‡b Washington Square Press, ‡c 1963.
300      ‡a x, 229 p. ; ‡c 17 cm.
440  0   ‡a ANTA series of distinguished plays
505 0    ‡a The sheep well / by Lope de Vega -- Life is a dream / by Calderón de la Barca -- None
         beneath the king / by Rojas Zorrilla.
700 1    ‡a Alpern, Hymen, ‡d 1895-1967
700 12   ‡a Vega, Lope de, ‡d 1562-1635. ‡t Fuente Ovejuna. ‡l English.
700 22   ‡a Calderón de la Barca, Pedro, ‡d 1600-1681. ‡t Vida es sueño. ‡l English.
700 22   ‡a Rojas Zorrilla, Francisco de, ‡d 1607-1648. ‡t Del rey abajo, ninguno. ‡l English.
740 02   ‡a Sheep well.
740 02   ‡a Life is a dream.
740 02   ‡a None beneath the king.
```

Title page	The ANTA Series of Distinguished Plays
	Three Classic Spanish Plays:
	The Sheep Well
	by Lope de Vega
	Life is a Dream
	by Calderón de la Barca
	None beneath the King
	by Rojas Zorrilla
	edited and with introductions by
	Hymen Alpern, Ph.D.
	Washington Square Press, Inc. • New York

21.7C. Item without a collective title

For an example of main entry and added entry for an item without a collective title, see figure 1-57. A name-title added entry is to be made for the second work in the item; entry is under the author of the first item.

The reader is reminded that *AACR2R* chapter 21 applies to all types of library materials equally. For further information on 21.7, particularly as it applies to sound recordings, see *LCRI* 21.7B and 21.7C (May 19, 1994).

Works of Mixed Responsibility

21.8A. Scope

Rules 21.1 through 21.7 cover works for which one or more persons or corporate bodies are responsible for the intellectual or artistic content of the item and have performed the same function, either as collaborators or as individuals working on separate parts of the item. Rules 21.8 through 21.27 deal with works in which different persons or corporate bodies have performed different kinds of functions on the same work: for example, one person has written a work; another has revised, adapted, illustrated, or

Figure 14-30.   More than three contributors named in chief source

245 00   ‡a Space exploration / ‡c Robert M.L. Baker, Jr. ... [et al.] ; edited by Donald P.
Le Galley, John W. McKee.
260   ‡a New York : ‡b McGraw-Hill, ‡c 1964.
300   ‡a xii, 467 p. : ‡b ill., maps ; ‡c 23 cm.
440   0   ‡a University of California engineering and sciences extension series
504   ‡a Includes bibliographical references
700   1   ‡a Baker, Robert M. L., ‡d 1930-
700   1   ‡a Le Galley, Donald P. ‡q (Donald Paul), ‡d 1901-
700   1   ‡a McKee, John W.

Title page	
	Space Exploration
	Robert M.L. Baker, Jr.
Herbert Corben
Paul Dergarabedian
Manfred Eimer
Louis B.C. Fong
A. Donald Goedeke
	edited by
Donald P. Le Galley
John W. McKee
	McGraw-Hill Book Company
New York, San Francisco, Toronto, London

translated it, or has acted in some other capacity that might lead library users to think of the latter person as being primarily responsible for the work's existence. The Paris Principles do not address themselves specifically to the problem of determining which of these several individuals or corporate bodies is actually principally responsible for the intellectual or artistic content of the work. Rules 21.8 through 21.27 give guidance so that the principle of authorship responsibility may be maintained even when responsibility is mixed.

Rules are divided into two types of mixed responsibility: (1) modifications of previously existing works and (2) new works to which different types of contributions have been made.

Works That Are Modifications of Other Works

21.9. GENERAL RULE

If a work has been rewritten or if the medium has been changed (i.e., a book made into a motion picture), in most cases the resulting product is regarded as a new work although the original author's ideas and even some of his or her words may have been kept. As such, it will be entered under the heading appropriate for the new work, with name-title added entry for the original work. Figure 1-94 is one example of a literary adaptation in which a story, retold by the adapter, is entered under the name of the adapter. The motion picture adaptation of *Alice in Wonderland* (figure 7-5) is a fairly obvious example of a motion picture made from a book, with the resultant motion picture definitely a new work.

However, a sound recording made from a book—as long as the original author's words are retained—will be entered under the heading appropriate to the original work (see *AACR2R* 21.23A1 and figure 6-2). Likewise, an updating, abridgment, revision, rearrangement, etc., will be entered in the same fashion as the original work as long as the original author (creator, etc.) is named in a statement of responsibility (for example, see figure 1-41; see also *AACR2R* 21.12A).

Modifications of Texts

21.10. ADAPTATIONS OF TEXTS

Examples of an adaptation covered by 21.10 would be a paraphrase in which the original author's ideas were kept but put into different words; a simplified, rewritten version of a work for children; or a novel rewritten as a play. Such works are to be entered under the name of the adapter if it is known (see figure 1-107). If the name of the adapter is not known, enter under title (see figure 7-5). In all cases, make a name-title added entry for the original work (see figures 14-31 and 14-32).

Compare rule 21.10 with rule 21.12, revision of texts.

Figure 14-31.   Adaptation entered under name of adapter—version rewritten for children

```
020      ‡a 0805030522
100 1    ‡a Highwater, Jamake.
245 10   ‡a Rama : ‡b a legend / ‡c Jamake Highwater ; with illustrations by Kelli Glancey.
250      ‡a 1st ed.
260      ‡a New York : ‡b Henry Holt and Co., ‡c 1994.
300      ‡a 226 p. : ‡b ill. ; ‡c 22 cm.
500      ‡a Based on Vālmīki's Rāmāyaṇa.
700 1    ‡a Glancey, Kelli.
700 0    ‡a Vālmīki. ‡t Rāmāyaṇa.
```

Title page

Rama
A Legend
Jamake Highwater
With illustrations by
Kelli Glancey
Henry Holt and Company
New York

Figure 14-32.   Adaptation entered under name of adapter—different literary medium

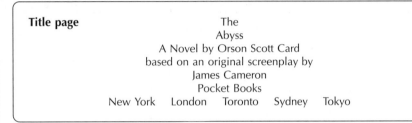

```
020        ‡a 0671676253
100 1      ‡a Card, Orson Scott.
245 10     ‡a The abyss : ‡b a novel / ‡c by Orson Scott Card ; based on an original screenplay by
           James Cameron.
260        ‡a New York : ‡b Pocket Books, ‡c 1989.
300        ‡a 363 p. : ‡b ill. ; ‡c 17 cm.
700 1      ‡a Cameron, James, ‡d 1954- ‡t Abyss.
```

Title page	The Abyss A Novel by Orson Scott Card based on an original screenplay by James Cameron Pocket Books New York London Toronto Sydney Tokyo

21.11. ILLUSTRATED TEXTS

An illustrated work is one in which the text was written first and illustrated later. The author of the text is primarily responsible for the work; entry will be under name of the author. See 21.30K2 for guidance in the matter of added entry under the name of the illustrator. In the example shown in figure 14-33, added entry will be made for illustrator because, as is the case with many books for children, illustrations occupy about half of the book and are an important feature of the work (see also figures 1-65 and 1-113). Illustrations are also usually "considered to be an important feature of the work" (21.30K2c) in modern fine press books (see, e.g., figures 1-20 and 2-6). Compare this rule with *AACR2R* 21.24, works of collaboration between a writer and an artist (photographer, etc.).

21.11B. Illustrations published separately

The artist is chiefly responsible for the content of a work consisting solely of illustrations. Under the principle of author (creator, artist, etc.) responsibility as defined in 21.1A1, main entry will be under the name of the artist (see figure 1-27).

An important example of this type of work is a reproduction of part of a medieval psalter or book of hours. Such a reproduction often emphasizes the illustrative material. By *LCRI* 21.11B (Feb. 1, 1989), the cataloger is to enter these incomplete psalters, etc., under the heading for the artist, or under title if the artist is unknown. Make an added entry for the heading for the original work (see figure 14-34).

Figure 14-33.   Illustrated work entered under author of text

```
020      ‡a 068931826X
100 1    ‡a Medearis, Angela Shelf, ‡d 1956-
245 10   ‡a Our people / ‡c by Angela Shelf Medearis ; illustrated by Michael Bryant.
250      ‡a 1st ed.
260      ‡a New York : ‡b Atheneum, ‡c 1994.
300      ‡a 1 v. (unpaged) : ‡b col. ill. ; ‡c 27 cm.
520      ‡a A father tells his daughter about the contributions made throughout history by Africans
         and African-Americans.
700 1    ‡a Bryant, Michael.
```

Title page	Our People
	by Angela Shelf Medearis
	illustrated by Michael Bryant
	Atheneum 1994 New York
	Maxwell Macmillan Canada
	Toronto
	Maxwell Macmillan International
	New York Oxford Singapore Sydney

Figure 14-34.   Illustrations published separately—Book of hours

```
020      ‡a 0714814202
100 0    ‡a Master of Mary of Burgundy, ‡d fl. 1475-1490.
245 12   ‡a A book of hours for Engelbert of Nassau, the Bodleian Library, Oxford / ‡c the Master
         of Mary of Burgundy ; introduction and legends by J.J.G. Alexander.
260      ‡a New York : ‡b G. Braziller, ‡c 1970.
300      ‡a 1 v. (unpaged) : ‡b 115 col. ill. ; ‡c 15 cm.
500      ‡a Facsims., except no. 1, are reproductions of illuminated pages from the ms. Douce
         219-220, Bodleian Library.
500      ‡a Issued in a case.
504      ‡a Includes bibliographical references.
700 1    ‡a Alexander, J. J. G. ‡q (Jonathan James Graham)
700 0    ‡a Engelbrecht ‡b II, ‡c Count of Nassau-Dillenburg-Dietz, ‡d 1451-1504.
710 2    ‡a Catholic Church. ‡t Book of hours (Ms. Engelbert of Nassau)
710 2    ‡a Bodleian Library. ‡k Manuscript. ‡n Douce 219-220.
```

Title page	The Master of
	Mary of Burgundy
	A Book of Hours
	for Engelbert of Nassau
	The Bodleian Library, Oxford
	Introduction and Legends by
	J.J.G. Alexander
	George Braziller/New York

21.12. REVISIONS OF TEXTS

Rule 21.12 deals with works that have been revised, enlarged, abridged, condensed, etc., but for which the text remains substantially in the words of the original author. The cataloger is not obliged to compare editions to determine whether or not that is the case; the wording of the title page will be the deciding factor in the choice of main entry.

21.12A. Original author considered responsible

This rule has been partially changed from that given in *AACR2* (1978). Under the revised *AACR2R* rule, main entry will be under the heading for the original author of a revised work only if the original author's name appears in the statement of responsibility of the work. The only exception is if the original author's name appears in the title proper and "no other person is named in a statement of responsibility or other title information," or, alternately, if the item does not include a statement of responsibility. In figure 1-59 the original author's name appears in the statement of responsibility. Main entry will therefore be under this author's name.

21.12B. Original author no longer considered responsible

If, in contrast to 21.12A, the original author's name no longer appears on the title page or other chief source of information, or if the original author's name appears only in the title proper "and some other person or body is named as being primarily responsible in the statement of responsibility or in the statement of responsibility relating to the edition," main entry will be under the name of the reviser, with a name-title added entry under the heading for the original author. See figure 1-60, which under *AACR2* (1978) would have had main entry under James Wilson Bright (see also figure 1-104).

21.13. TEXTS PUBLISHED WITH COMMENTARY

21.13A. Scope

This rule applies only to publications consisting of a work or group of works by a single author (personal or corporate) together with commentary on it by someone else. Use this rule only when both text and commentary are present.

21.13B. Commentary emphasized

If title page wording indicates that the publication is a commentary, enter it under the appropriate heading for the commentary according to 21.1A or 21.1B. In the example shown in figure 14-35, the commentary emanates from a corporate body. The publication is not one of the types listed under 21.1B2. Therefore, title main entry is appropriate, with an added entry for the corporate body as well as an added entry for the text of the law included as part of the publication (see also figure 1-83 for a further example of text with commentary emphasized).

Figure 14-35.   Commentary with text

245 00	‡a Civil Rights Act of 1964, with explanation : ‡b Public law 88-352, as approved by the President on July 2, 1964.
260	‡a Chicago : ‡b Commerce Clearing House, ‡c c1964.
300	‡a 108 p. ; ‡c 23 cm.
500	‡a Includes index.
500	‡a "Prepared for NAACP-Legal Defense & Education Fund by Commerce Clearing House, Inc."--Cover.
710 2	‡a Commerce Clearing House.
710 2	‡a NAACP Legal Defense and Educational Fund.
710 12	‡a United States. ‡t Civil Rights Act of 1964.

Title page	Civil Rights Act of 1964 With Explanation Public Law 88-352, as approved by the President on July 2, 1964

21.13C. Edition of the work emphasized

Catalog such a work as an edition of the work with added entry for commentator. Figure 2-11 is an example.

Note that for both 21.13B and 21.13C title page information and format will determine the main entry. If title page information is ambiguous, 21.13D gives some practical guidelines to aid in the decision. If these guidelines do not help, the work should be entered as an edition of the work, with added entry for the commentator.

21.14. TRANSLATIONS

A translation will be entered under the same heading as the original. Added entry will be made for the translator under the provisions of 21.30K1. That is to say, if the translation is in verse, if the translation is important in its own right, if it has been translated into the same language more than once, or if a library user might have reason to think from the wording of the title page that the translator was the author of the work, make an added entry for translator.

In the example shown in figure 14-36, both the original and the translation are in verse; the translation by a well-known American poet is important in its own right; and La Fontaine's fables have been translated into English more than once.

In the example shown in figure 14-37, Goethe's *Faust* has been translated into English by more than one translator; thus an added entry will be given to the translator.

Figure 14-36.   Translation

```
100 1    ‡a La Fontaine, Jean de, ‡d 1621-1695.
240 10   ‡a Fables. ‡l English
245 14   ‡a The fables of La Fontaine / ‡c translated by Marianne Moore.
260      ‡a New York : ‡b Viking, ‡c 1954.
300      ‡a x, 342 p. : ‡b ill. ; ‡c 24 cm.
500      ‡a Includes index.
700 1    ‡a Moore, Marianne, ‡d 1887-1972.
```

Title page	The Fables of La Fontaine
	Translated by Marianne Moore
	New York
	Viking Press • MCMLIV

Figure 14-37.   Translation

```
100 1    ‡a Goethe, Johann Wolfgang von, ‡d 1749-1832.
240 10   ‡a Faust. ‡l English
245 10   ‡a Faust : ‡b a tragedy / ‡c by Johann Wolfgang von Goethe ; translated by Alice
         Raphael ; with an introduction for the modern reader by Mark Van Doren and woodcuts
         by Lynd Ward.
260      ‡a New York : ‡b J. Cape, ‡c c1930.
300      ‡a xxi, 262 p. : ‡b ill. ; ‡c 23 cm.
700 1    ‡a Raphael, Alice Pearl, ‡d 1887-
```

Title page	Faust
	A Tragedy
	By Johann Wolfgang von Goethe
	Translated by Alice Raphael
	With an Introduction for the Modern Reader
	by Mark Van Doren and Woodcuts by Lynd Ward
	New York
	Jonathan Cape & Harrison Smith

A "free" translation or an adaptation, not a literal translation, should be treated according to the provisions of 21.10 and entered under the name of the translator-adapter, the translator being regarded in this instance as the author of an adaptation (see figure 14-38).

Figure 14-38.   Translation—adaptation

```
100 1    ‡a Phillips, Stephen, ‡d 1868-1915.
245 10   ‡a Faust / ‡c freely adapted from Goethe's dramatic poem by Stephen Phillips and
         J. Comyns Carr.
260      ‡a New York : ‡b Macmillan, ‡c 1908.
300      ‡a xix, 208 p. ; ‡c 19 cm.
700 1    ‡a Carr, J. Comyns ‡q (Joseph Comyns), ‡d 1849-1916.
700 1    ‡a Goethe, Johann Wolfgang von, ‡d 1749-1832. ‡t Faust.
```

Title page	Faust
	Freely Adapted from Goethe's Dramatic Poem
	By Stephen Phillips and J. Comyns Carr
	New York
	The Macmillan Company
	1908
	All rights reserved

Figure 14-39.   Collection of translations

```
245 03   ‡a An anthology of Old English poetry / ‡c translated into alliterative verse by Charles W.
         Kennedy.
260      ‡a New York : ‡b Oxford University Press, ‡c 1960.
300      ‡a xvi, 174 p. ; ‡c 21 cm.
500      ‡a Includes index.
700 1    ‡a Kennedy, Charles W. ‡q (Charles William), ‡d 1882-1969.
```

Title page	An Anthology of Old English Poetry
	Translated into Alliterative Verse by
	Charles W. Kennedy
	New York
	Oxford University Press
	1960

21.14B. A collection of translations of works by different authors will be entered as a collection under the provisions of 21.7, with added entry under the name of the translator (see figure 14-39).

21.15. TEXTS PUBLISHED WITH BIOGRAPHICAL/ CRITICAL MATERIAL

This rule applies to publications consisting of works, letters, etc., of an author together with biographical or critical material about this author by another person. Main entry for such a work, in essence, depends on the wording of the title page.

Figure 14-40.   Biographer as author

```
100 1    ‡a Dreiser, Theodore, ‡d 1871-1945.
245 10   ‡a Theodore Dreiser presents the living thoughts of Thoreau / ‡c cover photo, Bettman
         Archive.
246 30   ‡a Living thoughts of Thoreau.
250      ‡a New premier ed.
260      ‡a Greenwich, Conn. : ‡b Fawcett World Library, ‡c 1958, c1939.
300      ‡a 176 p. ; ‡c 18 cm.
440  0   ‡a Living thoughts series.
490 0    ‡a A premier book ; ‡c d63
700 1    ‡a Thoreau, Henry David, ‡d 1817-1862.
```

Title page   Theodore Dreiser
                                              presents the
                                      living thoughts of Thoreau
                                           A Premier Book
                                        The Living Thoughts Series
                                        cover photo: Bettman Archive
                                         Fawcett Publications, Inc.
                              Fawcett Bldg., Fawcett Place, Greenwich, Conn.

Verso of title page
                             Copyright MCMXXXIX, by David McKay Co., Inc.
            The Living Thoughts of Thoreau was originally published by David McKay Co.,
                  Inc., and this new Premier edition is reissued through arrangement
                                        with that company.
                             First Premier printing, February 1958
                         Premier Books are published by Fawcett World Library

21.15A. If the title page refers to the critic-biographer as author, main entry is under his or her name, with added entry for the other person. The example shown in figure 14-40 consists of a thirty-six-page section of biography-commentary by Dreiser, followed by selections from Thoreau's works.

21.15B. If the author of the biographical material is represented as an editor or compiler, main entry is under the name of the author of the text. Give an added entry to the editor, compiler, etc. The example shown in figure 14-41 consists of forty pages of biographical material about the diarist, followed by the diary, annotated by Mark A. Strang. Guided by the wording of the title page, main entry will be under the name of the diarist, James J. Strang.

Figure 14-41.   Author of text as author

```
100 1    ‡a Strang, James Jesse, ‡d 1813-1856.
245 14   ‡a The diary of James J. Strang / ‡c deciphered, transcribed, introduced and annotated by
         Mark A. Strang ; with a foreword by Russel B. Nye.
260      ‡a [East Lansing] : ‡b Michigan State University Press, ‡c c1961.
300      ‡a xlv, 78 p. : ‡b ill. ; ‡c 22 cm.
504      ‡a Includes bibliographical references (p. 65-78).
700 1    ‡a Strang, Mark A.
```

Title page	The Diary of James J. Strang Deciphered, Transcribed, Introduced and Annotated by Mark A. Strang With a Foreword by Russel B. Nye Michigan State University Press

Art Works

21.16. ADAPTATIONS OF ART WORKS

See *Handbook* chapter 8 ("Graphic Materials") for discussion and examples of this rule, which applies to a single art work.

21.17. REPRODUCTIONS OF TWO OR MORE ART WORKS

21.17A. Without text

Reproductions without text will be entered under name of the artist.

21.17B. With text

If the person who wrote the text is represented as the author (not editor), entry will be under the name of the author of the text, no matter how brief its extent. Fourteen pages of text is a small portion of the total extent of the example shown in figure 14-42. Nonetheless, entry will be under the name of the author of the text (see also 21.24).

If, on the other hand, the person who wrote the text is not represented as the author, but is, instead, listed as being an editor, entry will be under the name of the artist. Give added entry to the writer of the text (see figure 14-43).

Art catalogs present a special situation. If a catalog pertaining to a single artist contains reproductions of his or her works, 21.17B should be applied. If the catalog does not include reproductions of the artist's work, first 21.1B2a should be applied (entry under the corporate body issuing the catalog if it holds all the listed works); if that is not applicable, entry is under the author of the text of the catalog, if known; if neither of these is applicable, entry is under title (*LCRI* 21.17B, Jan. 5, 1989).

Figure 14-42. Art reproductions with text

```
020      ‡a 0714814857
100 1    ‡a Gaunt, William, ‡d 1900-
245 10   ‡a Turner / ‡c William Gaunt.
260      ‡a London : ‡b Phaidon, ‡c 1971.
300      ‡a 14 p., 48 p. of plates : ‡b col. ill. ; ‡c 32 cm.
500      ‡a Distributed in U.S.A. by Praeger Publishers, New York.
700 1    ‡a Turner, J. M. W. ‡q (Joseph Mallord William), ‡d 1775-1851.
```

Title page	William Gaunt
	Turner
	Phaidon

Figure 14-43. Writer of text as editor

```
100 1    ‡a Walcott, Mary Vaux, ‡d 1860-1940.
245 10   ‡a Wild flowers of America : ‡b 400 flowers in full color / ‡c based on paintings by Mary
         Vaux Walcott as published by the Smithsonian Institution of Washington ; with additional
         paintings by Dorothy Falcon Platt ; edited with an introduction and detailed descriptions
         by H.W. Rickett.
260      ‡a New York : ‡b Crown, ‡c c1953.
300      ‡a 71 p., 400 p. of plates : ‡b col. ill. ; ‡c 31 cm.
500      ‡a Walcott's ill. reproduced from: North American wild flowers / by Mary Vaux Walcott.
         Washington : Smithsonian, 1925.
700 1    ‡a Walcott, Mary Vaux, ‡d 1860-1940. ‡t North American wild flowers.
700 1    ‡a Platt, Dorothy Falcon.
700 1    ‡a Rickett, Harold William, ‡d 1896-
```

Title information on two facing pages

First page	400 flowers in full color
	based on paintings by
	Mary Vaux Walcott
	as published by the
	Smithsonian Institution of Washingon
	with additional paintings by
	Dorothy Falcon Platt
	edited with an introduction
	and detailed descriptions by
	H.W. Rickett
Second page	Wild Flowers of America
	Crown Publishers, Inc.
	New York

21.18–21.22. MUSICAL WORKS

See *Handbook* chapter 5 ("Music") for discussion and examples of rules for choice of access point for musical works.

21.23. SOUND RECORDINGS

See *Handbook* chapter 6 ("Sound Recordings") for discussion and examples of this rule.

Mixed Responsibility in New Works

Rules 21.1 through 21.8 give definitions, general principles, and rules for determining choice of main and added entry first for a work involving a single author and next for a work involving the collaboration of more than one author. Rules 21.9 through 21.23 deal with works that are modifications of previously published works—texts, art works, musical works, and sound recordings. Rules 21.24 through 21.28 address themselves to new works in which more than one person or corporate body has performed different functions and in which no one is clearly principally responsible for the intellectual or artistic content of the work.

21.24. COLLABORATION BETWEEN ARTIST AND WRITER

AACR2R 21.24 is based on *AACR1* rule 8A, which was clarified by the Library of Congress in *Cataloging Service Bulletin* 96 (Nov. 1970): "the word 'collaboration' as used in this rule means that the author and artist have worked *jointly* to produce the work. . . . If there is an indication, or a reasonable assumption, that the text has been illustrated after its completion, collaboration is not involved." Although this rule interpretation is no longer in force, it is still a good statement of the distinction between 21.24 ("Collaboration between Artist and Writer") and 21.11 ("Illustrated Texts"), as well as 21.17 ("Reproductions of Two or More Art Works").

The distinction between this rule and the previous rules mentioned is the matter of collaboration. Does the work in question seem to have been a joint effort, or was one part done independently of the other? The example shown in figure 14-44 is clearly a collaborative effort. Entry is under the name of the person listed first on the title page; an added entry is made for the other.

21.25. REPORTS OF INTERVIEWS OR EXCHANGES

21.25A. Under the stipulations of this rule, if the reporter simply records the words of the person(s) being interviewed without participating in the discussion, follow 21.6 ("Works of Shared Responsibility") to determine main entry. For an interview involving two participants, as shown in figure 14-45, entry will be under the first named. An added entry is to be made for the other participant, and also for a "prominently named" reporter (see 0.8 for definition of "prominently").

Figure 14-44.   Collaboration between artist and author

```
100 1    ‡a Molinard, Patrice.
245 10   ‡a Paris / ‡c photographies originales de Patrice Molinard ; texte d'Yvan Christ.
260      ‡a Paris : ‡b Éditions Mondiales, ‡c [1953?]
300      ‡a 1 v. (unpaged) : ‡b chiefly ill. (some col) ; ‡c 31 cm.
440  0   ‡a Couleurs du monde ; ‡v [3]
546      ‡a French and English.
500      ‡a English translation by Baird Hastings.
700 1    ‡a Christ, Yvan, ‡d 1919-
```

Title page

Les Éditions Mondiales
2, rue des Italiens, 2 Paris
présentent
Paris
Photographies Originales
de Patrice Molinard
texte d'Yvan Christ
"Couleurs du monde"
collection dirigée par J.-E. Imbert

Figure 14-45.   Interview

```
100 1    ‡a Twain, Mark, ‡d 1835-1910.
245 10   ‡a Abroad with Mark Twain and Eugene Field : ‡b tales they told to a fellow
         correspondent / ‡c by Henry W. Fisher.
260      ‡a New York : ‡b Nicholas L. Brown, ‡c 1922.
300      ‡a xxi, 246 p. ; ‡c 21 cm.
500      ‡a Edited by Merle Johnson.
700 1    ‡a Field, Eugene, ‡d 1850-1895.
700 1    ‡a Fischer, Henry W. ‡q (Henry William), ‡d 1856-1932.
700 1    ‡a Johnson, Merle De Vore, ‡d 1874-1935.
```

Title page

Abroad with Mark Twain
and Eugene Field
Tales They Told to a Fellow Correspondent
by Henry W. Fisher
New York   Nicholas L. Brown   MCMXXII

21.25B. This rule is related to 21.10 ("Adaptations of Texts"). If the reporter has restated the conversation rather than simply making a verbatim report or transcript, then he or she is considered to be responsible for the intellectual content of the interview. Make main entry under the name of the reporter (see figure 14-46).

Figure 14-46.   Interview

```
100 1    ‡a Henderson, Archibald, ‡d 1877-1963.
245 10   ‡a Table-talk of G.B.S. : ‡b conversations on things in general between George Bernard
         Shaw and his biographer / ‡c by Archibald Henderson.
260      ‡a New York : ‡b Harper, ‡c 1925.
300      ‡a 162 p. : ‡b ill. ; ‡c 20 cm.
700 1    ‡a Shaw, Bernard, ‡d 1856-1950.
```

Title page   Table-Talk of G.B.S.
Conversations on Things in General between
George Bernard Shaw
and his biographer
By Archibald Henderson, Ph.D., D.C.L., LL.D.
New York and London
Harper & Brothers Publishers
1925

21.26. SPIRIT COMMUNICATIONS

The predecessor of this rule was *AACR1* rule 13C, which, like its predecessor, ALA 1949 rule 11, called for main entry under the medium or "person reporting the communication" for communications "purporting to have been received from a spirit." Whether the editors of *AACR2* joined the society of true believers is not known; it is more likely that they decided that this rule, like all others, should be based on information presented in the work, which is ordinarily to be accepted at its face value, and that the catalog entry is simply to describe the work rather than to serve as a pejorative judgment of its truth or fiction. At any rate, under *AACR2* the earlier rule was reversed. Main entry will be under the name of the spirit, with added entry for the medium, as shown in figure 14-47.

Figure 14-47.   Spirit communication

```
100 1    ‡a Wilde, Oscar, ‡d 1854-1900 ‡c (Spirit)
245 10   ‡a Oscar Wilde from purgatory : ‡b psychic messages / ‡c edited by Hester Travers Smith
         ; with a preface by Sir William F. Barrett.
260      ‡a New York : ‡b Holt, ‡c 1926.
300      ‡a xii, 179 p. ; ‡b ill. ; ‡c 22 cm.
500      ‡a London ed. published as: Psychic messages from Oscar Wilde.
700 1    ‡a Smith, Hester Travers.
700 1    ‡a Wilde, Oscar, ‡d 1854-1900 ‡c (Spirit). ‡t Psychic messages from Oscar Wilde.
```

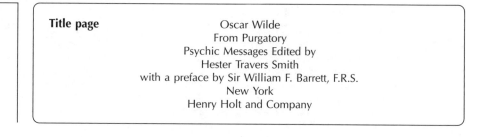

| Title page | Oscar Wilde
From Purgatory
Psychic Messages Edited by
Hester Travers Smith
with a preface by Sir William F. Barrett, F.R.S.
New York
Henry Holt and Company |

21.27. ACADEMIC DISPUTATIONS

This rarely used rule is mainly of historical interest, particularly in American libraries, because it applies to dissertations prepared in European universities before 1801. The rule is the same as in previous cataloging codes. The respondent is the candidate for a degree who defends his thesis against objections proposed by the *praeses,* or faculty moderator. The work is usually entered under the heading for the *praeses;* an added entry is given to the respondent (see figure 14-48). The rule interpretations of all four national libraries using *AACR2R* call for *not* applying the option of adding a designator to the headings (Howarth, at 21.27).

Related Works

21.28. RELATED WORKS

21.28A. Scope

A work that has a relationship to another work of the type given in the list under 21.28A1 may be cataloged under its own heading as a separate work, as already discussed at 1.5E1 and 1.9. The list is illustrative, not exclusive.

21.28B. General rule

The decision to describe a related work as an independent work is sometimes obvious. Although a concordance could not exist had not the "parent" work been written, the person who puts such a work together is clearly an author, under terms of the definition given in 21.1A1. Enter such works as independent entries, with added entry (name-title) for the related work (see figure 14-49).

Similar to concordances are indexes. *AACR2R* 21.28B calls for an added entry for the indexed work. The Library of Congress instructs its catalogers not to include such an entry in the record (*LCRI* 21.28B, Dec. 11, 1989). Instead, the cataloger should add a subject heading (6XX field) for the work followed by the subdivision "--Indexes" (see figure 14-50; topical subdivisions in subject headings are preceded by subfield ‡x).

Figure 14-48.   Academic disputation

```
100 1    ‡a Rinder, Leonhardus.
245 10   ‡a Dissertatio philosophico literaria de placitis quibusdam recentiorum philosophorum
         novitate falso suspectis / ‡c quam permittente amplissimo philosophorum ordine in
         Academia Altorfina d. XXVII Octobris a. MDCCLII publice ventilandam proponent
         praeses Leonhardus Rinder et respondens Wolfgangus Iaeger.
246 3    ‡a Dissertatio philosophico literaria de placitis qvibvsdam recentiorvm philosophorvm
         novitate falso svspectis
246 3    ‡a De placitis quibusdam recentiorum philosophorum nouitate falso suspectis
246 3    ‡a De placitis qvibvsdam recentiorvm philosophorvm novitate falso svspectis
260      ‡a Altorfii : ‡b Typis Ioh. Georgii Meyeri, Acad. Typogr., ‡c 1752.
300      ‡a 28 p. ; ‡c 21 cm.
700 1    ‡a Jaeger, Wolfgang, ‡d 1734-1795.
```

Title page	Dissertatio philosophico literaria de placitis qvibvsdam recentiorvm philosophorvm novitate falso svspectis qvam permittente amplissimo philosophorvm ordine in Academia Altorfina d. XXVII. Octobris a. MDCCLII. pvblice ventilandam proponent praeses M. Leonhardvs Rinder rev. min. Norimb. cand. et respondens Wolfgangus Iaeger Norimbergensis philos. cvltor. Altorfii Typis Ioh. Georgii Meyeri Acad. Typogr.

Figure 14-49.   Related work—concordance

```
100 1    ‡a Hudson, Gladys W.
245 10   ‡a Paradise lost : ‡b a concordance / ‡c compiled by Gladys W. Hudson.
260      ‡a Detroit : ‡b Gale Research Co., ‡c c1970.
300      ‡a viii, 361 p. ; ‡c 29 cm.
500      ‡a Based on the 2nd (1674) ed. in v. 3 (the second edition of Paradise lost) of Milton's
         Complete poetical works.
700 1    ‡a Milton, John, ‡d 1608-1674. ‡t Paradise lost.
```

Title page	Paradise Lost A Concordance Compiled by Gladys W. Hudson, Baylor University Gale Research Company Book Tower, Detroit, Michigan 48226

Figure 14-50. Related work—index

```
020      ‡a 0866980768 (alk. paper)
100 1    ‡a Bauman, Michael.
245 12   ‡a A scripture index to John Milton's De doctrina Christiana / ‡c by Michael Bauman.
260      ‡a Binghamton, N.Y. : ‡b Medieval & Renaissance Texts & Studies, ‡c 1989.
300      ‡a 179 p. ; ‡c 23 cm.
440  0   ‡a Medieval & Renaissance texts & studies ; ‡v v. 67
504      ‡a Includes bibliographical references and index.
600 10   ‡a Milton, John, ‡d 1608-1674. ‡t De doctrina Christiana ‡x Indexes.
```

Title page

A Scripture Index to
John Milton's
De doctrina Christiana
by
Michael Bauman
Medieval & Renaissance Texts & Studies
Binghamton, New York
1989

Figure 14-51. Related work—Bible

```
100 1    ‡a Walker, J. B. R. ‡q (James Bradford Richmond), ‡d 1821-1885.
240 10   ‡a Comprehensive Bible concordance
245 14   ‡a The comprehensive concordance to the Holy Scriptures : ‡b a practical, convenient,
         accurate text-finder ... based on the Authorized Version / ‡c by J.B.R. Walker.
260      ‡a New York : ‡b Macmillan, ‡c 1936, c1929.
300      ‡a vi, 957 p. ; ‡c 23 cm.
630 00   ‡a Bible ‡x Concordances, English.
```

Title page

The Comprehensive Concordance
to the Holy Scriptures
By Rev. J.B.R. Walker
A practical, convenient, accurate text-finder.
Unessential words omitted; all serviceable words retained. Only one alphabet for
all words, including proper names. Proper names accented. Fifty thousand more
references than in Cruden.

Based on the Authorized Version
New York
The Macmillan Company
1936

The Bible poses a special problem for 21.28B. Under the rule for Bible uniform titles (*AACR2R* 25.18), at least three elements are required: the name of the text, the language of the text, and the date of publication. Figure 14-51 shows cataloging for a Bible concordance. Because it is a concordance for any publication of the Authorized (King James) version, no year could be attached to a related works added entry. Furthermore, related works entries do not give language of translation. Because neither language nor date can be added to a desired Bible related works heading, it cannot be made. Instead, make a subject heading with the subdivision "--Concordances, English," as shown in the 630 field of figure 14-51.

Excerpts from periodicals are to be cataloged as independent works. In many cases these works will fall under the provisions of 21.7 ("Collections of Works by Different Persons or Bodies"), and will be given main entry under title. Added entry will be made under a prominently named compiler or editor, under the provisions of 21.7B, as well as under the name of the periodical to which the work is related (see figure 14-52).

Note that 21.28 applies to librettos and other texts set to music as well as to related works such as concordances, etc. Preferred treatment under 21.28 is entry under the individual responsible for the intellectual content of the work in hand, the librettist, with an added entry (name-title) for the musical work. An alternative rule given as a footnote to 21.28A1 allows entry under the heading appropriate to the musical work, with name-title added entry for the librettist. The Library of Congress, the British Library, the National Library of Canada, and the National Library of Australia all apply the alternative rule (see Howarth, at 21.28A; see figure 14-53).

Not quite as obvious as the examples shown in figures 14-49 through 14-53 is entry for a supplement, a teacher's manual, etc., particularly when, except for the generic terms *supplement, teacher's guide*, etc., the work has the same title, and often the same author, as the parent volume. If, in the cataloger's judgment, such a work is of minor importance, it may be entered as accompanying material, the fourth element of the physical description area (1.5E), or as a note (1.7B11) (see figure 14-54a).

Figure 14-52.   Related work—excerpts from periodical

245 00	‡a Youth's companion / ‡c edited by Lovell Thompson with three former Companion editors, M. A. DeWolfe Howe, Arthur Stanwood Pier, and Harford Powel.
260	‡a Boston : ‡b Houghton Mifflin, ‡c 1954.
300	‡a xii, 1140 p. : ‡b ill. ; ‡c 22 cm.
700 1	‡a Thompson, Lovell.
730 0	‡a Youth's companion (Boston, Mass. : 1827)

Title page

Youth's Companion
Edited by Lovell Thompson
With Three Former Companion Editors
M. A. DeWolfe Howe,
Arthur Stanwood Pier, and
Harford Powel
with illustrations
Houghton Mifflin Company Boston
The Riverside Press Cambridge
1954

If the cataloger feels that such a supplement, handbook, etc., warrants separate description, the work will be cataloged separately as a related work, with added entry for the parent work, as shown in figure 14-54b. For another example of separate description of a supplement, see figure 1-96.

Figure 14-53.   Related work—libretto

```
020        ‡a 0714541672 (pbk.)
100 1      ‡a Verdi, Giuseppe, ‡d 1813-1901.
240 10     ‡a Ballo in maschera. ‡s Libretto. ‡l English & Italian
245 12     ‡a A masked ball = ‡b Un ballo in maschera / ‡c Giuseppe Verdi.
260        ‡a London : ‡b J. Calder ; ‡a New York : ‡b Riverrun Press, ‡c 1989.
300        ‡a 96 p. : ‡b ill. ; ‡c 22 cm.
440  0     ‡a Opera guide ; ‡v 40
500        ‡a Includes libretto in Italian by Antonio Somma based on Scribe's libretto for Auber's
           Gustave III, with English translation by Edmund Tracey.
500        ‡a "Published in association with English National Opera."
504        ‡a Includes bibliographical references.
504        ‡a Discography: p. 93-95.
700 1      ‡a Somma, Antonio, ‡d 1809-1864.
700 1      ‡a Scribe, Eugène, ‡d 1791-1861. ‡t Gustave III.
```

Title page	40
	A Masked Ball
	Un ballo in maschera
	Giuseppe Verdi
	Opera Guide Series Editor: Nicholas John
	This guide is sponsored by Martini and Rossi Ltd
	Published in association with English National Opera
	John Calder • London
	Riverrun Press • New York

Figure 14-54a.   Independent work with accompanying material

```
020        ‡a 0393090728
245 04     ‡a The Norton anthology of short fiction / ‡c [compiled by] R.V. Cassill.
250        ‡a 1st ed.
260        ‡a New York : ‡b Norton, ‡c c1978.
300        ‡a xxxiv, 1437 p. ; ‡c 21 cm. + ‡e 1 instructor's handbook (xxiii, 215 p. ; 21 cm.)
500        ‡a Also available in shorter ed.
500        ‡a Includes index.
700 1      ‡a Cassill, R. V. ‡q (Ronald Verlin), ‡d 1919-
```

Title page	The Norton Anthology of
	Short Fiction
	R.V. Cassill
	W • W • Norton & Company • Inc.
	New York

Figure 14-54b.   Related work—Instructor's handbook (alternate practice)

```
020      ‡a 0393090507
100 1    ‡a Cassill, R. V. ‡q (Ronald Verlin), ‡d 1919-
245 14   ‡a The Norton anthology of short fiction. Instructor's handbook for the complete and
         shorter editions / ‡c R.V. Cassill.
250      ‡a 1st ed.
260      ‡a New York : ‡b Norton, ‡c c1977.
300      ‡a xxiii, 215 p. ; ‡c 21 cm.
730 0    ‡a Norton anthology of short fiction.
```

Title page	The Norton Anthology of Short Fiction Instructor's Handbook for the complete and shorter editions R.V. Cassill W • W • Norton & Company • Inc. New York

Added Entries

Rules 21.29 and 21.30 gather in one place all of the specific rules for added entry set forth in previous sections of *AACR2R* chapter 21, sorting them into categories according to function. These rules also make useful generalizations about the purpose of added entries as added points of access to the works included in a library catalog.

21.29. GENERAL RULE

An added entry should be made if the cataloger believes that catalog users might reasonably consider a person or corporate body not listed as main entry responsible for the work. *AACR2R* goes farther than previous cataloging codes in allowing added entries beyond those specifically prescribed in individual rules. For example, under 21.29D and 21.30H added entries may be made in addition to others suggested by 21.30, depending on the library's policy.

The cataloger is reminded that, in common with other rules in *AACR2R* chapter 21, rules 21.29 and 21.30 pertain equally to all types of library materials. However, because of the perceived difficulty of correctly assigning added entries to sound recordings and certain other types of audiovisual materials, the Library of Congress has set forth extensive guidelines in *LCRI* 21.29 (Jan. 5 and Feb. 1, 1989).

The conventional order in which added entries should be listed is as follows:

1. Personal name
2. Personal name/title
3. Corporate name

4. Corporate name/title
5. Uniform title (added entry for works entered under title)
6. Title traced as Title-period [i.e., the title proper]
7. Title traced as Title-colon, followed by a title [i.e., titles with different forms from that of the title proper]
8. Series (*LCRI* 21.29, Jan. 5, 1989).

This order is necessarily modified in MARC records. For example, titles (nos. 6 and 7) are generally traced from the the 245 and 246 fields, not 7XX fields; and series (no. 8) is traced from a 440 or 830 field. However, the first five categories *are* traced from 7XX fields, and it does make some sense to organize these in the conventional order.

21.30D. Editors and compilers

This rule calls for an added entry for a "prominently named" editor or compiler of a monographic work (see figure 14-55).

Note that an added entry for the editor of a serial is rarely made. See discussion of rule 12.1F3 in *Handbook*.

21.30E. Corporate bodies

Make an added entry for a prominently named corporate body that, under terms of 21.1B2, did not receive main entry (see, for example, figures 14-13, 14-14, and 14-15). In addition, an added entry will be made for a prominently named corporate body that sponsors a meeting (*LCRI* 21.30E, Feb. 25, 1993; see figure 14-6).

In case of doubt, make an added entry for a corporate body, unless it functions solely as a publisher, distributor, or manufacturer.

Figure 14-55.   Added entry for editor

```
020      ‡a 0521394694 (hardback)
020      ‡a 052139774X (pbk.)
100 0    ‡a Horace.
240 10   ‡a Epodi. ‡l English
245 10   ‡a Epodes / ‡c Horace ; edited by David Mankin.
260      ‡a Cambridge ; ‡a New York : ‡b Cambridge University Press, ‡c 1995.
300      ‡a vii, 321 p. ; ‡c 19 cm.
440  0   ‡a Cambridge Greek and Latin classics
504      ‡a Includes bibliographical references (p. 308-316) and indexes.
700 1    ‡a Mankin, David.
```

Title page

Horace
Epodes
edited by
David Mankin
Associate Professor of Classics, Cornell University
Cambridge University Press

21.30F. Other related persons or bodies

This rule specifies, but is not limited to, three examples for which an added entry would be appropriate. One of these is for the person honored by a Festschrift. A Festschrift is a publication consisting of a number of essays or short articles, generally on the honoree's subject interest, brought together to honor a person or to celebrate an anniversary, and normally written for the publication in question. As a collaborative effort of different persons or bodies, a Festschrift is an example of a work covered by 21.6. Because a Festschrift normally contains contributions of many more than three authors, it will usually be given title main entry (see figure 14-56).

The addressee of a collection of letters would, under normal provisions of the rules, not be given an added entry; that person in no way contributed to the intellectual or artistic content of the work being cataloged. In addition, ordinarily, a subject entry for the addressee would be inappropriate. But, obviously, the name of the addressee can serve as an important access point to the catalog entry for the work. An added entry for such an individual is stipulated by 21.30F (see figure 14-57).

Figure 14-56.   Festschrift

```
020       ‡a 0873581571
245 00    ‡a Voices from the Southwest : ‡b a gathering in honor of Lawrence Clark Powell / ‡c
          gathered by Donald C. Dickinson, W. David Laird, Margaret F. Maxwell.
250       ‡a 1st ed.
260       ‡a Flagstaff [Ariz.] : ‡b Northland Press, ‡c 1976.
300       ‡a xv, 159 p. : ‡b ill. ; ‡c 25 cm.
504       ‡a "A checklist of recently published works of LCP": p. 146-159.
505 0     ‡a Seventy suns : to L.C.P. / by William Everson -- History of the Spanish Southwest /
          Eleanor B. Adams -- Authors and books in colonial New Mexico / Marc Simmons --
          Voices from the Southwest / Sarah Bouquet -- The faces and forces of Pimería Alta /
          Bernard Fontana -- The fifth world : the ninth planet / Frank Waters -- An amateur
          librarian / Paul Horgan -- Give this place a little class / Ward Ritchie -- Richard J. Hinton
          and the American Southwest / Harwood Hinton -- J. Ross Browne and Arizona / Richard
          Dillon -- Reflections on the Powell-Harrison correspondence / Jake Zeitlin -- The making
          of a novel / L.D. Clark -- A chronology of LCP keepsakes / Al Lowman -- A checklist of
          recently published works of LCP / Robert Mitchell.
700 1     ‡a Powell, Lawrence Clark, ‡d 1906-
700 1     ‡a Dickinson, Donald C.
700 1     ‡a Laird, W. David, ‡d 1937-
700 1     ‡a Maxwell, Margaret F., ‡d 1927-
```

```
Title page              Voices from the Southwest
            A Gathering in Honor of Lawrence Clark Powell
                  Gathered by Donald C. Dickinson,
               W. David Laird, Margaret F. Maxwell
                    Northland Press • Flagstaff
                           MCMLXXVI
```

Figure 14-57.   Addressee of a collection of letters

```
100 1    ‡a Wise, Thomas James, ‡d 1859-1937.
245 10   ‡a Letters of Thomas J. Wise to John Henry Wrenn : ‡b a further inquiry into the guilt of
         certain nineteenth-century forgers / ‡c edited by Fannie E. Ratchford.
250      ‡a 1st ed.
260      ‡a New York : ‡b Knopf, ‡c 1944.
300      ‡a xiv, 591, xvi p. : ‡b ill. ; ‡c 25 cm.
500      ‡a "List of nineteenth-century forgeries in the Wrenn library, with the dates they were
         acquired and the prices Wrenn paid Wise": p. 578-583.
500      ‡a Includes index.
700 1    ‡a Wrenn, John Henry, ‡d 1841-1911.
700 1    ‡a Ratchford, Fannie Elizabeth, ‡d 1888-
```

> **Title page**   Letters of Thomas J. Wise to John Henry Wrenn
>   A Further Inquiry into the Guilt of Certain
>   Nineteenth-Century Forgers
>   Edited by
>   Fannie E. Ratchford
>   Alfred E. Knopf   New York   1944

21.30G. Related works

Make an added entry under the heading for a work to which the work being cataloged is closely related. For example, make an added entry to join editions (not translations) of a work with different titles (see figures 1-21 and 1-22). Relate a serial with a changed title to the earlier (or later) title by means of an added entry in a linking field (normally 780 or 785) for the related heading (see figures 12-7 and 12-8). See also discussion of related works in this *Handbook* at 21.28.

21.30J. Titles

A title added entry will be made for almost every work, except, obviously, those entered under title as main entry. Only rarely will the cataloger find that "the title proper is essentially the same as the main entry heading." If this is so, the cataloger will not make a title added entry. If the title proper has been composed by the cataloger, it would seem evident that such a title would not serve as a sought-for access point, and for this reason it should be omitted (see figure 10-4).

In the MARC record, the title proper is traced from the 245 field itself; this is controlled by the first indicator. If coded "1" the title will trace; if coded "0" the title will not trace.[6] If the cataloger needs to trace a part of the title other than the title proper, the 246 field is used (see figure 10-3 and discussion in this *Handbook* at 1.7B4). In the card system this was known as tracing the title explicitly (or "title colon," from the way it was noted on the card), and the desired tracing was found at the end of the card following the word "Title:". Parallel titles are traced in this fashion as well. As discussed at 1.7B4, when using the 246 field to trace titles, initial articles must be omitted (see figure 1-19). This is also true of the title in a name-title added entry (see figures 1-21 and 1-55).

Previous to 1995, titles (in MARC formats other than serials format) now traced from the 246 field were traced from the 740 field. Some titles are still traced from this field. These are uncontrolled related titles and uncontrolled analytical titles. "Uncontrolled" means "not in authority form." For example, in figure 14-29, the three plays are analyzed in 700 name-title added entries; however, the titles in these entries are in "controlled" or authority form, quite different from the titles as they appear in the book. A 740 field with indicators "02" (the second indicator "2" means "analytic entry") is used to give access to these forms of the title (see *USMARC Format for Bibliographic Data*, 1994 ed., 740, p. 2, Mar. 1995).

Examples of an uncontrolled *related* title (providing access to a work external to the item being cataloged) are seen in figures 1-82 and 7-1. The indicators for this 740 field are coded "0-blank." The first indicator of any 740 field, which shows nonfiling characters, should always be coded "0" and initial articles left off the title. This includes languages distinguishing by case: drop all initial articles, even those not in the nominative case (*CSB* 52, spring 1991, p. 26).

Extremely detailed guidelines for recording title added entries in 245, 246, 7XX name-title, and 740 fields will be found in *LCRI* 21.30J (Nov. 1995).

The MARC database may also trace other title fields, such as the 240 field and subfield ‡t in a 7XX field (name-title added entry). This depends on the local system parameters. Figures in this *Handbook* are cataloged under the assumption that such fields do trace. Therefore, in the *Handbook* figures, 740 and 246 fields that simply repeat the contents of other fields are not given.

21.30L. Series

The rule instructs the cataloger to make an added entry under the heading for a series "if it provides a useful collocation." This sounds as though the cataloger is to make a decision for each item on a case-by-case basis, but in fact the series area is one that falls under authority control; the decision whether to trace a series is made once for the entire series and thereafter every item in the series is traced by the series name or not depending on the decision recorded in the authority record (see detailed discussion in *Handbook* at 1.6).

The advent of computerized cataloging has caused many libraries to become more relaxed about tracing series (in the days when a complete card had to be typed for every added entry, including an added entry for the series, a reluctance to trace certain series was certainly understandable). More and more libraries now simply trace all series. For example, the Library of Congress's current policy is to "trace all analyzed series established after August 31, 1989" (*LCRI* 21.30L, Aug. 27, 1990). This replaces a policy with very elaborate rules for deciding whether or not to trace series (see *CSB* 41, summer 1988, p. 24–27). The decision whether to trace a given series is a policy decision entirely up to the library.

Special Rules

Certain Legal Publications

Rules 21.31 through 21.36 include laws, administrative regulations, constitutions and charters, court rules, and treaties. Previous cataloging rules for legal publications have been criticized because, in contradiction to general cataloging principles, they were based on form rather than authorship. Materials included were formerly entered under governmental jurisdiction, followed by a form subheading appropriate to the type of publication. A federal law of the United States would, under pre-*AACR2* rules, have taken the heading "United States. Laws, statutes, etc." Critics of the rules, led by Seymour Lubetzky, argued that these form subheadings were nothing but a kind of subject heading that served to gather material under the name of the governmental jurisdiction. The critics also said that the function could just as well be taken care of by true subject headings. Calling them "bastardized author entries," Lubetzky called for the elimination of these quasi-author, quasi-subject headings from rules that otherwise dealt with conditions of author responsibility.[7]

But the form subheadings, though they may have lacked consistency with principle, had custom on their side, going back at least as far as the 1908 Anglo-American code.[8] Those in favor of them argued that legal publications offered problems of authorship so complex that it was difficult to arrive at a valid statement of authorship. A law is an act of a particular political jurisdiction that comes into being by the agency of many different people acting as individuals, committees, etc. A law may be passed by Congress, but it is not valid until it is signed by the president. Who, then, is responsible for bringing it into being? In legal terms Congress and the president merely act as agents, not as authors. The United States is responsible for the law, and therefore the United States is author of the law.

Thus reasoned Seymour Lubetzky, as long ago as 1960, in his *Code of Cataloging Rules*. And yet in 1967, when the *AACR1* appeared, the traditional form headings were still a part of the code. Paul Dunkin, though speaking in a slightly different frame of reference, summed the problem up when he said, "The plain fact is that we have here an entry which we accept because it seems to be the practical thing to do. . . . Apparently we have grown so accustomed to the idea that we cannot change."[9]

In a victory for Seymour Lubetzky, and in a return to the stipulations of Paris Principle 9.5,[10] form subdivisions were eliminated from *AACR2*. Beginning with the 1978 code, laws, constitutions, court rules, and treaties formerly entered under the name of the governmental jurisdiction, followed by a form subheading, are to be entered under the name of the appropriate state or other territorial authority, with a uniform title interposed between the heading and the transcription of the title to aid in organizing the material.

21.31B. Laws of modern jurisdictions

Such laws will be entered under the heading for the jurisdiction governed. A uniform title will be interposed between the heading and the title transcription. Uniform titles will be discussed more fully in chapter 18 of this *Handbook*. Briefly, a uniform title serves to bring all the varying issues, editions, translations, etc., of a work together in one place in the catalog. Uniform titles for laws are to be constructed following rule 25.15.

The descriptive information for a legal publication is transcribed following appropriate rules in *AACR2R* Part I, chapter 1, etc. Added entries are to be made for persons or bodies responsible for compiling or issuing the law, but not for the legislative body that actually passed it. That is, as shown in figure 14-58, no added entry will be made for "United States. Congress." Nor will an added entry be made for "California. Legislature," the body responsible for the code illustrated in figure 14-59. But entry *is* made for the publishers, West Publishing Company and Legal Book Store.

Figure 14-58.   Federal law

110 1	‡a United States.	
240 10	‡a Employee Retirement Income Security Act of 1974	
245 10	‡a Pension reform act : ‡b (Employee Retirement Income Security Act of 1974) : with official legislative history : approved Sept. 2, 1974.	
260	‡a St. Paul, Minn. : ‡b West, ‡c c1974.	
300	‡a iii, xi, 833 p. ; ‡c 24 cm.	
440 0	‡a United States code congressional and administrative news ; ‡v 93rd Congress, second session, no. 8A	
500	‡a At head of title: 93rd Congress--Second session.	
500	‡a Issued Sept. 20, 1974.	
500	‡a Includes index.	
710 2	‡a West Publishing Company.	

Title page

No. 8A   September 20, 1974
United States Code
Congressional and Administrative News
93rd Congress—Second Session
Pension Reform Act
[Employee Retirement Income Security Act of 1974]
with official legislative history
approved Sept. 2, 1974
West Publishing Co.
50 West Kellogg Blvd.
St. Paul, Minn. 55102
Copyright © 1974 West Publishing Co.

Figure 14-59.   State law

```
020       ‡a 0910874522
110 1     ‡a California.
240 10    ‡a Penal Code of California
245 14    ‡a The Penal Code of the State of California : ‡b with amendments up to the end of the
          1963 regular session of the legislature.
250       ‡a Complete peace officers ed., with appendix of other penal laws, including rules of
          evidence, narcotic laws, juvenile court law, selected section from the alcoholic beverage
          control law, and titles 8, 18, 26 of the United States code.
260       ‡a Los Angeles, Calif. : ‡b Legal Book Store, ‡c c1963.
300       ‡a vii, 828 p. ; ‡c 23 cm.
710 2     ‡a Legal Book Store.
```

Title page

> The Penal Code of the State of California
> with amendments up to the end of the
> 1963 regular session of the legislature.
> The Complete Peace Officers Edition
> with appendix of other
> Penal Laws
> including
> Rules of Evidence
> Narcotic Laws
> Juvenile Court Law
> selected section from the
> Alcoholic Beverage Control Law
> and titles 8, 18, 26 of the United States Code
> Legal Book Store
> Law Book Seller and Publisher
> 122 South Broadway
> Los Angeles 12, California

The example shown in figure 14-60 is a work that includes both the code (laws) of a city and the charter. Heading and uniform title will be made for the material listed first on the title page. Name-title added entry is made for the charter.

21.32. ADMINISTRATIVE REGULATIONS, ETC.

21.32A. As explained in *LCRI* 21.32A (Jan. 5, 1989), this rule is to be applied only to administrative regulations, licenses, advisory opinions, and decisions for the United States or any other country in which such regulations, etc., are not laws. Do not apply 21.32A to rules or regulations, etc., from Great Britain or Canada, for instance. For regulations, etc., from these countries, use 21.32B.

Catalogers who catalog such materials will find the explanations and definitions in *LCRI* 21.32A extremely helpful. The National Library of Canada has also issued an explanation of implementation of 21.32B (Howarth, at 21.32B).

Figure 14-60.   Collection

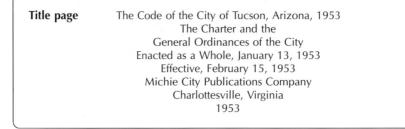

```
110 1    ‡a Tucson (Ariz.)
240 10   ‡a Laws, etc.
245 14   ‡a The code of the city of Tucson, Arizona, 1953 ; ‡b The charter and the general
         ordinances of the city, enacted as a whole, January 13, 1953, effective, February 15,
         1953.
260      ‡a Charlottesville, Va. : ‡b Michie City Publications Co., ‡c 1953.
300      ‡a 567 p. ; ‡c 24 cm.
710 12   ‡a Tucson (Ariz.). ‡t Charter.
710 2    ‡a Michie City Publications Company, Charlottesville, Va.
740 02   ‡a Charter and the general ordinances of the city, enacted as a whole, January 13, 1953,
         effective, February 15, 1953.
```

Title page   The Code of the City of Tucson, Arizona, 1953
The Charter and the
General Ordinances of the City
Enacted as a Whole, January 13, 1953
Effective, February 15, 1953
Michie City Publications Company
Charlottesville, Virginia
1953

21.33. CONSTITUTIONS, CHARTERS, AND OTHER FUNDAMENTAL LAWS

A constitution or charter will be entered under the heading for the jurisdiction with no further subdivision. Contrast this rule with previous codes
that stipulated entry under jurisdiction plus the form subheading "Constitution" or "Charter," as appropriate. When a constitution or charter is a
law of a jurisdiction other than the one the constitution or charter governs,
make an added entry for the one that promulgated the law and in this
added entry use a uniform title if appropriate according to 25.15A. The
general rule for uniform titles (25.1) may also need to be applied to the
question of a uniform title in the main entry.

If there is more than one constitution for the same jurisdiction, add in
parentheses the year of adoption to the uniform title for each. Figures
14-61 and 14-62 show two of the many French constitutions.

Figure 14-61.   Constitution

```
110 1    ‡a France.
240 10   ‡a Constitution (1848). ‡l German
254 14   ‡a Die französische Constitution, 1848.
260      ‡a Wien : ‡b C. Gerold, ‡c 1849.
300      ‡a 19 p. ; ‡c 21 cm.
```

Title page	Die französische Constitution. 1848. Wien Carl Gerold 1849.

Figure 14-62.   Constitution

```
110 1    ‡a France.
240 10   ‡a Constitution (1958). ‡l English
254 14   ‡a The constitution of the Fifth Republic : ‡b translation and commentary / ‡c Peter
         Campbell, Brian Chapman.
250      ‡a 2nd ed.
260      ‡a Oxford : ‡b Blackwell, ‡c 1959.
300      ‡a 61 p. ; ‡c 19 cm.
700 1    ‡a Campbell, Peter, ‡c 1926-
700 1    ‡a Chapman, Brian.
```

Title page	The Constitution of the Fifth Republic Translation and Commentary Peter Campbell Lecturer in Government, University of Manchester Brian Chapman Senior Lecturer in Government, University of Manchester Oxford Basil Blackwell 1959

21.34. COURT RULES

This rule stipulates entry of court rules under the name of the court. The rule is related to *AACR2R* 21.1B2b. According to this rule, court rules should be entered under the heading for the court governed by them. Rule 21.34 reinforces that practice (see figure 14-63).

Figure 14-63.   Court rules

```
110 1    ‡a Arizona. ‡b Supreme Court.
245 10   ‡a Rules of the Supreme Court of the State of Arizona.
260      ‡a Phoenix : ‡b Arizona State Press, ‡c 1912.
300      ‡a 15 p. ; ‡c 26 cm.
```

Title page

Rules of the
Supreme Court
of the State of Arizona
1912
Alfred Franklin - - - Chief Justice
D.L. Cunningham - - - Judge
H.D. Ross - - - Judge
J.P. Dillon - - - Clerk
The Arizona State Press

21.35. TREATIES, INTERGOVERNMENTAL AGREEMENTS, ETC.

21.35A1. Treaties are agreements between two or more governments. They pose special problems for catalogers because of their nature and because of the way in which they are drawn up. After representatives of the various governments at a treaty conference have met, they draw up an agreement, which is signed. Then the representatives return to their own countries, where the treaty is ratified by the government. Then the treaty is published by the government under a title that it creates, naming itself, of course, in first place on the title page. Each governing body involved does this, resulting in a number of different versions of the document. Although the text of the document should be the same, the title pages will vary. Under which name should a treaty be entered? ALA 1949 rule 88A called for entry under the party named first on the title page, with form subheading "Treaties, etc." *AACR1* rule 25A1 preferred entry under the country of the cataloging agency if it was a signatory; otherwise entry would be under the party on one side of a bilateral treaty if it is the only party on that side and there are two or more parties on the other side; or, under the party whose catalog heading is first in alphabetical order.

AACR2 rule 21.35A1 (identical in *AACR2R*) dropped the first provision of *AACR1* rule 25A1. It mandates entry for a treaty between two or three national governments according to the second and third preference of the 1967 code. Thus, the example shown in figure 14-64, which under 1967 rules was entered under "United States" (as the country of the cataloging agency), will now be entered under the country coming first in alphabetical order: Mexico. In addition, the *AACR1* form subheading "Treaties, etc." is dropped to uniform title position below the heading for the jurisdiction (see 25.16B1 for rules for form). Uniform title must be used. Added entry is made for the other government(s) involved; the form is name-[uniform]

Figure 14-64.   Bilateral treaty

```
110 1    ‡a Mexico.
240 10   ‡a Treaties, etc. ‡g United States, ‡d 1933 Feb. 1
245 10   ‡a Convención entre los Estados Unidos Mexicanos y los Estados Unidos de América para
         la rectificación del Rio Bravo del Norte (Grande) en el valle de Juarez-El Paso ...
260      ‡a México : ‡b Impr. de la Secretaría de Relaciones Exteriores, ‡c 1934.
300      ‡a 63 p. : ‡b ill. ; ‡c 24 cm.
546      ‡a Spanish and English in parallel columns.
710 1    ‡a United States. ‡t Treaties, etc. ‡g Mexico, ‡d 1933 Feb. 1.
```

Title page	Convención entre los Estados Unidos Mexicanos y los Estados Unidos de América para la rectificación del Rio Bravo del Norte (Grande) en el valle de Juarez-El Paso [8 lines of text describing the ratification] México Imprenta de la Secretaría de Relaciones Exteriores, 1934

title entry. Entry for the example shown in figure 14-65 is under the name of the country that comes first in alphabetical order, regardless of title page order or language of the text.

Instead of added entry for the other government, the Library of Congress would make an authority record for the main entry plus uniform title, with cross-reference(s) from the heading(s) for the other government(s) and uniform title(s). Thus, Library of Congress cataloging for figures 14-64 and 14-65 would omit the added entries for United States. Treaties, etc. . . .

21.35A2. Treaties involving four or more parties. In essence, this rule is based on the general rule governing diffuse authorship (21.6C2), which states that main entry will be under title if responsibility is shared between more than three corporate bodies (in this case, governments).

If the treaty has been issued under varying titles, do not use the title proper of the work for title main entry. Make main entry under a uniform title. See 25.16B2 for guidance on the proper construction of a uniform title for a treaty.

An example of a treaty involving four or more parties issued under differing titles is the Maastricht Treaty (see figure 14-66).[11] A U.S. cataloger would make no added entry for signatories, because the home government is not a signatory, the item is not published by any government, nor is any government named in the chief source of information. Since the U.K. is a signatory, a British cataloger would make an added entry for the U.K. with the uniform title of the treaty.

As with 21.35A1, the Library of Congress does not make the added entries called for in 21.35A2. Rather, its catalogers add appropriate cross-references to the authority record for the uniform title of the treaty.

In summary, the distinction between entry under one or the other of the governments involved in a treaty versus entry under title proper or a uniform title is based solely on the number of parties concerned. If two or three governments are involved, follow 21.35A1 and enter under one of the

Figure 14-65.   Bilateral treaty

```
110 1    ‡a Spain.
240 10   ‡a Treaties, etc. ‡g United States, ‡d 1898 Dec. 10
245 12   ‡a A treaty of peace between the United States and Spain : ‡b message from the President
         of the United States transmitting a treaty of peace between the United States and Spain :
         signed at the city of Paris on December 10, 1898 ...
260      ‡a Washington : ‡b G.P.O., ‡c 1899.
300      ‡a 3 v. in 2 : ‡b folded map ; ‡c 24 cm.
490 1    ‡a Doc. / 55th Congress, 3d sess., Senate ; ‡v no. 62
500      ‡a January 4, 1899, read; treaty read the first time and referred to the Committee on
         foreign relations, and, together with the message and accompanying papers, ordered to be
         printed in confidence for the use of the Senate.
500      ‡a January 11, 1899, injunction of secrecy removed.
500      ‡a January 13, 1899, ordered printed.
710 1    ‡a United States. ‡t Treaties, etc. ‡g Spain, ‡d 1898 Dec. 10.
710 1    ‡a United States. ‡b President (1897-1901 : McKinley)
830  0   ‡a Senate document (United States. Congress. Senate) ; ‡v 55th Congress, 3rd session,
         no. 62.
```

Title page   55th Congress, 3d Session, Senate Doc. No. 62, Part 1.
A Treaty of Peace between the United States and Spain.
Message from the President of the United States,
Transmitting a Treaty of Peace between the
United States and Spain,
Signed at the city of Paris on December 10, 1898
[6 lines of text describing the ratification]
Washington: Government Printing Office, 1899

Figure 14-66.   Treaty involving more than four parties

```
020      ‡a 9282409597
130 0    ‡a Treaty on European Union ‡d (1992). ‡l English.
245 00   ‡a Treaty on European Union.
260      ‡a Luxembourg : ‡b Office for Official Publications of the European Communities,
         ‡c 1992.
300      ‡a 253 p. ; ‡c 25 cm.
500      ‡a "Council of the European Communities, Commission of the European Communities"--
         Cover.
500      ‡a Includes the text of the treaty, the protocols, and the final act of the conferences of the
         representatives of the governments of the member states.
500      ‡a "RX-73-92-796-EN-C"--P. [4] of cover.
710 2    ‡a Council of the European Communities.
710 2    ‡a Commission of the European Communities.
```

Title page   Treaty
on European Union

governments, according to instructions. If four or more governments are involved, follow 21.35A2 and enter under either title proper or uniform title.

Certain Religious Publications

21.37. SACRED SCRIPTURES

Although 21.37 states that sacred scripture will be entered under title, problems of varying titles for different issues, editions, etc., will mean in almost every case that entry under uniform title rather than title proper will be made. See rules 25.17–25.18 for guidance in the formulation of a proper uniform title and for further examples of this rule. The example shown in figure 14-7 is of sacred scripture entered under uniform title.

21.39. LITURGICAL WORKS

A liturgical work will be entered under the heading for the denomination. A uniform title will be used to organize the file (see rules 25.19–25.23 for guidance and figure 2-8 for an example).

NOTES

1. General information about MARC coding is found in the introduction to this *Handbook*; details about coding the descriptive portion of the record are found throughout chapter 1. An explanation of the MARC authorities format is given in *Handbook* chapters 15, 17, and 18. Information about specific MARC fields may be found by consulting the index under "MARC fields."
2. *LCRI* 21.0D (Jan. 5, 1989). "Ill." will be added to headings for illustrators occurring in added entries for records in LC's annotated cards (AC) series.
3. *Corporate Headings* (London: IFLA Committee on Cataloguing, 1975), p. 3–7.
4. Ibid., p. 9.
5. Ibid., p. 13.
6. This, of course, depends on the setup of the library system. Many systems now trace all 245 fields, no matter how the first indicator is coded.
7. Seymour Lubetzky, *Code of Cataloging Rules: Author and Title Entry, an Unfinished Draft* . . . (Chicago: ALA, 1960), p. 56.
8. American Library Association, *Catalog Rules: Author and Title Entries*, comp. by committees of the American Library Association and the (British) Library Association, American ed. (Chicago: ALA, 1908), rule 62, p. 18.
9. In Lubetzky, *Code of Cataloging Rules*, p. 15.
10. "Constitution, laws and treaties . . . should be entered under the name of the appropriate state or other territorial authority, with formal or conventional titles indicating the nature of the material."
11. The reader may notice that the heading for this treaty is not "Maastricht Treaty," nor does this form appear in the cataloging example, even though this is the name by which the treaty is commonly known in the English-speaking world. The heading as established in the National Authority File is "Treaty on European Union (1992)," and this is therefore the heading used in the figure. The authority record includes a reference from "Maastricht Treaty," which will guide the user to the correct heading.

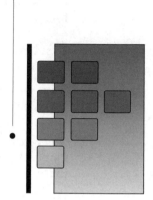

CHAPTER *15*

HEADINGS
FOR PERSONS

(*AACR2R* Chapter 22)

AACR2R is structured so that choice of entry and the form of the heading thus chosen are treated as separate problems. After the cataloger has determined the correct entry according to *AACR2R* chapter 21, he or she still must determine the correct form of the entry. This consideration is important because once the decision has been made, the same form of name will be used, in most cases, for every work by or about that author. This library practice is of long standing; a consistent heading brings together in one place in the library catalog all of the works by the author that the library holds and, in a library that has a dictionary catalog, all the books about the author.

In many cases, deciding on form for a personal author heading presents no problem. According to library custom, the entry element for most personal authors is the surname. It is a simple matter to take the name as it appears on the title page of the first book by a new author and to transcribe it as the main entry heading: surname first, followed by forenames and/or initials. But things are not always that easy. Personal names as they appear in library items present numerous problems. Most of these may be subsumed into three categories:

1. An author may not use the same name in all of his or her works. What name should be chosen when the author sometimes uses real name and sometimes pseudonym? And what about an author who seems unable to make up her or his mind about the fullness of name that she or he prefers? What is the cataloger to do when a woman who has written under her maiden name begins to use her married name in her works? Or, for that matter, when a formerly married woman resumes the use of her maiden name?
2. Some authors have compound surnames; others have a surname with a prefix; still others have no surname. Which part of the name will be used as the entry element?

3. How is one author to be distinguished from another of identical or similar name?

The rules included in *AACR2R* chapter 22 give guidance on these and other problems.

Authority

Integral to chapters 22–26 of *AACR2R* is the concept of authority. By long-standing library custom, all works by or about a single entity (whether a person or a corporate body) are brought together under a single heading; this heading is used anywhere needed in the catalog record, whether as main entry (1XX field), added entry (7XX field), subject (6XX field), or series (440/8XX field). In addition to names, it is desirable to standardize subject headings and certain title headings, so these are also included in authority work. This is done so that the user can look in a single place for the desired author or topic without having to guess all the possible forms the entry might have taken.

This goal is accomplished through the library catalog's authority structure. Ideally, the first time a heading appears in the library's catalog, the cataloger (using the rules found in chapters 22–26) "establishes" the heading's authorized form by creating a record in the library's authority file. Each heading has a single record, and any item received after the heading has been established uses the form exactly as found in the authority file. Any variants are recorded in the authority record as "search under" references, which are communicated to the library user via cards in the card catalog or displays in the on-line system.

Until recently most libraries kept a card file of authority records in the catalog department, to which catalogers referred when making decisions about headings. Most libraries now use an on-line authorities file as a part of their library automated system. Like the system for recording bibliographic records for individual items in the library, there is a MARC format for recording authority records. Details for coding are found in the latest edition of *USMARC Format for Authority Data* (Washington, D.C.: Cataloging Distribution Service, Library of Congress), but its basic structure is fairly simple.[1]

The core of the record is what appears in the 1XX field. This is the authorized form of the heading, established in accordance with chapters 22–26 of *AACR2R*. Because one and only one authorized form is made for any heading, there will never be more than one 1XX field in an authority record.

There are five types of 1XX fields that pertain to *AACR2R* (other 1XX fields are used for subject authority records):

100   Personal Name

110   Corporate Name

111   Meeting Name

130   Uniform Title (also used for series titles)

151   Geographic Name

References are generated from authority records through the 4XX and the 5XX fields. 4XX fields generate "search under" references and contain unauthorized forms of the heading in the 1XX field chosen mainly according to the stipulations of *AACR2R* chapter 26. 5XX fields generate "search also under" references, and must therefore themselves be the authorized form of headings related to the heading in the 1XX field. 4XX and 5XX fields exist in the same five types as listed above for 1XX fields:

400   Personal Name

410   Corporate Name

411   Meeting Name

430   Uniform Title (also used for series titles)

451   Geographic Name

500   Personal Name

510   Corporate Name

511   Meeting Name

530   Uniform Title (also used for series titles)

551   Geographic Name

Indicators are generally similar to the corresponding bibliographic MARC fields. The second indicator for 100, 110, 111, and their corresponding 4XX and 5XX fields has recently been eliminated from USMARC. Because it has not yet been implemented by the Library of Congress, RLIN, or OCLC, this change is *not* reflected in the figures given in this *Handbook*.

6XX fields are used in the MARC authorities format for notes. Among others, they include the 670 field, used to record where the data for the forms recorded in the record were found; the 667 field, used to record notes about the record internal to the catalog department; and the 663 field, used to record notes about the heading intended to display to the public.

Most of the figures in this and the following chapters will have authority records alongside the bibliographic records. Because they are for illustrative purposes, they have been simplified, showing only the 1XX field, pertinent 4XX and 5XX fields, and occasionally a 663 note field. Other note fields have not been included.

The Library of Congress and Authority Practice

The advent of shared machine-readable cataloging also brought about shared authority work. The Library of Congress has for some time now supervised and given access to its authority file, referred to as the National Authority File, and many libraries use these records for their own authority files. In the last few years a good number of libraries other than LC have become contributors to the National Authority File, making it more than just the Library of Congress's authority file. Indeed, negotiations and agreements are now underway for the alignment of international practice (both in MARC tagging and *AACR2R* rule interpretations) so that authority records will be able to be exchanged, for example, between the British Library and North American libraries. In fact, some British Library records are now contained in the National Authority File. Canadian libraries are also contributing. The eventual goal, not yet realized, is to create a single, unified authority file for the English-speaking world, to be called the Anglo-American Authority File (AAAF).

For the moment, however, because the National Authority File originates with the Library of Congress, contributors are expected to adhere strictly to the *Library of Congress Rule Interpretations* in choice of form and references. This *Handbook* takes these into account as far as possible in the discussion of *AACR2R* rules. In addition, the *Handbook* uses, for all "controlled" headings (i.e., those under authority control) in the figures, the forms found in the National Authority File at the time of its publication. This fact explains some headings that may be formulated differently than expected from the item illustrated in the figure. The usual case is that a form may already have been established that differs from the form found on the item. This is to be expected, because authors tend to use different forms of their names on their various works.

There is another category of "unexpected" headings, however, which stems from the Library of Congress's practice of declaring certain pre-*AACR2* headings "*AACR2* compatible." When *AACR2* was first introduced, the Library of Congress discovered that it was unable to make all the changes required by *AACR2* in its mammoth bibliographic catalog. It therefore declared that, while any new headings would be formulated strictly in accordance with *AACR2*, certain categories of headings established before *AACR2* would not be changed. Among these categories are the following:

> Hyphens: the existing heading lacked a hyphen between compound names, which would have been required under *AACR2* (e.g., Jean-Paul Sartre had already been established as "Sartre, Jean Paul." The hyphen required by *AACR2* was not added).
>
> Pseud.: the existing heading contained the term "pseud." (for "pseudonym"). This is not removed from the old heading.
>
> Extraneous or missing names or initials: certain names were established in a fuller or less full form than required under *AACR2*; these remained in the file as they were.
>
> The abbreviations "Bp." and "Abp.": if these abbreviated titles (standing for "Bishop" and "Archbishop") had been established with an otherwise acceptable form, the heading was not changed to include the spelled-out form as required by *AACR2*.

A full list of types of headings considered "*AACR2* compatible" will be found in *LCRI* 22.1 (Jan. 5, 1989). The list is of interest in explaining why certain forms are found in the National Authority File but is of no consequence in the establishment of new forms, and so it will not be discussed further in the *Handbook.*

It should be pointed out that the other national libraries issuing rule interpretations on *AACR2R* do *not* accept the Library of Congress's "*AACR2* compatible" headings (see Howarth, at 22 and 22.1). This is likely to be an important stumbling block to international agreement on shared authority records.

Choice of Name

22.1. GENERAL RULE

Catalogers should be aware that *AACR2R* chapter 22 distinguishes between choice and form of name even in the examples. General rule 22.1 addresses itself only to choice, not form, of name. Examples illustrating rules 22.1–22.3 are not in catalog entry format; they only indicate which of several names that a person may use should be chosen for the basis of the heading. For example, "Jimmy Carter" as listed under 22.1A would be entered in the catalog as "Carter, Jimmy." The example shows how the name would appear in a work by or about former President Carter. Not until rule 22.4 do the rules address themselves to the form that personal names should take in the catalog. Rule 22.1A considers the name only as the raw material from which the heading will be constituted.

The rules of chapter 22 are based on Paris Principle 7, which calls for entry under "the most frequently used name . . . appearing in editions of the work catalogued." Thus, in most instances, the cataloger will use the author's name as it appears on title pages of works issued in the language in which they were written, as long as the form of name is consistent. Both works published during and after the author's lifetime should be considered. In the case of authors active before 1801, the Library of Congress instructs its catalogers to prefer forms of names found in modern reference sources in the person's language to information taken from the chief source (*LCRI* 22.1B, Jan. 5, 1989).

If the person is commonly known by a nickname, this form will be chosen (see figure 15-1). Make references from the authority record to the full name if it is known.

If the person is commonly known by initials, the initials will be used, in direct order, as the access point in the catalog (see figure 15-2; see also *AACR2R* 22.10 and 22.18 for further explanation).

22.1B. The "commonly known" form of an author's name is determined very pragmatically. In almost all cases the name to be chosen will be that form appearing in the chief source (for a book, the title page) for the first item by that author cataloged by the library. No research need be done. If later works by the same author vary in form or fullness from the heading

Figure 15-1. Nickname

```
020      ‡a 0425134768 (pbk.)
100 1    ‡a Cosby, Bill, ‡d 1937-
245 10   ‡a Childhood / ‡c Bill Cosby ; introduction by Alvin F. Poussaint.
260      ‡a New York : ‡b Putnam, ‡c c1991.
300      ‡a 188 p. ; ‡c 22 cm.
```

Title page

Childhood
Bill Cosby
Introduction by Alvin F. Poussaint, M.D.
G.P. Putnam's Sons   New York

Authority

```
100 10   ‡a Cosby, Bill, ‡d 1937-
400 10   ‡a Cosby, William H. ‡d 1937-
```

Figure 15-2. Initials

```
020      ‡a 0822312409
020      ‡a 0822312425 (pbk.)
100 0    ‡a H. D. ‡q (Hilda Doolittle), ‡d 1886-1961.
245 10   ‡a Asphodel / ‡c H.D. ; edited with an introduction and biographical notes by Robert
         Spoo.
260      ‡a Durham : ‡b Duke University Press, ‡c 1992.
300      ‡a xxi, 215 p. ; ‡c 25 cm.
504      ‡a Includes bibliographical references.
700 1    ‡a Spoo, Robert E.
```

Title page

Asphodel
H.D.
Edited with an Introduction and Biographical Notes
by Robert Spoo
Duke University Press   Durham and London 1992

Authority

```
100 00   ‡a H. D. ‡q (Hilda Doolittle), ‡d 1886-1961
400 00   ‡a HD ‡q (Hilda Doolittle), ‡d 1886-1961
400 10   ‡a D., H. ‡q (Hilda Doolittle), ‡d 1886-1961
400 10   ‡a Aldington, Hilda Doolittle, ‡d 1886-1961
400 10   ‡a Doolittle, Hilda, ‡d 1886-1961
```

established by the cataloger, it may be necessary to change the heading. This will not happen very often, however. Virtually the only time it is necessary to go beyond the title page or other chief source of information is in establishing the "commonly known" name of a person who is not an author. In this case, the form listed in reference sources in the language and country of the person being established will be used. Caution: for purposes of this rule composers of music should be treated as authors and the form found in the chief source preferred to that found in reference sources (*LCRI* 22.1B, Jan. 5, 1989).

The rule explicitly includes "books and articles written about a person" as part of the definition of "reference sources" to be used in determining the commonly known name. The title page of the book used in the example shown in figure 15-3 was the primary source for the name of the colorful Johnny Appleseed. His name may also be found in such sources as James D. Hart's *Oxford Companion to American Literature*, 6th ed. (New York: Oxford University Press, 1995), p. 31, 119.

22.1C. If the name by which an author is commonly known includes a title of nobility (prince, etc.) or honor (sir, etc.), include it as part of the heading (see, for example, figures 1-36 and 1-37; note that these authors use their titles as part of their names in the chief source of information).

22.1D1. It would seem almost obvious that if an author's name includes accents and other diacritical marks, that they will be retained (see figure 1-27). A problem arises only in a few instances when a title page transcrip-

Figure 15-3.   Commonly known name—of a person who is not the author

```
020        ‡a 0807569097 (alk. paper)
100 1      ‡a Lawlor, Laurie.
245 14     ‡a The real Johnny Appleseed / ‡c Laurie Lawlor ; wood engravings by Mary Thompson.
260        ‡a Morton Grove, Ill. : ‡b A. Whitman, ‡c 1995.
300        ‡a 63 p. : ‡b ill., map ; ‡c 24 cm.
504        ‡a Includes bibliographical references (p. 55-59) and index.
600 10     ‡a Appleseed, Johnny, ‡d 1774-1845.
700 1      ‡a Thompson, Mary, ‡d 1947-
```

Title page

The Real
Johnny
Appleseed
Laurie Lawlor
Wood engravings by
Mary Thompson
Albert Whitman & Company • Morton Grove, Illinois

Authority
100 10   ‡a Appleseed, Johnny, ‡d 1774-1845
400 10   ‡a Chapman, John, ‡d 1774-1845

tion of an author's name—all in capital letters, for example—omits accents. If the cataloger knows that the author's name ordinarily includes accents, they should be supplied. No research needs to be done to determine this.

22.1D2. Hyphens. Again, it would seem obvious that if an author chooses to spell his or her name with a hyphen joining either given names or parts of a compound surname, this choice ought to be respected by the cataloger. And so it is, under *AACR2R* (see figure 15-4).

22.2. CHOICE AMONG DIFFERENT NAMES

22.2A. Predominant name

This rule deals with problems resulting when authors are not consistent about the way their names appear in the chief source of information in their works. If there is doubt about the name by which the person is "clearly" most commonly known, the cataloger makes a choice based on the following guidelines, in this order of preference:

1. Choose the name most frequently used by the author in his or her works. This includes forms of name found on works issued both during and after the person's lifetime.
2. Choose the form of name by which the author is generally identified in reference sources. This method could produce different answers, of course, depending on the reference sources available in a particular library.
3. Choose the latest name the author has used in her or his works. (This rule does not apply to persons using pseudonyms. For these individuals, see 22.2B.)

22.2B. Pseudonyms

22.2B1. One pseudonym. The rule for an author who writes consistently under a single name other than his or her real name is simply a reiteration

Figure 15-4.   Hyphen with given name

```
020        ‡a 2070707628
100 1      ‡a Léger, Jack-Alain, ‡d 1947-
245 10     ‡a Wanderweg : ‡b roman / ‡c Jack-Alain Léger.
260        ‡a [Paris] : ‡b Gallimard, ‡c c1986.
300        ‡a 541 p. ; ‡c 22 cm.
546        ‡a In French.
```

Title page	Jack-Alain Léger
	Wanderweg
	roman
	nrf
	Gallimard

of basic rule 22.1. Because the author chooses to be identified by this name, the cataloger should use it as any other name would be used. As a matter of fact, because catalogers are not required to search names of authors that do not present an obvious problem of identification and for which there is not a "conflict" (i.e., another author with an identical or very similar name) in the catalog, a pseudonym will not be recognized as such in most cases. The book or other material will simply be entered under the name as it appears in the chief source of information. This is a perfectly satisfactory way to catalog most material. As A. Jolley put it, "It is as impossible to count undiscovered pseudonyms as undiscovered murders."[2]

The example shown in figure 15-5 is that of a well-established author who consistently uses the same pseudonym on the title pages of her books. Cataloging, following 22.2B1, will be as shown. This author's real name is Lady Mary Dolling Sanders O'Malley. To aid library users who may know the author's real name and who may search under this name in the catalog, 22.2B1 calls for a reference from the real name, when this information is known. This reference will be incorporated into the authority record as shown and will appear to the catalog user as follows:

> O'Malley, Mary Dolling Sanders, Lady, 1889-1974
>   search under
> Bridge, Ann, 1889-1974

Such a reference guides the library user from a form of the name not used in the catalog to the "correct" form. See *AACR2R* chapter 26, "References," for further discussion, general principles, and guidelines for making references.

The cataloger will note that the Library of Congress has adopted the phrase "search under" rather than "see" for the directive in references as

Figure 15-5.   Entry under pseudonym

```
020       ‡a 0070077363
100 1     ‡a Bridge, Ann, ‡d 1889-1974.
245 10    ‡a Julia in Ireland / ‡c by Ann Bridge.
260       ‡a New York : ‡b McGraw-Hill, ‡c c1973.
300       ‡a 254 p. ; ‡c 22 cm.
```

Title page

Julia in Ireland
by Ann Bridge
McGraw-Hill Book Company
New York   St. Louis   San Francisco

Authority

```
100 10    ‡a Bridge, Ann, ‡d 1889-1974
400 10    ‡a O'Malley, Mary Dolling Sanders, ‡c Lady, ‡d 1889-1974
```

stipulated in *AACR2R* chapter 26. The display in any given system depends on the local system parameters. This *Handbook* follows Library of Congress usage.

Normally, the cataloger will not investigate a name found on the chief source for library material being cataloged unless the name presents a "conflict" (two or more authors with the same or similar names in the library's catalog). But if evidence points to something not quite usual about the name of the author, do a little sleuthing. The jacket of the book cataloged as figure 15-6 tells the identity of the two authors responsible for the work: "Whit Masterson . . . is actually Bob Wade and Bill Miller." Because jacket information is sometimes deliberately erroneous in order to preserve the ano-

Figure 15-6.   Joint pseudonym

```
100 1    ‡a Masterson, Whit.
245 10   ‡a Evil come, evil go / ‡c Whit Masterson.
260      ‡a New York : ‡b Dodd, Mead, ‡c c1961.
300      ‡a 185 p. ; ‡c 22 cm.
490 0    ‡a Red badge detective
```

Title page	Evil Come, Evil Go
	Whit Masterson
	Dodd, Mead & Company
	New York
	Red Badge
	Detective

Authorities (three records required)

```
100 10   ‡a Wade, Bob, ‡d 1920-
500 10   ‡w nnnc ‡a Miller, Wade
500 10   ‡w nnnc ‡a Masterson, Whit
500 10   ‡w nnnc ‡a Wilmer, Dale
663      ‡a For works of this author written together with Bill Miller under joint
         pseudonyms, search also under ‡b Miller, Wade, ‡b Masterson, Whit,
         ‡b Wilmer, Dale

100 10   ‡a Miller, Bill, ‡d 1920-1961
500 10   ‡w nnnc ‡a Miller, Wade
500 10   ‡w nnnc ‡a Masterson, Whit
500 10   ‡w nnnc ‡a Wilmer, Dale
663      ‡a For works of this author written together with Bob Wade under joint
         pseudonyms, search also under ‡b Miller, Wade, ‡b Masterson, Whit,
         ‡b Wilmer, Dale

100 10   ‡a Masterson, Whit
500 10   ‡w nnnc ‡a Miller, Bill, ‡d 1920-1961
500 10   ‡w nnnc ‡a Wade, Bob, ‡d 1920-
663      ‡a Joint pseudonym of Bill Miller and Bob Wade. For a listing of other
         pseudonyms used by these authors, search also under ‡b Miller, Bill,
         1920-1961, ‡b Wade, Bob, 1920-
```

nymity of a pseudonymous author, the cataloger will be well advised to check an appropriate reference source. *Who Done It? A Guide to Detective, Mystery, and Suspense Fiction* by Ordean A. Hagen (New York: Bowker, 1969) lists Whit Masterson as the pseudonym for Bill Miller and Bob Wade. With this corroborating evidence, we turn again to 22.2B1.

AACR2R 22.2B1 applies not only to a single author who consistently uses one pseudonym. It is closely related to 21.6D ("Shared pseudonyms"), which deals with two or more authors who collaborate and who consistently use a joint pseudonym. Because this is the form of name by which these authors wish to be identified, use the name as it appears in the chief source of information (see figure 15-6).

Make the three authority records shown, one for the pseudonym and (because each also wrote under other pseudonyms) one for each real name. Notes recorded in the 663 field will display to the public when the user searches under the name in the 100 field. Coding at the beginning of the 500 fields causes them not to display, because the "search also note" is taken care of by the explanatory reference in the 663 field. For details, see the latest edition of *USMARC Format for Authority Data* (Washington, D.C.: Cataloging Distribution Service, Library of Congress).

22.2B2. Separate bibliographic identities. This is a change from *AACR2* (1978) 22.2C2. Under the provisions of the earlier rule, the cataloger was to choose the name by which the author had come to be "identified predominantly" when such an individual did not always use the same name in editions of his or her works. Thus, all works, both mathematics and children's fantasy, of that split personality Charles L. Dodgson (better known as Lewis Carroll) were to be entered under "Lewis Carroll."

AACR2R 22.2B2 provides that if a person writes works of more than one type, and if that person chooses to use one bibliographic identity for one type and another name for works of other types, the cataloger will choose for each work "the name by which it is identified." Thus, the literary work *Alice's Adventures in Wonderland* will be entered under the heading Carroll, Lewis (see figure 6-2), whereas this author's mathematics and logic books will find entry under the name he used when writing in his academic discipline, Charles L. Dodgson (see figure 15-7).

When the works of an author, such as Dodgson/Carroll, are entered under two names, the cataloger makes a pair of authority records as shown. The 663 field displays to the public.

22.2B3. Contemporary authors. For a contemporary author (any author who has died since Dec. 31, 1900) who uses more than one name, enter each work under the name as it appears in the work regardless of whether 22.2B2 is applicable or not.

Evan Hunter, a writer of mystery novels, sometimes uses his real name and sometimes the pseudonym Ed McBain. His novel *Every Little Crook and Nanny*, written under the name Evan Hunter, gives a clue that the alert cataloger will follow up when he or she reads that "the jacket photo of Evan Hunter was graciously posed for by Ed McBain" (from the book, p. 228). Checking Hagen's *Who Done It?* the cataloger will discover that Evan Hunter is the real name of an author who writes under a number of pseu-

Figure 15-7. Separate bibliographic identity

```
020      ‡a 0486229688
100 1    ‡a Dodgson, Charles Lutwidge, ‡d 1832-1898.
245 10   ‡a Euclid and his modern rivals / ‡c by Lewis Carroll (Charles L. Dodgson) ; with a new
         introduction by H.S.M. Coxeter.
260      ‡a New York : ‡b Dover Publications, ‡c 1973.
300      ‡a xxxi, 275 p. : ‡b ill. ; ‡c 22 cm.
534      ‡p Reprint. Originally published: ‡b 2nd ed. ‡c London : Macmillan, 1885.
```

Title page

Euclid
and His
Modern Rivals
by Lewis Carroll
(Charles L. Dodgson, M.A.)
With a new introduction
by H.S.M. Coxeter
Professor of Mathematics
University of Toronto
Dover Publications, Inc.
New York

Authorities
```
100 10   ‡a Dodgson, Charles Lutwidge, ‡d 1832-1898
500 10   ‡w nnnc ‡a Carroll, Lewis, ‡d 1832-1898
663      ‡a For literary works of this author, search also under ‡b Carroll, Lewis,
         1832-1898

100 10   ‡a Carroll, Lewis, ‡d 1832-1898
500 10   ‡w nnnc ‡a Dodgson, Charles Lutwidge, ‡d 1832-1898
663      ‡a For mathematical works of this author, search also under ‡b Dodgson,
         Charles Lutwidge, 1832-1898
```

donyms, including the name Ed McBain. Each of Hunter's books will be entered under the name appearing on the title page, as shown in figures 15-8 and 15-9.

Connect the names used by this author that are represented in your library's catalog with authority records as shown. More 500 "search also under" fields may be added if the library has items written under any of Hunter's other pseudonyms.

22.2C. Change of name

This is the same as *AACR2* (1978) 22.2B. Apply this rule to names of all persons that have been changed, except for persons using pseudonyms. For pseudonyms, see *AACR2R* 22.2B.

Figure 15-8.   Contemporary author

```
100 1     ‡a Hunter, Evan, ‡d 1926-
245 10    ‡a Every little crook and nanny : ‡b a novel / ‡c by Evan Hunter.
250       ‡a 1st ed.
260       ‡a Garden City, N.Y. : ‡b Doubleday, ‡c 1972.
300       ‡a 229 p. ; ‡c 22 cm.
```

Title page	Every Little Crook and Nanny A Novel by Evan Hunter 1972 Doubleday & Company, Inc., Garden City, New York

Authority
100 10   ‡a Hunter, Evan, ‡d 1926-
500 10   ‡a McBain, Ed, ‡d 1926-

Figure 15-9.   Contemporary author

```
100 1     ‡a McBain, Ed, ‡d 1926-
245 10    ‡a Eighty million eyes : ‡b an 87th Precinct mystery novel / ‡c by Ed McBain.
260       ‡a New York : ‡b Delacorte Press, ‡c c1966.
300       ‡a 190 p. ; ‡c 22 cm.
```

Title page	Eighty Million Eyes An 87th Precinct Mystery Novel by Ed McBain Delacorte Press—New York

Authority
100 10   ‡a McBain, Ed, ‡d 1926-
500 10   ‡a Hunter, Evan, ‡d 1926-

Members of nobility sometimes change their names as they acquire new titles. If one begins to use his or her new title on title pages, headings for earlier works should be changed to reflect the changed usage. In addition, entries should be changed for married women who have written before their marriage and who use their changed name in their later works. The rule is based on general rule 22.1, inasmuch as the later form will usually become more "commonly known."

Clare Boothe Luce, American author and former American ambassador to Italy, wrote a number of works under her maiden name, Clare Boothe. She wrote at least one under an earlier married name, Clare Boothe Brokaw. After her marriage to Henry Luce, she used her married name, Clare Boothe Luce. She is clearly "commonly known" by her latest married name, both in reference sources such as *Current Biography* (Bronx, N.Y.: H. W. Wilson, 1940–) and in later books and articles by and about her. The heading for all of her works should be the latest form of her name (see figures 15-10 and 15-11).

Figure 15-10.   Changed name

```
100 1   ‡a Luce, Clare Boothe, ‡d 1903-1987.
245 10  ‡a Europe in the spring / ‡c Clare Boothe.
260     ‡a New York : ‡b Knopf, ‡c 1940.
300     ‡a xi, 324 p. ; ‡c 21 cm.
```

Title page

Europe in the Spring
Clare Boothe
Alfred • A • Knopf
New York 1940

Figure 15-11.   Changed name

```
100 1   ‡a Luce, Clare Boothe, ‡d 1903-1987.
245 10  ‡a Stuffed shirts / ‡c by Clare Boothe Brokaw ; illustrations by Shermund.
260     ‡a New York : ‡b Liveright, ‡c 1931.
300     ‡a 326 p. : ‡b ill. ; ‡c 21 cm.
```

Title page

Stuffed Shirts
by Clare Boothe Brokaw
Illustrations by Shermund
Horace Liveright • Inc., New York

Authority
```
100 10  ‡a Luce, Clare Boothe, ‡d 1903-1987
400 10  ‡a Brokaw, Clare Boothe, ‡d 1903-1987
400 10  ‡a Boothe, Clare, ‡d 1903-1987
```

The authority record shown will generate (from the 400 fields) two references for Luce:

Boothe, Clare, 1903-1987
  search under
Luce, Clare Boothe, 1903-1987

Brokaw, Clare Boothe
  search under
Luce, Clare Boothe, 1903-1987

Only one authority record is required because unlike the above cases with pseudonyms, only one heading will be used for Luce's works.

22.3. Choice among Different Forms of the Same Name

22.3A. Fullness

An author may consistently use the same name in works published during his or her lifetime, and yet may not be consistent in the form (fullness) of name as it appears on title pages or other chief sources. Fullness is determined by the number of elements in a name, not the length of the elements. Thus "R. E. A. Palmer" is a fuller form of the name than "Robert Palmer" even though the former consists solely of initials with the surname (cf. *LCRI* 22.3A, Feb. 15, 1994).

British playwright Bernard Shaw is an example of the kind of inconsistency often found. His name has variously been listed on title pages of his works published during his lifetime as Bernard Shaw, G. Bernard Shaw, and George Bernard Shaw. Rule 22.3A solves the question of which of these varying forms should be chosen for entry; the rule is consistent with general rule 22.1A in requiring the cataloger to choose "the form most commonly found." Choose the name by which the author is "commonly known" by quickly surveying bibliographic records in the library or in a national database such as RLIN or OCLC. Meticulous mathematical calculations are not necessary. Shaw will be listed as shown in figures 15-12, 15-13, and 15-14.

Following provisions of 26.2A2, the authority record shown will be made, which will generate the following references:

Shaw, G. Bernard (George Bernard), 1856-1950
  search under
Shaw, Bernard, 1856-1950

Shaw, George Bernard, 1856-1950
  search under
Shaw, Bernard, 1856-1950

Figure 15-12. Most common form of name

```
100 1   ‡a Shaw, Bernard, ‡d 1856-1950.
245 10  ‡a You never can tell : ‡b a comedy in four acts / ‡c by Bernard Shaw.
260     ‡a London : ‡b Constable, ‡c 1906.
300     ‡a 320 p. ; ‡c 18 cm.
```

Title page	You Never Can Tell A Comedy in Four Acts by Bernard Shaw Archibald Constable & Co. Ltd. London: 1906

Figure 15-13. Most common form of name

```
100 1   ‡a Shaw, Bernard, ‡d 1856-1950.
245 13  ‡a An unsocial socialist / ‡c by G. Bernard Shaw.
260     ‡a New York : ‡b Brentano, ‡c 1917.
300     ‡a 378 p. ; ‡c 17 cm.
```

Title page	An Unsocial Socialist by G. Bernard Shaw New York Brentano's 1917

Figure 15-14. Most common form of name

```
100 1   ‡a Shaw, Bernard, ‡d 1856-1950.
245 10  ‡a Love among the artists / ‡c by George Bernard Shaw.
260     ‡a New York : ‡b Brentano, ‡c 1910, c1900.
300     ‡a viii, 443 p. ; ‡c 19 cm.
```

Title page	Love Among the Artists by George Bernard Shaw Brentano's New York MCMX

Authority
```
100 10  ‡a Shaw, Bernard, ‡d 1856-1950
400 10  ‡a Shaw, G. Bernard ‡q (George Bernard), ‡d 1856-1950
400 10  ‡a Shaw, George Bernard, ‡d 1856-1950
```

22.3B. Language

This rule deals with the problem presented by an author whose works appear in more than one language and whose name appears in more than one form, due to translation or transliteration.

22.3B1. Persons using more than one language. This rule covers persons who write in more than one language and whose name therefore appears in different forms. Again, the principle of choice of the "most commonly known" form governs the rule, which states that the form corresponding to the "language of most of the works" should be used. In case of doubt, choose the form found in reference sources of the person's country of residence or activity.

Somhairle MacGill-Eain is an Irish poet who also writes in English under the English form of his name, Sorley Maclean. Because he primarily writes in Irish, the Irish form of his name is used for his heading, with a cross-reference from the English form (see figure 15-15).

22.3B2. Names in vernacular and Greek or Latin forms. This rule refers chiefly to medieval Latin and Greek authors, not to persons of the classical period (see 22.3B3).

22.3B3. Names written in the roman alphabet and established in an English form. This rule pertains to persons who have no surname and who are to be entered under given name (Horace) or byname (a word or phrase denoting place of origin, occupation, or other characteristic commonly associated with the person's given name in reference sources, e.g., John the

Figure 15-15.   Persons using more than one language

```
020       ‡a 0856358444
100 1     ‡a MacGill-Eain, Somhairle, ‡d 1911-
240 10    ‡a Poems. ‡l English & Irish
245 10    ‡a O choille gu bearradh / ‡c Somhairle MacGill-Eain = From wood to ridge : collected
          poems in Gaelic and English / Sorley Maclean.
246 31    ‡a From wood to ridge
260       ‡a Manchester : ‡b Carcanet, ‡c 1989.
300       ‡a xvi, 317 p. ; ‡c 23 cm.
546       ‡a Gaelic text with English translation; English preface and notes.
```

Title page	Somhairle MacGill-Eain
	O Choille gu Bearradh
	Sorley Maclean
	From Wood to Ridge
	Collected Poems in Gaelic and English
	Carcanet

Authority
100 20   ‡a MacGill-Eain, Somhairle, ‡d 1911-
400 10   ‡a Maclean, Sorley, ‡d 1911-

Baptist, Saint Francis of Assisi, etc.). The names of many such persons have become firmly established through common usage in English-speaking countries in an English form. Rule 22.3B3 calls for entry under the English form of the name as it is found in English-language reference sources. Prefer *Encyclopaedia Britannica, Encyclopedia Americana,* or *Academic American Encyclopedia.* Other major specialized English-language encyclopedias may be consulted (e.g., *New Catholic Encyclopedia, Oxford Classical Dictionary,* etc.) as appropriate (see *LCRI* 22.3C, Jan. 5, 1989).

This instruction is a change from ALA 1949 rule 60, which called for entry of all Latin authors under the Latin form. The rationale for the change is that in the case of a Roman of the classical period, it is difficult to establish his or her preference for form of name from "works by that person issued in his or her language" (22.1B). Establishing the preferred form of name for a classical non-author usually presents similar difficulties; reference sources in classical Greek and Latin are few and far between (22.1B). Rule 22.3B3 is a practical solution for librarians in most English-speaking countries; its retention from *AACR1* indicates its acceptance among library users despite the fact that in theory, at least, it would seem to be a stumbling block in the way of international exchange of cataloging information.

Catalogers can best determine common usage in English-speaking countries by checking English-language reference sources and by noting the spelling of the person's name in books written in English. At least a minimal amount of research is required on the part of the cataloger to establish the name heading, even though the name may not present a "conflict" in the catalog.

The decision about the form of heading to be used for figure 15-16 was fairly straightforward. The title page of the work being cataloged is one factor to be considered. In addition, the cataloger will find entry for the classical Roman author Virgil in *Encyclopaedia Britannica* (1993) and *Encyclopedia Americana* (1994) under the form Virgil, with references to the variant form Publius Vergilius Maro. The form Virgil will be used in the heading. Reference will be made according to 26.2A2 from the different language form not chosen for the heading in the authority record shown, which will display as follows:

Vergilius Maro, Publius
   search under
Virgil

Vergil
   search under
Virgil

22.3C. Names written in a nonroman script

22.3C1. Persons entered under given name, etc. This rule closely parallels 22.3B3. A person entered under given name or byname whose name is written in a nonroman script will be entered according to the form found in English-language reference sources. The Greek philosopher Plato is such an individual (see figure 15-17).

Figure 15-16.   Roman author of classical times

100 0	‡a Virgil
240 10	‡a Aeneis. ‡n Liber 9
245 10	‡a Aeneid. ‡n Book IX / ‡c Virgil ; edited by Philip Hardie.
260	‡a Cambridge ; ‡a New York : ‡b Cambridge University Press, ‡c 1994.
300	‡a vii, 259 p. ; ‡c 19 cm.
440 0	‡a Cambridge Greek and Latin classics
504	‡a Includes bibliographical references (p. 251-254) and index.
700 1	‡a Hardie, Philip R.

Title page

Virgil
Aeneid
Book IX
edited by
Philip Hardie
University Lecturer in Classics in the University of Cambridge
and Fellow of New Hall
Cambridge University Press

Authority
100 00   ‡a Virgil
400 20   ‡a Vergilius Maro, Publius
400 00   ‡a Vergil

22.3C2. Persons entered under surname. The Library of Congress, the National Library of Canada, and the National Library of Australia follow the alternative rule, footnote 4, which treats persons entered under surname essentially the same as those entered under given name, etc., in 22.3C1. The British Library follows the main rule, which takes the name as it is found in the original source(s) and romanizes it according to conventional romanization tables. As seen from the examples in *AACR2R*, the two rules lead to quite different results.

Entry Element

Rules 22.2–22.3 give guidance for the establishment of a personal name that appears in publications in more than one form. Once the form of the name has been determined, rules 22.4–22.11 tell the cataloger which part of the name will constitute the entry element (the first part of the name in the catalog entry). The overriding factor governing the rules is the preference of the person when it is known. Lacking that knowledge, the cataloger will choose the entry element according to linguistic usage, that is, "that part

Figure 15-17.   Greek author of classical times

```
020        ‡a 0521341825 (hardback)
020        ‡a 0521349818 (pbk.)
100 0      ‡a Plato.
240 10     ‡a Selections. ‡f 1996
245 10     ‡a Plato on poetry / ‡c edited by Penelope Murray.
260        ‡a Cambridge ; ‡a New York : ‡b Cambridge University Press, ‡c 1996.
300        ‡a ix, 250 p. ; ‡c 20 cm.
440 0      ‡a Cambridge Greek and Latin classics
546        ‡a Text in Greek; introd. and commentary in English.
504        ‡a Includes bibliographical references and index.
505 0      ‡a Ion -- Republic 376e-398b9 -- Republic 595-608b10.
700        ‡a Murray, Penelope.
```

Title page

Plato on Poetry
Ion; Republic 376e-398b9;
Republic 595-608b10
edited by Penelope Murray
Lecturer in Classics, University of Warwick
Cambridge University Press

Authority
100 00   ‡a Plato
400 00   ‡a Platon

of the name under which the person would normally be listed in authoritative alphabetic lists in his or her language or country" (22.4A).

The rules included in this section differ slightly from Paris Principle 12, under which entry element is to be based first on citizenship and second on the language in which the author writes. The editors of *AACR2* believed that principle 12 presented too many problems, particularly when dealing with the names of French origin in a country such as Belgium, where practices seem to be variable. *AACR2R* practice, therefore, is based on the language, not the citizenship, of the author.

A. H. Chaplin's *Names of Persons* was drawn up at the behest of the International Conference on Cataloguing Principles (1961) to expedite uniform entry of names internationally.[3] Chaplin's book is an indispensable guide to national usage; it should be referred to in cases in which the rules fail to give specific instructions.

22.4. GENERAL RULE

This rule stipulates that when a person's name consists of more than one part, the part chosen as the entry element by the cataloger will be determined by the way that person's name is given in alphabetical lists that show the custom of his or her country. See examples in *AACR2R* and further examples in this text.

22.5. ENTRY UNDER SURNAME

This rule is to be applied only to names that contain given name(s) and surname. For names consisting of a surname only, see 22.15A; for names consisting of a forename only, see 22.8 and 22.11B.

22.5A. General rule

Names formulated with a forename (or initial) and a surname will be entered under the surname, unless subsequent rules provide otherwise. Aside from conventional forename-surname names (Bernhardt, Sarah), the rule includes surnames represented by initials, when at least one forename is given in full. In this case, the initial is regarded as a surname, and entry is made under the initial. Include in the authority record a reference from the name in non-inverted form (see figure 15-18).

22.5B. Element other than the first treated as a surname

Some individuals are identified by made-up names that do not actually contain a surname. Malcolm X is one such individual. "X" is not an initial standing for a surname (see 22.5A). However, "X" identifies this person and functions as if it were a surname. Thus, entry will be made under this element (see figure 15-19).

Figure 15-18.   Entry under surname initial

```
100 1    ‡a Vachon, Georges André, ‡d 1926-
245 10   ‡a Esthétique pour Patricia / ‡c G.-André Vachon. Suivi d'un écrit de Patricia B.
260      ‡a Montréal, Qué. : ‡b Presses de l'Université de Montréal, ‡c 1980.
300      ‡a 144 p. ; ‡c 18 cm.
700 1    ‡a B., Patricia
```

Title page	
	G.-André Vachon
	Esthétique pour Patricia
	suivi d'un écrit de Patricia B.
	1980
	Les Presses de l'Université de Montréal
	C.P. 6128, Succ. «A», Montréal, Qué., Canada H3C 3J7

Authority
```
100 10   ‡a B., Patricia
400 00   ‡a Patricia B.
```

Figure 15-19.   Element other than the first treated as a surname

```
020      ‡a 0873486315
100 1    ‡a X, Malcolm, ‡d 1925-1965.
240 10   ‡a Speeches. ‡k Selections
245 10   ‡a Malcolm X talks to young people : ‡b speeches in the U.S., Britain, and Africa.
250      ‡a 1st ed.
260      ‡a New York : ‡b Pathfinder, ‡c 1991.
300      ‡a 110 p. : ‡b ill. ; ‡c 22 cm.
504      ‡a Includes bibliographical references (p. 101-106) and index.
```

Title page	Malcolm X talks
	to young people
	speeches in the U.S.
	Britain, and Africa
	Pathfinder

New York   London   Montréal   Sydney

Authority
100 10   ‡a X, Malcolm, ‡d 1925-1965
400 00   ‡a Malcolm X, ‡d 1925-1965
400 10   ‡a Little, Malcolm, ‡d 1925-1965

22.5C. Compound surnames

22.5C1. This rule encompasses the entry of surnames that include "two or more proper names" (e.g., C. Day-Lewis). It does not pertain to single surnames that consist of two or more words (e.g., Antoine de Saint Exupéry). The rule is divided into eight parts, which are to be applied in the order in which they are listed.

22.5C2. Preferred or established form known. Enter a person with a compound surname under the element of the surname that he or she prefers. Only rarely will the cataloger have information about the author's preference. The second part of the rule is more useful; in fact, it is the only way in most cases that the cataloger can be positive that he or she is dealing with a compound name rather than with a simple surname and one or more forenames that resemble surnames. The second part of the rule instructs the cataloger to check reference sources in the person's language and to list the person in the form found there. The cataloger will do well to be cautious, however. Some reference sources, such as the *Dictionary of National Biography* (London: Oxford University Press, 1921–22), enter all persons in a uniform style (in this case, under the last element of the name) regardless of personal preference.

22.5C3. Hyphenated surnames. Such names are to be entered under the first part of the name, with reference made from the second part (see figure 15-20).

Figure 15-20.   Compound surname

```
020      ‡a 0207130000 (hardbound)
020      ‡a 0207130213 (pbk.)
100 2    ‡a Wallace-Crabbe, Chris.
245 10   ‡a Melbourne or the bush : ‡b essays on Australian literature and society / ‡c Chris
         Wallace-Crabbe.
260      ‡a Sydney : ‡b Angus and Robertson, ‡c 1974.
300      ‡a 140 p. ; ‡c 22 cm.
440  0   ‡a Perspectives in Australian literature
```

```
Title page           Perspectives in Australian Literature
                            Melbourne or the Bush
                      Essays on Australian Literature
                               and Society
                          Chris Wallace-Crabbe
                     Angus and Robertson • publishers
```

```
Authority
100 20   ‡a Wallace-Crabbe, Chris
400 10   ‡a Crabbe, Chris Wallace-
```

Make reference as shown in the authority record from the second element (*AACR2R* 26.A3). This will display as follows:

Crabbe, Chris Wallace-
    search under
Wallace-Crabbe, Chris

22.5C4. Other compound surnames except those of married women. Check reference sources in the language of the person when you have reason to suspect that a name not hyphenated may be compound. Enter the person the way he or she is listed in such sources; make references from parts of the surname not used as entry element. Persons other than married women who use their maiden name followed by husband's name are to be entered under the first element of the compound name, whether hyphenated or not.

Many Spanish surnames are compounds consisting of the father's surname followed by the mother's maiden name. Those are to be entered under the first part of the compound, after checking references to be certain that the name is indeed compound. For more detailed information see Chaplin, *Names of Persons,* and Charles F. Gosnell, *Spanish Personal Names.*[4]

See figure 1-54 for an example of a compound Spanish name. Entry for Cotarelo y Mori is based on information from *Enciclopedia Universal Ilustrada* (Barcelona: Espasa, 1907–30), familiarly known as *Espasa.* Make an authority record with a reference from the final element (26.2A3):

100 20 ‡a Cotarelo y Mori, Emilio, ‡d 1857-1936
400 10 ‡a Mori, Emilio Cotarelo y, ‡d 1857-1936

This will display:

Mori, Emilio Cotarelo y, 1857-1936
   search under
Cotarelo y Mori, Emilio, 1857-1936

In the example shown in figure 15-21, the entry for Serafín and Joaquín Alvarez Quintero under the first part of their compound name is based on information from the Spanish-language encyclopedia *Hispanica* (Barcelona: Encyclopaedia Britannica, 1995). The authority records will cause the following references to display:

Quintero, Serafín Alvarez, 1871-1938
   search under
Alvarez Quintero, Serafín, 1871-1938

Quintero, Joaquín Alvarez, 1873-1944
   search under
Alvarez Quintero, Joaquín, 1873-1944

Compound Portuguese surnames are formed differently from Spanish. Generally speaking, the mother's name is the first part of the compound, the father's the last. For this reason, 22.5C4 specifies that such names are to be entered under the last element in the compound (see figure 15-22).

Figure 15-21.   Compound name—Spanish

100 2   ‡a Alvarez Quintero, Serafín, ‡d 1871-1938.
245 10 ‡a Tambor y cascabel : ‡b comedia en cuatro actos / ‡c Serafín y Joaquín Alvarez Quintero.
260   ‡a Madrid : ‡b Impr. Clásica Española, ‡c 1927.
300   ‡a 100 p. ; ‡c 19 cm.
700 2   ‡a Alvarez Quintero, Joaquín, ‡d 1873-1944.

Title page   Serafín y Joaquín Alvarez Quintero
                       Tambor y Cascabel
                       Comedia en Cuatro Actos
                       Madrid 1927

Authorities
100 20   ‡a Alvarez Quintero, Serafín, ‡d 1871-1938
400 10   ‡a Quintero, Serafín Alvarez, ‡d 1871-1938

100 20   ‡a Alvarez Quintero, Joaquín, ‡d 1873-1944
400 10   ‡a Quintero, Joaquín Alvarez, ‡d 1873-1944

Figure 15-22.   Compound name—Portuguese

```
100 1    ‡a Lima, Luiz Costa, ‡d 1937-
245 10   ‡a Lira e antilira : ‡b (Mário, Drummond, Cabral) / ‡c Luiz Costa Lima.
260      ‡a Rio de Janeiro : ‡b Civilização Brasileira, ‡c 1968.
300      ‡a 413 p. ; ‡c 21 cm.
440  0   ‡a Coleção Vera Cruz ; ‡v v. 127
504      ‡a Includes bibliographical references.
505 0    ‡a Introdução -- Permanência e mudança na poesia de Mário de Andrade -- O princípio :
         corrosão na poesia de Carlos Drummond -- A traição conseqüente, ou, A poesia de
         Cabral.
```

Title page   Luiz Costa Lima
                                Lira e Antilira
                            (Mário, Drummond, Cabral)
                                Civilização
                                 Brasileira

Authority
100 10   ‡a Lima, Luiz Costa, ‡d 1937-
400 20   ‡a Costa Lima, Luiz, ‡d 1937-

Reference from the first element will be made in the authority record as shown, displaying as follows:

Costa Lima, Luiz, 1937-
    search under
Lima, Luiz Costa, 1937-

Be wary of names consisting of two or more words not themselves surnames. Do not separate the parts of names such as Castelo Branco, Camilo or Espirito Santo, Vicente Antonio de. It is not necessary to give references from parts of a name not used for entry in such cases (see figure 15-23). However, do make a reference from the prefix (see 26.2A3).

22.5C5. Other compound surnames: married women. Follow general rule 22.1A in establishing the name of a married woman; use the name, either married or maiden name, by which the woman chooses to be known and by which she is most commonly identified. If she chooses to use, in addition to forenames, both her maiden name and her husband's surname, entry will be under the husband's surname, unless her language is Czech, French, Hungarian, Italian, or Spanish, or unless her name is hyphenated (for which see *AACR2R* 22.5C3). See figures 15-10 and 15-11 for examples of the entry of a married woman writing and best known by her married name.

22.5C6. Nature of surname uncertain. Some English- and Scandinavian-language names have the appearance of compound names when, actually,

Figure 15-23.   Surname not a compound name

```
100 2    ‡a Saint-Exupéry, Antoine de, ‡d 1900-1944.
240 10   ‡a Petit prince. ‡l English
245 14   ‡a The little prince / ‡c written and illustrated by Antoine de Saint-Exupéry ; translated
         from the French by Katherine Woods.
260      ‡a New York : ‡b Harcourt, Brace & World, ‡c c1943.
300      ‡a 113 p. : ‡b ill. ; ‡c 18 cm.
490 0    ‡a Harbrace paperbound library ; ‡v HPL 30
500      ‡a Translation of: Le petit prince.
```

Title page	The Little Prince
	Written and Illustrated by
	Antoine de Saint-Exupéry
	Translated from the French
	by Katherine Woods
	Harbrace Paperbound Library
	Harcourt, Brace & World, Inc.
	New York

Authority
```
100 20   ‡a Saint-Exupéry, Antoine de, ‡d 1900-1944
400 20   ‡a De Saint-Exupéry, Antoine, ‡d 1900-1944
```

the author simply has a family name or other surname as his or her middle name. Such names should be checked in reference sources. If the name cannot be found after reasonable search or, obviously, if the cataloger discovers that the name is not a compound surname, enter under the last part of the name. If there is a reasonable possibility that catalog users will think of the name as a compound name, make appropriate references.

The American author Ernest Thompson Seton has such a name; he is sometimes referred to as Thompson Seton. Information about Seton is to be found in Hart, *Oxford Companion to American Literature* (1995), which enters him as "Seton, Ernest [Evan] Thompson" with the further information that "his name was originally Ernest Seton Thompson," and his dates of birth and death.

Entry will be as shown in figure 15-24. References are made from 400 fields according to terms of 26.2A3.

22.5C8. Words indicating relationship following surnames. The word "junior" and any other word showing relationship is not to be included in the heading for English-speaking persons, even when such a term is used regularly by the person as a part of the name, unless the term is needed to distinguish between identical headings. (It is, however, included in transcribing the name in the body of the entry; see figure 1-42.) Portuguese and Brazilian surnames are exceptions to this rule. Such a name will have entry

Figure 15-24.   Nature of surname uncertain

```
100 1   ‡a Seton, Ernest Thompson, ‡d 1860-1946.
245 14  ‡a The biography of a grizzly, and 75 drawings / ‡c by Ernest Thompson Seton.
260     ‡a New York : ‡b Schocken Books, ‡c 1967.
300     ‡a 157 p. : ‡b ill. ; ‡c 21 cm.
490 0   ‡a Schocken paperbacks ; ‡v SB152
500     ‡a "First published in 1899."
```

Title page   The Biography of a Grizzly
                                and 75 Drawings
                           by Ernest Thompson Seton
                          Schocken Books • New York

Authority
100 10   ‡a Seton, Ernest Thompson, ‡d 1860-1946
400 10   ‡a Thompson, Ernest Seton, ‡d 1860-1946
400 20   ‡a Thompson Seton, Ernest, ‡d 1860-1946
400 20   ‡a Seton Thompson, Ernest, ‡d 1860-1946

as shown in figure 15-25. Reference is made from a 400 field under terms of 26.2A3, displaying as follows:

Filho, Antônio Martins
    search under
Martins Filho, Antônio

22.5D. Surnames with separately written prefixes

The guiding principle governing this part of the rule is the same as that for 22.5C (Compound surnames): enter a name with a separately written prefix under the element most commonly used as an entry element in alphabetical listings in the person's language.

22.5D1. Articles and prepositions. Rule 22.5D1 provides specific rules for various languages and countries to guide catalogers who are unsure of national customs governing entry in the various languages. Rules are applied to surnames that include a separately written prefix consisting of an article, a preposition, or a combination of the two. This section of *AACR2R* has drawn extensively on information contained in Chaplin, *Names of Persons.* For languages not covered under rule 22.5D1, see Chaplin.

English. Enter under the prefix (see figures 15-26 and 15-27). Rule 26.2A3 suggests reference under parts of the surname following a prefix for a name entered under prefix, as are English names. Thus, for Van der Post,

Figure 15-25.   Word indicating relationship

```
100 2    ‡a Martins Filho, Antônio.
245 12   ‡a O universal pelo regional : ‡b definição de uma política universitária / ‡c Antônio
         Martins Filho.
250      ‡a 2. edição.
260      ‡a Fortaleza : ‡b Imprensa Universitária do Ceará, ‡c 1966.
300      ‡a 329 p. : ‡b ill. ; ‡c 24 cm.
504      ‡a Includes bibliographical references.
```

Title page	Prof. Antônio Martins Filho
	O Universal Pelo Regional
	Definição de Uma Política Universitária
	(2.a edição)
	Fortaleza • Imprensa Universitária do Ceará • 1966

Authority
100 20   ‡a Martins Filho, Antônio
400 10   ‡a Filho, Antônio Martins

Figure 15-26.   English—enter under prefix

```
100 1    ‡a Van der Post, Laurens.
245 14   ‡a The dark eye in Africa / ‡c Laurens Van der Post.
260      ‡a New York : ‡b Morrow, ‡c 1955.
300      ‡a 224 p. ; ‡c 21 cm.
```

Title page	Laurens Van der Post
	The Dark Eye in Africa
	William Morrow & Company, Inc.
	New York 1955

Authority
100 10   ‡a Van der Post, Laurens
400 10   ‡a Der Post, Laurens Van
400 10   ‡a Post, Laurens Van der

Figure 15-27.   English—enter under prefix

```
100 2    ‡a Dos Passos, John, ‡d 1896-1970.
245 10   ‡a Airways, inc. / ‡c by John Dos Passos.
260      ‡a New York : ‡b Macaulay Co., ‡c c1928.
300      ‡a 148 p. ; ‡c 20 cm.
440  0   ‡a New playwrights' theatre production
```

Title page

Airways, Inc.
by
John Dos Passos
A New Playwright's Theatre Production
New York
The Macaulay Company

Authority
100 10   ‡a Dos Passos, John, ‡d 1896-1970
400 10   ‡a Passos, John Dos, ‡d 1896-1970

references are as seen in the 400 fields of the authority record, which display as follows:

Der Post, Laurens Van
    search under
Van der Post, Laurens

Post, Laurens Van der
    search under
Van der Post, Laurens

Reference for Dos Passos according to 26.2A3 is as seen in the authority record, displaying:

Passos, John Dos, 1896-1970
    search under
Dos Passos, John, 1896-1970

French. Enter under prefix if the prefix consists of an article (le, la) or of a contraction of an article and a preposition (du, des) (see figure 15-28). Reference for Des Cars displays:

Cars, Guy Des
    search under
Des Cars, Guy

A French name that includes an article (la, le) and a preposition (de) is to be entered under the part of the name following the preposition (see figure 15-29). The article in French, as well as a contraction of an article and

Figure 15-28.   French—enter under prefix (contraction)

```
100 1    ‡a Des Cars, Guy.
245 10   ‡a De cape et de plume : ‡b roman vécu / ‡c Guy Des Cars.
260      ‡a Paris : ‡b Flammarion, ‡c c1965.
300      ‡a 511 p. ; ‡c 20 cm.
```

> **Title page**
>
>   Guy Des Cars
>   De cape et de plume
>   roman vécu
>   Flammarion, Editeur
>   26, rue de Racine, Paris

> **Authority**
> 100 10   ‡a Des Cars, Guy
> 400 10   ‡a Cars, Guy Des

Figure 15-29.   French—enter under prefix (article)

```
100 1    ‡a La Boétie, Estienne de, ‡d 1530-1563.
245 10   ‡a Oeuvres complètes d'Estienne de La Boétie / ‡c publiées avec notice biographique,
         variantes, notes et index par Paul Bonnefon.
260      ‡a Genève : ‡b Slatkine Reprints, ‡c 1967.
300      ‡a lxxxv, 444 p. : ‡b ill. ; ‡c 24 cm.
504      ‡a Includes bibliographical references (p. [325]-382).
700 1    ‡a Bonnefon, Paul, ‡d 1861-1922.
```

> **Title page**
>
>   Oeuvres complètes
>   d'Estienne de La Boétie
>   Publiées avec Notice biographique, Variantes,
>   Notes et Index
>   par Paul Bonnefon
>   Slatkine Reprints
>   Genève
>   1967

> **Authority**
> 100 10   ‡a La Boétie, Estienne de, ‡d 1530-1563
> 400 10   ‡a Boétie, Estienne de La, ‡d 1530-1563
> 400 10   ‡a De La Boétie, Estienne, ‡d 1530-1563

preposition (des, du), is always capitalized in a proper name (*AACR2R* Appendix A [Capitalization] A.39C). References are to be made for La Boétie according to 26.2A3 as seen in the authority record, and display as follows:

> Boétie, Estienne de La, 1530-1563
>   search under
> La Boétie, Estienne de, 1530-1563

> De La Boétie, Estienne, 1530-1563
>   search under
> La Boétie, Estienne de, 1530-1563

If the French surname includes the preposition "de" with no article, enter the surname under the part of the name following the preposition (see figure 15-30). Reference for Balzac will appear:

> De Balzac, Honoré, 1799-1850
>   search under
> Balzac, Honoré de, 1799-1850

German. Entry of German surnames with prefix follows almost the same pattern as that for French. Enter under prefix if the prefix is an article (der, die, das) or a contraction of a preposition and an article (am, aus'm, vom, zum, zur) (see figure 15-31). Reference for Vom Brocke will be made according to 26.2A3 from the 400 field of the authority record, displaying as follows:

> Brocke, Bernhard vom, 1939-
>   search under
> Vom Brocke, Bernhard, 1939-

Figure 15-30.   French—enter under part of surname following preposition

```
020        ‡a 2862604216
100 1      ‡a Balzac, Honoré de, ‡d 1799-1850.
245 10     ‡a Albert Savarus / ‡c Honoré de Balzac ; postface par David Haziot.
260        ‡a Paris : ‡b Éditions Autrement, ‡c c1994.
300        ‡a 142 p. ; ‡c 21 cm.
490 1      ‡a Littératures, ‡x 1248-4873
830  0     ‡a Littératures (Éditions Autrement)
```

Title page
                    Honoré de Balzac
                    Albert Savarus
                    Postface par David Haziot
                    Éditions Autrement Littératures

Authority
100 10   ‡a Balzac, Honoré de, ‡d 1799-1850
400 10   ‡a De Balzac, Honoré, ‡d 1799-1850

Figure 15-31.   German—enter under contraction

```
100 1    ‡a Vom Brocke, Bernhard, ‡d 1939-
245 10   ‡a Kurt Breysig : ‡b Geschichtswissenshaft zwischen Historismus und Soziologie / ‡c von
         Bernhard vom Brocke.
260      ‡a Lübeck : ‡b Matthiesen, ‡c 1971.
300      ‡a 351 p. ; ‡c 24 cm.
490 1    ‡a Historische Studien ; ‡v Heft 417
504      ‡a Includes bibliographical references (p. 317-343).
830  0   ‡a Historische Studien (Matthiesen Verlag) ; ‡v Heft 417
```

Title page   Historische Studien
                                        Heft 417
                                      Kurt Breysig
                       Geschichtswissenshaft zwischen Historismus
                                    und Soziologie
                                          von
                                  Bernhard vom Brocke
                                         1971
                       Matthiesen Verlag • Lübeck and Hamburg

Authority
100 10   ‡a Vom Brocke, Bernhard, ‡d 1939-
400 10   ‡a Brocke, Bernhard vom, ‡d 1939-

If a German surname includes a preposition (von) or a preposition followed by an article, enter the name under the part following the prefix (see figure 15-32). Reference for Hentig will be made according to 26.2A3:

Von Hentig, Werner-Otto, b. 1886
   search under
Hentig, Werner-Otto von, b. 1886

Italian. Enter modern Italian names under prefix. Consult reference sources for medieval or early modern names, which ordinarily did not include an actual surname; the prefix was often part of a byname (e.g., Leonardo da Vinci) (see 22.8A for treatment of such names).

Figure 1-63 is an example of an Italian name entered under prefix. An authority record will be made including reference from the name without the prefix:

100 10   ‡a D'Annunzio, Gabriele, ‡d 1863-1938
400 10   ‡a Annunzio, Gabriele d', ‡d 1863-1938

This will display as follows:

Annunzio, Gabriele d', 1863-1938
   search under
D'Annunzio, Gabriele, 1863-1938

Figure 15-32.   German—enter under part of surname following prefix

```
100 1    ‡a Hentig, Werner-Otto von, ‡d b. 1886.
245 14   ‡a Der Nahe Osten rückt näher / ‡c Werner-Otto von Hentig.
260      ‡a Leipzig : ‡b P. List, ‡c c1940.
300      ‡a 117 p. : ‡b ill., map ; ‡c 22 cm.
```

> **Title page**
>
> Werner-Otto von Hentig
> Der Nahe Osten rückt näher
> Paul List Verlag Leipzig

> **Authority**
> 100 10   ‡a Hentig, Werner-Otto von, ‡d b. 1886
> 400 10   ‡a Von Hentig, Werner-Otto, ‡d b. 1886

It is, by the way, particularly important to make references from the part of the surname following the prefix to the name as established for cataloging purposes when, under older rules, the name would have been entered differently in the catalog. Such is the case with D'Annunzio, which under ALA 1949 rules was entered as ''Annunzio, Gabriele d'.''

Portuguese. The part of the surname following the prefix is used for entry (see figure 15-33). Reference, based on the authority record, will display:

Dos Santos, Francisco Marques
   search under
Santos, Francisco Marques dos

Figure 15-33.   Portuguese—enter under part of surname following prefix

```
100 2    ‡a Santos, Francisco Marques dos.
245 10   ‡a Louça e porcelana / ‡c Francisco Marques dos Santos ; direção e introdução, Rodrigo
         M.F. de Andrade.
260      ‡a Rio de Janeiro : ‡b Edições de Ouro, ‡c 1968.
300      ‡a 114 p. : ‡b ill. ; ‡c17 cm.
440  0   ‡a Artes plásticas no Brasil
440  0   ‡a Coleção brasileira de ouro ; ‡v 1047
504      ‡a Includes bibliographical references (p. 111-114).
```

> **Title page**
>
> Francisco Marques dos Santos
> As Artes Plásticas no Brasil
> Louça e Porcelana
> Direção e introdução
> Rodrigo M.F. de Andrade
> Rio de Janeiro
> Brasil

Authority
100 20   ‡a Santos, Francisco Marques dos
400 20   ‡a Dos Santos, Francisco Marques

Spanish. In almost all cases, entry will be under the part of the name following the prefix. Note that the rule states that if the prefix consists of an article *only*, the cataloger is to enter under the article. Thus, if the name includes an article (el, la, lo, los, las) and a preposition (de), entry will be under the part of the name following prefixes (see figure 15-34). References generated by the authority record display as follows:

De las Casas, Bartolomé, 1474-1566
    search under
Casas, Bartolomé de las, 1474-1566

Las Casas, Bartolomé de, 1474-1566
    search under
Casas, Bartolomé de las, 1474-1566

Figure 15-34.   Spanish—enter under part of name following prefix

100 1   ‡a Casas, Bartolomé de las, ‡d 1474-1566.
245 10   ‡a Doctrina / ‡c Bartolomé de las Casas ; prólogo y selección de Agustín Yáñez.
250   ‡a 2. ed.
260   ‡a México : ‡b Universidad Nacional Autónoma, ‡c 1951.
300   ‡a xxxvi, 178 p. : ‡b ill. ; ‡c 19 cm.
440   0   ‡a Biblioteca del estudiante universitario ; ‡v 22
700 1   ‡a Yáñez, Agustín, ‡d 1904-

Title page   Biblioteca del Estudiante Universitario
                          22
                   Fray Bartolomé de las Casas
                          Doctrina
                     Prólogo y selección
                          de
                       Agustín Yáñez
                      Segunda Edición
            Ediciones de la Universidad Nacional Autónoma
                      México   1951

Authority
100 10   ‡a Casas, Bartolomé de las, ‡d 1474-1566
400 10   ‡a De las Casas, Bartolomé, ‡d 1474-1566
400 10   ‡a Las Casas, Bartolomé de, ‡d 1474-1566

Another example of a Spanish surname with a prefix consisting of an article and a preposition is shown in figure 15-35. It is rare to find a name with only the article as a prefix. References display:

De la Maza, Francisco, 1913-1972
    search under
Maza, Francisco de la, 1913-1972

La Maza, Francisco de, 1913-1972
    search under
Maza, Francisco de la, 1913-1972

22.6. ENTRY UNDER TITLE OF NOBILITY

This rule, which should be compared to 22.12, is based on *AACR2R* rule 22.1A; that is, entry should be made under the form of the name by which the person is commonly known. If a nobleman or -woman uses title rather than family name in his or her works, or if such an individual who is not an author is known primarily by his or her title and is so listed in appropriate reference sources, such an individual should be listed under the proper name in the title of nobility rather than under family name. Check reference sources to identify the individual's rank and personal name accurately.

Two noblemen better known by title than by family name are the Duke of Wellington and the Earl of Lauderdale. The *Encyclopaedia Britannica* (1994) lists each of them under his title, followed by his family name and dates.[5] Entry should be under title, followed by the personal name in direct

Figure 15-35.   Spanish—enter under part of name following prefix

```
100 1     ‡a Maza, Francisco de la, ‡d 1913-1972.
245 13    ‡a El Palacio de la Inquisición (Escuela Nacional de Medicina) / ‡c Francisco de la Maza.
260       ‡a [México] : ‡b Instituto de Investigaciones Estéticas, ‡c 1951.
300       ‡a 81 p. : ‡b ill. ; ‡c 24 cm.
440   0   ‡a Edíciones del IV centenario de la Universidad de México ; ‡v v. 9
```

Title page	Francisco de la Maza
	El Palacio de la Inquisición
	(Escuela Nacional de Medicina)
	Instituto de Investigaciones Estéticas
	1951

Authority
```
100 10   ‡a Maza, Francisco de la, ‡d 1913-1972
400 10   ‡a De la Maza, Francisco, ‡d 1913-1972
400 10   ‡a La Maza, Francisco de, ‡d 1913-1972
```

order, and the term of rank excluding any numbers (e.g., not "2nd Earl of . . ."). The term of rank, as a title, is placed in subfield ‡c of the MARC field (see figure 15-36).

Rule 22.6A stipulates that a reference will be made from the family name for a person entered under name in nobility. References generated from the authority records for the example shown in figure 15-36 follow:

Maitland, James, Earl of Lauderdale, 1759-1839
   search under
Lauderdale, James Maitland, Earl of, 1759-1839

Wellesley, Arthur, Duke of Wellington, 1769-1852
   search under
Wellington, Arthur Wellesley, Duke of, 1769-1852

Very often application of rule 22.6A for persons to be entered under the proper name in the title of nobility, such as the Duke of Wellington and the Earl of Lauderdale, results in an entry that seems to violate the spirit of general rule 22.1, that the cataloger will choose as the basis of a heading for a person "the name by which he or she is commonly known." Often the name in nobility (Earl of Lauderdale, for example) is the only name found in chief sources of information of that person's works. Nonetheless, 22.6A directs the cataloger to add the personal name (forenames and family

Figure 15-36. Nobleman

```
100 1    ‡a Lauderdale, James Maitland, ‡c Earl of, ‡d 1759-1839.
245 10   ‡a Three letters to the Duke of Wellington / ‡c by the Earl of Lauderdale (1829).
260      ‡a New York : ‡b A.M. Kelley, ‡c 1965.
300      ‡a 138 p. ; ‡c 21 cm.
440  0   ‡a Reprints of economic classics
534      ‡p Reprint. Originally published: ‡c London : J. Murray, 1829.
700 1    ‡a Wellington, Arthur Wellesley, ‡c Duke of, ‡d 1769-1852.
```

Title page   Three Letters to the Duke of Wellington
by
the Earl of Lauderdale
[1829]
Reprints of Economic Classics
Augustus M. Kelley, Bookseller
New York 1965

Authorities
100 10   ‡a Lauderdale, James Maitland, ‡c Earl of, ‡d 1759-1839
400 10   ‡a Maitland, James, ‡c Earl of Lauderdale, ‡d 1759-1839

100 10   ‡a Wellington, Arthur Wellesley, ‡c Duke of, ‡d 1769-1852
400 10   ‡a Wellesley, Arthur, ‡c Duke of Wellington, ‡d 1769-1852

name) in direct order (e.g., James Maitland) followed by the term of rank
(e.g., Earl of). Application of this rule to the Earl of Lauderdale results in
the heading "Lauderdale, James Maitland, Earl of," despite the fact that
"Earl of Lauderdale" is the form of name by which he is commonly
known.[6]

Rule 22.6 specifies that the cataloger is to exclude unused forenames.
LCRI 22.6 (Jan. 5, 1989) clarifies this as follows: "If the person of nobility is
an author, use in the heading the forenames most commonly found in the
chief sources of information of the person's works. If no forenames are
found in the chief sources, or if the person is not primarily known as an
author, consult reference sources. If reference sources vary, use the least
number of forenames commonly found."

Reference sources uniformly list Lauderdale and Wellington as established in figure 15-36 (see also figure 1-66).

The following authority records show proper entry and references for
certain members of other ranks of British peerage.

    100 10 ‡a Queensberry, John Sholto Douglas, ‡c Marquis of, ‡d 1844-1900
    400 10 ‡a Douglas, John Sholto, ‡c Marquis of Queensberry, ‡d 1844-1900

    100 20 ‡a Grey of Fallodon, Edward Grey, ‡c Viscount, ‡d 1862-1933
    400 10 ‡a Grey, Edward, ‡c Viscount Grey of Fallodon, ‡d 1862-1933
    400 10 ‡a Fallodon, Edward Grey, ‡c Viscount Grey of, ‡d 1862-1933

    100 10 ‡a Lytton, Edward Bulwer-Lytton, ‡c Baron, ‡d 1803-1873
    400 20 ‡a Bulwer-Lytton, Edward, ‡c Baron Lytton, ‡d 1803-1873

The wife of a peer takes the title corresponding to that of her husband
(e.g., duchess, marchioness, countess, viscountess, baroness):

    100 10 ‡a Devonshire, Georgiana Spencer Cavendish, ‡c Duchess of, ‡d 1757-
        1806
    400 10 ‡a Cavendish, Georgiana Spencer, ‡c Duchess of Devonshire, ‡d 1757-
        1806

Entry under title of nobility for persons of other countries follows the
same pattern as that used for British nobility (follow, however, the rules in
AACR2R Appendix A for capitalization of the title):

    100 10 ‡a Cavour, Camillo Benso, ‡c conte di, ‡d 1810-1861
    400 10 ‡a Benso, Camillo, ‡c conte di Cavour, ‡d 1810-1861

    100 10 ‡a Alba, Fernando Alvarez de Toledo, ‡c duque de, ‡d 1508-1582
    400 20 ‡a Alvarez de Toledo, Fernando, ‡c duque de Alba, ‡d 1508-1582
    400 10 ‡a Toledo, Fernando Alvarez de, ‡c duque de Alba, ‡d 1508-1582

The cataloger should be aware that certain British titles below the rank
of baron and certain other titles for persons of other countries are simply
terms of honor. These persons are entered under family name, with the title
of honor added (see 22.12).

Figure 15-37. Nobleman

```
100 1   ‡a Tennyson, Alfred Tennyson, ‡c Baron, ‡d 1809-1892.
245 10  ‡a Tiresias and other poems / ‡c by Alfred, Lord Tennyson.
260     ‡a London : ‡b Macmillan, ‡c 1885.
300     ‡a viii, 203 p. ; ‡c 18 cm.
```

Title page

Tiresias and other poems
by
Alfred Lord Tennyson
London
Macmillan and Co.
1885

Sequential numbers are not used with a title of nobility; in case two or more of the bearers of such a title have the same personal name, they should be distinguished in the same fashion as other persons with identical names, by adding dates of birth and death (22.17).

Whatever the components of the name may be, if a nobleman uses his title, title name should be the entry word. Family name in direct order comes next, followed by the title. In the example shown in figure 15-37, no reference is needed from family name to surname in nobility, because they are the same.

22.8. ENTRY UNDER GIVEN NAME, ETC.

A person who is not commonly identified by a surname (or a name that appears to be a surname) and who is not identified by a title of nobility should be checked in an English-language reference source and entered accordingly. The 1993 amendments add the following phrase after the first sentence of this rule: "In case of doubt, enter under the last element, following the instructions in 22.5B." This means that if the name includes an element that appears to be a surname, and it is not clear (e.g., from reference sources, etc.) that it is not a surname, treat it as though it were.

Many names of this type include words or phrases denoting place of origin, etc. A name that includes such information will be entered in direct order, with the given name separated from the descriptive phrase by a comma. The descriptive phrase is entered in subfield ‡c (see figure 15-38). Henry of Huntingdon's name and dates are to be found in the *Dictionary of National Biography* (1921–22) and *Chambers' Encyclopedia* (1973) under "Henry of Huntingdon."

Figure 15-38.   Entry under given name

```
100 0    ‡a Henry, ‡c of Huntingdon, ‡d 1084?-1155.
245 14   ‡a The chronicle of Henry of Huntingdon / ‡c translated and edited by Thomas Forester.
260      ‡a New York : ‡b AMS Press, ‡c 1968.
300      ‡a xxviii, 442 p. : ‡b ill. ; ‡c 22 cm.
500      ‡a Originally issued in the series: Bohn's antiquarian library.
505 0    ‡a The history of England from the invasion of Julius Caesar to the accession of Henry II --
         The acts of Stephen, King of England and Duke of Normandy.
534      ‡p Reprint. Originally published: ‡c London : H. G. Bohn, 1853.
700 1    ‡a Forester, Thomas.
```

Title page

The Chronicle of
Henry of Huntingdon.
comprising
The history of England, from the invasion of
Julius Caesar to the accession of Henry II.
also,
The Acts of Stephen,
King of England and Duke of Normandy
translated and edited by Thomas Forester, A.M.
London:
Henry G. Bohn, York Street, Covent Garden
MDCCCLIII.
AMS Press
New York

22.9. ENTRY OF OTHER NAMES

22.9A. Roman names

This rule should be correlated with 22.3B3; as indicated under that rule, a Roman of classical times "whose name has become well established in an English form" will be searched in English-language reference sources. Entry will be under the part of the name "most commonly used" in such sources.

Ovid is entered as "Ovid" in the *Encyclopaedia Britannica* (1994), the *Encyclopedia Americana* (1994), and the *Oxford Classical Dictionary* (1996), with the added information that the Latin form of his name is Publius Ovidius Naso. Each of these sources also gives his dates. Entry will be as found in the reference sources (see figure 15-39).

Note that Latin names, as with all languages that decline nouns, should be given in headings and references in the nominative case only, not necessarily in the case in which they appear in the source. See figure 14-1. No reference should be made from the genitive form of Ovid's name (Publii Ovidii Nasonis).

Figure 15-39.   Roman name

```
020      ‡a 0151705291
100 0    ‡a Ovid, ‡d 43 B.C.-17 or 18 A.D.
240 10   ‡a Metamorphoses. ‡l English
245 14   ‡a The Metamorphoses of Ovid : ‡b a new verse translation / ‡c by Allen Mandelbaum.
250      ‡a 1st ed.
260      ‡a New York : ‡b Harcourt Brace, ‡c c1993.
300      ‡a 559 p. ; ‡c 29 cm.
700 1    ‡a Mandelbaum, Allen, ‡d 1926-
```

Title page   The
                               Metamorphoses
                                  of Ovid
                        A New Verse Translation by
                            Allen Mandelbaum
                         Harcourt Brace & Company
                     New York   San Diego   London

Authority
100 10   ‡a Ovid, ‡d 43 B.C.-17 or 18 A.D.
400 20   ‡a Ovidius Naso, Publius, ‡d 43 B.C.-17 or 18 A.D.

22.10. ENTRY UNDER INITIALS, LETTERS, OR NUMERALS

If an author consistently uses initials for identification in his or her works, the initials, in direct order, will be used as main entry. If the initials have been used by more than one author, see 22.18 for an addition to resolve a conflict.

If the name includes typographic devices (ellipses, asterisks, etc.), include them if they appear as part of a multi-letter abreviation of a name; omit them if they follow single letter initials. This is a change stemming from the 1993 amendments; previously all typographic devices were included, so long as they were not "primarily non-alphabetic or nonnumeric." Thus the form of the abbé de B... is now entered "B., abbé de," rather than "B..., abbé de."

Some attempt should be made, by looking in dictionaries of pseudonyms, anonyms, etc., to find the identity of the author. In the example shown in figure 15-40, William Cushing gives the information that "A.L.O.E." stands for "A Lady of England" and that the initials are the

Figure 15-40.   Initials

```
100 0    ‡a A. L. O. E., ‡d 1821-1893.
245 14   ‡a The giant-killer, or, The battle which all must fight / ‡c by A.L.O.E.
246 30   ‡a Battle which all must fight
260      ‡a London ; ‡a New York : ‡b Nelson, ‡c 1896.
300      ‡a 201 p. : ‡b ill. ; ‡c 19 cm.
```

Title page   The Giant-Killer;
                                        or,
                          The Battle Which All Must Fight
                                  by A.L.O.E.
                             with 40 engravings.
                                  London:
                    T. Nelson and Sons, Paternoster Row
                          Edinburgh; and New York.
                                    1896

Authority
100 00   ‡a A. L. O. E., ‡d 1821-1893
400 00   ‡a ALOE, ‡d 1821-1893
400 10   ‡a Tucker, Charlotte Maria, ‡d 1821-1893
400 00   ‡a Lady of England, ‡d 1821-1893
400 10   ‡a E., A. L. O., ‡d 1821-1893

pseudonym of Charlotte Maria Tucker.[7] Make references from those forms (26.2A2) in the authority record, causing the following displays:

> ALOE, 1821-1893
> search under
> A. L. O. E., 1821-1893

> Tucker, Charlotte Maria, 1821-1893
> search under
> A. L. O. E., 1821-1893

> Lady of England, 1821-1893
> search under
> A. L. O. E., 1821-1893

> E., A. L. O., 1821-1893
> search under
> A. L. O. E., 1821-1893

AACR2R calls for a name-title reference from the inverted form of the initials to the direct order form without the title. This would be accomplished by adding

> 400 10 ‡a E., A. L. O., ‡d 1821-1893. ‡t Giant-killer

to the authority record for A. L. O. E., which would produce the following reference:

E., A. L. O., 1821-1893. Giant-killer
    search under
A. L. O. E., 1821-1893

The Library of Congress will not make these name-title references. Instead, LC instructs its catalogers (and contributors to the National Authority File) simply to make a reference from the inverted form without title, as shown in the authority record accompanying figure 15-40. This sensible rule interpretation avoids unnecessary multiplicity of references (see *LCRI* 22.10, Feb. 15, 1994).

22.11. ENTRY UNDER PHRASE

22.11A. Sometimes a person may disguise his or her identity by using a phrase for identification. Following the general principles of 22.1, if this is the appellation by which the person is commonly known, this phrase will be used for the heading. The *AACR2* (1978) rule is unchanged, but the wording has been clarified in *AACR2R* 22.11A. If the phrase or appellation does not contain a forename, or consists of a forename preceded by a term other than a term of address or title, it will be entered in direct order. Thus, the cataloger selects "Old Sleuth" as the correct form for the main entry in figure 1-8 (see also figure 14-23).

  22.11B. If a person uses a forename plus a term of address or a title of position or office in his or her works, enter under forename, followed by the word or phrase. See figure 1-79, *The Boy's Book of Sports and Games*, with main entry as: John, Uncle. A reference is made from the direct form of name. The authority record for John, Uncle, would be constructed as follows:

100 00 ‡a John, ‡c Uncle
400 00 ‡a Uncle John

and would display:

Uncle John
    search under
John, Uncle

Note that 22.11B refers to a person using a forename plus term of address, etc. For a person who uses a surname plus term of address, see 22.15.

  22.11D. Correlate this rule with 21.5C, which deals with choice of entry for works identified by a characterizing word or phrase, etc. In figure 1-8, the author hides his identity under the words "Old Sleuth." Capitalization of the characterizing words or phrase is slightly different from *AACR2* (1978) practice; note that in contrast to *AACR2* (1978), each word of the phrase is capitalized (see also examples under *AACR2R* 22.11D).

  Rule 22.11D clearly states that a characterizing word or phrase is only to be used as the heading for a person "if that person is commonly identified by it in the chief sources of information of his or her works and in reference sources." This is particularly true if the author identifies himself or herself by a phrase including the title of another of his or her works. Thus, because it is known that *Memoirs of a Fox-Hunting Man* is by Siegfried Sassoon, the real name of the author is used as heading for his *Memoirs of an Infantry Officer* (see last example, *AACR2R* 22.11D). However, if the author's name is not known, the heading will be the phrase naming another work that is given in the statement of responsibility. Notice the capitalization of the statement of responsibility: the word "Author" is capitalized as the beginning of the identifying element, and the words in the title are capitalized as they would be in a title area transcription (see figure 15-41).

Additions to Names

The rules thus far have dealt with general principles governing the choice of names when these appear in different formats in various places and with the problem of determining which part of the name chosen according to *AACR2R* 22.1–22.3 to use as the entry element. Certain additions to personal names will be made under some circumstances. Rules 22.12 through 22.20 address themselves to these matters.

Figure 15-41.   Entry under phrase

```
100 0   ‡a Author of Evening amusement.
245 10  ‡a My young days / ‡c by the Author of Evening amusement, Letters everywhere, etc. etc.
        ; with twenty illustrations by Paul Konewka.
260     ‡a New York : ‡b Dutton, ‡c 1871.
300     ‡a 151 p. : ‡b ill. ; ‡c 18 cm.
```

Title page

My Young Days
by the
Author of "Evening Amusement,"
"Letters Everywhere," etc. etc.
with twenty illustrations by
Paul Konewka
New York:
E.P. Dutton & Co., 713 Broadway.
London: Seeley, Jackson, & Halliday.
1871.

Authority
```
100 00  ‡a Author of Evening amusement
400 20  ‡a Evening amusement, Author of
400 00  ‡a Author of Letters everywhere
400 20  ‡a Letters everywhere, Author of
```

22.12. TITLES OF NOBILITY AND TERMS OF HONOR

22.12A. Titles of nobility

This rule instructs the cataloger to add the title of nobility (in subfield ‡c) to a nobleman or -woman's heading, as already discussed at 22.6.

If a nobleman or noblewoman chooses to write using his or her family name instead of name in nobility, the person's preference is followed. See figure 15-42 for an example of such a practice. Although Dorothy Wellesley is the Duchess of Wellington, she chooses to identify herself by her family name. Because she does not use her title, no title will be added to her name. However, make reference from her name in nobility, as shown in the authority record. This will display:

> Wellington, Dorothy Wellesley, Duchess of, 1889-1956
>   search under
> Wellesley, Dorothy, 1889-1956

The German title "Fürst," meaning "prince," is a title of honor given the German statesman Bismarck in 1871. Because Bismarck was known by the title, it is used as part of the heading (see figure 15-43).

Compare 22.12A with 22.6 (Entry under title of nobility). Both rules follow general principles as set forth under *AACR2R* 22.1, inasmuch as each calls for entry under the name by which the individual chooses to identify himself or herself, either the name in nobility or the family name.

22.12B. British terms of honor

Following general principles of author preference, if a person includes the British titles of honor (Sir, Dame, Lord, or Lady) as part of his or her name on chief sources of information, the cataloger will include the title as part

Figure 15-42.   Name in nobility not used

100 1	‡a Wellesley, Dorothy, ‡d 1889-1956.
245 10	‡a Desert wells / ‡c Dorothy Wellesley.
260	‡a London : ‡b M. Joseph, ‡c 1946.
300	‡a 55 p. ; ‡c 21 cm.

Title page	Dorothy Wellesley Desert Wells Michael Joseph Ltd. 26 Bloomsbury Street, London, W.C.1

Authority
100 10   ‡a Wellesley, Dorothy, ‡d 1889-1956
400 10   ‡a Wellington, Dorothy Wellesley, ‡c Duchess of, ‡d 1889-1956

Figure 15-43.   Term of honor added

```
100 1    ‡a Bismarck, Otto, ‡c Fürst von, ‡d 1815-1898.
245 10   ‡a Fürst Bismarcks Briefe an seine Braut und Gattin / ‡c herausgegeben vom Fürsten
         Herbert Bismarck.
250      ‡a 4. Aufl., mit Erläuterungen und Register (Ergänzungsband) / ‡b von Horst Kohl ;
         Titelbild nach Franz von Lenbach und zehn weitere Porträt-Beilagen.
260      ‡a Stuttgart : ‡b J.G. Cotta, ‡c 1914.
300      ‡a xvi, 596 p. : ‡b ill. ; ‡c 24 cm.
700 1    ‡a Bismarck, Herbert, ‡c Fürst von, ‡d 1849-1904.
```

```
Title page              Fürst Bismarcks Briefe
                        an seine Braut und Gattin
                   Herausgegeben vom Fürsten Herbert Bismarck
                              Vierte Auflage
                Mit Erläuterungen und Register (Ergänzungsband)
                             von Horst Kohl
                    Titelbild nach Franz von Lenbach
                     und zehn weitere Porträt-Beilagen
                          Stuttgart und Berlin 1914
                   J.G. Cotta'sche Buchhandlung Nachfolger
```

```
Authority
100 1    ‡a Bismarck, Otto, ‡c Fürst von, ‡d 1815-1898
400 1    ‡a Von Bismarck, Otto, ‡c Fürst, ‡d 1815-1898
```

of the heading for that person. By Library of Congress (*LCRI* 22.12B, Jan. 5, 1989) and National Library of Canada (Howarth, at 22.12B) policy decision, in *all* cases the title of honor will be added at the end of the name. Thus, for instance, referring to the examples in *AACR2R* for this rule, the policy decision would establish these authors as

> Hess, Myra, Dame
>
> West, Rebecca, Dame
>
> Landseer, Edwin, Sir
>
> Beecham, Thomas, Sir
>
> Gordon, George, Lord
>
> Greaves, Rosamund, Lady
>
> Stanhope, Hester, Lady

This change not only eliminates a rather sticky distinction in the rule; it also facilitates filing in automated systems (see figure 15-44).

Figure 15-44.   British title of honor

```
100 1    ‡a Scott, Walter, ‡c Sir, ‡d 1771-1832.
245 14   ‡a The fortunes of Nigel / ‡c Sir Walter Scott ; edited with an introduction by Frederick
         M. Link.
260      ‡a Lincoln : ‡b University of Nebraska Press, ‡c c1965.
300      ‡a xli, 488 p. ; ‡c 21 cm.
500      ‡a "A bison book."
700 1    ‡a Link, Frederick M.
```

Title page

The Fortunes of Nigel
Sir Walter Scott
Edited with an introduction
by Frederick M. Link
A Bison Book
University of Nebraska Press • Lincoln

22.13. SAINTS

22.13A. The name of a saint will be established according to appropriate rules 22.1–22.11. The word "saint" is added to the name in subfield ‡c as it is thus established, unless the person was a pope, emperor, empress, king, or queen, in which case, see 22.16A–22.16B (see figure 1-98).

22.13B. A suitable word or phrase will be added following the word "saint" (still in subfield ‡c) and preceding dates (if any) to distinguish between two saints with identical names. This will be done even if dates are available. Determine uniqueness of saints' names by checking reference sources such as Holweck's *Biographical Dictionary of the Saints* (Detroit: Omnigraphics, 1990). This rule seems to be a curious exception to the general rules for distinguishing between identical names by the addition of dates (22.17) or, lacking dates, a distinguishing term in parentheses (22.18).

A distinguishing phrase was added to the example shown in figure 15-45 because "Cyril, Saint, Patriarch of Alexandria, ca. 370-444" has also been established. The form of Cyril's name, following *AACR2R* 22.3B3, is established according to citations found in such English-language reference sources as *Encyclopaedia Britannica* (1993) and *New Catholic Encyclopedia* (1967).

A reference will be made from the Latin and Greek forms of the author's name, as seen in the authority record.

For another example of this rule, see figure 1-39.

Figure 15-45.   Saint with identical name

```
020        ‡a 081320061X (v. 1)
020        ‡a 0813200644 (v. 2)
100 0      ‡a Cyril, ‡c Saint, Bishop of Jerusalem, ‡d ca. 315-386.
240 10     ‡a Works. ‡l English
245 14     ‡a The works of Saint Cyril of Jerusalem / ‡c translated by Leo P. McCauley and Anthony
           A. Stephenson.
260        ‡a Washington, D.C. : ‡b Catholic University of America Press, ‡c 1969-1970.
300        ‡a 2 v. ; ‡c 22 cm.
440   0    ‡a Fathers of the church ; ‡v v. 61, 64
504        ‡a Includes bibliographical references.
700 1      ‡a McCauley, Leo P.
700 1      ‡a Stephenson, Anthony A.
```

Title page   The Works of Saint Cyril of Jerusalem
                      Translated by Leo P. McCauley, S.J.
                      and Anthony A. Stephenson
                      The Catholic University of America Press
                      Washington, D.C. 20017

Authority
100 00   Cyril, ‡c Saint, Bishop of Jerusalem, ‡d ca. 315-386
400 00   Cyrillus, ‡c Saint, Bishop of Jerusalem, ‡d ca. 315-386
400 00   Kyrillos, ‡c Saint, Bishop of Jerusalem, ‡d ca. 315-386

22.14. SPIRITS

Purported communications from spirits are entered under the name of the spirit (see 21.26). If the spirit is supposed to have been a real person, follow *AACR2R* rules and establish the name of that person (if not already in the catalog). Add the word (Spirit) in subfield ‡c to the complete heading for the person. Note that if the name established for the living person includes dates, these will be retained (cf. *LCRI* 22.14, Jan. 5, 1989), e.g.,

100 10 ‡a Beethoven, Ludwig van, ‡d 1770-1827 ‡c (Spirit)

See figure 14-47 for an example of spirit communication.

22.15. ADDITIONS TO NAMES ENTERED UNDER SURNAME

Apply this rule to names of persons who identify themselves by their surname and a term of address (e.g., Mrs. Oliphant) (see figure 1-40). The heading will be entered under the surname, with the term in subfield ‡c. Caution: do not use this rule for persons of nobility who are entered under title of nobility. A title of nobility is not regarded as a surname. For such persons, see 22.6.

Rule 22.15 includes two types of names. One is phrase headings, most of which are pseudonymous. The author of books for children who identifies himself as Dr. Seuss is an example. Such headings will be entered under surname (real or pseudonymous) followed by the associated word (see figure 15-46). A reference will be made from the name in direct order via the authority record, and will display:

Dr. Seuss
    search under
Seuss, Dr.

The other type of name covered by 22.15 is that of a person who normally identifies himself or herself by actual surname plus term of address. This was a common practice particularly in the eighteenth and nineteenth centuries for women authors, Mrs. Oliphant being a typical example. The rule calls for entry of such individuals under the "commonly known" form of their name (e.g., Oliphant, Mrs.). Although it would seem from 22.15A that all names covered by 22.15 should have reference from the name in direct order, the Library of Congress has clarified this directive to apply only to phrase headings (i.e., those covered by type 1 above). A reference in direct order is *not* necessary for a name such as Mrs. Oliphant (*LCRI* 22.15A, Jan. 5, 1989).

See discussion under 22.18 for further additions to names covered by 22.15, type 2, such as Mrs. Oliphant.

Figure 15-46.   Surname with addition

100 1	‡a Seuss, ‡c Dr.
245 10	‡a One fish, two fish, red fish, blue fish / ‡c by Dr. Seuss.
250	‡a Book club ed.
260	‡a New York : ‡b Beginner Books, ‡c c1960.
300	‡a 62 p. : ‡b col. ill. ; ‡c 24 cm.

Title page

One fish two fish
red fish blue fish
by Dr. Seuss
Beginner Books
A Division of Random House, Inc.
© Copyright 1960 by Dr. Seuss.
Book Club Edition

Authority
100 10   ‡a Seuss, ‡c Dr.
400 00   ‡a Dr. Seuss

22.15B. Terms of address of married women

A married woman who chooses to identify herself in her works by her husband's name plus the term of address "Mrs." (or the equivalent in other languages) will be entered in that way. Note that the same Library of Congress/National Library of Canada policy decision that shifted British terms of honor to the end of the name (22.12B) shifts the term of address for a married woman to the end of her name (*LCRI* 22.15B, Jan. 5, 1989; Howarth, at 22.15B; see figure 1-41 for example). Do not add qualifiers or dates to the *husband's* name in this type of heading, even though they may have been added to the established form of his own heading (cf. *LCRI* 22.18A, exception 2, Feb. 1, 1989). If dates are to be added to the *wife's* heading, add them following "Mrs."

22.16. ADDITIONS TO NAMES ENTERED UNDER GIVEN NAME, ETC.

22.16A. Royalty

Correlate this rule with provisions of 22.8 that cover entry of persons under given name. The name will be given as it appears in English-language reference sources (cf. 22.3B3) and will include any roman numerals, recorded in subfield ‡b, appearing with the name in these sources. The title, recorded in subfield ‡c, will be in English if there is an English equivalent (see figure 15-47).

The 22.16A1 requirement to add the name of the state or people has been implemented in a rather confusing manner for British sovereigns.

Figure 15-47.   Royalty

```
020      ‡a 0304939691
100 0    ‡a Henry ‡b VIII, ‡c King of England, ‡d 1491-1547.
240 10   ‡a Correspondence. ‡k Selections
245 14   ‡a The letters of King Henry VIII : ‡b a selection, with a few other documents / ‡c edited
         by M. St. Clare Byrne.
250      ‡a New ed., reprinted.
260      ‡a New York : ‡b Funk & Wagnalls, ‡c c1968.
300      ‡a xxiii, 455 p. : ‡b ill. ; ‡c 22 cm.
504      ‡a Includes bibliographical references (p. 430-441).
700 1    ‡a Byrne, Muriel St. Clare, ‡d 1895-
```

Title page	The Letters of King Henry VIII A Selection, with a few other Documents edited by M. St. Clare Byrne Funk & Wagnalls New York

Therefore, given in the appendix to this *Handbook* is a list of headings for personal entry for British sovereigns, along with an explanation of the practice. In addition, see the appendix for a list of headings for British sovereigns acting in an official capacity.

To sum up provisions of 22.16A: use English-language reference sources to determine the name of the monarch. Use a roman numeral if the name of the monarch has such associated with it. Do not include epithets or the word "saint." Royalty takes precedence over all other titles.

The form for the Prussian king Frederick the Great illustrates provisions of the rule. Despite the fact that German-language reference sources such as *Der grosse Brockhaus* (Wiesbaden: Brockhaus, 1952–63) list him as "Friedrich II, der Grosse," his name is to be established according to the form found in English-language sources. *Encyclopaedia Britannica* (1994) lists him as monarch of Prussia, and gives his name, with dates, as "Frederick II, byname Frederick the Great, German Friedrich der Grosse." The English form of the name will be used, without epithets (see 22.16A2). Give references from the name by which he is commonly known in his home country and from forms with the epithet (see figure 15-48).

22.16A3. Consorts of royal persons. Appropriate title, as well as the phrase "consort of" and the name of the ruler, will be given for consorts of rulers. Prince Philip, Duke of Edinburgh and consort of Queen Elizabeth II of Great Britain, is an example of such a name. The *Encyclopedia Americana* (1994) lists him as "Philip, Duke of Edinburgh and consort of Elizabeth II, Queen of the United Kingdom of Great Britain and Northern Ireland." He is also referred to in the article as "Prince Philip, the duke of Edinburgh."

Figure 15-48.   Royalty

```
100 0     ‡a Frederick ‡b II, ‡c King of Prussia, ‡d 1712-1786.
245 10    ‡a Frederick the Great on the art of war / ‡c edited and translated by Jay Luvaas.
260       ‡a New York : ‡b Free Press, ‡c c1966.
300       ‡a xvi, 391 p. : ‡b ill., maps ; ‡c 22 cm.
504       ‡a Includes bibliographical references (p. 375-378) and index.
700 1     ‡a Luvaas, Jay.
```

Title page   Edited and Translated by
                                    Jay Luvaas
                    Frederick the Great on the Art of War
                        New York   The Free Press
                    London   Collier-Macmillan Limited

Authority
```
100 00    ‡a Frederick ‡b II, ‡c King of Prussia, ‡d 1712-1786
400 00    ‡a Friedrich ‡b II, ‡c King of Prussia, ‡d 1712-1786
400 00    ‡a Friedrich, ‡c der Grosse, ‡d 1712-1786
400 00    ‡a Frederick, ‡c the Great, ‡d 1712-1786
```

Thus, he has two titles, Prince and Duke of Edinburgh. The cataloger should list him by his higher title, Prince. See figure 1-37 for an example, with Philip as author.

In the example shown in figure 15-49, added entry is made for the consort, under the terms of 21.30F.

22.16B. Popes

A pope assumes a new name when he is elevated to the papacy. This name should be used, rather than his secular name, because it is the name by which he is commonly known. By the terms of 22.3B3, a person entered under given name whose name has become well established in an English-language form will be entered under this form, as found in English-language reference sources.

Pope John Paul II is listed in the *Encyclopaedia Britannica* (1993) as "John Paul II," with date of birth, his secular name, and his Latin name. By terms of 26.2A, references should be made as shown in the authority record. In addition, a "search also under" reference is made in a 510 field from his corporate name. Catalog entry will be as shown in figure 15-50.

Note that even though John Paul's secular and literary works are normally published under his secular name, for purposes of personal authorship all of his works are entered under John Paul. This is not a case of "separate bibliographic identities" (22.2B2), because neither name is a pseudonym.

Figure 15-49.   Consort of a ruler

```
100 0    ‡a Charles ‡b I, ‡c King of England, ‡d 1600-1649.
240 10   ‡a Correspondence. ‡k Selections
245 10   ‡a Charles I in 1646 : ‡b letters of King Charles the First to Queen Henrietta Maria / ‡c
         edited by John Bruce.
260      ‡a London : ‡b Printed for the Camden Society, ‡c 1856.
300      ‡a xxxi, 104 p. ; ‡c 22 cm.
490 1    ‡a Publications / Camden Society ; ‡v no. 63
700 0    ‡a Henrietta Maria, ‡c Queen, consort of Charles I, King of England, ‡d 1609-1669.
700 1    ‡a Bruce, John, ‡d 1802-1869.
830  0   ‡a Works of the Camden Society ; ‡v no. 63.
```

Title page   Charles I in 1646
                     Letters of King Charles the First
                     to Queen Henrietta Maria
                     Edited by John Bruce, Esq. F.S.A.
                     Printed for the Camden Society
                     M.DCCC.LVI.

Figure 15-50.   Pope

```
020      ‡a 0520052897
100 0    ‡a John Paul ‡b II, ‡c Pope, ‡d 1920-
240 10   ‡a Selections. ‡l English. ‡f 1987
245 14   ‡a The collected plays and writings on theater / ‡c Karol Wojtyła ; translated with
         introductions by Boleslaw Taborski.
260      ‡a Berkeley : ‡b University of California Press, ‡c c1987.
300      ‡a x, 395 p. ; ‡c 25 cm.
546      ‡a Translated from the Polish.
505 0    ‡a Job -- Jeremiah -- Our God's brother -- The jeweler's shop -- Radiation of fatherhood --
         Reflections on fatherhood -- On the theater of the word -- Drama of word and gesture --
         Rhapsodies of the millennium -- Forefather's eve and the twentieth century -- On The
         Divine comedy -- Foreword to Miecsyslaw Jitkarczjt's The art of the living word.
```

Title page	The
	collected
	plays
	and
	writings on
	theater
	Karol Wojtyła
	translated
	with introductions by
	Boleslaw Taborski
	University of California Press
	Berkeley Los Angeles London

```
Authority
100 00   ‡a John Paul ‡b II, ‡c Pope, ‡d 1920-
400 10   ‡a Wojtyła, Karol, ‡d 1920-
400 00   ‡a Joannes Paulus ‡b II, ‡c Pope, ‡d 1920-
510 20   ‡a Catholic Church. ‡b Pope (1978- : John Paul II)
```

22.16C. Bishops, etc.

Add the title, in English if possible, after the name of a high ecclesiastical official *who is entered under given name* (see figure 15-51). Note that bishops, etc., who are also saints are entered under 22.13, not 22.16C.

The cataloger will *not* add the designation after the name of a cardinal, bishop, etc., who is entered under surname. See for an example figure 1-44. Although Cardinal Newman consistently used his ecclesiastical title in his later writings, and although he is commonly known as Cardinal Newman, the fact that he is entered under surname means that his ecclesiastical title will not be retained in the heading.

Figure 15-51.   High ecclesiastical official

```
020      ‡a 0813207576
020      ‡a 0813207584 (pbk.)
100 0    ‡a Suger, ‡c Abbot of Saint Denis, ‡d 1081-1151.
240 10   ‡a Vita Ludovici Grossi Regis. ‡l English
245 14   ‡a The deeds of Louis the Fat / ‡c Suger ; translated with introduction and notes by
         Richard Cusimano and John Moorhead.
260      ‡a Washington, D.C. : ‡b Catholic University of America Press, ‡c c1992.
300      ‡a xiv, 223 p. : ‡b map ; ‡c 23 cm.
500      ‡a Translation of: Vita Ludovici Grossi Regis.
504      ‡a Includes bibliographical references and index.
700 1    ‡a Cusimano, Richard, ‡d 1939-
700 1    ‡a Moorhead, John, ‡d 1948-
```

Title page	Suger
	The Deeds of
	Louis the Fat
	Translated with Introduction
	and Notes by Richard Cusimano and
	John Moorhead
	The Catholic University of America Press
	Washington, D.C.

22.16D. Other persons of religious vocation

This rule applies *only* to persons of religious vocation who are commonly known by given name and who are thus entered. Add to such a name in the vernacular terms of honor, address, or title only if the term, etc., appears with the name in the chief source of information (see *LCRI* 22.16D, Jan. 5, 1989). If his or her secular name is known, make a reference from it. Do not add a religious title to the name of a person of religious vocation who is entered under surname. Figure 15-52 is an example of 22.16D.

Additions to Distinguish Identical Names

22.17. DATES

Dates (year of birth, death, etc.) will be added following a comma in subfield ‡d to distinguish between two or more authors if the headings are "otherwise identical."

According to the option in 22.17, dates may be added to personal names even when there is no need to distinguish between headings. The Library of Congress, the British Library, the National Library of Canada, and the National Library of Australia all apply this option when the dates are readily ascertainable (*LCRI* 22.17, May 21, 1990; Howarth, at 22.17).

Figure 15-52. Person of religious vocation

```
100 1    ‡a Cuthbert, ‡c Father, O.S.F.C., ‡d 1866-1939.
245 14   ‡a The Capuchins : ‡b a contribution to the history of the counter-reformation / ‡c Father
         Cuthbert, O.S.F.C.
260      ‡a New York : ‡b Longmans, Green, ‡c 1929.
300      ‡a 2 v. : ‡b ill. ; ‡c 22 cm.
500      ‡a Includes bibliographical references (p. 431-441).
```

```
Title page              Father Cuthbert, O.S.F.C.
                              The Capuchins
                    A Contribution to the History of the
                           Counter-reformation
                         Longmans, Green and Co.
                        55 Fifth Avenue, New York
                         210 Victoria St., Toronto
                                  1929
```

```
Authority
100 00   ‡a Cuthbert, ‡c Father, O.S.F.C., ‡d 1866-1939
400 10   ‡a Hess, Lawrence Cuthbert, ‡d 1866-1939
```

22.18. FULLER FORMS

One of the objects of the catalog is to provide a distinctive and uniform heading for each author represented in the library's collection. When two authors in the catalog have identical names, a "conflict" exists that must be resolved. The problem of "conflicts" in the catalog has been solved in various ways by the older cataloging codes. For example, consider the popular author T. H. White. ALA 1949 rule 36 stipulated the use of the author's name in full, with a search made for forenames represented by initials. Dates were added when available. Thus, regardless of whether the catalog included another author of the same name or not, White would have been searched and established as:

White, Terence Hanbury, 1906-1964

Few library users know T. H. White's forenames; the addition of such information often served to complicate rather than to solve problems of catalog use, particularly with a common name such as White. The next code, *AACR1*, brought a distinct improvement with rule 40 being almost the same as *AACR2* rule 22.1A, calling for entry under the name "by which [the person] is commonly identified."

The provision seemed sensible. However, *AACR1* rule 43A stipulated the use of "the fullest form that has appeared in a prominent position" on any of the author's publications, even if that form only appeared once, with the author clearly preferring to use initials on other works. Additionally, 43B directed the cataloger "always [to] spell out a first forename represented by an initial if the surname is a common one." Thus, T. H. White would have been established

> White, Terence H., 1906-1964

It seemed to critics of *AACR1* that this violated the spirit of the code, because it disregarded the author's preference and usage. The rationale behind the provision was that although the catalog may not now contain another A. S. Jones or T. J. Smith (or other author with common surname), eventually a conflict may arise. Better to resolve it now than recatalog later. Against such a spirit of "borrowing trouble," Michael Gorman said that the rule "represents a failure of nerve, a failure to carry through the logical consequence of the general rule."[8]

The problem of constructing an entry under the commonly known form of the author's name for a person whose name consists of or contains initials has been solved in a highly satisfactory manner under 22.18. If no conflict exists in the catalog, the cataloger will establish such a person according to the provisions of 22.1 under the name by which he or she is commonly known (e.g., White, T. H.). If necessary to distinguish between identical names in the library's catalog, the cataloger will add full forenames (or the entire name in direct order, as appropriate) in parentheses following the initials. This "qualifier" is preceded by subfield ‡q in the MARC record. White, T. H. (figure 15-53), will be qualified as

> White, T. H. (Terence Hanbury), 1906-1964

Figure 15-53.   Fuller form of name

100 1	‡a White, T. H. ‡q (Terence Hanbury), ‡d 1906-1964.
245 10	‡a Mistress Masham's repose / ‡c by T.H. White ; illustrations by Fritz Eichenberg.
260	‡a New York : ‡b G.P. Putnam's Sons, ‡c c1946.
300	‡a 255 p. : ‡b ill. ; ‡c 21 cm.
520	‡a Ten-year-old Maria, heiress to the Palace of Malplaquet, triumphs over her wicked guardian and governess while befriending a colony of Lilliputians.

Title page

Mistress
Masham's
Repose
By T.H. White
Illustrations by Fritz Eichenberg
G.P. Putnam's Sons
New York

Authority
100 10   ‡a White, T. H. ‡q (Terence Hanbury), ‡d 1906-1964
400 10   ‡a White, Terence Hanbury, ‡d 1906-1964

In searching for the forenames, dates of birth are often found as well. The four national libraries will apply the optional provision of 22.17 and add dates of birth to these headings (cf. discussion at 22.17).

Optionally, a library may make additions according to provisions of 22.18 to all names containing initials, whether a conflict exists or not. The national libraries' unanimous position on this option is the same as is their practice in the matter of adding dates of birth, death, etc., to an author's name. Except to resolve a conflict, the cataloger should not search reference sources to try to find information about an author's forenames (etc.) represented by initials. Use the information as it appears in the chief source of information. But if further information is "readily available" it seems only sensible to add it (*LCRI* 22.18A, Jan. 5, 1989; Howarth, at 22.18). Thus, if the cataloger knows further information about T. H. White's name, this will be used, regardless of whether a conflict exists or not. Reference will be made from the fuller form of the name, as shown in the authority record.

A problem that was not addressed in the 1978 version of *AACR2* was what to do about resolving conflicts in names covered by 22.15, those persons who are commonly identified only by surname and term of address. Rule 22.18 option extends the provisions of the rule to include such names. By applying the option, the forenames that belong with the surname will be added in parentheses following the term of address. Thus, Oliphant, Mrs., will become Oliphant, Mrs. (Margaret), 1828-1897 (see figure 1-40). Note: this situation is *not* covered by the modification of rule 22.15B by *LCRI*, which calls for giving the term of address as the *last* element of the name (see discussion in this *Handbook* at 22.15B).

Mrs. Oliphant's authority record will be formulated as follows:

```
100 10 ‡a Oliphant, ‡c Mrs. ‡q (Margaret), ‡d 1828-1897
400 10 ‡a Oliphant, Margaret, ‡d 1828-1897
```

The reference from the fuller form displays:

Oliphant, Margaret, 1828-1897
   search under
Oliphant, Mrs. (Margaret), 1828-1897

Caution: the option to 22.18A allows qualifiers to be added to headings consisting of surnames *without forenames*. In the case of a woman using a term of address (e.g., Mrs.) plus her husband's name, no qualifier with her own forenames may be added because a forename (her husband's) is present. "Ward, Humphry, Mrs., 1851-1920" may *not* be established "Ward, Humphry, Mrs. (Mary Augusta Arnold), 1851-1920."

22.19. DISTINGUISHING TERMS

Obviously, if a person's name is the same as another name in the catalog, the cataloger will need to make every reasonable effort to provide dates, or a fuller form of name, if not for the new heading, then for the existing one. But if the cataloger cannot find either of these elements to resolve a conflict, a suitable, brief descriptive designation may be added. More lee-way about terminology is given in the case of names entered under given name; when distinguishing between two names entered under surname, the rule stipulates that the cataloger is to confine distinguishing terms to statements appearing on the title page of the work cataloged or taken from reference sources (see *LCRI* 22.19, Nov. 1995, for details). This rule is used only in the few cases in which a conflict cannot otherwise be resolved.

22.20. UNDIFFERENTIATED NAMES

If no addition can be found to break the conflict, 22.20A permits the cata-loger to use the same heading for all persons with the same name (this is called "undifferentiated names"). According to *AACR2R* rules, this is a so-lution only to be used as a last resort. However, in deciding whether to use an undifferentiated name or to attempt to qualify it in some way, the cat-aloger should consider the effect of qualifying the heading on the index. Sometimes artificial qualifiers such as those suggested by *AACR2R* 22.19 serve only to cause a heading, particularly if is a common one, to be lost in the index when a user attempts to find it. Will the user be able to guess that the Johannes he or she wants is filed under "N" for "Notary," or that George Brown is filed under "C" for "Captain" (cf. the examples to *AACR2R* 22.19)? If not, it may be better to leave the name undifferentiated under rule 22.20.

NOTES

1. General information about MARC coding is found in the introduction to this *Handbook;* details about coding the descriptive portion of the record are found throughout chapter 1; information about the coding of main and added access points is found at the beginning of chapter 14. Further explanation of the MARC authorities format is given in *Handbook* chapters 17 and 18. Information about specific MARC fields may be found by consulting the index under "MARC fields."
2. *The Principles of Cataloguing* (London: Lockwood, 1960), p. 52.
3. *Names of Persons: National Usage for Entry in Catalogues* (Sevenoaks, Kent, Eng.: IFLA, 1967).
4. *Spanish Personal Names* (New York: H. W. Wilson, 1938; reprint, Detroit: Blaine-Ethridge, 1971).
5. *The Dictionary of National Biography* lists all individuals under family name. There-fore, it is not a good source for determining the preferred entry of a British nobleman or -woman. *Encyclopedia Americana* and *Encyclopaedia Britannica* list members of the British nobility under title when they are best known by title, under family name when they are best known by it. *Who's Who* is another source of information for living British noblemen and -women.
6. Note that italics are used in *AACR2R* to set off titles of nobility and for other purposes. The Library of Congress does not use italics in headings. This text follows LC practice.
7. William Cushing, *Initials and Pseudonyms: A Dictionary of Revealed Disguises,* 2 vols. (New York: Crowell, 1885–88).
8. "A-A 1967: The New Cataloguing Rules," *Library Association Record* 70 (Feb. 1968): 29.

CHAPTER 16

GEOGRAPHIC NAMES

(*AACR2R* Chapter 23)

23.1. INTRODUCTORY NOTE

Geographic names are needed to represent governments as headings (24.3E); in addition, many government bodies are entered subordinately to such geographic names (24.17–24.26). Other geographic names are used to differentiate between identical corporate names (24.4C). *AACR2R* chapter 23 gives guidance about the form of name that should be used.

23.2. GENERAL RULES

The English form of geographic name is to be used, rather than the form used by residents of the place, if there is a common English form. In some cases this instruction may prove to be a barrier to international exchange of cataloging information, but it is an easy and satisfactory rule for English-language libraries. It will certainly lead to a "sought" heading in such libraries. Note the examples under 23.2A1.

The heading Union of Soviet Socialist Republics will not be used by the Library of Congress. LC will use the short form, Soviet Union. The republics of the former Soviet Union are now established independently under their own names. Another important decision: the Library of Congress will use "Great Britain" instead of "United Kingdom" everywhere this heading appears (including qualifiers and titles for monarchs; see *Handbook* at 22.16A and appendix) (*LCRI* 23.2, "Special decisions" 3 and 6, Nov. 1995).

23.4. ADDITIONS

With certain exceptions, the cataloger is instructed to add to the name of a place the name of a larger place, as instructed in specific rules. This addition will be made in parentheses. Use abbreviations as found in Appendix B.14

when making the addition: for example, New York (N.Y.). However, if the name of the larger place qualifier is not found in B.14, do not abbreviate: for example, London (England).

Do *not* qualify the name of a country or a state, etc., in the United States, Canada, Australia, Malaysia, U.S.S.R., or Yugoslavia by adding the name of a larger place. For example, United States stands without a qualifier. So do the states of the United States: Arizona. (Note that the cataloger uses the abbreviations found in B.14 *only* when using these terms as geographic qualifiers. Spell out Arizona when using the name as a geographic heading.)

An exception to the above directions: if a state (etc.) has a name that is the same as that of a city (etc.), the name of the state will be qualified by a term that indicates the jurisdiction. For example, New York (State) (see *AACR2R* 24.6B for instructions).

23.4D. Places in the British Isles

Under *AACR2* (1978) catalogers were instructed to add the name of a county in the British Isles to names of cities in England, Wales, or the Republic of Ireland. For catalogers outside of the British Isles, this rule was difficult to apply and led to headings that were cumbersome and less than helpful to library users. The rule has been modified under *AACR2R*. If a place is located in England, Ireland, Northern Ireland, Scotland, Wales, the Isle of Man, or the Channel Islands, add one of those terms as appropriate (see examples under 23.4D2).

23.4E. Other places

For places not covered in the discussion above, add the name of the country, for example, Paris (France) or Helsinki (Finland). In case of conflict between identical place names formulated under 23.4E, make further additions to the qualifier as instructed in 23.4F or 24.6B.

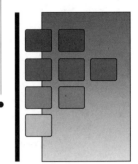

CHAPTER 17

HEADINGS FOR CORPORATE BODIES

(*AACR2R* Chapter 24)

Once the cataloger has determined, according to *AACR2R* chapter 21, that a corporate body is to serve as either main or added entry in a catalog, the problem of proper form of name remains to be decided. In many respects the chapter giving rules for corporate names parallels that for personal headings. Each chapter starts with a general rule (22.1 for personal headings, 24.1 for corporate headings). The principle behind each rule is the same: enter either the person or the corporate body under the name most likely to be known by the library user (i.e., the heading by which it is commonly identified).

General information about MARC coding is found in the introduction to this *Handbook;* details about coding the descriptive portion of the record are found throughout chapter 1; information about the coding of main and added access points is found at the beginning of chapter 14. Further explanation of the MARC authorities format is given in *Handbook* chapters 15 and 18. Information about specific MARC fields may be found by consulting the index under "MARC fields."

Library of Congress Practice

As discussed in *Handbook* chapter 15, the Library of Congress has designated certain pre-*AACR2* headings which were not formulated according to *AACR2* to be "*AACR2* compatible." While such headings are not used in the figures in this *Handbook*, the cataloger should be aware of them. They include the following:

> Quotation marks: the heading omits quotation marks that would be present under *AACR2R*.
>
> Acronyms: the heading contains a lowercase acronym where the body's predominant usage is uppercase.

Terms of incorporation: the heading contains a term of incorporation (e.g., inc.), which either is not capitalized according to *AACR2R* or would not have been retained; or it lacks a term of incorporation that would have been retained.

For more information, see *LCRI* 24.1, Nov. 1995. As pointed out in *Handbook* chapter 15, no other national library accepts the Library of Congress's "*AACR2* compatible" forms.

24.1. GENERAL RULE

With certain exceptions that are necessary because of the complexity of corporate structure and that are treated later in the rules, the cataloger is to enter a corporate body directly under its name. *AACR2R* has changed one word in this rule; the name is to be the one by which the body is "commonly" identified (formerly "predominantly"). Rule 24.1 is now exactly parallel to its counterpart, 22.1, for personal headings. Both rules are based on the principle that the name that will be selected will be the name by which the entity identifies itself.

As with a personal heading (22.1B), the cataloger will determine the "common" form of name from works issued by the corporate body in its own language (see figure 17-1). Note, however, the form in this figure. In languages such as German that have case endings, the name is always established in the nominative case. Hence, this body's name is established as "Deutsches Bucharchiv München", *not* "Deutschen Bucharchiv München".

The rule for a corporate body that consists of or contains initials parallels the stipulations of *AACR2R* 1.1B6. Do not leave a space between initials, or between a full stop and a following initial. Include or omit full stops between initials according to the body's usage. However, precede or follow abbreviations consisting of two or more letters with a space (e.g., W. Va.; Ph. D. Associates) (*LCRI* 24.1, Nov. 1995). See figures 17-2 and 17-3 for examples of corporate headings that contain initials.

Figure 17-1.   Form of name in language of body

```
245 04   ‡a Das Verlagswesen in der Bundesrepublik Deutschland / ‡c dargestellt vom Deutschen
         Bucharchiv München.
260      ‡a Rastatt : ‡b Verlag für Zeitgeschichtliche Dokumentation, ‡c 1971.
300      ‡a 71 p. : ‡b ill. ; ‡c 20 cm.
440  0   ‡a Deutschland Report ; ‡v 4
710 2    ‡a Deutsches Bucharchiv München.
```

Title page

Das Verlagswesen
in der Bundesrepublik Deutschland
Dargestellt vom Deutschen Bucharchiv München
Verlag für Zeitgeschichtliche Dokumentation

Figure 17-2.   Initials as part of name

```
245 14   ‡a The teachers' library : ‡b how to organize it and what to include / ‡c AASL-TEPS
         Coordinating Committee for the Teachers' Library Project ; Margaret Nicholsen, chairman
         ... [et al.].
250      ‡a 1968 ed.
260      ‡a Washington : ‡b American Association of School Librarians : ‡b National Education
         Association, ‡c 1968.
300      ‡a 208 p. ; ‡c 23 cm.
700 1    ‡a Nicholsen, Margaret.
710 2    ‡a AASL-TEPS Coordinating Committee for the Teachers' Library Project.
```

Facing title page   AASL-TEPS Coordinating Committee
for the Teachers' Library Project
Margaret Nicholsen, chairman
Ruth Bauner
Don Davies
Lawrence A. Lemons

Title page   The Teachers' Library
How to Organize It and What to Include
American Association of School Librarians
National Commission for Teacher Education
and Professional Standards
National Education Association

Authority
110 20   ‡a AASL-TEPS Coordinating Committee for the Teachers' Library Project
410 20   ‡a American Association of School Librarians-Teacher Education and
         Professional Standards Coordinating Committee for the Teachers' Library
         Project

Make references from variant forms of the name, including the spelled-out form of an initialism. The reference from the 410 field of the authority record for figure 17-2 would display:

American Association of School Librarians-Teacher Education and
    Professional Standards Coordinating Committee for the Teachers'
    Library Project
    search under
AASL-TEPS Coordinating Committee for the Teachers' Library Project

24.1C. Changes of name

This rule is the same as *AACR1* rule 68. The *AACR1* rule was an important change from ALA 1949 rules 91 and 92, which called for entry of societies and institutions under the latest form of name. The ALA rules, which were similar to *AACR2R* 22.2C for personal names, served, as does 22.2C for

Figure 17-3.   Initials as part of name

245 10   ‡a Du Pont : ‡b the autobiography of an American enterprise : the story of E.I. du Pont de Nemours & Company : published in commemoration of the 150th anniversary of the founding of the company on July 19, 1802.

260   ‡a Wilmington, Del. : ‡b The Company ; ‡a New York : ‡b Distributed by Scribner, ‡c c1952.

300   ‡a 138 p. : ‡b ill. (some col.) ; ‡c 32 cm.

710 2   ‡a E.I. du Pont de Nemours & Company.

Title page   Du Pont
                         The Autobiography of an American Enterprise
                        The Story of E. I. du Pont de Nemours & Company
                       Published in commemoration of the 150th anniversary
                            of the founding of the company on July 19, 1802
                             E.I. Du Pont de Nemours & Company
                                    Wilmington, Delaware
                        Distributed by Charles Scribner's Sons, New York

Authority
110 20   ‡a E.I. du Pont de Nemours & Company
410 20   ‡a Du Pont de Nemours & Company
410 20   ‡a Du Pont (Firm)

personal authors, to bring together in one place in the catalog all of the publications of a corporate body, no matter how many names it had used during the course of its history. However, it remained for Seymour Lubetzky, in his *Cataloging Rules and Principles,* to point out that corporate bodies as authors are not at all like personal authors. A person, even though he or she may change names, remains the same person. On the other hand, said Lubetzky,

> The life of a corporate body may be considerably longer than that of a personal author and it is always subject to various organizational and constitutional changes. These changes are normally reflected in changes in its name. The question arises, therefore, whether a body whose name has been changed should be regarded, for purposes of entry, as the same body or as a different body.[1]

The present rules take the position that a corporate body that has changed its name is, indeed, a different entity. Entry will be made under successive names used by the body. References will be made between the various names (for examples, see figures 12-3 and 12-4). A reader seeking all of the publications of the center under its various names would be aided by explanatory references from both names, included in the authority records:

110 20 ‡a Midwest Inter-Library Center (U.S.)
510 20 ‡w b ‡a Center for Research Libraries (U.S.)

110 20 ‡a Center for Research Libraries (U.S.)
510 20 ‡w a ‡a Midwest Inter-Library Center (U.S.)

As explained in *Handbook* chapter 15, the 1XX field in the authority record contains the established form of the name. 5XX fields generate "search also under" references. If the field begins with the control subfield ‡w, the field can be made to display a more complex reference, as, for example, earlier and later headings. Code "a" in subfield ‡w indicates that the heading in the 5XX field is an earlier heading than that in the 1XX field; code "b" indicates that it is a later heading. The 5XX references from the above two authority records would display:

Midwest Inter-Library Center (U.S.)
    search also under the later heading:
Center for Research Libraries (U.S.)

Center for Research Libraries (U.S.)
    search also under the earlier heading:
Midwest Inter-Library Center (U.S.)

"Search also under" links are only made to the immediately previous and subsequent bodies.

24.2. VARIANT NAMES. GENERAL RULES

24.2A. As long as the name of a corporate body appears in a consistent form in its publications, the name is to be used as it appears. But sometimes a corporate body, although it has not changed its name, lists it in different forms in its publications. Rules 24.2–24.3 give guidance about which of the varying forms to choose as heading. Caution: these rules are to be used to establish the name in the library's authority file. Once the name has been so established, the cataloger should always use the form found there no matter how the body appears in the item in hand, unless there is strong evidence that the form in the authority file is incorrect, in which case both the authority record and all associated bibliographic records should be changed.

24.2B. Prefer the form of a corporate name that is found in the chief source of information (e.g., the title page of a book) rather than forms found elsewhere in the item (the verso of the title page, a page preceding the title page, the cover, the running title, etc.). The book cataloged as figure 1-77 in this *Handbook* is an example of this rule. The name American Philosophical Society appears on the title page (chief source). The half title (page preceding the title page) lists the society's full name, American Philosophical Society Held at Philadelphia for Promoting Useful Knowledge. The cataloger will choose the title-page form for entry.

24.2D. If the chief source of information gives the name in more than one form, prefer a "formal" presentation (i.e., at the head of the title, in the imprint, in the statement of responsibility) rather than another form, such as might be presented in the title of the work. If both the full form and an initialism or acronym appear formally, following Library of Congress policy the cataloger will choose the full form for the heading (*LCRI* 24.2D, Jan. 5, 1989). U.S. catalogers will follow this practice rather than that prescribed by *AACR2R* 24.2D (see figure 17-4).

Following 26.3A3, reference will be made in the authority record as shown, which displays:

ERIC
   search under
Educational Resources Information Center (U.S.)

In contrast to ERIC, Unesco is a corporate body that predominantly uses a brief form of name on its publications (see figure 17-5).

The reference from the 410 field of the authority record will display:

United Nations. Educational, Scientific, and Cultural Organization
   search under
Unesco

Figure 17-4.   Full form of name

```
110 2   ‡a Educational Resources Information Center (U.S.)
245 10  ‡a How to use ERIC / ‡c U.S. Department of Health, Education, and Welfare, National
        Institute of Education, Educational Resources Information Center.
250     ‡a Rev.
260     ‡a Washington, D.C. : ‡b ERIC, ‡c 1972.
300     ‡a 14 p. : ‡b ill. ; ‡c 20 × 26 cm.
440  0  ‡a DHEW publication ; ‡v no. (OE) 72-129
```

Title page
How to Use ERIC
U.S. Department of Health, Education, and Welfare
National Institute of Education
Educational Resources Information Center

Authority
110 20   ‡a Educational Resources Information Center (U.S.)
410 20   ‡a ERIC

Figure 17-5.   Brief form of name

```
020      ‡a 9231027301 (Unesco)
020      ‡a 0907706045 (BHTC)
245 00   ‡a Book promotion, sales and distribution : ‡b a management training course / ‡c Book
         House Training Centre/Unesco.
260      ‡a London : ‡b The Centre, ‡c 1991.
300      ‡a x, 166 p. ; ‡c 30 cm.
710 2    ‡a Book House Training Centre.
710 2    ‡a Unesco.
```

Title page	Book Promotion, Sales and Distribution A Management Training Course Book House Training Centre/Unesco

Authority
110 20   ‡a Unesco
410 20   ‡a United Nations. ‡b Educational, Scientific, and Cultural Organization

In regard to corporate bodies such as ERIC and Unesco, note that the cataloger will establish the name or references to the name with capitalization according to the body's preference (e.g., ERIC consistently appears in all capital letters; Unesco, in contrast, is written as a word, with an initial capital and the rest lowercase letters) (see figure 17-5). See also *AACR2R* 24.7B4 example, Conference "Systematics of the Old World Monkeys"; if the name of a corporate body is consistently presented with all or part of its name in quotation marks, the quotation marks will be retained (*LCRI* 24.1, "Punctuation," Nov. 1995).

Sometimes the brief form of the name used by a corporate body in some of its publications is the same as the name of another organization, or it does not provide adequate identification for cataloging. If this is the case, the last paragraph of 24.2D directs the cataloger to use the form found in reference sources or "the official form."

The National Research Council of Canada sometimes is so listed in its publications; sometimes it appears as National Research Council. The brief form is not sufficient to identify the body, because there is another organization of the same name based in Washington, D.C. *World of Learning* (London: Allen & Unwin, 1947–) gives the official form of the Canadian body as National Research Council of Canada.

This is the form, rather than the brief form, that will be used for entry (see figure 1-99).

24.3. VARIANT NAMES. SPECIAL RULES

24.3A. Language

When the name of a corporate body appears in its publications in different languages, the official language of the body is used for the heading. In countries such as Canada, where there is more than one official language, if one of the languages is English, use the English-language form. The Canadian School Library Association is an example of such a corporate body (see figure 17-6).

None of the national libraries issuing rule interpretations applies the alternative rule (footnote 7) (Howarth, at 24.3A).

24.3B. Language. International bodies

Use the English form, if one exists, for works issued by an international body (see, for example, the International Federation of Library Associations, figure 2-11).

24.3C. Conventional name

24.3C2. Ancient and international bodies. This rule is limited to bodies of ancient origin or those international in character with names that have become established in an English form in English-language usage. With a directive that is analogous to that given in 22.3B3 for a similar situation,

Figure 17-6.   One of official languages is English

110 2	‡a Canadian School Library Association.
245 10	‡a Standards of library service for Canadian schools / ‡c recommended by the Canadian School Library Association.
260	‡a Toronto : ‡b Ryerson Press, ‡c c1967.
300	‡a xii, 68 p. ; ‡c 23 cm.
504	‡a Includes bibliographical references.

Title page

Standards of Library Service
for Canadian Schools
recommended by the
Canadian School Library Association
Association canadienne des bibliothèques scolaires
The Ryerson Press

Authority
110 20 ‡a Canadian School Library Association
410 20 ‡a Canadian Library Association. ‡b Canadian School Library Association
410 20 ‡a Association canadienne des bibliothèques scolaires
410 20 ‡a Canadian Library Association. ‡b Association canadienne des bibliothèques scolaires

the cataloger is told to enter such a body in the English-language form of its name. Check English-language reference sources to determine the name when in doubt.

The Council of Trent is such a body. It is listed in *Encyclopedia Americana* (1993) and the *New Catholic Encyclopedia* (1967) as the "Council of Trent." The heading for this body will be the one found in these sources (see figure 17-7). References will be made from its original Latin name and its name entered subordinately to its parent body, the Catholic Church. The references in the 4XX fields of the authority record will display:

Concilium Tridentinum (1545-1563)
    search under
Council of Trent (1545-1563)

Catholic Church. Council of Trent (1545-1563)
    search under
Council of Trent (1545-1563)

Catholic Church. Concilium Tridentinum (1545-1563)
    search under
Council of Trent (1545-1563)

Figure 17-7.   Ancient and international body

111 2	‡a Council of Trent ‡d (1545-1563)
240 10	‡a Canones et decreta. ‡l English & Latin
245 10	‡a Canons and decrees of the Council of Trent : ‡b original text / ‡c with English translation by H. J. Schroeder.
260	‡a St. Louis, Mo. : ‡b B. Herder, ‡c 1941.
300	‡a xxxiii, 608 p. ; ‡c 24 cm.
700 1	‡a Schroeder, H. J. ‡q (Henry Joseph), ‡d 1875-1942.

Title page

Canons and Decrees
of the
Council of Trent
original text
with English translation
by
Rev. H. J. Schroeder, O.P.
B. Herder Book Co.
15 & 17 South Broadway, St. Louis, Mo.
and
33 Queen Square, London, W.C.

Authority
111 20 ‡a Council of Trent ‡d (1545-1563)
411 20 ‡a Concilium Tridentinum ‡d (1545-1563)
410 20 ‡a Catholic Church. ‡b Council of Trent ‡d (1545-1563)
410 20 ‡a Catholic Church. ‡b Concilium Tridentinum ‡d (1545-1563)

24.3D. Religious orders and societies

As with other ancient and international bodies, the English-language form should be chosen for entry. The Redemptorists are such a body. Although they originated in Italy, they should be entered in the conventional English form rather than the language of their country of origin. The *Encyclopaedia Britannica* (1993) lists them as "Redemptorists," and also as "Congregation of the Most Holy Redeemer," as well as "C. SS. R." The title page of figure 17-8 has a Latin form. All these forms should be given as 4XX cross-references in the authority record. Note that as in all languages that decline nouns (see figure 17-1 and corresponding text), Latin names should be given in headings and references in the nominative case only, not necessarily in the case in which they appear in the source. In this case, references are made for "Congregatio . . ." not "Congregationi . . ." (as the name appears on the title page).

Figure 17-8.   Religious orders and societies

```
110 2    ‡a Redemptorists.
245 10   ‡a Documenta authentica facultatum et gratiarum spiritualium : ‡b quas Congregationi
         SS. Redemptoris S. Sedes concessit sive directe, sive per communicationem cum aliis
         institutis in usum presbyterorum ejusdem congregationis ad integrum descripta et in unum
         collecta.
260      ‡a Ratisbonae : ‡b F. Pustet, ‡c 1903.
300      ‡a xi, 642, 231 p. ; ‡c 21 cm.
500      ‡a Includes index.
```

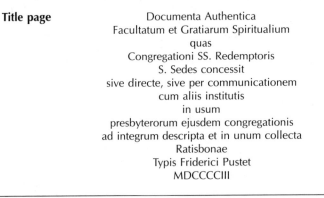

```
Title page               Documenta Authentica
                  Facultatum et Gratiarum Spiritualium
                              quas
                   Congregationi SS. Redemptoris
                        S. Sedes concessit
              sive directe, sive per communicationem
                       cum aliis institutis
                            in usum
                 presbyterorum ejusdem congregationis
              ad integrum descripta et in unum collecta
                          Ratisbonae
                      Typis Friderici Pustet
                          MDCCCCIII
```

```
Authority
110 20   ‡a Redemptorists
410 20   ‡a Congregation of the Most Holy Redeemer
410 20   ‡a Congregatio SS. Redemptoris
410 20   ‡a Congregatio Sanctissimi Redemptoris
410 20   ‡a C. SS. R.
```

24.3E. Governments

If the name of a government appears in varying forms, use the conventional name rather than the official name. Thus, the cataloger will use ''France'' rather than ''République Française''.

A word of caution: because a government is regarded as a corporate body, if its name changes, following 24.1C the cataloger will use the heading appropriate to the date of the original issue of a publication. Note, however, the LC decision, based on British Library practice, regarding the British Isles. Although the name ''Great Britain'' changed to ''United Kingdom'' in 1801, ''Great Britain'' will continue to be used as the name of the government (see *LCRI* 23.2, ''Special decision 3,'' Nov. 1995; and *Handbook*, appendix).

The opposite problem occurs when the jurisdiction changes but the name remains the same. The Library of Congress instructs its catalogers to use one heading for all jurisdictions in such a situation (*LCRI* 24.6, Feb. 4, 1991). The book cataloged in figure 17-9 emanates from the territory of Utah and was published three decades before Utah became a state. Nevertheless, it is entered under ''Utah'', not ''Utah (Territory)''.

Figure 17-9.   Change of jurisdiction

110 1	‡a Utah.
240 10	‡a Laws, etc. (Session laws : 1862-1863)
245 10	‡a Acts, resolutions and memorials passed by the Legislative Assembly of the Territory of Utah, during the twelfth annual session, for the years 1862-63.
260	‡a Palo Alto, Calif. : ‡b R.A. Ogg, ‡c 1936.
300	‡a 15 p. ; ‡c 20 cm.
534	‡p Facsimile reprint: Originally published: ‡c Great Salt Lake City : Elias Smith, public printer, 1863.
710 1	‡a Utah. ‡b Legislative Assembly.

Title page

Acts,
Resolutions and Memorials
passed by the
Legislative Assembly
of the
Territory of Utah
during the
Twelfth Annual Session
for the years 1862-63
Elias Smith, Public Printer
Great Salt Lake City

24.3F. Conferences, congresses, meetings, etc.

This rule is directed to choice among varying names of conferences. For conferences, see the discussion in this *Handbook* under 24.7.

24.3G. Local churches, etc.

Use the name of the church as it appears in its publications in the chief source of information. If the names varies, use the predominant form. If there is no predominant form, choose a name according to order of preference as given under 24.3G. For examples and discussion of the entire rule, see under 24.10 in this *Handbook*.

Additions, Omissions, and Modifications

The foregoing rules have dealt with basic problems of entry. The basic rule is constructed on the same principle as that governing personal names: use the name by which the body is commonly identified. If this name changes, see 24.1C for guidance. If, without actually changing its name, the body uses varying forms of the same name in its publications, 24.2–24.3 give directions for choosing among varying forms. But sometimes the name of the body as it appears in its publications is the same as that of another corporate body. Sometimes the name as it appears does not clearly give the idea that it belongs to a corporate body. Other problems may also enter into the formation of corporate headings that necessitate additions, omissions, and modifications of the name. The following rules give guidance in such cases.

24.4. ADDITIONS

All additions to corporate names will be enclosed in parentheses.

24.4B. Names not conveying the idea of a corporate body

For such bodies, in a ruling analogous to that for the addition of distinguishing terms to personal names (22.19), a suitable general designation or qualification will be added, simply for clarification. The example given in figure 17-10 includes entries for two ships, "Mascarin" and "Marquis de Castries." Neither of these names sounds particularly like that of a corporate body. Therefore, a general designation "Ship" should be added.

Note the last example given under 24.4B1: Friedrich Witte (Firm). Except for the addition of the qualifying word, it would appear to be a personal name. Use this form for subjects or for main or added entry headings only, not for the name of such a firm appearing in the publisher statement.

The Library of Congress has amplified the rules for adding a general designation qualifier to a corporate name containing a personal name.

Figure 17-10.   Addition to name

```
020        ‡a 0908702027
110 2      ‡a Mascarin (Ship)
245 10     ‡a Extracts from journals relating to the visit to New Zealand in May-June 1772 of the
           French ships Mascarin and Marquis de Castries under the command of M.-J. Marion du
           Fresne / ‡c transcriptions and translation by Isabel Ollivier ; with an appendix of charts
           and drawings compiled by Jeremy Spencer.
260        ‡a Wellington : ‡b Alexander Turnbull Library Endowment Trust with Indosuez New
           Zealand, ‡c 1985.
300        ‡a viii, 396 p. : ‡b ill. ; ‡c 26 × 30 cm.
440    0   ‡a Early eyewitness accounts of Maori life ; ‡v 2
546        ‡a English and French.
700 2      ‡a Marion Du Fresne, M.-J. ‡q (Marc-Joseph)
700 1      ‡a Ollivier, Isabel.
710 2      ‡a Marquis de Castries (Ship)
710 2      ‡a Alexander Turnbull Library Endowment Trust.
```

Title page	Extracts from Journals
	relating to the visit to New Zealand
	in May-June 1772 of the French ships
	Mascarin and Marquis de Castries
	under the command of
	M.-J. Marion du Fresne
	Transcriptions and translation
	by Isabel Ollivier
	with an Appendix of charts and drawings
	compiled by Jeremy Spencer
	Alexander Turnbull Library Endowment Trust
	with Indosuez New Zealand Limited
	Wellington 1985

When such a corporate name contains two or more surnames, without fore-names or forename initials, a qualifier need not be added, because such a heading does not resemble a personal name. *LCRI* 24.4B (Jan. 5, 1989) contrasts the heading "Morgan and Morgan" (no qualifier needed) with "B. Morgan and D. Morgan (Firm)" (qualifier needed as the heading could be a pair of personal names).

24.4C. Two or more bodies with the same or similar names

24.4C1. General rule. This rule is disarmingly similar to its predecessor in *AACR2*. In fact, it begins with an identical stipulation, based on general *AACR2R* principles for resolving conflicts in the library catalog. As enunciated in *AACR2R* chapter 22, when two persons have the same name or names so similar that they are likely to be confused, the names are distinguished by spelling out forenames in parentheses (22.18), by adding dates of birth and death (22.17), or by adding a distinguishing term (22.19). Similarly, to distinguish between corporate bodies with identical or similar names, a word or phrase will be added to each name.

A single sentence has been added to the general rule in *AACR2R*, however, which means that, in many instances, qualifiers will be added to corporate headings even when they do not conflict. The rule now states, "Add such a word or phrase to any other name [other than identical names] if the addition assists in the understanding of the nature or purpose of the body." To do this, the cataloger must make a distinction between a government and a nongovernment heading.

Government bodies: If, according to *AACR2R* 24.17, a government body is to be entered directly under its own name rather than as a unit subordinate to the name of the government (see discussion under 24.17), the cataloger will add the name of the government as a qualifier (see *LCRI* 24.4C, "non-conflicts 1b," Feb. 11, 1992; see figure 17-4). Use abbreviations authorized by *AACR2R* Appendix B.14.

Exceptions: a qualifier need not be added to a subordinate government body entered under its own name (24.17) if

1. The name of the government (or an understandable surrogate) is already present in the name. See, for example, figure 17-11 (Arts Council of Great Britain).
2. The government body is an institution (school, library, laboratory, hospital, archive, museum, prison, etc.).

Thus, the heading "Library of Congress" needs no qualifier (see figure 14-5). Nor does the name of a state university such as the University of Arizona or Arizona State University—as long as the name has not been

Figure 17-11.   Government body entered under its own name, not qualified

245 00	‡a Daumier : ‡b paintings and drawings : an exhibition / ‡c organized by the Arts Council of Great Britain at the Tate Gallery.
260	‡a [London] : ‡b The Council, ‡c 1961.
300	‡a 70 p., 36 p. of plates : ‡b ill. ; ‡c 25 cm.
504	‡a Includes bibliographical references (p. 24-25).
700 1	‡a Daumier, Honoré, ‡d 1808-1879.
710 2	‡a Arts Council of Great Britain.
710 2	‡a Tate Gallery.

Title page

Daumier
Paintings and Drawings
An exhibition organized by
the Arts Council of Great Britain
at the Tate Gallery
The Arts Council of Great Britain 1961

Authority
110 20   ‡a Arts Council of Great Britain
410 10   ‡a Great Britain. ‡b Arts Council of Great Britain

replicated, or as long as it is not likely to be. State university systems with schools in many locations, such as the University of California, generally do not need qualifiers either, because the local place name is normally a part of the name of the branch of the University, as "University of California, Irvine" (figure 17-12; compare the form of the name on the title page with the established heading).

All other corporate bodies: Add a qualifier to names of nongovernment bodies or government institutions (schools, libraries, etc.) when such names are entered directly "if the addition assists in the understanding of the nature or purpose of the body" (24.4C1). In a full discussion of this rule, the Library of Congress has stated that "the use of the undefinable phrase 'nature or purpose' is deliberate, with the intention of letting the cataloger judge the situation—does the addition of a qualifier really improve the heading? In case of doubt, do not add the qualifier" (*LCRI* 24.4C, "non-conflicts 2a," Feb. 11, 1992).

Such exercise of "cataloger judgment" will lead to variations in headings. Catalogers may or may not choose to be influenced by such factors as the distinctiveness of a nonconflicting corporate body's name (a corporate name is distinctive if it includes a personal name or if it includes a geographic term or place name). If it seems useful to show the location of the body, the name of the city or town in which the body is located may be added (see, for example, figures 17-13 and 17-14). Note that when local place name is added, its catalog entry form should be used as shown in 23.4A1, second example. This means that even if the established heading contains the name of the larger geographic entity, the name of the town or city will be qualified by the larger entity. Abbreviation should be used for

Figure 17-12.   Local place name

```
245 00   ‡a Computers and education : ‡b a workshop conference at University of California,
         Irvine / ‡c edited by R.W. Gerard with the assistance of J.G. Miller.
260      ‡a New York : ‡b McGraw-Hill, ‡c c1967.
300      ‡a xxi, 307 p. : ‡b ill. ; ‡c 24 cm.
500      ‡a "Organized by University of California, Irvine, with support of U. S. Office of
         Education ... project no. 5-0997, contract no. OE-5-16-022."
700 1    ‡a Gerard, R. W. ‡q ( Ralph Waldo), ‡d 1900-
700 1    ‡a Miller, J. G.
710 2    ‡a University of California, Irvine.
710 1    ‡a United States. ‡b Office of Education.
```

Title page

Computers and Education
A Workshop Conference at
University of California, Irvine
Edited by R.W. Gerard
With the Assistance of J.G. Miller
McGraw-Hill Book Company
New York   St. Louis   San Francisco
Toronto   London   Sydney

Figure 17-13.   Addition of place

```
020      ‡a 1882723104
100 1    ‡a Bess, Stacey.
245 10   ‡a Nobody don't love nobody : ‡b lessons on love from the School With No Name /
         ‡c Stacey Bess.
260      ‡a Carson City, NV : ‡b Gold Leaf Press, ‡c c1994.
300      ‡a x, 226 p. : ‡b ill. ; ‡c 24 cm.
710 2    ‡a School With No Name (Salt Lake City, Utah)
```

Title page	Nobody Don't Love Nobody Lessons on Love from the School With No Name Stacey Bess Gold Leaf Press

Figure 17-14.   "Inc." omitted in heading—place added

```
100 1    ‡a Carr, William H. ‡q (William Henry), ‡d 1902-
245 14   ‡a The desert speaks : ‡b the story of the Arizona-Sonora Desert Museum, Inc., 1951-
         1973 / ‡c by William H. Carr.
250      ‡a 4th rev. ed.
260      ‡a Tucson, Ariz. : ‡b The Museum, ‡c 1973.
300      ‡a 44 p. : ‡b ill. (1 col.) ; ‡c 23 cm.
710 2    ‡a Arizona-Sonora Desert Museum (Tucson, Ariz.)
```

Title page	The Desert Speaks The Story of the Arizona-Sonora Desert Museum, Inc. 1951-1973 by William H. Carr Founder and Director Emeritus, Arizona-Sonora Desert Museum Fourth Revised Edition, 1973 Arizona-Sonora Desert Museum, Inc. Tucson, Arizona

the larger entity if found in Appendix B.14 (see *LCRI* 24.4C, "non-conflicts 2c," May 19, 1994). Thus, Arizona-Sonora Desert Museum (Tucson, Ariz.) will be the heading rather than Arizona-Sonora Desert Museum (Tucson) (figure 17-14).

Particularly if a nonconflicting corporate heading is not "distinctive," the cataloger may choose to add a local place name qualifier (see figure 1-34 for an example of a nondistinctive corporate name that might be so qualified).

Although the local place name is perhaps the most frequently used qualifier, the cataloger may choose to qualify a corporate heading by the name of a larger place or jurisdiction that reflects the scope of the body's activities. Thus, in figure 17-15, Great Britain may be added as a qualifier to the heading Folklore Society.

In many instances, *AACR2R* 24.12 calls for direct entry of a nongovernment subordinate body (see discussion under 24.12). If in the cataloger's judgment a qualifier is needed, the name of the higher or related body will normally be added as the qualifier. The Edwin A. Fleisher Collection of Orchestral Music is such a body. The name of the higher body (Free Library of Philadelphia) will be used as the qualifier (see figure 17-16).

24.4C6. Year(s). Date may also be used as a qualifier, if the name has been used by two or more bodies that cannot be distinguished by place or related institution. This is rather rare. On the other hand, date(s) should always be added as a qualifier to a named expedition, if available (*LCRI* 24.4C6, Feb. 16, 1994; see figure 17-17).

In summary, the cataloger will add a qualifier (with exceptions noted in discussion above) to the headings for all subordinate government bodies entered directly under their own names. For nongovernment headings, except in the case of a conflict with another identical or similar heading in the catalog, the cataloger will add a qualifier "if the addition assists in the understanding of the nature or purpose of the body" or if such an addition provides useful information. The Library of Congress advises that, in case of doubt, the cataloger should not add the qualifier (*LCRI* 24.4C, "nonconflicts 2a," Feb. 11, 1992). Normally, a qualifier will not be added to the name of an international organization (e.g., International Federation of Library Associations). A national association with a distinctive name will not

Figure 17-15. Qualification by place of jurisdiction

```
020        ‡a 1850752435
245 00     ‡a Aspects of British calendar customs / ‡c edited by Theresa Buckland and Juliette Wood.
260        ‡a Sheffield, England : ‡b Sheffield Academic Press, ‡c 1993.
300        ‡a 188 p. ; ‡b ill., map ; ‡c 24 cm.
440  0     ‡a Mistletoe series ; ‡v 22
500        ‡a "The papers contained in this publication are drawn from the Calendar Customs
           Conference organized by the Folklore Society and the English Folk Dance and Song
           Society in September 1984"--Pref.
700 1      ‡a Buckland, Theresa.
700 1      ‡a Wood, Juliette.
710 2      ‡a Folklore Society (Great Britain)
710 2      ‡a English Folk Dance and Song Society.
```

Title page	Aspects of British Calendar Customs edited by Theresa Buckland and Juliette Wood

Figure 17-16.   Subordinate body entered under its own name

```
020      ‡a 0816179425
110 2    ‡a Edwin A. Fleisher Collection of Orchestral Music (Free Library of Philadelphia)
245 10   ‡a The Edwin A. Fleisher Collection of Orchestral Music in the Free Library of
         Philadelphia : ‡b a cumulative catalog, 1929-1977 / ‡c the Fleisher Collection in the
         Free Library of Philadelphia.
260      ‡a Boston : ‡b G.K. Hall, ‡c c1979.
300      ‡a xix, 956 p. : ‡b ill., music ; ‡c 28 cm.
500      ‡a Includes index.
```

Title page   The Edwin A. Fleisher Collection
                                          of Orchestral Music
                              in the Free Library of Philadelphia
                               a cumulative catalog, 1929-1977
                          The Fleisher Collection in the Free Library
                                          of Philadelphia
                                         G.K. Hall & Co.
                                70 Lincoln Street, Boston, Mass.

Authority
110 20   ‡a Edwin A. Fleisher Collection of Orchestral Music (Free Library of
         Philadelphia)
410 20   ‡a Fleisher Collection of Orchestral Music (Free Library of Philadelphia)
410 20   ‡a Free Library of Philadelphia. ‡b Edwin A. Fleisher Collection of
         Orchestral Music

be qualified (e.g., American Library Association; National Council of Teachers of English). In instances where the rules do not provide specific guidance, the question should be: does the addition of a qualifier clarify or in some other way improve the heading? If not, it probably should not be added.

24.5. OMISSIONS

24.5A. Initial articles

Omit an initial article unless the heading is to file under the article. Thus, the name "The University of Michigan" becomes "University of Michigan"; "The School With No Name" (figure 17-13) becomes "School With No Name." However, "La Jolla (Calif.)," because the name of this city files under the article, retains the article in the heading.

24.5C. Terms indicating incorporation and certain other terms

In most instances, terms indicating incorporation will be omitted from the heading for a corporate body (see Arizona-Sonora Desert Museum, figure 17-14).

Figure 17-17.   Named expedition qualified by date

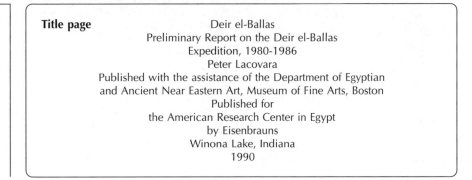

```
020      ‡a 0936770244
111 2    ‡a Deir el-Ballas Expedition ‡d (1980-1986)
245 10   ‡a Deir el-Ballas : ‡b preliminary report on the Deir el-Ballas Expedition, 1980-1986 /
         ‡c [edited by] Peter Lacovara.
260      ‡a Winona Lake, Ind. : ‡b Published for the American Research Center in Egypt by
         Eisenbrauns, ‡c 1990.
300      ‡a ix, 67 p., xvii p. of plates : ‡b ill., maps ; ‡c 29 cm.
440  0   ‡a American Research Center in Egypt reports ; ‡v v. 12
500      ‡a Five plans on 5 folded leaves in pocket.
504      ‡a Includes bibliographical references.
700 1    ‡a Lacovara, Peter.
```

Title page

Deir el-Ballas
Preliminary Report on the Deir el-Ballas
Expedition, 1980-1986
Peter Lacovara
Published with the assistance of the Department of Egyptian
and Ancient Near Eastern Art, Museum of Fine Arts, Boston
Published for
the American Research Center in Egypt
by Eisenbrauns
Winona Lake, Indiana
1990

If such a term is necessary to make it clear that the name is that of a corporate body, include the term (see figure 17-18). If the term indicating incorporation cannot be omitted, follow the punctuation and capitalization customarily used by the corporate body, either including or omitting the comma preceding the term, as appropriate (see figure 17-19).

24.6. GOVERNMENTS. ADDITIONS

24.6A1. Names of governments are used for official publications of the government. See *AACR2R* chapter 23 for general discussion on establishing the name of a government. In some instances, the name of a government requires further differentiation from another identical name than that prescribed in chapter 23. This rule gives guidance on further additions the cataloger may make.

24.6B. When further differentiation is needed, add the type of jurisdiction in English in parentheses following the heading:

Washington (State)
Washington (D.C.)

For further examples and discussion, see 24.17 in this *Handbook*; see also *AACR2R* 21.31–21.36.

Figure 17-18.   "Inc." included

245 00	‡a Flavor research and food acceptance : ‡b a survey of the scope of flavor and associated research / ‡c compiled from papers presented in a series of symposia given in 1956-1957 ; sponsored by Arthur D. Little, Inc.
260	‡a New York : ‡b Reinhold, ‡c c1958.
300	‡a vi, 391 p. : ‡b ill. ; ‡c 24 cm.
504	‡a Includes bibliographical references and index.
710 2	‡a Arthur D. Little, Inc.

Title page

Flavor Research and Food Acceptance
sponsored by Arthur D. Little, Inc.
A survey of the scope of flavor
and associated research
compiled from papers presented in a series of symposia
given in 1956-1957
Reinhold Publishing Corporation
New York
Chapman & Hall, Ltd., London

Authority
110 20   ‡a Arthur D. Little, Inc.
410 20   ‡a Little, Inc.

Figure 17-19.   "Ltd." included

020	‡a 0950245542
245 00	‡a Handbook on Irish genealogy : ‡b how to trace your ancestors and relatives in Ireland / ‡c Heraldic Artists Ltd.
260	‡a Dublin : ‡b Heraldic Artists Ltd., ‡c c1978.
300	‡a 145 p. : ‡b ill., maps ; ‡c 24 cm.
710 2	‡a Heraldic Artists Ltd.

Title page

Handbook on
Irish Genealogy
How to trace your ancestors
and relatives in Ireland
Heraldic Artists Ltd.

Heraldic Artists Ltd., Trinity Street, Dublin

24.7. CONFERENCES, CONGRESSES, MEETINGS, ETC.

A conference, workshop, institute, etc., is a meeting convened "for the purpose of discussing and/or acting on topics of common interest" (*AACR2R*, Appendix D [Glossary]). By terms of 21.1B2d, a named conference may be the main entry for works that record the collective activity of the conference (e.g., its proceedings or collected papers). To be used as the main entry heading, however, the conference name must appear *prominently* in the item being cataloged (see *AACR2R* 0.8 for definition of "prominently").

Before making main entry under the name of a conference, the cataloger must determine whether the conference is a named conference. *AACR1* included guidelines that may still be helpful to the cataloger in deciding whether a conference has a name. According to these guidelines (p. 134), "A conference is considered to have a name if the words referring to it partake more of the character of a specific appellation than of a general description. Such factors as capitalization of initial letters, consistency in wording, and the use of the definite article in references to the conference in the text are evidence supporting the presence of a name" (see also *LCRI* 21.1B1, Nov. 1995). Thus, the workshop-conference cataloged under figure 17-12 is not regarded as having a name, nor is the symposium in figure 17-20. In contrast, see figure 14-6 for an example of a named conference. Named conferences entered directly under the name are recorded in MARC field X11, with the name in subfield ‡a.

Figure 17-20.   Unnamed conference

```
020      ‡a 0931146186
245 00   ‡a Islands, plants, and Polynesians : ‡b an introduction to Polynesian ethnobotany :
         proceedings of a symposium / ‡c sponsored by the Institute of Polynesian Studies,
         Brigham Young University--Hawaii Campus, Laie, Hawaii ; edited by Paul Alan Cox
         and Sandra Anne Banack.
260      ‡a Portland, Or. : ‡b Dioscorides Press, ‡c c1991.
300      ‡a 228 p. : ‡b ill. ; ‡c 27 cm.
504      ‡a Includes bibliographical references and indexes.
700 1    ‡a Cox, Paul Alan.
700 1    ‡a Banack, Sandra Anne.
710 2    ‡a Brigham Young University--Hawaii Campus. ‡b Institute for Polynesian Studies.
```

Title page

Islands, Plants,
and Polynesians
An Introduction to Polynesian Ethnobotany
Edited by
Paul Alan Cox
and
Sandra Anne Banack
Department of Botany and Range Science
Brigham Young University
Provo, Utah 84602
Proceedings of a Symposium Sponsored by
the Institute of Polynesian Studies
Brigham Young University-Hawaii Campus
Laie, Hawaii
Dioscorides Press
Portland, Oregon

The concept of a named conference has been expanded by *AACR2R* to include generic terms, so long as the generic-term name "designates a meeting *of* a body (as opposed to one merely sponsored by a body)" (*LCRI* 21.1B1, Nov. 1995). Generically named meetings of a corporate body will be entered as a conference heading subordinate to the heading for the corporate body (see figure 17-21). Because such meetings are entered subordinately to the corporate body, they will be recorded in MARC field X10; the generic term will follow the name of the body, preceded by full stop - subfield ‡b.

Many conferences do not include the word "conference" as part of their name. In addition, a smaller seminar, symposium, conference, etc., held in conjunction with a larger meeting may be treated as a corporate body if it is a "named" meeting, according to *AACR2R* 21.1B (see figure 17-22).

24.7A. Omissions

The number of the conference is omitted from the name and given in parentheses as the first addition to the name of the conference (24.7B2) (see figure 17-23). Also omitted are terms indicating frequency or date of convocation.

24.7B. Additions

24.7B1. Additions must be in the following order: number of conference, year, and place. The entire addition is enclosed within parentheses and elements are separated by space - colon - space.

24.7B2. Number. If a conference has a number, it is the first of the additions that follow the name of the conference (see figure 17-23). The

---

Figure 17-21.   Meeting of an organization

```
110 2    ‡a Society of American Foresters. ‡b Meeting ‡d (1958 : ‡c Salt Lake City, Utah)
245 10   ‡a Proceedings / ‡c Society of American Foresters meeting, September 28-October 2,
         1958, Hotel Utah, Salt Lake City, Utah.
260      ‡a Washington, D.C. : ‡b The Society, ‡c c1959.
300      ‡a 215 p. : ‡b ill. ; ‡c 23 cm.
```

Title page

Proceedings
Society of American Foresters
Meeting
September 28-October 2, 1958
Hotel Utah
Salt Lake City, Utah
Published by the Society of American Foresters
Mills Building
Washington 6, D.C.
Copyright 1959, by Society of American Foresters

Figure 17-22.   Named conference

```
111 2    ‡a Graduate Record Examinations Board Research Seminar ‡d (1972 : ‡c New Orleans,
         La.)
245 10   ‡a Papers / ‡c presented at the Graduate Record Examinations Board Research Seminar at
         the 12th annual meeting of the Council of Graduate Schools.
260      ‡a Princeton, N.J. : ‡b Educational Testing Service, ‡c 1973.
300      ‡a 38 p. : ‡b ill. ; ‡c 28 cm.
505 0    ‡a Background, purpose, and scope of the GRE Board research program / Bryce Crawford,
         Jr. -- Predicting success in graduate education / Warren W. Willingham -- Research on
         testing and the minority student / Roland L. Flaugher.
710 2    ‡a Council of Graduate Schools in the United States.
```

```
Title page          Papers Presented at the
              Graduate Record Examinations Board Research Seminar
                    at the 12th Annual Meeting of the
                       Council of Graduate Schools
                       Educational Testing Service
                        Princeton, N.J. 08540
                             May, 1973
```

Figure 17-23.   Named conference (omit number from the name, add to qualifier)

```
111 2    ‡a Lunar Science Conference ‡n (5th : ‡d 1974 : ‡c Houston, Tex.)
245 10   ‡a Lunar science V : ‡b abstracts of papers submitted to the Fifth Lunar Science
         Conference / ‡c sponsored by NASA through the Lunar Science Institute and the
         Johnson Space Center, March 18-22, 1974 ; compiled by the Lunar Science Institute.
260      ‡a Houston, Tex. : ‡b The Institute, ‡c 1974.
300      ‡a 2 v. (xxv, 900 p.) : ‡b ill. ; ‡c 28 cm.
504      ‡a Includes bibliographical references.
710 2    ‡a Lunar Science Institute.
710 1    ‡a United States. ‡b National Aeronautics and Space Administration.
710 2    ‡a Lyndon B. Johnson Space Center.
```

```
Title page            Lunar Science V
              Abstracts of Papers Submitted to the
                  Fifth Lunar Science Conference
                     Sponsored by NASA through
                     The Lunar Science Institute
                             and
                     The Johnson Space Center
                        March 18-22, 1974
                Compiled by The Lunar Science Institute
              3303 NASA Road 1, Houston, Texas 77058
```

English ordinal number is recorded in subfield ‡n, following the opening parenthesis. Not all conferences are numbered. Simply omit this element if the conference has no number (cf. figure 17-22). Note, however, that a number may be inferred when information available to the cataloger clearly indicates the position of the meeting within a series of meetings of the same name.

If a conference is an ongoing one (e.g., numbered, occurring biennially, etc.), the Library of Congress will only make a single authority record for the name of the conference, and not make separate authority records for the individual conferences (*LCRI* 24.7B, Nov. 27, 1990).

24.7B3. Date. In almost all cases, the date to be added is the *year only* (see figure 17-24). This is recorded in subfield ‡d. Add specific dates as shown in the last example under 24.7B3 in *AACR2R* only if more than one conference of the same name was held in the same year. Such a coincidence will occur only rarely.

24.7B4. Location. The last element added to the name of the conference, etc., is local place or the institution where the conference was held, recorded in subfield ‡c. An "institution" includes such organizations as schools, libraries, museums, hospitals, etc. A hotel or other similar meeting place is not an institution. If an institution's name appears with the name of the conference in the source from which the conference name was taken, use

Figure 17-24.   Named conference (add year)

020	‡a 0882570978
020	‡a 0882570986 (pbk.)
111 2	‡a Larc Institute on Automated Serials Systems ‡d (1973 : ‡c St. Louis, Mo.)
245	‡a Proceedings of the Larc Institute on Automated Serials Systems held May 24-25, 1973 at the Chase Park Plaza, St. Louis, Missouri / ‡c coordinated by Estelle Brodman ; edited by H. William Axford.
246 18	‡a Automated serials systems
260	‡a Tempe, Ariz. : ‡b Larc Association, ‡c c1973.
300	‡a 128 p. ; ‡c 23cm.
504	‡a Includes bibliographical references.
700 1	‡a Brodman, Estelle, ‡d 1914-
700 1	‡a Axford, H. William.
710 2	‡a Larc Association.

Title page	Proceedings of the Larc Institute on Automated Serials Systems Held May 24-25, 1973 at the Chase Park Plaza St. Louis, Missouri Coordinated by Estelle Brodman Edited by H. William Axford Copyright © 1973 — The Larc Association P.O. Box 27235 Tempe, Arizona 85282 Hardbound ISBN 0-88257-097-8

the institution's name as the qualifier (see figure 14-6). Otherwise prefer the name of the local place where the conference was held (see figure 17-24; *LCRI* 24.7B, Nov. 27, 1990).

A final word of caution regarding conferences: if a conference does not have a name, treat the publication as though no conference were involved. The example shown in figure 17-25 is an unnamed conference sponsored by the Graduate Library School, University of Chicago. The meeting has a generic-term name (annual conference) but is not a meeting *of* the Library School, but rather "one merely sponsored" by it. The nature of the contents of the publication excludes it from consideration as a work to be entered under the heading for the Graduate Library School (see 21.1B2). Instead, it should be regarded as a work by different persons or bodies (21.7B), to be entered under title.

24.8. EXHIBITIONS, FAIRS, FESTIVALS, ETC.

A named exhibition, like a named conference, is regarded as the author of its publications that fall within the scope of 21.1B2d. Rules for exhibitions parallel those for conferences in elements to be added to the name of the

Figure 17-25.   Unnamed conference

020	‡a 0226777316
245 00	‡a Library catalogs : ‡b changing dimensions : the twenty-eighth annual conference of the Graduate Library School, August 5-7, 1963 / ‡c edited by Ruth French Strout.
260	‡a Chicago : ‡b University of Chicago Press, ‡c 1964.
300	‡a 127 p. : ‡b ill. ; ‡c 25 cm.
440 0	‡a University of Chicago studies in library science
500	‡a "Papers ... published originally in the Library quarterly, January 1964"--T.p. verso.
504	‡a Includes bibliographical references.
505 0	‡a Introduction / Ruth French Strout -- The information needs of current scientific research / Herbert Menzel -- The changing character of the catalog in America / David C. Weber -- The catalog in European libraries / Felix Reichmann -- Duplicate catalogs in regional and public library systems / William Spence Geller -- Duplicate catalogs in university libraries / George Piternick -- The National Union and Library of Congress catalogs / John W. Cronin -- Studies related to catalog problems / Henry J. Dubester -- The relation of library catalogs to abstracting and indexing services / Frank B. Rogers -- Dialogues with a catalog / Don R. Swanson.
700 1	‡a Strout, Ruth French, ‡d 1906-
710 2	‡a University of Chicago. ‡b Graduate Library School.

Title page	Library Catalogs
	Changing Dimensions
	The Twenty-Eighth Annual Conference
	of the Graduate Library School
	August 5-7, 1963
	Edited by Ruth French Strout
	The University of Chicago Press
	Chicago and London

exhibition, etc. (see figure 14-11 for an example of a named exhibition). Despite the wording of *AACR2R* 24.8B1, the Library of Congress adds date as a qualifier even if it is a part of the name (*LCRI* 24.8B, Jan. 5, 1989).

24.9. CHAPTERS, BRANCHES, ETC.

See figure 14-13 for an example of a chapter as an addition to the name of a corporate body.

24.10. LOCAL CHURCHES, ETC.

See 24.3G for rules on variant forms of the name of a local church. Entry is to be made under the name by which the church is predominantly identified.

24.10A. Add a general designation if the name of the local church does not convey the idea of a church, as was done to indicate the nature of other corporate bodies (see figure 17-26). The Library of Congress instructs its

Figure 17-26.   Local church

110 2	‡a St. Mary at Hill (Church : London, England)
245 14	‡a The medieval records of a London city church (St. Mary at Hill), A.D. 1420-1559 / ‡c transcribed and edited with facsimiles and an introduction by Henry Littlehales.
260	‡a London : ‡b Published for the Early English Text Society by K. Paul, Trench, Trübner, ‡c 1904-1905.
300	‡a 2 v. : ‡b ill. ; ‡c 23 cm.
490 1	‡a Early English Text Society. Original series ; ‡v no. 125, 128
500	‡a Includes glossarial index.
700 1	‡a Littlehales, Henry, ‡d 1859-
830 0	‡a Early English Text Society (Series). ‡p Original series ; ‡v no. 125, 128.

Title page	The Medieval Records of a London City Church (St. Mary at Hill) A.D. 1420-1559 Transcribed and Edited With Facsimiles and an Introduction by Henry Littlehales London: Published for the Early English Text Society by Kegan Paul, Trench, Trübner & Co., Limited Dryden House, 43, Gerrard Street, Soho, W. 1904

Authority
110 20   ‡a St. Mary at Hill (Church : London, England)
410 20   ‡a Saint Mary at Hill (Church : London, England)

catalogers to add the place in which the church is located even if it is clear from the name of the church (see figures 17-26 and 17-27, and *LCRI* 24.10B, Nov. 17, 1994).

Subordinate and Related Bodies

In many respects the rules governing corporate bodies are analogous to those for personal authors. But in one important respect corporate bodies are unlike personal authors: corporate bodies may have subdivisions, units subordinate or related in some way to the parent body. When dealing with a subordinate body, one of two options is open to the cataloger:

1. If the name of the subordinate body is of such a nature that it implies subordination, the subordinate body will be entered as a subheading under the name of the higher body to which it is related (24.13).

Figure 17-27.   Local church

110 2	‡a St. Bartholomew's Church (London, England)
245 14	‡a The book of the foundation of St. Bartholomew's Church in London, the church belonging to the priory of the same in West Smithfield / ‡c edited from the original manuscript in the British Museum, Cotton Vespasian B IX, by Sir Norman Moore.
260	‡a London : ‡b Published for the Early English Text Society by H. Milford, Oxford University Press, ‡c 1923.
300	‡a xii, 72 p. : ‡b ill. ; ‡c 23 cm.
490 1	‡a Early English Text Society. Original series ; ‡v no. 163
500	‡a From a manuscript formerly belonging to the Priory of St. Bartholomew by an Augustinian canon of the Priory. Of the two versions, Latin (ca.1174-1189) and English (ca. 1400), only the English is printed here.
700 1	‡a Moore, Norman, ‡d 1847-1922.
830 0	‡a Early English Text Society (Series). ‡p Original series ; ‡v no. 163.

Title page

The Book of the Foundation of
St. Bartholomew's Church in London,
The Church Belonging to the Priory
of the Same in West Smithfield.
Edited from the Original Manuscript in the
British Museum,
Cotton Vespasian B IX.
by Sir Norman Moore, Bart., M.D.,
London:
Published for the Early English Text Society
By Humphrey Milford, Oxford University Press,
1923

Authority
110 20   ‡a St. Bartholomew's Church (London, England)
410 20   ‡a Saint Bartholomew's Church (London, England)

2. If the subordinate body has a distinctive name that is sufficient to identify it in the catalog, it will be entered as an independent unit under its own name (24.12).

24.12. GENERAL RULE

This rule is actually only a restatement of the general rule governing headings for corporate bodies (24.1). If a subordinate body has a distinctive, self-sufficient name that it consistently uses in its publications, enter it directly under that name. The Edwin A. Fleisher Collection of Orchestral Music, at the Free Library of Philadelphia, has such a name (see figure 17-16). Note the qualifier, made under the provisions of 24.4C1 (see discussion, *Handbook*).

If a subordinate body is entered directly under its own name, 24.12 calls for a reference from the name of the body as a subheading under the parent organization; the reference for figure 17-16, recorded in the second 410 field of its authority record, displays:

> Free Library of Philadelphia. Edwin A. Fleisher Collection of Orchestral Music
> search under
> Edwin A. Fleisher Collection of Orchestral Music (Free Library of Philadelphia)

24.13. SUBORDINATE AND RELATED BODIES ENTERED SUBORDINATELY

This rule enumerates six types of subordinate bodies that are to be entered as subheadings under the name of a higher body. These types have their origin in Paris Principle 9.61, which calls for entry of a corporate body under a higher body "if this name itself implies subordination or subordinate function, or is insufficient to identify the subordinate body." If the body being entered subordinately includes the name of the parent body, omit this from the subordinate heading. The parent body is recorded in subfield ‡a of the X10 field; the subordinate body in subfield ‡b.

Type 1. A subordinate body whose name includes a word such as "department," "division," etc., or some other word implying that the body is a component part of something else will be entered as a subheading under the higher body. Do not repeat the name of the higher body or any words that link the lower to the higher body.

Figure 17-28 includes an example of Type 1, a subordinate body whose name contains the word "department." The Library of Congress, by policy decision, abbreviates the word "Department" to "Dept." in headings, regardless of the spelling used by the subordinate body (*LCRI*, Appendix B.9, Jan. 5, 1989). This is also the policy of the National Library of Canada (Howarth, at chapter 24, p. 1). This abbreviation occurs in the *heading only*. When transcribing the title and statement of responsibility area, the cata-

Figure 17-28.   Subordinate body—Type 1

```
020      ‡a 0824084594 (alk. paper)
110 20   ‡a American Museum of Natural History. ‡b Dept. of Library Services.
245 10   ‡a Catalog of the American Museum of Natural History film archives / ‡c American
         Museum of Natural History, Department of Library Services ; edited by Nina J. Root.
260      ‡a New York : ‡b Garland Pub., ‡c 1987.
300      ‡a xxiv, 410 p. : ‡b ill. ; ‡c 23 cm.
440  0   ‡a Garland reference library of the humanities ; ‡v vol. 723
504      ‡a Includes bibliographical references and index.
700 1    ‡a Root, Nina J.
```

Title page	Catalog of the American Museum of Natural History Film Archives American Museum of Natural History Department of Library Services edited by Nina J. Root Garland Publishing, Inc. • New York & London 1987

loger will follow spelling as it is found in the prescribed source (see figure 17-28; compare the name in the statement of responsibility with the heading).

Type 2. If the name of a committee, etc., is worded in such a fashion that it implies administrative subordination to a higher body, it will be entered as a subheading under the name of the higher body (for an example, see figure 17-29).

The Library of Congress has issued a supplementary list of words in English, French, and Spanish that normally imply administrative subordination, in addition to "committee" and "commission" as given under *AACR2R* 24.13 "Type 2." If a subordinate body's name includes one of the words on the following list, it is probably governed by this rule (*LCRI* 24.13, "Type 2," Nov. 1995).

English

administration

administrative . . .
    (e.g., administrative office)

advisory . . . (e.g., advisory panel)

agency

authority

board

bureau

directorate

executive

. . . group (e.g.,
    work group)

inspectorate

office

panel

secretariat

service

task force

working party

French

administration

agence

bureau

cabinet

comité

commissariat

commission

délégation

direction

groupe de . . .

inspection

mission

office

secrétariat

service

Spanish

administración

agencia

asesoría

comisaría

comisión

comité

consejería

coordinación

delegación

diputación

dirección

directoria

fiscalía

gabinete

gerencia

grupo de . . .

jefatura

junta

negociado

oficina

secretaría

secretariado

servicio

superintendencia

For bodies with names in English, French, or Spanish, only names containing one or more of the words listed above are to be treated according to Type 2 (*LCRI* 24.13, "Type 2," Nov. 1995).

Type 3. Some subordinate or related bodies have names so general that the name of a higher body is needed for identification. The Library of Congress interprets "general in nature" to mean containing neither distinctive elements (e.g., proper nouns or adjectives) nor subject words. "Friends of the Libraries" is an example (see figure 17-30). Enter such a body as a subheading under the name of the higher body. On the other hand, by the Library of Congress definition, "Fine Arts Museum" and "Music Archive" are *not* general in nature and should be entered directly (probably with qualifiers) (*LCRI* 24.13, "Type 3," Jan. 5, 1989).

Type 4. Although somewhat akin to Type 3, this type of corporate body, which is to be entered as a subdivision under the name of the body to which it is subordinate, is new to *AACR2R*. Occasionally the name of a subordinate unit does not suggest the idea that it is a corporate body at all. Referring to the examples in *AACR2R*, "Collection Development" and "Corporate Public Relations" sound like concepts or processes rather than names of organized units of an institution or corporation. Although such names are relatively rare, it is well to have them delineated. When they occur, they will be added as subordinate bodies under the name of the higher body to which they belong.

Figure 17-29. Subordinate body—Type 2

245 10 ‡a Adventuring with books : ‡b a book list for elementary schools / ‡c prepared by Elizabeth Guilfoile, editorial chairman, and the Committee on the Elementary School Book List of the National Council of Teachers of English.
260 ‡a New York, N.Y. : ‡b New American Library, ‡c c1966.
300 ‡a 256 p. : ‡b ill. ; ‡c 18 cm.
490 0 ‡a A Signet book ; ‡v T2914
504 ‡a Includes bibliographical references.
700 1 ‡a Guilfoile, Elizabeth.
710 2 ‡a National Council of Teachers of English. ‡b Committee on the Elementary School Book List.

Title page

Adventuring with Books
A Book List for Elementary Schools
Prepared by
Elizabeth Guilfoile, Editorial Chairman
and the Committee on the Elementary School Book List
of the
National Council of Teachers of English
A Signet Book
Published by The New American Library
P.O. Box 2310, Grand Central Station
New York, N.Y. 10017

Figure 17-30. Subordinate body—Type 3

022 0 ‡a 0010-8669
245 00 ‡a Coranto.
260 ‡a Los Angeles : ‡b Friends of the Libraries, University of Southern California, ‡c 1963-
300 ‡a v. : ‡b ill. ; ‡c 25 cm.
310 ‡a Annual, ‡b 1981-
321 ‡a Semiannual, ‡b 1963-1977
362 0 ‡a Vol. 1, no. 1 (Fall 1963)-
500 ‡a Title from cover.
515 ‡a Vol. 11, no. 2 never published; vol. 12, 1983 not numbered.
515 ‡a Publication suspended 1978-1980.
550 ‡a Journal of the Friends of the Libraries, University of Southern California.
710 2 ‡a University of Southern California. ‡b Friends of the Libraries.

Title page

Coranto
Journal of the Friends of the Libraries
University of Southern California : Fall 1963

Contents page

Coranto
Volume 1 • Los Angeles, Fall 1963 • Number 1
Ruth Pryor, Editor
Published twice a year

Type 5. As with the headings covered by Type 3, those covered by Type 5 would be incomplete, ambiguous, and insufficient to provide proper identification for the subordinate unit if they were entered independently. Type 5 is limited to names of university schools or colleges that simply are descriptive of the field of study (see figure 17-20).

Type 6. If the subordinate body uses in its publication a name that includes the *entire* name of the higher body, it will be entered as a subheading under the name of the higher body. The "entire name" means the name that was selected for the heading, *excluding* additions made by the cataloger, such as qualifiers, etc. (*LCRI* 24.13, "Type 6," Feb. 1, 1989). The name of the higher body is not repeated as part of the subheading (see figure 17-31).

Notice two of the examples in *AACR2R* under 24.12. "BBC Symphony Orchestra" is not a name that includes the entire name of the body (British Broadcasting Company). See also the example "Harvard Law School." As with BBC, the name of the Law School does not include the entire name of the higher body (Harvard University). Therefore, these subordinate bodies are entered under their own names directly; a reference is made, however, from the name of the higher body with the lower body entered subordinately.

24.14. DIRECT OR INDIRECT SUBHEADING

Sometimes a corporate body that is to be entered as a subdivision is part of a whole chain or hierarchy of agencies, each dependent on the one above it. Entry of the lowest link of the chain, the most subordinate of the subordinate units, can present problems. Sometimes it is necessary to give the entire hierarchy, as in the third example under 24.14 in *AACR2R*. In the example, each of the elements in the hierarchy depends directly on the one above it: "Board of Directors" is a Type 3 name; "Resources and Technical Services Division" is a Type 1 name; the board's name is meaningless with-

Figure 17-31.   Subordinate body—Type 6

```
110 2    ‡a University of New Mexico. ‡b Library.
245 10   ‡a Manuscripts and records in the University of New Mexico Library / ‡c by Albert James
         Diaz.
260      ‡a Albuquerque : ‡b The Library, ‡c 1957.
300      ‡a 57 p. ; ‡c 24 cm.
700 1    ‡a Diaz, Albert James.
```

Title page

Manuscripts and Records
in the University of New Mexico Library
by Albert James Diaz
University of New Mexico Library • Albuquerque
1957

out the name of the division to which it is attached; the division has a name that implies subordination and so it must be attached to that of the parent organization, American Library Association.

But as the above example demonstrates, such a practice often results in a very long heading. More important, over the years the intervening bodies between the first and last link of the hierarchy may change, or control of the subordinate agency may be shifted from one higher body to another. When this happens, if all of the links of the hierarchy have been displayed in the heading, the heading must be changed. Such a change often means extensive recataloging. Rule 24.14 offers a good solution to the problem. Enter the subdivision at hand directly under the first larger body that can stand independently. Leave out the intermediate units as long as they are not needed to clarify the function of the smaller body. Figure 14-9 is a good example of this practice. The hierarchy for this body, as shown on the title page of the book, is

American Library Association

Resources and Technical Services Division

Copying Methods Section

Library Standards for Microfilm Committee.

The lowest element of the hierarchy that can be entered independently is "American Library Association." The name "Library Standards for Microfilm Committee" is not likely to be used by any other body that is a subordinate unit of the American Library Association. In addition, the intermediate links of the hierarchy are not needed to identify or clarify the function of the committee. Therefore, the heading will be "American Library Association. Library Standards for Microfilm Committee."

The first added entry in figure 17-32 is another illustration of 24.14. The hierarchy for this heading is

American Library Association

Division of Cataloging and Classification

Board on Cataloging Policy and Research.

The heading is "American Library Association. Board on Cataloging Policy and Research." The intermediate link was dropped because the function of the committee and its identity are clear without it. Also, no other division of ALA is likely to have a Board on Cataloging Policy and Research.

Notice the difference between the subheading "Board on Cataloging Policy and Research" and the subheading that is the lowest element in the hierarchy of the second example given under 24.14 in *AACR2R*, "Policy and Research Committee." Any of the sections or divisions, etc., of the American Library Association might have a Policy and Research Committee. Its function and identity are not clear without the addition of the next higher unit, the "Cataloging and Classification Section." However, no other ALA division is likely to have a unit called "Board on Cataloging Policy and Research." Thus, the name of the division may be omitted.

As just shown, the cataloger cannot always drop all of the intervening links of a hierarchy. If the bottom link is of a type that is dependent on the

Figure 17-32.   Direct subheading

```
100 1    ‡a Lubetzky, Seymour.
245 10   ‡a Cataloging rules and principles : ‡b a critique of the A.L.A. rules for entry and a
         proposed design for their revision / ‡c prepared for the Board on Cataloging Policy and
         Research of the A.L.A. Division of Cataloging and Classification by Seymour Lubetzky.
260      ‡a Washington : ‡b Processing Department, Library of Congress, ‡c 1953.
300      ‡a ix, 65 p. ; ‡c 24 cm.
504      ‡a Includes bibliographical references.
710 2    ‡a American Library Association. ‡b Board on Cataloging Policy and Research.
710 2    ‡a Library of Congress. ‡b Processing Dept.
```

Title page
```
                      Cataloging Rules and Principles
                 A Critique of the A.L.A. Rules for Entry
                  and a Proposed Design for their Revision
         Prepared for the Board on Cataloging Policy and Research
            of the A.L.A. Division of Cataloging and Classification
                          by Seymour Lubetzky
                Consultant on Bibliographic and Cataloging Policy
                 Processing Department, Library of Congress
                          Washington : 1953
```

Authority
```
110 20   ‡a American Library Association. ‡b Board on Cataloging Policy and
         Research
410 20   ‡a American Library Association. ‡b Division of Cataloging and
         Classification. ‡b Board on Cataloging Policy and Research
```

next link according to the stipulations of 24.13 Types 1–6, that link must be included. For example, referring once more to figure 17-32, suppose the cataloger has a publication of the Program Committee of ALA's Board on Cataloging Policy and Research. If all of the intervening links between Program Committee and American Library Association were dropped, the entry would be "American Library Association. Program Committee." It would give the impression that this body was a Program Committee for the entire association, not just for the Board on Cataloging Policy and Research. Therefore, the cataloger would need to include the name of the subdivision that identifies which Program Committee this one is. The heading would be "American Library Association. Board on Cataloging Policy and Research. Program Committee."

If the cataloger has omitted some of the connecting links in a hierarchy in setting up a heading, a reference must be made that includes at least the immediately superior body. Although 24.14A is a sensible rule, the user of the catalog cannot be expected to know which intermediate bodies have been dropped, and so help is given in the form of a reference. The authority record for the Board on Cataloging Policy and Research (figure 17-32) should contain a reference including the intermediate body in a 410 field, as shown. It will display:

> American Library Association. Division of Cataloging and Classification. Board on Cataloging Policy and Research
> search under
> American Library Association. Board on Cataloging Policy and Research

Special Rules

24.15. JOINT COMMITTEES, COMMISSIONS, ETC.

24.15A. A joint committee will be entered under its own name if it is made up of representatives of two or more *separate, independent* corporate bodies. A joint committee sponsored the conference in the example shown in figure 17-33.

Figure 17-33.   Joint committee entered under its own name

```
020      ‡a 0838901492
111 2    ‡a Conference on Total Community Library Service ‡d (1972 : ‡c Washington, D.C.)
245 10   ‡a Total community library service : ‡b report of a conference / ‡c sponsored by the Joint
         Committee of the American Library Association and the National Education Association ;
         edited by Guy Garrison.
260      ‡a Chicago : ‡b ALA, ‡c 1973.
300      ‡a x, 138 p. ; ‡c 23 cm.
504      ‡a Includes bibliographical references (p. 116-121).
700 1    ‡a Garrison, Guy Grady, ‡d 1927-
710 2    ‡a Joint Committee of the American Library Association and the National Education
         Association.
```

Title page

Total Community Library Service
Report of a Conference
Sponsored by the
Joint Committee of the American Library Association and the
National Education Association
Edited by Guy Garrison
American Library Association
Chicago 1973

Authority
110 20   ‡a Joint Committee of the American Library Association and the National Education Association
410 20   ‡a American Library Association. ‡b Joint Committee of the American Library Association and the National Education Association
410 20   ‡a National Education Association (U.S.) ‡b Joint Committee of the American Library Association and the National Education Association

Make reference from each of the corporate bodies involved in the joint committee, with the name of the joint committee as subdivision, as long as not more than three corporate bodies are involved. The reference generated from the first 410 field of the authority record will display:

> American Library Association. Joint Committee of the American Library
> Association and the National Education Association
> search under
> Joint Committee of the American Library Association and the National
> Education Association

A similar reference displays from the heading for the National Education Association.

When a joint committee, commission, etc., is composed of representatives of more than three corporate bodies, make a reference as shown above only from the name of the first corporate body mentioned in the item (*LCRI* 24.15A, Jan. 5, 1989).

24.15B. If the bodies making up a joint committee are themselves subordinate to a single larger body, the joint committee will be entered as a subordinate heading under the name of the larger body. The many joint committees of the United States Congress are entered as subdivisions under "United States. Congress." See also the example in *AACR2R* under 24.15B.

Government Bodies and Officials

Under the 1949 ALA rules, governments and their agencies, with certain specified exceptions, were regarded as authors of publications for which they were responsible. Such publications were to be entered under the name of the government, with the agency as a subheading (ALA 1949 rules 71–72). Catalogers were required to determine whether there was any administrative or financial link between the name of a corporate body and a government jurisdiction in order to be certain that this rule was followed. All such headings had to be looked up in official manuals such as (for the United States government) the *United States Government Organization Manual* or another appropriate reference source. The rule caused catalogers much grief, and it was difficult to apply consistently.

In an attempt to solve the difficulties and inconsistencies of the 1949 rules, the editors of *AACR1* arrived at a general rule for government headings, which, in its own way, was even more complex than the ALA 1949 rules it replaced. The rule was based on the function of the agency rather than type of name; an agency that exercised legislative, judicial, or executive functions was to be entered as a subheading under the name of the government. All other agencies were to be entered under their own names. To aid catalogers in determining agencies that were not regarded as legislative, judicial, or executive, the editors drew up an elaborate list of seven types of agencies with numerous examples, all to be entered under their own names (rule 78). But almost immediately the cumbersome rule fell into difficulties; exceptions were made for government agencies whose names included terms suggesting subordination, such as "bureau . . . administration," etc., regardless of the function of the body. The rule proved too complex to be satisfactory.

The present rule adheres to the same principles governing nongovernment bodies as set forth in 24.12 and 24.13; in fact, these two rules closely parallel 24.17 and 24.18 and should be compared. As with the rule for nongovernment bodies, the general rule for choice of entry either subordinately or independently may be summarized: if the government agency has a unique name not likely to be duplicated elsewhere and one that does not include terms that suggest dependent status, it should be entered under its own name. If the name of the agency includes terms that suggest dependent status or that need the name of the government to identify the agency, the agency should be entered as a subordinate unit under the name of the government.

24.17. GENERAL RULE

Enter a subordinate government agency under its own name if its name is unique and if it does not contain terms that suggest dependent status.

The Library of Congress has a name that is unique. Rule 24.17 stipulates that a reference will be made from the name of the agency entered as a subheading, generated by its authority record:

110 20 ‡a Library of Congress
410 20 ‡a United States. ‡b Library of Congress

This displays:

United States. Library of Congress
　　search under
Library of Congress

This reference is particularly important because under 1949 rules most of these agencies were entered as subheadings under the name of the government; many library users may seek them under government headings.

Likewise, the National Gallery of Art has a name that does not contain words suggesting dependent status (see figure 17-34). Reference will be made from the authority record as shown, which displays:

United States. National Gallery of Art
　　search under
National Gallery of Art (U.S.)

The British government-controlled Bank of England also has a name that sounds independent (see figure 17-35). Reference will be made from the authority record; this displays:

Great Britain. Bank of England
　　search under
Bank of England

Note the addition of the name of the governmental jurisdiction as a qualifier at the end of headings for certain subordinate government bodies

Figure 17-34.   Government body entered under its own name

```
110 2    ‡a National Gallery of Art (U.S.)
245 10   ‡a American paintings and sculpture : ‡b an illustrated catalogue / ‡c National Gallery of
         Art.
260      ‡a Washington : ‡b The Gallery, ‡c 1970.
300      ‡a 192 p. : ‡b ill. ; ‡c 23 cm.
500      ‡a Includes index.
```

Title page   National Gallery of Art
                        American Paintings and Sculpture
                          an Illustrated Catalogue
                             Washington 1970

Authority
110 20   ‡a National Gallery of Art (U.S.)
410 10   ‡a United States. ‡b National Gallery of Art

Figure 17-35.   Government body entered under its own name

```
245 00   ‡a United Kingdom overseas investments, 1938 to 1948.
260      ‡a London : ‡b Bank of England, ‡c 1950.
300      ‡a 33 p. ; ‡c 25 cm.
500      ‡a Cover title.
710 2    ‡a Bank of England.
```

Title page   United Kingdom Overseas Investments
                               1938 to 1948
                            Bank of England, 1950

Authority
110 20   ‡a Bank of England
410 10   ‡a Great Britain. ‡b Bank of England

entered under their own names. See discussion in this *Handbook* at 24.4C for explanation of this practice. Jurisdictional qualifiers need not be added to governmental *institutions* with names that are unique or that are highly unlikely to be duplicated. The Library of Congress is such an institution; on the other hand, the National Gallery of Art is a name that is likely to be duplicated in other English-speaking countries. Therefore, despite the fact that it, like the Library of Congress, is an "institution" (see discussion under 24.4C and definition at *LCRI* 24.4C, "non-conflicts 2a," Feb. 11, 1992), U.S. should be added as a qualifier.

The Arts Council of Great Britain, controlled by the British government, has a distinctive name that sounds independent (see figure 17-11). Reference in its authority record will display:

> Great Britain. Arts Council of Great Britain
>   search under
> Arts Council of Great Britain

The government agency that calls itself the Ontario Geological Survey is a further example of a name that does not contain terms implying subordination. It will be entered directly under its own name. Because the name contains the name of the government, no qualifier is needed. Furthermore, there is no equivalent of 24.13 Type 6 (name that includes the entire name of the higher body) in 24.18, so although the name includes "Ontario," it is not entered subordinately (*LCRI* 24.18, Jan. 5, 1989; see figure 17-36).

Figure 17-36.   Government body entered under its own name

020	‡a 0772989761 (pt. 1)
020	‡a 077298977X (pt. 2)
020	‡a 0772989753 (2 v. set)
245 00	‡a Geology of Ontario / ‡c edited by P.C. Thurston ... [et al.].
260	‡a [Toronto] : ‡b Ontario Ministry of Northern Development and Mines, ‡c 1991-1992.
300	‡a 2 v. (vii, 1525 p.) : ‡b ill., maps ; ‡c 29 cm. + ‡e 34 maps in case (29 cm.)
490 1	‡a Special volume / Ontario Geological Survey, ‡x 0827-181X ; ‡v 4
500	‡a "This publication celebrates the centenary of the Ontario Bureau of Mines ... later ... the Ontario Geological Survey"--p. 3.
504	‡a Includes bibliographical references and index.
700 1	‡a Thurston, P. C.
710 1	‡a Ontario. ‡b Ministry of Northern Development and Mines.
710 2	‡a Ontario Geological Survey.
830 0	‡a Special volume (Ontario Geological Survey) ; ‡v 4.

Title page	Ontario Geological Survey Special Volume 4 Part 1 Geology of Ontario Edited by P.C. Thurston, H.R. Williams, R.H. Sutcliffe and G.M. Stott 1991 Ontario Ministry of Northern Development and Mines

Authority
110 20   ‡a Ontario Geological Survey
410 10   ‡a Ontario. ‡b Division of Mines. ‡b Geological Survey

The full hierarchy of the survey is:

Ontario

Ministry of Natural Resources

Division of Mines

Ontario Geological Survey

Reference will be made, following the stipulations of 26.3A7, from the next body up, as shown in the authority record. This displays:

Ontario. Division of Mines. Geological Survey
    search under
Ontario Geological Survey

24.18. GOVERNMENT AGENCIES ENTERED SUBORDINATELY

This rule parallels 24.13; the types of corporate bodies that will be entered as subheadings under the name of a higher body as given in 24.13 are closely correlated, and in some cases identical, to the types of government agencies that will be entered under the name of the government. In both instances, the principle is the same: if the name of the subordinate unit contains terms that imply subordination, or that are incomplete or not clearly identified without the name of the governmental jurisdiction, the agencies will be entered as subordinate bodies under the name of the government. The rule is based strictly on the way the agency's name is formulated.

Type 1. If an agency's name includes a word, such as "department," "section," "service," "bureau," etc. (or foreign equivalents), that implies that the agency is subordinate to a higher body, enter the agency subordinately. Figure 17-37, a publication of the State of Virginia's Department of Historic Resources includes an example of such a heading (see discussion, *Handbook*, under 24.13 "Type 1" for abbreviation of "Dept.").

Type 2. Notice the exact parallel between this rule and 24.13 "Type 2." A good rule of thumb for a decision about whether "the name of the government is required for the identification of the agency" or not is if the name of the commission, committee, etc., is made up simply of generic words signifying its function or if (as with government agencies covered by 24.17) it has a distinctive name. The Commission on Obscenity and Pornography (figure 17-38) needs the name of the government for identification.

As it did with nongovernment agencies subsumed under 24.13 "Type 2," the Library of Congress has issued a list of terms in English, French, and Spanish to help catalogers determine whether a subordinate government agency falls under the jurisdiction of 24.18 "Type 2." For bodies with names in these languages, only those containing one or more of the words

Figure 17-37.   Subordinate agency—Type 1

```
020      ‡a 0813916003
020      ‡a 0813916011 (pbk.)
245 00   ‡a Virginia landmarks of Black history : ‡b sites on the Virginia Landmarks Register and
         the National Register of Historic Places / ‡c prepared by the Virginia Department of
         Historic Resources ; edited by Calder Loth.
260      ‡a Charlottesville : ‡b University Press of Virginia, ‡c 1995.
300      ‡a xx, 201 p. : ‡b ill. ; ‡c 28 cm.
440   0  ‡a Carter G. Woodson Institute series in Black studies
500      ‡a Includes index.
700 1    ‡a Loth, Calder, ‡d 1943-
710 1    ‡a Virginia. ‡b Dept. of Historic Resources.
```

Title page

Virginia Landmarks of
Black history
Sites on the Virginia Landmarks Register
and the National Register of Historic Places
Prepared by the Virginia Department of Historic Resources
Edited by Calder Loth
University Press of Virginia
Charlottesville and London

Figure 17-38.   Subordinate agency—Type 2

```
110 1    ‡a United States. ‡b Commission on Obscenity and Pornography.
245 14   ‡a The report of the Commission on Obscenity and Pornography / ‡c special introduction
         by Clive Barnes.
260      ‡a Toronto ; ‡a New York : ‡b Bantam Books, ‡c 1970.
300      ‡a xviii, 698 p. : ‡b ill. ; ‡c 18 cm.
500      ‡a "A New York Times book."
504      ‡a Includes bibliographical references.
```

Title page

A New York Times Book
The Report of the Commission on
Obscenity and Pornography
Special Introduction by Clive Barnes of
the New York Times
Bantam Books
Toronto • New York • London

listed below will be treated according to this type (*LCRI* 24.18, "Type 2," Nov. 1995).

English
administration
administrative . . .
   (e.g., administrative office)
advisory . . . (e.g., advisory
   panel)
agency
authority
board
bureau
directorate
executive
. . . group (e.g., work group)
inspectorate
office
panel
secretariat
service
task force
working party

French
administration
agence
bureau
cabinet
comité
commissariat
commission
délégation
direction
groupe de . . .

inspection
mission
office
secrétariat
service

Spanish
administración
agencia
asesoría
comisaría
comisión
comité
consejería
coordinación
delegación
diputación
dirección
directoria
fiscalía
gabinete
gerencia
grupo de . . .
jefatura
junta
negociado
oficina
secretaría
secretariado
servicio
superintendencia

Type 3. An agency with a name that is general in nature or that does no more than indicate a geographic, chronological, or numbered or lettered subdivision of the government or one of its agencies is entered subordinately.

The Library of Congress has interpreted the word "general" to mean a name that contains no proper nouns, adjectives, or subject words. Such terms as "Research Center, "Library," or "Technical Laboratory" are examples of general names that should be entered under the name of the government. On the other hand, in headings established since 1988, such general words and phrases plus the term "national" or "state" or their equivalents in foreign languages are *not* considered to be examples of 24.18 "Type 3" (*LCRI* 24.18, "Type 3," Jan. 5, 1989) (previously the interpretation was the opposite to this, so headings have been established both ways in the National Authority File) (see figure 17-39 for an example).

Type 4. This subsection of 24.18 is, like its exact parallel under 24.13 "Type 4," new to *AACR2R*. It includes subordinate government agencies whose names do not convey the idea of a corporate body (see examples in *AACR2R* and discussion under 24.13 "Type 4").

Type 5. A top-level executive agency in a *national* government (cf. *LCRI* 24.18, "Type 5," Jan. 5, 1989) will be entered as a subordinate heading under the name of the government, regardless of whether its name includes words such as "department," "ministry," "administration," or not. However, names of most such agencies do include such terms; in most cases, these agencies are also examples of 24.18 "Type 1," having names that imply that the body is a part of another.

In the example shown in figure 17-40, the heading in the first 710 field is for a Type 5 government agency. Note that according to stipulations of 23.2A, the cataloger will use the English form of name for the government: Austria, rather than Österreich. But the name of the government agency (translated as "Federal Ministry of Agriculture and Forestry") is always to be given in the vernacular. Make reference from the vernacular form of the

Figure 17-39.   Subordinate agency—Type 3

110 1	‡a Great Britain. ‡b Foreign Office. ‡b Library.
245 12	‡a A short title catalogue of books printed before 1701 in the Foreign Office Library / ‡c compiled by Colin L. Robertson.
260	‡a London : ‡b Her Majesty's Stationery Office, ‡c 1966.
300	‡a vii, 176 p. ; ‡c 25 cm.
700 1	‡a Robertson, Colin L.

Title page

Foreign Office
A short Title Catalogue of
Books printed before 1701
in the Foreign Office Library
compiled by
Colin L. Robertson
London
Her Majesty's Stationery Office
1966

Figure 17-40.   Subordinate agency—Type 5

245 00 ‡a Österreichische Waldstandsaufnahme, 1952/56 : ‡b Gesamtergebnis / ‡c
        herausgegeben vom Bundesministerium für Land- und Forstwirtschaft und von der
        Forstlichen Bundes-Versuchsanstalt Mariabrunn in Schönbrunn.
260   ‡a Wien : ‡b Der Bundes-Versuchsanstalt, ‡c 1960.
300   ‡a 323 p. : ‡b ill., maps (some col.) ; ‡c 27 cm.
500   ‡a Final summary report for: Ergebnisse der österreichischen Waldstandsaufnahme,
        1952/56 / herausgegeben vom Bundesministerium für Land- und Forstwirtschaft.
710 1   ‡a Austria. ‡b Bundesministerium für Land- und Forstwirtschaft.
710 2   ‡a Forstliche Bundesversuchsanstalt Mariabrunn.

Title page   Österreichische
                                  Waldstandsaufnahme
                                     1952/56
                                  Gesamtergebnis
                                   herausgegeben
                                       vom
                     Bundesministerium für Land- und Forstwirtschaft
                                   und von der
                     Forstlichen Bundes-Versuchsanstalt Mariabrunn
                                 in Schönbrunn
                                      1960

name of the government, according to the provisions of 26.3A1 in the authority record for the government:

    151 0   Austria
    451 0   Österreich

This displays:

    Österreich
        search under
    Austria

24.19. DIRECT OR INDIRECT SUBHEADING

This rule is parallel to 24.14. It applies only to agencies entered as subheadings of the government according to 24.18. As with nongovernment
corporate bodies, sometimes a government agency is a part of a chain or
hierarchy of agencies, each dependent on the one above it. Also, as with
nongovernment corporate bodies, sometimes one or more of the links in
the chain may be omitted in the heading. See discussion in this *Handbook*
under 24.14 for full explanation.

Figure 17-41 shows a government agency that may be entered directly
under the name of the government. In 1968, the United States Office of

Figure 17-41. Direct subheading

```
245 00   ‡a Criteria for technician education : ‡b a suggested guide.
260      ‡a Washington, D.C. : ‡b U.S. Dept. of Health, Education, and Welfare, Office of
         Education : ‡b For sale by the Supt. of Docs., U.S. G.P.O., ‡c 1968.
300      ‡a vi, 84 p. ; ‡c 24 cm.
504      ‡a Includes bibliographical references (p. 77-78).
500      ‡a OE-80056; Supt. of Docs. catalog no. FS5.280:80056.
710 1    ‡a United States. ‡b Office of Education.
```

Title page

OE-80056
Criteria for Technician Education
A Suggested Guide
U.S. Department of Health, Education, and Welfare
Wilbur J. Cohen, Secretary
Office of Education
Harold Howe II, Commissioner

Verso of title page

November 1968   Superintendent of Documents
Catalog no. FS5.280:80056
United States Government Printing Office
Washington: 1968
For sale by the Superintendent of Documents
U.S. Government Printing Office
Washington, D.C. 20402

Authority

```
110 10   ‡a United States. ‡b Office of Education
410 10   ‡a United States. ‡b Dept. of Health, Education, and Welfare. ‡b Office of
         Education
```

Education was an agency under the control of the Department of Health, Education, and Welfare. The name of the department is not needed to identify or clarify the function of the Office of Education. Furthermore, the name of the agency has not been, nor is it likely to be, used by another agency entered under the United States government. Therefore, the heading will be "United States. Office of Education." Following stipulations of 26.3A7, make reference from the full hierarchy, as shown in the authority record. This displays:

> United States. Dept. of Health, Education, and Welfare. Office of
> Education
> search under
> United States. Office of Education

Special Rules

24.20. Government Officials

This rule covers form of heading for official messages, proclamations, etc., that will be entered under the heading for a head of a government according to 21.4D.

24.20B. Heads of state, etc.

This rule includes governors as well as sovereigns and presidents. Headings for such individuals include the inclusive years of reign or incumbency and the name of the individual (see figure 17-42).

For an example of a corporate heading for the United States president, see figure 1-75. See figure 14-18 for an example of the collective heading used for more than one United States president. See *Handbook* at 21.4D for a discussion of entries and references and the *Handbook* appendix for a list of headings for presidents acting in an official capacity. See also the *Handbook* appendix for an explanation of practice with respect to corporate headings for British sovereigns, as well a list of those headings.

Figure 17-42.   Governor

110 1	‡a California. ‡b Governor (1967-1975 : Reagan)
245 10	‡a Environmental goals and policy / ‡c Ronald Reagan, governor ; John S. Tooker, director, Office of Planning and Research, Governor's Office.
260	‡a Sacramento : ‡b State of California, Governor's Office, ‡c 1972.
300	‡a 86 p. : ‡b ill., maps (some col.) ; ‡c 28 cm.
500	‡a Transmitted to the California Legislature, Apr. 26, 1972.
700 1	‡a Reagan, Ronald.
700 1	‡a Tooker, John S.
710 1	‡a California. ‡b Legislature.
710 1	‡a California. ‡b Office of Planning and Research.

Title page

State of California
Environmental Goals and Policy
Ronald Reagan
Governor
John S. Tooker
Director, Office of Planning and Research
Governor's Office
March 1, 1972

First preliminary page

Ronald Reagan
Governor
State of California
Governor's Office
Sacramento 95814

24.20C. Heads of governments and of international intergovernmental bodies

Official statements from heads of governments aside from those covered by 24.20B are entered under a heading similar in form to that given heads of state, except that dates and names of incumbents are not included in the subheading. As is done for heads of state entered under official title, an added entry will be made for the incumbent (see figure 1-108 for an example).

As previously discussed, by policy decision based on British Library practice, headings for *all* corporate entries dealing with the United Kingdom will be "Great Britain" (*LCRI* 23.2, "Special decision 3," Nov. 1995). The Library of Congress will use the heading "Great Britain. Prime Minister," for example, rather than "United Kingdom. Prime Minister," as shown in *AACR2R* 24.20C. Examples in this text follow LC policy.

24.20E. Other officials

Official statements from a government official who is not a head of a government will be entered under the heading for the agency he or she represents (see figures 17-43 and 17-44). Added entry will be made for the name of the person if the person is prominently named in the publication. An added entry is also to be made, when appropriate, for the name of the

Figure 17-43.   Head of an agency

110 2	‡a Library of Congress.
245 10	‡a Report of the Librarian of Congress on the Bryant memorandum / ‡c submitted to the Joint Committee on the Library.
260	‡a Washington, D.C. : ‡b The Library, ‡c 1962.
300	‡a 54 leaves ; ‡c 27 cm.
500	‡a Signed: L. Quincy Mumford, Librarian of Congress.
700 1	‡a Mumford, L. Quincy ‡q (Lawrence Quincy), ‡d 1903-1982.
710 2	‡a United States. ‡b Congress. ‡b Joint Committee on the Library.

Title page	Report of the Librarian of Congress on the Bryant Memorandum Submitted to the Joint Committee on the Library September 1962 Washington, D.C.

Authority
110 20   ‡a Library of Congress
410 10   ‡a United States. ‡b Library of Congress
410 20   ‡a Librarian of Congress
410 20   ‡a Library of Congress. ‡b Librarian of Congress

Figure 17-44.   Head of an agency

```
110 1    ‡a United States. ‡b General Accounting Office
245 10   ‡a Report to the Congress of the United States : ‡b need to reexamine planned
         replacement and augmentation of high-endurance vessels, western area, United States
         Coast Guard, Treasury Department / ‡c by the Comptroller General of the United States.
260      ‡a Washington : ‡b U.S. General Accounting Office, ‡c 1966.
300      ‡a 28 p. ; ‡c 27 cm.
500      ‡a Cover title.
710 1    ‡a United States. ‡b Congress.
```

Title page

Report to
The Congress of the United States
Need to Reexamine
Planned Replacement and Augmentation of
High-Endurance Vessels
Western Area
United States Coast Guard
Treasury Department
by the Comptroller General
of the United States
February 1966

Authority
110 10   ‡a United States. ‡b General Accounting Office
410 10   ‡a United States. ‡b Comptroller General of the United States

body to which an official report, statement, etc., is transmitted. Reference is made from the title of the official, generated from the 410 fields in the authority records. These (among others) display:

Librarian of Congress
    search under
Library of Congress

United States. Comptroller General of the United States
    search under
United States. General Accounting Office

The Library of Congress has commented on rule 24.20E, stating, "If the chief source gives only the name of the official, nevertheless use the name of the ministry or agency that the official represents in the heading. If necessary, determine the latter from reference sources" (*LCRI* 24.20E, Jan. 5, 1989).

24.21. LEGISLATIVE BODIES

24.21A. Pre-*AACR2* cataloging rules called for "United States. Congress. House of Representatives" to be shortened to "U.S. Congress. House." This practice will be discontinued by a library following *AACR2R*. However, the Library of Congress continues to shorten "House of Representatives" to "House" (*LCRI* 24.21B, Jan. 5, 1989). Examples in this text follow LC policy (see figure 17-45).

24.21B. A committee will be entered as a subheading under the chamber of the legislature to which it is related or under the whole legislature, as appropriate (see figures 17-43 and 17-45).

24.21C. Legislative subcommittees of the U.S. Congress and U.S. state legislatures are an exception to provisions of 24.19 that otherwise call for entry directly under either Congress or the appropriate chamber. Such subcommittees are to be entered under the name of the committee to which each is subordinate (see figure 14-4 as well as 17-46). References should be made from the name subordinated directly, as seen in the authority record for figure 17-46.

24.21D. Apply this rule only if the number of the session is named in the chief source. The required order is as shown in figure 17-47. Do not add number and year unless (1) an entry must be made for the U.S. Congress or one of its chambers as a whole, (2) no entry is appropriate for any subordinate unit (e.g., a committee), *and* (3) the number of the session is named in the chief source (*LCRI* 24.21D, Jan. 5, 1989). Thus, because entry

Figure 17-45.   Legislative committee

```
020      ‡a 0670701653
110 1    ‡a United States. ‡b Congress. ‡b House. ‡b Committee on Un-American Activities.
245 10   ‡a Thirty years of treason : ‡b excerpts from hearings before the House Committee on
         Un-American Activities, 1938-1968 / ‡c edited by Eric Bentley.
260      ‡a New York : ‡b Viking, ‡c c1971.
300      ‡a xxviii, 991 p. ; ‡c 24 cm.
500      ‡a Includes index.
700 1    ‡a Bentley, Eric, ‡d 1916-
```

Title page	Thirty Years of Treason Excerpts from Hearings Before the House Committee on Un-American Activities, 1938-1968 Edited by Eric Bentley New York / The Viking Press

Figure 17-46. Legislative subcommittee

110 1 ‡a United States. ‡b Congress. ‡b Senate. ‡b Committee on the Judiciary.
‡b Subcommittee on Patents, Trademarks, and Copyrights.
245 10 ‡a Copyright law revision : ‡b hearings before the Subcommittee on Patents, Trademarks
and Copyrights of the Committee on the Judiciary, United States Senate, Ninety-third
Congress, first session, pursuant to S. Res. 56 on S. 1361, July 31 and August 1, 1973.
260 ‡a Washington : ‡b U.S. G.P.O., ‡c 1973.
300 ‡a v, 675 p. ; ‡c 23 cm.

Title page	Copyright Law Revision
	Hearings before the Subcommittee on
	Patents, Trademarks and Copyrights
	of the
	Committee on the Judiciary
	United States Senate
	Ninety-third Congress
	First Session
	Pursuant to S. Res. 56
	on
	S. 1361
	July 31 and August 1, 1973
	U.S. Government Printing Office
	Washington : 1973

Authority

110 10 ‡a United States. ‡b Congress. ‡b Senate. ‡b Committee on the Judiciary.
‡b Subcommittee on Patents, Trademarks, and Copyrights
410 10 ‡a United States. ‡b Congress. ‡b Senate. ‡b Subcommittee on Patents,
Trademarks, and Copyrights

is under a subordinate unit in figure 17-46, the number and year of the congress are not used in the heading.

24.23. COURTS

This rule stipulates that the name of the court is to be entered as a sub-heading under the name of the governmental jurisdiction whose authority it exercises. In the example shown in figure 17-48, added entry is made for the United States Supreme Court under the provisions of 21.30F. Note that the Attorney General and the Solicitor General are entered, according to the provisions of 24.20E, under the heading for the agency they represent, the Department of Justice.

Figure 17-47. Numbered session of Congress

```
245 00   ‡a Memorial addresses and other tributes in the Congress of the United States on the life
         and contributions of Carl T. Hayden, Ninety-second Congress, second session.
260      ‡a Washington : ‡b U.S. G.P.O., ‡c 1972.
300      ‡a vii, 174 p. : ‡b ill. ; ‡c 24 cm.
490 1    ‡a 92d Congress, 2d session, Senate document ; ‡v no. 92-68
700 1    ‡a Hayden, Carl Trumbull, ‡d 1877-1972.
710 1    ‡a United States. ‡b Congress ‡n (92nd, 2nd session : ‡d 1972).
830  0   ‡a Senate document (United States. Congress. Senate) ; ‡v no. 92-68.
```

Title page	92d Congress, 2d Session Senate Document No. 92-68
	Memorial Addresses and Other Tributes in the
	Congress of the United States
	on the Life and Contributions of
	Carl T. Hayden
	Ninety-second Congress
	Second Session
	U.S. Government Printing Office
	Washington : 1972

Figure 17-48. Court

```
020      ‡a 083712221X
110 10   ‡a United States. ‡b Dept. of Justice.
245 10   ‡a Prejudice and property : ‡b an historic brief against racial covenants / ‡c submitted to
         the Supreme Court by Tom C. Clark, Attorney General of the U.S., and Philip B. Perlman,
         Solicitor General of the U.S.
260      ‡a Washington, D.C. : ‡b Public Affairs Press, ‡c 1948.
300      ‡a 104 p. ; ‡c 21 cm.
504      ‡a Includes bibliographical references (p. 86-104).
700 1    ‡a Clark, Tom C. ‡q (Tom Campbell), ‡d 1899-1977.
700 1    ‡a Perlman, Philip B. ‡q (Philip Benjamin), ‡d 1890-1960.
710 1    ‡a United States. ‡b Supreme Court.
```

Title page	Prejudice and Property
	An Historic Brief against Racial Covenants
	Submitted to the Supreme Court
	by Tom C. Clark
	Attorney General of the U.S.
	and
	Philip B. Perlman
	Solicitor General of the U.S.
	Public Affairs Press
	Washington, D.C.

24.26. DELEGATIONS TO INTERNATIONAL AND INTERGOVERNMENTAL BODIES

This rule is the same as *AACR1* rule 86. It differs from ALA 1949 rule 79, which formulated a conference heading with the name of the delegation as a subheading following the name of the conference for such a group. Under ALA 1949 rule 79, the example shown in figure 17-49 would have received the heading:

> Inter-American Conference for the Maintenance of Peace, Buenos Aires, 1936. Delegation of the United States of America

Rule 24.26, as well as its predecessor *AACR1* rule 86, represents a return to 1908 rules.

The Mexican delegation to the Inter-American Conference also made a report to its home country. According to ALA 1949 rule 79 the heading, like the previous one, would have been the name of the conference followed by the name of the delegation in the vernacular:

> Inter-American Conference for the Maintenance of Peace, Buenos Aires, 1936. Delegación de Mexico

Figure 17-49.   Delegation to international conference

110 1	‡a United States. ‡b Delegation to the Inter-American Conference for the Maintenance of Peace, 1936, Buenos Aires, Argentina.
245 10	‡a Report of the Delegation of the United States of America to the Inter-American Conference for the Maintenance of Peace, Buenos Aires, Argentina, December 1-23, 1936.
260	‡a Washington : ‡b U.S. G.P.O. : ‡b For sale by the Supt. of Docs., ‡c 1937.
300	‡a vi, 280 p. ; ‡c 24 cm.
490 1	‡a Department of State publication ; ‡v 1088. ‡a Conference series ; ‡v 33
711 2	‡a Inter-American Conference for the Maintenance of Peace ‡d (1936 : ‡c Buenos Aires, Argentina)
830 0	‡a Department of State publication ; ‡v 1088.
830 0	‡a Department of State publication. ‡p Conference series ; ‡v 33.

Title page	Report of the Delegation of the United States of America to the Inter-American Conference for the Maintenance of Peace Buenos Aires, Argentina December 1-23, 1936 United States Government Printing Office Washington : 1937

As can be seen, such a heading served to gather all of the various reports together in one place in the catalog.

Rule 24.26 calls for main entry under the name of the government of the delegation, with the subheading in the vernacular (see figure 17-50).

Figure 17-50.   Delegation to international conference

110 1   ‡a Mexico. ‡b Delegación a la Conferencia Interamericana de Consolidación de la Paz, 1936, Buenos Aires, Argentina.
245 10   ‡a Informe de la Delegación de México a la Conferencia Interamericana de Consolidación de la Paz, reunida en Buenos Aires, Republica Argentina, del 1. al 23 de diciembre de 1936.
260   ‡a México : ‡b D.A.P.P., ‡c 1938.
300   ‡a xiv , 308 p. ; ‡c 23 cm.
500   ‡a At head of title: Conferencia Internacional de Consolidación de la Paz.
711 2   ‡a Inter-American Conference for the Maintenance of Peace ‡d (1936 : ‡c Buenos Aires, Argentina)

Title page   Conferencia Internacional
                                    de Consolidación de la Paz
                              Informe de la Delegación de México
                                            a la
                  Conferencia Interamericana de Consolidación de la Paz
                                 Reunida en Buenos Aires
                                    Republica Argentina
                              del 1. al 23 de diciembre de 1936
                                          D•A•P•P
                                        México, 1938

Authorities
111 20   ‡a Inter-American Conference for the Maintenance of Peace ‡d (1936 : ‡c Buenos Aires, Argentina)
411 20   ‡a Conferencia Internacional de Consolidación de la Paz ‡d (1936 : ‡c Buenos Aires, Argentina)

111 20   ‡a Inter-American Conference for the Maintenance of Peace ‡d (1936 : ‡c Buenos Aires, Argentina). ‡b Delegations
663   ‡a Delegations to the Inter-American Conference for the Maintenance of Peace are entered under the name of the nation followed by the name of the delgation, e.g., ‡b United States. Delegation to the Inter-American Conference for the Maintenance of Peace, 1936, Buenos Aires, Argentina; Mexico. Delegación a la Conferencia Interamericana de Consolidación de la Paz, 1936, Buenos Aires, Argentina

A general explanatory reference serves to bring together in the catalog all of the names of the various delegations to the conference. Under the stipulations of 24.3B, the name of the conference will be given in English. Reference from the Spanish form of the name will be made under provisions of 26.3A3, as seen in the authority record. This displays:

> Conferencia Internacional de Consolidación de la Paz (1936: Buenos
>   Aires, Argentina)
>   search under
> Inter-American Conference for the Maintenance of Peace (1936: Buenos
>   Aires, Argentina)

The general explanatory reference may be made in a general authority record for the delegations. The note recorded in the 663 field of the second authority record accompanying figure 17-50 displays to the public.

Note

1. Seymour Lubetzky, *Cataloging Rules and Principles* (Washington, D.C.: Library of Congress, 1953), p. 50.

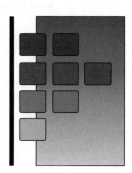

CHAPTER 18

UNIFORM TITLES

(*AACR2R* Chapter 25)

25.1. USE OF UNIFORM TITLES

Many works appearing in library catalogs are published in varying issues, translations, etc., with different titles. Because one of the objects of the library catalog is to show what works the library has by a given author, some method must be devised to bring these works issued with varying titles together in the catalog.[1] Probably the best way to do it is for the cataloger to choose one title and to gather all of the manifestations of the work together under this one title. Such a title is known as a uniform title.

Uniform titles are used for various purposes. *AACR2R* 25.1A listed two:

1. to bring together all entries for a work when various manifestations have appeared under various titles, and
2. to provide identification for a work when its title proper differs from that by which it is commonly known.

The 1993 amendments added two more purposes:

3. to differentiate between two or more works published under identical title proper, and
4. to organize the bibliographic file.

The use of uniform titles in library catalogs is not new. Such works as sacred scriptures (the Bible, etc.) have long been entered under uniform title. So-called anonymous classics (epics, folktales, etc., whose authors are unknown) are likewise by long-standing custom entered under uniform title. *AACR2R* chapter 25 brings together not only these long-established and familiar uses of uniform titles but also utilizes uniform titles to bring together varying titles for modern works (those published after 1501).

Most libraries use uniform titles for sacred scriptures and anonymous classics. The use of uniform title for modern works aside from music has

475

not had similar widespread acceptance. This practice is recognized by the editors of *AACR2R* with their statement under 25.1A, "The need to use uniform titles varies from one catalogue to another and varies within one catalogue." Illustrations and discussion in this chapter are based on the policy that all uniform titles are displayed as part of the catalog entry.

AACR2R chapter 25 is organized similarly to previous chapters. It begins with a general rule (25.2), followed by some general rules for choice and form of title. These are followed by special rules for particular types of works that may be arranged using uniform titles.

MARC Coding of Uniform Titles

It goes without saying that a work for which a uniform title may be provided will be entered, like any other work, in the catalog according to the rules in *AACR2R* chapter 21, "Choice of Access Points." Accordingly, if a work should be entered under author, the uniform title will be recorded in the 240 field, between the author main entry heading (1XX field, as discussed in *Handbook* chapter 14) and the transcription of the title page (245 field) (see figure 18-1).[2] Because it must always be accompanied by an author, this type of uniform title will be referred to as an "author-title uniform title" in the following paragraphs.

The first indicator of the 240 field tells the system whether to display the uniform title or not. Generally, this should be coded "1" (display). The second indicator gives the number of nonfiling characters (the number of

Figure 18-1.   Uniform title

```
100 1    ‡a Dickens, Charles, ‡d 1812-1870.
240 10   ‡a Oliver Twist
245 14   ‡a The adventures of Oliver Twist / ‡c by Charles Dickens ; illustrated by Barnett
         Freedman.
260      ‡a New York : ‡b Heritage Illustrated Bookshelf, ‡c c1939.
300      ‡a 431 p. : ‡b ill. (some col.) ; ‡c 22 cm.
```

Title page	The Adventures of Oliver Twist By Charles Dickens Illustrated by Barnett Freedman New York The Heritage Illustrated Bookshelf

Authority
100 10   ‡a Dickens, Charles, ‡d 1812-1870. ‡t Oliver Twist
400 10   ‡a Dickens, Charles, ‡d 1812-1870. ‡t Adventures of Oliver Twist

characters that the system should skip before beginning to file the title). Because under *AACR2R* 25.2C1 initial articles are omitted from uniform titles, this indicator should always be coded "0." Initial articles are dropped whether they appear in the nominative case or not, for languages that distinguish by case (*CSB* 52, spring 1991, p. 26). The uniform title itself is recorded in subfield ‡a. Other subfield codes will be discussed later in the chapter. Do *not* enclose the uniform title in brackets; these are supplied by the system.

The MARC authority record for author-title uniform titles is a bit tricky, because it must combine two fields (the 1XX and the 240 fields) in one heading. This is accomplished by using the established form for the author in the expected 1XX authority field (see *Handbook* chapter 15), and adding the uniform title following the author's established form - full-stop - subfield ‡t. Further title-related subfields may be added as necessary. Obviously, the established form of the author's name in this authority record is the same as the established form without the uniform title.

The trick to interpreting a MARC authority record for an author-title uniform title is to remember that everything preceding subfield ‡t will go into the 1XX field of the bibliographic record; that following subfield ‡t goes into the 240 field exactly as in the authority record, with the exception that the 240 field begins with subfield ‡a, not subfield ‡t.

Author-title uniform titles used in other areas of the record (6XX fields for subject headings, 7XX fields for added entries, 8XX fields for series) are entered exactly as they appear in the authority record.

An example of an authority record for an author-title uniform title accompanies figure 18-1. The established form for Dickens appears in subfields ‡a and ‡d of the 100 field; the uniform title appears in subfield ‡t. The 400 field contains a reference from the form of the title that appears on the book, as stipulated by *AACR2R* 25.2E2 and 26.4B1, because it differs from the uniform title. This field will generate the following display:

Dickens, Charles, 1812-1870. Adventures of Oliver Twist
    search under
Dickens, Charles, 1812-1870. Oliver Twist

If according to the provisions of *AACR2R* chapter 21 a work is to be entered under title as main entry and the title varies in different versions, such a work may also be given a uniform title. In this case the uniform title becomes the main entry (and thus will be referred to in the following paragraphs as a "main-entry uniform title") and is recorded in the 130 field of the bibliographic record. The first indicator, nonfiling characters, should be coded "0" (*AACR2R* 25.C1 calling for the omission of initial articles); the second is left blank. The title is recorded in subfield ‡a, with other title-related subfields as explained later in this chapter. If used as an added entry, it will be recorded in the 730 field; if used as a subject, in the 630 field; if used as a series, in the 830 field. A main-entry uniform title is recorded in a 130 field of the authority record in the same manner. The pattern of the indicators is reversed, however, in the authorities format: the first indicator is blank, the second is "0."

Do not enclose main-entry uniform titles in brackets. The system will supply brackets if the cataloging agency chooses to use them (cf. *AACR2R* 25.2A option).

25.2. GENERAL RULE

25.2A. If a work appears under various titles, select one of the titles as the uniform title under which all manifestations of the work will be cataloged. The rules for selection (25.3–25.4) are based on the first sentence of Paris Principle 7:

> The uniform heading should normally be the most frequently used name (or form of name) or title appearing in editions of the work catalogued or in references to them by accepted authorities.[3]

25.2B. Uniform title is *not* to be used to connect revised editions of a work that appear under different titles. Relate these titles with a note and an added entry for the title of the earlier edition (see figure 1-21).

25.2C. Initial articles

The Library of Congress has given a full discussion of the deletion of initial articles from certain access points in the catalog record (*LCRI* 21.30J, Nov. 1995). Initial articles are to be omitted from uniform titles. This includes languages distinguishing by case: drop all initial articles, even those not in the nominative case (*CSB* 52, spring 1991, p. 26). An exception is made when such titles begin with an article that forms a part of a personal, geographic, or corporate name (La Fontaine, Los Angeles, El Cajon) or "when the title begins with an article in a situation in which meaning and cataloger's judgment require its retention" (*LCRI* 21.30J, Nov. 1995).

25.2E. Added entries and references

25.2E1. Works entered under title. Figure 18-2 is a work entered under a uniform title. As noted above, such uniform titles are entered in the 130 field. Such a work will have an added entry under the title proper as it appears in the chief source of information of the item being cataloged, unless it is "essentially the same as the main entry [i.e., the uniform title] heading" (*AACR2R* 25.2E1, 1993 amendments). A reference to the uniform title *(Mother Goose)* will also be made the first time this "variant" title (i.e., title other than the uniform title) appears in the catalog, as shown in the authority record. This displays:

> Book of nursery songs and rhymes
>   search under
> Mother Goose

Like other references, this reference is made one time only; it does not refer to a specific issue of *Mother Goose* but simply to the work in all of its variant

Figure 18-2.   Uniform title as main entry

```
130 0    ‡a Mother Goose.
245 12   ‡a A book of nursery songs and rhymes / ‡c edited by S. Baring-Gould ; with illustrations
         by members of the Birmingham Art School under the direction of A.J. Gaskin.
260      ‡a Detroit : ‡b Singing Tree Press, ‡c 1969.
300      ‡a xvi, 159 p. : ‡b ill. ; ‡c 23 cm.
534      ‡p Reprint. Originally published: ‡c London : Methuen, 1895.
504      ‡a Includes bibliographical references.
700 2    ‡a Baring-Gould, S. ‡q (Sabine), ‡d 1834-1924.
710 2    ‡a Birmingham Art School.
```

```
Title page          A Book of Nursery Songs and Rhymes
                   Edited by S. Baring-Gould: with illustrations by
                     Members of the Birmingham Art School
                       Under the direction of A.J. Gaskin
                         London: Methuen & Company
                        Essex St. Strand: MDCCCXCV
                             Detroit: Reissued by
                             Singing Tree Press
                             Book Tower, 1969
```

```
Authority
130   0   ‡a Mother Goose
430   0   ‡a Book of nursery songs and rhymes
430   0   ‡a Mother Goose nursery rhymes
```

manifestations. A similar reference will be made from any other variant of the uniform title in the library's collection. For the example shown in figure 18-3, make a second reference, shown in the authority record accompanying figure 18-2. This will display:

> Mother Goose nursery rhymes
>   search under
> Mother Goose

25.2E2. Works entered under a personal or corporate heading. Figure 18-1 is an example of a work entered under personal heading. Also given above is the format for the reference that will be made the *first time* the work known as *Oliver Twist* appears with the variant title *The Adventures of Oliver Twist*. The reference refers not to the Heritage Illustrated Bookshelf edition of Dickens' tale, but simply to the work *Oliver Twist* generally. In contrast, the title added entry traced from the 245 field, an added entry for the *title proper (The Adventures of Oliver Twist)* of this edition, refers specifically to this edition and to no other. The rule stipulates that a title added entry will be made for each new edition of such a work; a reference will be made *once* for each varying title.

Figure 18-3.   Uniform title as main entry

```
130 0    ‡a Mother Goose.
245 10   ‡a Mother Goose nursery rhymes / ‡c illustrations by Esmé Eve.
260      ‡a New York : ‡b Grosset & Dunlap, ‡c c1958.
300      ‡a 200 p. : ‡b col. ill. ; ‡c 27 cm.
700 1    ‡a Eve, Esmé.
```

Title page	Mother Goose Nursery Rhymes Illustrations by Esmé Eve Grosset & Dunlap • New York

Individual Titles

25.3. WORKS CREATED AFTER 1500

25.3A. When editions of a modern work (i.e., one first created after 1500) have appeared under varying titles, use the best-known title in the original language of the work. "Best-known title" should be determined either by checking reference sources to see how they refer to the work or by examining issues and editions of the work to see which title is most frequently used. Obviously, for an author such as William Shakespeare, examination of citations to his individual plays, etc., in reference sources would be appropriate.

The first time an edition of *Macbeth* with the title *The Tragedy of Macbeth* is received in the library, a reference will be made in an authority 400 name-title field, as shown in the authority record for figure 18-4. This will display:

> Shakespeare, William, 1564-1616. Tragedy of Macbeth
>   search under
> Shakespeare, William, 1564-1616. Macbeth

This reference simply refers to the work *Macbeth* in general, not to a specific edition. The title added entry given for figure 18-4 (traced from the 245 field) refers specifically to the Folio Society's 1951 edition.

25.3B. If no title is clearly best known, choose the title proper of the original edition of a work as the uniform title.

If a statement of responsibility has been transcribed as part of the title proper (particularly if this statement of responsibility obscures the actual title proper), a uniform title may be used to properly identify the work (see figures 1-60 and 18-5). The uniform title should not include the statement of responsibility ("Bright's" or "Plato's"). This *Handbook* itself has a uniform title of this type; cf. the cataloging in publication data on the verso of the title page.

Figure 18-4.   Best-known title

```
100 1    ‡a Shakespeare, William, ‡d 1564-1616.
240 10   ‡a Macbeth
245 14   ‡a The tragedy of Macbeth / ‡c by William Shakespeare ; introduction by Sir Lewis
         Casson ; designs by Michael Ayrton and John Minton.
250      ‡a 2nd ed.
260      ‡a London : ‡b Folio Society, ‡c 1951.
300      ‡a 96 p. : ‡b col. ill. ; ‡c 23 cm.
500      ‡a "Authoritative text of 'The New Temple Shakespeare', edited by M.R. Ridley."
700 1    ‡a Ridley, M. R. ‡q (Maurice Roy), ‡d 1890-
```

Title page	The Tragedy of Macbeth By William Shakespeare Introduction by Sir Lewis Casson Designs by Michael Ayrton and John Minton The Folio Society : London : 1951

Authority
```
100 10   ‡a Shakespeare, William, ‡d 1564-1616. ‡t Macbeth
400 10   ‡a Shakespeare, William, ‡d 1564-1616. ‡t Tragedy of Macbeth
```

Figure 18-5.   Statement of responsibility omitted from uniform title

```
020      ‡a 092952456X
100 0    ‡a Plato.
240 10   ‡a Apology
245 10   ‡a Plato's Apology / ‡c [commentary by] Gilbert P. Rose.
260      ‡a Bryn Mawr, Pa. : ‡b Thomas Library, Bryn Mawr College, ‡c c1989.
300      ‡a 2 v. ; ‡c 22 cm.
440   0  ‡a Bryn Mawr Greek commentaries
504      ‡a Includes bibliographical references (v. 2, p. 53) and indexes.
546      ‡a Text in Greek; commentary and notes in English.
505 0    ‡a [1] Text -- [2] Commentary.
700 1    ‡a Rose, Gilbert P. ‡q (Gilbert Paul), ‡d 1939-
```

Title page to vol. 1	Bryn Mawr Greek Commentaries Plato's Apology Text Gilbert P. Rose Thomas Library, Bryn Mawr College Bryn Mawr, Pennsylvania

25.4. WORKS CREATED BEFORE 1501

25.4A. General rule

Most works created before 1501 exist in many varying versions, editions, etc., with almost as many variant titles. The cataloger is to identify the best-known title, using modern reference works, in the language of the original work, if possible.

Some of these works are known to be the responsibility of a particular author. Entry for such works is governed by general rule 21.1A2; uniform title is added, following 25.2A, in a 240 field between the name of the author and transcription of the title proper from the chief source of information (see figure 18-6).

Many works created before 1501 have no known author. Of these, many epics, poems, romances, tales, plays, chronicles, etc., have been retold, re-printed, published, translated, etc., many times in many versions over the centuries. Catalogers have given the name "anonymous classic" to the genre. Because anonymous classics find a place, often in translation, even in small general libraries, the cataloger should have some familiarity with some of the better-known anonymous classics and should know the rules for entry of such works.

Figure 18-6.   Entry under known author

020	‡a 0195087402
100 0	‡a Dante Alighieri, ‡d 1265-1321.
240 10	‡a Divina commedia. ‡l English & Italian
245 14	‡a The divine comedy of Dante Alighieri / ‡c edited and translated by Robert M. Durling ; introduction and notes by Ronald L. Martinez and Robert M. Durling ; illustrations by Robert Turner.
260	‡a New York : ‡b Oxford University Press, ‡c 1996-
300	‡a v. : ‡b ill., maps ; ‡c 25 cm.
504	‡a Includes bibliographical references and indexes.
505 1	‡a v. 1. Inferno -- v. 2. Paradiso
700 1	‡a Durling, Robert M.

Title page to vol. 1

The Divine Comedy
of
Dante Alighieri
Edited and Translated by
Robert M. Durling
Introduction and Notes by
Ronald L. Martinez and Robert M. Durling
Illustrations by Robert Turner
Volume 1
Inferno
New York   Oxford
Oxford University Press
1996

Following the rule for entry for anonymous works, title main entry is appropriate (21.5A). Because the title varies from one edition to the next, the cataloger will identify the best-known title, according to general prescriptions in 25.4A, and will give main entry to this title for all editions of the work. *Mother Goose* (figures 18-2 and 18-3) is an example of an anonymous classic. No one knows the author of most of the traditional rhymes usually included in such collections; titles vary with the ingenuity of the compiler or editor. The best-known title, *Mother Goose,* will serve as the uniform title for all manifestations of this work.

A list of a few of the common anonymous classics with uniform headings found in the National Authority File, which may be helpful to the beginning cataloger, is given in this *Handbook,* appendix.

A uniform heading will be used alone for an edition of the work in the language of the original. If the edition being cataloged is a translation, the name of the language of the translation is to be added after the uniform title (25.5C) in subfield ‡l. The language of the original is also added if the original text accompanies the translation (see figure 18-7). A reference will be made from the authority record, which displays:

Song of Roland
   search under
Chanson de Roland. English & French (Old French)

Figure 18-7.   Anonymous classic

```
020      ‡a 0271005165
130 0    ‡a Chanson de Roland. ‡l English & French (Old French)
245 14   ‡a The Song of Roland : ‡b an analytical edition / ‡c Gerard J. Brault.
260      ‡a University Park : ‡b Pennsylvania State University Press, ‡c 1978.
300      ‡a 2 v. : ‡b ill. ; ‡c 24 cm.
504      ‡a Includes bibliographical references (v. 1, p. 479-510) and index.
505 0    ‡a v. 1. Introduction and commentary -- v. 2. Oxford text and English translation.
700 1    ‡a Brault, Gerard J.
```

Title page to vol. 1	The
	Song
	of
	Roland
	An Analytical Edition
	I. Introduction and Commentary
	Gerard J. Brault
	The Pennsylvania State University Press
	University Park and London

Authority
130   0   ‡a Chanson de Roland. ‡l English & French (Old French)
430   0   ‡a Song of Roland

In cataloging anonymous classics, the cataloger should be wary of publications presented as adaptations. These are to be entered under the name of the adapter, following provisions of 21.10. Give added entry to the uniform title in a 730 field for the original work as shown in figure 18-8. Note that as a "related works" added entry, no language is added to the title, even though English is not the original language of *Cuchulain*.

25.4B. Classical and Byzantine Greek works

The rule for uniform title for a work in classical or Byzantine Greek is an exception to the general rule of using a uniform title in the original language of the work. Rule 25.4B is analogous to 22.3C1, which directs the cataloger to make entry for persons whose names were written in a non-roman script in the form in which they are found in English-language reference sources. As with anonymous classics, if the edition being cataloged is a translation, the cataloger will add the name of the language of the translation to the uniform title (see figure 18-9).

25.4C. Anonymous works written neither in Greek nor in roman script

This rule is closely related to 25.4B, which directs the use of an English-language title for classical and Byzantine Greek works. Likewise, the cataloger is to prefer a title in English for an anonymous work created before 1501 whose original language is not written in Greek or in roman script (see figure 18-10).

The Arabian Nights is an anonymous work originally written in Arabic script. The cataloger is directed to prefer an established title in English as

Figure 18-8.   Adaptation of anonymous classic

```
100 1    ‡a Hull, Eleanor, ‡d 1860-1935.
245 14   ‡a The boys' Cuchulain : ‡b heroic legends of Ireland / ‡c by Eleanor Hull ; with sixteen
         illustrations in colour by Stephen Reid.
260      ‡a New York : ‡b Crowell, ‡c [1910]
300      ‡a 279 p. : ‡b col. ill. ; ‡c 22 cm.
730 0    ‡a Cuchulain.
```

Title page	The Boys' Cuchulain Heroic Legends of Ireland by Eleanor Hull with sixteen illustrations in colour by Stephen Reid Thomas Y. Crowell & Company New York Publishers

Figure 18-9.   Greek work

```
100 0    ‡a Homer.
240 10   ‡a Odyssey. ‡l English
245 14   ‡a The Odyssey / ‡c Homer ; a new verse translation by Albert Cook.
250      ‡a 1st ed.
260      ‡a New York : ‡b Norton, ‡c c1967.
300      ‡a xi, 340 p. ; ‡c 22 cm.
700 1    ‡a Cook, Albert, ‡d 1925-
```

Title page	Homer The Odyssey
	A New Verse Translation by Albert Cook
	W. W. Norton & Company • Inc. • New York

Figure 18-10.   Anonymous work not in roman or Greek script

```
130 0    ‡a Book of the dead. ‡l English & Egyptian.
245 14   ‡a The book of the dead : ‡b the papyrus of Ani in the British Museum : the Egyptian text
         : with interlinear transliteration and translation, a running translation, introduction, etc. /
         ‡c by E. A. Wallis Budge.
246 14   ‡a Egyptian book of the dead
260      ‡a New York : ‡b Dover, ‡c 1967.
300      ‡a clv, 377 p. : ‡b ill. ; ‡c 24 cm.
534      ‡p Reprint. Originally published: ‡c London : British Museum, 1895.
504      ‡a Includes bibliographical references (p. [371]-377).
700 1    ‡a Budge, E. A. Wallis ‡q (Ernest Alfred Wallis), ‡c Sir, ‡d 1857-1934.
730 0    ‡a Papyrus of Ani.
```

Title page	The Book of the Dead
	The Papyrus of Ani
	in the British Museum
	The Egyptian Text with interlinear transliteration
	and translation, a running translation, introduction, etc.
	by E. A. Wallis Budge
	Dover Publications, Inc., New York

uniform title. As shown in the authority record accompanying figure 18-11, reference from the romanized form of the original title should be made to the English-language title chosen under 25.4C. Figure 2-9 shows an English translation of *The Arabian Nights*. The language of the translation is added to the uniform title. Reference will be made from the variant title in the authority record:

```
130  0 ‡a Arabian Nights. ‡l English
430  0 ‡a Book of the thousand nights and a night
```

Figure 18-11.   Adaptation

```
100 2    ‡a Williams-Ellis, Amabel, ‡d 1894-1984.
245 14   ‡a The Arabian nights : ‡b stories / ‡c retold by Amabel Williams-Ellis ; illustrated by
         Pauline Diana Baynes.
260      ‡a New York : ‡b Criterion Books, ‡c c1957.
300      ‡a 348 p. : ‡b ill. (some col.) ; ‡c 23 cm.
730 0    ‡a Arabian nights.
```

Title page   The Arabian Nights
                          Stories retold by Amabel Williams-Ellis
                           Illustrated by Pauline Diana Baynes
                             Criterion Books   New York

Authority
130 0 ‡a Arabian nights.
430 0 ‡a Alf laylah wa-laylah

This displays:

Book of the thousand nights and a night
    search under
Arabian nights. English

In contrast to the entry shown in figure 2-9, an adaptation of *The Arabian Nights* will be entered under the name of the adapter, with a "related works" added entry for the uniform title of the original work (21.10) (see figure 18-11), without the addition of language.

25.5. ADDITIONS TO UNIFORM TITLES

25.5B. Conflict resolution

25.5B1. This rule provides for the addition in parentheses of a word or phrase to distinguish a uniform title from an identical or similar heading in the catalog. Provisions of this rule have been expanded by the 1993 amendments to include the use of a uniform title made up of title proper plus a parenthetical qualifier for any serial entered under title if the title proper is identical to the title proper of another serial in the catalog. For discussion of this rule as it applies to serial and series titles, see chapter 12 in this *Handbook,* including discussion of title main entry for serials; figures 12-9 and 12-10; and *LCRI* 25.5B (Aug. 27, 1990).

25.5C. Language

25.5C1. Translations. For an item in which the language is different from the original, add the name of the language to the uniform title. Separate the uniform title from the name of the language by a full stop and subfield ‡l (see figure 18-7 for an example of language added to uniform title for an anonymous classic). Uniform title plus language is used to bring translations into the same place in the library catalog as the original work (see figure 18-12 for a translation of a modern work).

Although libraries customarily use uniform headings for anonymous classics, not all libraries will choose to use uniform titles to collect translations of modern works under a single heading in the catalog. For a non-research library, which is unlikely to acquire works such as those illustrated in figures 1-9, 14-36, 14-37, and 18-12 in the original language, the addition of a uniform title to the entry may actually be confusing and undesirable. For this reason, the use of uniform titles is subject to the policy of the cataloging agency (25.1).

25.5D. Optionally, the cataloger may add a GMD (see 1.1C) as the last element in the uniform title. No national library will make this optional addition (*LCRI* 25.5D, Jan. 5, 1989; Howarth, at 25.5D).

25.6. PARTS OF A WORK

25.6A. One part

One of the problems that the cataloger must solve is the question of how to handle separately published parts of a work, particularly if library policy is to relate such parts to the main work from which they have been taken. One way to accomplish this is by the use of uniform title. The title of the part by itself serves as uniform title. Orson Scott Card's *Tales of Alvin Maker* is an example of a whole work, each of whose parts may be handled in

Figure 18-12.   Translation

100 1	‡a Hürlimann, Bettina, ‡d 1909-
240 10	‡a Europäische Kinderbücher in drei Jahrhunderten. ‡l English
245 10	‡a Three centuries of children's books in Europe / ‡c Bettina Hürlimann ; translated and edited by Brian W. Alderson.
250	‡a 1st U.S. ed.
260	‡a Cleveland : ‡b World Pub. Co., ‡c c1969.
300	‡a xviii, 297 p. : ‡b ill. (some col.) ; ‡c 25 cm.
500	‡a Translation of: Europäische Kinderbücher in drei Jahrhunderten.
504	‡a Includes bibliographical references.
700 1	‡a Alderson, Brian.

Title page	Three Centuries of Children's Books in Europe Bettina Hürlimann Translated and edited by Brian W. Alderson The World Publishing Company Cleveland and New York

such a fashion (see figure 18-13a). Note that in this case, because the complete uniform title (Prentice Alvin) is identical to the title proper, it is not included in the bibliographic record (cf. *LCRI* 25.1, "Applicability," Feb. 15, 1994).

An authority record is created for this uniform title, giving as a reference in subfield ‡a of a 400 field the author's name followed by the title of the whole in subfield ‡t, subdivided by the number in subfield ‡n and title of the part in subfield ‡p.

Another way to handle this situation is to treat the whole work as a series, as shown in figure 18-13b.

Figure 18-13a.   Parts of a work (treated with uniform title)

```
020        ‡a 0812502124 (pbk.)
100 1      ‡a Card, Orson Scott.
245 10     ‡a Prentice Alvin / ‡c Orson Scott Card.
250        ‡a 1st ed.
260        ‡a New York : ‡b T. Doherty Associates, ‡c 1989.
300        ‡a x, 342 p. : ‡b ill. ; ‡c 18 cm.
500        ‡a Distributed by St. Martin's Press.
500        ‡a "A Tor book"--T.p. verso.
500        ‡a Maps on lining papers.
```

Title page

Orson Scott Card
Prentice
Alvin
The Tales of Alvin Maker III
TOR fantasy
A Tom Doherty Associates Book
New York

Authority
100 10   ‡a Card, Orson Scott. ‡t Prentice Alvin
400 10   ‡a Card, Orson Scott. ‡t Tales of Alvin Maker. ‡n 3, ‡p Prentice Alvin

Figure 18-13b.   Parts of a work (treated with series)

```
020        ‡a 0812502124 (pbk.)
100 1      ‡a Card, Orson Scott.
245 10     ‡a Prentice Alvin / ‡c Orson Scott Card.
250        ‡a 1st ed.
260        ‡a New York : ‡b T. Doherty Associates, ‡c 1989.
300        ‡a x, 342 p. : ‡b ill. ; ‡c 18 cm.
490 1      ‡a The tales of Alvin Maker ; ‡v 3
500        ‡a Distributed by St. Martin's Press.
500        ‡a "A Tor book"--T.p. verso.
500        ‡a Maps on lining papers.
800 1      ‡a Card, Orson Scott. ‡t Tales of Alvin Maker ; ‡v 3.
```

The Library of Congress does not generally use explanatory references such as those illustrated at *AACR2R* 25.6A1 (Raven, Simon; and Sinbad the Sailor), preferring instead to use simple "search under" and "search also under" references (see *LCRI* 26.2D, Feb. 1, 1989, and 26.3B–26.3C, May 21, 1990).

25.7. TWO WORKS ISSUED TOGETHER

Not too infrequently two works by an author will be issued together in one physical volume, with or without a collective title. This is the case with the example of the two Horatio Alger novels, which may be cataloged as shown in figure 18-14a. An alternate method of cataloging this item would be to use a uniform title, thus arranging the work under the author's name by the title of the first item. Name-title added entry will be given for the uniform title of the second work (see figure 18-14b). The practice illustrated in

Figure 18-14a.   Two works by the same author

```
100 1    ‡a Alger, Horatio, ‡d 1832-1899.
245 10   ‡a Strive and succeed : ‡b two novels / ‡c by Horatio Alger ; introduction by S.H.
         Behrman.
260      ‡a New York : ‡b Holt, Rinehart and Winston, ‡c c1967.
300      ‡a xii, 173 p. : ‡b ill. ; ‡c 22 cm.
505 0    ‡a Julius, or, The street boy out West -- The store boy, or, The fortunes of Ben Barclay.
740 02   ‡a Julius.
740 02   ‡a Store boy.
```

Title page	Strive and Succeed
	Julius or The Street Boy Out West
	The Store Boy or The Fortunes of Ben Barclay
	Two Novels by Horatio Alger
	Introduction by S.H. Behrman
	Holt, Rinehart and Winston
	New York Chicago San Francisco

Figure 18-14b.   Two works by the same author—alternative cataloging

```
100 1    ‡a Alger, Horatio, ‡d 1832-1899.
240 10   ‡a Julius
245 10   ‡a Strive and succeed : ‡b two novels / ‡c by Horatio Alger ; introduction by S.H.
         Behrman.
250      ‡a 1st ed.
260      ‡a New York : ‡b Holt, Rinehart and Winston, ‡c c1967.
300      ‡a xii, 173 p. : ‡b ill. ; ‡c 22 cm.
505 0    ‡a Julius, or, The street boy out West -- The store boy, or, The fortunes of Ben Barclay.
700 12   ‡a Alger, Horatio, ‡d 1832-1899. ‡t Store boy.
```

18-14b is particularly useful when, as in the example, the title proper is not the same as the uniform title.

Collective Titles

25.8. COMPLETE WORKS

In a library in which it seems advantageous to gather all editions of an author's complete works together in the catalog, regardless of the title proper appearing on the various chief sources of information, a conventional uniform title in English, "Works," may be used. Add language in subfield ‡l if the item is a translation. Although not called for in *AACR2R*, the Library of Congress adds the date of publication in subfield ‡f at the end of the uniform title, whether it appears in a 240 field or a 7XX name-title entry (*LCRI* 25.8, Jan. 5, 1989, and 21.30M, Nov. 10, 1993). This addition is made because the collective uniform title "Works" is used so frequently as to make it advisable, in the judgment of the Library of Congress, to further subdivide the file. LC has chosen to do this by date of publication. This reasoning may not be applicable to the majority of libraries, which will not have the mammoth collections of the Library of Congress. As with the policy decision on whether and when to use uniform titles at all (*AACR2R* 25.1), the decision on whether to add dates to collective uniform titles is up to the local cataloging agency. LC policy has been followed in this *Handbook* (see figure 18-15).

Figure 18-15.   Complete works

```
100 0     ‡a Persius.
240 10    ‡a Works. ‡f 1956
245 10    ‡a A. Persi Flacci Saturarum liber : ‡b accedit vita / ‡c edidit W.V. Clausen.
246 10    ‡a Saturarum liber
260       ‡a Oxford : ‡b Clarendon Press, ‡c 1956.
300       ‡a xxviii, 43 p. ; ‡c 22 cm.
504       ‡a Includes bibliographical references.
700 1     ‡a Clausen, Wendell Vernon, ‡d 1923-
```

Title page	A. Persi Flacci
	Satvrarvm Liber
	Accedit Vita
	Edidit W.V. Clausen
	Oxford
	At the Clarendon Press
	1956

25.9. SELECTIONS

As with the conventional uniform title "Works," the conventional uniform title in English "Selections" may be used if it seems advantageous to gather various editions of selections from a voluminous author's work in one place in the library's catalog (see figure 18-16). See discussion in this *Handbook* at 25.8 on the addition of the date to the uniform title and *LCRI* 25.9 (Feb. 25, 1993) (the same reasoning applies to the collective title "Selections" as to "Works").

25.10. WORKS IN A SINGLE FORM

If an author has written in only one literary form, the conventional uniform titles listed under 25.10 may be used to gather various editions into one place in the library's catalog. Note that the list is not exclusive. Other appropriate specific collective titles may be used (see *LCRI* 25.10, May 28, 1993, for helpful comments).

25.11. TRANSLATIONS, ETC.

This rule pertains to translated works entered under uniform title according to rules 25.8 through 25.10. See figure 18-16 for an example of name of language added to the uniform title "Selections." Note that the language

Figure 18-16.   Selections

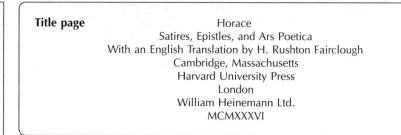

```
100 0    ‡a Horace.
240 10   ‡a Selections. ‡l English & Latin. ‡f 1936
245 10   ‡a Satires ; ‡b Epistles ; and, Ars poetica / ‡c Horace ; with an English translation by
         H. Rushton Fairclough.
260      ‡a Cambridge, Mass. : ‡b Harvard University Press, ‡c 1936.
300      ‡a xxx, 508 ; ‡c 17 cm.
440  0   ‡a Loeb classical library
546      ‡a Latin and English on opposite pages.
504      ‡a Includes bibliographical references (p. xxii-xxx).
700 1    ‡a Fairclough, H. Rushton ‡q (Henry Rushton), ‡d b. 1862.
```

Title page

Horace
Satires, Epistles, and Ars Poetica
With an English Translation by H. Rushton Fairclough
Cambridge, Massachusetts
Harvard University Press
London
William Heinemann Ltd.
MCMXXXVI

of translation precedes that of the original in this bilingual text, and the names of the languages are separated by "&", not "and."

Take careful note of the order prescribed in 25.11 for the name of the language and the subdivision "Selections." When added as a subdivision to a uniform title, this must follow the name of the language (if present) rather than precede it. In addition, when "Selections" is used to further subdivide a uniform title (rather than used as a collective title itself), it is placed in subfield ‡k. To illustrate these two points, if the book cataloged in figure 18-9 contained only translated selections of the *Odyssey* rather than the complete work, its uniform title would be

240 10 ‡a Odyssey. ‡l English. ‡k Selections,

　　not

240 10 ‡a Odyssey. ‡k Selections. ‡l English.

Special Rules for Certain Types of Work

25.13. MANUSCRIPTS AND MANUSCRIPT GROUPS

Use this rule when cataloging a manuscript that contains (a) more than one work and that lacks a title, or a manuscript group that lacks a title, and (b) the situation would not be covered by any of the rules previous to 25.13. Use 25.13 also to formulate headings when an added entry is wanted for the manuscript(s) as a physical entity (without regard to its contents) (see figure 18-10 for the distinction between uniform title for the text [Book of the dead] and that for the manuscript as a physical entity [Papyrus of Ani]). Many such manuscript groups have acquired titles subsequent to their writing; if this is so, use the title that has been assigned to the manuscript or that title by which the manuscript is commonly known. If the manuscript has no "commonly known" title, create a uniform title according to directions under 25.13B1c.

The Dead Sea scrolls qualify as an example of a manuscript group that has come to be identified in reference sources by a familiar name. Use this name as the uniform title. Add the name of the language of the translation, if any, following the uniform title (see figure 18-17).

If a manuscript has not acquired a title by which it is commonly known, enter it under its repository, as follows:

‡a [name of repository]. ‡k Manuscript. ‡n [repository's designation for the manuscript].

See figure 14-34 for an example.

Figure 18-17.   Manuscript group

```
020      ‡a 0140135448 (pbk.)
130 0    ‡a Dead Sea scrolls. ‡l English.
245 14   ‡a The Dead Sea scrolls in English / ‡c G. Vermes.
250      ‡a 3rd ed.
260      ‡a London, England ; ‡a New York, N.Y., USA : ‡b Penguin, ‡c 1987.
300      ‡a xvi, 320 p. ; ‡c 20 cm.
504      ‡a Includes bibliographical references (p. [313]-316) and index.
700 1    ‡a Vermès, Géza, ‡d 1924-
```

Title page	The
	Dead Sea Scrolls
	in English
	G. Vermes
	Third Edition
	Penguin Books

Laws, Treaties, etc.

25.15. LAWS, ETC.

25.15A1. Collections. The collective title "Laws, etc." is used as a uniform title for general collections of laws of a jurisdiction. The effect of this uniform title, new to *AACR2,* has been to create enormous files all under a single uniform title, especially for jurisdictions like the United States and other large countries and states. Therefore, the Library of Congress has prescribed the addition of certain qualifiers to this collective title. For collections of laws from jurisdictions other than U.S. states, add an "appropriate designation" in parentheses. This will usually be the title proper of the collection, and may be further qualified by year, edition, etc. (see figure 18-18).

For laws enacted by a state legislature at its annual session(s), use the qualifier "Session laws" followed by the date(s) covered (see figure 18-19). This may be further qualified by type of law if necessary. Collections of codified legislation of a state are qualified by "Compiled statutes" followed by the date of the code (see figure 18-20). For a full discussion of this issue, see *LCRI* 25.15A1 (Jan. 5, 1989, and Feb. 1, 1989).

25.15A2. Single laws, etc. Publications of single laws of other enactments are given a uniform title based on the title of the law, preferably its official title. This may be the same as the title proper. For examples, see figures 14-58 and 14-59.

Figure 18-18.   Compilation of laws on a national level

```
110 1   ‡a Canada.
240 10  ‡a Laws, etc. (Revised statutes of Canada, 1985). ‡l English & French
245 10  ‡a Revised statutes of Canada, 1985 / ‡c prepared under the Authority of the Statute
        Revision Act = Lois révisées du Canada (1985) / révision réalisée sous le régime de la
        Loi sur la révision des lois.
246 31  ‡a Lois révisées du Canada (1985)
260     ‡a Ottawa : ‡b Queen's Printer for Canada, ‡c 1985.
300     ‡a 8 v. ; ‡c 26 cm.
500     ‡a Includes unnumbered Table of concordance and Appendices volumes.
500     ‡a Kept up to date by supplements.
```

Title page

Revised Statutes	Lois révisées
of Canada, 1985	du Canada (1985)
prepared under the Authority	révision réalisée sous le régime de la
of the Statute Revision Act	Loi sur la révision des lois
Queen's Printer for Canada	Imprimeur de la reine pour le Canada
Ottawa, 1985	Ottawa, 1985

Figure 18-19.   State session laws

```
110 1   ‡a Idaho.
240 10  ‡a Laws, etc. (Session laws : 1865-1866)
245 10  ‡a Laws of the territory of Idaho, third session : ‡b convened on the fourth day of
        December, 1865, and adjourned on the twelfth day of January, 1866, at Boise City.
260     ‡a Boise City : ‡b F. Kenyon, ‡c 1866.
300     ‡a xiii, 329 p. ; ‡c 23 cm.
500     ‡a Includes index.
```

Title page

Laws
of the
Territory of Idaho
Third Session:
Convened on the fourth day of December, 1865, and adjourned on the twelfth day
of January, 1866,
at
Boise City

Boise City:
Frank Kenyon, territorial printer
1866.

Figure 18-20.   State code

```
110 1    ‡a Utah.
240 10   ‡a Laws, etc. (Compiled statutes : 1988- )
245 10   ‡a Utah code unannotated.
260      ‡a Charlottesville, Va. : ‡b Mitchie Co., ‡c 1988-
300      ‡a v. ; ‡c 26 cm.
310      ‡a Annual
362      ‡a 1988-
515      ‡a Issued in parts.
710 2    ‡a Mitchie City Publications Company, Charlottesville, Va.
```

Title page	Utah Code
	Unannotated
	1988
	vol. 1
	Mitchie Company
	Charlottesville, Virginia

25.16. TREATIES, ETC.

See 21.35 for rules governing entry of treaties and other intergovernmental agreements. See discussion in this *Handbook* under 21.35 and figures 14-64 and 14-66 for examples of use of uniform headings for treaties.

Sacred Scriptures

25.17. GENERAL RULE

This rule should be correlated with rule 21.37, which stipulates that sacred scriptures will be entered under title. However, because of the nature of sacred scripture, such works have, in almost all cases, been issued many times, with varying titles, over a long period of time. Main entry under a uniform title is thus appropriate (see figures 18-21 and 14-7). Uniform title will be the title by which the scripture is most commonly known in English-language reference sources—if possible, official sources authorized by the religious group involved. As with other uniform titles, add the language of the translation to a translated work (see figure 18-22).

25.18. PARTS OF SACRED SCRIPTURES AND ADDITIONS

It is indicative of the broader frame of reference on which *AACR2R* is based that special rules for the Bible are no longer emphasized virtually to the exclusion of the sacred scriptures of other religions as they were in previous

Figure 18-21.   Sacred scripture—original language

```
130 0    ‡a Book of Mormon.
245 14   ‡a The Book of Mormon : ‡b an account / ‡c written by the hand of Mormon upon plates
         taken from the plates of Nephi ; translated by Joseph Smith, Jun.
260      ‡a Salt Lake City, Utah, U.S.A. : ‡b Church of Jesus Christ of Latter-day Saints, ‡c 1961.
300      ‡a 558 p. : ‡b ill. ; ‡c 18 cm.
500      ‡a Includes index.
700 1    ‡a Smith, Joseph, ‡d 1805-1844.
710 2    ‡a Church of Jesus Christ of Latter-day Saints.
```

Title page

The Book of Mormon
An Account Written by
The Hand of Mormon
Upon Plates
Taken from the Plates of Nephi
Translated by Joseph Smith, Jun.
Published by
The Church of Jesus Christ of Latter-day Saints
Salt Lake City, Utah, U.S.A.
1961

Figure 18-22.   Sacred scripture in translation

```
130 0    ‡a Book of Mormon. ‡l French.
245 13   ‡a Le Livre de Mormon : ‡b récit / ‡c écrit de la main de Mormon sur des plaques prises
         des plaques de Néphi ; traduit en anglais par Joseph Smith, Junior ; traduit de l'anglais par
         John Taylor et Curtis E. Bolton.
250      ‡a 2. éd. / ‡b divisé en chapitres et en versets, et pourvu de renvois, d'après l'édition
         anglaise, par James L. Barker et Joseph E. Evans.
260      ‡a Zurich : ‡b S.F. Ballif, ‡c 1907.
300      ‡a 39, 623 p. ; ‡c 17 cm.
500      ‡a Includes index.
700 1    ‡a Smith, Joseph, ‡d 1805-1844.
700 1    ‡a Taylor, John, ‡d 1808-1887.
700 1    ‡a Bolton, Curtis E.
```

Title page

Le Livre de Mormon
Récit écrit de la main de Mormon
sur des plaques prises des plaques de Néphi
Traduit en anglais par Joseph Smith, Junior
Traduit de l'anglais par John Taylor
et Curtis E. Bolton
Deuxième édition
Divisé en chapitres et en versets
et pourvu de renvois
d'après l'édition anglaise
par James L. Barker et Joseph E. Evans
Publié par
Serge F. Ballif, Zurich
1907

codes. Rules for uniform heading for special parts, versions, etc., of the Koran, Talmud, etc., are worked out in a parallel fashion to those for the Bible and subsumed as parts of the same rule governing headings for the Bible.

25.18A. Bible

The uniform title for the Bible will be the word "Bible." To this the cataloger will add (in this order) language (subfield ‡l), name of version (subfield ‡s), and year of publication (subfield ‡f):

    130 0　‡a Bible. ‡l English. ‡s Authorized. ‡f 1969.

25.18A2. Testaments. Parts of the Bible are treated as subheadings following the uniform title "Bible." These subheadings are recorded in subfield ‡p, which is repeatable if necessary. "O.T." stands for Old Testament; "N.T." stands for New Testament. These designations will be used when cataloging a separate edition of the Old Testament or the New Testament (see figure 18-23). Make a reference from the authority record for the Old Testament to guide the user to the correct heading:

    130　0 ‡a Bible. ‡p O.T.
    430　0 ‡a Old Testament

This displays:

    Old Testament
      search under
    Bible. O.T.

Figure 18-23.　　Old Testament

```
130 0    ‡a Bible. ‡p O.T. ‡l English. ‡s Gordon, et al. ‡f 1927.
245 14   ‡a The Old Testament : ‡b an American translation / ‡c by Alexander R. Gordon ...
         [et al.] ; edited by J.M. Powis Smith.
260      ‡a Chicago : ‡b University of Chicago Press, ‡c c1927.
300      ‡a xii, 1712 p. ; ‡c 23 cm.
700 1    ‡a Gordon, Alexander R. ‡q (Alexander Reid), ‡d 1872-1930.
700 1    ‡a Smith, J. M. Powis ‡q (John Merlin Powis), ‡d 1866-1932.
```

Title page	The Old Testament An American Translation by Alexander R. Gordon • Theophile J. Meek J.M. Powis Smith • Leroy Waterman Edited by J.M. Powis Smith The University of Chicago Press Chicago, Illinois

25.18A3. Books. A separate book of the Bible will be entered, as appropriate, as a subheading to "Bible. O.T." or "Bible. N.T." (see figure 18-24). Make reference from the authority record:

```
130   0 ‡a Bible. ‡p N.T. ‡p Mark
430   0 ‡a Mark (Book of the New Testament)
430   0 ‡a Bible. ‡p Mark
```

The 430 fields generate the displays:

Mark (Book of the New Testament)	Bible. Mark
search under	search under
Bible. N.T. Mark	Bible. N.T. Mark

25.18A4. Groups of books. The list of groups of books of the Bible commonly identified by a group name given under 25.18A4 includes all of the groups that can be gathered in this manner. Do *not* add to this list.

25.18A9. Other selections. The word "selections" will be inserted as a subheading in subfield ‡k between the version and the date for combinations of three or more books that cannot be encompassed by any of the groupings given in 25.18A4. The word is also used for condensations, abridgments, etc., of the Bible (see figure 18-25).

25.18A10. Language. Add the name of the language of the text after the word "Bible" or the part being cataloged, in subfield ‡l (see figures 18-23, 18-24, and 18-25). In a departure from normal rules for uniform titles, language is always added, even if the text is in the original language.

25.18A11. Version. Record version in subfield ‡s. The following list gives some of the commonly used English versions (see figures 18-26, 18-27, and 18-28 for examples).

> Rheims—Rheims New Testament, originally translated in 1582
>
> Douai—Douai Old Testament and the Rheims New Testament
>
> Authorized—King James Version of 1611
>
> Revised—Revised Version (N.T. 1881, O.T. 1885)
>
> American Revised—American Revised Version (1901)
>
> Revised Standard—Revised Standard Version (N.T. 1946, O.T. 1962, Apocrypha 1957)
>
> New English—New English Bible (N.T. 1961, O.T. 1966)
>
> Today's English—Today's English Version, 1966

Figure 18-24.   Book of the Bible

```
130 0    ‡a Bible. ‡p N.T. ‡p Mark. ‡l English. ‡s New English. ‡f 1965.
245 14   ‡a The Gospel according to Mark / ‡c commentary by C.F.D. Moule.
260      ‡a Cambridge [England] : ‡b University Press, ‡c 1965.
300      ‡a x, 133 p. : ‡b map ; ‡c 21 cm.
440  0   ‡a Cambridge Bible commentary, New English Bible
700 1    ‡a Moule, C. F. D. ‡q (Charles Francis Digby), ‡d 1908-
```

Title page	The Gospel According to Mark
	Commentary by
	C.F.D. Moule
	Cambridge
	At The University Press
	1965

Figure 18-25.   Bible—selections

```
130 0    ‡a Bible. ‡l English. ‡s Revised Standard. ‡k Selections. ‡f 1964.
245 12   ‡a A shortened arrangement of the Holy Bible, Revised Standard Version / ‡c edited by
         Robert O. Ballou.
250      ‡a 1st ed.
260      ‡a Philadelphia : ‡b A.J. Holman Co. for Lippincott, ‡c c1964.
300      ‡a xxxii, 773 p. ; ‡c 22 cm.
700 1    ‡a Ballou, Robert Oleson, ‡d 1892-
```

Title page	A Shortened Arrangement of
	The Holy Bible
	Revised Standard Version
	Edited by Robert O. Ballou
	Published by A.J. Holman Company
	for J.B. Lippincott Company
	Philadelphia

Figure 18-26.   Bible—version

```
130 0    ‡a Bible. ‡l English. ‡s Authorized. ‡f 1948.
245 14   ‡a The Holy Bible : ‡b containing the Old and New Testaments and the Apocrypha /
         ‡c translated out of the original tongues ; and with the former translations diligently
         compared and revised, by His Majesty's special command ; appointed to be read in
         churches.
260      ‡a Cambridge [England] : ‡b University Press ; ‡a New York : ‡b Distributed by Dryden
         Press, ‡c 1948.
300      ‡a xxii, 662, 870 p. : ‡b maps ; ‡c 20 cm.
```

Title page	The Holy Bible
	Containing the Old and New Testaments
	and the Apocrypha
	Translated out of the original tongues
	and with the former translations
	diligently compared and revised
	by His Majesty's Special Command
	Appointed to be read in Churches
	Cambridge
	At The University Press
	Distributed in
	American Colleges and Universities by
	The Dryden Press, Publishers, New York

Figure 18-27.   Bible—version

```
130 0    ‡a Bible. ‡l English. ‡s American Revised. ‡f 1929.
245 14   ‡a The Holy Bible : ‡b containing the Old and New Testaments / ‡c translated out of the
         original tongues ; being the version set forth A.D. 1611, compared with the most ancient
         authorities and revised A.D. 1881-1885 ; newly edited by the American Revision
         Committee, A.D. 1901.
250      ‡a Standard ed.
260      ‡a New York : ‡b T. Nelson, ‡c c1929.
300      ‡a viii, 814, vi, 252 p. : ‡b maps (some col.) ; ‡c 18 cm.
500      ‡a Includes index.
710 2    ‡a American Revision Committee.
```

Title page

The Holy Bible
Containing the Old and New Testaments
Translated out of the Original Tongues
Being the Version set forth A.D. 1611
Compared with the most ancient Authorities and revised
A.D. 1881-1885
Newly Edited by the American Revision Committee
A.D. 1901
Standard Edition
New York
Thomas Nelson & Sons
385 Madison Ave.

Figure 18-28.   Bible—version

```
130 0    ‡a Bible. ‡p N.T. ‡l English. ‡s Today's English. ‡f 1966.
245 10   ‡a Good news for modern man : ‡b the New Testament in Today's English Version.
260      ‡a New York : ‡b American Bible Society, ‡c c1966.
300      ‡a vii, 599 p. ; ‡c 18 cm.
710 2    ‡a American Bible Society.
```

Title page

Good News
for Modern Man
The New Testament
in Today's English Version
American Bible Society
New York

Some versions are identified by the name of the translator. Use the translator's name in place of version if identification is by translator (see figure 18-23). Some names commonly used in headings for the Bible are

Kleist-Lilly—New Testament by James A. Kleist and Joseph Lilly

Knox—translation by Ronald Knox

Moffatt—translation by James Moffatt

Montgomery—translation of the New Testament by Helen Barrett Montgomery

Lamsa—translation by George M. Lamsa

Phillips—J. B. Phillips translation

Schonfield—New Testament translation by Hugh Schonfield

Smith-Goodspeed—O.T. translation by J. M. Powis Smith; N.T. translation by Edgar Goodspeed.

For further information about versions of the English Bible, see a Bible encyclopedia or dictionary, such as *The HarperCollins Bible Dictionary* (New York: HarperCollins, 1996).

25.18A12. Alternatives to version. Another term can be substituted for the name of the version when the text is the original language, when the version is unknown, when it has been altered, when it cannot be identified by translator's name, or when more than two versions are involved. The use of the surname of the person who has altered the text as an alternative to use of name of version is analogous to using the name of a translator in place of version (see figure 18-29).

25.18A13. Year. The year of publication is the last element of the uniform heading for the Bible. It is recorded in subfield ‡f. In the case of a facsimile edition, use the original date for the main entry heading; make an otherwise identical added entry in a 730 field, using the date of the facsimile.

Liturgical Works, Theological Creeds, Confessions of Faith, etc.

Compare rules for liturgical works, 25.19–25.23, with 21.39, the rule for entry. Liturgical works were formerly entered under the name of the denomination followed by the form subheading "Liturgy and ritual." Under *AACR2R* rules, entry is to be under the name of the denomination, with a uniform title for the work interposed between the heading and the transcription of the title proper (see figure 2-8 for an example of catalog entry for a liturgical work).

Figure 18-29.   Alternative to version

```
020      ‡a 0830900322
130 0    ‡a Bible. ‡l English. ‡s Smith. ‡f 1970.
245 10   ‡a Joseph Smith's "new translation" of the Bible : ‡b a complete parallel column
         comparison of the Inspired Version of the Holy Scriptures and the King James Authorized
         Version / ‡c introduction by F. Henry Edwards.
260      ‡a Independence, Mo. : ‡b Herald Pub. House, ‡c 1970.
300      ‡a 523 p. ; ‡c 23 cm.
700 1    ‡a Smith, Joseph, ‡d 1805-1844.
730 0    ‡a Bible. ‡l English. ‡s Authorized. ‡f 1970.
```

Title page	
	Joseph Smith's
	"New Translation"
	Of The Bible
	A complete parallel column comparison of the
	Inspired Version of the Holy Scriptures and the
	King James Authorized Version
	Introduction by F. Henry Edwards
	1970
	Herald Publishing House, Independence, Missouri

25.19B. This new rule, from the 1993 amendments, calls for entry under a well-established English title for a theological creed, confession of faith, etc., accepted by one or more denominational bodies (see figure 18-30). If there is no well-established English title, use a title in the original language.

Music

Rules for uniform titles for music have been extensively reworked and reorganized in *AACR2R* (see 25.25–25.35). The formulation of uniform titles for music is often an extremely complex operation, one requiring an extensive background in music bibliography. Several sources of information may be recommended for the general cataloger who only occasionally must catalog music. The best general guide is Richard P. Smiraglia's *Cataloging Music,* second edition, which does not, however, take into account the *AACR2R* revision of music uniform title rules.[4] The Library of Congress's *Cataloging Service Bulletin* provides general information about cataloging rules and interpretations. Specialized information concerning interpretations of rules for music cataloging is given in *Music Cataloging Bulletin,* issued monthly by the Music Section, Descriptive Cataloging Division, Library of Congress.

For discussion and examples of uniform titles for musical works, see chapter 5 ("Music") in this *Handbook.* See also chapter 6 ("Sound Recordings"), especially figures 6-1, 6-4, 6-9, 6-12, 6-13, and 6-15.

Figure 18-30.   Confession of faith

```
020      ‡a 0800613856
130 0    ‡a Augsburg Confession. ‡l English.
245 14   ‡a The Augsburg Confession : ‡b a confession of faith presented in Augsburg by certain
         princes and cities to his imperial majesty Charles V in the year 1530 / ‡c translated from
         the German text.
250      ‡a Anniversary ed.
260      ‡a [Philadelphia] : ‡b Fortress Press, ‡c 1980.
300      ‡a 64 p. : ‡b ill. ; ‡c 18 cm.
500      ‡a "From the Book of Concord, translated and edited by Theodore G. Tappert"--T.p. verso.
700 1    ‡a Tappert, Theodore G. ‡q (Theodore Gerhardt), ‡d 1904-1973.
```

Title page   The Augsburg Confession
                 A Confession of Faith Presented in Augsburg
                    by certain Princes and Cities to His
                       Imperial Majesty Charles V
                          in the year 1530
                   (translated from the German text)
                          Fortress Press

Notes

1. Charles Ammi Cutter's objectives of the library catalog are still the basis of cataloging theory. As he saw it, the library catalog had three objectives:
   1. To enable a person to find a book of which one of the following is known:
      A. the author
      B. the title
      C. the subject
   2. To show what the library has:
      D. by a given author
      E. on a given subject
      F. in a given kind of literature
   3. To assist in the choice of a book:
      G. as to its edition (bibliographically)
      H. as to its character (literary or topical)

   (*Rules for a Dictionary Catalog*, 4th ed. [Washington, D.C.: GPO, 1904], p. 12).
2. General information about MARC coding is found in the introduction to this *Handbook;* details about coding the descriptive portion of the record are found throughout chapter 1; information about the coding of main and added access points is found at the beginning of chapter 14. Further explanation of the MARC authorities format is given in *Handbook* chapters 15 and 17. Information about specific MARC fields may be found by consulting the index under "MARC fields."
3. International Conference on Cataloguing Principles, Paris, 1961; *Statement of Principles,* annotated edition with commentary and examples by Eva Verona (London: IFLA Committee on Cataloguing, 1971), p. 23.
4. Lake Crystal, Minn.: Soldier Creek Press, 1986.

APPENDIX

LISTS

HEADINGS FOR BRITISH SOVEREIGNS

Although the rules for the fomulation of royal names, both personal (22.16A) and corporate (24.20B), are relatively straightforward, their implementation for British sovereigns in the National Authority File is not. The country commonly referred to as "England" has actually gone through four name changes according to cataloging rules. To Henry VII, "England" is used. In 1536, under Henry VIII, Wales joined England to become "England and Wales." In 1707, under Anne, England and Wales officially merged with Scotland to become "Great Britain." Finally, in 1801, under George III, Ireland was joined to Great Britain to form the "United Kingdom."

According to *AACR2R*, one would expect the personal and corporate names of British sovereigns to be formed using the appropriate one of these four official names of the country. However, at the time *AACR2* was officially adopted by the Library of Congress in 1981, LC established these headings as supplied to them by the British Library. For personal forms, the qualifying phrase reads: "King [or Queen] of England" through William III; beginning with Anne and continuing to the present, "King [or Queen] of Great Britain" should be used.

Corporate headings, too, are not formed as expected; however, neither are they consistent with the form used in the personal name. To Henry VII, use "England. Sovereign . . ." From Henry VIII to William III, use "England and Wales. Sovereign . . ." From Anne to the present, use "Great Britain. Sovereign . . ." "United Kingdom" is used neither in the corporate nor the personal form of the name of British sovereigns (cf. *LCRI 23.2*, "Special decision 3," Nov. 1995). A list of correctly formed headings for these names beginning with William I follows, formatted according to MARC format for authorities.

Headings for personal entry of British sovereigns

```
100 00 ‡a William ‡b I, ‡c King of England, ‡d 1027 or 8-1087
100 00 ‡a William ‡b II, ‡c King of England, ‡d 1056?-1100
100 00 ‡a Henry ‡b I, ‡c King of England, ‡d 1068-1135
100 00 ‡a Stephen, ‡c King of England, ‡d 1097?-1154
100 00 ‡a Henry ‡b II, ‡c King of England, ‡d 1133-1189
100 00 ‡a Richard ‡b I, ‡c King of England, ‡d 1157-1199
100 00 ‡a John, ‡c King of England, ‡d 1167-1216
100 00 ‡a Henry ‡b III, ‡c King of England, ‡d 1207-1272
100 00 ‡a Edward ‡b I, ‡c King of England, ‡d 1239-1307
100 00 ‡a Edward ‡b II, ‡c King of England, ‡d 1284-1327
100 00 ‡a Edward ‡b III, ‡c King of England, ‡d 1312-1377
100 00 ‡a Richard ‡b II, ‡c King of England, ‡d 1367-1400
```

100 00 ‡a Henry ‡b IV, ‡c King of England, ‡d 1367-1413
100 00 ‡a Henry ‡b V, ‡c King of England, ‡d 1387-1422
100 00 ‡a Henry ‡b VI, ‡c King of England, ‡d 1421-1471
100 00 ‡a Edward ‡b IV, ‡c King of England, ‡d 1442-1483
100 00 ‡a Edward ‡b V, ‡c King of England, ‡d 1470-1483
100 00 ‡a Richard ‡b III, ‡c King of England, ‡d 1452-1485
100 00 ‡a Henry ‡b VII, ‡c King of England, ‡d 1457-1509
100 00 ‡a Henry ‡b VIII, ‡c King of England, ‡d 1491-1547
100 00 ‡a Edward ‡b VI, ‡c King of England, ‡d 1537-1553
100 00 ‡a Mary ‡b I, ‡c Queen of England, ‡d 1516-1558
100 00 ‡a Elizabeth ‡b I, ‡c Queen of England, ‡c 1533-1603
100 00 ‡a James ‡b I, ‡c King of England, ‡d 1566-1625
100 00 ‡a Charles ‡b I, ‡c King of England, ‡d 1600-1649
100 10 ‡a Cromwell, Oliver, ‡d 1599-1658
100 10 ‡a Cromwell, Richard, ‡d 1626-1712
100 00 ‡a Charles ‡b II, ‡c King of England, ‡d 1630-1685
100 00 ‡a James ‡b II, ‡c King of England, ‡d 1633-1701
100 00 ‡a Mary ‡b II, ‡c Queen of England, ‡d 1662-1694
100 00 ‡a William ‡b III, ‡c King of England, ‡d 1650-1702
100 00 ‡a Anne, ‡c Queen of Great Britain, ‡d 1665-1714
100 00 ‡a George ‡b I, ‡c King of Great Britain, ‡d 1660-1727
100 00 ‡a George ‡b II, ‡c King of Great Britain, ‡d 1683-1760
100 00 ‡a George ‡b III, ‡c King of Great Britain, ‡d 1738-1820
100 00 ‡a George ‡b IV, ‡c King of Great Britain, ‡d 1762-1830
100 00 ‡a William ‡b IV, ‡c King of Great Britain, ‡d 1765-1837
100 00 ‡a Victoria, ‡c Queen of Great Britain, ‡d 1819-1901
100 00 ‡a Edward ‡b VII, ‡c King of Great Britain, ‡d 1841-1910
100 00 ‡a George ‡b V, ‡c King of Great Britain, ‡d 1865-1936
100 00 ‡a Edward ‡b VIII, ‡c King of Great Britain, ‡d 1894-1972[1]
100 00 ‡a George ‡b VI, ‡c King of Great Britain, ‡d 1895-1952
100 00 ‡a Elizabeth ‡b II, ‡c Queen of Great Britain, ‡d 1926-

Headings for British sovereigns acting in an official capacity

110 10 ‡a England. ‡b Sovereign (1066-1087 : William I)
110 10 ‡a England. ‡b Sovereign (1087-1100 : William II)
110 10 ‡a England. ‡b Sovereign (1100-1135 : Henry I)
110 10 ‡a England. ‡b Sovereign (1135-1154 : Stephen)
110 10 ‡a England. ‡b Sovereign (1154-1189 : Henry II)
110 10 ‡a England. ‡b Sovereign (1189-1199 : Richard I)
110 10 ‡a England. ‡b Sovereign (1199-1216 : John)
110 10 ‡a England. ‡b Sovereign (1216-1272 : Henry III)
110 10 ‡a England. ‡b Sovereign (1272-1307 : Edward I)
110 10 ‡a England. ‡b Sovereign (1307-1327 : Edward II)
110 10 ‡a England. ‡b Sovereign (1327-1377 : Edward III)
110 10 ‡a England. ‡b Sovereign (1377-1399 : Richard II)
110 10 ‡a England. ‡b Sovereign (1399-1413 : Henry IV)
110 10 ‡a England. ‡b Sovereign (1413-1422 : Henry V)

110 10 ‡a England. ‡b Sovereign (1422-1461 : Henry VI)
110 10 ‡a England. ‡b Sovereign (1461-1483 : Edward IV)
110 10 ‡a England. ‡b Sovereign (1483 : Edward V)
110 10 ‡a England. ‡b Sovereign (1483-1485 : Richard III)
110 10 ‡a England. ‡b Sovereign (1485-1509 : Henry VII)
110 10 ‡a England and Wales. ‡b Sovereign (1509-1547 : Henry VIII)
110 10 ‡a England and Wales. ‡b Sovereign (1547-1553 : Edward VI)
110 10 ‡a England and Wales. ‡b Sovereign (1553-1558 : Mary I)
110 10 ‡a England and Wales. ‡b Sovereign (1558-1603 : Elizabeth I)
110 10 ‡a England and Wales. ‡b Sovereign (1603-1625 : James I)
110 10 ‡a England and Wales. ‡b Sovereign (1625-1649 : Charles I)
110 10 ‡a England and Wales. ‡b Lord Protector (1653-1658 : O. Cromwell)
110 10 ‡a England and Wales. ‡b Lord Protector (1658-1659 : R. Cromwell)
110 10 ‡a England and Wales. ‡b Sovereign (1660-1685 : Charles II)
110 10 ‡a England and Wales. ‡b Sovereign (1685-1688 : James II)
110 10 ‡a England and Wales. ‡b Sovereign (1689-1694 : William and Mary)
110 10 ‡a England and Wales. ‡b Sovereign (1694-1702 : William III)
110 10 ‡a Great Britain. ‡b Sovereign (1702-1714 : Anne)
110 10 ‡a Great Britain. ‡b Sovereign (1714-1727 : George I)
110 10 ‡a Great Britain. ‡b Sovereign (1727-1760 : George II)
110 10 ‡a Great Britain. ‡b Sovereign (1760-1820 : George III)
110 10 ‡a Great Britain. ‡b Sovereign (1820-1830 : George IV)
110 10 ‡a Great Britain. ‡b Sovereign (1830-1837 : William IV)
110 10 ‡a Great Britain. ‡b Sovereign (1837-1901 : Victoria)
110 10 ‡a Great Britain. ‡b Sovereign (1901-1910 : Edward VII)
110 10 ‡a Great Britain. ‡b Sovereign (1910-1936 : George V)
110 10 ‡a Great Britain. ‡b Sovereign (1936 : Edward VIII)
110 10 ‡a Great Britain. ‡b Sovereign (1936-1952 : George VI)
110 10 ‡a Great Britain. ‡b Sovereign (1952-   : Elizabeth II)

HEADINGS FOR U.S. PRESIDENTS ACTING IN AN OFFICIAL CAPACITY

110 10 ‡a United States. ‡b President (1789-1797 : Washington)
110 10 ‡a United States. ‡b President (1797-1801 : Adams)
110 10 ‡a United States. ‡b President (1801-1809 : Jefferson)
110 10 ‡a United States. ‡b President (1809-1817 : Madison)
110 10 ‡a United States. ‡b President (1817-1825 : Monroe)
110 10 ‡a United States. ‡b President (1825-1829 : Adams)
110 10 ‡a United States. ‡b President (1829-1837 : Jackson)
110 10 ‡a United States. ‡b President (1837-1841 : Van Buren)
110 10 ‡a United States. ‡b President (1841 : Harrison)
110 10 ‡a United States. ‡b President (1841-1845 : Tyler)
110 10 ‡a United States. ‡b President (1845-1849 : Polk)
110 10 ‡a United States. ‡b President (1849-1850 : Taylor)
110 10 ‡a United States. ‡b President (1850-1853 : Fillmore)
110 10 ‡a United States. ‡b President (1853-1857 : Pierce)
110 10 ‡a United States. ‡b President (1857-1861 : Buchanan)

110 10 ‡a United States. ‡b President (1861-1865 : Lincoln)
110 10 ‡a United States. ‡b President (1865-1869 : Johnson)
110 10 ‡a United States. ‡b President (1869-1877 : Grant)
110 10 ‡a United States. ‡b President (1877-1881 : Hayes)
110 10 ‡a United States. ‡b President (1881 : Garfield)
110 10 ‡a United States. ‡b President (1881-1885 : Arthur)
110 10 ‡a United States. ‡b President (1885-1889 : Cleveland)
110 10 ‡a United States. ‡b President (1889-1893 : Harrison)
110 10 ‡a United States. ‡b President (1893-1897 : Cleveland)
110 10 ‡a United States. ‡b President (1897-1901 : McKinley)
110 10 ‡a United States. ‡b President (1901-1909 : Roosevelt)
110 10 ‡a United States. ‡b President (1909-1913 : Taft)
110 10 ‡a United States. ‡b President (1913-1921 : Wilson)
110 10 ‡a United States. ‡b President (1921-1923 : Harding)
110 10 ‡a United States. ‡b President (1923-1929 : Coolidge)
110 10 ‡a United States. ‡b President (1929-1933 : Hoover)
110 10 ‡a United States. ‡b President (1933-1945 : Roosevelt)
110 10 ‡a United States. ‡b President (1945-1953 : Truman)
110 10 ‡a United States. ‡b President (1953-1961 : Eisenhower)
110 10 ‡a United States. ‡b President (1961-1963 : Kennedy)
110 10 ‡a United States. ‡b President (1963-1969 : Johnson)
110 10 ‡a United States. ‡b President (1969-1974 : Nixon)
110 10 ‡a United States. ‡b President (1974-1977 : Ford)
110 10 ‡a United States. ‡b President (1977-1981 : Carter)
110 10 ‡a United States. ‡b President (1981-1989 : Reagan)
110 10 ‡a United States. ‡b President (1989-1993 : Bush)
110 10 ‡a United States. ‡b President (1993-   : Clinton)

UNIFORM HEADINGS FOR COMMON ANONYMOUS CLASSICS[2]

130   0 ‡a Arabian nights

Collection of ancient stories from the Middle East, originally in Arabic, compiled about A.D. 1450. Some of the tales are well known and are often published separately; these are entered under their own names with references to Arabian Nights, such as:

130   0 ‡a Sindbad the sailor
430   0 ‡a Arabian nights. ‡p Sindbad the sailor

This displays:

Arabian nights. Sindbad the sailor
    search under
Sindbad the sailor

130   0 ‡a Avesta

Zoroastrian and Parsee sacred book, consisting of writings and oral traditions of Zoroaster before 800 B.C., in five parts: Yasna (Gathas or hymns); Vispered; Vendidad (laws); Yashts (stories of gods); and Khordah (private devotions). Sometimes called "Zend-Avesta" (interpretation of the Avesta).

130   0 ‡a Beowulf

Anglo-Saxon epic dating from early eighth century. Concerns a hero-warrior, Beowulf, who rescues Hrothgar, king of the Danes, from Grendel and Grendel's mother, two monsters whom Beowulf wrestles single-handedly and unarmed, in the best heroic tradition.

130   0 ‡a Chanson de Roland

French *chanson de geste* (song of deeds) (mid-eleventh century). Its 4,002 lines are divided into stanzas of unequal length. Charlemagne's nephew Roland, fighting under Charlemagne in Spain, is betrayed by Ganelon and ambushed by 400,000 Saracens at the pass of Roncesvalles. Roland refuses to sound his horn and recall the main body of Charlemagne's army; the unequal contest between his small group and the Saracens occupies most of the poem. When he finally does sound his horn, it is too late; Roland and his army are dead when Charlemagne reaches them.

130   0 ‡a Cid (Epic cycle)

Cycle of poems in Spanish, similar in form to the *Chanson de Roland*. Concerns the adventures of Rodrigo or Ruy Diaz de Bivar (c. 1043-1099), known as *el Cid* (the Lord) and *el Campeador* (the champion), who fought on both sides in the struggle with the Moors and was active in the conquest of Valencia (1094). The cycle includes much legendary detail. El Cid is presented as the model Castilian warrior. Individual titles in the cycle are entered under their own name, as

> 130   0 ‡a Cantar de mío Cid

130   0 ‡a Cuchulain

Legendary Irish warrior and hero, sometimes described as "the Achilles of the Gael." As a child, he was attacked by a ferocious dog and killed it. When he saw the grief of its owner, Culain, he acted as watchdog until a replacement could be found; thus his name, which means "the hound of Culain." Stories about his heroic exploits in love and war are favorite subjects for many modern Irish poets, including William Butler Yeats (see his "On Baile's Strand"). The form of the name is also found as Cu Chulainn, Cuculain, Cuchulin, Cu Cullin, and Setana.

130   0 ‡a Domesday Book

A Latin census and survey of England compiled for William the Conqueror in 1086. It served as basis for tax assessments until 1522. Also known as Doomsday Book.

130   0 ‡a Edda Samundar
130   0 ‡a Edda Snorra Sturlusonar

Two collections of early Icelandic mythology. "Edda Samundar" is the uniform heading used to refer to the Elder (or Poetic) Edda, erroneously attributed to Saemund Sigfusson (1056-1133) and thus called the "Edda of Saemund" (Edda Samundar), mythological stories of Norse gods and heroes. "Edda Snorra Sturlusonar" is the uniform heading used to refer to the Younger (or Prose) Edda (early thirteenth century), also called "Snorra Edda." It was written by Snorri Sturluson (1179-1241), an Icelandic historian. The Prose Edda tells of the creation of the world and of poetry; it includes the Skalda (rules of ancient prosody) and Hattatal (technical analysis of meters). It also gives early Scandinavian myths and legends of the gods not included in the Poetic Edda.

130   0 ‡a Gesta Romanorum

A popular medieval collection of Latin stories. First printed in England in 1473, it included one hundred to two hundred tales. The unhistorical episodes are arbitrarily assigned to various Roman emperors. Each tale concludes with a moral. Chaucer, Shakespeare, and other English writers drew on these tales, and they were favorite reading for English children until the eighteenth century.

130   0 ‡a Grettis saga

The story of Grettir the Strong, a historical Icelandic hero who lived during the late tenth and early eleventh centuries. The saga was set down in the fourteenth century. Parts bear strong resemblance to *Beowulf.* Translated into English by William Morris.

130   0 ‡a Kalevala

The Finnish national epic, compiled by Elias Lönnrot (1802-1884). It includes an account of the origin of the world and the adventures of various heroes. Longfellow's "Hiawatha" (1855) was influenced by a German translation of the poem.

130   0 ‡a Kudrun

An anonymous German epic poem written about 1210 in Austria, influenced by the *Nibelungenlied.* There are three sections: Hagen, king of Ireland; Hetel's courtship of Hagen's daughter, Hilde, and their marriage; the abduction of their daughter, Kudrun (also known as Gudrun), by Hartmut of Normandy and her rescue by her betrothed and her brother.

130   0 ‡a Mabinogian

A collection of twelve Welsh tales, first written down in the fourteenth century but probably originating much earlier. Concerned with Celtic mythology and folklore, they were first translated into English by Lady Charlotte Guest in 1839; "Mabinogian" is her term for the collection. J. R. R. Tolkien (*The Lord of the Rings; The Hobbit*) and Lloyd Alexander (*The High King; The Black Cauldron,* etc.) draw heavily on these Welsh medieval legends for the spirit and flavor of their works.

130   0 ‡a Mahābhārata

With the *Rāmāyaṇa,* the *Mahābhārata* is one of the two main ancient Indian epic poems. The story concerns the five Pandavas, or sons of Pandu, and their struggle with the Kauravas (the family of Pandu's brother), who refuse to give up the throne to the Pandavas, the rightful heirs. It also concerns the exploits of two of the brothers, Yudhishthira, the eldest, who finally gains the kingdom, and Arjuna, who wins the hand—for all five brothers—of Draupadi in open contest and brings her home.

Evidently they all live happily ever after; the end of the epic concerns the journey of the five brothers, their wife, and their dog, to seek admission to the heaven of Indra on Mount Meru. The *Mahābhārata* has been called "an encyclopaedia of Hindu life, legend, and thought."

130   0 ‡a Nibelungenlied

An anonymous medieval German epic poem, probably written about 1190 or 1200. Based in part on the *Edda Samundar* (Poetic Edda) and the Völsunga saga, it includes much more German legendary material and omits much of the supernatural aspects of the two earlier sources. The story of Siegfried—who killed the Nibelung kings and took their name, their treasure of gold, and their cape of darkness, which makes the wearer invisible—and his exploits in wooing Kriemhild and in duping the fabulously strong Queen Brunhild of Iceland into marrying Kriemhild's brother, Gunther, make up the first part of the Nibelungenlied. Seigfried—like Achilles, Baldur, and other heroes invulnerable except for one spot on their bodies—is killed by treachery. The story ends in a general bloodbath, with none of the main characters left alive. Wagner drew on this material in part for *Der Ring des Nibelungen*.

130   0 ‡a Panchatantra

A collection of Sanskrit fables, dating from about the fifth century A.D. Arthur W. Ryder translated them into English (1955).

130   0 ‡a Reynard the Fox

A collection of medieval beast tales from French, Flemish, and German folklore. Episodes in various versions differ. Most of the tales concern the cunning fox Reynard and his struggle for power with the physcially powerful (but stupid) wolf Isengrim. Other episodes involve Reynard with King Noble the Lion, Sir Bruin the Bear, Tibert the Cat, and Chanticleer the Cock (see Chaucer's "Nun's Priest's Tale").

Because a number of distinct variants or versions of these tales exist, each with an individuality all its own, the heading "Reynard the Fox" is not used as a main entry. Instead, a separate uniform title is used for each. "Reynard the Fox" is used as a subject heading for critical discussions of the cycle and may also be used for added entries (see below). Some examples of the individual titles follow:

Ecbasis cujusdam captivi	(Early Latin version)
Reinaert	(Flemish version)
Reinke de Vos	(Low German version)
Roman de Renart	(French version)
Renart le contrefait	(French sequel to original French version)
Reinaerts historie	(Dutch version)

When cataloging any version of Reynard the Fox, make an added entry under "Reynard the Fox," with language as subheading. See *AACR2R* 25.12.

130   0 ‡a Second shepherd's play

A miracle play (also called "Secunda Pagina Pastorum") written in England about the end of the fourteenth century, the second in the Towneley cycle of plays (see Towneley Plays, below). It deals with the Nativity in terms of Yorkshire life, full of rollicking, farcical fun. The best-known episode deals with Mak the sheep stealer, who disguises a stolen sheep as his wife's newborn baby.

130   0 ‡a Towneley Plays

Also known as "Towneley Mysteries" and "Wakefield Mysteries" because they were probably acted near Wakefield. Mystery and miracle plays were medieval dramas based on the Old and New Testaments and on the lives of the saints. Individual plays in the cycle are entered under their own names. Other well-known cycles are "Chester Plays," "Coventry Plays," and "York Plays."

130   0 ‡a Vedas

The four sacred books of the Hindus composed about 2500 B.C.: the Rig Veda, the Yajur Veda, the Sama Veda, and the Atharva Veda. Prayers and hymns in verse and prose; formulas for consecration, imprecation, expiation, etc.

130   0 ‡a Völsunga saga

A Scandinavian prose cycle of legends, the major source of the German epic poem *Der Niebelungenlied* (q.v.) and of Wagner's *Der Ring des Nibelungen*. The saga takes its name from Völsung, grandson of the god Odin and father of Sigmund. The hero Sigurd (Siegfried) is Sigmund's son. William Morris's *Sigurd the Völsung* (London: Ellis & White, 1876) is based on the story.

Notes

1. Edward VIII is actually established in the National Authority File as:

   100 10 ‡a Windsor, Edward, ‡c Duke of, ‡d 1894-1972

2. Most of the factual information about the anonymous classics has been taken from *Benét's Reader's Encyclopedia*, 4th ed., ed. Bruce Murphey (New York: HarperCollins, 1996). A more extensive list of uniform headings for anonymous classics is contained in International Federation of Library Associations, *Anonymous Classics: A List of Uniform Headings for European Literatures*, ed. Rosemary C. Hewett (London: IFLA International Office, 1978). The titles given here are in the form found in the National Authority File at the time of publication of this *Handbook*.

INDEX